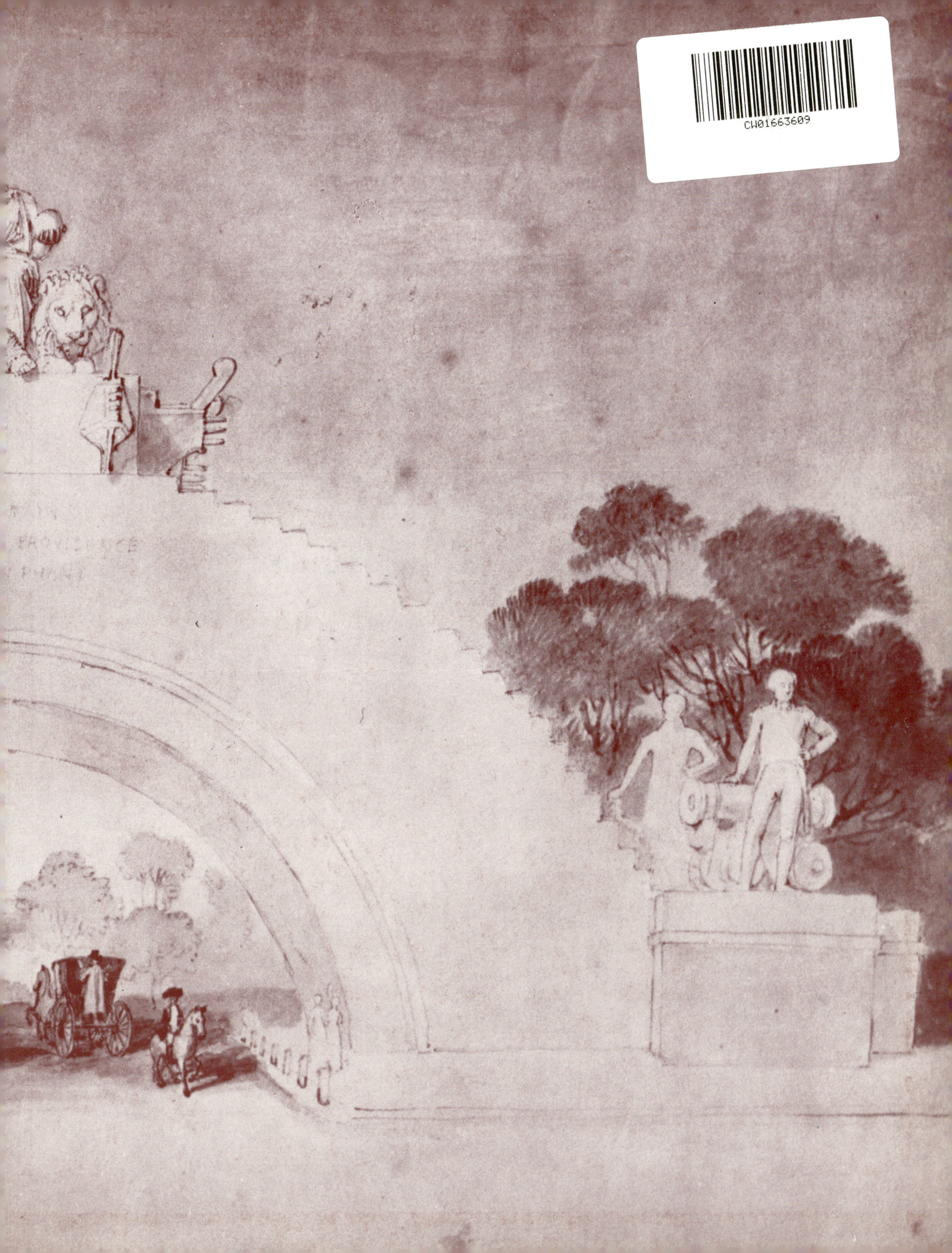

John Flaxman 1755–1826

SCULPTOR ILLUSTRATOR DESIGNER

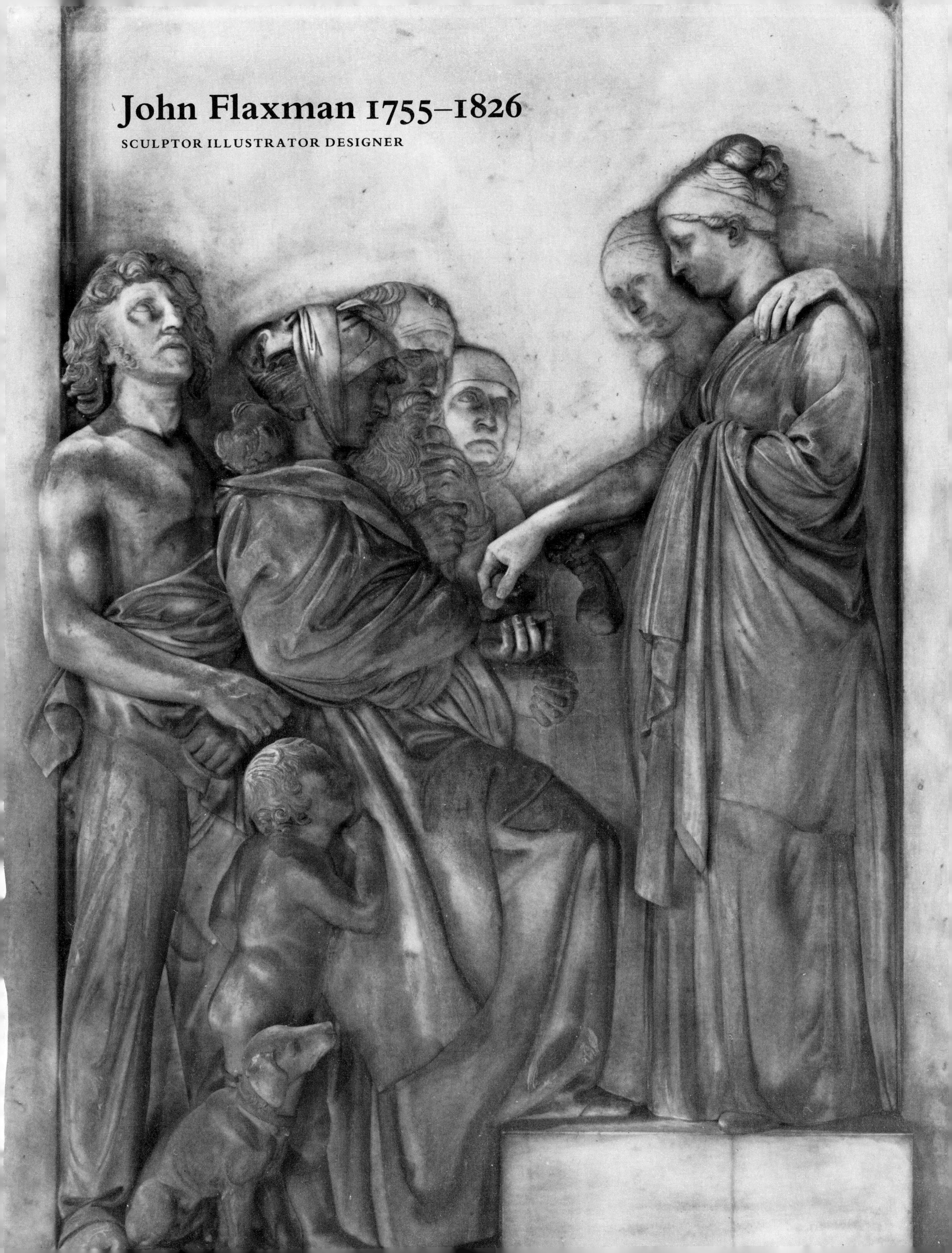

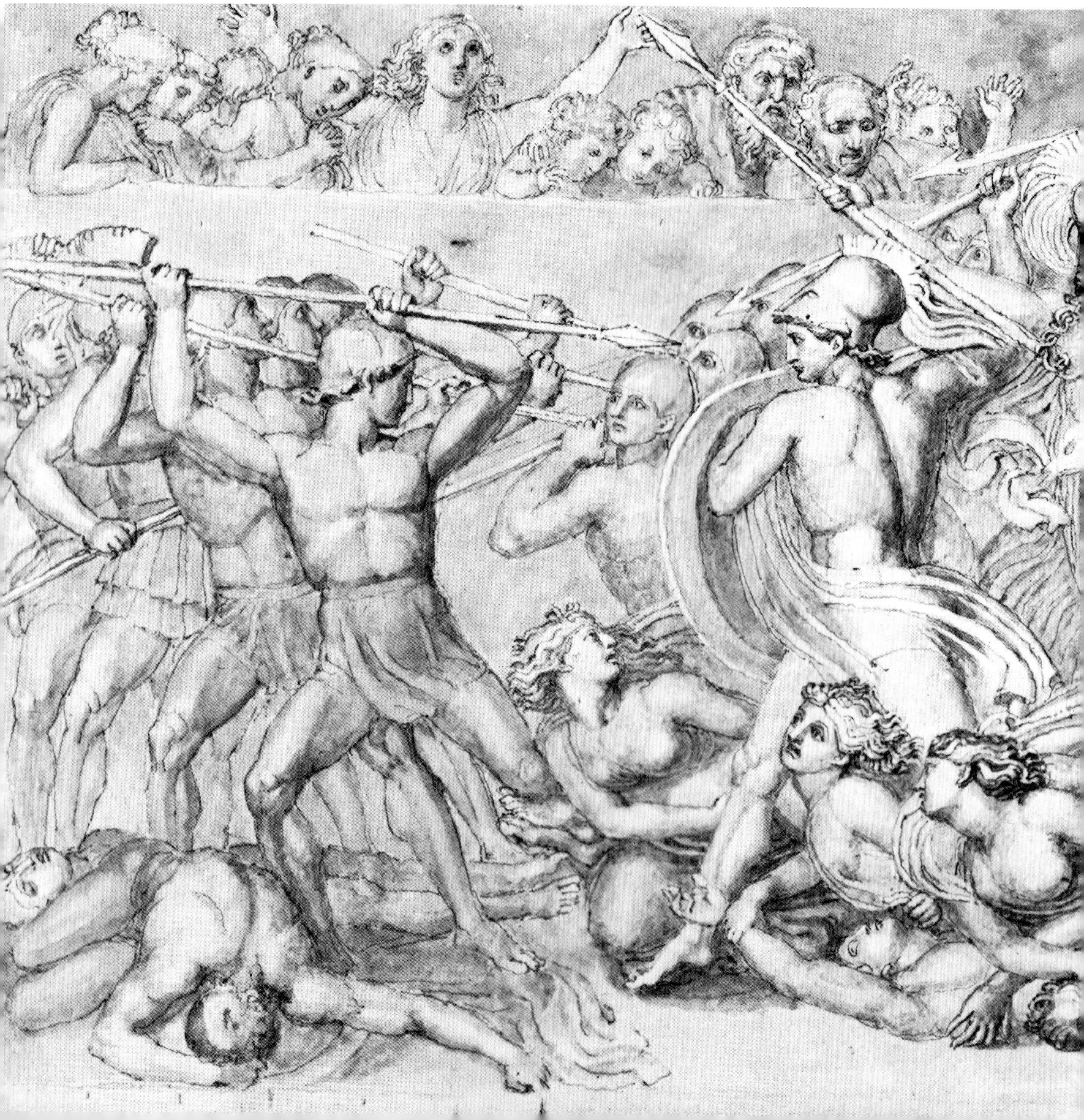

John Flaxman 1755–1826

SCULPTOR ILLUSTRATOR DESIGNER

DAVID IRWIN

Studio Vista / Christie's London 1979

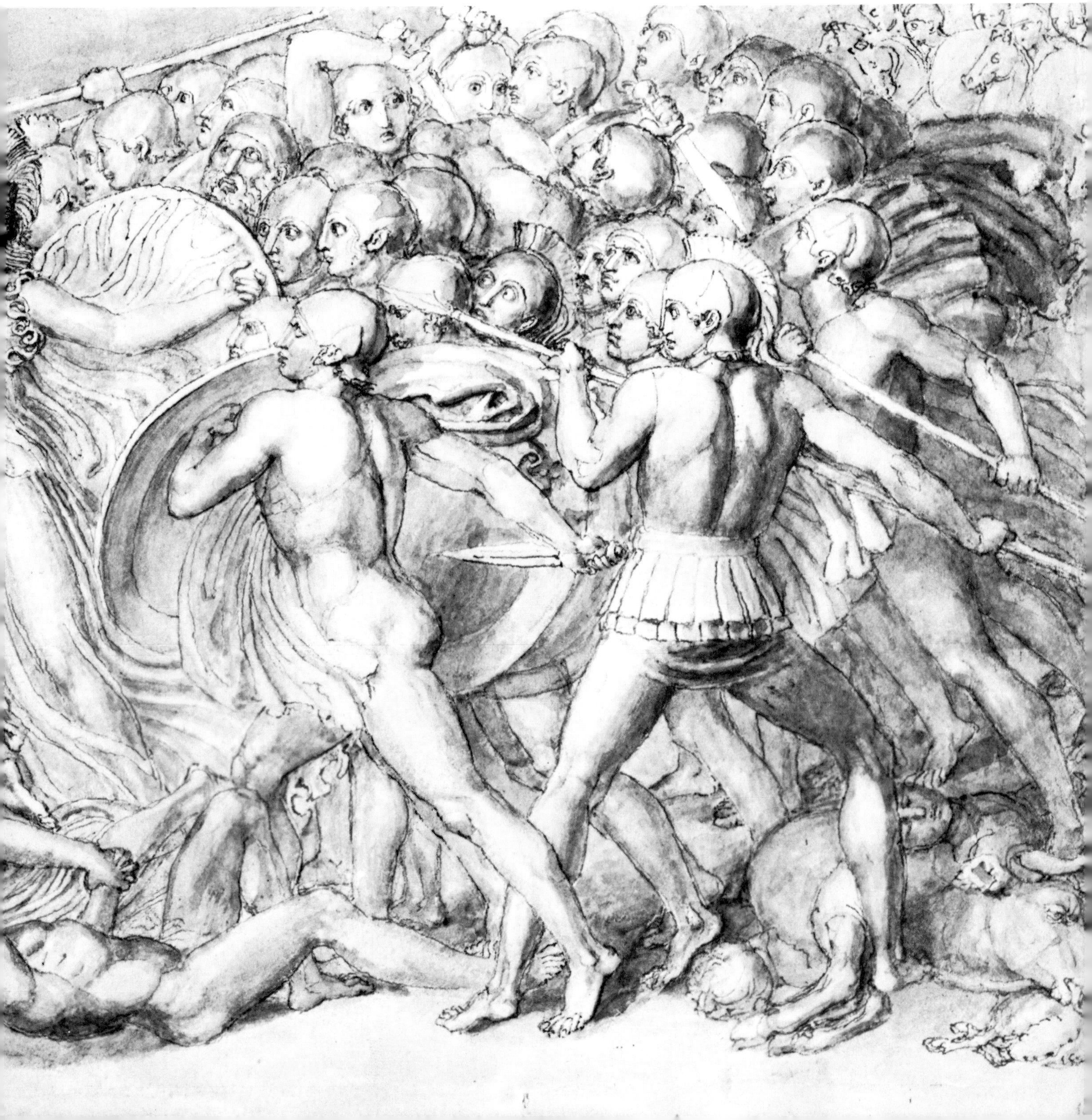

to Francina

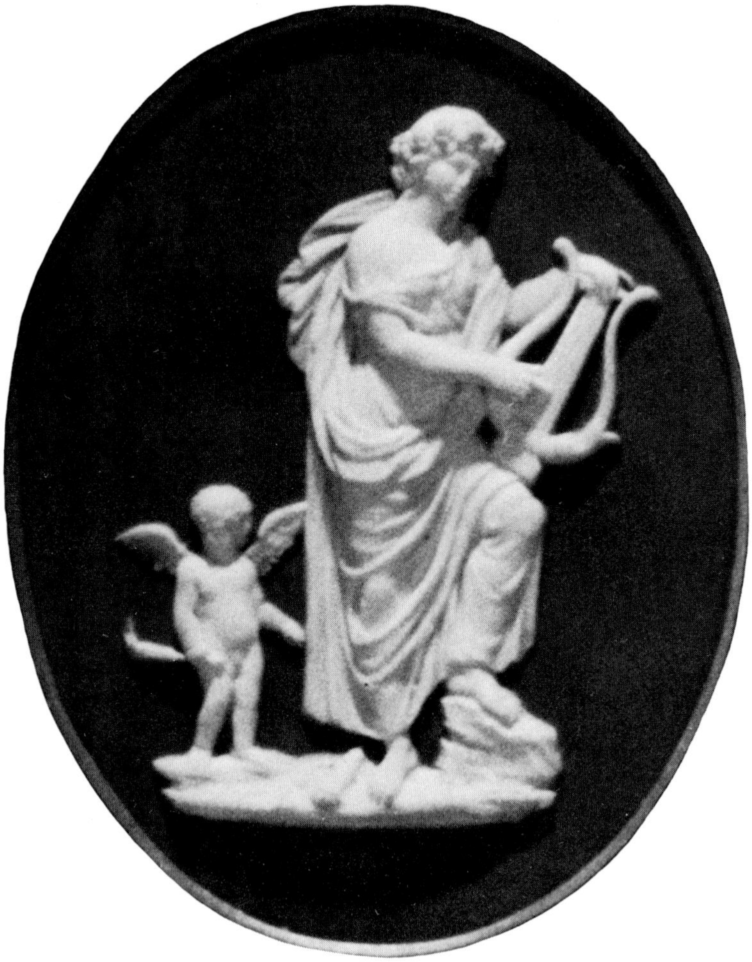

A Studio Vista book published
by Cassell Ltd,
35 Red Lion Square, London, WC1R 4SG
and at Sydney, Auckland, Toronto, Johannesburg,
an affiliate of
Macmillan Publishing Co., Inc., New York

ISBN 0 289 70885 0

Filmset and printed by BAS Printers Limited,
Over Wallop, Hampshire

Contents

Chronology

1755 Born in York on 6 July, the second son of John Flaxman, maker of plaster casts and models. The family moves to London six months later.

1769 Becomes a student at the Royal Academy School; the same year wins an Academy silver medal. About the same year the start of a friendship with the Reverend and Mrs Mathew.

1770 Starts exhibiting at the Royal Academy's annual exhibition.

1775 Thomas Bentley recommends to Wedgwood that Flaxman be employed by the firm. First designs for jasperware this year.

1775 (approx) Start of lifelong friendships with George Romney and Thomas Stothard.

1779 (approx) Start of lifelong friendship with William Blake.

1782 Marries Nancy Denman, daughter of a gunstock-maker in Whitechapel, London. The Flaxmans live in Wardour Street, Soho, London.

1783 Start of friendship with William Hayley.

1784 Joins the Theosophical Society.

1784 (approx) *Sarah Morley* monument.

1787 John and Nancy Flaxman travel through France to Italy, where they stay until 1794.

1789 *Cephalus and Aurora* commissioned by Thomas Hope; completed next year.

1790 *Fury of Athamas* commissioned by the Earl-Bishop of Bristol and Derry; completed 1794.

1792 *Mansfield* monument; completed 1801.

1792 *William Collins* monument; completed 1795.

1793 *Iliad and Odyssey* illustrations, commissioned by Mrs Hare-Naylor, published.

1793 *Dante* illustrations, commissioned by Thomas Hope, published privately; first public English edition in 1807.

1794 The Flaxmans return to London, where they live for the rest of their lives, in Buckingham Street, off Fitzroy Square.

1795 *Aeschylus* illustrations, commissioned by the Dowager Countess Spencer, published.

1796 *The Knight of the Blazing Cross*, unpublished, illustrated poem.

1796 *Sir William Jones* monument.

1797 Elected an Associate of the Royal Academy.

1798 *Agnes Cromwell* monument; completed 1800.

1799 Colossal *Britannia* statue proposed as a naval memorial on Greenwich Hill.

1800 Elected a full Royal Academician.

1800 *Reverend Dr Joseph Warton* monument; completed 1804

1802 Visits Paris during the Peace of Amiens.

1803 *Howe* monument; completed 1811.

1803 *Yarborough* monument; completed 1806.

1805 Flaxman's association with the silversmiths Rundell, Bridge and Rundell forged by his *Trafalgar Vase*.

1806 *Baring Family* monument; completed about 1810.

1807 *Nelson* monument; completed 1818.

1809 *Abraham Balme* monument; completed 1812.

1809 Friezes for Covent Garden Theatre.

1810 Appointed the Royal Academy's first Professor of Sculpture; delivers his first lecture in 1811.

1810 Joins the Swedenborg Society; twice a committee member in 1815 and 1817.

1812 *The Casket*, unpublished illustrated poem.

1816 *Viscountess Fitzharris* monument; completed 1817.

1816 Elected a Member of the Accademia di San Luca in Rome.

1817 *Hesiod* illustrations published, without a patron.

1819 *St Michael overcoming Satan* commissioned by the Earl of Egremont; completed 1824.

1820 Candidate in the election for the President of the Royal Academy; defeated by Sir Thomas Lawrence.

1820 Flaxman's wife dies.

1821 *Achilles Shield* executed by Rundell, Bridge and Rundell.

1822 *Robert Burns* statue; completed 1826.

1826 Buckingham Palace decorative sculptures, designs begun but not executed.

1826 Dies in London on 7 December. Buried in the churchyard of St. Giles-in-the-Fields.

Preface

WHEN JOHN FLAXMAN died in 1826, one diarist at the time noted that 'the country has lost one of its greatest best men. As an artist he had done more than any other man of the age to spread her fame; as a man, he exhibited a rare specimen of moral and Christian excellence' (Henry Crabb Robinson).

Flaxman was a seminal figure who created a wide and unusually varied range of works. His illustrations were of interest to artists as diverse as Blake, Ingres, Goya and the Nazarenes, and later the Pre-Raphaelites and Walter Crane. His monuments represented a major contribution to contemporary sculpture, and were to be an important influence on tomb design in the Victorian period. His secular commissions would have culminated in sculptures for George IV's new palace. In the field of the decorative arts, Flaxman was one of the principal artists employed by Wedgwood, and later produced silverwork designs for Rundell and Bridge. He was the Royal Academy's first Professor of Sculpture. Posthumously he shared with Turner the unusual distinction of having a group of his works permanently on display in the capital, when the Flaxman Gallery was opened at University College in London.

This exhibition space helped to make amends for the absence of a near-contemporary biography, lavishly illustrated with line engravings, as had been accorded to Canova and to Thorvaldsen. Near Flaxman's own lifetime the only long account of his work, without any illustrations, was the chapter in Allan Cunningham's *Lives* published in 1830, which still remains a useful biography. The only extensively illustrated account of Flaxman's work in the course of the nineteenth century were the articles published in the *Art Journal* between 1867 and 1872 by G. F. Teniswood, who discussed a large number of sculptures and many of the illustrations. Sidney Colvin published the drawings at University College in 1876, reproducing them as an invaluable collection of small-scale photographs. Talfourd Ely produced a catalogue of the College's collection in 1900.

The only full-scale book on this many-faceted artist has been W. G. Constable's study published in 1927. More recently scholars have made further contributions by editing catalogues of plaster models, drawings and an account-book, sorting out various editions of his published illustrations and producing an invaluable dictionary entry. For all this work I am much indebted to the publications of the late Margaret Whinney, the late Rupert Gunnis, G. E. Bentley, Edward Croft-Murray and Robert Wark.

Exhibitions have encouraged a growing interest in Flaxman's work; in Newcastle in 1958, and a dealer's show in London in 1976. Flaxman was included in both of the Council of Europe's London exhibitions spanning his lifetime, *The Romantic Movement* in 1959 and more extensively in *The Age of Neoclassicism* in 1972, an exhibition which I helped to plan. By the time this book is published, the first major one-man exhibition of Flaxman's art will have been held in 1979 in Hamburg, and will have subsequently travelled to Copenhagen and London.

My own researches on Flaxman began in 1957 as part of a doctoral dissertation for London University, under the supervision of Margaret Whinney and Anthony Blunt, with additional tuition from Leopold Ettlinger. My debt to them has always been great, especially as my researches into Neoclassicism began at a time when few scholars showed much interest in the style. Fortunately the picture has changed in the late two decades. My thesis, in a much revised form, was published as *English Neoclassical Art* in 1966, in which Flaxman appeared throughout. In 1959 I had published extracts from Flaxman's Italian journals and correspondence for the first time, in an article in the *Burlington Magazine*. Since my postgraduate days I have continued to collect material with a view to eventually writing a separate monograph. My aim has been a comprehensive examination of all aspects of Flaxman's career between the covers of one book. Different areas of his work are interdependent, thus making separate studies by their very nature incomplete. I have not traced his influence abroad, nor included his influence on Victorian artists. I have tried, however, to discuss as many of Flaxman's works as possible, short of producing a *catalogue raisonné*. Since new tombs keep turning up, such a catalogue of sculptures would at present be impossible until every church in Britain and those countries abroad that used to form the British Empire have been fully examined. For similar reasons a catalogue of all the drawings would also be impossible. Even whilst I was writing this preface an interesting and hitherto unknown drawing came to light in one of the London auction-houses. However, one of the indexes of this book has been planned to serve as an almost complete listing of his works.

In the early stages of my researches I received a much-valued grant for photographs and travel from the Central Research Fund of London University. More recently the Carnegie Trust for the Universities of Scotland has generously provided grants for study in Italy and in the U.S.A. I am also grateful to the University of Aberdeen for making it possible to purchase photographs, some of which have been specially taken, as well as for providing me with periods of sabbatical leave during which much of the book has been written.

My work has been helped by many people over the years, in addition to the scholars already named who apart from their publications or supervision have provided me with guidance on many points. I would also like to thank: Keith Andrews, Mildred Archer, Geoffrey de Bellaigue, Shirley Bury, David Bindman, the late T. S. R. Boase, Walter Brandt, R. J. Charleston, Catherine Cruft, Lorenz Eitner, John des Fontaines, Ian H. C. Fraser, Ernst Gombrich, Terence Hodgkinson, Michael Kitson, Mary Lightbown, John McManners, Ulrich Middeldorf, Hamish Miles, Jennifer Montagu, Peter Murray, the late Benedict Nicolson, Graham Pollard, John Pope-Hennessy, Robert Rosenblum, Mary Sorabji, John Sunderland, Gerald Taylor, Pamela Tudor-Craig, Philip Ward-Jackson, and the late Edgar Wind.

This book could not have been written, or at least would have been considerably more difficult to write, without the photographic resources of the Witt and Conway Libraries of the Courtauld Institute of Art. I have also been helped by the special photographs taken for me by the Paul Mellon Centre for Studies in British Art. Of the many other libraries I have used I would like to thank the staffs of the British Library, Victoria and Albert Museum, Warburg Institute, Society of Antiquaries, Bodleian Library, John Rylands University Library, National Library of Scotland, the libraries of Aberdeen, Edinburgh and Glasgow Universities, and abroad the British School, Biblioteca Vaticana and Biblioteca Hertziana in Rome, and the Kunsthistorisches Institut in Florence.

Museum and gallery staffs in Britain and abroad, as well as private owners, have also provided invaluable help in showing me their resources, and I am also grateful to them for their permission to publish works in their possession. Her Majesty The Queen has graciously granted permission to reproduce works in her collection.

Throughout my work I have had the continuous support and encouragement of my wife, and I dedicate this book to her with both gratitude and affection.

Aquhorthies *January 1979*

List of Illustrations

61 *A Roman Girl going to Church.* Pen and ink and wash. John Murray, London (Photo Godfrey New)

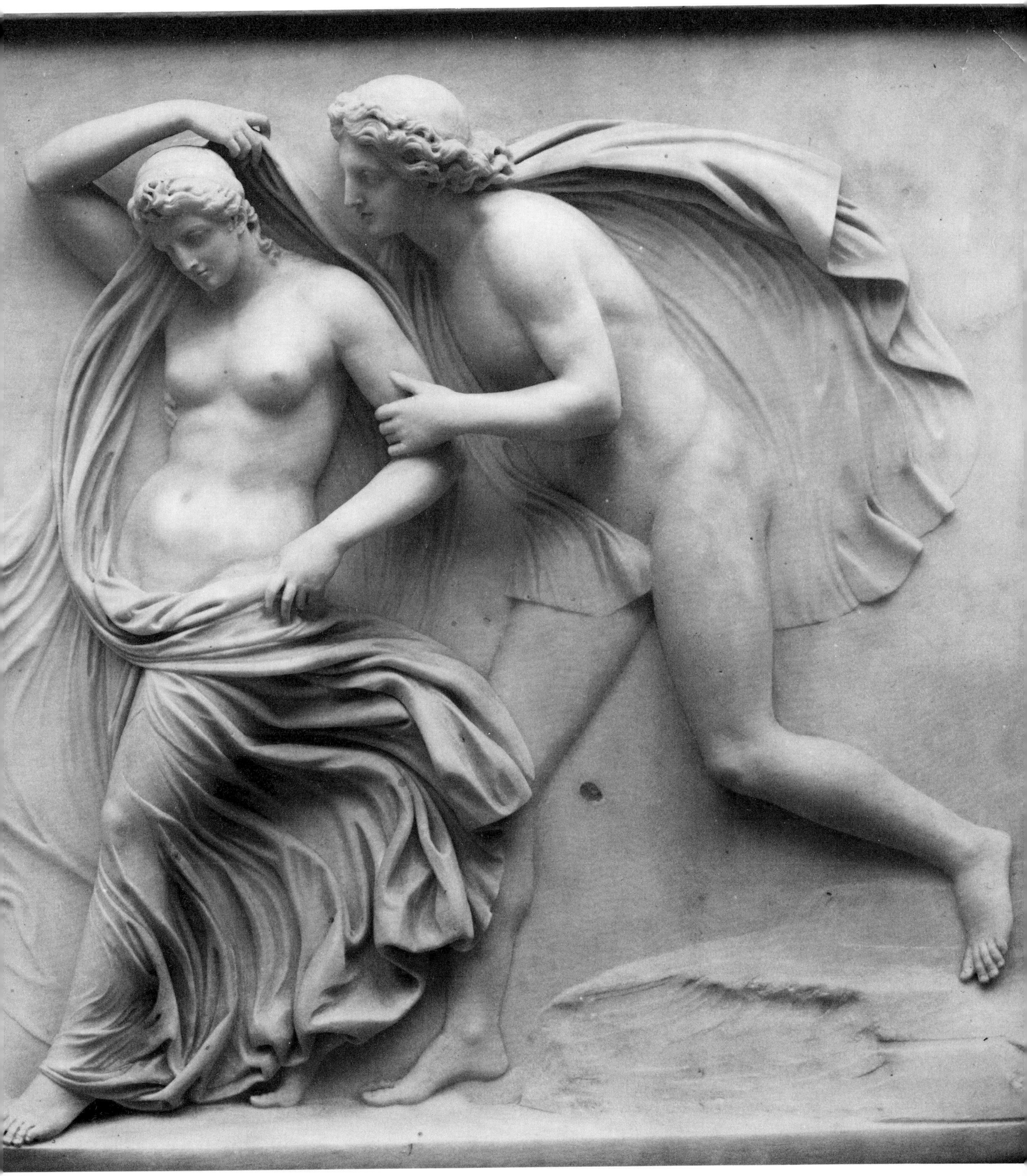

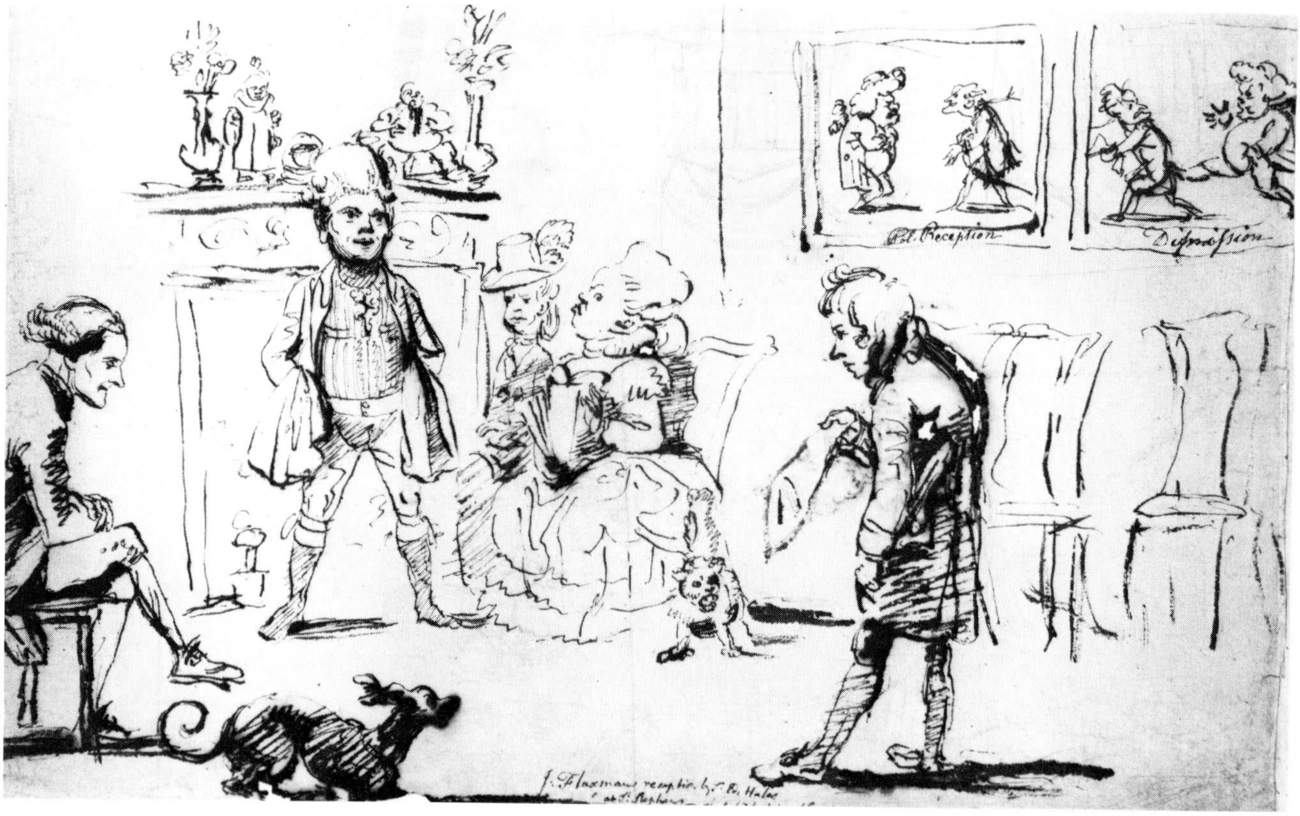

2 *Waiting to see Sir Edward Hales at St. Stephen's*, c. 1775. Pen and ink, 30·5 × 51·4 cms.

CHAPTER I

Early Career

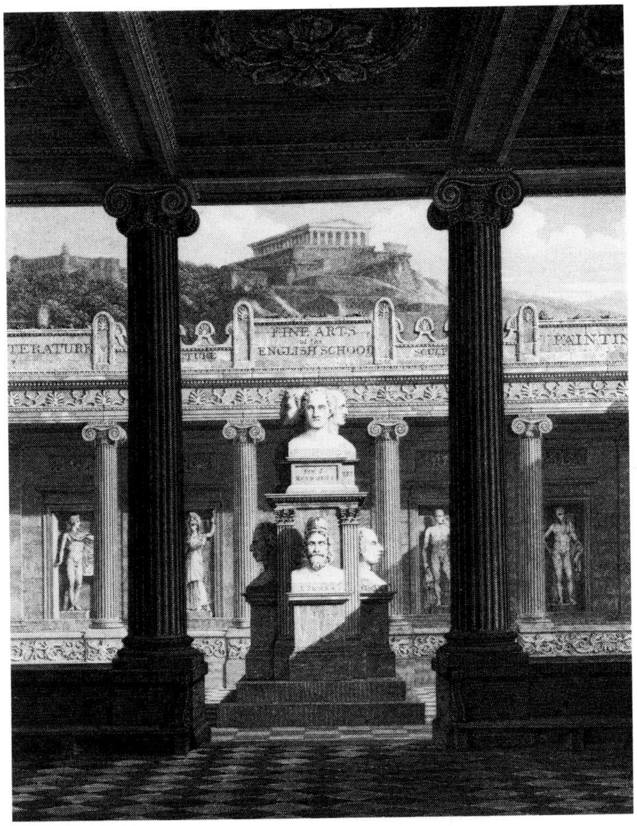

1 Joseph Gandy: *Design for a National Institution*. Frontispiece to John Britton, *Fine Arts of the English School*, Volume I, 1812, detail.

Throughout the nineteenth century, John Flaxman was often amongst the famous artists chosen for commemoration in public buildings and elsewhere, such as the new Houses of Parliament, the 1851 Exhibition commemorative shield and the Albert Memorial. Flaxman's name also appeared in more personal catalogues, such as the Pre-Raphaelites' list of Immortals. When a novelist wished to describe a particularly fine work, as Disraeli did on one occasion, he might say that it was 'hardly inferior to Flaxman'. But by the end of the century, Yeats was able to write that 'Flaxman even at his best has not yet touched me very deeply', and after the turn of the century his name was to become less prominent, although his illustrations to Homer continued to be used in popular editions, and some of his Wedgwood designs were still in production.[1]

Already by 1812 Flaxman was being canonised in one of Joseph Gandy's typically visionary designs, contributed as a frontispiece to the first volume of John Britton's *Fine Arts of the English School* (Plate 1). It shows an imaginary 'National Institution appropriated to the Fine Arts, the Sciences and Literature of the Kingdom', with a monument in the centre of a classical courtyard, on which are grouped together busts of such artists as Inigo Jones, Sir Joshua Reynolds, Benjamin West (the current President of the Royal Academy) and John Flaxman.

1 Character, Training and Friends

Most contemporary accounts of Flaxman describe a sympathetic and respected personality. He was enthusiastic, generous, kind and hard-working.[2] He always rose early, usually at six, breakfasted at eight, and was generally in his studio before any of his assistants. He spent the rest of the morning either drawing or modelling, and then dined at one or two o'clock.[3] He then started work again in the studio, sometimes having passages read to him, including the Greek Testament, by a pupil.[4] After his afternoon work, he would either walk through the fields in the direction of Hampstead[5] and perhaps visit his friend George Romney, or would have tea in his own house with his wife, sisters and friends. When the pressure of finishing commissions became great, he would devote part of the evening to again working in his studio. Supper would be at nine, and on winter evenings he sometimes composed light and amusing stories and verses, illustrated by sketches.[6] He was a cheerful man and occasionally drew caricatures (Plate 2), and was fond of company. More than one contemporary records that he sang beautifully, contributing much to

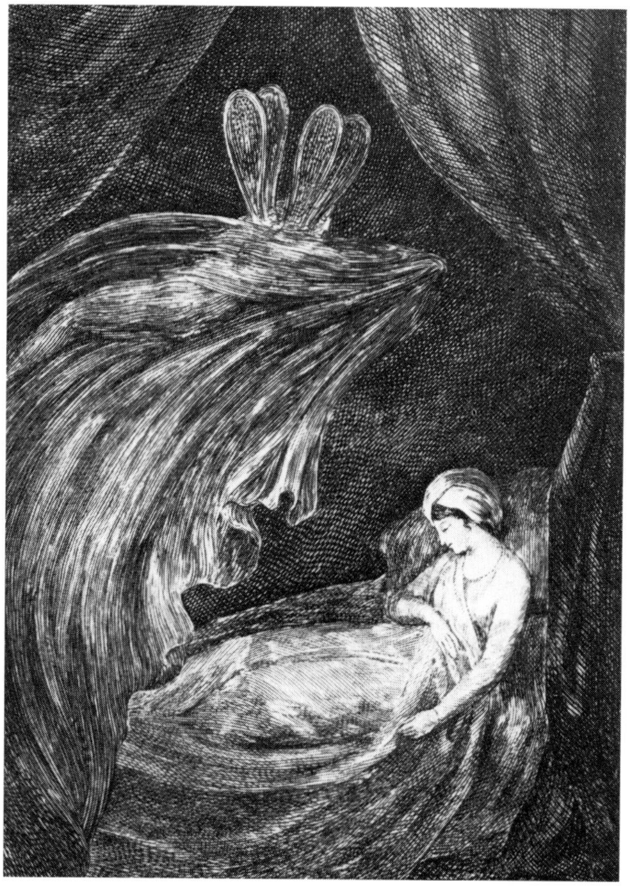

3 Mary Ann Flaxman: *The figure of Quiet visits the sleeping maid.* Illustration to William Hayley, *The Triumphs of Temper*, 1803, engraved by William Blake.

convivial evenings, with the music of Mozart, Cimarosa and other eighteenth-century composers.[7]

His serene temper, and what some contemporaries described as a 'purity of mind'[8], derived to some extent from his religious beliefs as a practising Christian of the Protestant faith, who became interested in Swedenborgianism.[9] He is often described as pious, contemplative and modest. He wrote with some passion once in a letter that the present 'age of affectation prefers glare and tinsel to beauty and feeling',[10] and he would retire into his work in a way that some contemporaries remarked as 'unworldly'.[11] He told one correspondent that he 'always avoided popularity and retreated from the notice of the world',[12] a belief which is reflected not only in the many hours he spent at his work, but also in the consideration he gave to those immediately around him, and at the Royal Academy. By the time he was successful, Flaxman employed ten to fifteen men, and treated them to dinners and jaunts out into the country, and always looked after them when ill, continuing to pay their wages in addition to the doctor's bills.[13] He kept neither carriage nor servant in livery, so that at Academy dinners Flaxman's marble polisher (Plate 261) would stand behind his master's chair dressed in his Sunday clothes.[14] Flaxman was just as thoughtful about students, showing unbounded kindness to them, and devoting much time to giving them advice. At the Academy School he treated students with the 'affection of a parent', as Sir Thomas Lawrence put it in his obituary comments,[15] and scrupulously performed his duties there as Professor of Sculpture.

Flaxman was never financially greedy, with a result that he died leaving far less money than one might expect of a successful sculptor. His prices for commissions were reasonable without being exorbitant, and he apparently even returned part of the money for a monument if he thought the price in the end too high.[16] When one of the friends of the poet Cowper died leaving his family in straitened circumstances, Flaxman said any money should be spent on the widow and orphans rather than on a monument.[17] When the actor John Kemble retired from the stage, Flaxman designed the silvergilt cup which was presented to him, free of charge as his contribution to the subscription.[18] Traders liked doing business with Flaxman as he did not haggle over prices, whether it was the charge for hiring a hackney-coach, or the cost of a block of marble.[19] His benevolence extended to supporting charities, and giving alms to the poor in the street.[20]

Such was the man who by the age of ten had overcome a boyhood physical weakness, which had meant that he could not play with other children of his own age. He had been a solitary child, grave but nonetheless cheerful. Physically however he was never able to remedy the curvature of his spine, which had been slightly deformed from birth, leaving him short and hump-backed: 'so unhappily formed by nature', as his friend the architect C. R. Cockerell described him.[21] The contrast between his physical appearance and his intelligent and benign face made it seem when he laughed 'as if he were mocking himself', recorded another friend later in life, Henry Crabb Robinson.[22]

Throughout most of his career, Flaxman had the sympathetic support of his wife, Nancy Denman, the daughter of a Whitechapel gunstock-maker. They married in 1782, after a largely secret courtship because her father had objected to her marrying a young man with such an uncertain future.[23] They lived together in what seems to have been a state of domestic happiness, until her death in 1820. The marriage was childless, but

Flaxman was very fond of children and often drew them. His household included Flaxman's sister Mary Ann and his sister-in-law Maria Denman, both of whom were amateur artists (Plate 3). Flaxman also employed in the studio his brother-in-law Thomas Denman, a modest sculptor in his own right, who was to complete some of the unfinished marbles in the studio after Flaxman's death. Mrs. Flaxman was an ideal wife for the sculptor, cheerful and intelligent, enjoying the same friends, reading the same books, and collecting drawings and sketches.[24] Contemporaries agreed that they were perfectly matched.

After their marriage, the young Flaxmans lived in Wardour Street, Soho, the part of London favoured by artists throughout the century. Reynolds lived on the southern edge of Soho in Leicester Fields, and other artists in the locality included William Blake, Thomas Stothard, Benjamin West, James Tassie, and the elder John Bacon. Wedgwood had his first London showroom there. The Flaxmans lived in a small house which they made neat and elegant, and which had an 'air of devout quiet', as one early biographer put it.[25] After their visit abroad, the Flaxmans set up house on a larger, but still modest, scale a little further north in a recently built area, off Fitzroy Square, in Buckingham Street (now Grafton Way). This house and studio Flaxman retained up to his death, in a part of London that was to supersede Soho in popularity with artists.

Flaxman's earliest acquaintance with art was in his father's shop, which acted as his boyhood academy, as he received no additional training until he went to the Academy School.[26] John Flaxman senior (Plate 4) made plaster casts and models, often of antique subjects, and in his original pieces worked in a late Baroque style that showed the influence of Roubiliac and Scheemakers (Plate 5).[27] He was living in York at the time his second son John, the future sculptor, was born in 1755, but six months later went south to London. There he opened premises in New Street, Covent Garden, and subsequently moved into a larger shop in the Strand, where he continued to trade until after the turn of the century.[28] The father's customers included such sculptors as Roubiliac and Scheemakers, and the industrialists Josiah Wedgwood and Matthew Boulton, clients that reflect the high esteem in which the elder Flaxman's work was held. It was whilst he was in his father's shop that Flaxman made some of his earliest friendships.

In 1769 he became a student at the newly established Royal Academy School, at the age of fourteen, where he found himself among the first year enrolments together with equally young students such as the painter William Hamilton and the future diarist Joseph Farington, working alongside more experienced artists such as Thomas Banks, the elder John Bacon, James Tassie and Biagio Rebecca.[29] Flaxman showed great promise as a student, winning one of the Academy's silver medals in his first year, in 1769.

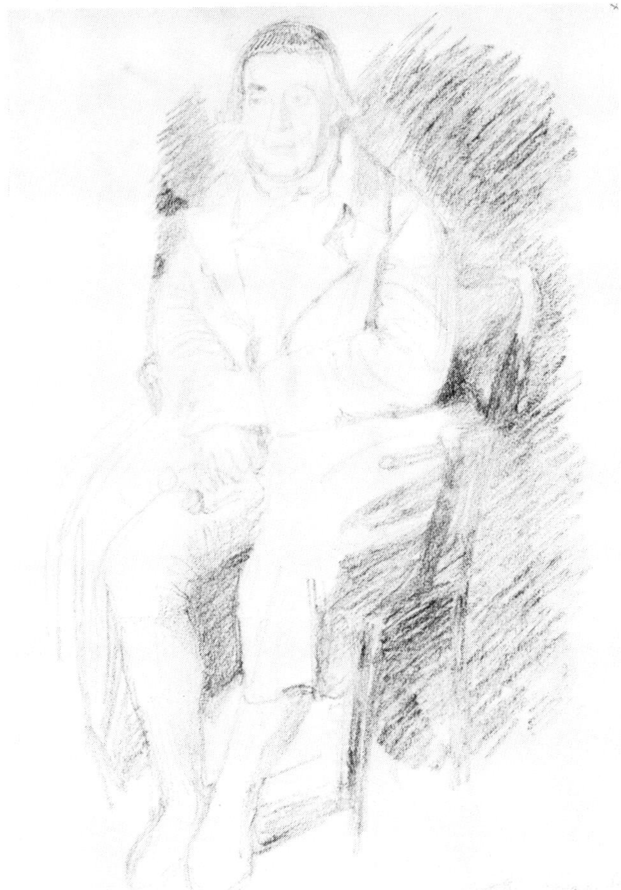

4 *John Flaxman the elder.*
Pencil, 21·8 × 18 cms.

In the Academy School students received general instruction in drawing and modelling from antique casts and life models, but Flaxman was too young to be allowed to draw from the female nude. He would also have had access to the Academy's library, and heard lectures given by the Professors of Painting (Edward Penny), Architecture (Thomas Sandby), Perspective (Samuel Wale) and Anatomy (Dr. William Hunter). There was no Professor of Sculpture until 1810, when Flaxman himself was appointed, and there was also in the eighteenth century no specialised training in either painting or sculpture. Hunter's lectures and demonstrations were popular with the students, and his stress on the 'superiority of nature over art' which 'seems to shine forth in almost everything',[30] must have led to lively discussions amongst the students in Flaxman's day as Hunter's views clashed with those of the President. Hunter was telling the students categorically, in 1770, that 'in the fine arts the more precise the imitation of nature is, . . . the more striking I should suppose the effect will be; and therefore the more pleasing'. But Reynolds believed, as he told his Academy students later that year, that 'nature herself is not to be too closely copied', she must be idealised. The artist must remember that it is the mind, not the eye, that he is addressing. The student, said Reynolds, should make 'a careful study of the works of the ancient sculptors; who, being indefatigable in the school of nature, have left models of that perfect form behind them, which an artist would prefer as supremely beautiful'. The young Flaxman would also have heard Reynolds's advice the following year when he stressed the importance of 'mental labour', that is the use of literature as a source of inspiration: Greek and Roman myths and history, as well as the Bible. Reynolds praised Raphael, Michelangelo and Correggio in terms that are to be reflected later in Flaxman's own writings on art, especially the stress on the 'simplicity' of Raphael, and the grace, elegance and 'simplicity' of Correggio.

One of Flaxman's early self-portraits, a meticulous drawing executed a few years after he had finished his studies at the Academy School, sums up the teaching he had received there (Plate 6). It shows him with one hand on a skull as a reminder of nature, an elbow on a pile of books representing 'mental labour', a small plaster of the *Apollo Belvedere* as a record of classical antiquity, and a pilaster decorated with acanthus scrolls suggesting his interest in ornament.

A few early patrons and friends provided the necessary encouragement that any young artist needs. He first met one of his lifelong friends, the painter George Romney, in his father's shop, soon after Romney had returned from Italy in 1775. They shared similar interests, including not only classical antiquity, but also medieval art. The two artists, together with the poet William Hayley, spent the whole of one afternoon and evening together in the summer of 1783, looking at the sculptures in Westminster Abbey.[31] Flaxman always retained a great admiration for the older artist, who was just over twenty years his senior, from the time he had 'first come to see my father's casts. I was a little boy, and as he frequently found me employed in modelling, he would stand by me a long while together giving me encouragement in a manner so obliging and affectionate that he won my heart, and confirmed my determination in the pursuit of sculpture', as Flaxman wrote shortly after the painter's death in 1802.[32] In the same letter Flaxman also reminisced that Romney had offered him £200 when he was setting out for Italy, to help him with expenses. He had been very much encouraged in his desire to go to Italy by the older artist, who knew from his own experience how invaluable a stay in Italy could be.[33] Much later in life he was able to tell Romney's son that he remembered the painter's 'original and striking conversation', and felt that he was still—as late as 1821—benefiting from his friendship and suggestions.[34]

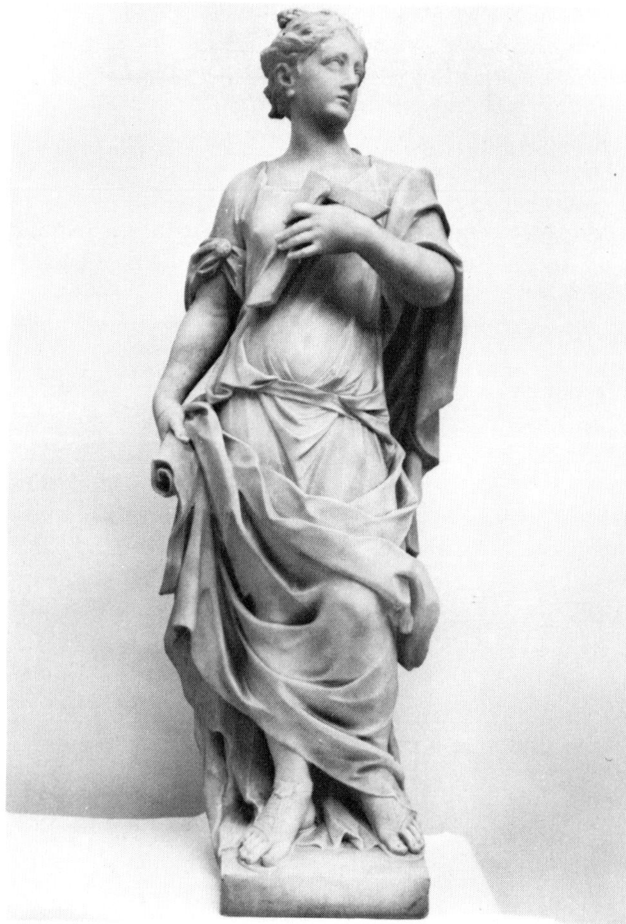

5 John Flaxman the elder: *Architecture*. Marble, 117·7 cms. high.

The other artists who were Flaxman's chief companions in his youth were of his own age, William Blake and Thomas Stothard. It was Stothard who introduced Blake and Flaxman to each other. All three artists were to remain lifelong friends.[35] Flaxman met Stothard about the middle of the 70's as a result of seeing some of his early designs published in the *Novelist's Magazine* and asking his father if he could meet the artist.[36] They seem to have remained on good terms throughout their friendship. They shared common interests in classical and medieval art, sometimes chose similar subjects, and evolved styles of drawing which are at times close (so much so that Stothard's drawings have sometimes been erroneously catalogued as the work of Flaxman). It is impossible to say whether they influenced each other; it is more likely that their similarities evolved from the use of the same sources in the past and from the same contemporary attitudes to nature and sentiment. Both artists were also very varied in their activities, designing for the decorative and applied arts as well as doing book illustrations, in addition to their paintings or sculptures. They also both eventually held posts at the Royal Academy, where Stothard was to be the Librarian (from 1814 onwards). Mrs. Flaxman found Stothard's

6 *Self-Portrait with skull*, c. 1778. Pen and ink and watercolour, 18 × 18·5 cms.

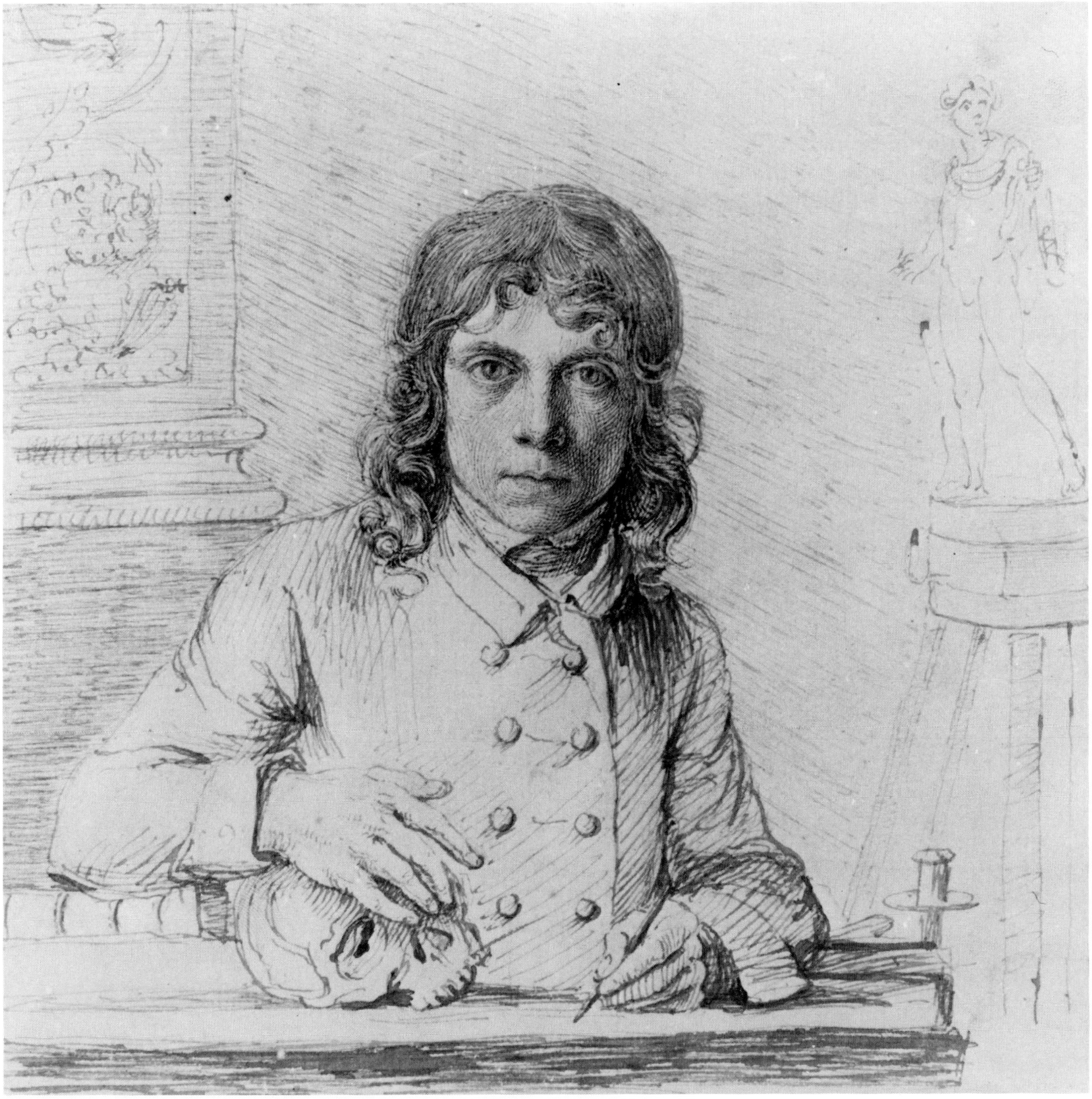

art particularly sympathetic, building up a large collection of his drawings and engravings.[37]

More is known about the relationship between Flaxman and his other friend, the temperamental Blake. The two artists seem to have met for the first time about 1779,[38] and maintained a friendship which sometimes on Blake's side could be cool and even hostile. In one of his more irascible moments later in life Blake claimed in his *Public Address* (about 1810) that he had designed one of Flaxman's first monuments for him: a fascinating claim but it cannot be substantiated. Flaxman admired Blake's art, later defending it against adverse criticism, and commissioned work from him. Even whilst in Italy, Flaxman was able to make a hasty sketch which he labelled 'from memory of three drawings of Blake'.[39] Such a drawing, executed in the midst of classical antiquity and other art, might suggest a strong influence of Blake on Flaxman, but this does not seem to be the case, as Blake did not noticeably provide any of Flaxman's imagery; the resemblances between their two styles derive from shared interests. Where an influence can be detected it is usually Flaxman on Blake, especially as a result of the Homer and Aeschylus illustrations in the 1790's.[40] A more likely area of early, generalised influence of Blake on his friend can be found in their mutual interest in medieval art, to which Blake may have introduced Flaxman (a point to be discussed later in this chapter).

Flaxman was willing to promote Blake's cause from as early as 1783, when he may have helped with the costs of printing the *Poetical Sketches*.[41] Flaxman sent a copy to Hayley a year after it was printed saying that 'they are the writings of a Mr. Blake you have heard me mention', and reporting in the same letter that Romney 'thinks his historical drawings rank with those of Michelangelo'.[42] At the same period, Flaxman was encouraging acquaintances to commission works from Blake, including John Hawkins from Cornwall, who was so delighted with what he saw that he tried to raise funds to send Blake to Italy, an ambitious but abortive scheme.[43] After his return from Italy, Flaxman himself was to order work from Blake. He commissioned, for example, a series of watercolour illustrations to Gray's *Poems* to give to Mrs. Flaxman as a birthday present in 1797; the engraving of additional plates for the edition of Homer in 1805; and later the engraving of his plates to Hesiod. Flaxman subscribed for a copy of Blake's illustrations to Blair's *Grave*, and owned the preliminary drawing for the late *Arlington Court Pictures* as well as a copy of the *Book of Job*.[44] Some of Blake's letters, especially in the years around 1800, show that he appreciated Flaxman's efforts on his behalf, particularly

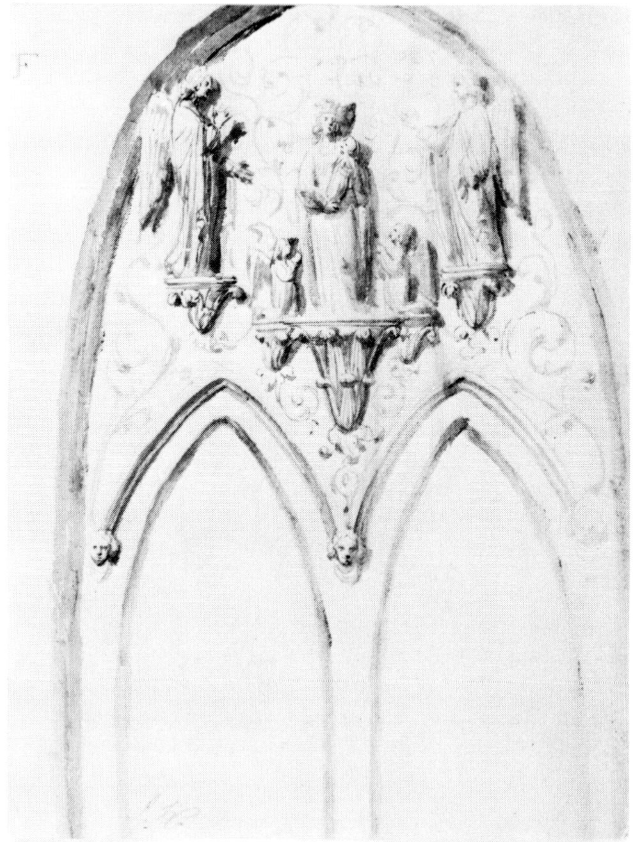

7 *Virgin, Child and Angels above a Gothic Arch.* Wash and pencil, 19·1 × 17·5 cms.

when Hayley took Blake under his wing as a result of Flaxman introducing them to each other. Flaxman was thanked profusely in Blake's correspondence, who even wrote ecstatically, 'I bless thee, O Father of Heaven and Earth, that I ever saw Flaxman's face'.[45]

However, Flaxman's encouragement of Blake, both directly and indirectly, could not hide the fact that as far as Blake's inner world of the imagination was concerned, Flaxman remained, like Hayley, an outside observer, sympathetic but not comprehending. Even in the same letter as the one in which he sent Hayley a copy of the *Poetical Sketches*, Flaxman said rather condescendingly of Blake that 'his education will plead sufficient excuse to your liberal mind for the defects of his work'. If one accepts the suggestion that Flaxman is Steelyard the Lawgiver in Blake's satire *An Island in the Moon*,[46] Blake realised that Flaxman was not capable of understanding him fully. Later, after the turn of the century, Flaxman is pilloried in some of Blake's epigrams, on one occasion together with Stothard: 'I found them blind: I taught them how to see; / And now they know neither themselves nor me'.

Apart from painters and sculptors, Flaxman's most important early friends and patrons were the Reverend and Mrs. Mathew, William Hayley and Josiah Wedgwood. Flaxman first met the Mathews in about 1769, when Anthony Stephen Mathew came into the Strand shop. He was then minister of Percy Chapel in Charlotte Street, and he introduced the young Flaxman to his blue-stocking wife, Harriet. She conducted a modest salon at their house in Rathbone Place, where their circle of friends included Stothard and, briefly, Blake who may have had this salon in mind when writing *An Island in the Moon*, in which Mrs. Sicknacker may be Mrs. Mathew. Blake broke off his relations with Mrs. Mathew's salon, but Flaxman retained and valued this friendship until after the turn of the century, when the aged Reverend Mathew pleasantly observed to Flaxman (in 1806) that 'while making monuments for others, he was raising his own'.[47] Whilst in Italy Flaxman arranged for Angelica Kauffmann to paint for the Mathews a pair of ovals of *Modesty* and *Vanity*, as well as two larger paintings of classical subjects.[48] In one of his letters from Rome Flaxman described Mrs. Mathew as 'my honoured friend, to whom I owe great obligations' referring to unspecified 'benefits I have received by her means'.[49] The obligations would certainly have included Mrs. Mathew's support and encouragement when Flaxman was in his teens, and her shepherding of John Flaxman and Nancy Denman to a happy marriage.[50] When a youth he had often spent evenings at their house, listening to Mrs. Mathew read Homer and Virgil, and discussing sculpture and poetry. She had also encouraged him to learn Latin and Greek. There is ample evidence amongst Flaxman's later writings and inscriptions on his drawings, including some of the preliminary ones to Homer executed whilst in Italy, that Flaxman was conversant with the classical languages, and his knowledge of Greek could well have started as a result of Mrs. Mathew's evenings.

Flaxman's earliest drawings of Homeric subjects seem to have been executed during his visits to the Mathews. They inspired Jeremiah Crutchley, a member of Parliament and friend of Henry Thrale, to give Flaxman his first commission for six black chalk drawings of Homeric and other classical subjects.[51] Portrait drawings by Flaxman of the Mathew family survive as examples of their active encouragement of his art. There is unfortunately no record left—except perhaps one drawing which might be connected with the scheme (Plate 7)—to show us what Flaxman's decoration of the Mathews' library looked like. It was executed in a Gothic manner, with figures in niches, whilst another artist painted the windows in imitation of stained glass.[52]

William Hayley was a friend of Romney as well as Flaxman, and their association is perpetuated in Romney's lifesize portrait of the poet (Plate 8). Flaxman encouraged Hayley to give the commission to Romney,[53] which may have suggested the multiple portrait. It not only depicts the poet, but also the sculptor modelling a bust of him (now lost), the painter himself looking out quizzically at the left, as well as Hayley's son Thomas aged fifteen, a pupil of Flaxman who was to die as a result of illness only five years later. As Flaxman is seen standing, the picture shows clearly his short stature and hump back. Romney had in-

8 George Romney: *Flaxman modelling the Bust of William Hayley, watched by Thomas Hayley and the Painter*, begun 1795. Oil on Canvas, 226 × 144·75 cms.

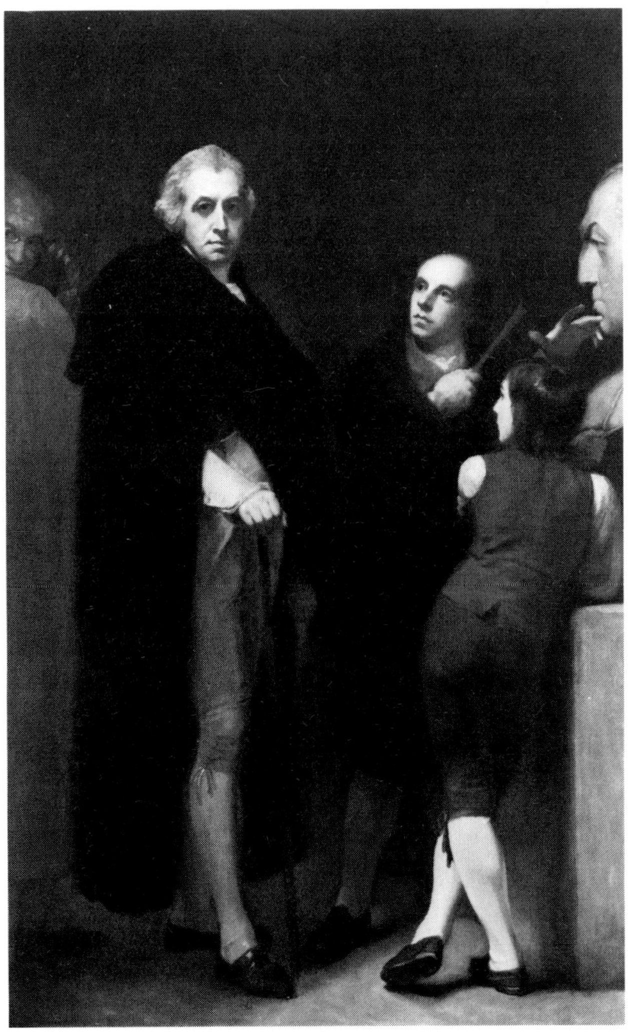

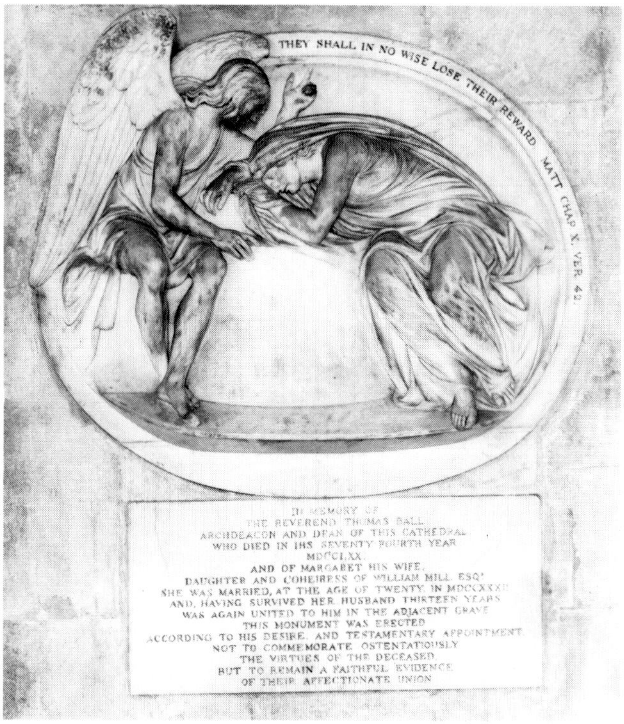

9 *Reverend Thomas and Mrs. Ball: monument*, 1784–86. Chichester Cathedral.

troduced the sculptor to Hayley in 1783,[54] an association that was to last until Hayley's death in 1820. The introduction had probably been made because the poet wanted to commission a monument in nearby Chichester Cathedral to his wife's parents, the Reverend and Mrs. Thomas Ball (Plate 9).[55] The *Ball* monument established an important link between Flaxman and Chichester Cathedral that was to lead to several more monuments there, including one to the poet William Collins, a commission which Hayley obtained for Flaxman (see Plate 75).[56]

During the 80's the Flaxmans spent several holidays at Hayley's small country-house in Sussex, Eartham, which he enlarged with a new library, to which Flaxman in 1784 contributed a chimney-piece and Romney some decorative paintings.[57] Hayley had a boundless, but uncritical, enthusiasm for Flaxman's work, and the long poem accompanied by extensive footnotes published in 1800 with the title *An Essay on Sculpture* was dedicated to Flaxman, and written with him in mind. It was conceived as a pair to Hayley's earlier *Essay on Painting* (1781) which had been dedicated to Romney, and had been similarly didactic. Amongst the notes at the end of the *Essay on Sculpture* Hayley printed a sonnet he had sent to Flaxman before he visited Italy, in which he expressed the hope that as England had produced a Milton to match the glory of Homer, she could now produce in Flaxman a match for Phidias: 'Flaxman! young artist of an ardent mind! / Whose just ambition, by the Greeks inspir'd, / Thirsts for pure Attic glory'. Such heady praise, typical of the more flowery writing of the period, would not have been taken by Flaxman too literally.

2 Classical and Gothic: Sculptures and Drawings

Flaxman had started to exhibit as early as 1767 at the Free Society of Artists, at the age of twelve, when he showed plasters of *Hercules* and *Omphale*. In the year after he became a student, he began exhibiting at the Royal Academy's own annual exhibition with two portraits and a figure of *Neptune* in 1770. He was to continue to exhibit there regularly most years for the rest of his career, the longest gap being the period he spent in Italy. Nearly all these early works, executed in terracotta, plaster or wax, and shown in London exhibitions before Flaxman set off for the Continent in 1787, have disappeared. The titles of the classical pieces show a young artist working in a well-established tradition, choosing the subjects of most of his exhibited works from ancient Roman history and literature. Titles of these early sculptures include *The Death of Julius Caesar* (1768, and again in 1781),[58] *Pompey after his defeat at Pharsalia* (1777) and *Acis and Galatea* (1781). Flaxman's early sculptures were both freestanding and in relief, and he was presumably refering to these two aspects of his work when he included in the inscriptions around his self-portrait medallion of 1778 the words 'Artifex statuarum et cœlator' (Victoria and Albert Museum).[59] Flaxman also used Greek sources, but only in drawings, as when executing the series commissioned privately for Jeremiah Crutchley mentioned earlier. Flaxman was therefore aware as a young artist of both the older use of Roman sources and the newer one of Greek literature, that had already become important in the early development of Neoclassicism in the 60's, in the canvases of Gavin Hamilton.

Flaxman often exhibited portraits amongst his early works, an aspect of his sculpture that was to play only a minor role later in his career. The enchanting wax medallion of his sister Mary Ann, holding a doll, and knocking over a mug underneath her chair (Plate 10), was probably exhibited at the Royal Academy in 1772 as *Figure of a child*. The delightfully informal pose shows Flaxman as a master of natural observation, an important characteristic of his work which sometimes later

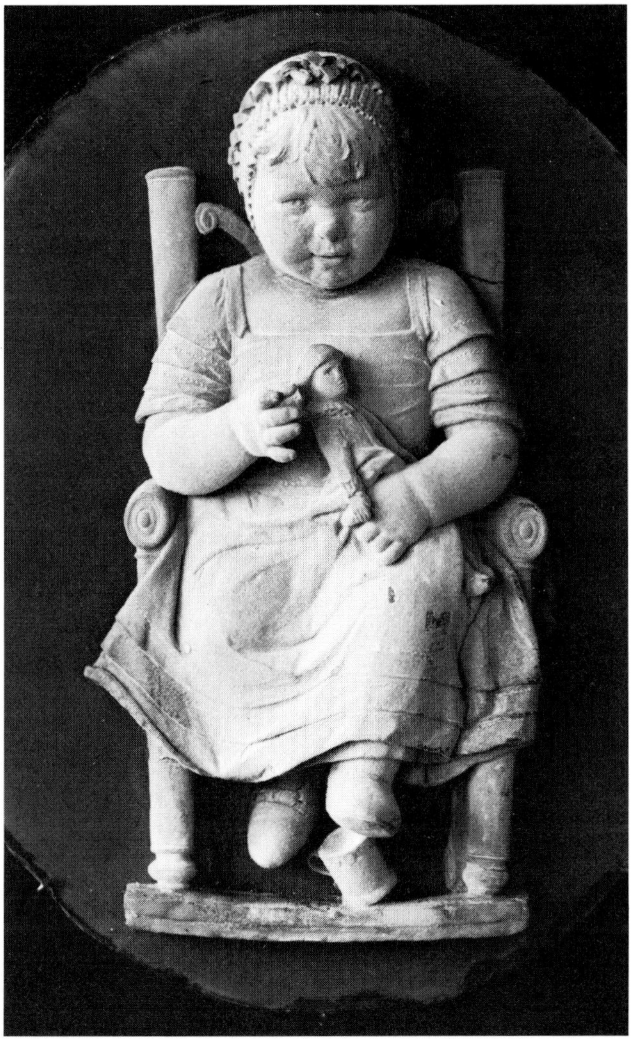

10 *Flaxman's Sister, Mary Ann, holding a Doll*, c. 1772. Wax, 15·3 × 8·3cms.

becomes overlaid with a classical rhetoric, but which is nevertheless evident in many of his sculptures, as well as in his drawings of genre scenes and of children.

Before going to Italy, Flaxman received few commissions for monuments, so he was particularly excited in the summer of 1783 when he was able to write to his young wife that 'I have nothing but good news to send' because clients had just been into his studio to order a monument and had paid £35 on account (probably for the *Ball* monument), and another client had called wanting a small monument for Westminster Abbey. But Flaxman was not so hard up that he felt obliged to take on this latter commission since he regarded it as 'a Scotch job': a cheap, economical commission. Barely a week later he was writing again to his wife to say that yet another monument had been ordered, and a further order was likely.[60] Two to three commissions in one year would have made 1783 unusually fruitful for Flaxman's studio, because, unless there remain large numbers of unidentified tombs in churches throughout Britain, his entire output in the 1780's seems to have totalled less than about a dozen monuments, which would account for the enthusiasm of his letters in the summer of 1783. One monument of 1784 to *Jean-Jacques Rousseau*, erected on a private estate, seems unfortunately to have disappeared.[61]

The design of the few identifiable tombs shows a lack of confidence in their style, using latter-day Baroque elements, newer Neoclassical ones, as well as unexpected Gothic ideas, and also straightforward naturalism and contemporary sentiment. For Flaxman a clearer sense of direction was only to be attained during his visit to Italy. He could give the impression that he was dogmatic about his beliefs on art in conversation, but these strong convictions were not necessarily carried over into his art. At the beginning of the year that Flaxman was to set out for Rome, one of his friends, Dr. Benjamin Bates (who was to accompany the Flaxmans on their journey) recorded in a letter that 'according to the text of Flaxmanus', the sculptor 'seems to assert that straight lines, simplicity and antiquity are the constituent principles of beauty'. This strict dogma, of the most puritanical Neoclassical school, was fortunately not to dominate Flaxman's own style, but as a guiding principle could have helped him more through the earlier 80's.[62]

Tombs by his father's late clients Roubiliac and Scheemakers helped to influence the style of some of the young sculptor's earliest commissions, such as his monument to *Barbara Bourchier* who died in 1784 (Plate 11). Like some of his contemporaries in the 70's and 80's, including Joseph Nollekens, Flaxman turned to a well-tried formula. He has modified a Baroque angel on a cloud, shown with an open book inscribed with an appropriate text. These words could easily be altered from one commission to the next, and were one of the few changes Flaxman made to the design when he used it for several different clients. Even after he came back from Italy he reused the composition, when one would have expected him to be reluctant to do so.[63] His most elaborate attempt to rework Baroque angels, with only a limited Neoclassical restraint, can be seen in his monument to Ann Russell and her only son (Plate 12). The mother had died in 1780, and is shown on the monument receiving the body of her child who had died the following year. By retaining a Baroque formula but trying to eliminate Baroque space, Flaxman created a confused composition in the right half of

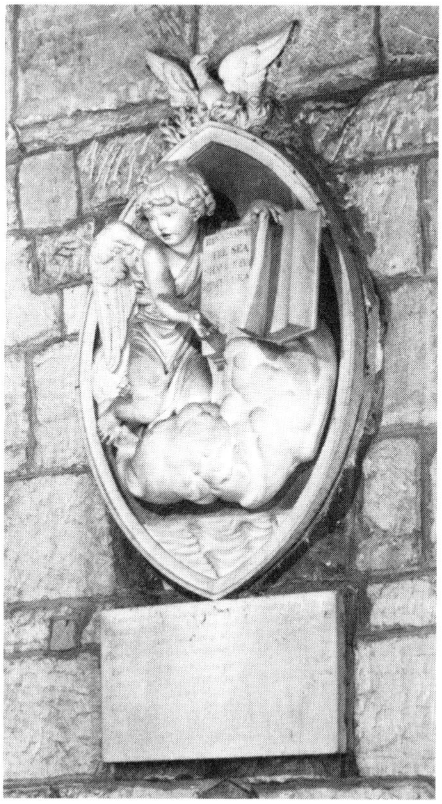

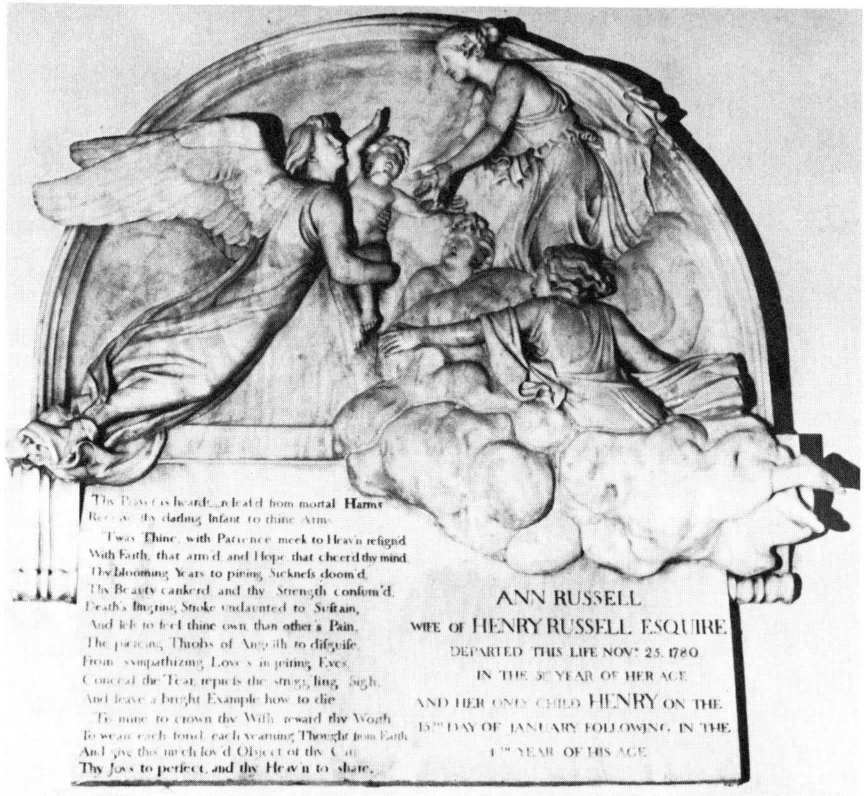

11 *(left) Barbara Bourchier: monument.* Died 1784. St. Mary, Newent, Gloucestershire.

12 *(right) Ann Russell and her son Henry: monument.* Died 1780–81. All Saints, Lydd, Kent.

the *Russell* monument. Some of the lessons he learnt on this commission however, were to be put into practice on his most ambitious early monument, to *Mrs. Sarah Morley*, in Gloucester Cathedral (Plates 13 and 14).

As medical conditions in late eighteenth-century India were primitive, and educational facilities unsatisfactory, Mrs. Morley had embarked whilst pregnant from Bombay with her young family to bring them home. After giving birth at sea she had died, in 1784, aged only twenty-nine. Her husband, who had stayed out in Bombay, paid for the erection of a handsome monument in the cathedral of her native county.[64] There is a clear allusion to her death at sea in the main relief, and also to her self-sacrifice for her children in the lefthand medallion showing a pelican.

In the composition Flaxman has retained a diluted Baroque style, but combined it with more dominant un-Baroque elements than he had used in the *Russell* monument. His combination of a number of disparate elements in the *Morley* design shows the variety of his interests before he set out on his Grand Tour, but he has failed to unite these elements into a harmonious composition. By selecting the theme of resurrection, Flaxman's monument is an unmistakably Christian one unlike many contemporary tombs, on which the symbolism is not specifically Christian. The angels above clouds, and the suggestion of transcendentalism, are clearly Baroque in origin, via Roubiliac. The draperies, clinging to reveal the underlying human form and fluttering outwards in exaggerated, linear movement, are classical in origin, deriving most directly from engravings of the Tower of the Winds in Athens (Plate 15), which Flaxman could easily have known in the first volume of Stuart and Revett's *Antiquities of Athens* (1762). On the other hand, the arch and clustered columns, as well as the angels' bodies and wings, are medieval in origin, the angels probably deriving from thirteenth-century ones in Westminster Abbey, in the transept spandrels. Yet another stylistic characteristic can be seen in the expression on the faces of the mother and the angels, which is unmistakably contemporary in its sentiment.

The stylistic muddle of the *Morley* monument however seems not to have worried contemporaries, if we accept Cunningham's later comments that capture the mood which Flaxman presumably intended to evoke: 'She perished with her child at sea, and is poetically represented called up by angels, with her babe, from the waves, and ascending into heaven; the effect is inexpressibly touching—it elevates the mind and not without tears. In this as in all his works, there is that serene simplicity which accords with holy thoughts'.[65]

Flaxman grew up at a time when the last vestiges of the weakened Baroque and debased Rococo styles were being replaced by a vigorous injection of renewed inspiration from classical antiquity. He belonged to a generation which was forming a new style, that of Neoclassicism. The name of the style however is only a late nineteenth-century invention,[66] and its implication of an unmitigated diet of Greek and Roman forms would not have been recognised in the eighteenth century. Like many of his contemporaries, Flaxman looked at the art of the past and present with eyes trained on classical imagery, but that imagery was not all-exclusive. He also loved the art of the Middle Ages, and he always asserted that his prime source of inspiration was nature itself.

At the same time as he was working on the *Morley* monument, Flaxman was sculpting the one to Hayley's parents-in-law, the Reverend Thomas Ball, a Dean of Chichester Cathedral who died in 1770, and his wife who had died more recently, in 1783 (Plate 9). The monument is a simple relief of an angel comforting a mourning female figure stretched across a sarcophagus, fulfilling as the inscription says, a wish for a commemoration that is not ostentatious. Within the oval panel Flaxman has blended the elements of the composition into a pleasing rhythmic curve. It is also, like the *Morley* monument, cut with a nice attention to detail and surface, which suggests that Flaxman may have executed all the carving himself. As a young sculptor who had still not established his reputation and income, he presumably had little studio assistance at this stage of his career. This suggestion is borne out by a letter he wrote to Hayley when the *Ball* monument was finished and ready for transportation, in which he apologised for the length of time he had taken (just over two years), hoping that Hayley would not only be

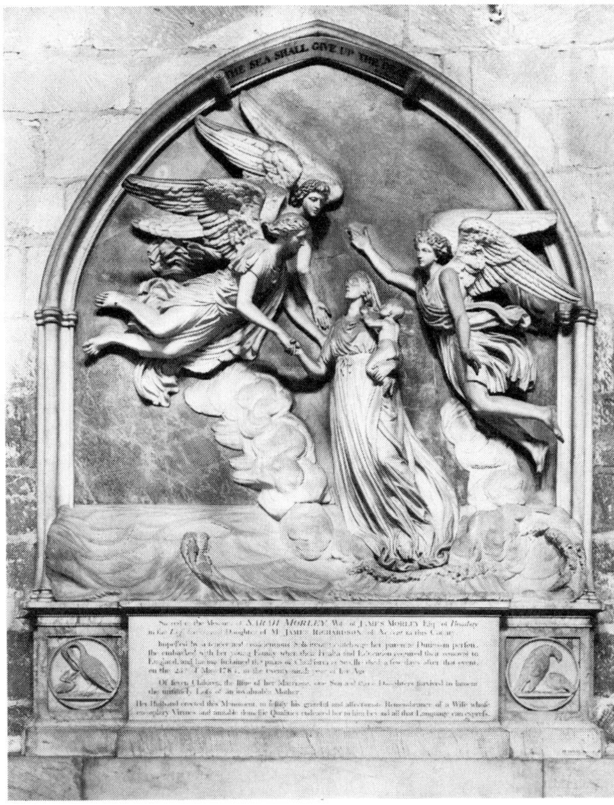

13 *Mrs. Sarah Morley: monument.* Died 1784. Gloucester Cathedral.

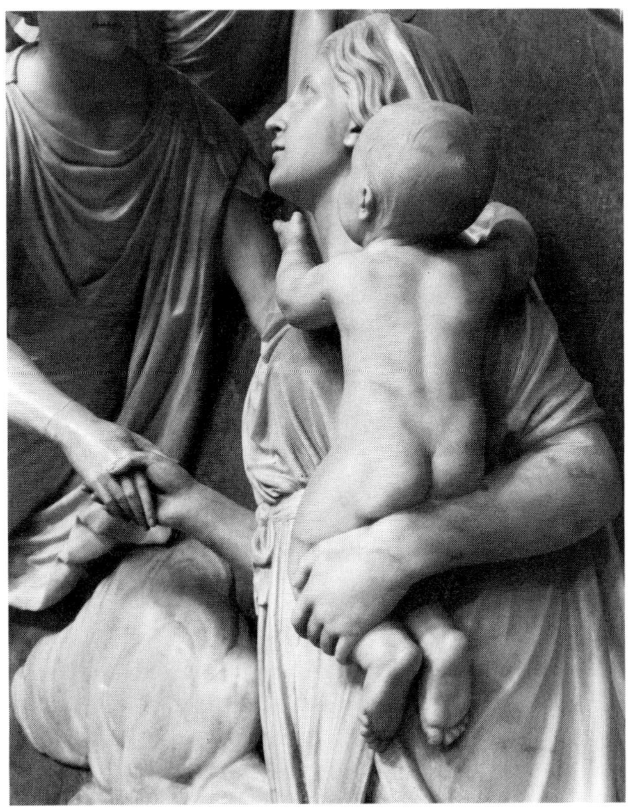

14 *Mrs. Sarah Morley: monument: detail of Mother and Child.*

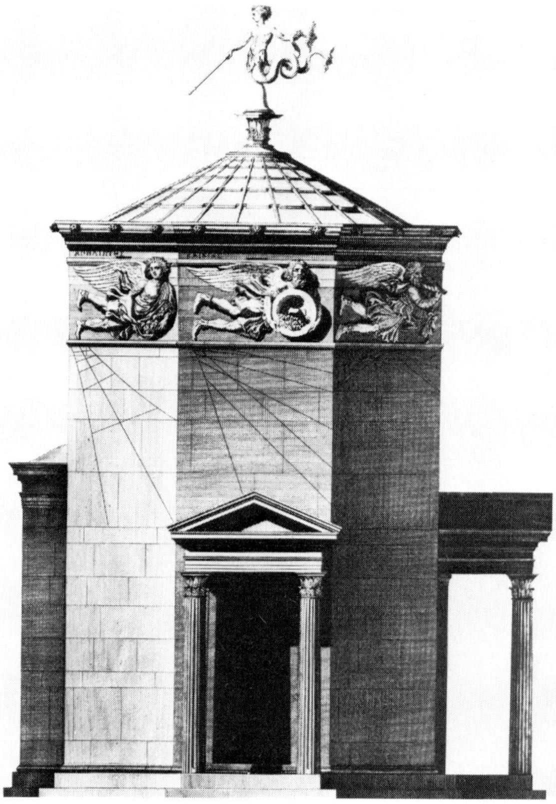

15 James Stuart and Nicholas Revett: *The Antiquities of Athens*. Volume I, 1762, *The Tower of the Winds, Athens.*

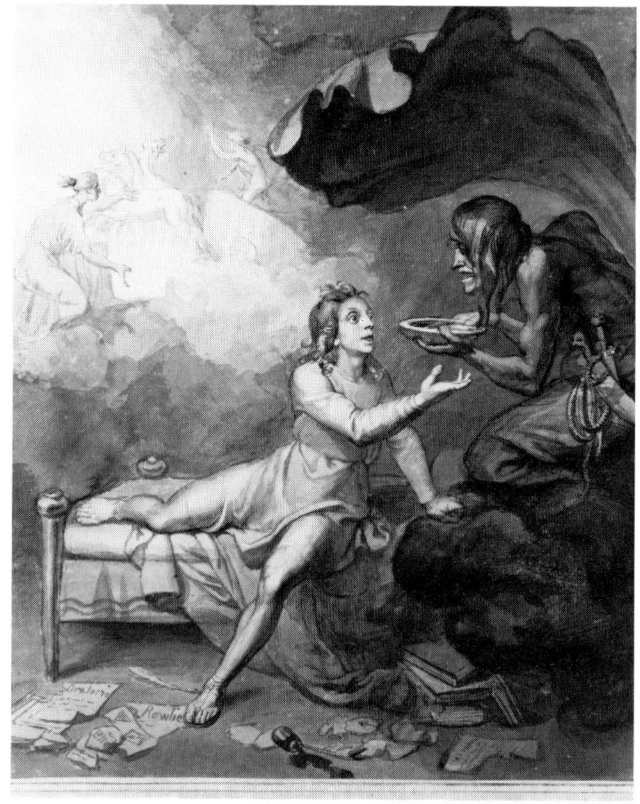

16 *Thomas Chatterton taking the Bowl of Poison from the Spirit of Despair*, c. 1780. Pen and ink and wash, 32·1 × 26·7 cms.

'satisfied with the execution' but also bear in mind 'the slow operation of cutting marble'.[67]

Flaxman's interest in the medieval period in Britain extended to reading books of medieval history and poetry, both genuine and spurious, and this wider concern for the Gothic Revival in literature is reflected in his work from 1780 onwards. In that year he exhibited at the Royal Academy what seems to have been his earliest example in this field, a sketch for a monument to the young writer whose pseudo-medieval poetry had played such a dominant part in the Gothic Revival, namely Thomas Chatterton.[68] The sketch is lost, but a group of drawings in the British Museum, including the carefully finished one reproduced in Plate 16, must have been produced about the same time, illustrating *Thomas Chatterton taking the Bowl of Poison from the Spirit of Despair*. The poet's suicide at the age of seventeen, here conceived by Flaxman in an exaggeratedly theatrical manner with all the horror of Burkian sublimity, is an appropriately Romantic image of an imaginative writer influential in the early development of Romanticism. Flaxman was also interested about this time in the equally popular and controversial poetry of Ossian, and drew a head of Fingal.[69] He gave a copy of another important Gothic Revival book to his future wife in 1780, Bishop Percy's *Reliques of Ancient English Poetry*, and in the accompanying letter praised its 'heroic virtue, the constant love and every noble quality which exalts the human soul, which is expressed in a way so simply natural'.[70]

Flaxman found other heroic and noble qualities in scenes from British medieval as well as pre-medieval history, and also in the Old Testament, which he illustrated in a series of carefully finished drawings in the early 1780's, most of them on an unusually large scale for him. These drawings seem not to have been commissioned, do not have a consistent theme or source, and relate to no known project. Most of the series is in the Fitzwilliam Museum, Cambridge. As a young man Flaxman executed a few paintings, and some of these wash drawings presumably give an indication of what his lost pictures may have looked like.[71] Stylistically these drawings belong to the school of history-painting of the 1770s and 1780s that included Benjamin West and Angelica Kauffmann, who were also interested in scenes from early English history as well as from classical antiquity. Amongst Flaxman's most immediate circle of friends Blake was working on a series of illustrations derived from English history from about 1779, at the same time as the two artists probably first met.

Blake was already very familiar with the medieval period as a result of his apprenticeship to the engraver James Basire, from 1772 onwards for seven years, during which time Blake worked for him on some of the plates for Richard Gough's *Sepulchral Monuments of Great Britain*, drawing Gothic monuments in Westminster Abbey and elsewhere. These lavishly illustrated folios were eventually to be published in 1786 and 1796, when they became one of the most important works devoted to medieval art published in the late eighteenth and early nineteenth centuries. The only comparable work of importance was the richly illustrated *Antiquities* of Francis Grose, which covered in several volumes England, Wales and Scotland and was published between 1773 and 1791. In addition, there were other sources of inspiration behind the medieval revival, including the Society of Artists in London which had been offering premiums for early English history subjects from the 1760's onwards. The popular and widely read *History of England* by David Hume had been published in 1763, superseding the *History* by the French historian Rapin (available in English from 1725–31). Earlier historical sources were also available, such as Bede and Geoffrey of Monmouth, and there had been several recent editions of the *Itinerary in England and Wales* by the sixteenth-century antiquarian John Leland, a work largely devoted to descriptions of medieval antiquities. Ballads could also be used as a source; Flaxman chose for instance the story of *Sir Cauline and the Fair Christabelle* from Percy's *Reliques*.[72]

Two of the Fitzwilliam Museum series illustrate *The Massacre of the Britons by Hengist's Party at Stonehenge* (Plate 18), one of which is dated 1783. The two drawings are conceived as a continuous frieze of naked, fighting men organised into a composition that shows a familiarity with Roman sarcophagi panels, both in the poses and in the shallow space. The drawings reproduced in Plates 19 and 20 belong to the same series, and are conceived on an identically large scale. The massiveness and heavy musculature of the seated men in the Old Testament drawing show an early admiration for Michelangelo, as well as providing a clear indication that the young Flaxman believed (as did Shaftesbury and others in English writing) that art had a moral purpose, choosing on this occasion a story of righteousness. The monumental simplicity of the kneeling woman is to be echoed in later works by Flaxman.[73] The other drawing reproduced here, of *Saint Ethelburga*, is unusual amongst Flaxman's illustrations because it is set in a landscape, which he rarely used outside his Dante plates of a few years later. The figures are walking in a frieze-like procession, their bodies have been elongated like late medieval tomb figures, and the piety and sentiment of the facial expressions is modern, closely akin to the contemporaneous *Morley* monument. The other early drawing reproduced here in Plate 17 was executed on a smaller scale, and illustrates a later incident in English medieval history, when in Richard II's reign Lord Cobham was impeached and sentenced as a traitor. Perhaps Flaxman chose this incident for moral reasons, as an example of an unjust punishment eventually corrected, when Cobham was recalled from banishment by Henry IV. The drawing shows Flaxman's lively observation of facial expressions, and a meticulous recording of realistic

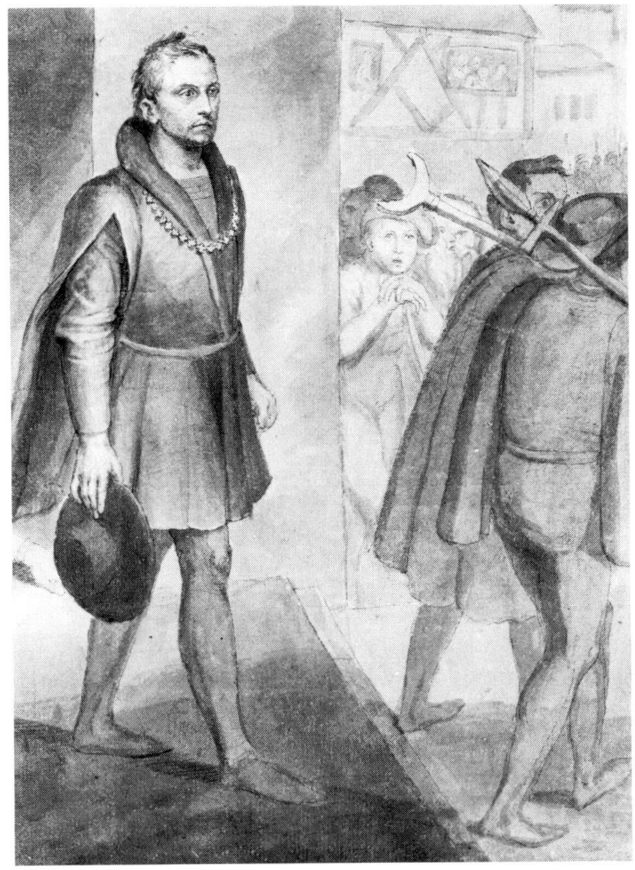

17 *The Punishment of John de Cobham*, c. 1780. Pen and ink and wash, 24·8 × 18·4 cms.

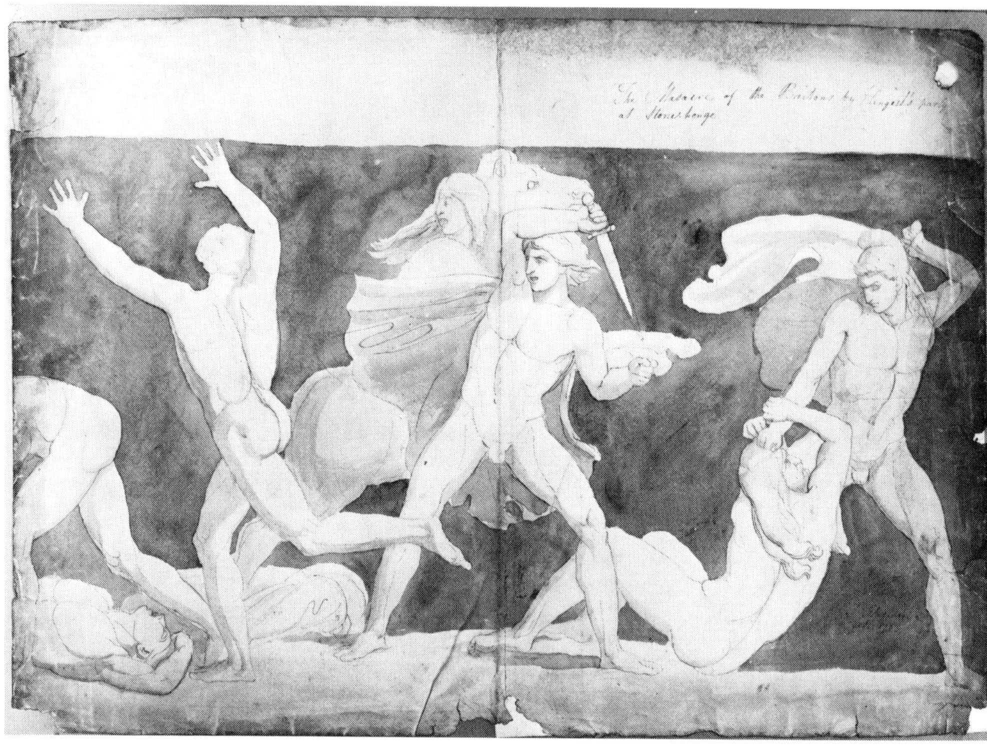

18 *The Massacre of the Britons by Hengist's Party at Stonehenge.* 1783.
Pen and ink and wash, 47 × 66 cms.

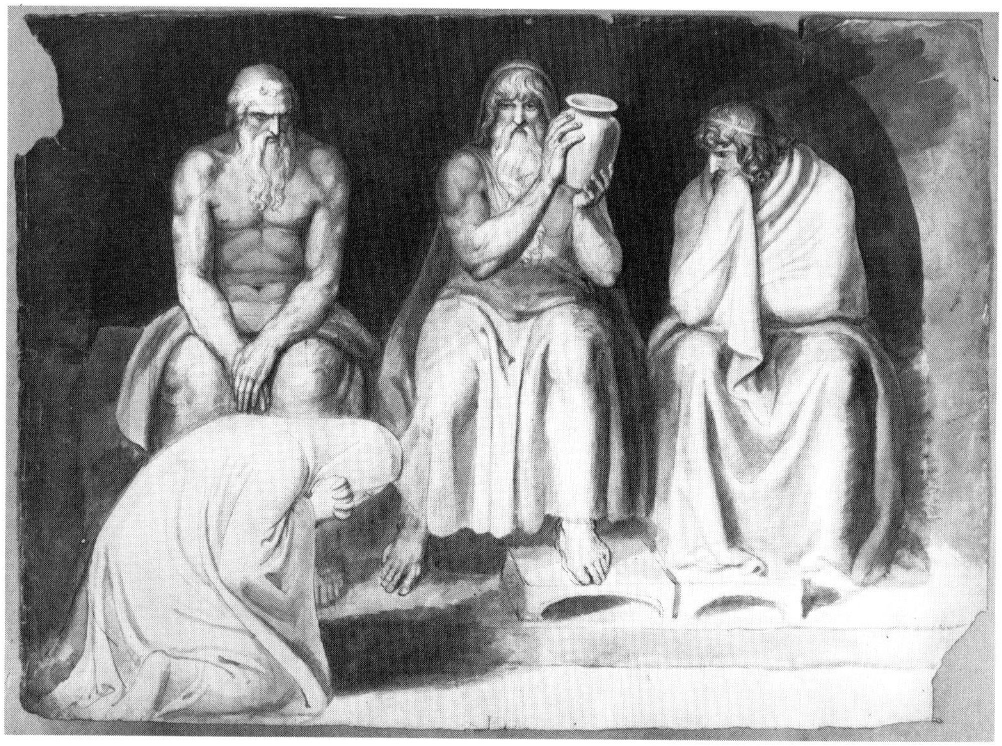

19 *Tamar kneeling before Judah*, c. 1783.
Pen and ink and wash, 47 × 66 cms.

details based on a close observation of nature, especially in the elderly Lord Cobham's tousled hair and the veins on his right hand.

The few drawings surviving from the period before Flaxman went abroad suggest a breadth of subject-matter and choice of styles comparable to that of his

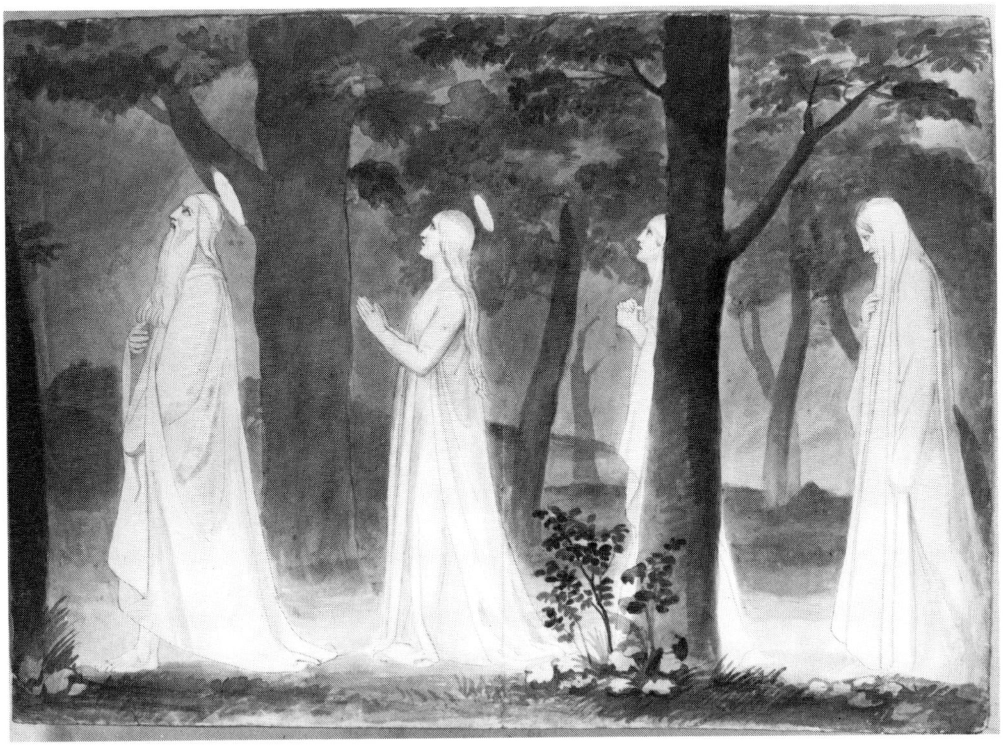

20 *St. Ethelburga with her chaplain St. Paulinus of Rochester bringing Christianity to Northumbria*, c. 1783.
Pen and ink and wash, 47 × 66 cms.

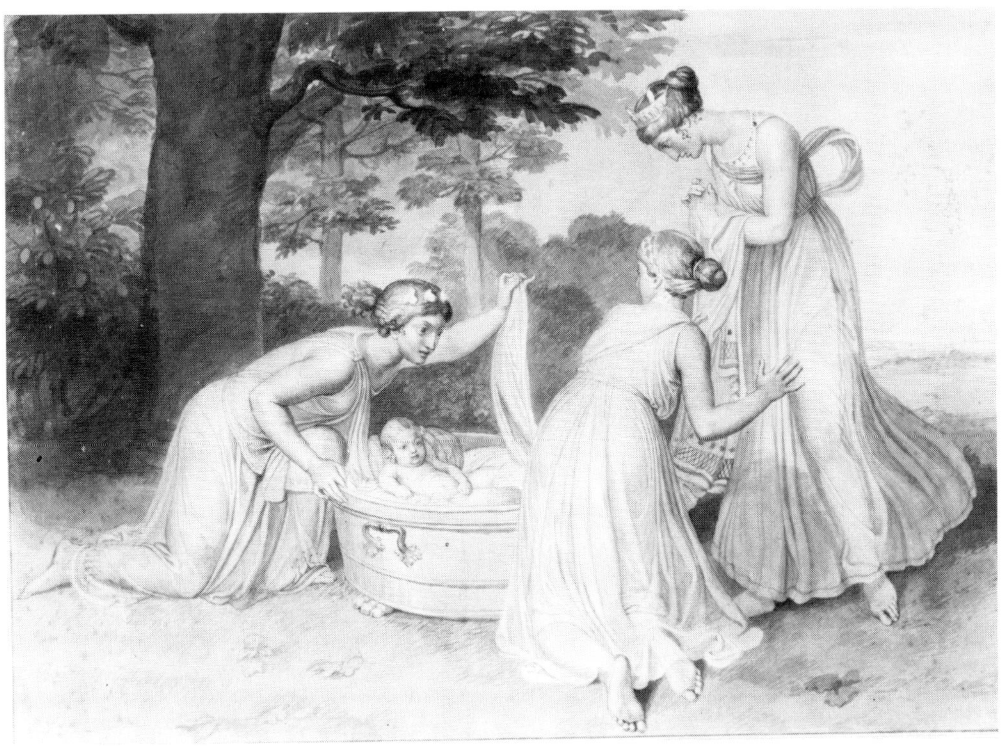

21 *The Nurturing of Bacchus*. c. 1780.
Pen and ink and wash, 42 × 58·7 cms.

sculptures. Apart from the medieval drawings just discussed, one of his few early classical subjects to survive is the one, reproduced in Plate 21, depicting the *Nurture of Bacchus*, which is in a fairly strict Neoclassical style. He had now laid firm foundations for his later career and established lasting interests, but he was only to reach artistic maturity whilst in Italy.

CHAPTER II

Artist and Industry: Wedgwood

After Wedgwood's death in 1795, Flaxman lamented that he had lost an 'old and valued friend', who 'for his taste, his knowledge, his virtues, and the extensive good desired to his country and humanity . . . it were to be wished that he had lived longer than Nestor'.[1] A few years later, when plans were being discussed for the erection of a Gallery of National Glory, Flaxman drafted an address to the King, during the course of which he specifically mentioned the great achievement of the first Josiah Wedgwood.[2] Before Flaxman went to Italy, he had been provided with more work by Wedgwood and his partner Thomas Bentley than by any one else. Flaxman had good reason to be grateful to them at a time in his career when he was under-employed. Only by 1785 was he becoming so busy with other commissions that he had to apologise to Wedgwood for delays in supplying a relief, saying that in order to fulfill his commissions from Wedgwood, he had to work at night and occasionally take 'a day from some large monuments I have in hand which are in great haste'.[3]

Wedgwood had been in the pottery business since the 1750's, but it was the partnership with Bentley and the opening of his new Staffordshire factory named Etruria in 1769 that marked the real beginning of his success. Wedgwood's early reputation and the foundation of his fortune had grown on the basis of his creamware products, usually intended for everyday household use, but to these products Wedgwood and Bentley were now to add an ever-expanding range of decorative, and more costly, products, especially after the invention of jasper in 1774. With an astute business sense, which saw a potentially profitable market in the mass-production of decorative objects in the newly fashionable Neoclassical style, the two men not only visited collections of antiquities together, but also set about acquiring a small library of antiquarian books and engravings which could be used as source material in their factory. They also bought plaster casts, including examples after the antique, some of which came from the shop of Flaxman's father. It was not an unusual practice in the eighteenth century for factories to provide small-scale art museums and reference libraries on the spot for the use of their designers. Wedgwood's friend Matthew Boulton provided such facilities not far away in Birmingham; other examples at the time can be found in Paris, Florence and Vienna.[4]

Bentley, until his death in 1780, seems to have been the main person in the firm who sought out artists and was responsible for the firm's bias towards classicism. It was Bentley, and not Wedgwood, who recommended that the young Flaxman be employed by the firm,[5] presumably partially because Flaxman's father had already been providing plasters for Wedgwood and Bentley over about a five-year period.

Wedgwood was the first industrialist to use such modern methods of publicity as a London showroom and a printed catalogue. The intention was not only to make the knowledge of his products more widespread, but by so doing 'to diffuse a good taste through the arts', which he believed could be done by the 'power of multiplying copies of fine things', as he says in a didactic passage which is repeated from one catalogue to the next. This mass-production of good taste, largely in the Neoclassical idiom, he achieved partially by commissioning painters and sculptors to produce designs for him, chiefly Flaxman. But he also employed other artists such as George Stubbs and Lady Elizabeth Templeton.

In Wedgwood and Bentley, Flaxman acquired enterprising and level-headed patrons who were men both of culture and of business. They not only knew what they wanted but also how to achieve it, if necessary as economically as possible. Wedgwood on one occasion even expressed a preference for using existing designs at Etruria, rather than employing Flaxman, as it would be cheaper.[6] Other letters show Wedgwood keeping not only a strict control over the quality of the designs, but also over technical matters, grumbling for example that one model was too thin and could not be carried out in jasperware.[7]

Although Wedgwood was justifiably proud of the high standard of design of his products, he did not usually give the names of his designers in his catalogues. In Wedgwood's 1779 catalogue, in which he listed in great detail his new range of jasperware, he included under the heading of cameos of the 'Heads of Illustrious Moderns' those of the eminent English naturalist Sir Joseph Banks, one of Wedgwood's friends, and his Swedish librarian and companion on his voyages, Dr. Daniel Charles Solander. Both portrait medallions, catalogued anonymously, had been modelled by Flaxman in 1775, and seem to be the first works which he executed for Wedgwood (Plate 22). Flaxman's medallion of Captain Cook, which would logically have accompanied the ones to Banks and Solander, did not follow until later, payment being made in 1784.[8]

Flaxman seems to have been asked by Wedgwood to sculpt mostly 'illustrious moderns' of his own century. He executed medallions of twenty-two eighteenth-century personalities, including two of himself and one of his wife (Plate 23). The design of each medallion seems to have usually earned him two or three guineas.[9] In addition to the firmly documented examples by

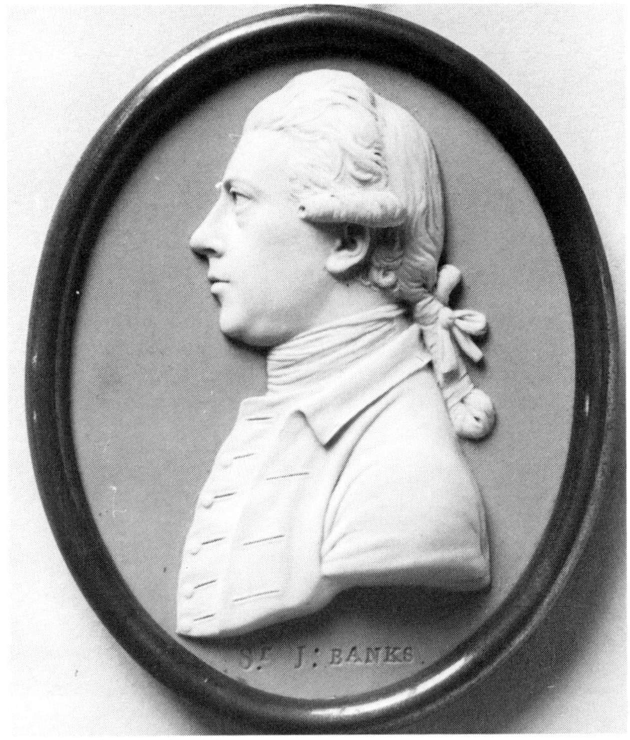

22 *Sir Joseph Banks*, 1775. Jasperware, 9·5 × 8·0 cms.

23 *Mrs. Flaxman*, c. 1790. Jasperware, 15·2 cms. diameter.

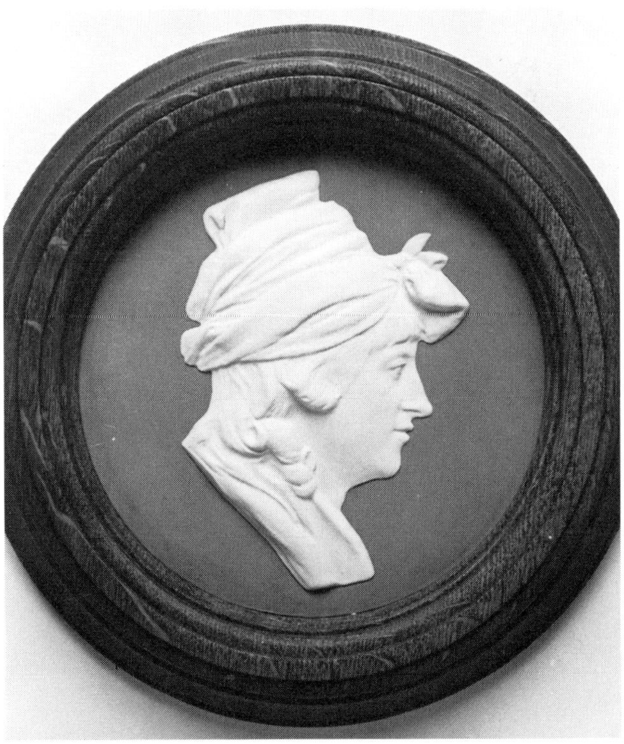

Flaxman, there are about nineteen more attributed to him with varying degrees of certainty, together with about eight further attributions of earlier historical figures, such as Caesar and Alexander the Great, as well as a head of Medusa.

The reason for the choice of personalities by Wedgwood for inclusion amongst the medallions is usually self-evident. Famous or popular writers, actors, politicians and contemporary sovereigns are obvious candidates, but some of the figures included appear less significant. After the first commission of 1775, Flaxman's documented medallions included the Earl of Chatham and Samuel Johnson, both modelled as commemorative pieces in the years of their deaths (1778 and 1784); Warren Hastings when he was still out in India as Governor of Bengal (1784); and Dr. William Buchan (1783), a contemporary Scottish doctor who wrote a best-seller entitled *Domestic Medicine, or the Family Physician*. Contemporary rulers modelled by Flaxman include one of George IV when still Prince of Wales (about 1782), monarchs abroad who contributed to the development of the arts, science, commerce or agriculture, such as Ferdinand I, King of the Two Sicilies (1781) and Gustavus III of Sweden (1784), but other rulers were included as well, presumably for the sake of completeness, such as Paul I of Russia (1782) and Maria I of Portugal (1787).

Like other designers working for Wedgwood, Flaxman used a variety of sources for his likenesses. Occasionally they were probably modelled from life, such as the medallion of Mrs. Siddons (1782), which has been convincingly attributed to Flaxman,[10] and the earlier medallions of Banks and Solander were presumably drawn from life, as both men were settled in London at the time. But Flaxman often had to resort to the use of engravings, paintings, medals and busts; even for the portrait of Samuel Johnson he used a print. For the medallion of the famous early 18th-century physician and collector, Richard Mead, he used a cast of a contemporary ivory carving which had been sent to Etruria for the purpose in 1778.[11]

In the case of medallions only attributed to Flaxman, it is difficult always to be confident about the attribution, since the style is identical with that of other Wedgwood medallions known to be the work of other designers, such as James Tassie. By the time a fairly naturalistic head had been translated from the designer's original model into a jasper mould, individual traits in modelling have disappeared. Some of the most famous of the eighteenth-century personalities on Wedgwood's medallions have been attributed in the past to Flaxman, but there is no documentation to

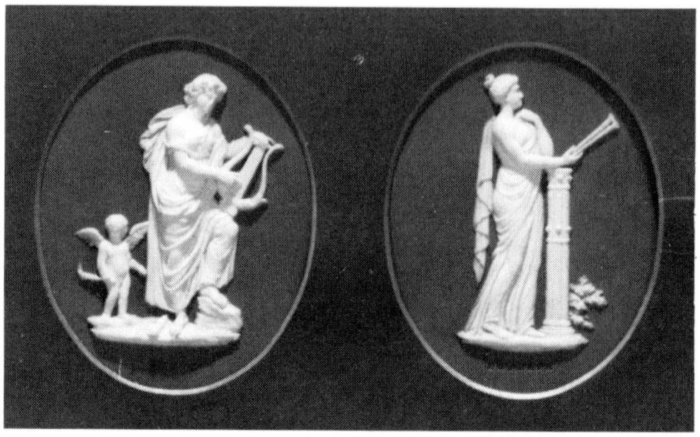

24 *Erato and Euterpe*. Designed 1777. Jasperware medallions, each 9 × 6·8 cms.

prove, for example, that he was actually responsible for the medallions of such men as Charles James Fox, the younger Pitt, Reynolds, the actor Kemble, or Goethe (whom he could have modelled from life in Rome, since the visits of the two men to Italy overlapped).[12] Any attempts to attribute such medallions to Flaxman solely on the basis of stylistic analysis can only lead to insecure conclusions.

As the use of profile in many of the portrait medallions is a continuation of a tradition in medallion and coin portraiture going back to classical times, some of the Wedgwood portraits inevitably look as if they have been borrowed from antique sources. The influence of the art of ancient Rome and Greece is however much more direct on the other work Flaxman designed for Wedgwood, namely the jasperware bas-reliefs. Apart from the medallions, Wedgwood was building up a large and flourishing part of his business in vases and other ornamental objects as well as a wide range of plaques from large ones for incorporation into chimneypieces, to very small ones which could be set into steel jewellery by Matthew Boulton. The bas-relief designs which Flaxman produced for Wedgwood would therefore appear in a variety of sizes, and also be adapted sometimes to curved as well as to flat surfaces. The six Muses which Flaxman modelled in 1777 were put into production in four different ways. Firstly, they were made as oval medallions which could be purchased individually (Plate 24) or added to other Muses and an Apollo which Wedgwood already had in production (but which had not been designed by Flaxman). Secondly, they could be put together with the other Muses in a pair of rectangular bas-relief panels, with the arrangement of the figures varied sometimes between castings. Thirdly, Flaxman's Muses could be combined with the already existing ones and

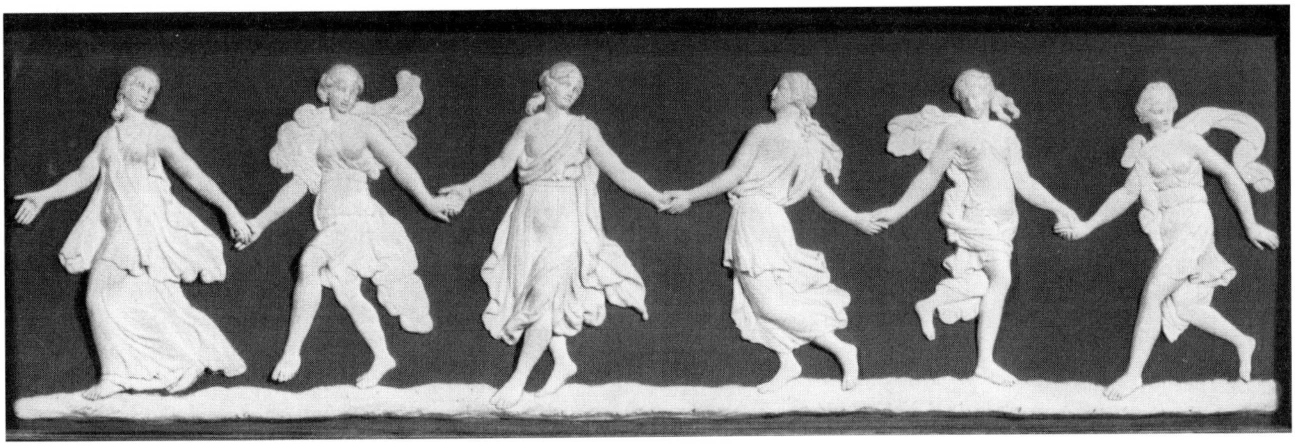

25 *Dancing Hours*. Designed 1778. Jasperware panel, 14·3 × 45·7 cms.

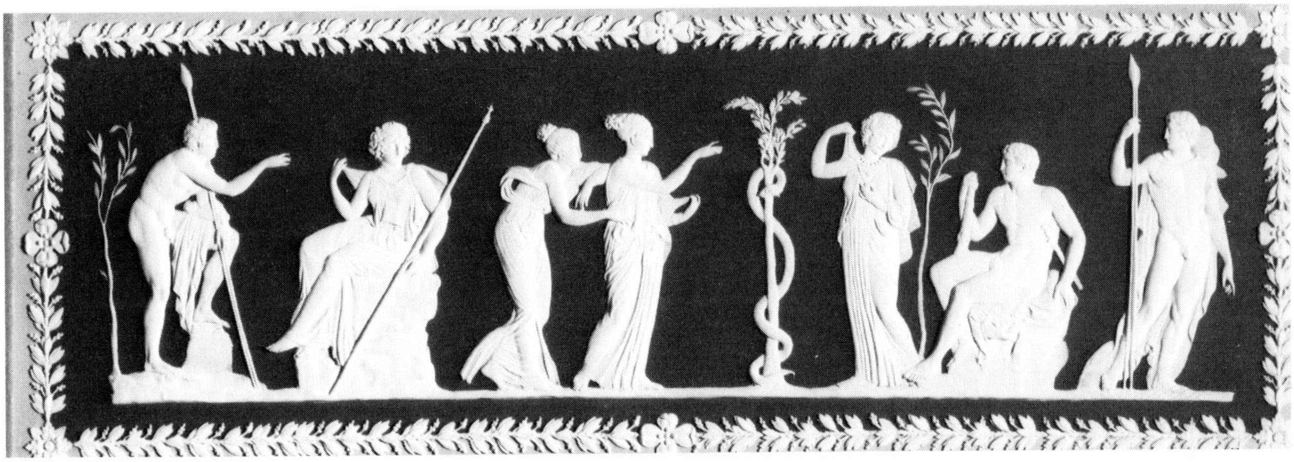

25a *Hercules in the Garden of Hesperides*. Jasperware panel, 20·2 × 51·4 cms.

Apollo around a vase. And, fourthly, on a larger scale, the Muses could be grouped together for insertion as panels into chimneypieces. Wedgwood would have known that the Muses were a common theme in contemporary ceramic figures being made both in Britain and on the Continent, and he was successfully capitalising on current taste both in theme and in style. The source of Wedgwood's Muses were clearly classical, derived from the easily available engravings of bas-reliefs, gems and other works of ancient Roman art. Some of the poses could have been borrowed from a sarcophagus relief showing all the Muses reproduced in Montfaucon's *L'Antiquité expliquée*.[13]

Even when assembled into a continuous relief, the Muses are static, and lack the elegant rhythm which Flaxman achieved in the following year with his panels of the *Dancing Hours* (1778) (Plate 25). Many classical prototypes again existed, the most likely source being that invaluable compendium of antique bas-reliefs in Bartoli's *Admiranda Romanorum Antiquitatum* (1685) in which two plates reproduce a relief then in the Borghese collection (Plate 26), and now in the Louvre. The Bartoli plates were re-engraved for inclusion in Montfaucon. The use of the Borghese source may well have been encouraged by a chimneypiece imported from the same collection by one of Wedgwood's clients, Sir Laurence Dundas, for installation in one of his houses, Moor Park, in Hertfordshire. The white marble and lapis lazuli chimneypiece (now in Lady Lever Art Gallery, Port Sunlight) incorporates copies of the same frieze of dancing female figures. The flanking pilasters on the Roman original have been removed in Flaxman's adaptation thus increasing the sense of continuous movement, and Flaxman's draperies fall in

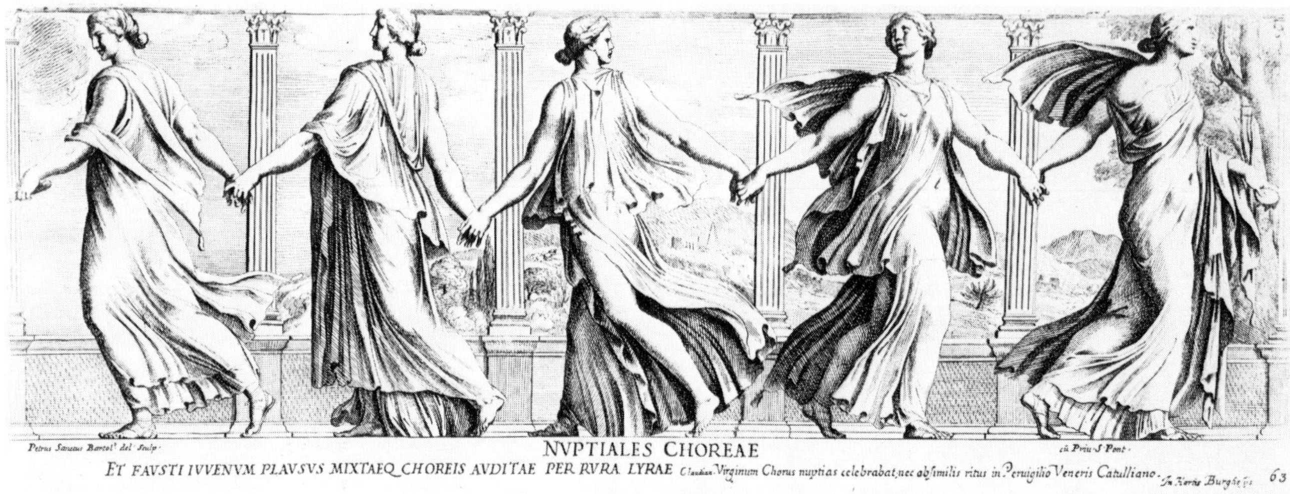

26 Pietro Santi Bartoli: *Admiranda Romanorum Antiquitatum*, 1693 edition. Plate 63, *Dancing Hours.*

27 *Apotheosis of Homer*. Designed 1778. Jasperware fireplace panel, 20·5 × 46 cms. Haddo House, Aberdeenshire.

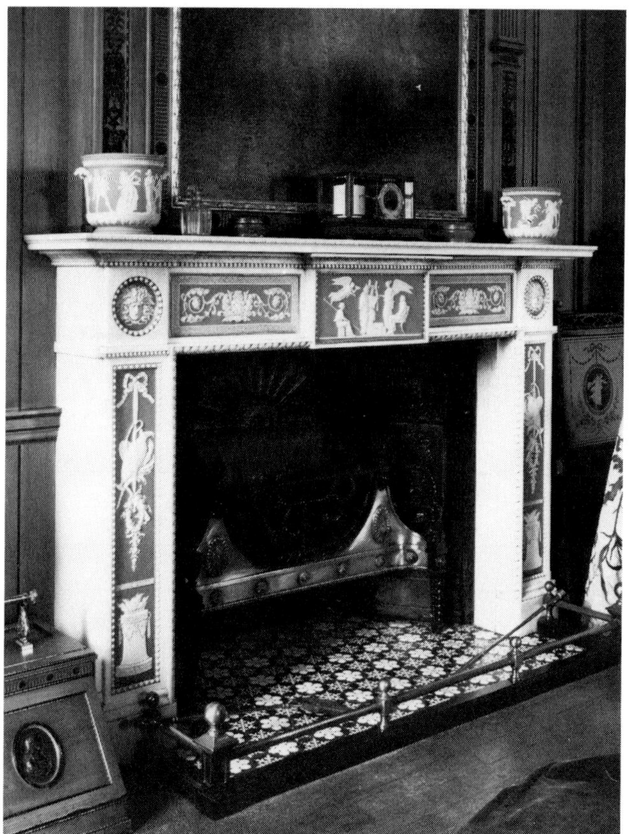

softer curves. Although he was heavily indebted to classical antiquity, Flaxman's *Dancing Hours* are more elegant than his source, and ideally suited in spirit to the Neoclassical interiors in which they would have been placed, especially if incorporated into chimneypieces, flanking a central panel, as was Wedgwood's original intention.

Other chimneypiece panels designed by Flaxman in the same year were more playful in mood, including one of a *Sacrifice to Hymen*, also called *Cupids with a Goat*, taken from a design by Cipriani, and echoing the charm of the late Roman cameo known as the Marlborough Gem depicting the *Marriage of Cupid and Psyche* (now in the Museum of Fine Arts, Boston), which Wedgwood had had copied for use on fireplaces about three years earlier.

Flaxman turned to Greek vases for the inspiration of his most important jasperware panel in 1778, the *Apotheosis of Homer* (Plate 27), again initially intended for chimneypieces.[14] Later, in 1786, the design was also used on a vase, the example which Wedgwood gave to the British Museum being reproduced in Plate 28.

Greek vases—or Etruscan vases as they were incorrectly called until later in the eighteenth century—were to be vital for the development of the Neoclassical style, especially in the emphasis on outline in design. Few examples were known and collected until the middle of the eighteenth century, when large numbers, many of Southern Italian make, were discovered in central Italy. As early as 1766 Wedgwood had recognised the importance of Sir William Hamilton's large collection in Naples, and wanted to use the vases as possible sources for his factory. In that year, Wedgwood had acquired proof plates from the forthcoming catalogue, the lavish folio volumes of the *Collection of*

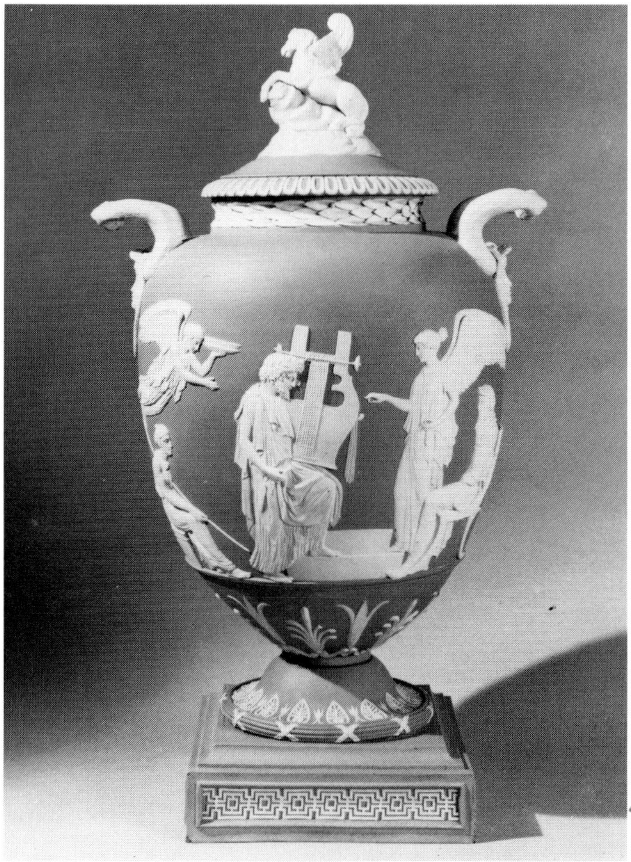

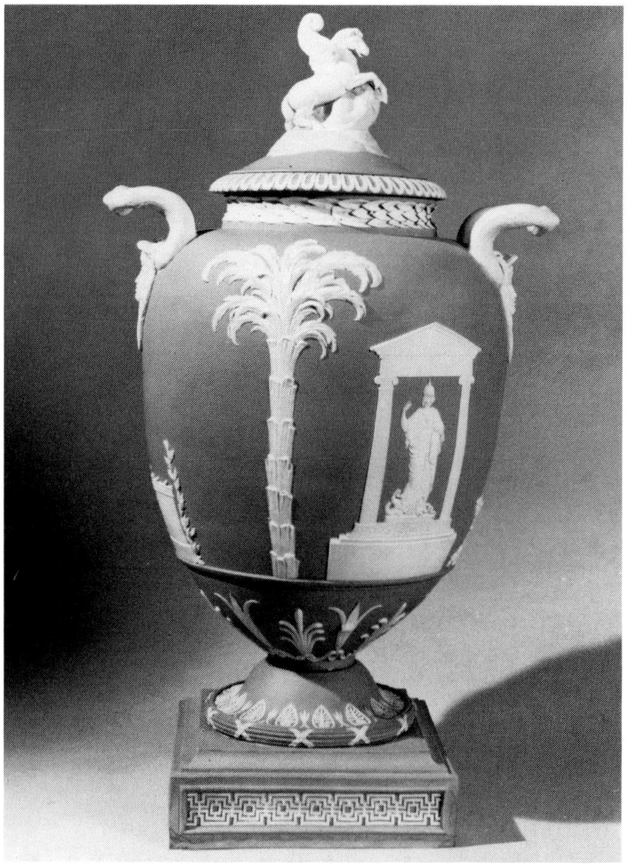

28a *Apotheosis of Homer*, 1786. Designed 1778. Jasperware vase, 45·7 cms. high. **28b** Reverse side.

Etruscan, Greek and Roman Antiquities from the Cabinet of the Honorable William Hamilton. The volumes themselves were eventually to be included on the record of books owned by Wedgwood and Bentley drawn up in 1770, a list which includes the main archaeological publications of the century.[15] The plates in these volumes, catalogued by the French antiquarian d'Hancarville, were mostly coloured and provided a reasonably accurate visual record of Hamilton's first collection, which only a few years later, in 1772, he was to sell to the newly established British Museum. Either in the Museum, or from the published engravings, or perhaps even from a drawing supplied by Hamilton's cataloguer,[16] Flaxman copied fairly closely the composition of the painted decoration, and retained the contrast in the original between light figures and a dark ground (Plate 29). However, he made many subtle alterations, ranging from a more detailed treatment of hair styles, feathered wings and arm muscles to larger changes in facial features, with the provision of a seat for the figure on the left. Flaxman has absorbed the ideas of the Greek painter, but has transformed them, and in the process seems to have looked at nature for himself. The seated figure of the defeated Hesiod on the right could easily be mistaken for a study from life; there is an ease and naturalism in his pose that is absent in the stiffer treatment of the same figure on the vase and in the engraving. As Wedgwood himself said about his products in general, 'I only pretend to have attempted to copy the fine antique forms, but not with absolute servility. I have endeavoured to preserve the style and spirit, or if you please, the elegant simplicity of the antique forms'.[17]

Wedgwood was very proud of the *Apotheosis of Homer* plaque, and hastened to send one to Italy as a present for Sir William Hamilton. He responded with an enthusiastic letter in which he said, 'I was sure that your industry would produce in time something excellent in the way of basreliefs from the specimens I saw before I left England, but I really am surprised and delighted to the highest degree with this proof of the hasty strides you have made towards perfection in your art', and he continued to tell Wedgwood that 'your bas-relief astonishes all the artists here, it is more pure and in

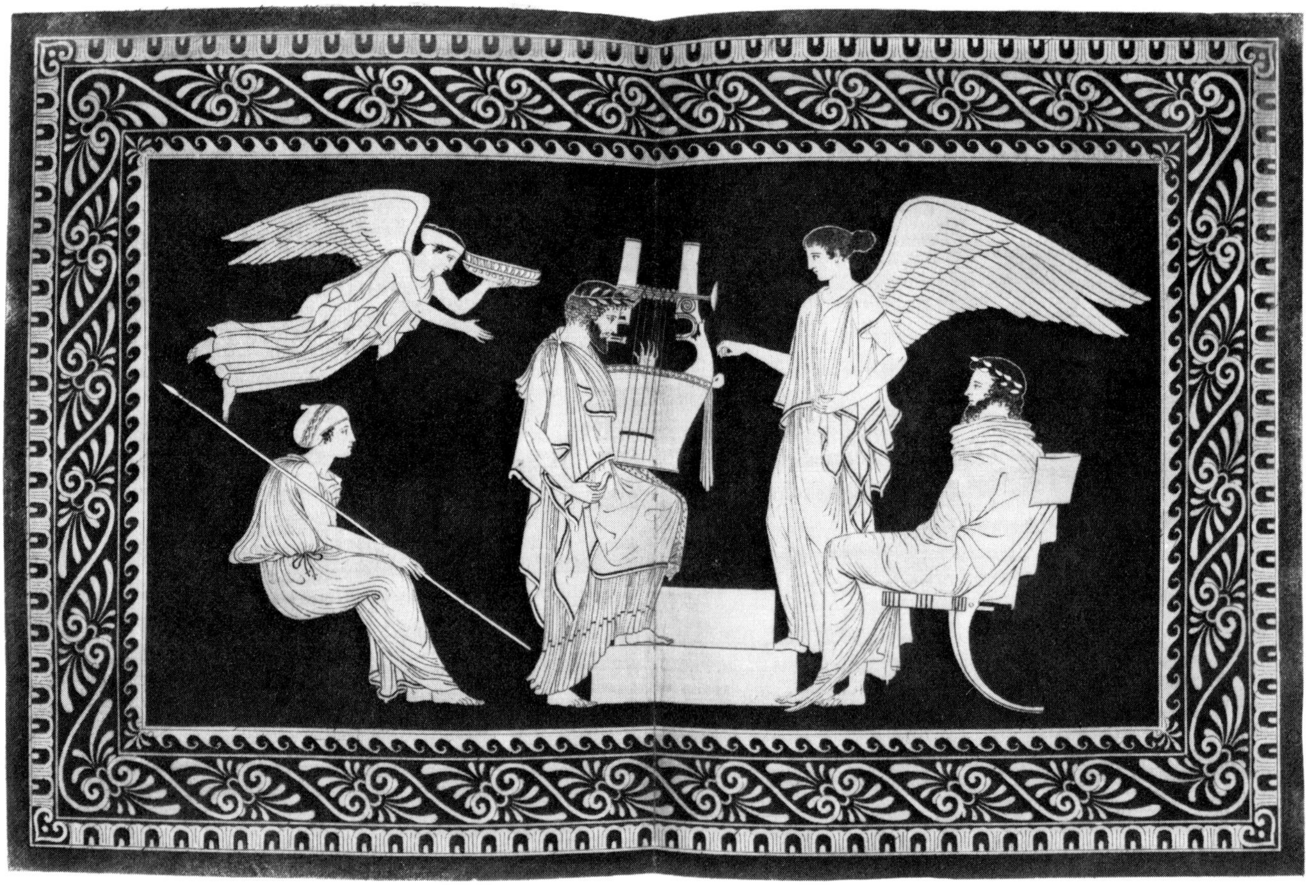

29 Pierre François D'Hancarville: *Collection of Etruscan . . . Antiquities . . . of the Honorable William Hamilton*, 1766–67. Volume III, Plate 31, *Apotheosis of Homer* (or *Crowning of a Kitharist*).

a truer antique taste than any of their performances though they have so many fine models before them'.[18] Purity and a true antique taste were the main aesthetic points made in the preface to the folios publishing Hamilton's first collection, and similar adjectives were to be used later when he published his second collection between 1791 and 1795. It is a 'purity' and true taste' seen, inevitably, with late eighteenth-century eyes, and which the Greek painter of the original vase would not have recognised as a straight copy. But in jasperware panels of this kind, and its pair *The Apotheosis of Virgil* which was produced later, between about 1783 and 1785, and which Flaxman probably also designed, Wedgwood was manufacturing some of the most successful pieces of Neoclassical art, perfect accompaniments to the fashionable interiors and furnishings of Robert Adam and his contemporaries. The success of Wedgwood's jasperware plaques can also be measured by the sincerest form of flattery, namely the extent to which they were plagiarised by other firms both in Britain and on the Continent. The Meissen factory, for instance, imitated the *Apotheosis of Homer* in a large medallion.

Hamilton's collection was to provide a further design for one of Flaxman's panels and vases for Wedgwood, *Hercules in the Garden of the Hesperides*, commissioned in 1785 (Plate 30).[19] The source chosen this time by Wedgwood was one of his favourite items in the collection, since Wedgwood had chosen to copy figures from it on the very first encaustic-painted, basalt vase that his firm had produced at Etruria in 1769. The vase, a fifth-century red figure hydria decorated by the Meidias Painter (Plate 31), is covered with a wealth of figures in a variety of scenes, and occupied four double-page spreads in the first volume of d'Hancarville's catalogue. Of the three scenes devoted to Hercules, Flaxman has chosen the engraving with the greatest variety of incident and the best grouping of the figures (Plate 32). As on other occasions Flaxman's correspondence with Wedgwood is very practical. After thanking him for the commission for the *Hercules* plaques (of which there were originally going to be

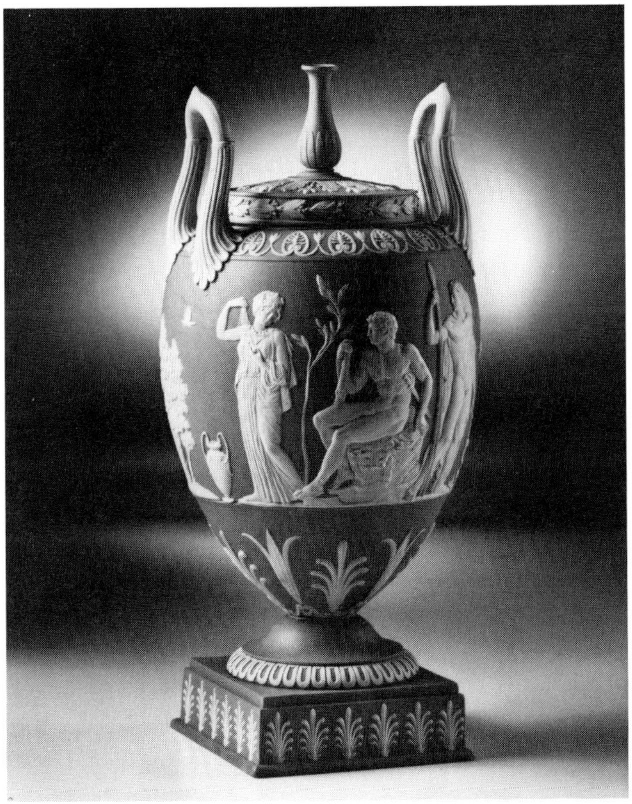

30 *Hercules in the Garden of the Hesperides*, c. 1790. Designed 1785. Jasperware vase, 35·7 cms. high.

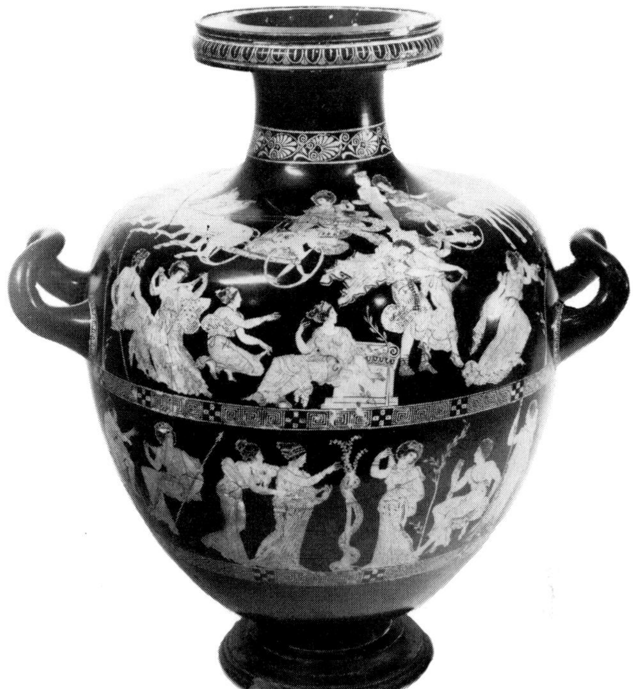

31 Meidias Painter: *Attic Red-Figure Hydria*, c. 410 BC.

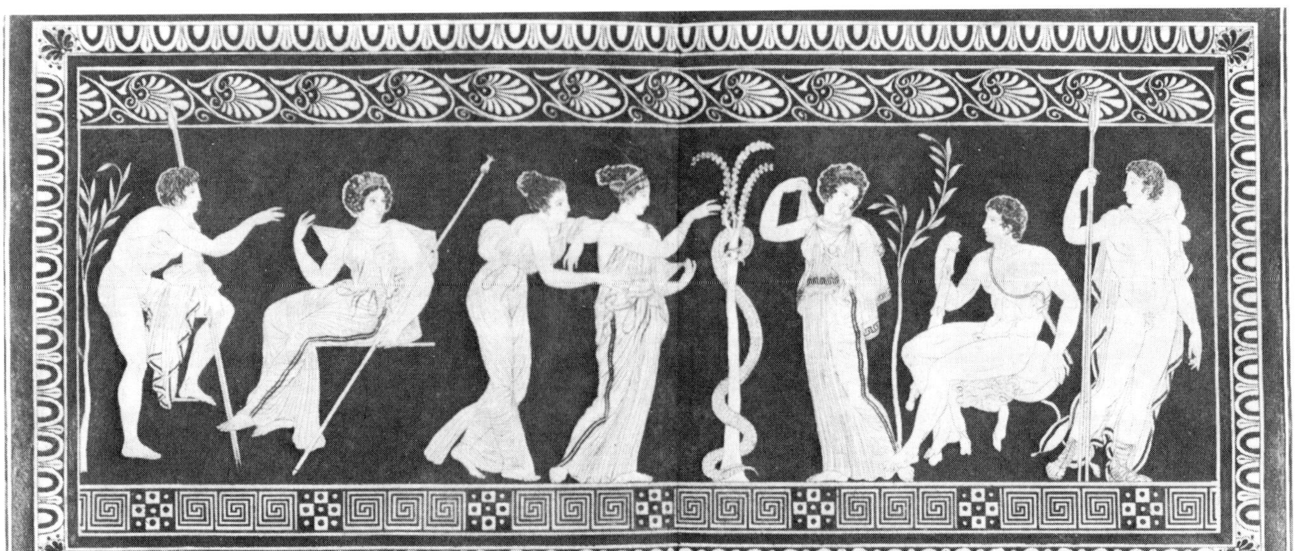

32 Pierre François D'Hancarville: *Collection of Etruscan . . . Antiquities . . . of the Honorable William Hamilton*, 1766–67. Volume II, Plate 127, *Hercules in the Garden of the Hesperides*.

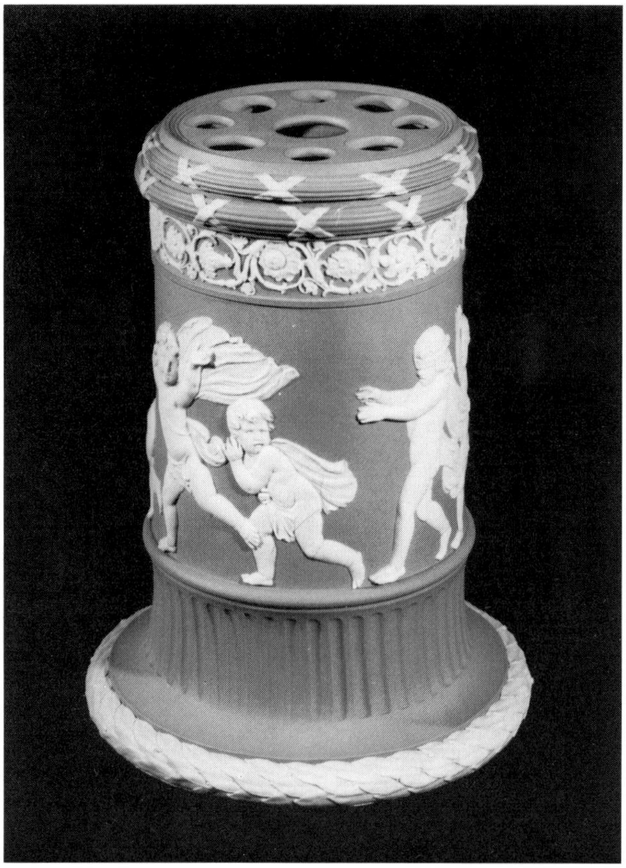

33 *Blind Man's Buff*. Designed 1782. Jasperware jardinière, 17·3 cms. high.

two) and one of *Coriolanus*, Flaxman said that 'the figures in the print are 4 inches and ⅝ths high, and I have modelled my figure 5 inches and ⅜ths which allows one seventh for shrinking in the bisque.'[20] Flaxman's design repeats the composition of the original engraving with only minor adjustments, such as the removal of a tree and the placing of rocks underneath Hercules so that he has something on which to sit. Like the *Homer* design, the *Hercules* was used for both plaques and vases.

Other work in the 1780's included reliefs for use on teapots and other objects (Plate 33). One of Flaxman's letters to Wedgwood in 1782 shows very clearly how carefully he considered the practical application of his ideas: 'I have designed some groups of children proper for bas-reliefs to decorate the sides of teapots. No. 1 and 2 are intended to go entirely round a teapot of a flat shape except where the handles and spout interrupt them, I have therefore made separate stories for each side, the 1st is Blind's Man's Buff, the 2nd is the game of marbles, 3 and 4 are the Triumph [of] Cupid to be disposed in a similar manner on the sides of round and upright teapots. When you return the sketches to be modelled from, be pleased to give instructions concerning the size and other necessary particulars'.[21]

In 1786 Wedgwood seized the opportunity to capitalise on the commercial treaty between Britain and France and commissioned a design from Flaxman, who at first produced ideas for one plaque. Wedgwood however asked Flaxman to rework the design as two plaques because he thought they would look better, but he presumably also had an eye on the possibility of doubling his profits. The plaques were finally marketed in 1787 as *Peace preventing Mars from bursting open the Gates of the Temple of Janus* and *Mercury uniting the hands of England and France*.[22]

One commission in the 1780's was to be designed by Flaxman in a different style from that of all his other Wedgwood ware. In 1783 Wedgwood asked for a set of chessmen, which was put into production the following year (Plate 34). This commission coincided with the period when Flaxman was showing an interest in medieval English history and sculpture, which is reflected in some of the chess pieces. By the late eighteenth century, chess was a long-established game, growing increasingly in popularity, with an expanding range of literature about it. The rules of the game had established the names of each piece, but the characters could be cast or carved either in contemporary or in historical dress. Wedgwood, ever a far-sighted business man, spotted a potential new market for a mass-produced, jasperware set, that was to be marketed at the sum of five guineas, a modest price when compared with prices for ivory or silver sets. Flaxman's choice of medieval dress for his pieces was therefore not predetermined by the tradition of the game, but shows rather his own interest in English history. As this was Wedgwood's only venture into the Gothic Revival, it shows him willing to benefit from an aspect of fashionable taste, but not pursue it very far, doubtless recognising the dominance of Neoclassicism. For the same reason probably his son was to dabble cautiously in the Egyptian Revival at the turn of the century, producing a few pieces in that new style. In designing his chess pieces, Flaxman combined his own knowledge of medieval sculptural figures with theatrical roles on the contemporary stage. According to tradition (and there is no good reason to doubt it) the piece of the king was based on John Kemble, that of the queen on Sarah Siddons (Plate 35.)

The treatment of some of the figures, especially the heavy folds of the draperies, as well as the attempt at accurate costume in some of the pieces, show a knowledge of late medieval sculpture, studied both at

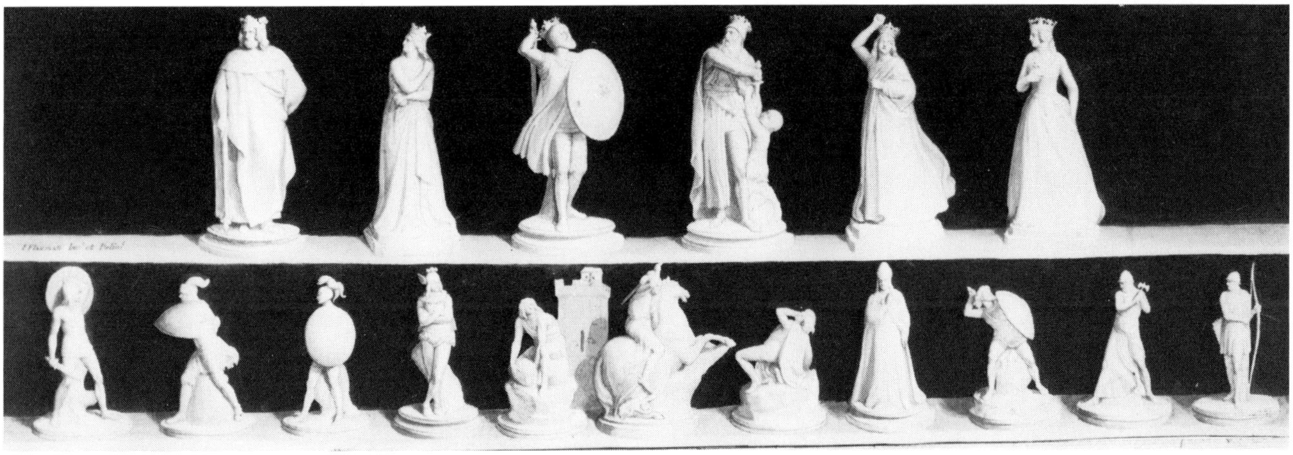

34 *Chessmen: design*, 1783. Pen and ink and wash, 12·7 × 25·5 cms.

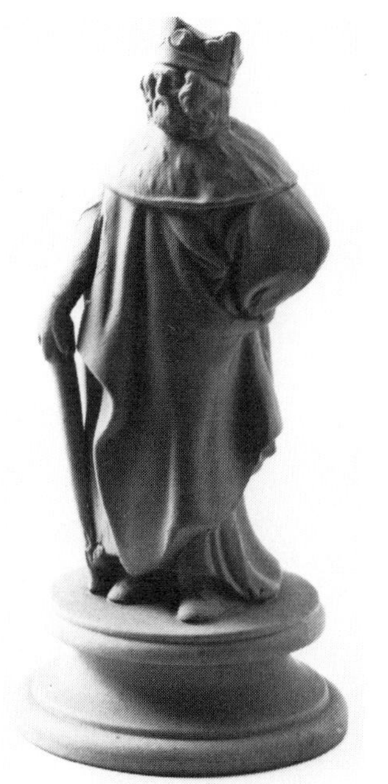

35a *Chess piece: King*. 1783 Wax, 8·5 cms. high.

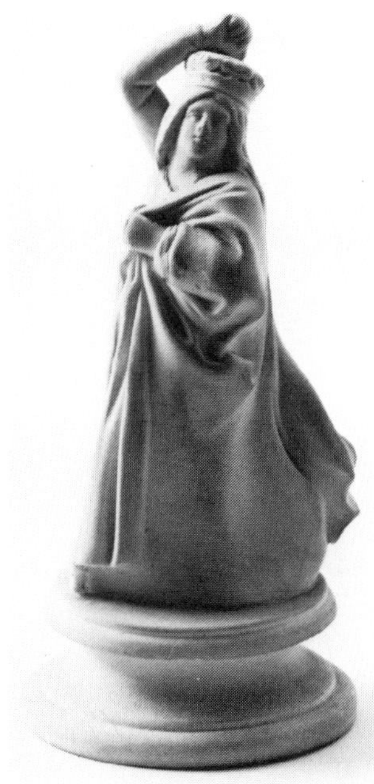

35b *Chess piece:* Queen. 1783. Wax, 9 cms. high.

firsthand, and also through engravings, especially of the kind of material being collected by Richard Gough for his *Sepulchral Monuments of Great Britain*, to which Flaxman may well have had access before its publication, through his friendship with Blake (Plate 36). The chess pieces, however, are not entirely medieval in inspiration, since some of the variations of the king and queen, as well as of the knight, have a vitality that comes more directly from nature itself, and not through the intermediary of an earlier art form.

Shortly after his arrival in Rome, Flaxman had written to Wedgwood's nephew saying that 'I shall employ all the time I can for Mr. W',[23] but most of Flaxman's work for Etruria came to an end after he had set out for the Continent. He had executed a great deal of work for the factory at Etruria, including a wide range of commissions from designing expensive jasper-ware pieces to a menial task such as grinding the edges of snuff-boxes for an ambassador.[24] Flaxman had also been involved throughout the 1780's in designing chimneypieces, cornices, friezes and even ceiling paintings for Wedgwood's own house.[25] After his arrival in Italy, Flaxman was to maintain only occasional links with Wedgwood, including a few commissions and the supervision of work by other artists to be sent back to England. Shortly before Flaxman's departure, Wedgwood wrote to Sir William Hamilton telling him that Flaxman 'has promised to employ for me all the time he can spare at Rome, and to superintend a modeller, who I have engaged to accompany him and to employ the whole of his time for me at Rome'.[26] The modeller was John Devaere, who on his return to England in 1790 went back for a time into Wedgwood's employment. In the meantime he worked under Flaxman's supervision on a copy of the relief on the *Borghese Vase*,

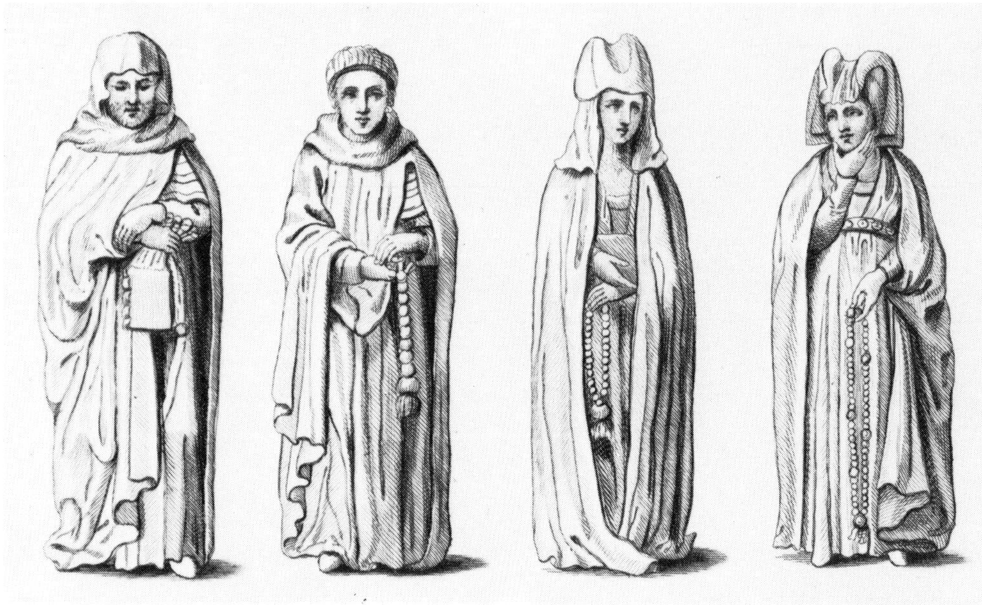

36 Richard Gough: *Sepulchral Monuments of Great Britain*, 1786–96. Vol. III, Plate 38, *Monument to Richard, Earl of Warwick*: detail of statues.

copied other reliefs in Rome collections, and designed jasperware plaques with Homeric and other classical themes. Apart from conscientiously looking after Devaere's progress, Flaxman executed a few commissions for Wedgwood himself. In 1788, for instance, he modelled a medallion of Victor Amadeus III, King of Sardinia and Duke of Savoy, taking the portrait from a miniature. Also whilst in Rome he added to Wedgwood's collection of engravings by purchasing for him the plates of the Museo Capitolino collection.

Josiah Wedgwood himself died shortly after Flaxman returned to England. Flaxman by now was an established, busy sculptor, also with a reputation for book illustrations, and he did not resume his connection with the firm, except briefly in 1815, when he introduced Blake to Josiah Wedgwood II, an introduction that led to Blake's engraving the plates for the 1816 catalogue, one of several hack jobs that he undertook about that time. Flaxman was to continue his links with the decorative and industrial arts, but not in the field of pottery. He had, however, already contributed some of the most famous pieces to Wedgwood's jasperware, a range which Wedgwood regarded as the finest that his factory produced. Some of Flaxman's designs continued in production long after his death; some are still being made today. His *Dancing Hours* has probably been manufactured more times than any other of the firm's classical designs.

Flaxman's work for Wedgwood's factory and for other workshops later, is one of the outstanding examples, in the latter part of the eighteenth and early nineteenth century, of an artist becoming involved in the decorative and industrial arts. Painters, sculptors and architects usually remained aloof from industry. Design connected in any way with commerce was not taught at the Royal Academy School, and in the early days of its foundation the Academy itself would not even elect engravers as members. The Society of Arts in London and the Trustees' Academy in Edinburgh were the main bodies concerned with the closing of the gap between industrial design and the fine arts in the second half of the eighteenth century, looking forwards to the Schools of Design and the fundamental change of attitude after the 1830's. In Britain and on the Continent in Flaxman's day there was a small group of artists who did not recognise a barrier between art and industry, performing an important pioneering role; the group included in Britain the elder Bacon, Stothard and David Allan, and abroad such figures as Falconet and, a little later, Schinkel.[27] In the field of industrial design, Flaxman's work for Wedgwood was to be of lasting importance, especially in the middle of the nineteenth century, when the Battle of the Styles had reached the point of chaotic confusion exemplified in many of the exhibits in the 1851 Exhibition. Then perceptive critics valued Flaxman's classicism in his Wedgwood designs; as one of them wrote, 'it is still seemingly the great prerogative of Messrs. Wedgwood to exhibit pure specimens of the Greek style; and still for the most part in the exquisite productions of Flaxman'.[28]

CHAPTER III

To Italy

By the autumn of 1787 Flaxman and his wife had saved up enough money to go to Italy; their costs were to be aided by contributions from Mrs. Flaxman's family.[1] Their intention was to stay for a period of two years.[2] As early as 1771 one of his father's friends had been encouraging the young artist to go to Rome, but presumably at that stage there were insufficient funds available as Flaxman's father would not have been prosperous enough to support such a project.[3] Although Flaxman had to wait longer than usual for a period of study abroad, he was to benefit from the maturer experience. In the end, Flaxman and his wife stayed on the Continent nearly eight years, returning to England in 1794; the longer visit having been made possible by commissions received whilst in Rome for both sculptures and illustrations.[4]

The Flaxmans sent the bulk of their luggage ahead direct to Rome so that they could travel less encumbered. Apart from clothing, Flaxman would have found waiting for him such essential requirements as ten and a half dozen lead pencils, a folio of sketches, a trunk of modelling tools, some painting sticks and classical books.[5]

The Flaxmans crossed the Channel to Dieppe and started their Grand Tour in Normandy. From then onwards Flaxman recorded much of what he saw in sketchbooks, journals and letters, so providing a fairly full coverage of his stay abroad. He visited many of the main buildings and collections on his route, looking at works of art in all styles as a conscientious and avid tourist. Although some of his comments are terse, it is possible to gain a clear idea about his artistic likes and dislikes, and also learn about his patrons, friends and daily life.[6]

Apart from drawings, notebooks, models and sculptures, Flaxman brought back from his Italian visit a small collection of purchases which reflects his interests. His books included some of the publications dealing with the Herculaneum antiquities as well as a recent archaeological publication by the Abbate Carlo Fea. He also bought like many another tourist at the time impressions of gems, as well as engravings after Michelangelo. But his purchases also include some unexpected items, such as prints by Dürer, whose art was not encompassed by the accepted canons of taste. He also bought Renaissance medals,[7] mostly of the Quattrocento, and continued to add to them after his return to England, although the best examples he found in Rome. He always regarded his group of medals, which included the work of Pisanello, as 'the richest treasure in art he could possibly possess', and he much enjoyed talking about them.[8] Flaxman could obviously not afford any larger original works of art from the Quattrocento, because they were either not for sale or would be too expensive, and these miniature forms of Renaissance art were beautiful reductions of the kind of linear, low relief sculpture that he admired so much.

Of all his drawings and comments, those concerned with Italian Trecento art onwards are the most revealing and often the most unexpected. He was generally interested in Christian rather than pagan works of this period; for secular subjects he usually went directly to the antique. The exceptions, apart from a Signorelli grisaille at Orvieto (and even that fresco in its context is arguably religious), are his drawings in Florence from statues in the Piazza della Signoria, which would have been relevant to him from the point of view of his own secular commissions. The bulk of his Renaissance drawings could be regarded, partially at least, as possible sources of inspiration by a Christian artist who was both a sculptor of tombs and an illustrator of religious subjects, including Dante's epic. Flaxman would have seen few examples of early Italian art in the form of engravings before he left England, and these, together with the rough sketches which Romney had made after such early works in Italy and which almost certainly Flaxman would have seen, could hardly have prepared him for the relevation that Italian art was to be.

In many works including Jacopo della Quercia's reliefs on the facade of San Petronio in Bologna, Ghiberti's first Baptistry doors and Donatello's San Lorenzo pulpits, Flaxman saw major examples of Christian works of art conceived within the context of a classical revival, a fusion of traditions that reflected Flaxman's own dual interests, and for which he would have found practically no visual stimulus back in England. Flaxman was responding to such works not only as an artist collecting data on compositions and styles, but also as a practising Christian reacting emotionally.

Flaxman was not looking at Italian art, however, with a completely open mind. Although very receptive to it, he was not a young, impressionable artist readily succumbing to influences. He was now in his mid-thirties, already aware to some extent of the direction in which his art was going, and thus looking at Italian works very selectively. The 'simplicity' and linearity which he had found on sarcophagi and Greek vases, he was now able to find in what was then called 'primitive' Italian art, and he rejected the scientific side of the Renaissance exemplified in the use of perspective. Apart from the collection of Christian imagery, Flaxman singled out certain characteristics from the works of only those artists to whom he responded. His ideal painters and sculptors included Duccio and Giotto, Ghiberti, Jacopo della Quercia, Luca della Robbia and Masaccio, on to Raphael, Michelangelo, Correggio and Andrea del Sarto. In his taste Flaxman was thus a major forerunner of the new approach to Italian art which was to develop in the nineteenth century, from the Nazarenes to Lord Lindsay and Dyce.

Without the impact that Italian art from the late Ducento to the High Renaissance made on Flaxman, the style of his own art both in Italy and when back in England would presumably have been more conventionally Neoclassical, compounded mainly of the antique and of nature, and as a result far less individual.

Flaxman accepted the generally recognised importance of both the art of classical antiquity and of the High Renaissance, which he combined with a personal taste for the unfashionable earlier period leading up to the High Renaissance. In all this art of the past he sought what he called 'simplicity' or purity, which he joined with qualities of gracefulness and delicacy. Occasionally he showed his approval of works of art by the use of such terms as 'affecting', 'noble' or 'sublime', and sometimes 'powerful greatness'. Only when some of these characteristics were present would Flaxman apply the word 'beauty'. He would also expect some evidence of imagination, together with a proper attention to contour or outline, and also perhaps to light and revealing drapery. He therefore admired forms of art far removed from that of the Baroque; only calmer works by such artists as Puget, Guercino and Orazio Gentileschi were acceptable from an otherwise much-hated period. Otherwise the seventeenth century exemplified bad taste, and its works were dismissed with a range of adjectives that included 'extravagant', 'affected', 'bombastic' and 'hard'. In general Flaxman disliked anything that was 'rich' or 'splendid'.

1 Through France

In Normandy Flaxman looked at many of the Gothic churches in which he admired altars 'magnificently decorated with statues', but did not go into details.[9] Travelling south through Rouen, he noted of the elaborate decoration of the cathedral's west facade, dating from the twelfth to the sixteenth centuries, that it was similar to 'the Saxon Gothic, the statues and ornaments so entirely cover this part of the building that it has the appearance of rockwork of petrification'. The Flaxmans travelled to Evreux, where they stayed for a week with the Duc de Bouillon, with whom Flaxman had already been in correspondence in 1786.[10]

The duke, a soldier and man of liberal ideas, wanted the sculptor whilst in France to execute two marble busts for him, but Flaxman declined as he did not wish to delay his journey.[11] Having reached Paris, he went to the abbey of St. Denis, noting many details about the monuments and the treasury, and making a drawing of the tomb of *Francis I* by Philibert de l'Orme and Pierre Bontemps, commenting that its bas-reliefs were of the 'grandest gusto like Michelangelo, they border a little on the extravagant'. Throughout his tour, Flaxman made few sketches of entire tombs. That of *Francis I* must have been particularly interesting to him; perhaps he found in its blending of Christian and classical forms a combination which he would find relevant to his own work, giving him a foretaste of a kind of imagery of which he was to see many more Renaissance examples when he reached Italy. Other excursions from Paris included one to the Sèvres porcelain factory, which unfortunately he does not record in detail, merely describing the products as 'beautiful'.[12]

He also went to Versailles, where the richness of the decorations of the apartments and of the theatre seem to have overwhelmed him; in a letter he described the works by Lebrun and his contemporaries as 'splendid', and the theatre as 'wonderfully rich',[13] but these words when used by Flaxman are not ones of praise, since in his journal he described the same theatre as 'barbarous'. He found more to say about the garden sculptures, as one might expect. The restrained group of *Milo* by Puget in the Allée Royale (now in the Louvre) he regarded as the best modern work, admiring the 'genius in the thought and attention to nature in the execution', but continuing his comments with a typical qualification that the *Milo* 'wants the purity of some of the neighbouring statues copied from the antique. It is unlucky for Puget that his group of *Perseus and Andromeda* is placed next to a good copy of *Paetus and Arria*' (both these sculptures are also now in the Louvre).

Flaxman then continued his journey down the Rhône valley, noting in Lyon that in a church such as the Primatiale St-Jean, begun in the eleventh century, one could see that 'architecture of the time of our Saxon Gothic, though exceedingly barbarous, has retained something more of the Greek ornaments'. This comment indicates that although Flaxman already admired Gothic works before he left England, he was not visually receptive to the more primitive forms of Romanesque, and felt it needed justifying as a style by showing that at least chronologically Romanesque was nearer to classical sources.

2 Northern Italy and Tuscany: Early Italian and later art

As Flaxman was travelling by the overland route to Italy, and not by sea to Leghorn, his comments in the peninsula start with Turin. There he found the Baroque palaces and churches very disagreeable, showing that 'bad taste of architecture which succeeded the age of Michelangelo', with carved facades and interiors 'as rich in gold, silver and fine marble as they were poor in taste'. Even amongst the large collection of paintings in the Palazzo Reale he found very little he liked, as the collection was 'mostly Dutch, not three of which pleased me'. The one painting that 'pleased me best' was Orazio Gentileschi's *Annunciation* (now in the Pinacoteca, Turin), a graceful composition that would appeal to Flaxman's taste (Plate 37).

He next passed through Milan, where he naturally looked at Leonardo's *Last Supper*, admiring its 'noble

37 Orazio Gentileschi: *Annunciation.*

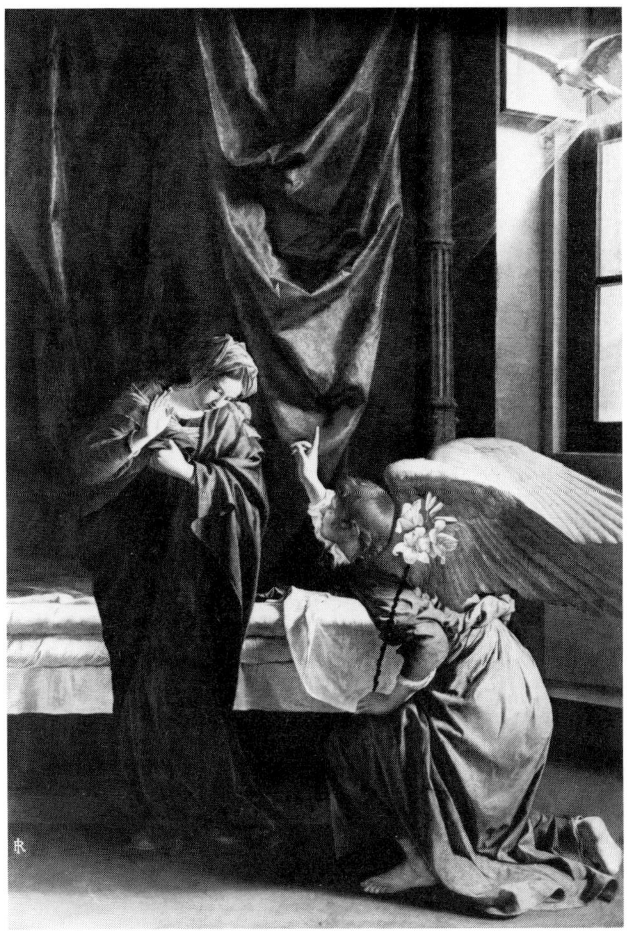

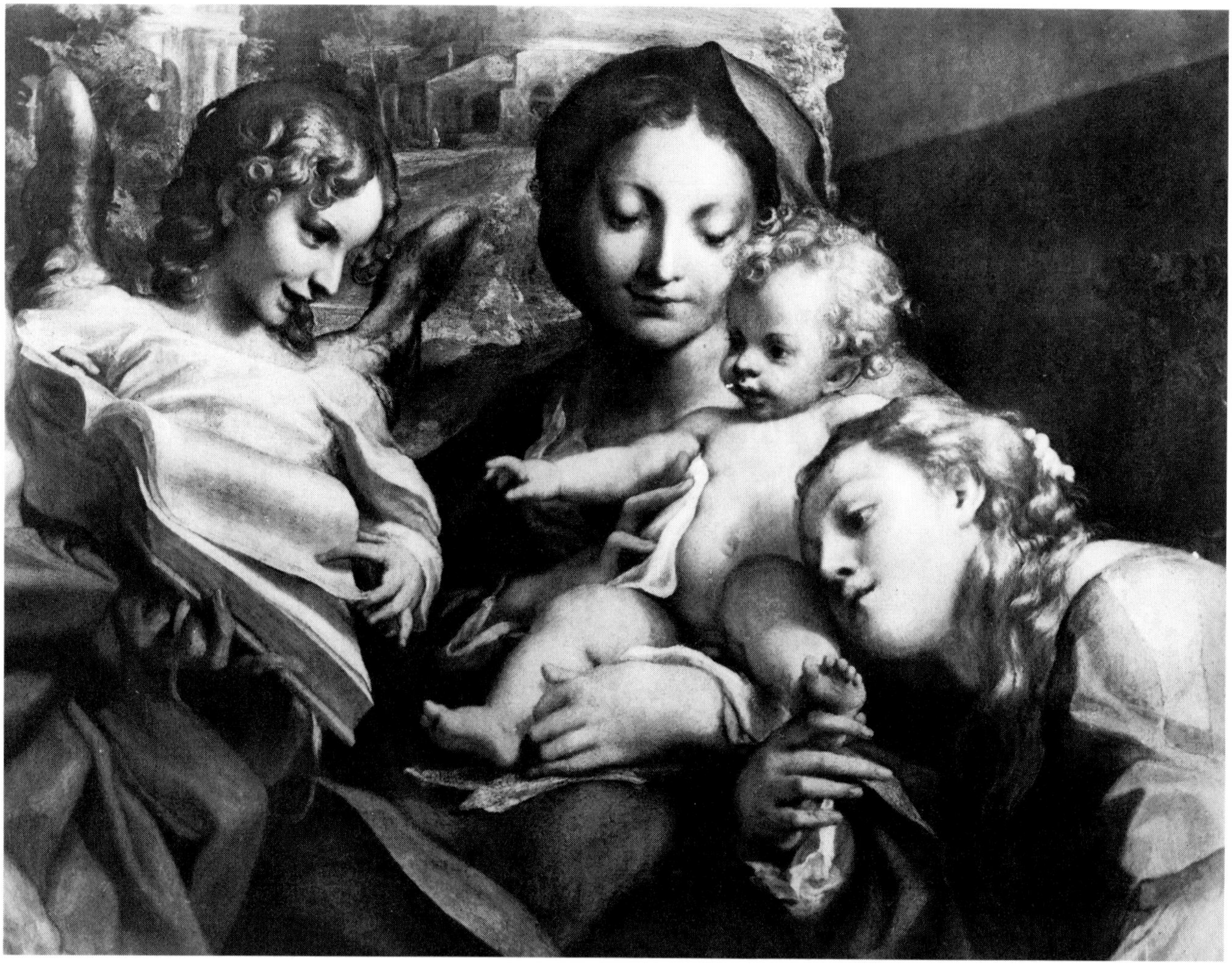

38 Correggio: *Virgin of St. Jerome (Il Giorno)*: detail.

and affecting manner', and hoping that some who travelled to Italy 'for improvement' would make copies of it. By the time he had been in Rome several months he still regarded the *Last Supper* even in its decayed state as a finer picture than any he had seen in Rome, with the exception of Michelangelo's Sistine Chapel frescoes.[14] Flaxman also commented in his diary on Milan cathedral, and made rough drawings of the bas-reliefs over the west doors, which he describes as being built in the 'grecian manner'. The general effect of the cathedral he found 'exquisitely light and beautiful', and he particularly admired the sixteenth-century wooden bas-reliefs in the choir: 'nothing can excell some of the compositions for imagination and beauty, and I would advise [any] artist who visits this church to observe them with attention'. The one work in the cathedral which Flaxman disliked intensely was the mid-sixteenth-century sculpture of a flayed *St. Bartholomew*. This piece by Marco d'Agrate he thought 'stiff, and though the artist might be considered a great anatomist in his time, his work would do no credit to a sculptor of the present age'.

Travelling south to Piacenza, he admired the frescoes in the cathedral dome by Guercino and Morazzone, noting that 'the design is bold, the execution is grand', approving of this more restrained aspect of the seventeenth century. It was usually the more extravagant element in the Mannerist and Baroque styles which prompted Flaxman's adverse comments, especially when those works could be examined at closer quarters, such as Mochi's equestrian Farnese statues also in Piacenza. He noted that these were the works of a pupil of Giambologna, who 'has followed the style of his master, whom Winckelmann judiciously calls the destroyer of art'.

Although Flaxman admired the Piacenza dome, when he came to Parma he disliked Correggio's dome of the *Ascension of Christ* in San Giovanni Evangelista because the artist was 'out of his element' in representing figures which need 'a powerful greatness and simplicity of manner he was not master of'. He much preferred Correggio's easel paintings, both when in Italy and when at home. Before going abroad he had already bought an engraving of Correggio's *Virgin of St. Jerome (Il Giorno)*, and when he saw it in Steccata he wrote in his journal that 'there is some grace, some affectation and very fine colouring, with an originality of thought in the composition' (Plate 38). In this context he is probably using the word 'affectation' in its better contemporary sense of 'fondness' or 'a high degree of liking', as defined in Samuel Johnson's *Dictionary*. Flaxman's great admiration for this altarpiece may have influenced the sentiment as well as the general composition, if not the details, of one of his own Italian drawings inscribed 'The Golden Age' (Plate 39), which also captures some of the grace and charm which both Flaxman and his contemporaries saw in the work of Correggio.

In Bologna, Flaxman was to find two major Renaissance works which appealed to his taste. The earliest were the bas-reliefs on the west facade of San Petronio, in particular the central portal by Jacopo della Quercia (Plate 40). Flaxman described these panels in detail in his journal, showing he wanted to remember as clearly as possible works which had aroused in him great enthusiasm. He praised them for 'the force, beauty and intelligence of their composition and execution', which he found 'very little inferior to the greatness of Michelangelo or the delicacy of Raphael', the highest praise that the eighteenth century could bestow on any work of art, apart from making a favourable comparison with classical antiquity. Flaxman responded wholeheartedly to an early Renaissance series of reliefs in which the principal stylistic feature was linearity, avoiding solid modelling and spatial illusion. The impression that these reliefs by Jacopo della Quercia made on Flaxman must have been profound, as he was not only looking with fresh eyes at a major series of works of Christian art whose compositions he might find subsequently relevant to his own art, but also at works whose style must have helped to confirm the direction in which he himself was already moving.

Also whilst in Bologna he went to San Giovanni in Monte to see Raphael's famous large altarpiece of *St. Cecilia* (Plate 41). He was already familiar with the work from Strange's engraving, but when he saw the original painting for the first time isolated in its own side chapel, the experience prompted some of the highest praise to be found anywhere in Flaxman's Italian journals or letters. 'This picture', he notes, 'shows the superiority of Raphael over the other painters in the delicacy of expression, the noble character and air of the figures, the fine turn of the heads, the intelligence of the limbs and the perfection of the folds of the drapery, but above all in the simple and poetical composition of the whole'. Flaxman's stress on the 'delicacy of expression', and his choice of such adjectives as 'simple' and 'poetical' are particularly relevant to his own art. Flaxman disliked some elements in a larger altarpiece in the same church by Raphael's master Perugino of the *Madonna and Saints* (also now in the Pinacoteca, Bologna), which he thought showed 'a little stiffness, poverty and want of understanding in the drawing of the drapery and limbs'. As a whole, however, he found the painting had 'great purity and beauty'. The expression on the face of St. Catherine he found 'beautiful and ecstatic', presumably attracting his attention as she is one of the most Raphaelesque figures in the composition.

The work that Flaxman disliked most in Bologna was the Fontana del Nettuno with its bronzes by Giambologna, only a few yards across the square from San Petronio. The figure of Neptune he at first dismissed as 'extravagant', but crossed the word out to write the stronger one of 'bombastic'. He continued his adverse assessment by saying that the Neptune was 'affected in its action and knobby in the manner of making out the anatomy'; an unfair comment since he is no more 'knobby' than the *Torso Belvedere* or the *Farnese Hercules*. As to the four mermaids at the corners, Flaxman's purer—or more prudish—sensibilities found them quite unacceptable; the act of 'squeezing water from their breasts is whimsical and indelicate', he noted. The contrast between such 'whimsical', profane art and Jacopo della Quercia's sacred art would have seemed all the more marked after looking at the church.

Flaxman's general assessment of the Bolognese School of painters is in keeping with his comments on the Fontana del Nettuno. He dismissed all late sixteenth and seventeenth century paintings in general terms, presumably after seeing some of the many altarpieces (which he does not specify) by the Carracci, Guido Reni and others. Their works are all banished from his canon because of their 'twisted heads, full bodies, fluttering draperies, small wrists and ankles, and bombastic attitudes', which Flaxman contrasts un-

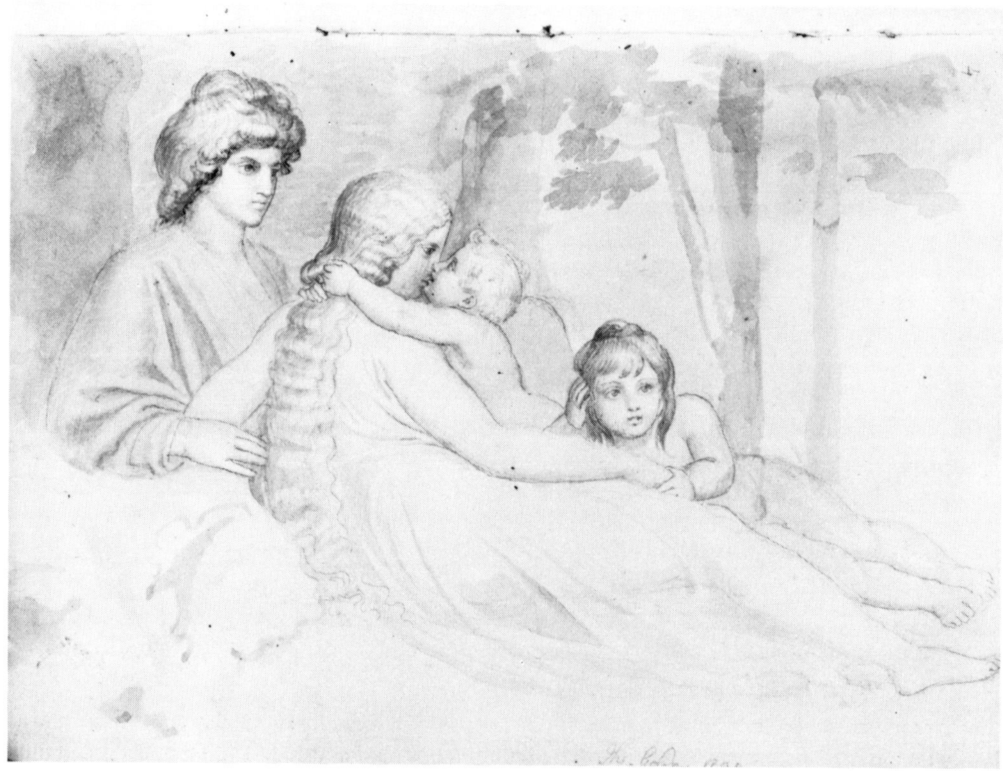

39 *The Golden Age*. Pen and ink and wash, 22·6 × 16·4 cms.

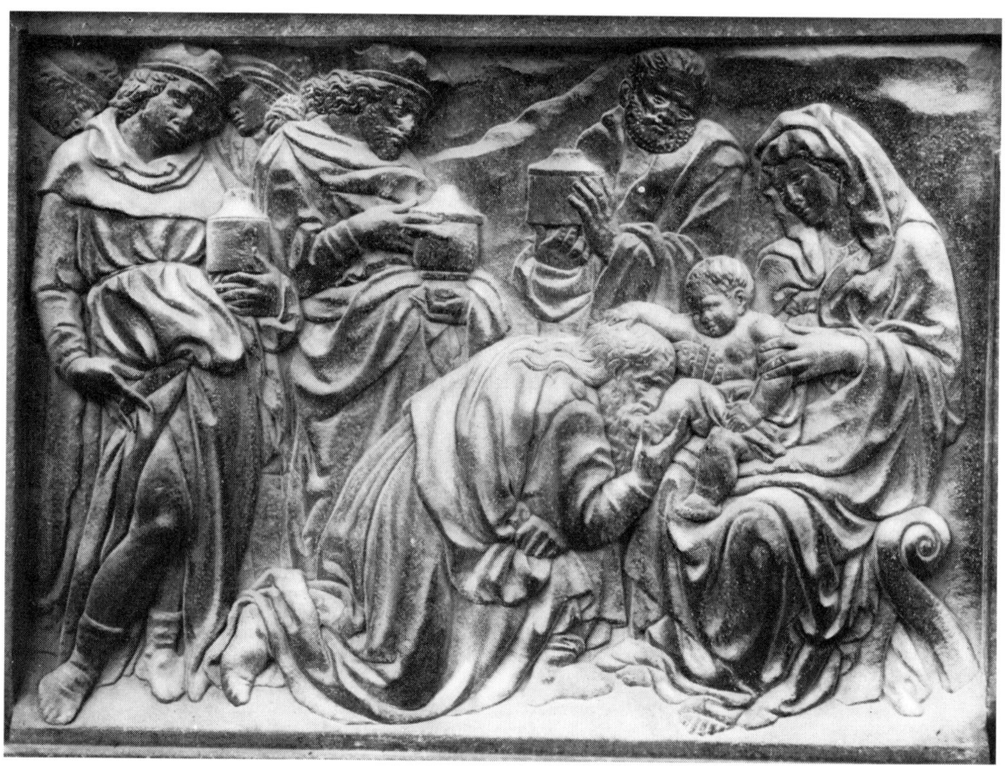

40 Jacopo della Quercia: *The Adoration of the Magi*.

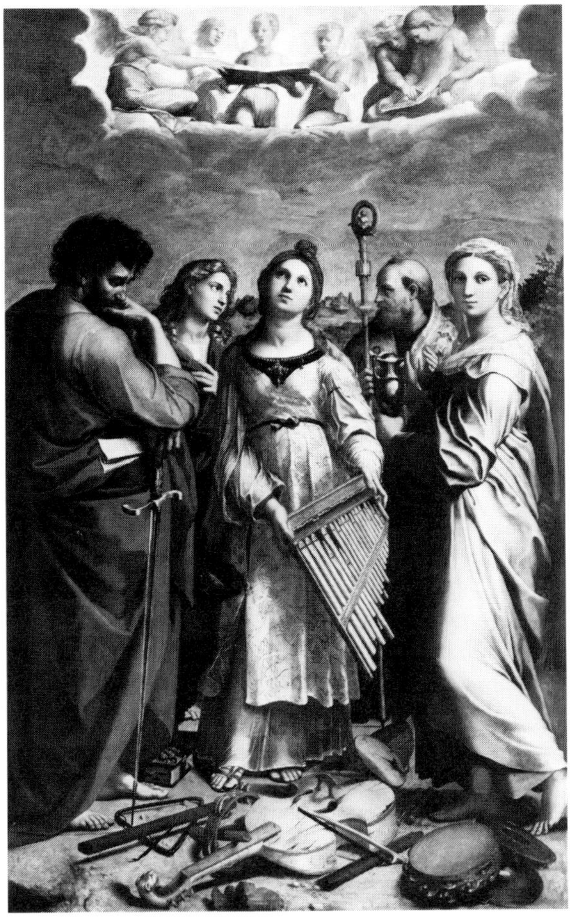

41 Raphael: *St. Cecilia.*

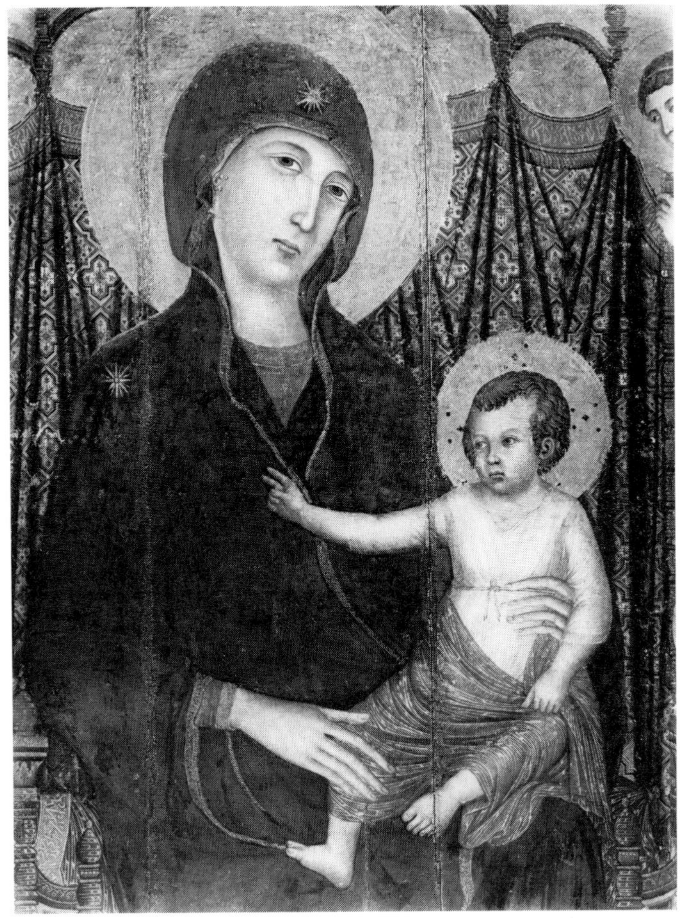

42 Duccio: *Rucellai Madonna:* detail.

favourably with 'the simple natural characters and expression of Masaccio [and] Andrea del Sarto'.

On arrival in Florence, where Flaxman made a more prolonged stay, his comments on works of art become more detailed and his sketches more extensive, including not only rough drawings but also more carefully worked ones, sometimes using a wash. Flaxman started a Florentine notebook with a drawing after a Luca della Robbia, a revealing choice of artist since Flaxman would have found in works by all the della Robbia family that Christian piety and delicate sentiment which were amongst the characteristics in Renaissance art which Flaxman found sympathetic. The drawing is a prelude to several pages largely devoted to comments on sculpture of the fifteenth and sixteenth centuries, followed by a few pages on earlier paintings.[15]

The longest comment on a painting in his Florence journal is devoted to the *Rucellai Madonna*, then still in its chapel in Santa Maria Novella (Plate 42). Flaxman's detailed comments are particularly interesting not only in the light of his own work, but also in the context of the gradual revival of interest at the end of the eighteenth century in the so-called 'primitives'. He wrote that although the painter had retained the 'general appearance' of his predecessors' works, he gave the Virgin 'a beautiful, simple face, an easy turn to the head, he paid considerable attention to the folds and their joints in the drapery, he left out the hard outlines the Greeks [i.e. Byzantine artists] used to express the features, and rounded them and the folds of drapery with tender shadows'. He concluded his description by making an interesting parallel with a work he knew well in London, the panel of *Richard II* in Westminster Abbey.

Like his admiration for the *Rucellai Madonna*, some of Flaxman's other comments on Trecento and Quattrocento works as well as his sketches after works of these periods, show an independence in taste which marks him out from most of his contemporaries. Other artists noticed how important this early Italian period was for Flaxman. Thomas Unwins, for example, was to write from Naples to a friend in 1827 observing that 'it was in this school even more than in the antique that Flaxman studied, and it is following soundings left by Flaxman, that the Germans are now making such discoveries.'[16]

Gradually in the last quarter of the eighteenth century a few discerning artists, collectors and curators in Britain and on the Continent were beginning to appreciate the merits of Italian art created before the days of the High Renaissance, which had been either ignored or barely mentioned in the literature earlier in the century, such as the Richardsons' widely used guidebook, their *Account* from 1722 onwards, or Joseph Addison's *Remarks on Several Parts of Italy* (1705 onwards). Romney might have opened Flaxman's eyes to this period of Italian art,[17] and before the sculptor had arrived in Italy Thomas Patch had published his series of prints in the early 70's after Giotto, Masaccio and Ghiberti. As early as the late 1760's and the 70's Grand Duke Pietro Leopoldo had reorganised the display of his collection in the Uffizi galleries, bringing out of neglect and putting on public display works by such artists as Fra Angelico and Piero della Francesca. Before Flaxman arrived in Italy, Luigi Lanzi had published his *Real Galleria di Firenze* (1782), one of several late eighteenth-century guidebooks to the Uffizi which list works hanging that are attributed to Trecento and Quattrocento artists. Only gradually, however, was this new revolutionary arrangement in the Uffizi going to have a broad influence on taste. Initially, only a small number of Flaxman's contemporaries shared the Duke's and Lanzi's enthusiasm. In the 90's Flaxman would undoubtedly have found Canova's taste sympathetic, since he too was looking at the time at early Italian art.[18]

Flaxman admired Giotto as a 'prodigy of genius',[19] and other painters of the Trecento and Quattrocento whose art he saw and admired in Florence include Taddeo Gaddi, Andrea and Bernardo Orcagna, and Fra Angelico, whose works he praised in general terms, without specifying examples, for their 'simplicity' and their 'beauty'. In Santa Croce, he said that he found some of the compositions of the frescoes 'distinct and striking, the perfection of the character, the force of action and expression is astonishing'. At the time he could not have seen Giotto's frescoes in the Bardi and Peruzzi chapels, nor those by Agnolo Gaddi in the Castellani Chapel, all of which had been painted over. Flaxman does not specify which frescoes he admired in the church, but he presumably had in mind Taddeo Gaddi's cycle in the Baroncelli chapel, and other Trecento works in the sacristy. He would also have seen Cimabue's *Crucifixion*.

His sketches after paintings include two scenes from the life of Abraham by dello Delli in Santa Maria Novella, and also in the same church, Uccello's *Flood*.[20] He would presumably also have been interested in the large cycle in the Spanish Chapel by Andrea di Bonaiuto. Like all his drawings after Trecento and Quattrocento art, Flaxman shows in his sketches after dello Delli and Uccello a desire to record the story-telling elements of the compositions to the exclusion of important stylistic traits. This is particularly evident in the drawing after *The Flood* since Flaxman has completely eliminated Uccello's striking perspective and clear articulation of space. He has translated the statuesque original into the terms of a bas-relief. Santa Maria Novella seems to have been one of the more significant Florentine churches for Flaxman since he drew from two series of frescoes there, commented at length on the *Rucellai Madonna*, and might even perhaps have derived inspiration from Masaccio's *Trinità*, which could perhaps have suggested in the majestic, monumental figure in the foreground of the donor's wife, Flaxman's later series of figures symbolising Resignation (Plates 173 and 175).

His sketches after early Italian sculptures in Florence include Andrea Pisano's relief of the *Creation of Eve* on the lower register of the Campanile (in the Mellon sketchbook). His drawing, which almost entirely excludes the dominant background trees, is a simple record in outline of a compact composition neatly fitted in to a hexagon. Other sketches after early Italian sculptures include two of the front panels from Tino da Camaino's tomb of *Gastone della Torre* in Santa Croce (now re-assembled in the church's museum). In choosing the *Resurrection* and *Noli Me Tangere* panels, and not recording the whole composition of the monument, Flaxman again shows a very definite interest in the story-telling aspect of Christian subjects.

Ghiberti's reliefs on his first Baptistry doors were to have a profound influence on Flaxman's style, and it is not surprising to find him writing in a letter from Italy that 'I could never quit Ghiberti's brass gates to the Baptistry of St. John's so much studied by Raphael and Michelangelo'.[21] Flaxman preferred Ghiberti above all other Quattrocento sculptors, a preference he was to maintain throughout his life. Later in his lectures at the Royal Academy he made it clear that he liked the first set of doors because they lacked the complex perspectival settings of the later ones,[22] and it is therefore not surprising to find him concentrating in his sketches on the earlier bronzes (Plates 43 and 186). He con-

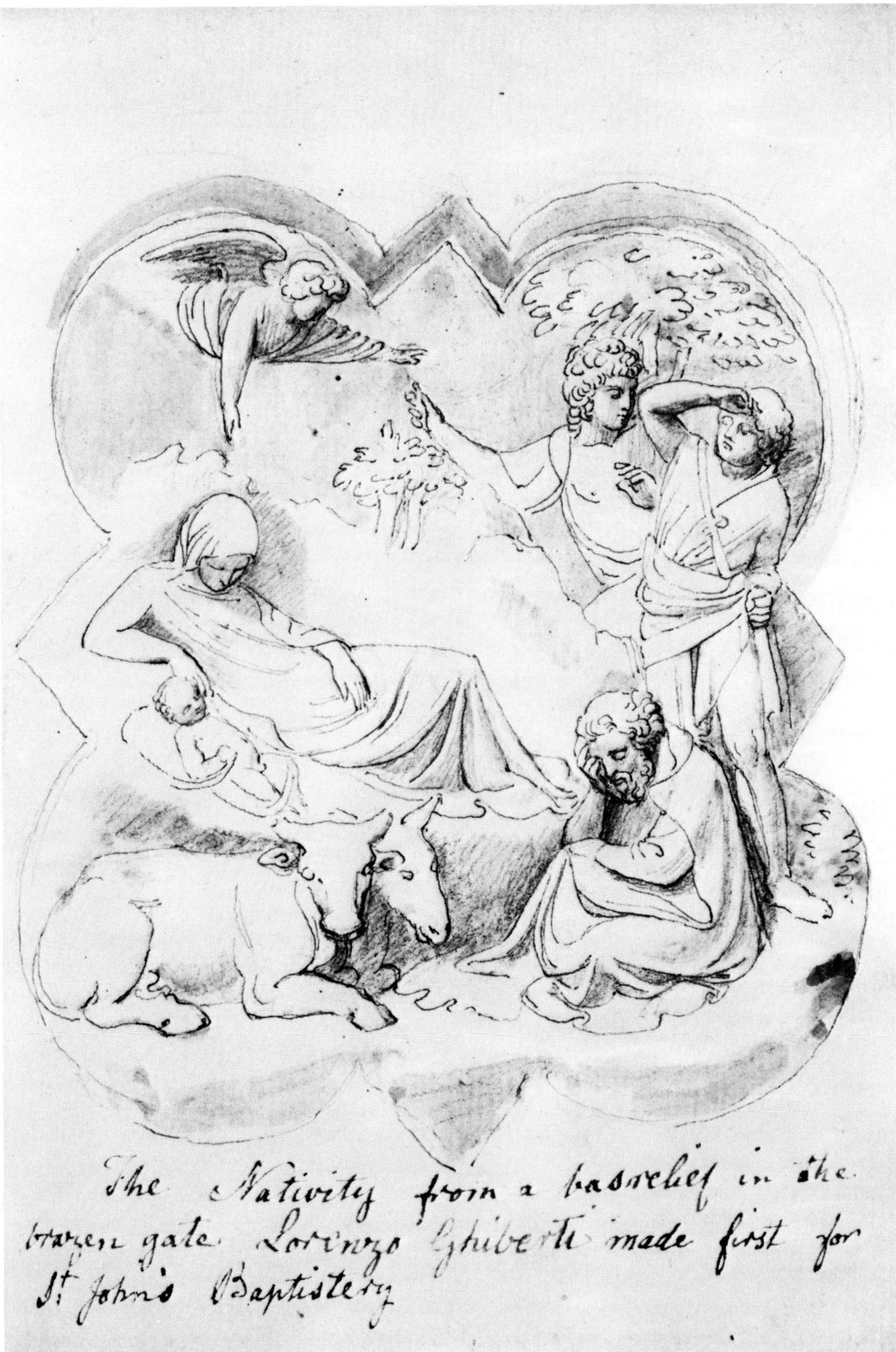

43 *The Nativity, after Ghiberti, Baptistry, Florence.* Pen and ink and wash, 22 × 15·4 cms.

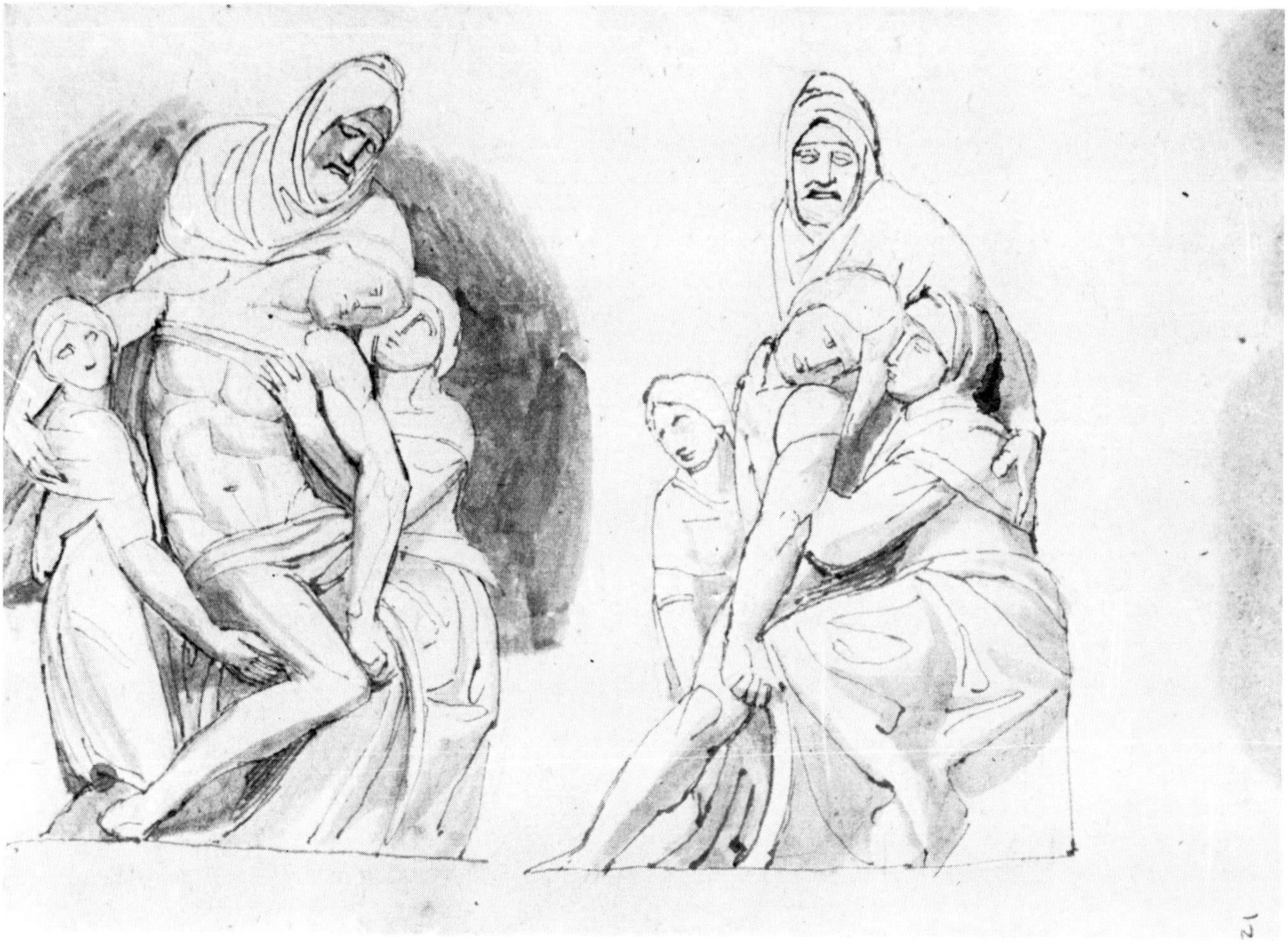

44 *Pietà, after Michelangelo, Duomo, Florence.* Pen and ink and wash, 26·8 × 21 cms.

sistently exaggerated in his drawings the linear qualities inherent in Ghiberti's reliefs, to the extent that he omitted or barely suggested the more illusionistic elements in the composition and eliminated the Renaissance sense of space. In his copy of *Christ among the Doctors* Flaxman has left out the architectural background which helps to create the original spatial setting, merely executing a rough record of the arrangement of the figures. In his drawing of the *Nativity* he has omitted the projecting rocks and minimised the trees. Some years later it is possible that Flaxman had this latter panel in mind when designing the monument to *Lady Shuckburgh-Evelyn* (Plate 202), although the main source for the monument is a Roman sarcophagus.

In San Lorenzo Flaxman drew Brunelleschi's competition panel of the *Sacrifice of Abraham* (now in the Bargello), dividing the composition horizontally between two pages of a sketchbook, recording the details fairly accurately. The drawings show a greater interest in the upper half with the sacrifice, than in the lower half of the composition. As in the instances of the Ghiberti and della Quercia panels, Flaxman chose a relief which portrays an incident with a minimum number of elements, set against a fairly plain background.

The reliefs on Donatello's pulpits in the same church, on the other hand, are more complex compositions in the original bronzes, but Flaxman's sketches simplify them in his customary manner. He was only interested in isolated scenes on the pulpit, not its whole design, and in rendering Donatello's reliefs he again exaggerates the linearity of the originals. He drew the *Entombment* from one pulpit, and chose three scenes from the other, the *Harrowing of Hell* and *Ascension* from one side, and the *Three Maries at the Sepulchre* from the end. However, Flaxman disliked other aspects of Donatello's work, confiding to his journal an attack on the *Judith and Holofernes* because it was not only 'poor' in composition, but also because Judith's attitude was 'tame', the drapery 'ill conceived' and the naked parts 'excessively poor'. By the time he was writing a few pages later he had seen the bronze *David*, which is also dismissed as a 'copy of mean nature in a hard, poor Gothic manner', an unexpected use of the word 'Gothic' as one of censure although commonly used in this way in the eighteenth century.

Michelangelo was one of Flaxman's heroes both whilst in Italy and when in England. The *Medici* tombs seem to have fascinated him and he made drawings of them in two of his sketchbooks (in the Victoria and Albert Museum and Mellon Collection). Many of the details of the tombs as rendered by Flaxman are inaccurate, or even omitted, suggesting that his prime interest in the two monuments was as specimens of a particular type. The *Medici* tombs were supreme examples of a kind of monument that combined a contemporary portrait, allegorical figures and a sarcophagus, conceived within a Christian context. This mixture of elements had become common on monuments—of the more expensive kind—by Flaxman's day, and he must have been excited to see at first hand some of the examples from which the tradition had stemmed. That Flaxman was collecting practical information is clearly evident in one drawing in which he shows the *Giuliano de'Medici* tomb from a very oblique and unusual angle. The drawing suggests that he wishes to remember how such large, freestanding figures could nonetheless be contained within the limited space of a wall monument and not need the great area of a freestanding design: a practical requirement for Flaxman in the overcrowded interiors of late eighteenth century churches. In the same sketchbook he drew Michelangelo's *Pietà* in the Duomo from two different angles (Plate 44). He fails to capture the essence of Michelangelo's style, but shows an interest in how he has arranged his forms within the confines of a block of marble. Flaxman sketches the masses but not the details; the general forms of the composition he has recorded fairly accurately, whereas he has barely drawn the faces.

Flaxman's taste in architecture is similar to that in the other arts, as is shown by a few summary comments in his Florence journal. He admired the Baptistry because it was 'very handsome', a general assessment in which he would presumably have included the mosaics and Andrea Pisano's doors, as well as his known admiration for Ghiberti's early reliefs. He mentioned the 'perfection' of the Duomo and of the Palazzo Vecchio. The church of Santo Spirito he thought was 'truly beautiful', a strongly worded description for Flaxman who presumably not only enjoyed Brunelleschi's architecture, but also the wealth of sympathetic altarpieces dating from the Trecento and Quattrocento by Filippino Lippi and others, as well as Andrea Orcagna's fresco in the refectory.

His first written comments in the Florence journal were on four of the principal sculptures outside the Palazzo Vecchio and in the Loggia dei Lanzi. In Cellini's *Perseus* he found that 'the contour is grand, the attitude is natural and noble, the parts are made out with great intelligence, the figure of Medusa is finely composed'. In his sketchbooks he made more drawings of this sculpture from different angles than from any other piece, (Plate 64) and even drew a plan of the group's compositional complexities. The colossal group of *Hercules and Cacus* by Bandinelli was dismissed as 'tame, bombastical and bad', but Flaxman nevertheless made a drawing of it (in the Mellon sketchbook). He drew six of the low relief figures by the same sculptor on the choir screen in the Duomo, presumably preferring this more restrained and linear side of Bandinelli's work. Flaxman made drawings from different angles of both Giambologna's *Hercules and the Centaur* (in the Mellon sketchbook) and his *Rape of the Sabines* (Plate 72). In both sketches after the *Rape* he has chosen angles from which the faces cannot be seen suggesting as in his drawings after Michelangleo's *Pietà* that one of his concerns was to learn how great sculptors of the past had organised complex compositions within the confines of a block of marble, very basic information of obvious practical application.

Elsewhere in Tuscany, and in other parts of Italy, Flaxman made notes and comments which provide even further examples of his admiration for the art of the Trecento and the Quattrocento.[23] In the north, he made six rough sketches on one page of the Scaligeri tombs in Verona, mostly dating from the Trecento, showing an interest in the variety amongst the designs of the tombs, which he has drawn complete in each case. Whilst in Lucca he drew from the facade of the Duomo Nicola Pisano's lunette of the *Deposition* (Plate 45).

In Siena he again drew from Nicola Pisano, sketching the overall composition of his pulpit in the Duomo, and also selecting a vigorously expressive detail from the panel depicting the damned being pushed down to Hell by an angel. From Duccio's *Maestà*, then still in the Duomo, he sketched a rough outline from part of the scene of *Christ in the Garden of Gethsemane*. Flaxman's collection of Christian imagery continued in the Duomo with the *Resurrection* panel from Tino da

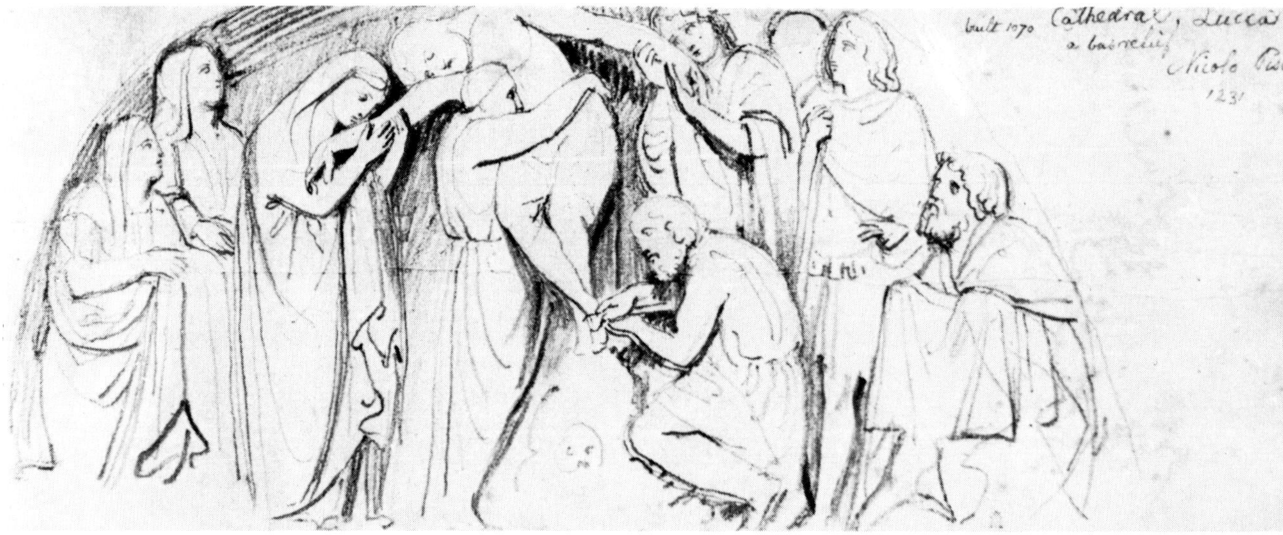

45 *Deposition, after Nicola Pisano, Duomo, Lucca.* Pencil, 15·2 × 36·2 cms.

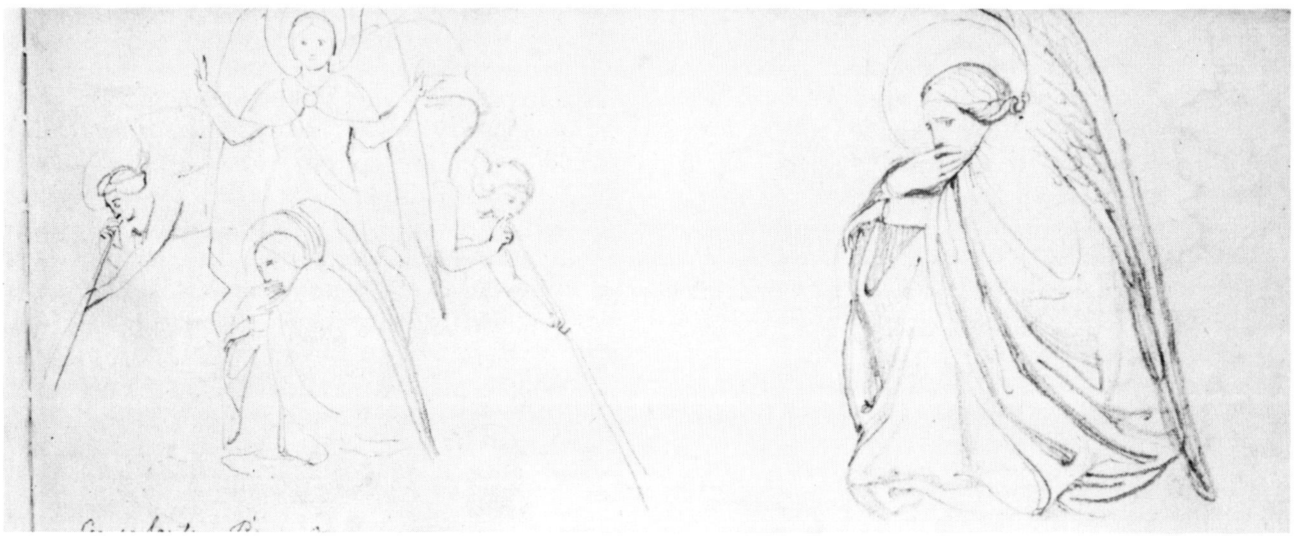

46 *Angels, after the Master of the Triumph of Death (? Francesco Traini), Camposanto Pisa.* Pencil, 15·2 × 36·2 cms.

Camaino's *Petroni* tomb, as well as a drawing of the whole monument. When he went below to the Baptistry he sketched two panels from the font, believing them both to be the work of Ghiberti, *St. John led to Prison* and *Dance of Salome*. The former is by Ghiberti, the latter in fact by Donatello. In both his drawings Flaxman eliminated architectural backgrounds which contributed towards the sense of space, and flattened the compositions into classical bas-reliefs. The base of the throne in the prison scene, which Ghiberti set at an angle, is even made parallel to the picture plane in Flaxman's copy.

In Pisa, Flaxman made very rough sketches from two panels of the bronze doors by Bonanno Pisano, the *Raising of Lazarus* and the *Transfiguration*. He did not normally draw works as early as these, belonging to the late Ducento, but was presumably attracted by what he would have called their 'simplicity'. The *Transfiguration* panel is one of the most symmetrically balanced compositions on the doors, a sparse and neatly arranged design which Flaxman obviously found sympathetic

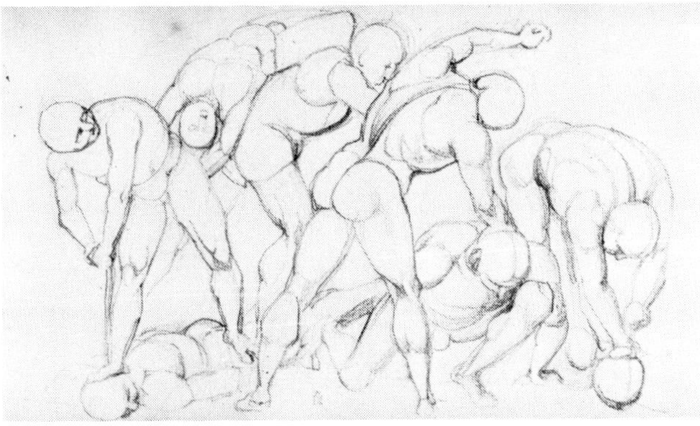

48 *Battle of the Nudes, after Signorelli, Duomo, Orvieto.* Pencil, 15·2 × 36·2 cms.

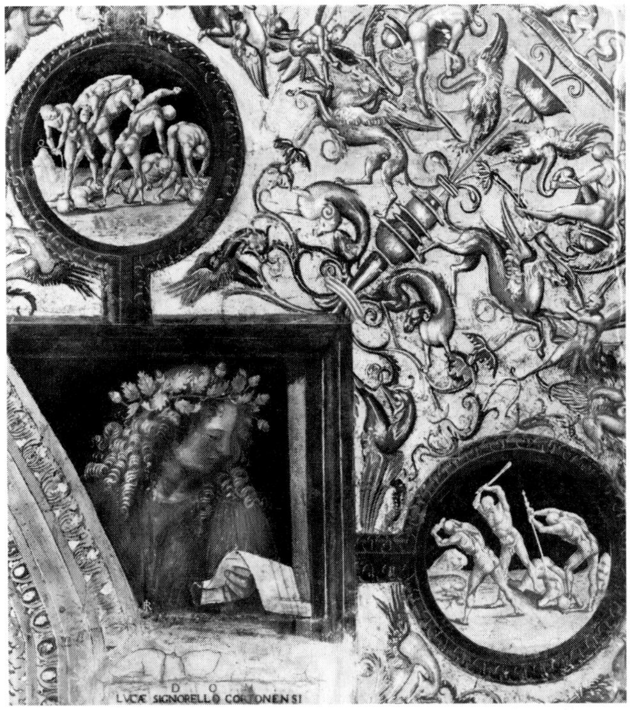

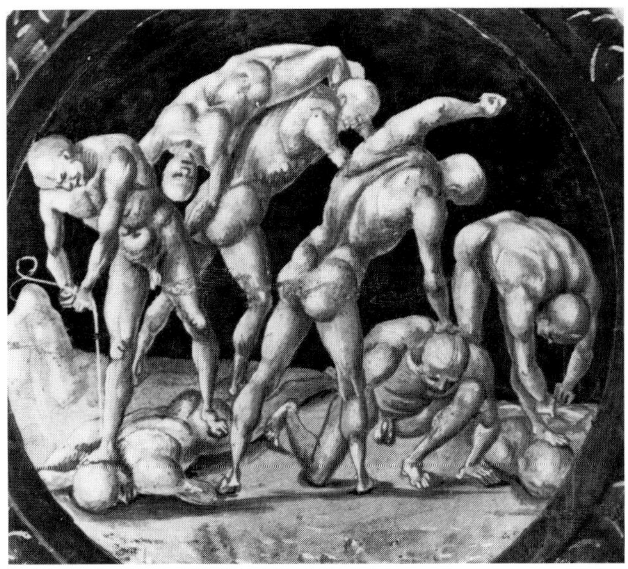

47a Signorelli: *Battle of the Nudes.*
47b *Battle of the Nudes:* detail.

and which was later to be included amongst the plates of his *Lectures*.

In the same sketchbook in the Camposanto he made two drawings from the large frescoes of the *Triumph of Death* and the *Last Judgment and Hell* then attributed to Andrea Orcagna (but nowadays to an anonymous Master of the Triumph of Death, perhaps Francesco Traini). From the *Triumph* he chose the most anguished set of heads in the whole composition, seen at eye level, those of the lepers imploring for mercy. In choosing this detail rather than the hermits, aristocratic riders or pastoral musicians, Flaxman was obviously wishing to record a more emotionally charged aspect of late Trecento art. On the other hand, he selected from the *Last Judgment* the group of angels forming the central, focal point of the vast and tumultuous composition, a point of tranquillity that is symmetrically balanced. On the same page he even drew one of the angels a second time, with greater care, obviously finding it an attractive detail (Plate 46). The same detail was to be selected a few years later, about 1798, by Humbert de Superville and reproduced amongst Ottley's illustrations in his *Early Florentine School* (1826).

Orvieto cathedral was another of the major early Italian buildings that Flaxman studied. From the famous series of frescoes by Signorelli, Flaxman chose to sketch not from one of the large scenes relating to the *Last Judgment*, but rather after one of the small grisaille roundels on the walls below, one of those depicting fighting male nudes (Plate 47). It would have been difficult to record adequately part of one of the elaborate compositions, and even more difficult to extract a satisfactory group from the whole. Flaxman therefore very sensibly chose a scene that is not at first sight obvious, but one which epitomises Signorelli's style in miniature, and which is complete in itself (Plate 48). The treatment of a scene of struggling figures would have interested him as a theme as it related to one in his own works at the time, the *Fury of Athamas*.[24] (Plate 69)

Also whilst at Orvieto, Flaxman drew from Maitani's marble relief sculptures on the main facade of the cathedral, selecting the panel from the lowest of the

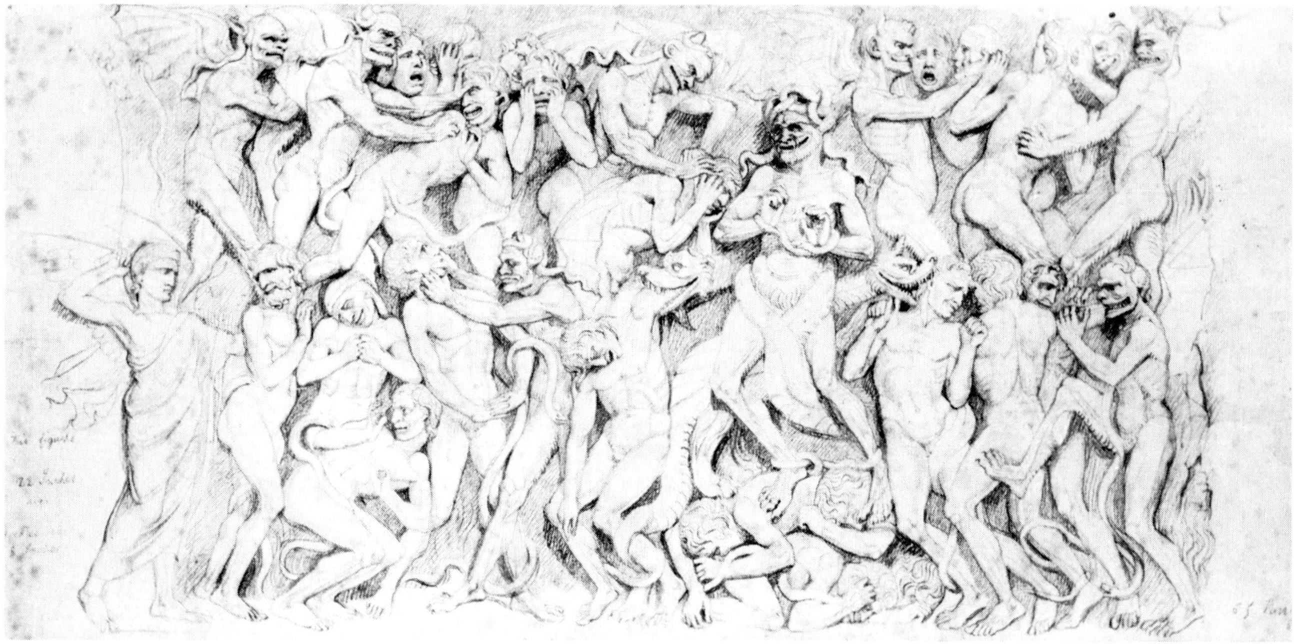

49 *Last Judgment, after Maitani, Duomo, Orvieto.* Pencil, 23·5 × 49·4 cms.

scenes showing the *Last Judgment*, the one illustrating the separation of the saved from the damned souls. Flaxman split the scene, which is divided in the original in any case by trailing vines, into two separate drawings, executing only the bottom half of each scene. Both of the drawings in the British Museum (Plate 49) he completed on a larger scale than usual, not in his small sketchbooks. The drawings are fairly accurate copies of the sculptures, completed with careful shading and not left merely as simple outlines. He even recorded on one of the drawings—the one reproduced here—the size of the original sculpture, this too is contrary to his normal practice. Flaxman chose, as with the lepers from the fresco at Pisa, the most emotional scene on the facade, in which he must have been impressed both by the intensity of expression and the vigour of execution.

At Orvieto and at Pisa Flaxman shared one of his sketchbooks with William Young Ottley.[25] A young man just turned twenty, Ottley arrived in Italy in 1791 and was to remain after the Flaxmans left until 1801, spending much of his time gathering material for his important future publications, such as *The Italian School of Design* (to be published between 1805 and 1823). His lifelong enthusiasm for early Italian art, which one sees in these later pages, was presumably either kindled or at least strengthened by this early association with Flaxman. Ottley's own drawing style shows the influence of Flaxman in its linearity (Plate 50), and he has also left a pleasantly intimate record of the sculptor at work on a model by candlelight (Plate 51).

The sculpture and frescoes of the *Last Judgment* which Flaxman saw in Italy must have come as a revelation to him, since he would have seen no such works on a grand scale in England. His drawings from various *Last Judgments* therefore surely record an emotional response of some excitement both in visual and in Christian terms. In so far as he was collecting information for future possible use, scenes of Hell in tomb designs would have been theologically unacceptable in the late eighteenth century, whereas angels and compositions of the Blessed would not. Such scenes as well as those of the damned, however, would have been relevant when designing plates for Dante, and it is even possible that some of his studies after *Last Judgments* were undertaken because of or suggested by Thomas Hope's commission for a set of *Divine Comedy* illustrations.[26] One of the reasons for Flaxman going to Orvieto may have been that he would have known that Signorelli had used Dante's epic as a source for some of his scenes, but Flaxman was not to borrow directly from them in his own interpretation. On the other hand, the large centralised figure of Lucifer in the fresco of *Hell* in the Camposanto at Pisa, is the kind of image that almost certainly lies behind Flaxman's own Lucifer in his *Dante* illustration (see Plates 121 and 122).

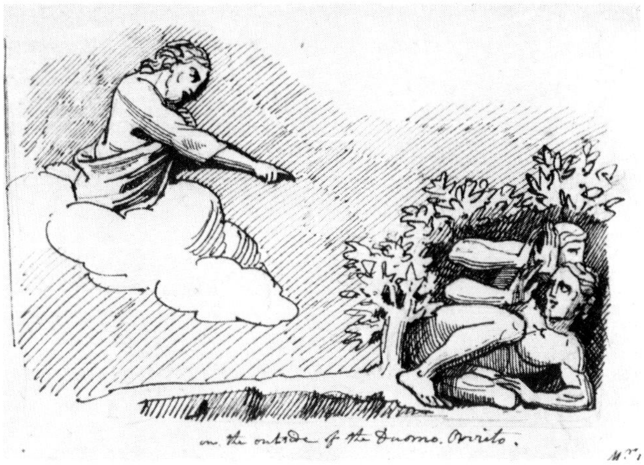

50 William Young Ottley: *Adam and Eve hiding from the Lord, after Maitani, Duomo, Orvieto.*
Pen and ink, 15·2 × 36·2 cms.

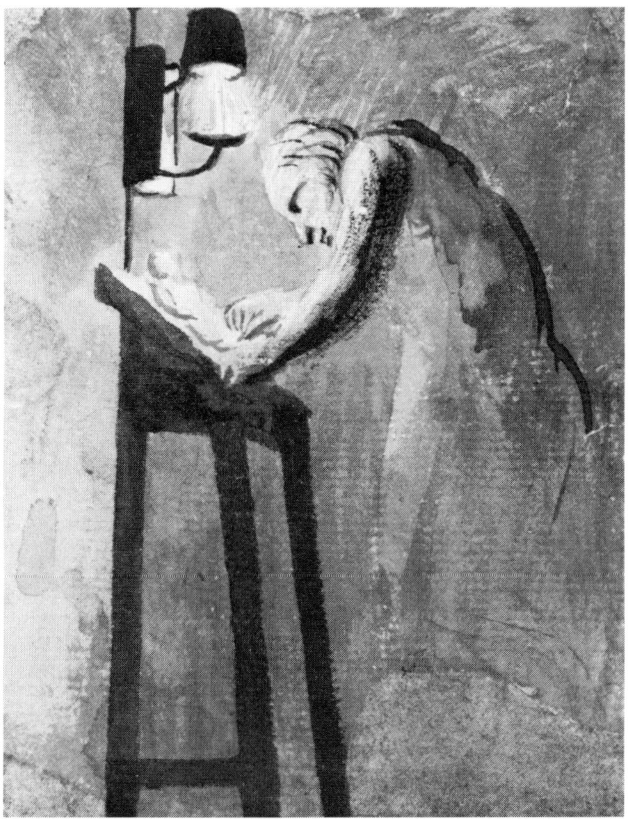

51 William Young Ottley: *John Flaxman at work on a model by candlelight.* Watercolour and bodycolour, 9·5 × 7·2 cms.

3 The Antique: Rome and elsewhere

Whenever Flaxman had an opportunity he looked at antique sculpture, long before he arrived in Rome. After leaving Turin, he regretted he had not known about the collection which was on display at the university, making amends when he reached Milan by visiting the fine collection of casts in the Accademia. Antique sculptures which Florence he sought 'everywhere', and also in the Camposanto in Pisa, in Rome and Portici, contributed many items to his journals and sketchbooks.

His longest comments on sculpture whilst in Florence are reserved in his journal for works of classical antiquity, especially the two most famous works in the Uffizi, the *Medici Venus* and the *Niobe* group. The *Niobe* group fascinated him. He not only made drawings of several of the different figures (in the Mellon sketchbook) but he was probably influenced by the largest and most impressive figures of the group, that of *Niobe with a clinging daughter* (see Plate 71), which may have been one of the many possible sources for his own *Fury of Athamas* (see Plate 69). The basis for his great admiration of classical art comes out clearly in his general description of the various *Niobe* group figures. 'There is no affectation of style', he wrote, by which he presumably meant on this occasion Dr. Johnson's definition of no 'artificial show'. Flaxman continued: 'beautiful nature was chosen by the artist and copied with so much spirit, judgment and truth of anatomy and outline, with a delicacy of execution, that when seen in proper light the naked parts seem capable of motion, the draperies are of fine cloths, light, beautifully disposed to contrast the limbs and shew them, as well as to add dignity to the figures'. Flaxman's comment does however show that he was not careful in distinguishing between the merits of the different pieces of this group, since some are fine but others mediocre.

He did not confine his drawings, however, to the largest pieces in the Uffizi. He found time to draw a lifesize *Infant Hercules strangling a Serpent*, a delightful standing *Cupid* who has just thrown an arrow at Jupiter which is as charming and pretty in the original marble as Flaxman's record of it (Plate 52), and a small-scale *Bathing Venus* of great elegance (all in the Mellon sketchbook). Flaxman drew the playful and almost sentimental aspect of antique sculpture, as well as the heroic and grand.

In Rome, where he arrived in December 1787, Flaxman showed the same interest in a wide variety of styles as he did elsewhere on his tour, drawing not only works of art accepted within the academic canon but also unfashionable ones such as the New Testament

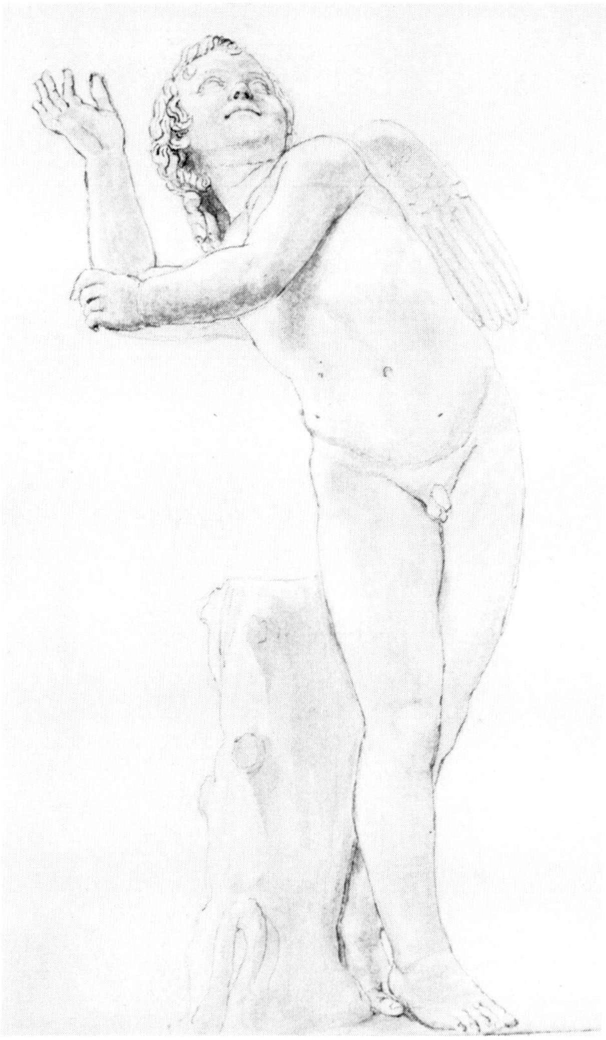

52 *Cupid throwing an Arrow, after antique sculpture, in Uffizi.* Pen and ink and wash, 22 × 15·4 cms.

scenes in the apse mosaic in Santa Maria Maggiore and Santa Maria in Trastevere, by Torriti and Pietro Cavallini respectively, from the late Ducento and the Trecento. Most of the drawings he executed in Rome after works of art of the past seem to have been done shortly after his arrival in the city, and he probably was so busy studying and drawing that he allowed his journal to lapse, writing down few comments (unless, of course, a Rome journal is lost). He was eventually to become extremely busy as a result of commissions, and during the latter part of his stay in Rome he would have had little time to spare for historical studies.

Farington reported that Flaxman was disappointed by his first impressions of Rome and its ruins because they did not look like the engravings of Piranesi,[27] but many travellers must have had this reaction. Flaxman was soon active visiting sites, churches and collections, scrupulously recording in his account-books the amounts of the gratuities he had to disburse. Much time was spent, as might be expected, in studying the major collections of antiquities in the Vatican, the Museo Capitolino, and the Villas Albani and Borghese, to which he paid frequent visits. Collections also included the Ludovisi, Pamfili, Mattei and others. He also made the well-established pilgrimage to Tivoli.[28]

Flaxman devoted more pages of his sketchbooks to drawings after works of classical antiquity, both statues and reliefs, than to works from the Ducento onwards. But whereas these later works represented fresh revelations to him, the antique sculptures would already in many instances have been familiar either from engravings in the archaeological literature, or from prints of similar examples. In these cases the visual impact would be derived from at last seeing the originals of works known for so long only at second-hand. Where engravings did not exist, however, there were obviously still some fresh encounters to be made.

Greek vase paintings hardly feature amongst his Italian drawings, perhaps because he was already very familiar with such source material before he went abroad, both in the British Museum and in the form of engravings. He also knew that Hamilton's second collection was going to be published as engravings, which would have eliminated the necessity of making drawings.[29] Although by the same token many of the antique sculptures he drew had also been published as engravings, the impact of seeing these in the originals would have been much stronger than in the case of vases which suffer less by being transposed onto the printed page.

The drawings he executed in Italy after the antique are fairly predictable, including many examples that one would expect to find in the work of a classically-trained and partially classically-orientated artist. Some of the most obvious examples are the *Apollo Belvedere*, the *Laocoon* and the *Horsetamers* of Monte Cavallo, the last drawn from several different angles (in both the Victoria and Albert Museum and Mellon sketchbooks). Because of their expectedness, Flaxman's drawings after the antique merit a less detailed discussion than that devoted to drawings after post-classical art.

His sketches, especially those after sarcophagi panels, usually accentuate the linearity inherent in the style of the original marbles. He often recorded many details of a composition so that he would be able to recall accurately how a story had been told. The bas-reliefs he

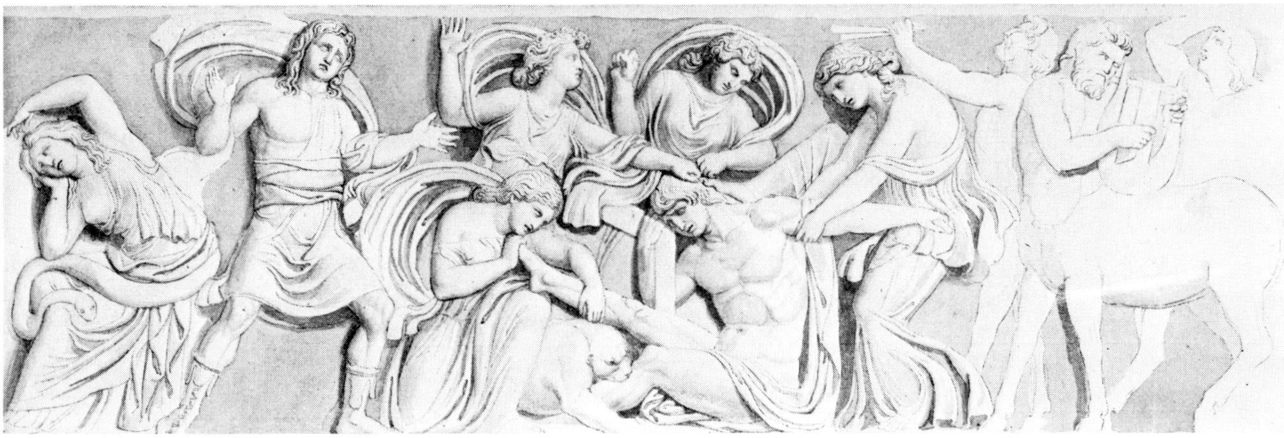

53 *Death of Orpheus, after antique relief in Giustiniani Collection*, c. 1791. Pen and ink and wash, 24·4 × 65·8 cms.

drew were mostly sarcophagi panels from the pre-Christian era devoted to incidents in classical mythology. He chose a variety of subjects, sometimes imbuing them in his drawings with a slight sentiment not evident in the original marble. Violent themes selected included the death of Orpheus, the struggle of Hercules with the Nemean Lion, and the battle of the Amazons (Plates 53 and 99). Heroic subjects included a fine sarcophagus panel of Achilles then in the Borghese collection (and now in the Louvre). Gentler subjects included the famous relief panel of Orpheus and Eurydice in the Villa Albani collection (Plate 54).

The drawing after a bas-relief is more elaborately finished than usual in Plate 53, showing the two main stories of the death of Orpheus on a sarcophagus panel in the Giustiniani collection. In the centre Orpheus is being torn to pieces by the women of Thrace, whilst on the left Eurydice dies in the coils of a snake. The careful finish of the drawing suggests it may be related to a commission from Edward Knight in London, who had already been one of Flaxman's patrons. This drawing cannot be the actual commission, however, since Flaxman would not have left it unfinished, but in May 1791 he despatched to Knight ten drawings after bas-reliefs ranging from tranquil scenes such as *The Marriage of Bacchus and Ariadne* and *The Triumph of Neptune*, to the terrifying scene of *The Death of Orpheus*.[30]

From Rome Flaxman went briefly further south, to visit Naples, Herculaneum, Pompeii, Portici and risked the malarial swamps to go as far as Paestum. His remarks about his visit to Paestum in a letter to Hayley show how much he valued what he regarded as simplicity in ancient civilisations. 'The simple greatness of their effect', he wrote, 'elevated and delighted my mind more than all the other architecture I have seen in Italy'.[31] When he wrote to Romney about the temples he enclosed a sketch, called them the 'sublime of architecture' and placed them, correctly, in the same period as the Greek vases he admired, 'both the work of Greek colonies'.[32] The stylistic link he made between the Doric of the Paestum temples and the decoration of Greek vases is further confirmation of his love of elemental forms. The Paestum temples would also have been a relief after the baroque churches of Naples which he had found—as in Turin—'in bad taste'.[33]

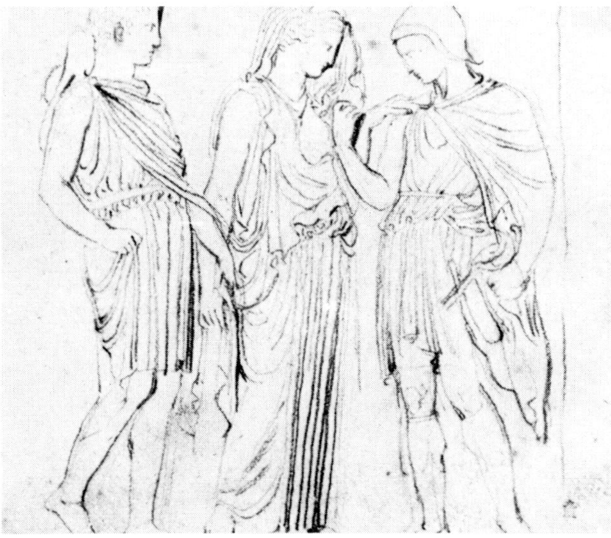

54 *Orpheus and Eurydice, after antique relief in Albani Collection:* detail. Pencil 15·2 × 36·2 cms. (whole page).

He started to keep a journal in Naples at the beginning of 1788, which is largely devoted to the great variety of antiquities in the museum at Portici and to what he saw at Pompeii.[34] A recurring theme in his comments on classical art both at Portici and elsewhere is the ancients' fidelity to nature, not the theme of idealisation which perhaps one might expect. Flaxman's comments thus run counter to academic theory as exemplified in Winckelmann's stress on the ideal. Flaxman was particularly impressed at Portici by the sculpture of horses. Writing in his journal from memory after the visit (as visitors were not allowed to make notes in the museum) Flaxman praised the equestrian statues of *Appius Claudius* and *Marcus Nonnius*, because 'both the human figures and the horses are most perfect and beautiful copies of nature', and a few pages later he describes in detail the horse of the equestrian statue of *Nonnius Balbus*, concluding that 'this piece of sculpture together with many others in the Vatican museum and other places are permanent refutations to those who maintain an opinion that the ancients did not excell in the imitation of animals'.

Like many visitors before him Flaxman was impressed by the considerable variety of objects at Portici, commenting on a wide range of items that embraced coins, small bronzes, larger statuary, mosaics and frescoes. The one part of the collection which he found disappointing, as other commentators had before him (including Winckelmann), was the frescoes from Herculaneum. Apart from *Marsyas teaching the young Olympus to play on two pipes* which he thought 'so extremely natural that it seems to me the production of a great master', he dismissed the scenes of *Chiron teaching Achilles*, *Telephus discovered in Arcadia by Hercules* and others with the words: 'In general I think the fire evident in original works is wanting in these, there is little intelligence in the outline drawing or drapery of the figures, the heads are made out in a manner not much superior to sign painting, the effect is produced by strong hatchings, and on the whole the chief merit of execution is the boldness of manner.'

When he visited the other part of the Bourbon collection nearby in Capo di Monte, Flaxman entered a disappointingly brief comment on the 'fine collection of pictures', but wrote in more detail about Etruscan frescoes removed from a tomb at Nola, depicting a procession of men on horseback and on foot. The figures 'are in proper colours but without light and shade', he wrote, 'so they resemble Indian [presumably Moghul] paintings, but there is so much of the spirit of nature both in the outline and action that they really seem as if they had been traced from living figures'. He then noted briefly that there was a 'fine' collection of Greek vases and Greek and Roman coins. The remaining pages of the Neapolitan notebook are devoted to frescoes, buildings and tombs which he drew at Pompeii, which he visited at least twice in February 1788. His drawings include the courtyard of the Temple of Isis, one of the baths with a relief, a fresco of a bacchante and some pots.

Plaster casts formed an important part of the furnishings of studios and academies, and played an essential role in the art trade. Whilst in Italy therefore it is not surprising to find Flaxman active not only on Romney's behalf in collecting casts, but also on his own and that of his elderly father, who would have found casts useful stock for his shop in the Strand. Flaxman reported in one letter to his parents that some particularly good casts had been made of the busts of the *Apollo Belvedere* and of the *Laocoon*, and in another letter he regrets he cannot find a good cast of the *Medici Venus*.[35] In the same letter he reports that he has heard that Romney wants him to spend £100 on casts, for an academy he is establishing, and Flaxman is going to suggest that his father make moulds for Romney from those sent from Italy to avoid any unnecessary duplication.[36] Late in 1791 he wrote to his parents to say that Romney's casts were to be despatched in the spring, and confirms that 'I shall desire in my letter that he will let my father mould such of them as he chooses.' Also by the following spring it is clear from another letter why Flaxman is anxious that his father should improve his stock of casts: 'I find from what I see of the English nobility and gentry here that the taste increases in England for plaster casts as well as other articles of sculpture.'[37] This growing interest is reflected, for instance, in the large collection assembled by the Prince Regent which he was to present to the Royal Academy. In September 1792 Flaxman wrote to Romney saying that ten large cases of casts had been despatched from Leghorn, some of which he had had specially moulded. 'I think I have sent you the cream of the finest things in Rome, as far as the money would go', he wrote, listing some of the choicest items which included famous works in the Papal and Borghese collections.[38] The casts arrived safely, Romney was delighted and Flaxman offered late in 1793 to buy more for him, which he did the following March, shortly before leaving Rome.[39]

4 Studies from Nature

The art of the past played a major part in Flaxman's studies whilst in Italy, but it was not the only form of study to which he devoted his time. As he wrote in a letter early in his visit, 'I am studying nature and the works of antiquity with all the diligence I can'.[40] In another letter his wife reports that in order to 'fit' himself for all the work he has on hand for Lord Bristol and for Thomas Hope, Flaxman was studying 'anatomy, attitudes and draperies'.[41] When he sent advice to his sister on how to draw, he was most explicit on the importance of nature: 'I earnestly recommend to her attention that she will always choose some affecting action or sentiment for the subject on her composition, that she will observe attentively the actions of people engaged in conversation or employed in any other way that affects the passions or affections, to consider their countenances, the contour of their figures and their draperies, and particularly to habituate herself in making perfect sketches from nature in a few minutes; that when she makes a drawing she may get some of her friends to sit for each of the figures, never to produce anything without studying nature in this manner'.[42] These rules are the kind that Flaxman himself would have put into practice. In other letters he mentions the importance of nature when designing his sculptures, such as the figures reading the Bible on the *Collins* monument 'making many studies from nature for it', and, in an unspecific way, when working on his *Athamas*.[43] Nature also formed an important basis for his classical illustrations.

He never forgot nature and even paid in Rome in 1792 for a course in anatomy.[44] His Italian sketchbooks and loose sheets contain many drawings from nature, ranging from academic nudes and drapery studies to genre scenes. He also made detailed studies of arms and legs, as well as executing innumerable drawings of drapery (Plates 55, 56, and 57). The abundance of these academic life studies, and the care with which they have sometimes been drawn and shaded, indicate that many hours must have been devoted to such drawings with the enthusiasm and thoroughness of a student. Flaxman was, however, now in his mid-thirties, still keeping in practice the basic kind of drawing which he had learnt earlier at the Royal Academy School. Such drawing was to remain a vital part of his working method and was not to be totally supplanted by antique statuary, Greek vases or any other art of the past.

He also drew many domestic and genre scenes, including everyday street life and peasant activities, as well as the occasional landscape, and even a few

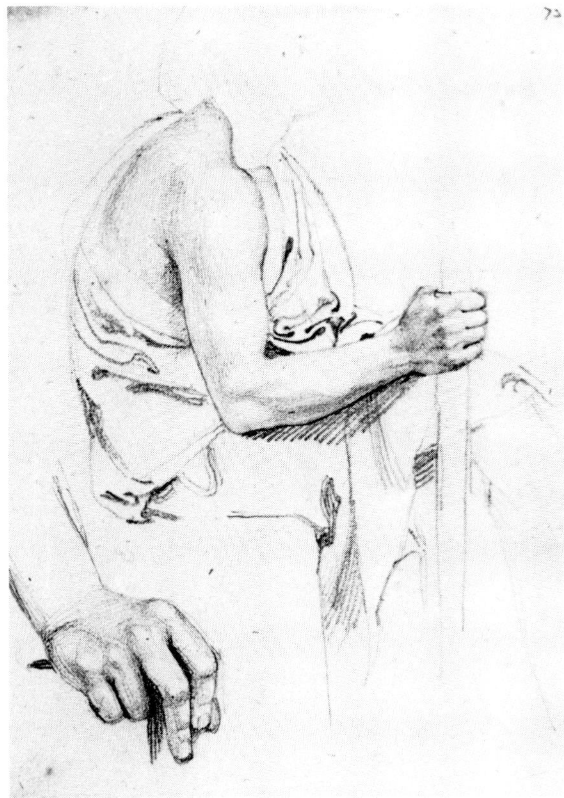

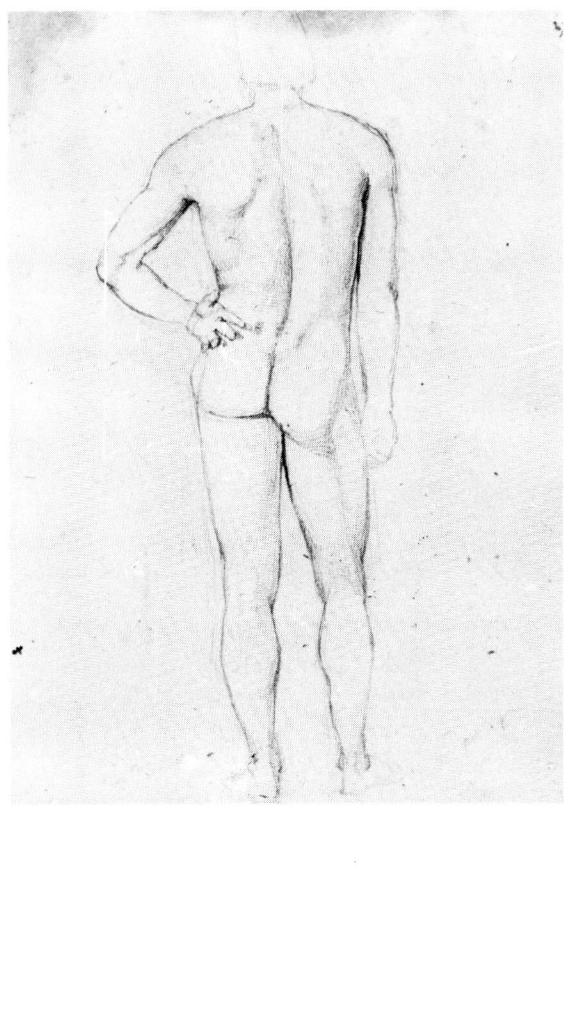

55 (*above*) *Life Studies: Seated figure, and hand.* Pencil 26·8 × 21 cms.

56 *Life Study: Male nude, from behind.* Pencil, 26·8 × 21 cms.

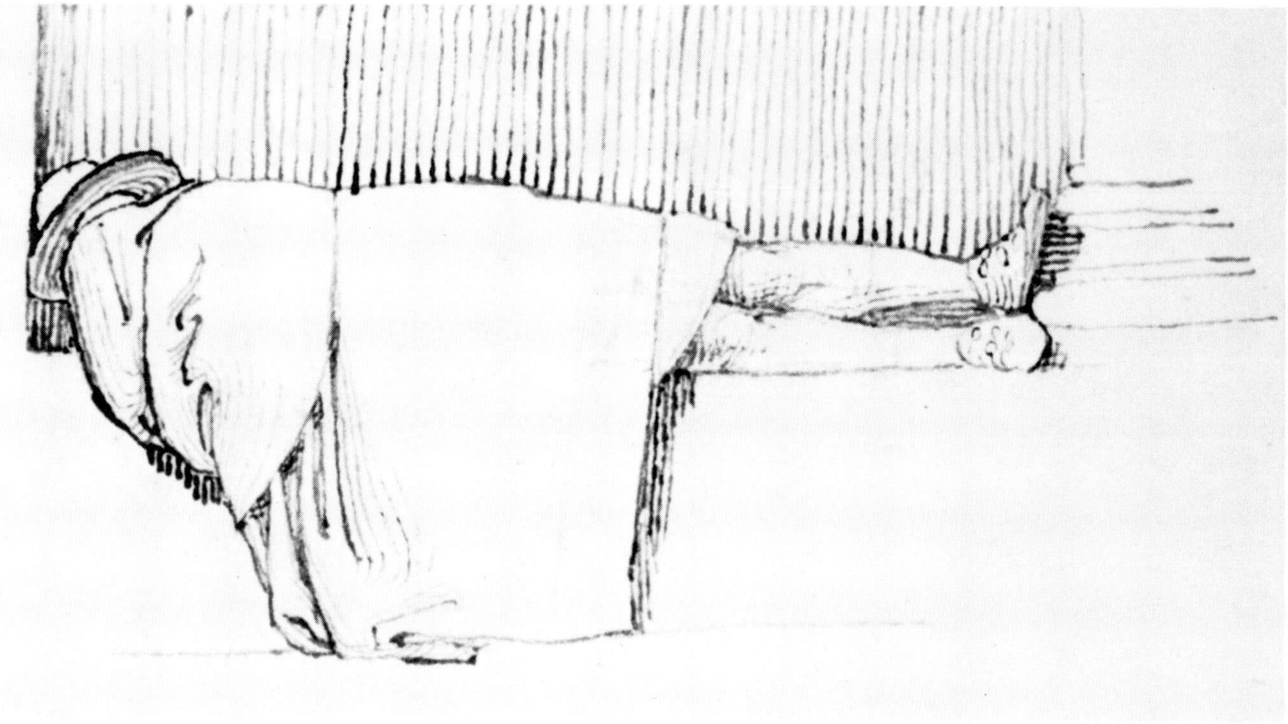

57 *Peasant asleep on the plinth of a building.* Pen and ink, 5·8 × 10·5 cms.

caricatures. One of his Italian sketchbooks[45] contains a particularly good range of everyday scenes, starting with one of a lady looking out of a window inscribed 'Looking out of [the] window after din[ner]'. A few pages later is a drawing of a family group entitled 'The Golden Age' which has already been mentioned (see Plate 39). Later there are 'The Pope going in procession on the Corpus Domini', a priest saying mass, several very attractive drawings of peasant women at work (Plates 58, 59 and 60), and a pretty watercolour—an unusual medium for Flaxman—of a Sienese woman with her servant. The same sketchbook also includes a charming girl with billowing skirts walking to church, which is a contemporary echo of the fluttering draperies of the maidens at Herculaneum, one of which he drew into his Naples journal (Plates 61 and 62). This range of drawings executed in Italy, and others similar to them, represent a little-known aspect of Flaxman's art of which only a small part appeared in his more public works. It is a vein of naturalistic genre, however, which fits quite logically into his attitude to nature as a whole. It shows Flaxman's art from an unfamiliar angle that can be related to the attractive genre scenes executed by other artists whilst staying in Italy, notably David Allan before him, and Wilkie later.

5 Social life

Flaxman was hardworking and retiring whilst in Italy, disinclined to waste time on social gatherings as he was temperamentally an industrious artist. In that he had also had to save for a long time in order to be able to afford the visit, he presumably did not want to waste his time, more especially as he had a great deal he wanted to see and study.

Within a year of settling in Rome, he was writing in a letter that he never went to the nearby Caffé Inglese in the Piazza di Spagna, in the same square in which he had lodgings (in the house of the engraver Cunego). Although the Caffé was the principal meeting place for British artists in Rome (as they had no Academy or other focal point), Flaxman did not like it because 'here is always some party, some disagreement and the flame is continually kept up: when winter comes and the people of quality come here, they are then ready to tear each other in pieces for business'. But, he continued, 'there are however some worthy men here who set a better example'.[46] At the same time, Flaxman's wife confirmed their dislike of fashionable habits by pouring scorn on the English gentry's practice in winter of looking at the Colosseum by moonlight and the Papal collection in the Museo Capitolino by torchlight, the former leading to 'coughs and consumption', and the

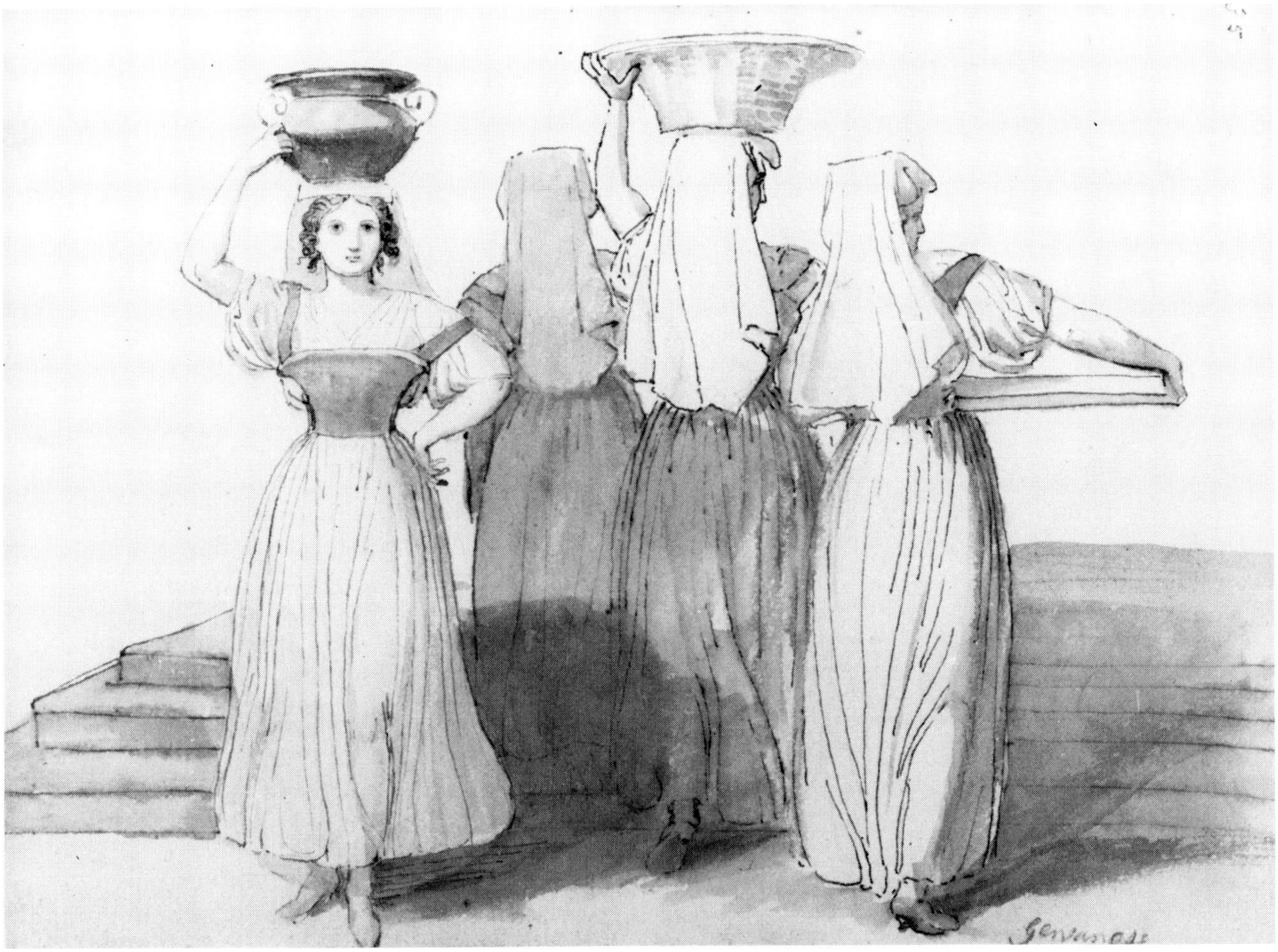

58 *Italian Peasant Women at Work.* Pen and ink and washes, 22·6 × 16·4 cms.

latter to the loss of 'much of the true beauty of antiquity'.[47] It is perhaps because Flaxman was so serious and scholarly that a later letter shows that his company was much valued as an antiquarian guide, when the pressing requests of English gentry 'almost hurried him off his legs'.[48]

The increasing burden of commissions was to leave him little spare time. He devoted daylight hours largely to sculpture, and evenings to drawing.[49] For entertainment he liked to dine occasionally with friends, just as in London he had preferred small gatherings of friends for entertainment in the evenings. But if a special cause merited his attention he devoted time to it, contributing funds, for example, to the campaign being organised by artists in Rome to have the customs duty repealed on works of art they brought back into Britain.[50]

Writing home to his parents in January 1790, Flaxman optimistically recorded that 'I have no reason to be discontented with Rome, for I have been treated with particular attention by most of the artists of the first eminence, both Englishmen and foreigners.'[51] Foreign contemporaries who befriended him included Antonio Canova (a relationship which will be discussed in the next chapter) and the French architect Charles Percier, then studying in Rome having won the Grand Prix for architecture in the year before Flaxman set out for Italy. The record of the friendship with Percier includes drawings in one of Flaxman's sketchbooks, to which the architect contributed a restoration of part of the Forum of Nerva and a sketch of some French guardsmen, as well as a wash drawing of a catacomb which Flaxman stuck into the book.[52] Flaxman gave Percier a letter of introduction to Sir William Hamilton in the last year of Percier's visit in 1790, in which Percier was described as 'a French architect of the first talent', and the hope was expressed that Hamilton would allow Percier to make some sketches in his collection.[53]

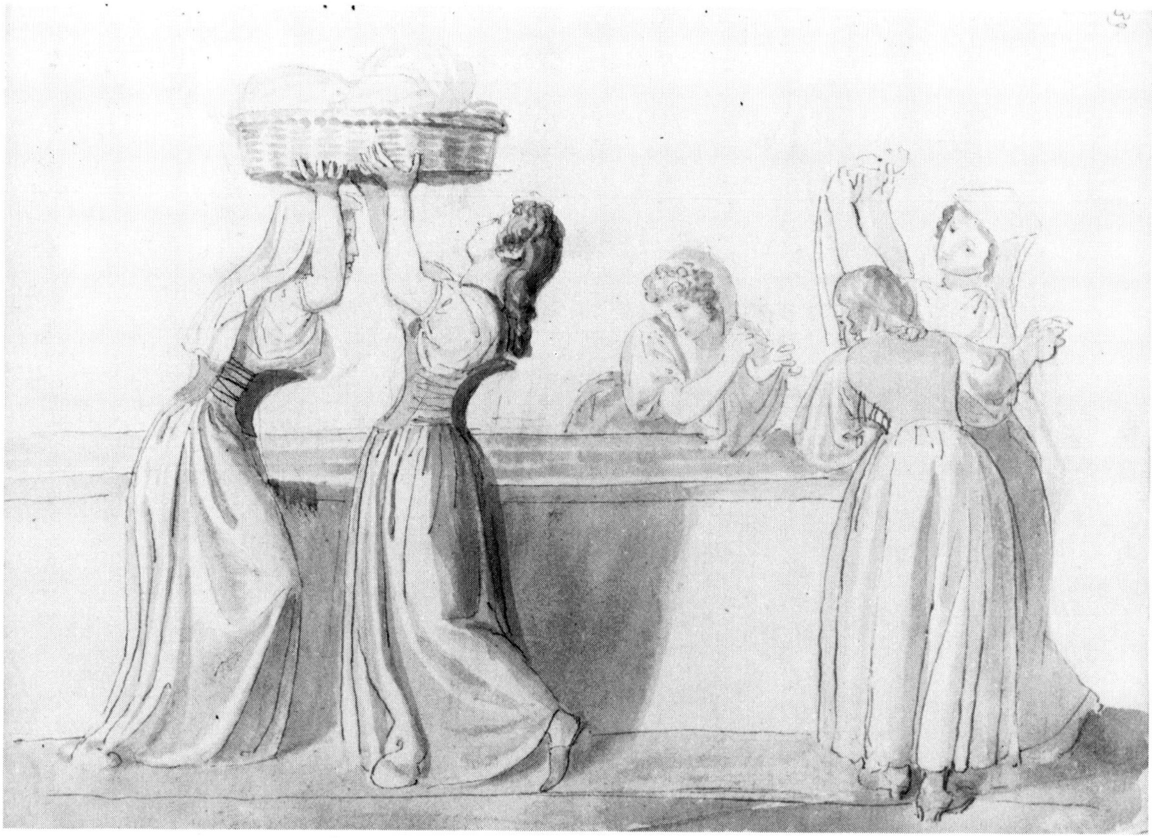

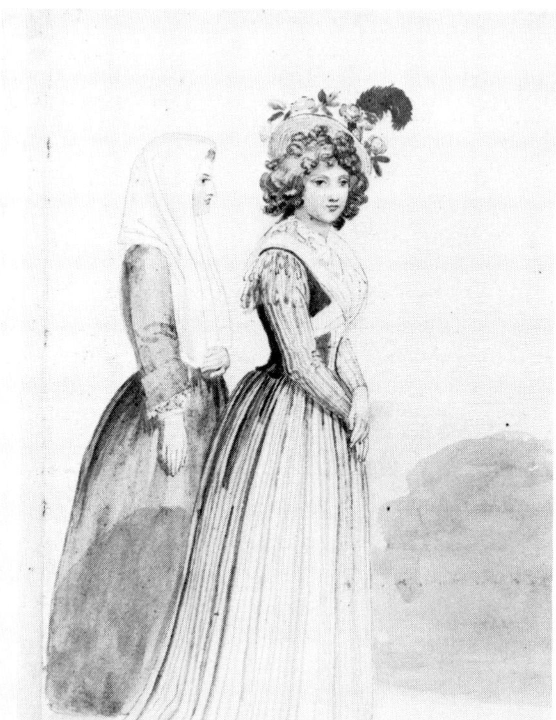

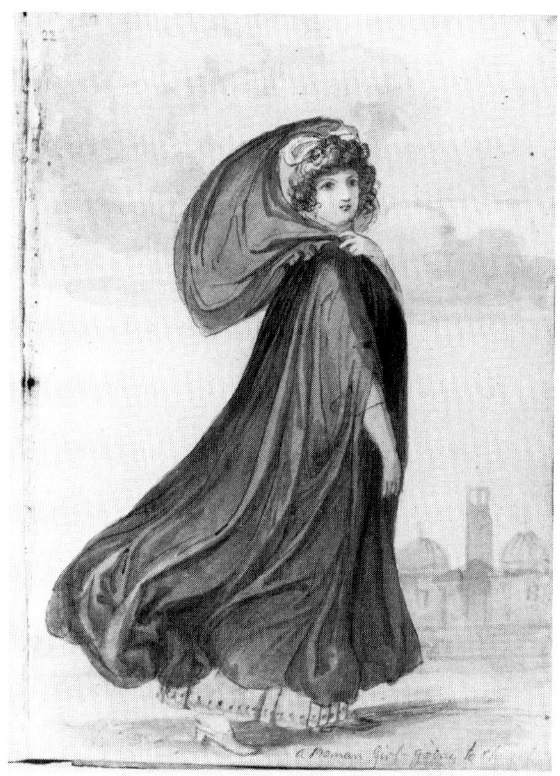
a Roman Girl going to Church

Subsequently Flaxman kept in touch with Percier by letter, calling him some years later '*carissimo amico*'.[54] Whilst in Paris during the Peace of Amiens Flaxman drew Percier's portrait, and was given a couple of chalk drawings by the architect.[55] Flaxman was also on sufficiently friendly terms with the French landscape-painter Ducros, for him too to contribute to the same sketchbook as Percier a characteristic watercolour of the Temple of the Sybil at Tivoli.

The Irish portrait-painter Hugh Douglas Hamilton was described as the Flaxmans' 'best friend in Rome' early in their stay,[56] and Flaxman encouraged him to take up oils, which he did on returning to Ireland in 1791. The history-painter Guy Head, who had arrived in Italy about a couple of years after Flaxman, painted the sculptor's portrait whilst in Rome in 1792 (it is now in the National Portrait Gallery, London) (Plate 63). He formed part of a dinner party together with the architect James Playfair and Canova at Flaxman's apartment one evening in April that same year, after which they all went together to a firework display.[57] Flaxman had written a letter of introduction on Playfair's behalf to Sir William Hamilton, and Playfair had also contributed to the same sketchbook as Percier.[58] Another architect mentioned amongst Flaxman's acquaintances is Samuel Bunce, a minor pupil of Wyatt, whose moral character and abilities as an architect Flaxman greatly admired, twice referring to him as 'my most esteemed friend in Rome'.[59] The Flaxmans might also have made the acquaintance of Angelica Kauffmann, Maria Cosway and Vigée Le Brun,[60] all of whom were in Italy at the time, a fact mentioned in one of Mrs. Flaxman's letters.

Flaxman was in frequent contact with antiquaries and collectors such as Sir William Hamilton and Pierre d'Hancarville, as well as travellers such as Mariana Starke (who was shortly to publish a record of her tour in her *Letters from Italy*[61]) and also travellers en route to or from Greece. During his first winter in Rome 'the learned Greek' Nicolaides passed through the city on his way back to Greece, 'he enquired for me, and as we

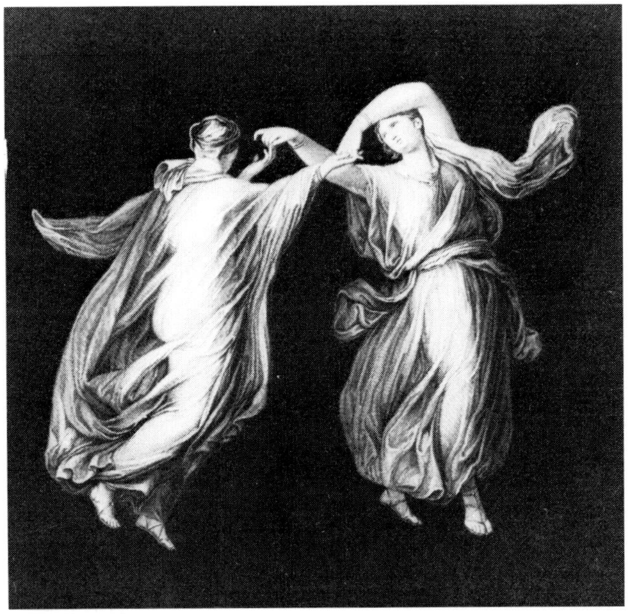

62 Accademia Ercolanese: *Le Pitture antiche d'Ercolano*, 1757–79. Volume I, Plate 17, *Bacchante*.

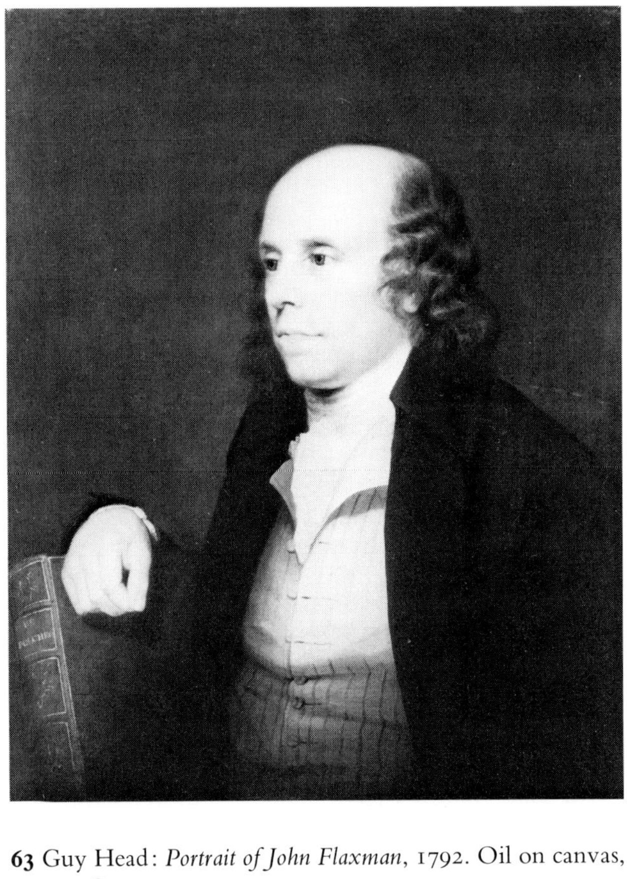

63 Guy Head: *Portrait of John Flaxman*, 1792. Oil on canvas, 72·4 × 58·4 cms.

59 *(facing below left) A Lady of Siena with her Servant.* Watercolour and ink, 22·6 × 16·4 cms.

60 *(facing top) Italian peasant women washing clothes* Pen and ink and wash, 16·4 × 22·6 cms.

61 *(facing below left) A Roman Girl going to Church.* Pen and ink and wash, 22·6 × 16·4 cms.

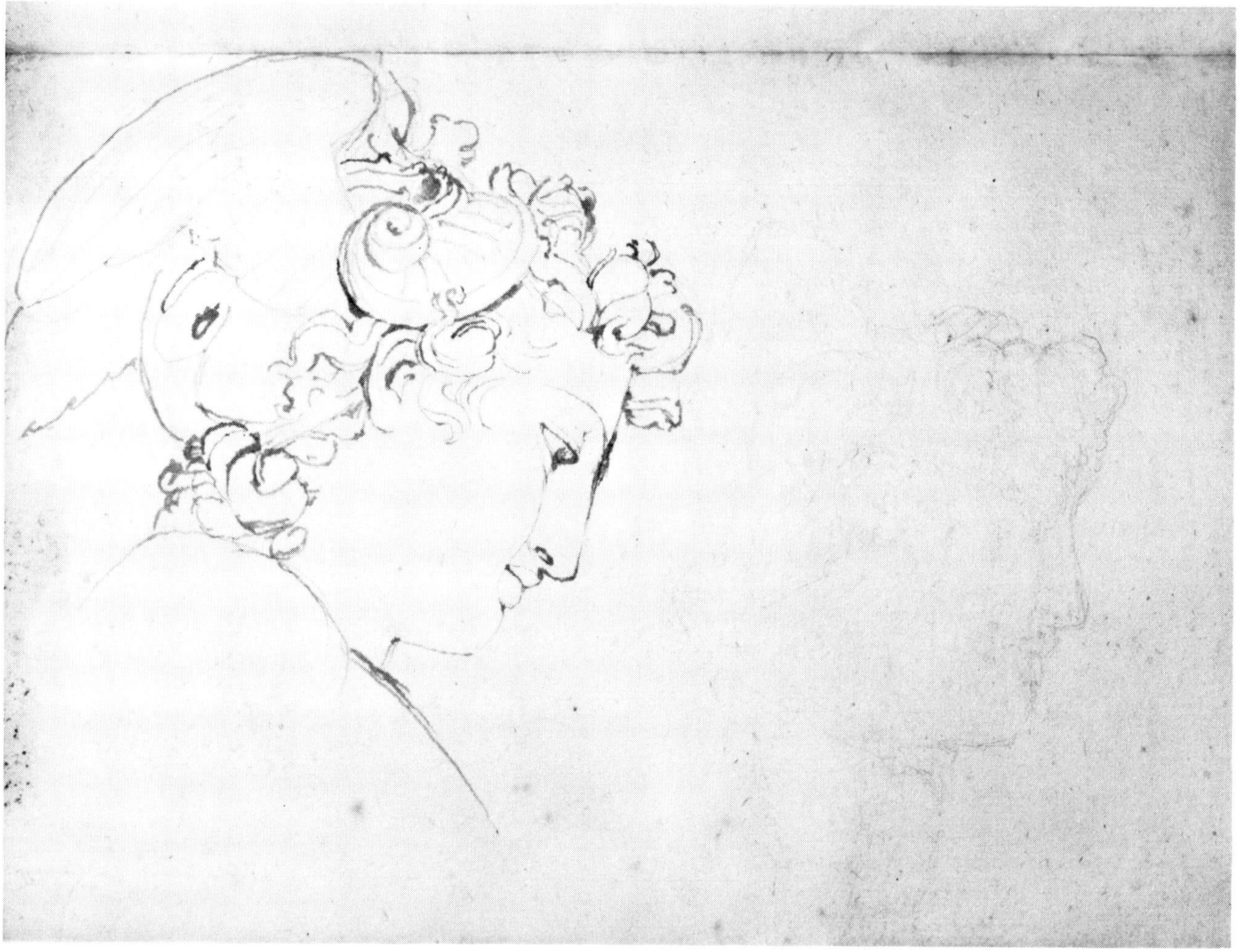

64 *Head of Perseus: detail after Cellini.* Pen and ink and pencil, 26·8 × 21 cms.

had been acquainted in England, we exchanged four or five visits to our mutal satisfaction', discussing, amongst other matters, their common friend Mrs. Mathew.[62] This was presumably the same Nicolaides who was a nephew of the patriarch of Constantinople and who, on an earlier visit to England, had become acquainted with Samuel Johnson. Flaxman met John Hawkins on his return from Greece in May 1788. He was one of the growing number of Englishmen at the end of the century who were making careful studies of Greece and contributing to British Philhellenism. The acquaintance with Hawkins was not a passing one, since it continued when both men were back in England. Flaxman was later to see examples of pottery that Hawkins had excavated in Mycenae and Delos, and also a fine bas-relief he had brought back from Greece and which he may well have had with him in Rome.[63] Flaxman was recognised as an authority on matters of classical antiquity. Towards the end of his stay in Rome he was approached by Guglielmo della Valle, who had just published an edition of Vasari and was one of the small group who admired the 'primitives', having published an article on the Sienese school in 1788.[64] Father della Valle asked Flaxman for assistance over passages in Pliny devoted to art,[65] and the debt was to be acknowledged by the author in his *Vite dei Pittori antichi Greci e Latini* (1795).

Flaxman's circle of friends and acquaintances in Italy seems to have been small, a few artists (including the painter Henry Howard in addition to those already mentioned), archaeologists, scholars and collectors whose occasional company was sufficient relief from the rigours of sculpting and drawing.

To only a limited extent did Flaxman keep in touch with friends back in England. Apart from his parents, he wrote most regularly to Hayley and occasionally to

Romney. In a letter to his father in 1792 Flaxman enquired after Stothard, Blake and Barry.[66] The engraver William Sharp also features in his correspondence[67]. Apart from these occasional references, Flaxman seems to have largely forgotten about his English friends whilst abroad.

Sculptures and illustrations commissioned by Thomas Hope, Lord Bristol, Countess Spencer, Mrs. Hare-Naylor and a few other clients had made it financially feasible for Flaxman and his wife to remain abroad longer than originally intended. However apart from a natural desire to return to their native country, expressed in a letter in 1793, the return home would have been precipitated by the events of the French Revolutionary Wars and the increasing military successes of France's new leader.[68] Shortly before leaving Rome, Flaxman attended an evening party at which the French ambassador proudly showed his medal of Bonaparte. The image reminded the sculptor of Augustus Caesar, but the political connotation of Flaxman's comparison was not lost on the diplomat: 'Image of a tyrant! no indeed . . .—he is a young and enthusiastic hero'[69]. Flaxman and his wife left the peninsula before travelling became difficult for foreigners.

The Flaxmans left Rome in June 1794, intending on the way to visit Florence again for only five days but staying as many weeks. As his wife wrote: 'The beauties of that little city were like sirens to poor Flaxman, and though he worked like a slave from morning to night, he could not finish the drawings from them in five weeks.'[70] Flaxman was also to be detained in Florence because he wanted to present a copy of his *Divine Comedy* illustrations to the Duke, and also his patron Lord Bristol unexpectedly arrived in the city.[71] Because of the French Revolutionary Wars, the Flaxmans left Italy via Venice, in order to avoid the main areas of battle. Flaxman himself seems not to have recorded his impressions of Venice, but his wife (who often shared his views) found St. Mark's 'bad Gothic, it is the most ornamented'[72]. Their return route then passed through Innsbruck (where he drew the tomb of the Emperor Maximilian), Augsburg and Kassel.[73] Possibly a detour was made to Vienna, but this is not certain.

The Flaxmans were back in London by late in November, and moved to a new address, leasing a house in Buckingham Street, off Fitzroy Square. Workshops were erected, models unpacked and arranged, and the house furnished, perhaps including a carpet designed from an ancient Roman mosaic which had been embroidered for them in Italy by their friend and patroness Mrs. Hare-Naylor.[74] Flaxman was finally settled in when he engaged assistants. He was back in business in the capital as a sculptor.

He was not to go abroad again except briefly to Paris in 1802, like so many of his fellow artists during the Peace of Amiens, where he was to admire many works of art he had previously seen elsewhere in Europe now assembled as part of the Napoleonic plunder[75].

CHAPTER IV

Sculptures in Italy

Once he had settled in Rome, Flaxman started fairly soon to sculpt again, and was then onwards to find himself often occupied with clay and marble. He began by spending three months in 1788 on a terracotta copy of the relief on the *Borghese Vase* for Edward Knight in London,[1] a task which was followed by a commission for a bust of Hugh Douglas Hamilton's daughter.[2] Flaxman intended to start work next on a large bas-relief of *Hercules delivering Alcestis from Orcus*, with figures four feet high, but it is not certain if he actually did.[3]

He was busy in the winter of 1789–90 on a group of *Aurora visiting Cephalus on Mount Ida* (Plate 65), originally intended to be cast in bronze but finally executed in marble.[4] Conceived on a modest scale just under five feet high, it was ideally suited for Hope's newly furnished house in Duchess Street, London, in which a room was to be specially designed around it, to be known as the Flaxman or Star Room (Plate 66). The engraving that appeared in Hope's *Household Furniture* (1807) shows Flaxman's marble group as the focal point, reflected in mirrors over the fireplace and sideboard. The iconography and colouring of the room was entirely devoted to the theme of Aurora, and the completed scheme must have been one of the most attractive examples of Regency-period decoration.

Flaxman used Ovid's *Metamorphoses* for his literary source, choosing the moment when Aurora is about to kiss Cephalus on her daily visit to him, but he is showing some reluctance as he still remembers his wife Procris from whom he has been abducted. Whilst Flaxman was in Rome Canova chose a similar moment before an embrace when he designed his group of *Cupid and Psyche*, both sculptors showing a similar delicacy and charm in rather pretty treatments of love scenes. For artistic inspiration Flaxman seems to have gone for his Cephalus no further than the *Apollo Belvedere*, rendering this already gentle and idealised image still gentler and more youthful (Plate 67). Flaxman's Aurora seems to derive from a Nike or winged Victory, of which there are several drawings amongst his Italian sketches (Plate 68), relating to the cast of such a figure which he bought whilst in Rome (and which is now in the Soane Museum).[5]

Flaxman's sculptural activities in Italy were to be overshadowed by his only major commission for a marble whilst abroad that was actually to be completed. The enlightened, if eccentric and mean, Earl-Bishop of Bristol and Derry commissioned *The Fury of Athamas* for the sum of six hundred guineas (Plate 69).[6] But this apparently handsome figure had to cover all costs including that of the marble itself, and as the group was

65 *(facing page) Aurora visiting Cephalus on Mount Ida*, 1789–90. Marble, 184 cms. high.

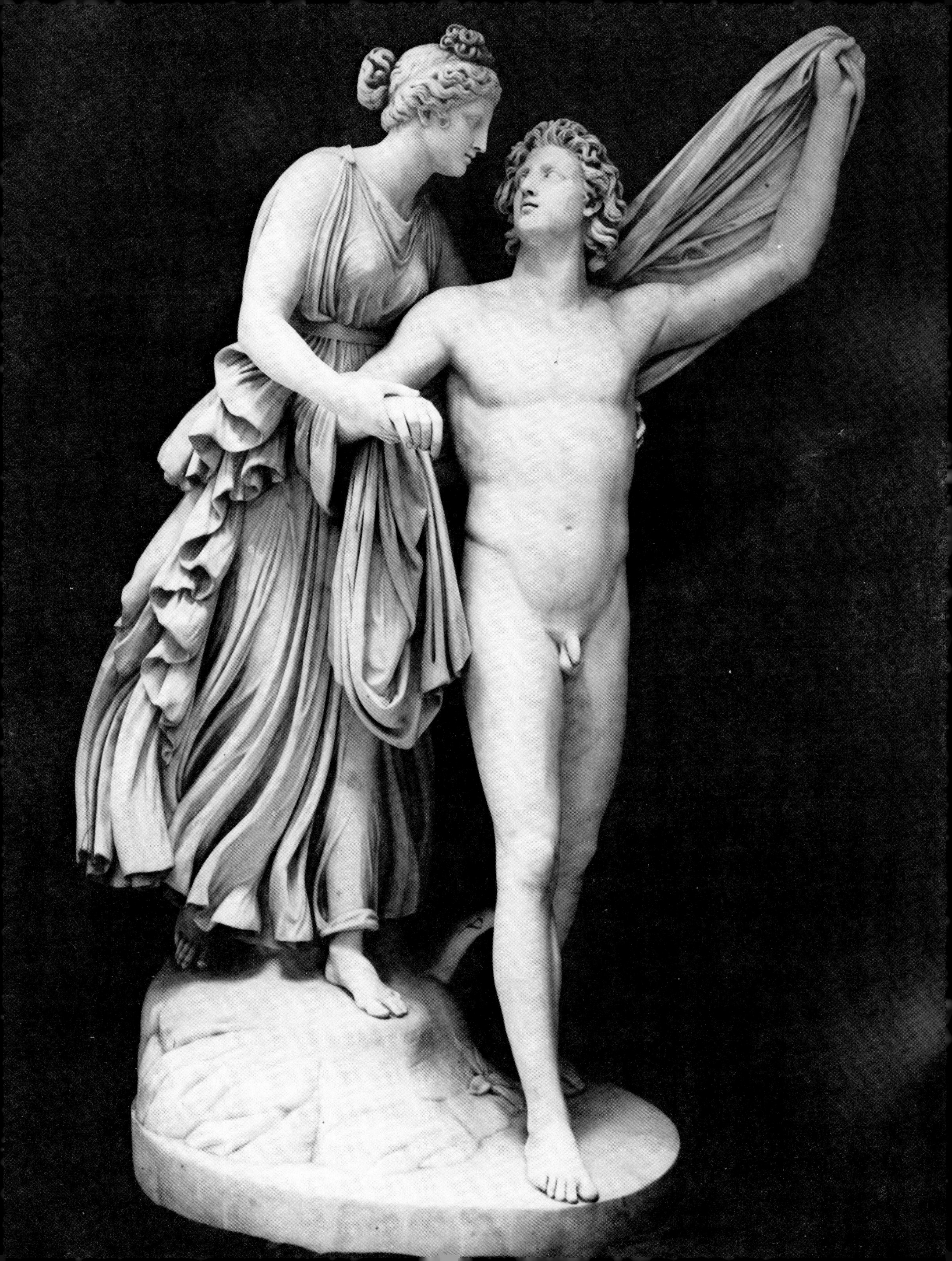

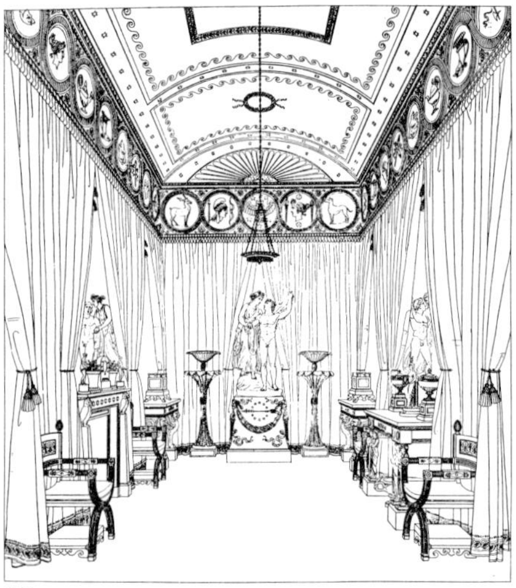
66

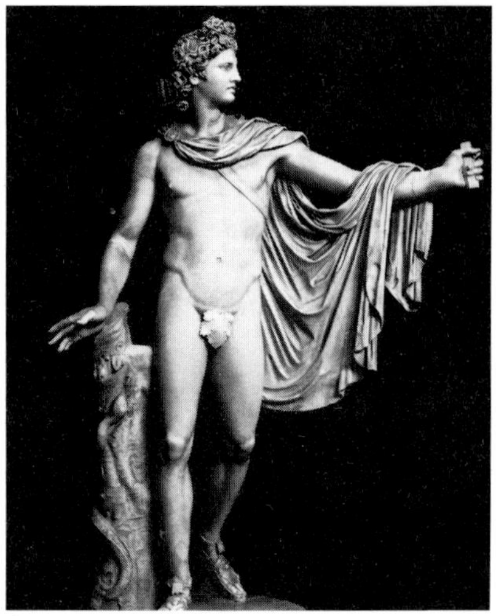
67

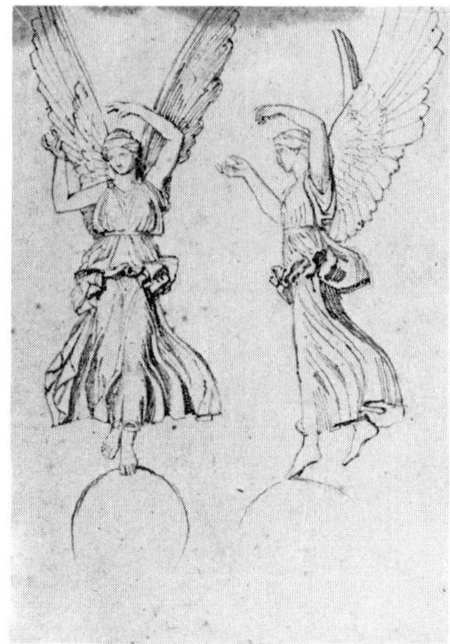
68

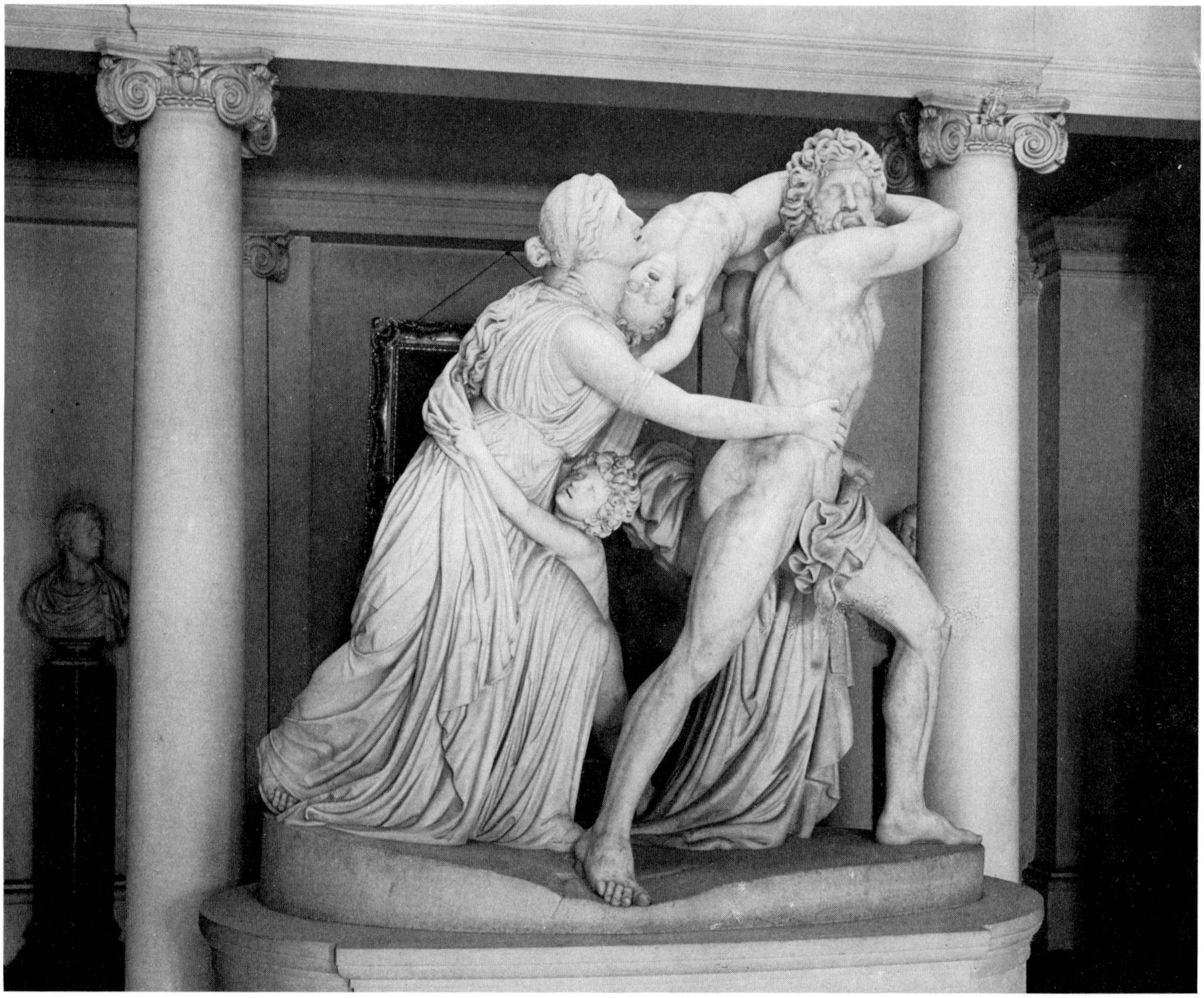
69

to be lifesize Flaxman eventually found himself out-of-pocket. He undertook the commission because he particularly wanted to execute a work in Italy 'that might establish my reputation as a sculptor',[7] and for this reason enlarged a small-scale model he had already made in terracotta of the Athamas subject. He refused to comply with Bristol's request that he should make instead a marble bas-relief nearly five feet high and eight to nine feet wide from another existing terracotta, depicting *Amphion and Zethus delivering their mother Antiope from the fury of Dirce and Lycus*, 'my own composition, taken from a different point of time, but the same story as the group of the Toro Farnese'.[8] But although Flaxman did not execute this project, he was to retain the theme of mythological violence in his choice of *The Fury of Athamas*, which like the Thomas Hope commission was based on a story in Ovid's *Metamorphoses*. Flaxman chose the incident when Athamas, driven insane by Hera, is about to kill one of his own sons, whilst his wife Ino is struggling with him and beseeching him to stop.

Lord Bristol confirmed the commission in a letter written in March 1790. That October the sculptor reported to his parents that 'my great group in clay is on the point of finishing, two or three weeks more will complete it, and I think for a group as large as the Laocoon, finished every part from Nature in the best manner that I am able.'[9] Later in the letter Flaxman wrote that 'if I ever expect to be employed on great works, it is but reasonable that I should show the world some proof of my abilities, otherwise I cannot reasonably expect employment of that kind'. This grand project was to be spread over the next three years.[10]

Although Flaxman stressed that his *Fury of Athamas* was based on nature, it is obvious that he was also heavily indebted to the past, especially to sculptures of classical antiquity. Both artist and patron compared the size of the group with that of the *Laocoon*, and Bristol enthusiastically claimed that Flaxman's sculpture 'even exceeded the Laocoon in expression'.[11] The *Laocoon* is undoubtedly Flaxman's main point of departure, as it too illustrates a struggle against impending disaster and is conceived on a similar scale (Plate 70). The classical group also provided Flaxman with his modelling of the head and torso of Athamas himself. But Bristol was wrong when he said that the expression of the *Athamas* exceeded that of its prototype. The fury on Athamas's face and the horror on that of his wife are as controlled as the anguish shown by Laocoon and his sons. In neither group is passion allowed to burst forth, a point which Winckelmann, for example, had stressed when he analysed the *Laocoon*.

The famous antique group of a *Gaul killing his wife and himself* then in the Ludovisi collection where Flaxman drew it several times (now it is in the Museo dei Terme, Rome), may have suggested the general pose of Athamas, including the position of his raised arm. The pose of Ino might derive from that of Niobe with her clinging daughter, one of several figures from the famous group which Flaxman drew in Florence (Plate 71). In a more general way, the *Toro Farnese* in

66 *Aurora visiting Cephalus on Mount Ida: in original setting.* Plate 7 from Thomas Hope, *Household Furniture*, 1807.

67 Roman copy: *Apollo Belvedere*, original c. 350–320 BC.

68 *Nike, after antique sculpture.* Pencil 26·8 × 21 cms.

69 *Fury of Athamas*, 1790–94. Marble, 208·5 cms. high.

70 Hagesandros, Athanadoros and Polydoros: *Laocoon*, c. 150 BC.

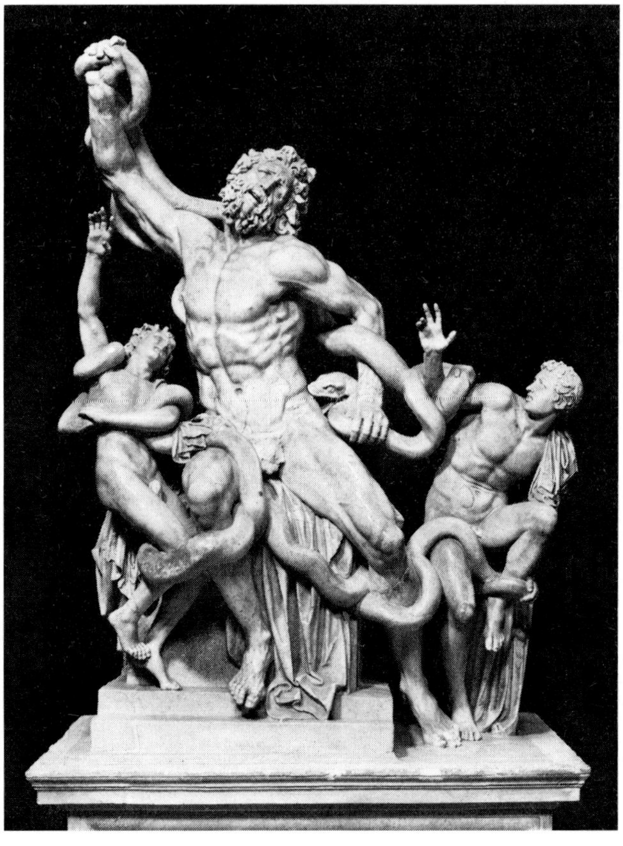

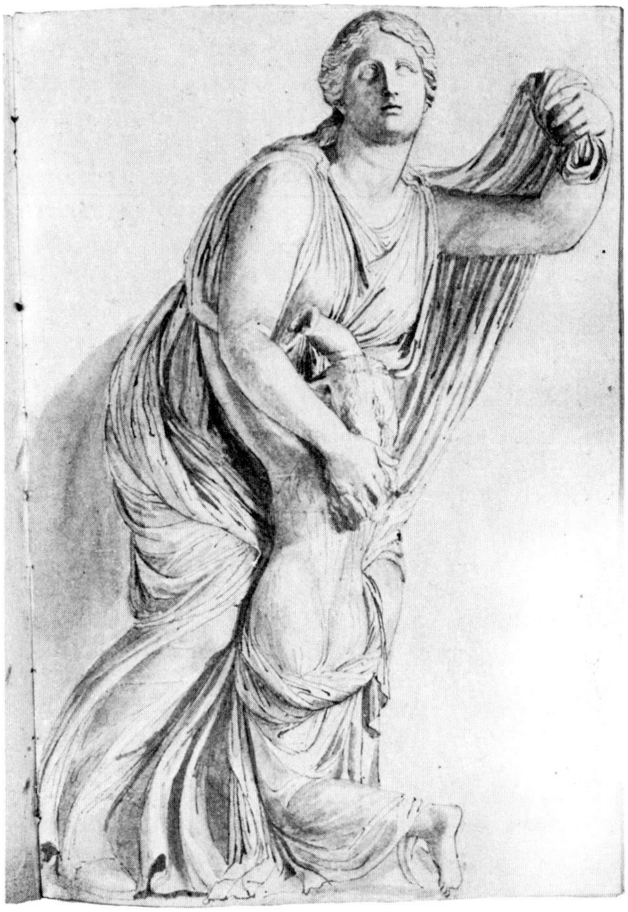

71 *Niobe and a daughter, after antique sculpture, in Uffizi.* Pen and ink and wash, 22 × 15·4 cms.

its choice of a brutal struggle could have inspired Flaxman's interest in the arrangement of freestanding figures. Amongst examples of more recent art, his drawings in the Loggia dei Lanzi after the struggling groups of Giambologna's *Hercules and the Centaur* and *Rape of the Sabine Women* (Plate 72) might also have further stimulated an interest in showing violence and anguish in large, freestanding sculptures.

In his *Fury of Athamas* Flaxman made a bold attempt at a Neoclassical work on a grand scale. Subjects of violence play a minor role in Flaxman's *oeuvre* as a whole, and the choice of such a theme for a large marble on which he hoped to build his reputation as a sculptor shows how high his ambitions were, by choosing a heroic or tragic subject in the first category of the academic canon. Another reason for his choice of the Athamas story may have been a desire to carve a subject diametrically opposite to the gentler ones of *Cephalus and Aurora* already executed from Ovid and the relief of *Apollo and Marpessa* (Plate 233), derived from Apollodorus, on which he was working at the same time (and which will be discussed in Chapter VII). That Flaxman never again received a commission similar in character to the *Athamas* suggests that contemporaries, especially potential patrons, valued Flaxman's achievement more highly in the area of gentler themes.

The owner of the *Athamas* was never to see it installed in his new country house of Ickworth in Suffolk because it only reached there after Bristol had died. He was convinced, however, that Flaxman had shown by this group that he was the greatest artist that had ever lived, superior to Canova.[12] The comparison with Canova is unfortunate since the Italian was more successful with scenes of violence, both in his *Hercules and Lycas* on which he was shortly to start work in 1795 (Plate 73), and in his later *Theseus and the Centaur* (Kunsthistorisches Museum, Vienna). Canova's *Hercules* is the first of his colossal marbles and it is possible that the *Athamas* might have inspired Canova's selection of a subject also involving a murderous action in which a victim is hurled to his death. Canova's two groups might border on the histrionic in their expression, but in the *Hercules and Lycas* Canova has enhanced the composition of his drama by a rhythmical sweep in the protagonist's gestures, whereas Flaxman's movement is cramped and seems to be still contained within the cube of the marble.

Whilst working on *The Fury of Athamas* Flaxman expressed his determination in several letters not to accept any more commissions whilst in Italy, as he wanted to return home soon, certainly no later than 1793. Nonetheless he was working simultaneously on designs for monuments to *William Collins* and to *Lord Mansfield*, both of which he intended to finish after his return home, and he also undertook to execute a marble of *Hercules and Hebe* for Thomas Hope. He was also working at the same time on his classical and Dante illustrations.

The *Hercules and Hebe* (Plate 74) was intended to be an ambitious recreation of a lost classical group, based on a suggestion made to him by Sir William Hamilton's archaeological friend, d'Hancarville, a man of dubious scholarship,[13] who was at the time editing for publication Hamilton's second collection of vases. Flaxman accepted d'Hancarville's idea that the *Torso Belvedere* had originally formed part of a group representing the marriage of Hercules and Hebe, a gentler side of the Hercules myth that should have appealed to Flaxman's taste, especially as he had already, when working for Wedgwood, executed an incident similar in mood in the garden of the Hesperides (Plate 30), to which he

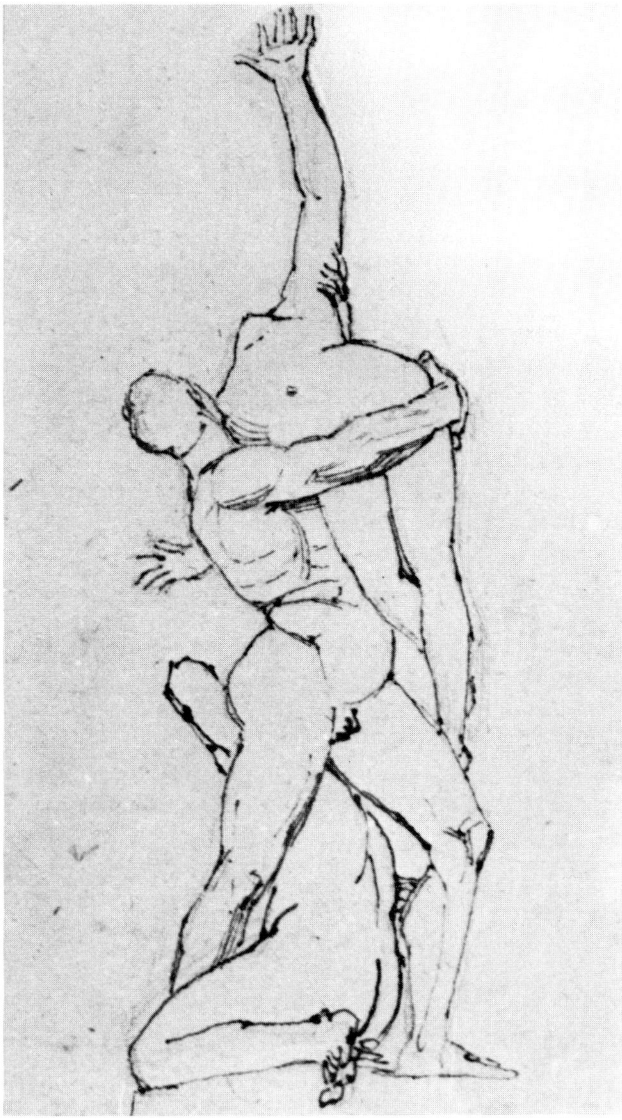

72 *Rape of the Sabines, after Giambologna, in Loggia dei Lanzi, Florence*: detail. Pen and ink and pencil, 26·8 × 21 cms. (whole page).

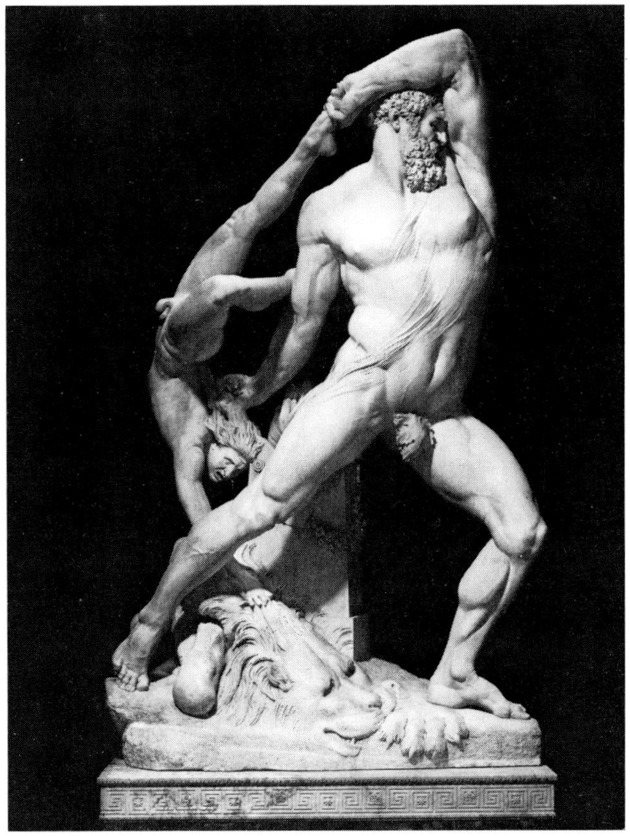

73 Antonio Canova: *Hercules and Lycas*. 1795–1815.

was to return later when designing candelabra for Rundell and Bridge (Plate 263). Flaxman decided to make his recreation of the 'lost' Hercules and Hebe group on the same scale as that of the original marble, with Hercules eight feet high, and got as far as making a full-scale plaster model. But he was never to execute the marble, although Thomas Hope made two advance payments totalling £341, towards the 700 guineas promised.[14] It is a mark of Hope's generosity as a wealthy patron that he was to remain on good terms with an artist who failed to complete a commission for which he had already received so much money. When completed Flaxman had intended to exhibit the marble publicly in Rome, his wife optimistically hoping that it would gain Flaxman 'immortal credit'.[15] Those who saw the model, on which he worked from March to December 1792, were very impressed by it, and Lord Camelford was in 'great grief', because Thomas Hope had bespoken a work which 'Michelangelo might have been afraid to undertake' but in which Flaxman had nonetheless 'succeeded'.[16] Flaxman did not complete the commission because he felt it would not turn out right.[17] In his life of the sculptor, Cunningham wrote that the 'Hercules was certainly too ponderous a companion for so tender a lady, and some surly critic compared it to Milton's lion dandling the kid'.[18] Such contemporary adverse criticisms are fair, and one agrees with Flaxman that the *Hercules and Hebe* was doomed to be a failure.[19]

The two monuments that Flaxman started to design whilst in Italy were both very different in character, one to the poet William Collins, and the other to the late Lord Chief Justice, Lord Mansfield. The *William*

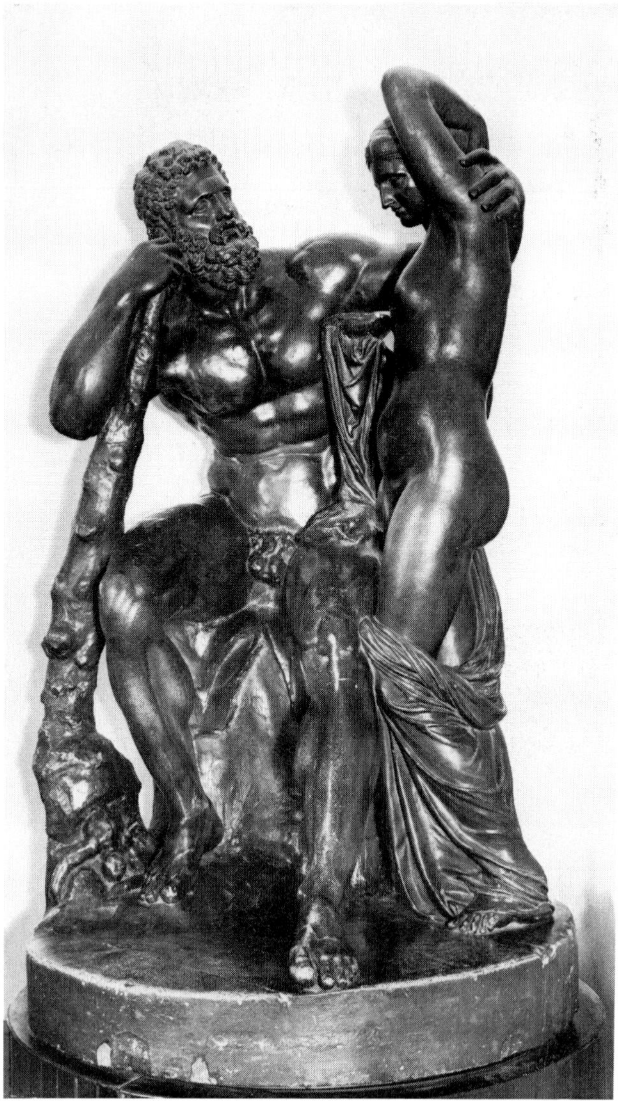

74 *Hercules and Hebe*, 1792. Plaster, coloured, 190·5 cms. high.

Collins memorial in Chichester Cathedral (Plate 75) was to lay the foundation of a series of slab monuments which include some of Flaxman's most successful and original sculptures. The other monument to *Mansfield* in Westminster Abbey (Plate 76) was to be Flaxman's first freestanding tomb, a rare type not only in his work but also in that of other sculptors at the time. It was to influence the Napoleonic monuments in St. Paul's Cathedral, as well as firmly establishing Flaxman's reputation as a sculptor.

The contemplative intimacy and Christian sentiment of the *Collins* monument is in marked contrast to the public statement and pagan symbolism of the *Mansfield*. But the elements of both compositions came largely from the same source: classical antiquity. So varied were the prototypes available, as earlier artists had found, that antiquity could produce almost any motif required.

The elements of the *Collins* composition were to be repeated many times throughout Flaxman's career. The overall form is that of a stele, a form derived ultimately from ancient Greece but known to Flaxman through Roman examples, with the main panel filled with a bas-relief. It is possible that Flaxman's composition for the roundel may have been suggested by a late Quattrocento altarpiece which he would have seen when visiting Siena cathedral. There, forming part of the entrance to the Piccolomini Library, Lorenzo Vecchietta carved a roundel with a seated John the Baptist, with an open Bible on a stand before him. Although the details are different, the general arrangement is similar to Flaxman's. Collins is shown in casual contemporary dress reading the beginning of St. Matthew's gospel; at his feet is the manuscript of his famous poem *The Passions*, together with a lyre. Surmounting the monument is a pediment showing Pity embracing Love.[20]

In his design Flaxman followed Hayley's instructions that the poet should be shown reading the Bible in his study, and thus perpetuate the image drawn in Samuel Johnson's *Life*, in which the poet is described as a man whose 'morals were pure and his opinions pious'. The lines of verse which Hayley provided for the main inscription panel also conclude by stressing the paramount importance of Christianity in Collins's life. These lines together with Flaxman's composition create an unmistakably Christian memorial. But if the most ambitious of Flaxman's original designs for the monument had been chosen, it would have given equal prominence to pagan and to Christian imagery. The plinth would have been enlarged to accommodate a bas-relief illustrating a passage from Collins's *Passions*, with Hope in the centre clutching a lyre, separating Revenge, Anger, Fear and Despair from Love, Joy and Mirth (Plate 77). Flaxman also worked out, in less detail, an alternative relief showing Music and Painting placing a garland on the altar of Pity. Had the panel of the *Passions* been included, however, the monument would have been a more complete commemoration of the poet, since although he was a profound Christian, his poetry does not express that faith, but treats themes such as the passions as well as death with a humanistic paganism within a mid-century framework of sentimentalism.

75 *(facing page) William Collins: monument*, 1792–95. Chichester Cathedral

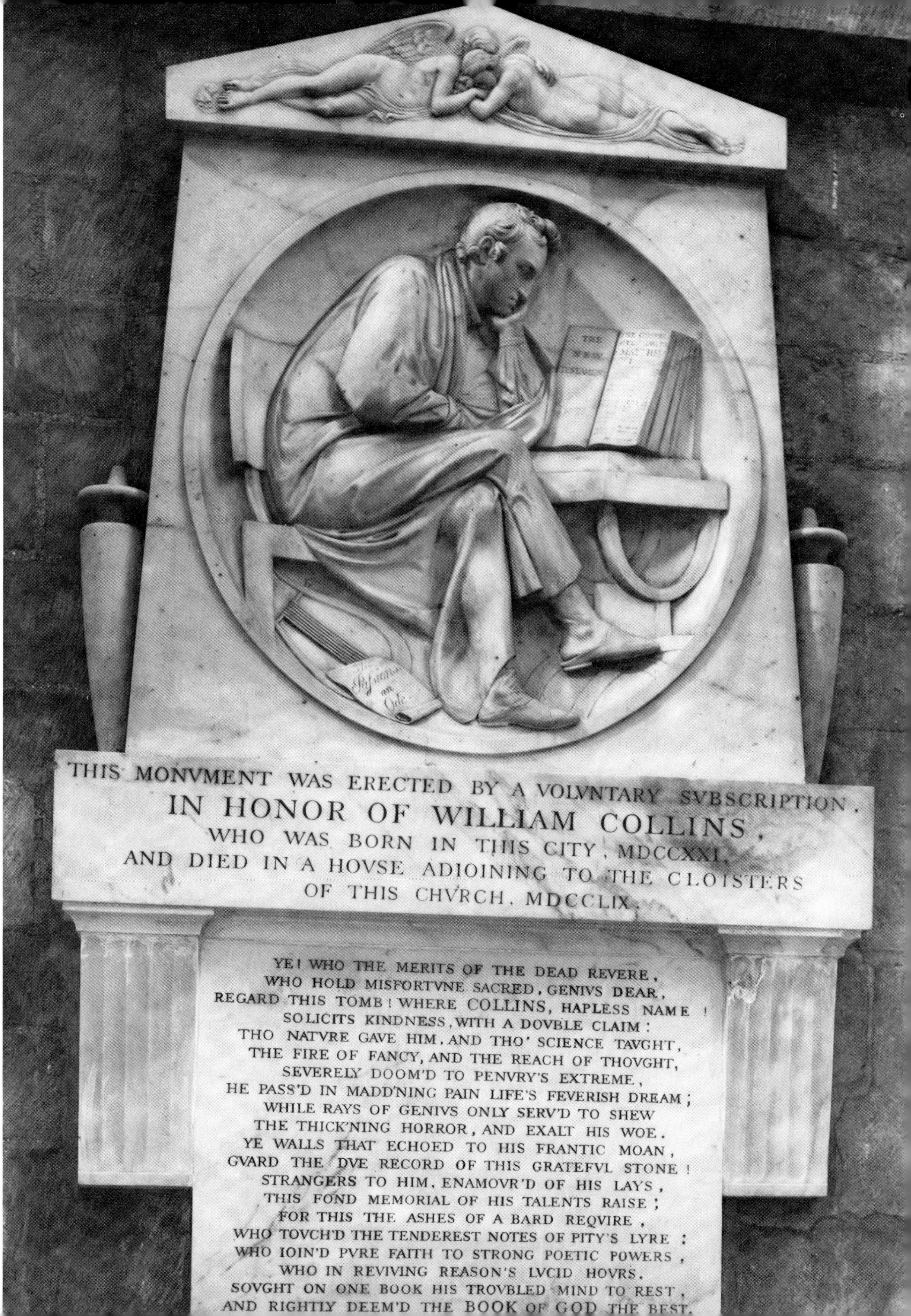
THIS MONVMENT WAS ERECTED BY A VOLVNTARY SVBSCRIPTION,
IN HONOR OF WILLIAM COLLINS,
WHO WAS BORN IN THIS CITY, MDCCXXI,
AND DIED IN A HOVSE ADIOINING TO THE CLOISTERS
OF THIS CHVRCH, MDCCLIX.
YE! WHO THE MERITS OF THE DEAD REVERE,
WHO HOLD MISFORTVNE SACRED, GENIVS DEAR,
REGARD THIS TOMB! WHERE COLLINS, HAPLESS NAME!
SOLICITS KINDNESS, WITH A DOVBLE CLAIM:
THO NATVRE GAVE HIM, AND THO' SCIENCE TAVGHT,
THE FIRE OF FANCY, AND THE REACH OF THOVGHT,
SEVERELY DOOM'D TO PENVRY'S EXTREME,
HE PASS'D IN MADD'NING PAIN LIFE'S FEVERISH DREAM;
WHILE RAYS OF GENIVS ONLY SERV'D TO SHEW
THE THICK'NING HORROR, AND EXALT HIS WOE.
YE WALLS THAT ECHOED TO HIS FRANTIC MOAN,
GVARD THE DVE RECORD OF THIS GRATEFVL STONE!
STRANGERS TO HIM, ENAMOVR'D OF HIS LAYS,
THIS FOND MEMORIAL OF HIS TALENTS RAISE;
FOR THIS THE ASHES OF A BARD REQVIRE,
WHO TOVCH'D THE TENDEREST NOTES OF PITY'S LYRE;
WHO IOIN'D PVRE FAITH TO STRONG POETIC POWERS,
WHO IN REVIVING REASON'S LVCID HOVRS,
SOVGHT ON ONE BOOK HIS TROVBLED MIND TO REST,
AND RIGHTLY DEEM'D THE BOOK OF GOD THE BEST.

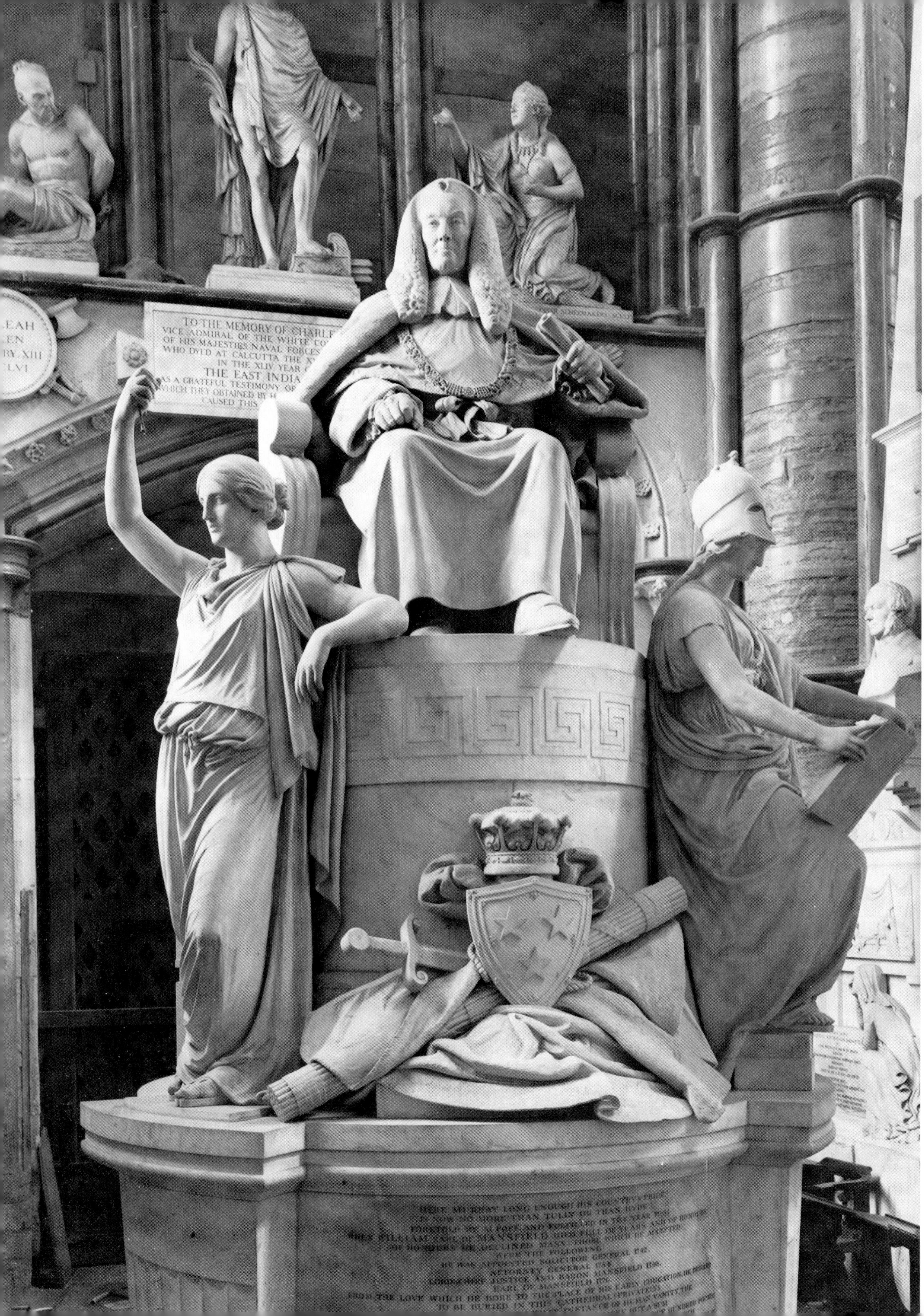

TO THE MEMORY OF CHARLE
VICE ADMIRAL OF THE WHITE
THE EAST INDIA
SCHEEMAKERS SCULP
HERE MURRAY LONG ENOUGH HIS COUNTRY'S PRIDE
IS NOW NO MORE THAN TULLY OR THAN HYDE
WILLIAM EARL OF MANSFIELD
WERE THE FOLLOWING
HE WAS APPOINTED SOLICITOR GENERAL 1742.
ATTORNEY GENERAL 1754.
LORD CHIEF JUSTICE AND BARON MANSFIELD 1756.
EARL OF MANSFIELD 1776
TO BE BURIED IN THIS CATHEDRAL (PRIVATELY)

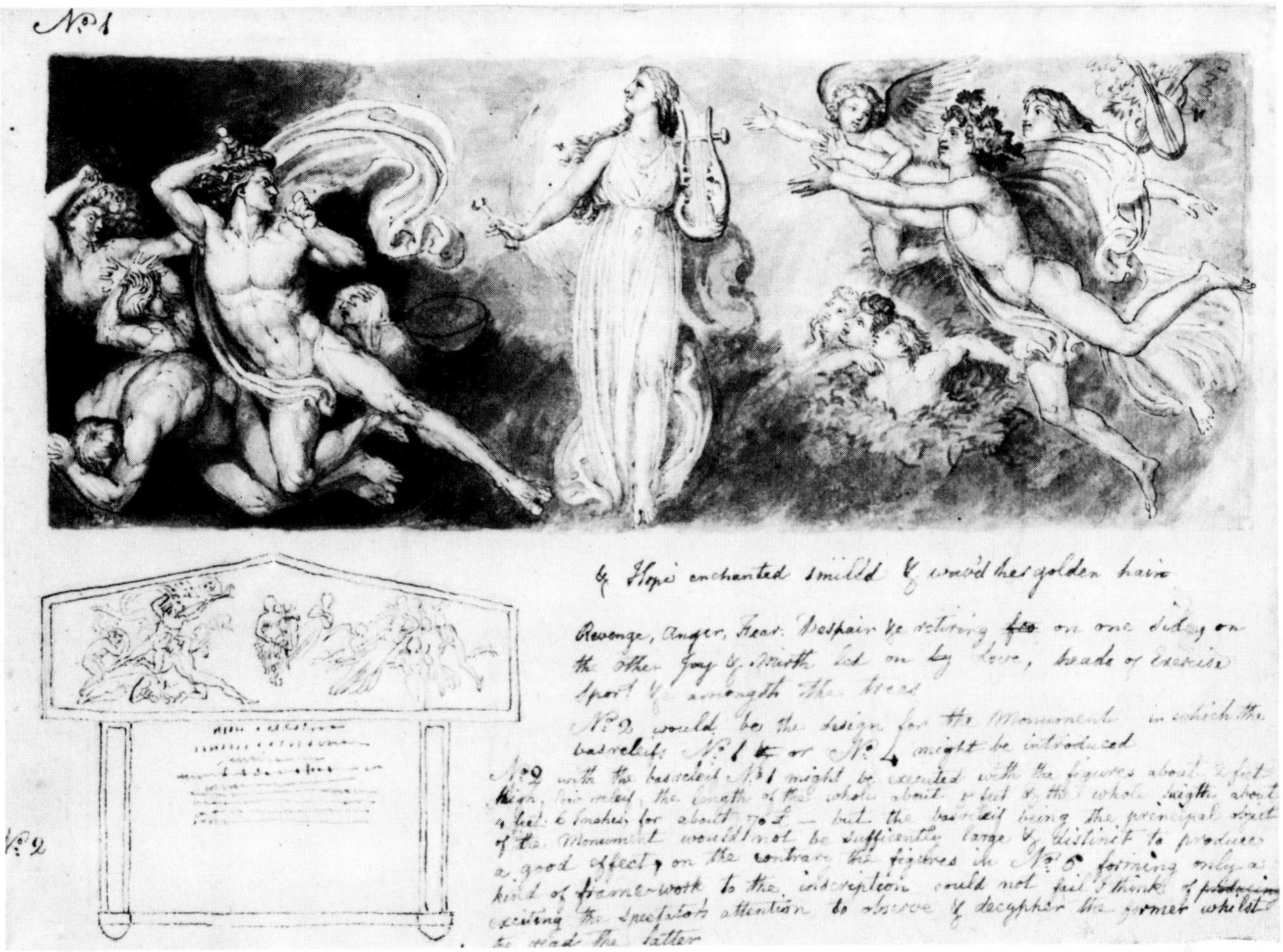

77 *William Collins: monument: design:* detail. Pen and ink and wash, 39·5 × 27 cms. (whole sheet).

Payment for the *Collins* monument, commemorating a death in penury earlier in the century (1729), came from a voluntary subscription, and Flaxman's more elaborate ideas would have cost up to £225. A more economical version at £90 was the one chosen, which although modest by comparison is nevertheless a successful design, which the sculptor was to regard as one of his 'favourite' works.[21]

The tomb of the 1st Earl of Mansfield was commissioned by his nephew and heir, Viscount Stormont, in the year his uncle died, 1793.[22] Lord Mansfield had expressed a wish to be buried privately in Westminster Abbey, but a suitor who had benefited from one of Mansfield's judgments had bequeathed money for a monument, which now amounted with interest to £2,500. Flaxman was to receive the whole sum in installments, the first in 1795. The marble alone cost him £600.

The monument was completed in 1801 and placed in a prominent position in the Abbey at the west corner of the north transept and aisle. Unfortunately it was moved in 1933 to its present site seriously diminishing the artist's intention. But even in its original position the sculptor did not regard it as ideal, since he wanted to reduce daylight glare from the windows by changing some of the panes to grey glass, a request which the Dean refused.[23]

Although Nollekens had already sculpted a good bust of Mansfield, his nephew in choosing Flaxman to execute the monument was making a bold decision, because not only had Flaxman up to then not executed a monument on the scale envisaged, but also he had scarcely even begun his career as a designer of monu-

76 *(facing page) William, 1st Earl of Mansfield: monument,* 1793–1801. Westminster Abbey.

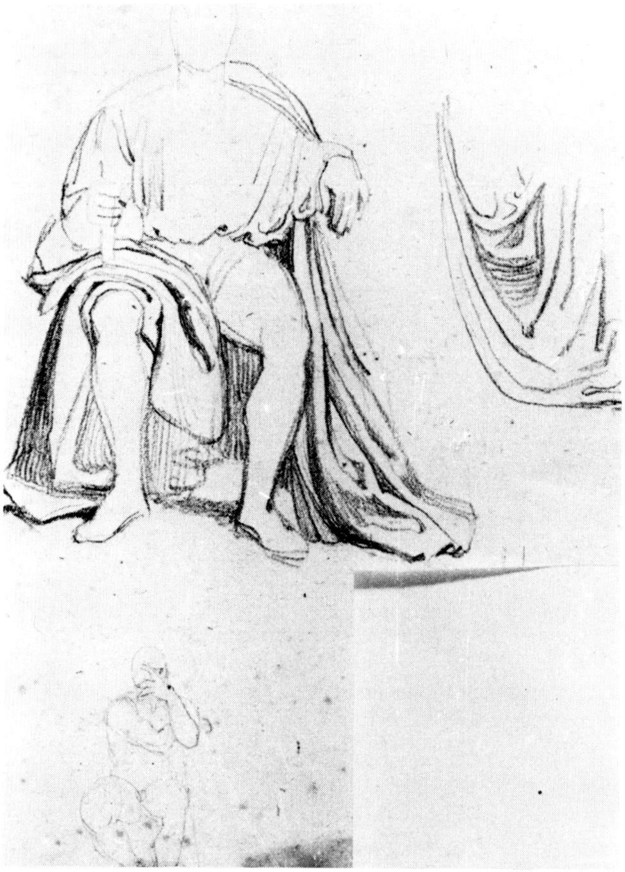

78 *William, 1st Earl of Mansfield: monument: preliminary design for the seated figure.* c. 1793.
Pencil, 26·8 × 21 cms.

ments. Stormont, a diplomat, learned and cultured, with an interest in contemporary art, was presumably impressed by the young artist's growing reputation. Whatever the reason for choosing Flaxman, since the sculptor was abroad it was agreed that the design should be approved by Sir William Hamilton.

From the first, Flaxman seems to have conceived the broad details of the design that was to be finally executed. Already by the end of June 1793 the new Lord Mansfield was writing from London to say that he approved of 'your general idea of having three figures', and that once Hamilton had given his approval to the sketch, Flaxman was to 'begin the model as soon as you conviently can'.[24] Next month Flaxman was in contact with Hamilton as instructed, showing him a design with Lord Mansfield seated high above Justice and Wisdom, the latter wearing Minerva's helmet, 'to mark his Lordship's attic wit', but the figure could be changed to one of the Christian virtue of Prudence if Hamilton preferred.[25] Above Mansfield's head were to be swords of Justice and Mercy bound together by a civic crown, a detail not included in the final design, their position showing that the monument at this stage of planning was to be sited against a wall.

The idea of combining a contemporary portrait with classically-inspired allegorical figures was a well established formula in tomb design by the end of the eighteenth century. Flaxman's most immediate source was the series of papal monuments in St. Peter's and it may have been in connection with the *Mansfield* commission that he drew in the same sketchbook as the one in which some rough ideas for this monument appear (Plate 78), four of the papal tombs in St. Peter's: Canova's monument to *Clement XIII* which had been completed as recently as 1792 (Plates 79 and 80), Bernini's *Alexander VII* (as well as his *Countess Matilda*), Rusconi's *Innocent XI*, and the monument to *Alexander VIII* by Arrigo di San Martino and others (in a Victoria and Albert Museum sketchbook). The papal monuments are set in niches against walls, and it is possibly this form that Flaxman first envisaged for his *Mansfield*. His sketches are little more than rough compositional reminders, lacking any details of the Baroque characteristics which he would have hated. His *Mansfield* is as restrained as Canova's *Clement XIII*, whilst rejecting the Italian's asymmetry in favour of a more formally balanced composition. Flaxman has kept his pyramid of figures simple. His details are minimal; the pedestal, for instance, is ornamented only with a band of Greek key pattern unlike the pretty borders used by Canova. The figure of the elderly Mansfield has an impressive dignity based on Reynolds' portrait. This part of the monument was cut by Flaxman himself, but he left the rest to assistants (including the competent, if uninspired, James Smith) with the result that the flanking figures are rather lifeless. Flaxman also left his assistants to make the enlargements from his small scale model (now in the Soane Museum).

The figures that one sees from the front of Flaxman's monument are devoid of any of the contemporary sentiment so frequently found in his work. But the artist used the freestanding position of the tomb to introduce a naked boy at the back, crouching at the base of the pedestal and clutching an inverted torch. This figure has been interpreted as a condemned youth,[26] but is almost certainly a wingless Genius of Death (Plate 81), whose sentimental melancholy parallels that of the Genius of Death seated in a more languid pose to the right of the *Clement XIII* tomb.

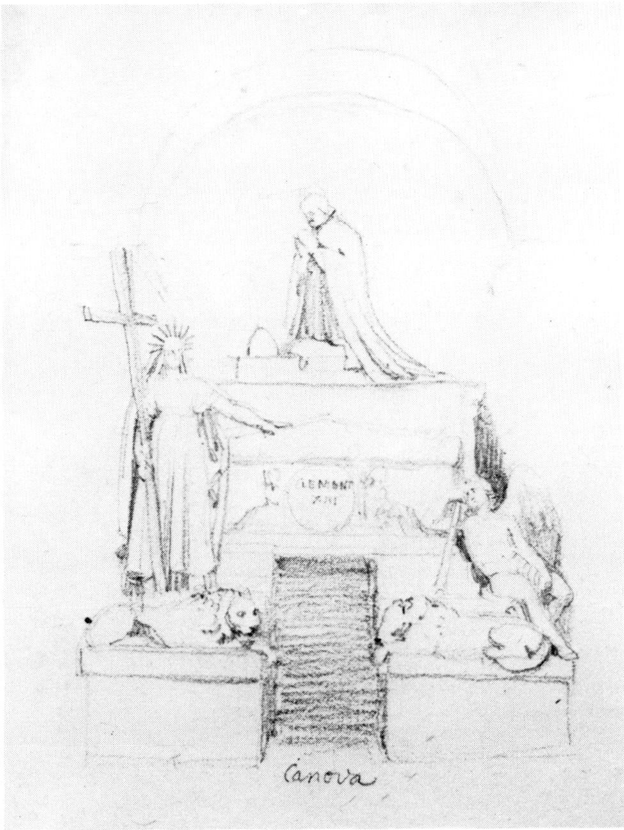

79 *Clement XIII monument, after Canova.* Pencil, 26·8 × 21 cms.

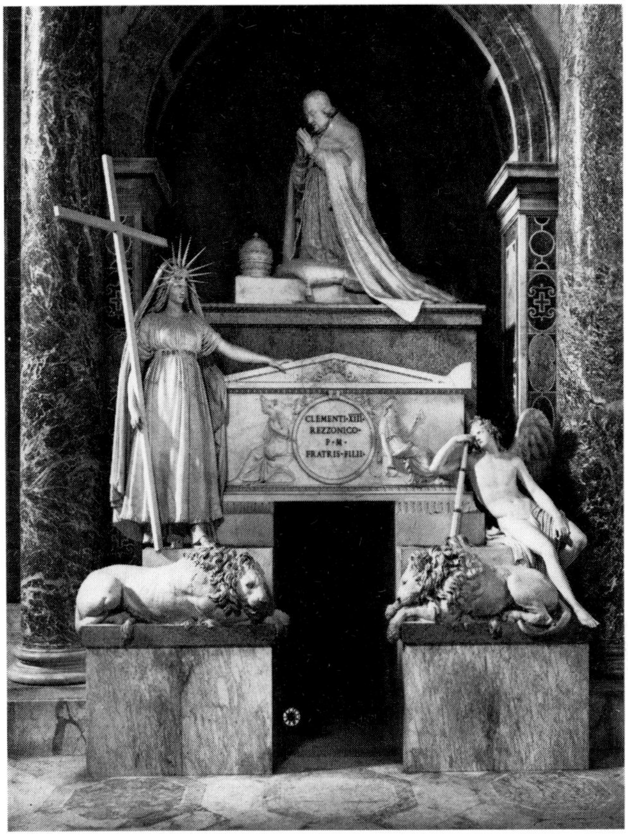

80 Antonio Canova: *Clement XIII: monument.* 1783–92. St. Peter's, Rome.

The relationship between Canova and Flaxman in Rome is not very well documented, but enough clues exist to create an outline beyond the hypothetical influence of the *Clement XIII* monument and the *Cupid and Psyche* in one direction, and that of the *Fury of Athamas* in the other. By the time Flaxman arrived in Italy, Canova was beginning to emerge as the leading sculptor there, having just completed the monument to *Clement XIV* in Santi Apostoli. Canova was friendly and welcomed artists in his studio, and it was therefore natural that he and Flaxman should become acquainted. Canova liked his work and it was on his recommendation that Lord Bristol approached Flaxman with a view to commissioning a sculpture, which materialised as the *Athamas*. Flaxman's account-books[27] show that in 1790 he had clay carried to Canova's studio, indicating that he was at least using his facilities, and perhaps receiving some help or instruction. The following year he paid a 'carter to Mr. Canova's', but for what purpose is unspecified, perhaps more clay. Later that year he paid for a repair to Canova's carriage, which had broken a beam whilst he had borrowed it. And in 1792 the accounts show a sum debited to 'Mr. Canova for [a] gold chain', presumably a present as a sign of gratitude. The account-book entries are only scraps, but they indicate that the two sculptors were not merely formal acquaintances but on good terms with each other.

The subsequent careers of the two sculptors were to develop along different lines. Whilst in Italy they seemed close, because Flaxman's sculptures were predominantly classical subject-pieces with few tombs, a proportion of secular to religious work similar to Canova's at the time. Later, however, whilst Canova's output was to retain the same balance between the two types of commission, Flaxman's secular sculptures were to take second place to his religious works. Although the nature of their work was different, contemporaries often praised and joined the names of these two leading Neoclassical sculptors. One typical example occurs in 1808, when a patron of the arts in Scotland lamented that Edinburgh had 'no Flaxman or Canova'.[28] One of

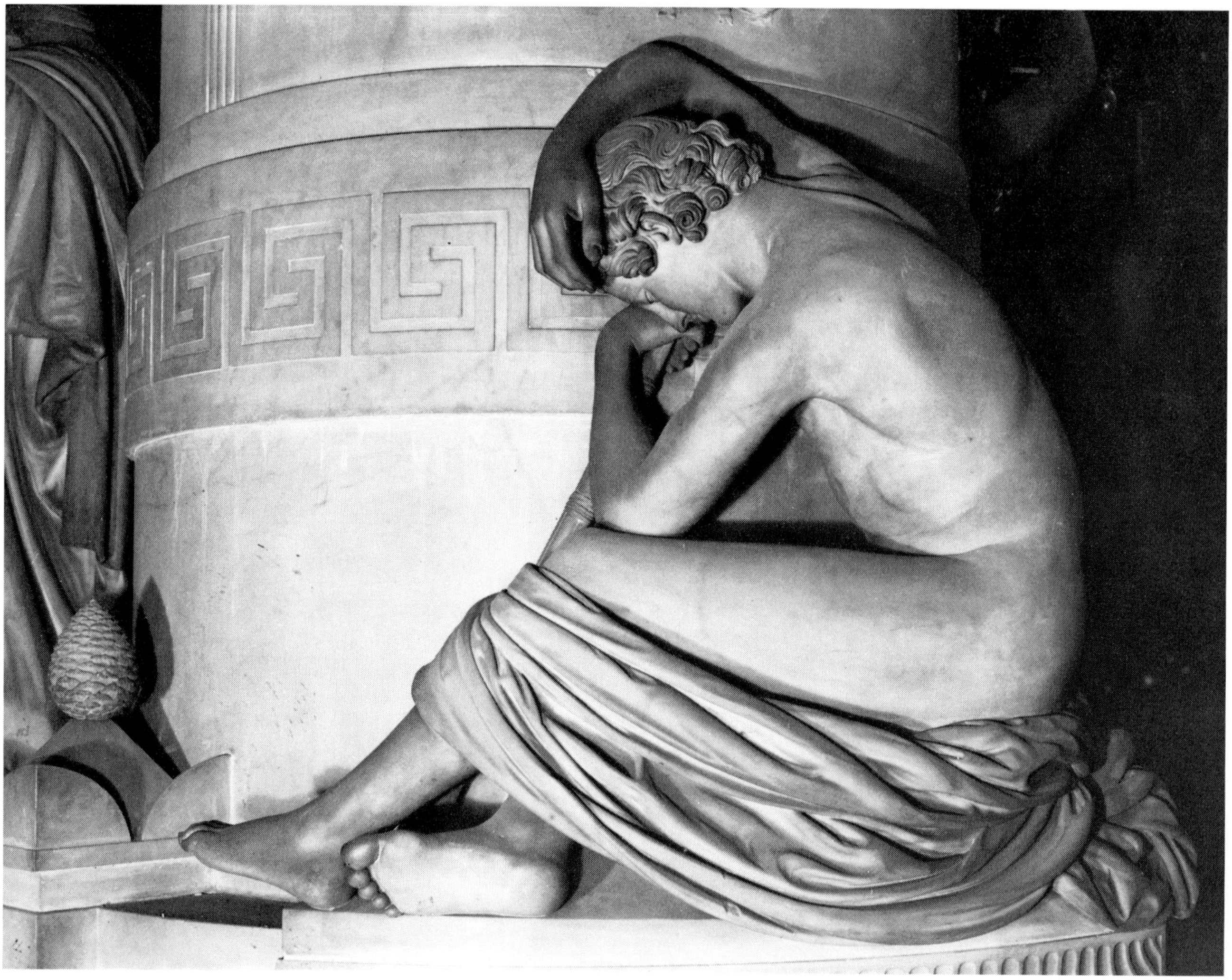

81 *William, 1st Earl of Mansfield: monument: detail of Genius of Death.* Westminster Abbey.

the contemporary biographies of Canova contains an interesting comparison of the work of the two artists, in the course of which the writer makes many valid points. 'The name of Flaxman alone will divide with his the applause of posterity', wrote J. S. Memes. 'Flaxman had already displayed a judicious and fearless disregard of the conventional modes by which art was enslaved, being distinguished at Rome for devotion to the study of the antique, and for that deep feeling of its simplicity and severe beauties, which have since characterised his productions. Equal to, perhaps, in some respects, surpassing Canova in fertility of invention, and in strength of original conception; he falls beneath him in facility of execution, in beauty and grace of expression, and in exquisite delicacy of finish. Had the English artist remained in Italy, he certainly would have proved a rival to be feared, and would have shared with the Venetian the glory of reforming modern sculpture'.[29]

CHAPTER V

Illustrations

Flaxman became 'the idol of all the dilettanti' on the Continent because of his illustrations, according to Goethe in an enthusiastic article he wrote in 1799.[1] Another German critic even went so far as to write in a history of art that in John Flaxman 'a shining star has risen in England's artistic heaven. May his arrival announce the dawn of a marvellous period of art'.[2]

These comments are typical of the contemporary praise which Flaxman received from writers and artists on the Continent. Flaxman's sculptures were largely unknown abroad, since very few were published as engravings in his own lifetime; therefore the Continent knew Flaxman mainly through his illustrations to Homer, Aeschylus and Dante, and, to a lesser extent, Hesiod. The earlier engravings were so well received that Flaxman's name joined those of the small group of British artists who in the eighteenth and early nineteenth centuries achieved a reputation beyond the shores of Britain. This rare, European reputation Flaxman shared with other Neoclassicists, Gavin Hamilton, Angelica Kauffmann and Jacob More, all of whom, unlike Flaxman, spent most of their lives in Italy.

1 Homer

Flaxman arrived in Italy already well read in Greek and Latin authors, and familiar with illustrations of classical scenes on bas-reliefs and vases. This knowledge together with the rigorous stylistic discipline developed whilst working for Wedgwood, were soon to be put to use in several sets of illustrations. Even before he received the commissions that were to establish his fame, Flaxman was busy in Rome in 1789 producing drawings inspired by Euripides which already bear the hallmark of the linear style he was shortly to use for his published illustrations. In the *Alcestis* drawing reproduced in Plate 82 Flaxman has chosen the poignant moment of the reunion of Admetus and his wife after she had been brought back to life by Hercules, who stands to one side watching the scene. An Italian friend commenting at the time on the Euripides drawings, which were never engraved, singled out their 'simple outlines,' which would not have been 'disapproved of in Greece at the time of Timanthes'.[3] These comments are representative of many, in which critics stressed the linearity of Flaxman's illustrations, describing how appropriate they would have been in fifth century Greece. One particularly perceptive critic, A. W. von Schlegel, in a long essay in 1799, devoted to all Flaxman engravings, went so far as to say that outline was better than a fully detailed drawing for literary illustrations.

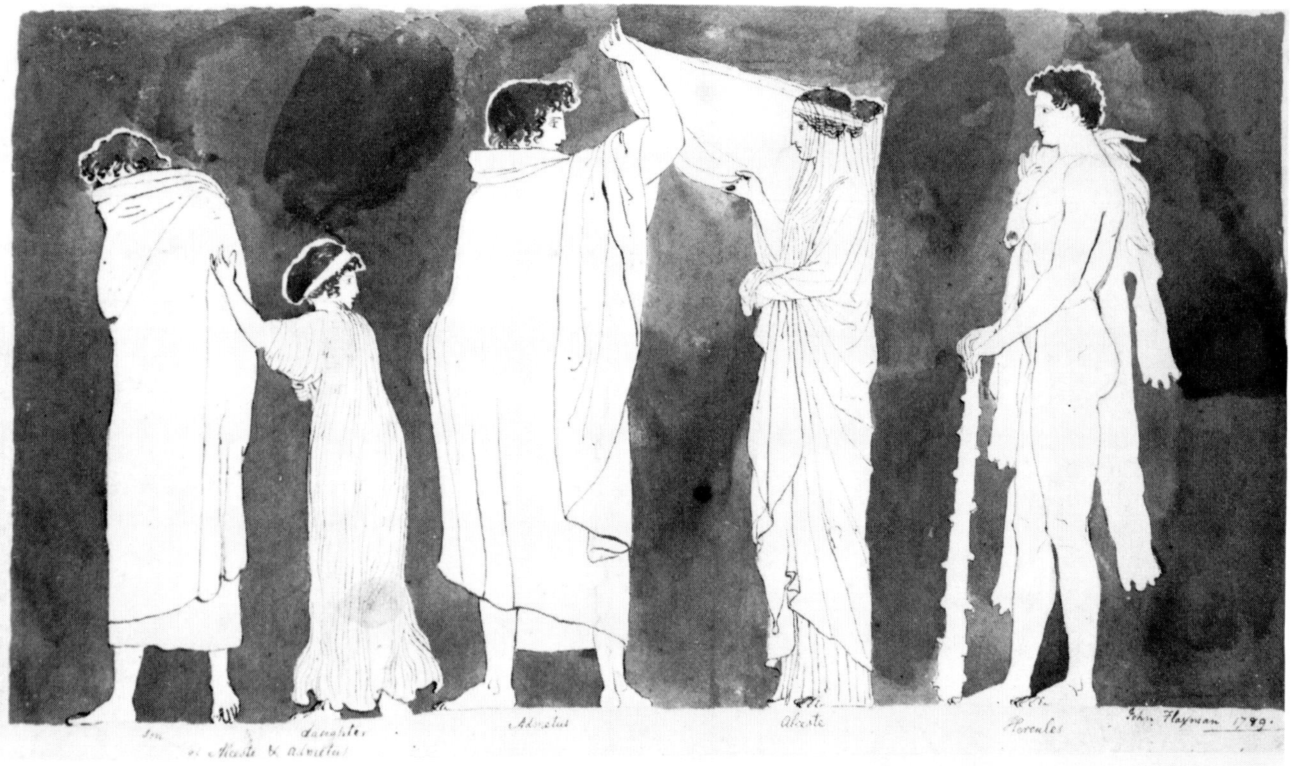

82 *The Reunion of Admetus and Alcestis (Euripides).* Pen and ink and wash, 23·8 × 41·6 cms.

'Just as the words of the poet are formulae for life and beauty,' he wrote, 'whose secret power one does not recognise according to their component parts, so the successful sketch produces a true magic, that so much soulfulness can inhabit a few gentle strokes'. But 'the fondness for mere contour drawings', he admits, 'is much more unusual' than a love of more fully finished drawings, in which the general public 'can only imagine a blue or green dress if they see it with their own eyes'.[4]

In 1792 Flaxman was working on two sets of illustrations to Homer, only one of which was intended for publication. Mrs. Hare-Naylor (a cousin of the dowager Countess Spencer who was to order the *Aeschylus* illustrations) commissioned the *Homer* drawings that were to be published in two volumes in 1793, engraved by Piroli. The order for the other set was placed by a 'Mr. Udny', who was probably Robert Fullerton Udney, a connoisseur and collector, and Fellow of both the Royal Society and the Society of Antiquaries.[5] The double commission might account for the existence of drawings for *Homer* in two markedly different styles, one as linear as the final engravings, the other modelled and completed with a wash. The latter type of drawings that survive could either have formed part of, or at least relate to, Udney's set, because as they were not intended for reproduction as engravings they may have been more elaborately worked as pictures (see Plate 89).

None of Flaxman's volumes of illustrations was published with the complete text of the poem or play, as his drawings were not conceived as visual accompaniments to the typography but as a replacement for the text itself: 'my intention is to show how any story may be represented in a series of compositions on the principles of the ancients', he wrote in a letter in 1793.[6] Several years later he was to stress his objections to conventional book illustrations in another letter, when Hayley was trying to persuade him to make designs for his edition of Milton's Latin poems (Hayley only succeeded in his aim because he was a friend). Flaxman wrote: 'I have already stated my objections to making designs for the decoration of printed books—that I never have made any for such purposes; that it is a branch of art in which I am not likely to succeed for want of practice, and the productions in which will be regarded with a jealous eye by those to whom that department belongs.'[7] Flaxman's volumes were therefore published either without any quotations at all or with only a minimal number of lines under each plate. This novel form of publication undoubtedly contributed to their contemporary visual impact, and their far-reaching influence.

The lines of English text that appear under the plates of some of the *Homer* editions were chosen from Alexander Pope's famous translation. This version had been reprinted frequently throughout the century. It had not been superseded by the more recent translation of William Cowper (1791), which Flaxman did not use presumably because contemporary critics regarded it as inferior to Pope's. Although Dante is quoted in the original tongue on the *Divine Comedy* plates, Homer is not, although Flaxman read Greek, acquired a Greek lexicon whilst in Italy,[8] and inscribed some of the preparatory drawings in the original language.

The *Homer*, *Aeschylus* and *Dante* illustrations, together with the sculptures executed and planned in Italy, show Flaxman tackling the widest range of actions and emotions in his entire career, within the short space of time between about 1792 and 1794. The dominant role of funerary monuments after his return home was to leave little time for the treatment of themes of violence and passion in his sculpture, and only one more set of illustrations was to be published in addition to those commissioned whilst abroad. After 1794 therefore, Flaxman's art was to become primarily concerned with themes of compassion and gentleness. But whilst in Italy both the tranquil and the passionate are important themes in his art.

When the first edition of Flaxman's *Iliad* illustrations appeared, he divided the thirty-four scenes evenly between tranquil and violent scenes. When he added five more plates in 1805 he changed the balance by adding only one scene involving any violence: Minerva repressing the anger of Achilles (Plate 83). In the *Odyssey* the balance was in favour of gentle scenes from the first edition onwards, accounting for eighteen out of a total of twenty-eight plates (Plates 84 and 85).

In choosing his scenes from Homer, Flaxman showed a bias both in his choice of subjects and in his treatment of them. Although he did not avoid the more passionate and horrific moments in Homer's lines,

83 *Minerva repressing the anger of Achilles.* Engraving, 18·2 × 31·5 cms., after Flaxman by William Blake. *Iliad*, 1805, Plate 2.

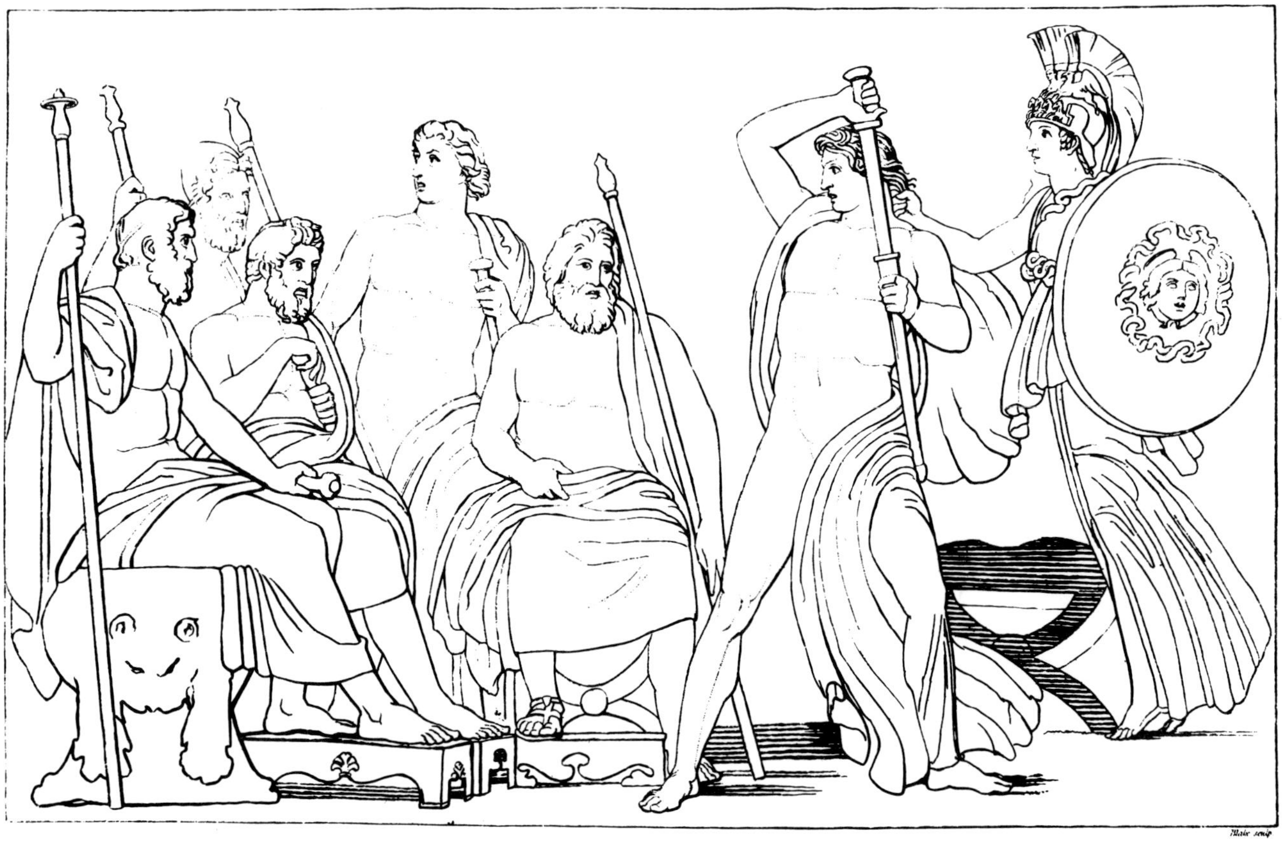

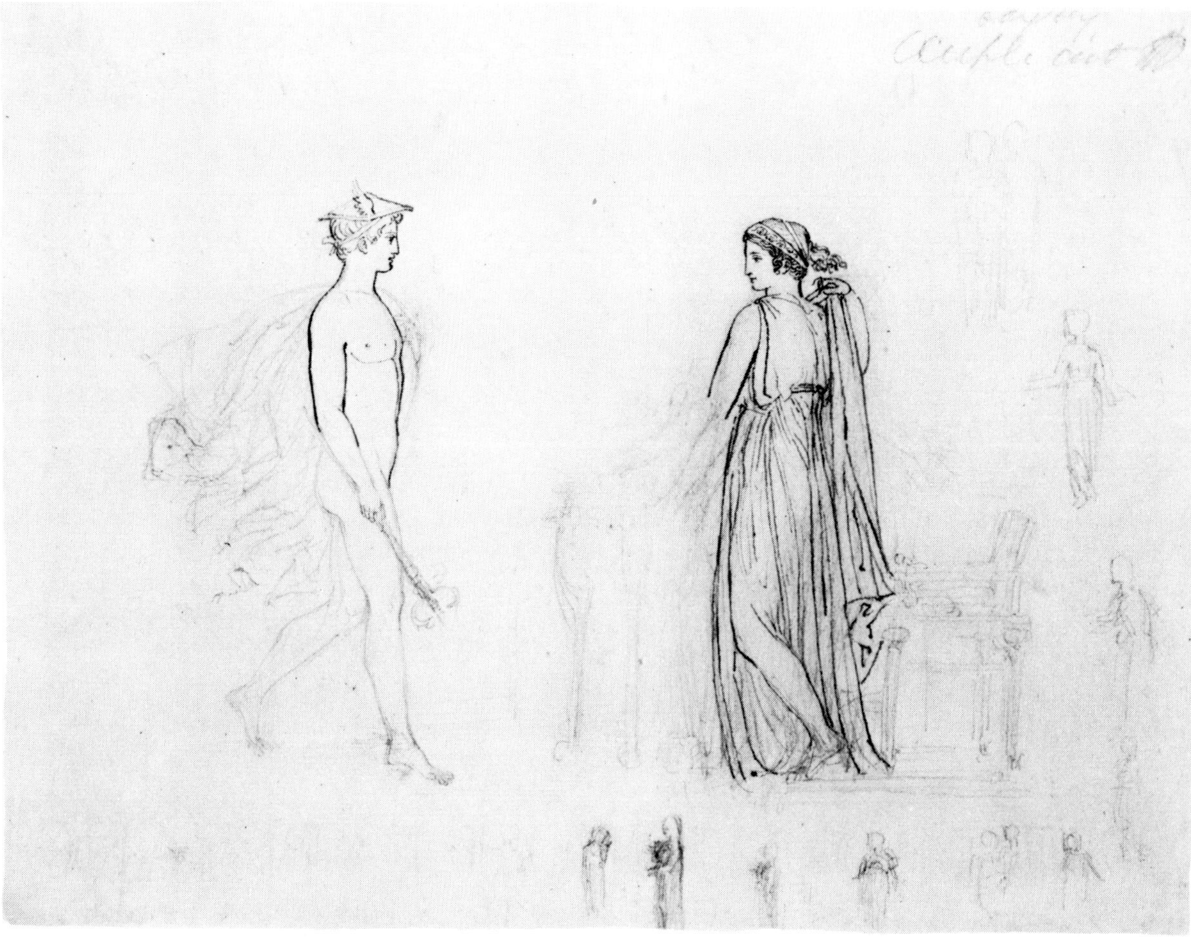

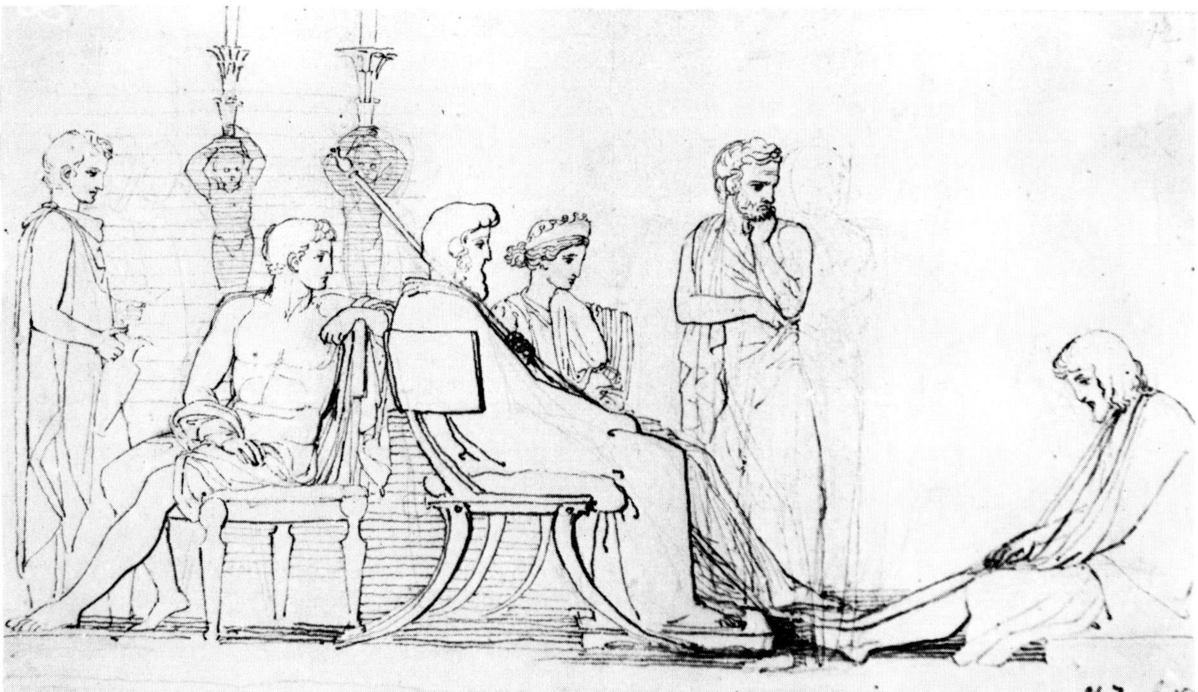

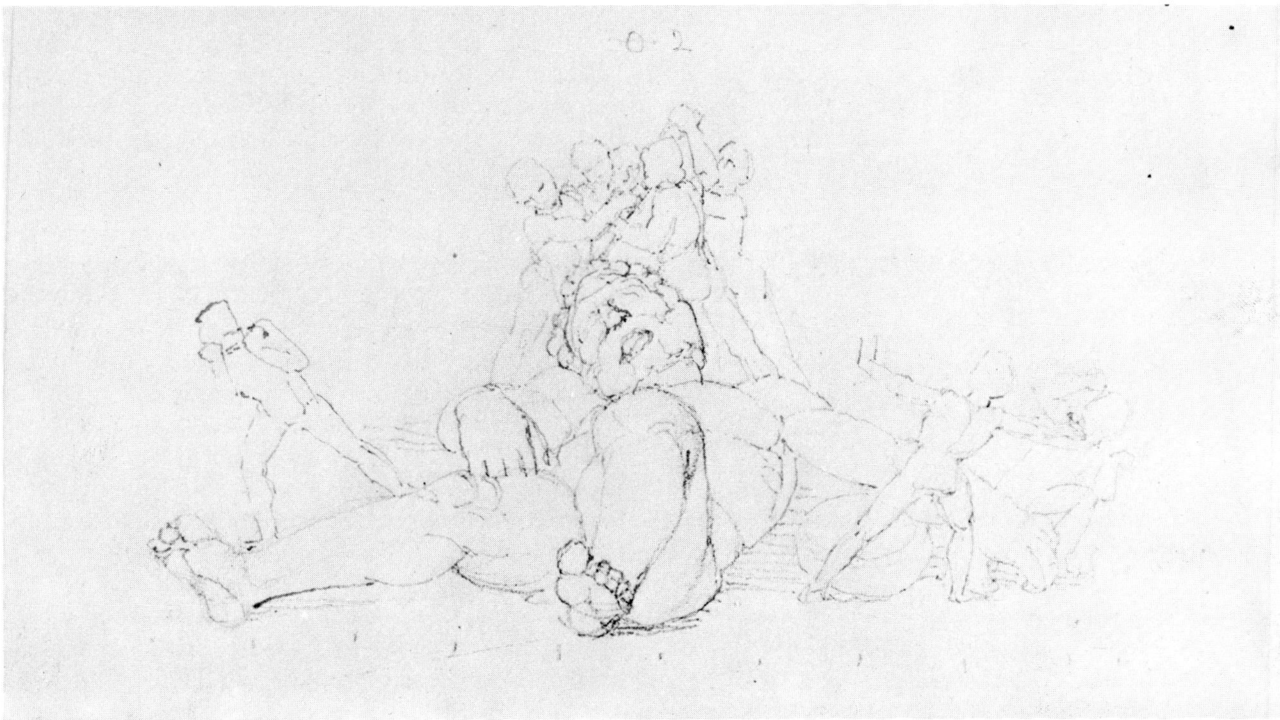

86 *Cyclops (Odyssey).* Pen and ink 14·4 × 17·5 cms.

Flaxman tended to minimise them. The horror that one might expect in the scene of Achilles dragging Hector's body around the walls of Troy, which had been exploited to great dramatic effect even by an earlier Neoclassicist, Gavin Hamilton, becomes in Flaxman's illustration disappointingly timid. Potential anguish is removed by the dominant presence of Apollo as the dead warrior's divine guide who hovers elegantly over the corpse. Amongst Flaxman's unused Homer designs is a vigorous image in the *Odyssey* showing the blinding of the *Cyclops*, with a group of Ulysses's companions poised with their heated stake (Plate 86).

This withdrawal from violence can be partly explained by a contemporary comparison between the *Iliad* and *Odyssey*. As recently as 1785, Henry Boyd in the introduction to his translation of the *Inferno* (the edition which Flaxman used in the captions to his own Dante plates) had written: 'It is this that sets the *Odyssey*, in point of sentiment, so far above the *Iliad*. We feel the injuries of Ulysses; . . . we seem to feel the generous indignation of the young Telemachus, and we tremble at the dangers of the fair Penelope, . . . we can go along with the resentment of Ulysses, because it is just, but our feelings must tell us that Achilles carried his resentment to a savage length, a length where we cannot follow him.'

Such a comment helps to explain the omission of some of the scenes in Flaxman's designs, but not all of them. Even with the extra plates added in 1805, the five just mentioned to the *Iliad* and six to the *Odyssey*, Flaxman's two Homer volumes still omitted some of the scenes frequently illustrated by other artists, including Neoclassicists. Whilst he took the opportunity in 1805 to add popular scenes as the meeting of Hector and Andromache (Plate 87) and the judgement of Paris, he started the *Iliad* with a new first plate of an attractive but not essential image of Homer invoking a Muse. Yet Flaxman still left out important and popular scenes such as the one of the death of Hector and one of Priam coming to redeem his dead body from Achilles. Preparatory drawings exist for these two scenes[9] but they were rejected. Also excluded was an illustration of the dream of Achilles, in which he stretches out his arms in an attempt to grasp the spirit of Patroclus as it floats through the sky, which would have been one of the most exaggeratedly elongated images in the whole

84 *(facing above) Hermes visiting Calypso (Odyssey).*
Pen and ink and pencil, 21 × 27·3 cms.

85 *(facing below) Ulysses on the Hearth presenting himself to Alcinous and Arete (Odyssey).*
Pen and ink and pencil 17·2 × 30·6 cms.

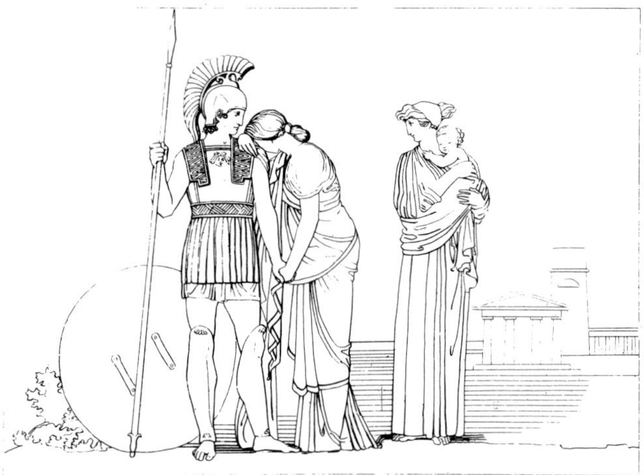

87 *The Meeting of Hector and Andromache*. Engraving, 18 × 25 cms., after Flaxman by James Parker. *Iliad*, 1805, Plate 14.

series, and was perhaps for that reason not included. The dream of Achilles might also have been excluded because it would have been visually repetitive, since Flaxman had included another scene of a dead body floating in the sky in the illustration of Sarpedon. But the deliberate minimising of Hector's role in the story cannot be explained on grounds of visual repetition, since there are few death scenes and there is no design compositionally similar to the redemption of Hector's body. Apart from the playing down of the element of horror Flaxman's rejections suggest that he was determined to make his volumes as compositionally varied as possible, even if this meant altering the emphasis in the story itself.

The action in Flaxman's designs is reduced to the smallest number of figures necessary to illustrate the particular incident. Superfluous details are excluded, furnishings are kept to the minimum, and landscape settings are hardly ever employed. His compositions are as elemental as is necessary to relate the story: a characteristic that Goethe aptly described as 'naïvety'.[10]

Amongst the many surviving drawings for the *Iliad* and *Odyssey* it is sometimes possible to trace the development of an illustration from the first rough sketch through several intermediate stages to the final outline ready for the engraver. The process is normally one of continual minor modifications, usually retaining the first general idea. When the change in a composition was more fundamental, it was sometimes made to heighten the drama. In some scenes passion is undoubtedly played down, but in others, Flaxman uses the emotional intensity in Homer's lines to the utmost.

The first plate of the 1793 edition of the *Iliad* shows the departure of Briseis from the tent of Achilles (Plate 88). Patroclus stands in the centre, gently pushing the captured Briseis before him, whilst she is being handed over to Agamemnon's heralds. She looks over her shoulder at Achilles, grieving at her misfortunate but in a more restrained manner than that described by Homer. In the engraving the five figures appear in a single line along the shore, but Flaxman had also been working on the idea of placing one of the heralds in the background, whilst making the other turn away from the spectators as he grasps Briseis's hand (Plate 89). By removing the contrapposto and the spatial depth in this drawing the engraved version becomes more two-dimensional. The figure of Achilles has also been changed between the two versions. In the unpublished version he is standing, with his head turned away from the departing Briseis, and the whole composition is very close to one Canova had used for the same scene in a gesso panel completed in 1790 (Plate 90) which Flaxman could easily have known. Even in the engraved version, the centre and righthand parts of the composition remain close to Canova's. But by changing the pose of his Achilles, Flaxman altered the emotional intensity of the scene. Achilles no longer turns his back on Briseis, they still look at each other even in the moment of separation, making the scene more poignant. Homer's description is not detailed, leaving a great deal of scope for artistic invention.

Another example of a fundamental change between a preparatory drawing and a final engraving is provided by the illustration in the *Odyssey* showing Penelope surprised by the suitors. Flaxman at first drew Penelope seated (Plate 91), so intent on her weaving on a small horizontal loom—one that looks more suitable for embroidery—that she is unaware of the suitors' arrival behind her. Only the servant on the right has seen their entry. Flaxman kept close to the text, which reads in Pope's translation: 'We saw, as unperceiv'd we took our stand, / The backward labours of her faithless hand'. But in the final version, although these two lines are printed underneath the engraving in the editions that quote the English translation, Penelope stands staring at

88 *(facing above) The Departure of Briseis from the Tent of Achilles*. Engraving, 18·2 × 31·5 cms., after Flaxman by Thomas Piroli. *Iliad*, 1793, Plate 1.

89 *(facing below) The Departure of Briseis from the Tent of Achilles (Iliad)*. Pen and ink and wash, 19·7 × 27 cms.

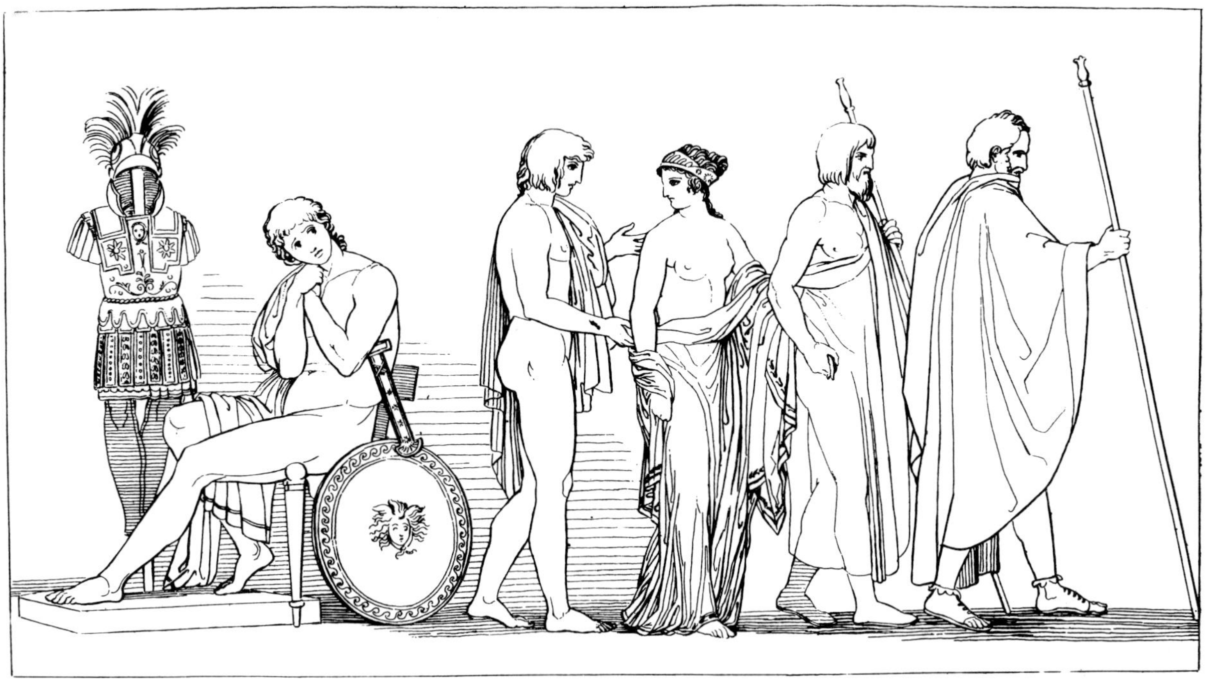

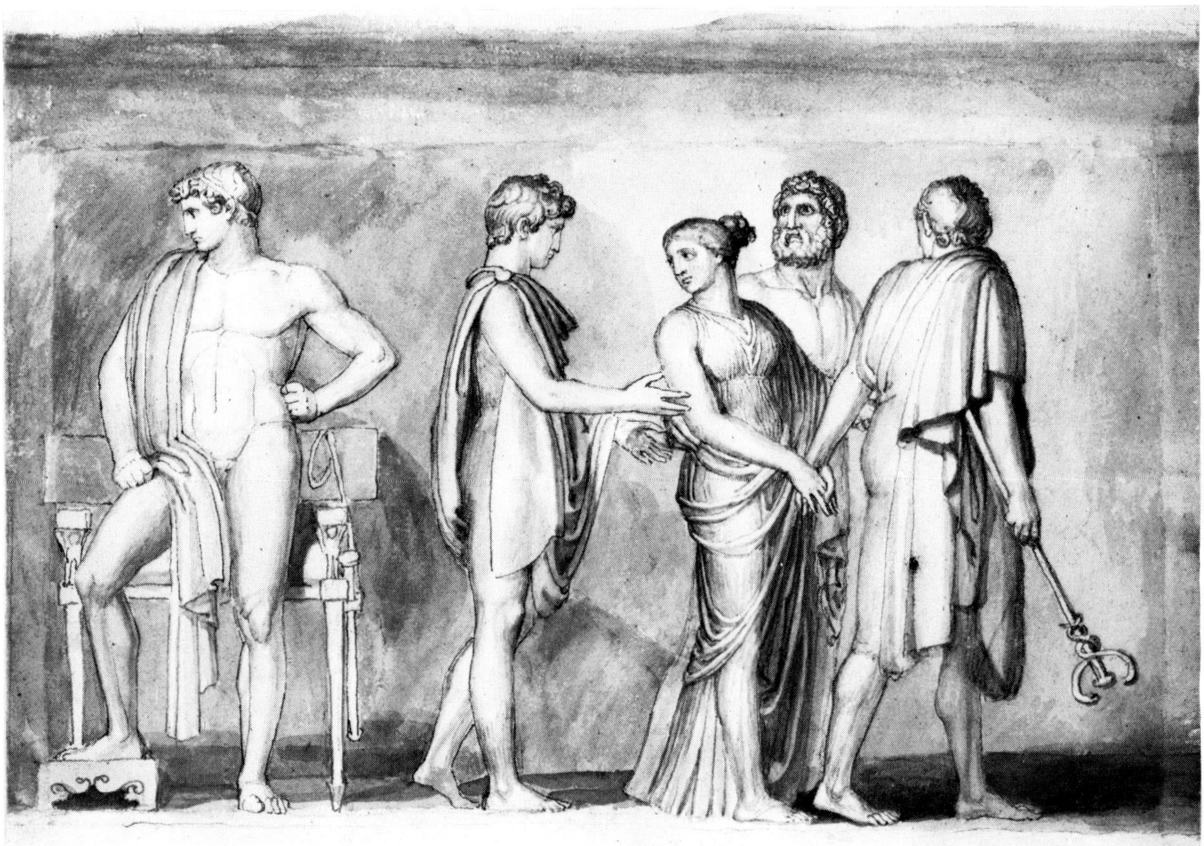

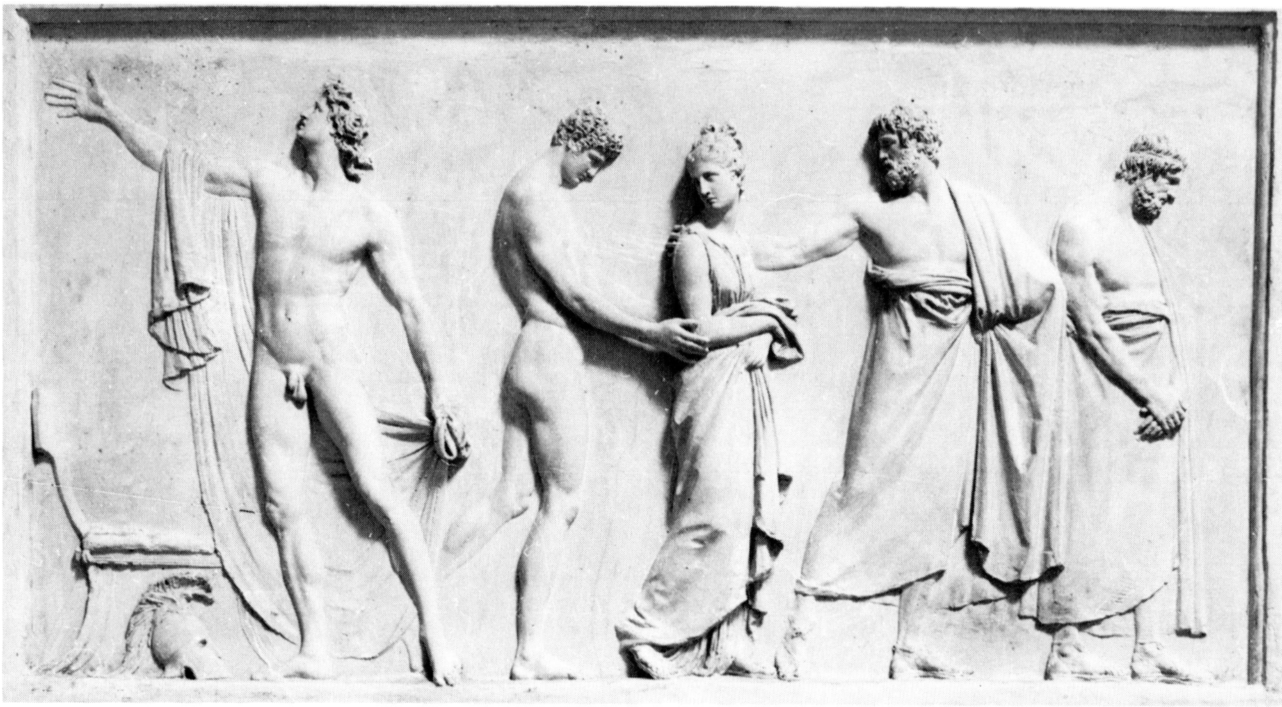

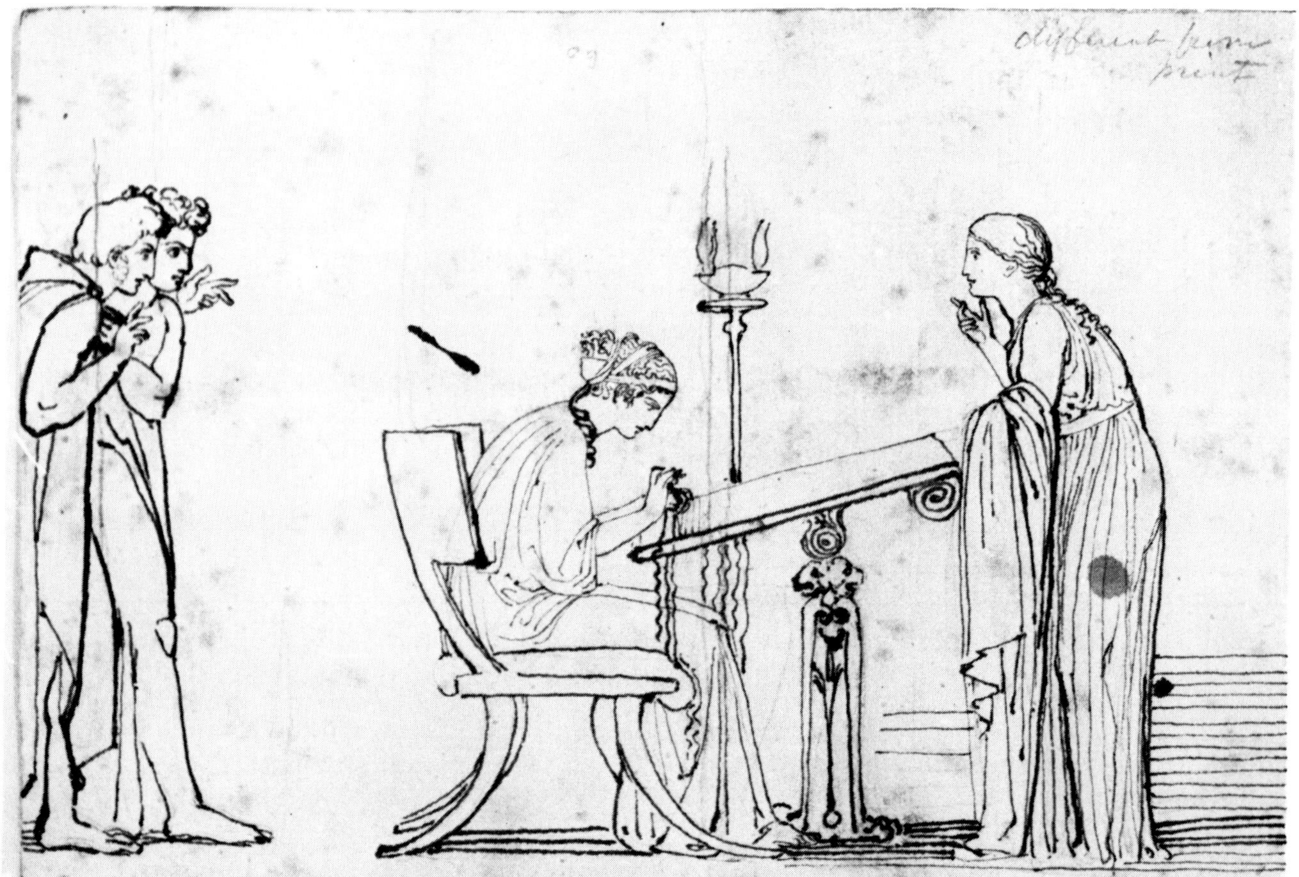
different from
print

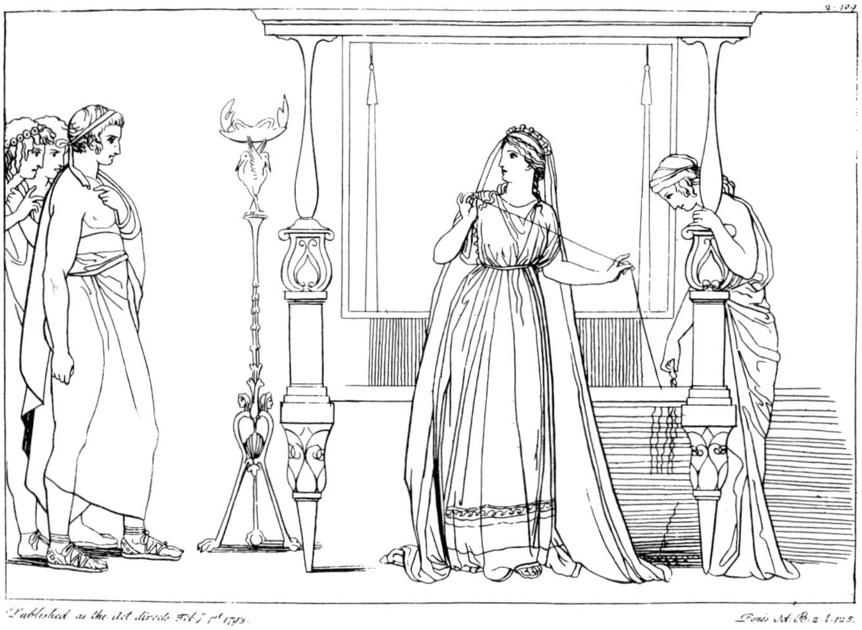

92 *Penelope surprised by the Suitors.* Engraving, 17·8 × 25·5 cms. After Flaxman by Thomas Piroli. *Odyssey*, 1793, Plate 2.

the suitors in amazement (Plate 92). Between her hands is stretched a thread from her loom, which has now become a larger construction unmistakably intended for weaving, which frames her like an arch. The servant no longer records surprise, but concentrates on the process of unpicking her mistress's work. The first version had been almost a domestic genre scene, as if based on his observations of his wife or sister-in-law embroidering, an intimate pose which on different occasions he did actually draw (Plate 93). But in the engraved version Penelope's pose is more dramatic and the element of surprise is intensified, making a more effective illustration. Sometimes a preliminary drawing contained too many figures, which Flaxman reduced in number. In the illustration showing Ulysses fighting the suitors, Flaxman originally included in the background the distracting figure of a musician hurrying away to safety, which is removed in the engraving. Sometimes Flaxman's economy of imagery led to the removal of a figure as important as Minerva herself, who in a preliminary drawing is shown standing behind Ulysses to guide him in his fight with Irus. But in the engraving Ulysses stands alone confronting the reluctant Irus, who is being dragged into the fight by two other men. The figure of Ulysses now fighting without visible signs of divine intervention appears more striking than in the preparatory drawing.

Each plate in the *Iliad* and *Odyssey* shows a meticulous attention to detail, not only in terms of archaeological accuracy but also in many minor changes in the course of perfecting a composition. When Ulysses sits at the table of Circe, in a preliminary drawing he is confronted simply with a basin and some bread. But by the stage of the engraving (Plate 94) the bread has been replaced by some elegant ewers, more suggestive of the attractive meal which Circe had laid before her guest. Such small alterations abound throughout the drawings, creating the impression of an artist who is very precise in the effect he wishes to achieve. He might change a hair style or the type of a helmet from one drawing to the next, alter a chair or a cushion. Furnishings such as candelabra or a tripod are sometimes removed if thought irrelevant or distracting, regardless of how attractive these objects may be in their own right.

Flaxman used architectural and landscape backgrounds very sparingly. When Briseis is removed from Achilles one might expect some indication of the encampment on the shore, at least Achilles's tent. But Flaxman included none of these details and only suggested the tent by including some of its furnishings: a chair and a stand on which armour has been placed. When 'swarms of spectres rose from deepest hell' to terrify Ulysses, they fill a large area of the composition

90 *(facing above)* Antonio Canova: *The Departure of Briseis from the Tent of Achilles (Iliad)*, 1787–90.

91 *(facing below) Penelope Surprised by the Suitors (Odyssey).* Pen and ink and pencil, 16·5 × 24·2 cms.

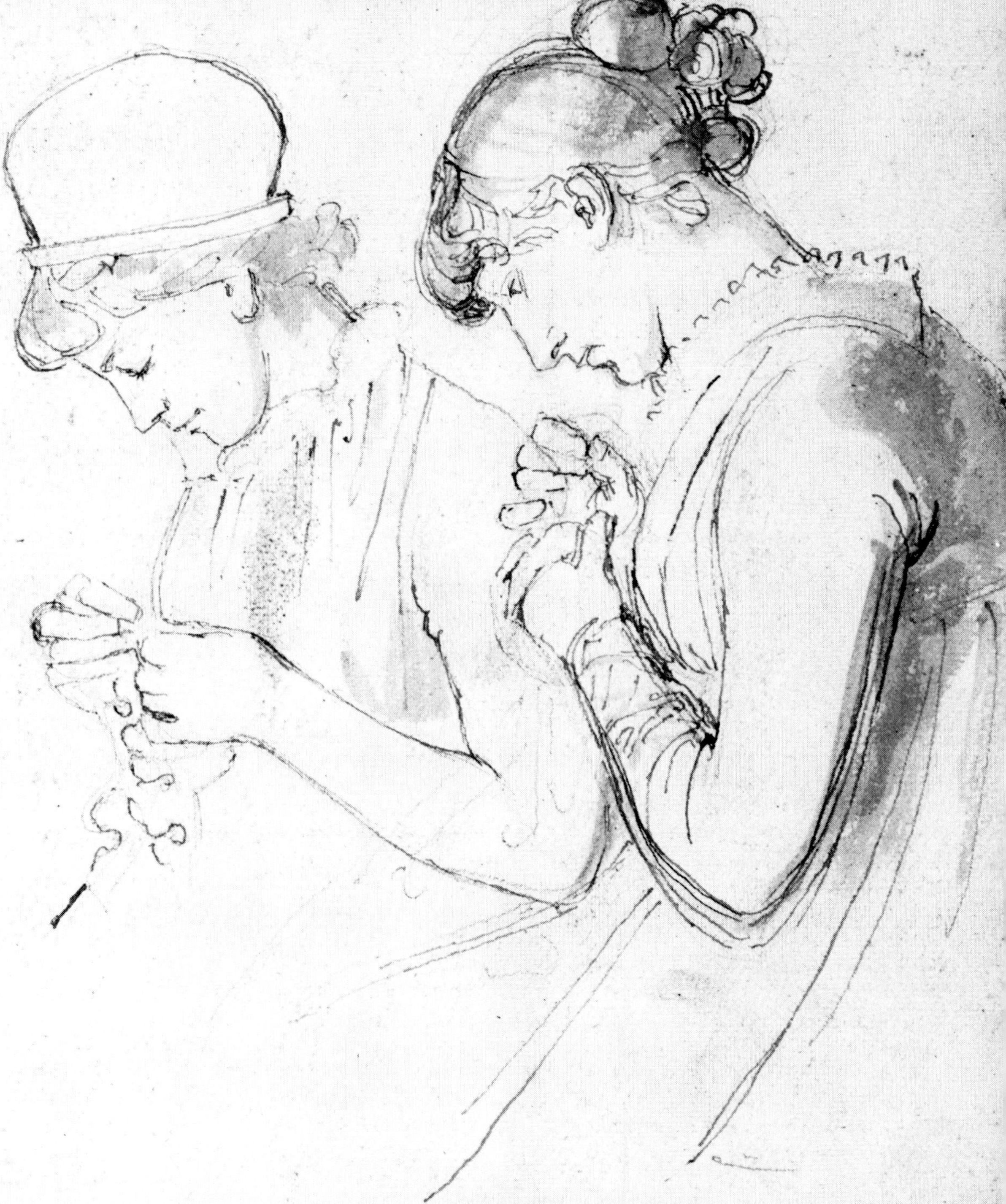

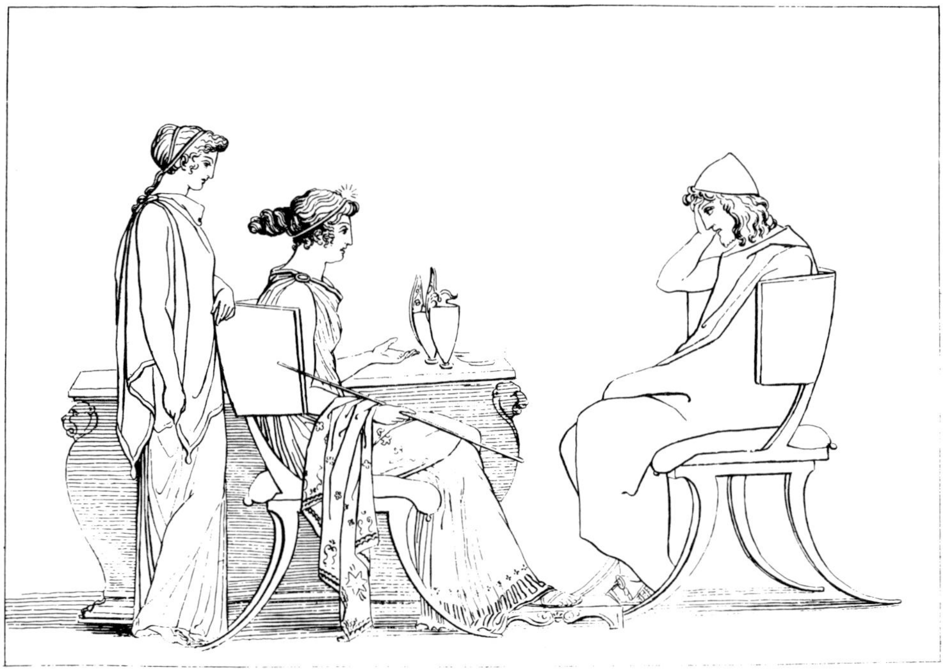

94 *Ulysses at the Table of Circe.* Engraving, 19 × 27·2 cms., after Flaxman by Thomas Piroli. *Odyssey,* 1793, Plate 12.

and leave no room for any scenery beyond a suggestion of bare rock on which Ulysses is standing (Plate 95).

Several illustrations include clouds, always used functionally as settings for divine or supernatural activities, never as mere background decoration. Flaxman's most ambitious use of clouds is in the plate showing the funeral pyre of Patroclus, where the billowing smoke fanned by the winds envelops much of the composition, producing one of the artist's most ambitious and complex outdoor settings (Plate 96).

The sea is an important element in the story, used effectively in a very stylized, almost unnatural manner in several plates. The representation of sea ranges from gentle ripples in the illustration of Thetis ordering the Nereids to descend into the sea, to violent waves just before the quelling of the storm that nearly drowned Ulysses (Plates 97 and also 169). In the *Iliad* a very dramatic undulation of water provides the basis for the beautifully stylized linear rhythm of the composition showing Achilles's fight with the river gods, who themselves almost become the waves (Plate 98).

The only plate in the Homer series that approaches a more conventional use of landscape is the one showing the Sirens wooing Ulysses, a plate added to the 1805 edition. They are shown seated on an apparently idyllic island covered with flowers, but in the foreground—invisible from Ulysses's boat—is a macabre still-life of skulls and bones. The composition, however, is spatially unconvincing, as Flaxman has introduced perspective but not been able to resolve the contradiction between traditional space and pure outline.

Architecture is used on an elaborate scale once in the *Odyssey*, in the scene showing Apollo and Diana discharging their arrows on the inhabitants of the isle of Syria. The lower part of Flaxman's composition is filled with a harbour, temples and a background acropolis, in a very elemental style of architecture that attempts to recreate a pre-Doric period. Normally Flaxman included only the barest suggestion of architecture, the best use of which in the *Iliad* occurs in the scene (added in 1805) in which Hector unexpectedly meets his wife as he is about to leave the gates of Troy (Plate 87). The contrast between the uncertainties of war outside the city's perimeter and the safety and comfort within seems to be highlighted by an architectural background representing security. Flaxman has again tried to recreate a simple, stark architecture with a colonnade, a Doric temple and what is presumably a reconstruction of the Tower of Ilium. The elemental, primitive quality of the architecture is a perfect accompaniment to the simplicity and purity of form he was achieving in his human figures.

Flaxman drew many Roman bas-reliefs whilst in Italy and these, together with those he already knew

93 *Two Ladies Sewing (? Mrs. Flaxman and Maria Denman).* Pen and ink, wash and pencil, 32 × 23 cms.

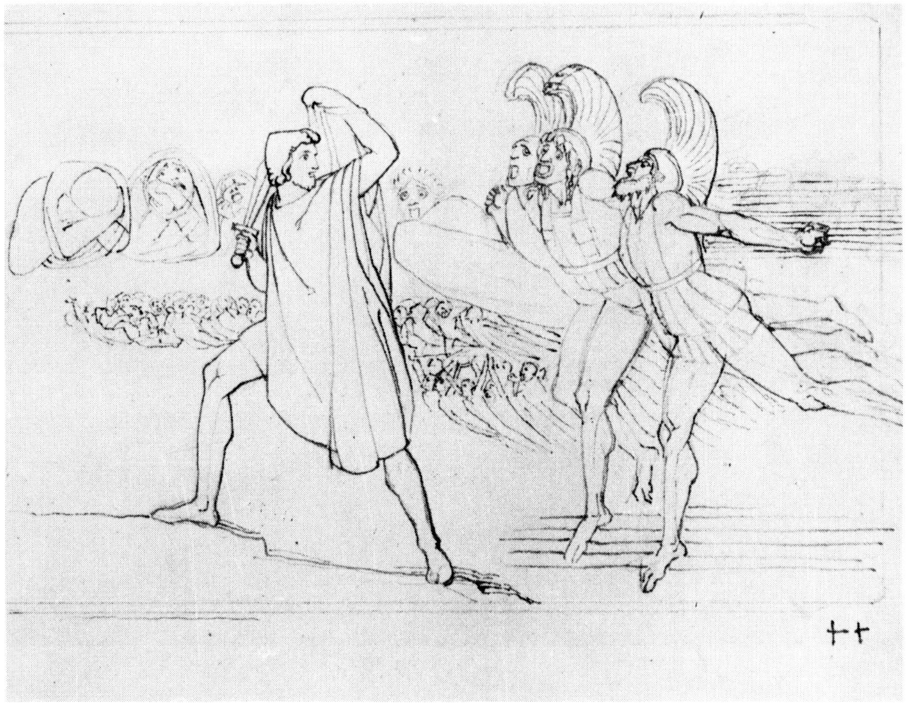

95 *Ulysses terrified by the Ghosts (Odyssey).* Pencil, pen and ink, 23 × 36 cms.

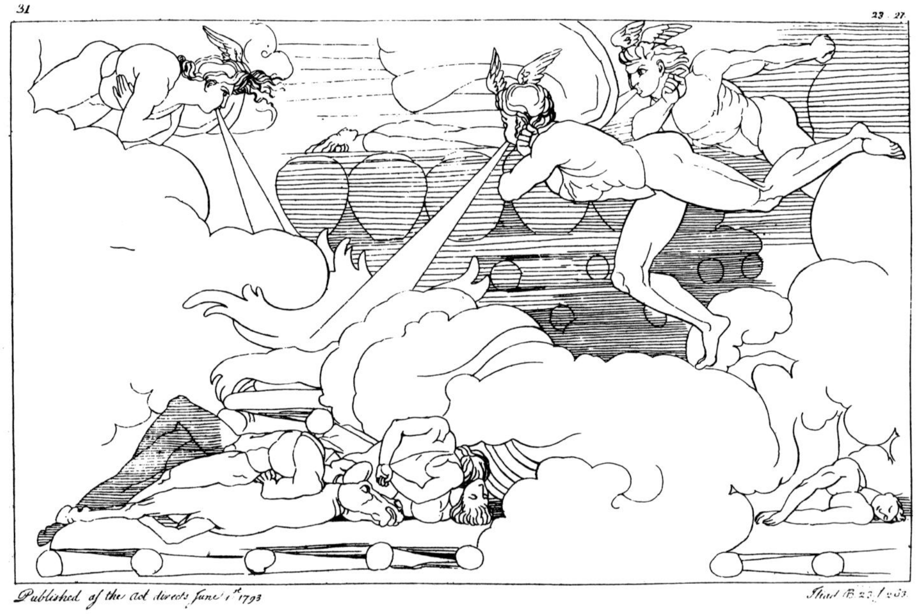

96 *The Funeral Pyre of Patroclus.* Engraving, 19 × 28 cms., after Flaxman, by Thomas Piroli. *Iliad*, 1793, Plate 31.

before he went abroad, provided a useful repertoire of compositions which could be consulted for reference, as well as in a more general way influencing his style, as these drawings usually ignore the deep undercutting and stress the linearity. Only in a very few instances can a particular relief be shown to have influenced a specific illustration in his *Iliad* or *Odyssey*, as the relationship between his sources and the uses to which they are put is more imprecise.

Amongst his sketches is a rough outline, omitting all details, of a well known sarcophagus panel depicting the battle of the Amazons in the Vatican collections (Plate 99), which he seems to have used as the basis for his composition in the *Iliad* showing the fight for the

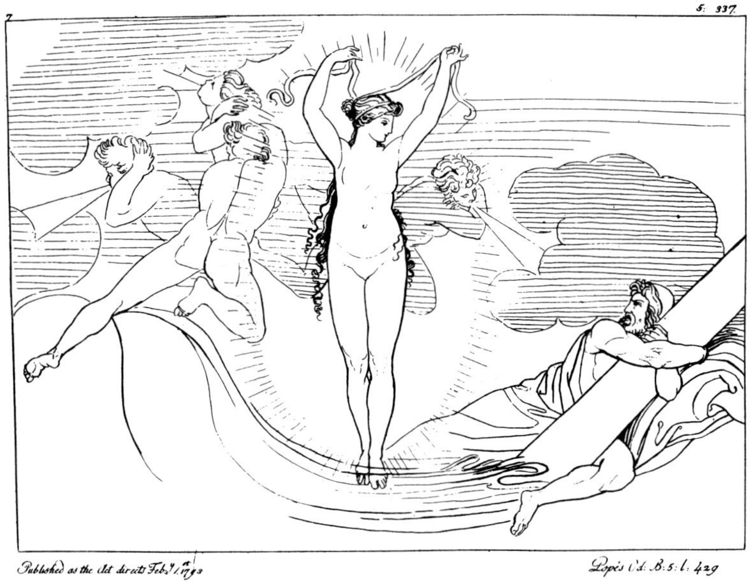

97 *Lucothea preserving Ulysses*. Engraving, 19·2 × 27·1 cms., after Flaxman by Thomas Piroli. *Odyssey*, 1793, Plate 7.

98 *Achilles contending with the Rivers (Iliad)*. Pen and ink and pencil, 21·2 × 27·5 cms.

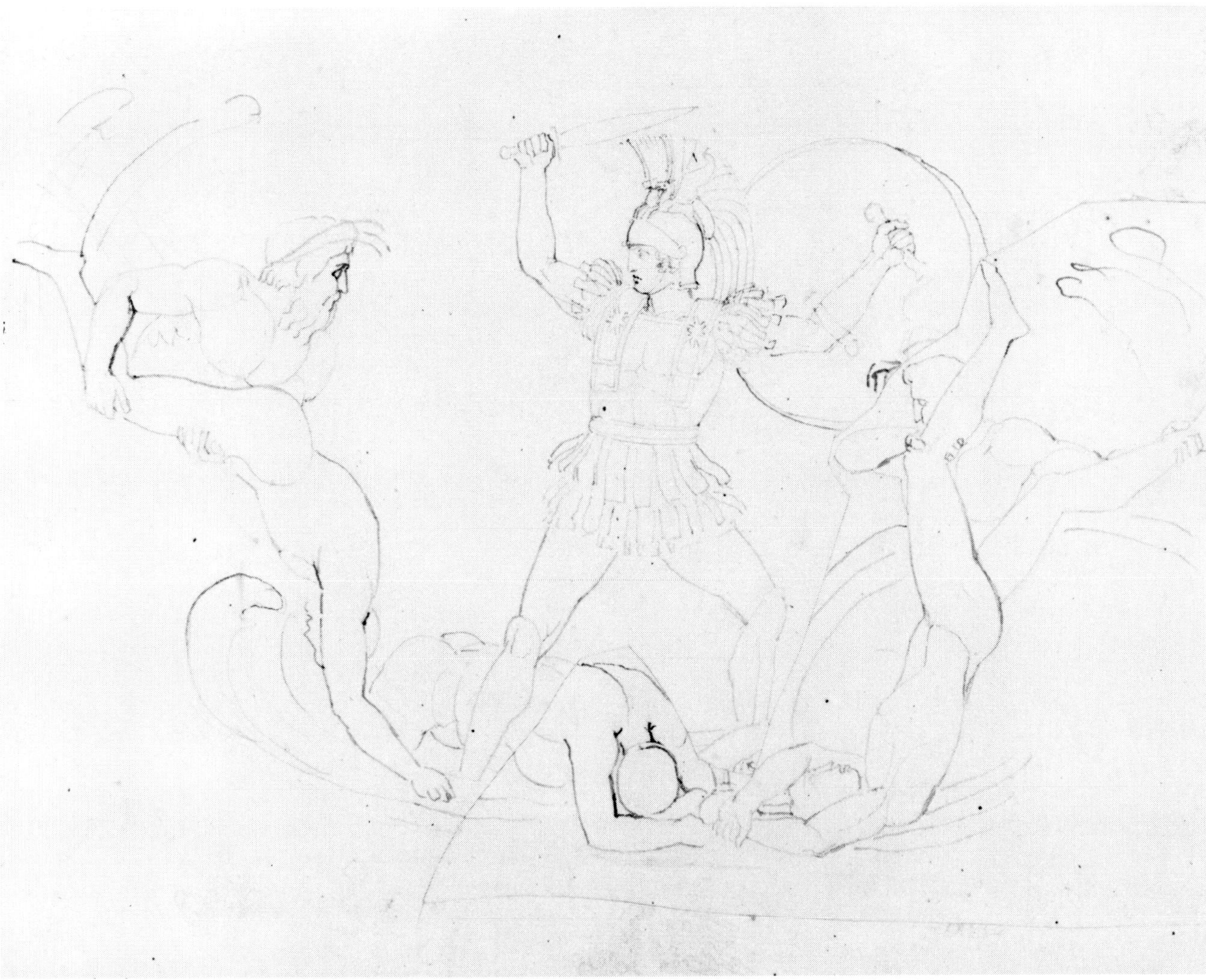

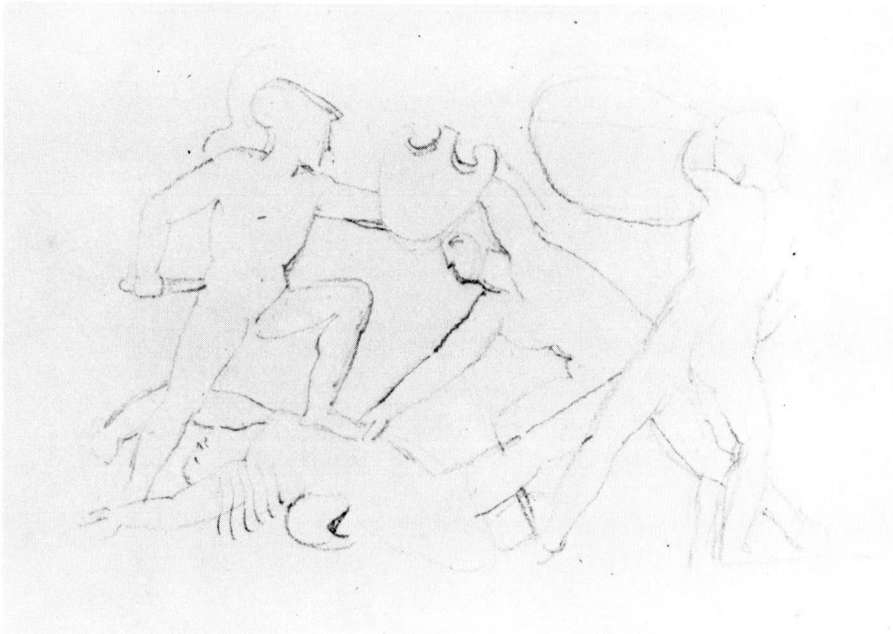

99 *Battle of the Amazons, after antique relief in Vatican.* Pencil, 24 × 16·5 cms.

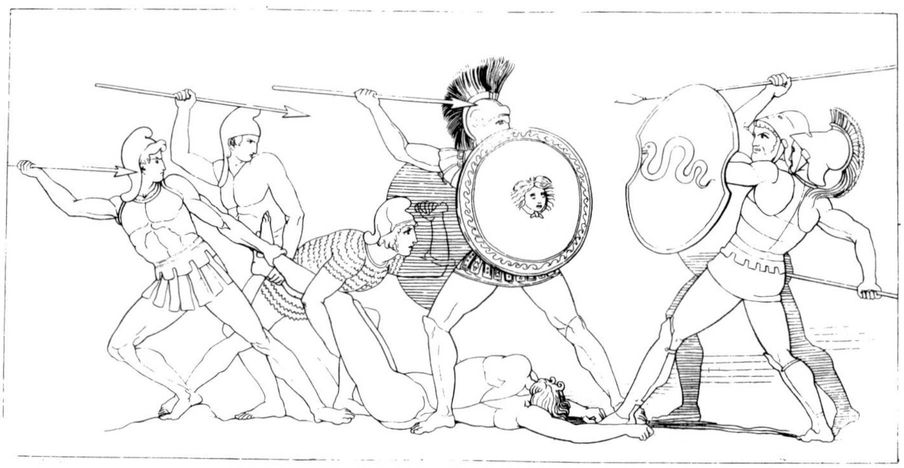

100 *The Fight for the Body of Patroclus.* Engraving, 18·8 × 34·3 cms. after Flaxman by Thomas Piroli. *Iliad*, 1793, Plate 22.

body of Patroclus, but making many changes in the poses and types of armour (Plate 100).

Further ideas were provided by a bas-relief (Plate 101), placed at the time above a fountain in the garden of the Villa Mattei in Rome (but since 1802 in the Vatican collections). The scene of the battle of the giants suggested compositions both for an *Odyssey* illustration showing Leucothea coming to Ulysses's rescue at sea (Poseidon had nearly succeeded in drowning him), and also, in a much looser way, for the proposed relief for the *Collins* monument (Plates 75 and 97). In all three a centrally-placed female figure divides the composition into two parts, separating opposing forces or people: Ulysses is separated by Leucothea from the destructive winds that have been wildly tossing his boat and on the *Collins* panel Hope separates Revenge and Anger from Joy and Mirth. Some of Flaxman's poses have also been adapted from the bas-relief: one of the righthand figures provides the basis for Ulysses, and (in reverse) the belligerent figure of Revenge.

A few instances amongst the Homer plates suggests that Flaxman is also still looking at engravings. The wind-blown figure of Discord flying through the sky with her torches, as she descends on the Achaean ships, in one of the *Iliad* plates, suggests that Flaxman has been

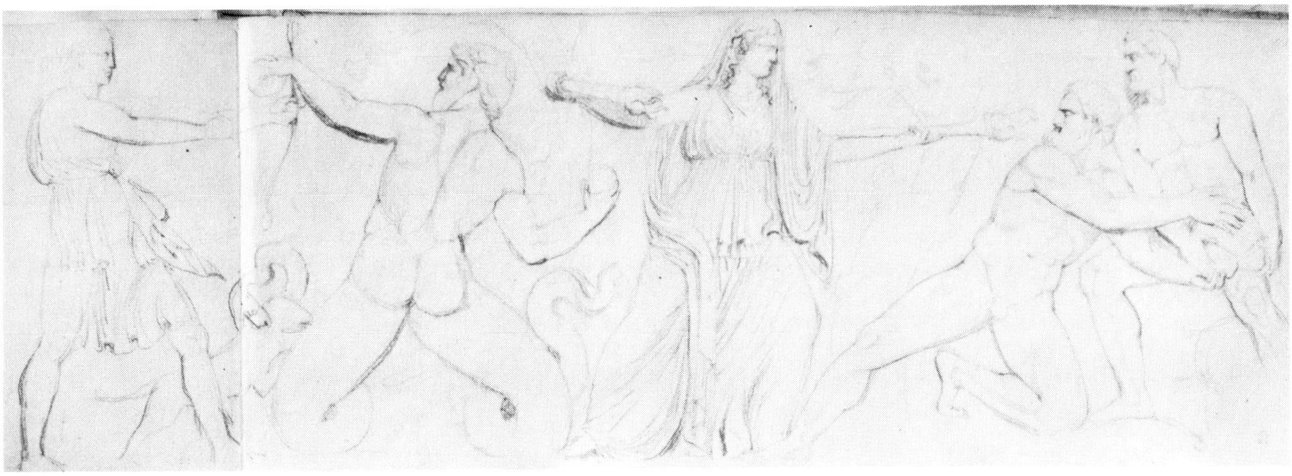

101 *Apollo and Ceres fighting the Giants, after an antique relief, Villa Mattei, Rome (now in Vatican collections).* Pencil, 15·2 × 36·2 cms.

looking afresh at a source with which he was already familiar, namely the Tower of the Winds as it appeared in the first volume of Stuart and Revett's *Antiquities of Athens* (Plate 15).

One of Flaxman's early biographers claimed that he derived whole compositions for his Homer plates from Greek vase paintings, a claim that was subsequently denied by his sister-in-law.[11] Greek vases had provided compositions for Flaxman when he was working for Wedgwood but now this source, rather than supplying actual compositions, had a more fundamental and pervading influence on his style of drawing, which showed he had absorbed the spirit of Greek vase painting. Many contemporaries recognised the link with Greek vases, and often mentioned them in association with the illustrations. Runge in one of his letters wrote: 'My God, I have never seen this kind of thing before in my life; the drawings on Etruscan vases completely pale by comparison'.[12]

Early in his Italian visit even before the Euripides drawings, he was using a linear style. Writing to Romney from Rome in May 1788, he told him that 'my drawings have surprised some of the best English artists here, who thought they were copied from the stories on Greek vases'.[13] The examples of vases that Flaxman would have known were mostly red and black figure vases of the fifth and fourth centuries BC, of both Greek and Southern Italian manufacture. From them Flaxman absorbed a style that eliminated modelling and spatial depth, pared down settings and furnishings to an absolute minimum, and portrayed figures and detailing in pure line. Flaxman already knew Hamilton's first collection, and whilst in Italy familiarised himself with the second one before it too was published. He wrote to Hamilton in 1790 asking for 'some few particulars of the Greek stories represented on those beautiful Etruscan vases which you have added to your collection since I was last at Naples, and which I have so great a longing to see':[14] a letter which shows clearly not only that he kept in close touch with the collector and was aware of his continuing acquisitions, but also that he was interested in the iconography of the vases, not necessarily the precise copying of compositions.

The merits of Greek vase painting were enthusiastically extolled in 1791 in the text of Hamilton's second collection. 'There are no monuments of antiquity', Hamilton wrote, 'that should excite the attention of modern artists more than the slight drawings on the most excellent of these vases; they may from them form a just idea of the spirit of the ancient Greek artists, of their conception and of their facility in the execution of them.' A few pages later he noted that 'artists will here have an opportunity of seeing how very justly Winckelmann has observed, that the first grand style of the art was founded on a system which consisted of rules borrowed from nature only; afterwards artists have plunged beyond measure into the ideal, abandoned truth in their forms and worked more after the adopted system than after nature of which they ought never to have lost sight'.[15] Winckelmann had written enthusiastically about Greek vase painting in his *History of Ancient Art* (1764), comparing their quality to that of a drawing by Raphael, whilst Mengs had been 'persuaded that the ancients began the art of designing with forms very simple, long and straight, after the manner

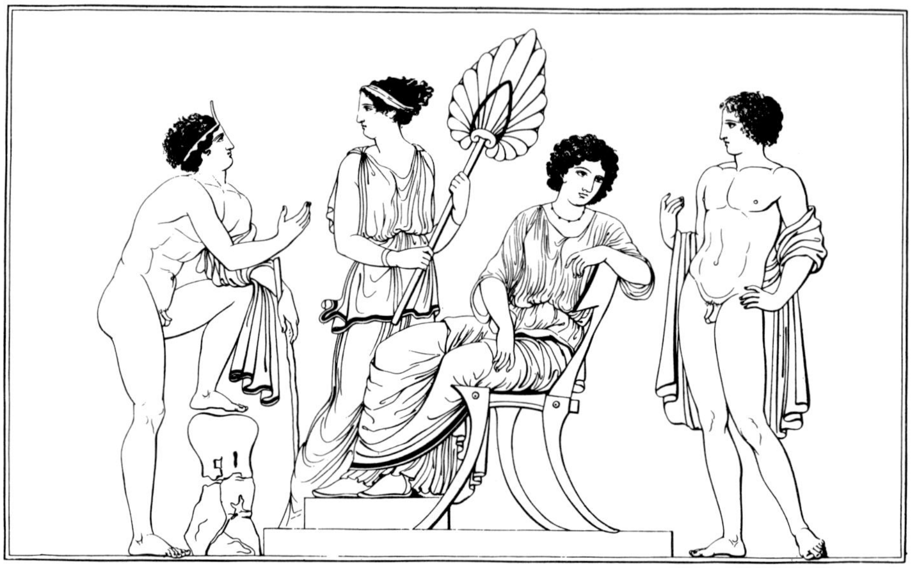

102 Sir William Hamilton: *Ancient Vases*, 1791–95. Volume I, Plate 18, Scene from Euripides, *Iphigenia in Tauris*.

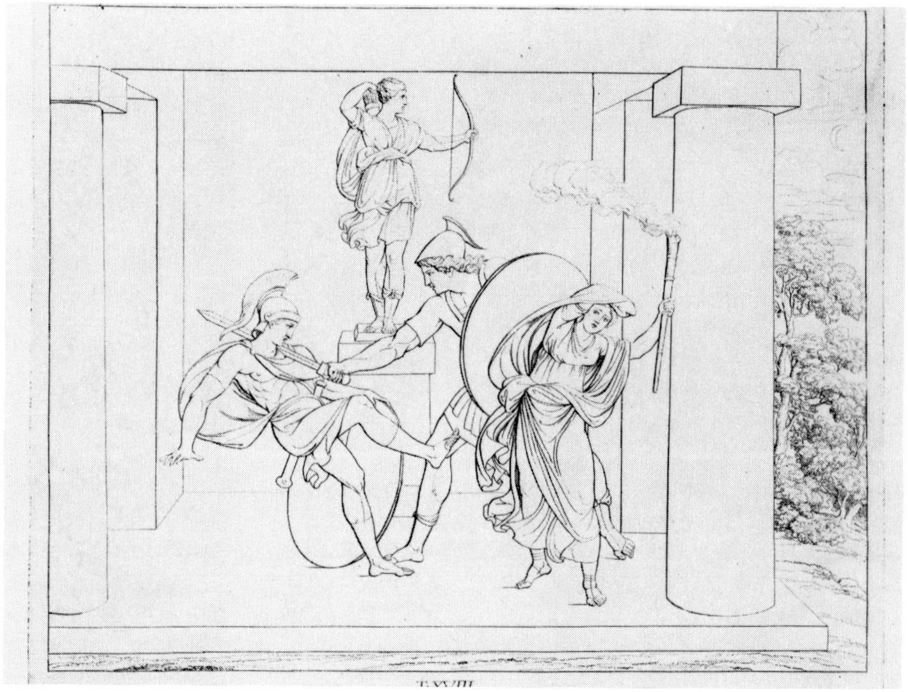

104 Asmus Jacob Carstens: *Les Argonautes*, 1799. Plate 18, *Jason Killing Medea's Brother*.

of the figures which we see in the Etruscan vases'.[16]

Hamilton's folios of 1791-95 were the first major archaeological publication to be illustrated almost entirely by line engravings (Plate 102). The reader was presented with a succession of images (by Wilhelm Tischbein) of the utmost simplicity, as nearly all the engravings lack the shading used in most of the plates in the publication of Hamilton's first collection (1766–67), which had in addition been coloured by hand.[17] The most important influence of the 1791 folio on Flaxman must have been the confidence it would have given him to develop a linear style beyond the mere depiction of archaeological specimens into an area of original invention.[18] Flaxman's confidence would have been reinforced by the occasional use of outline engravings in some of the earlier archaeological publications,

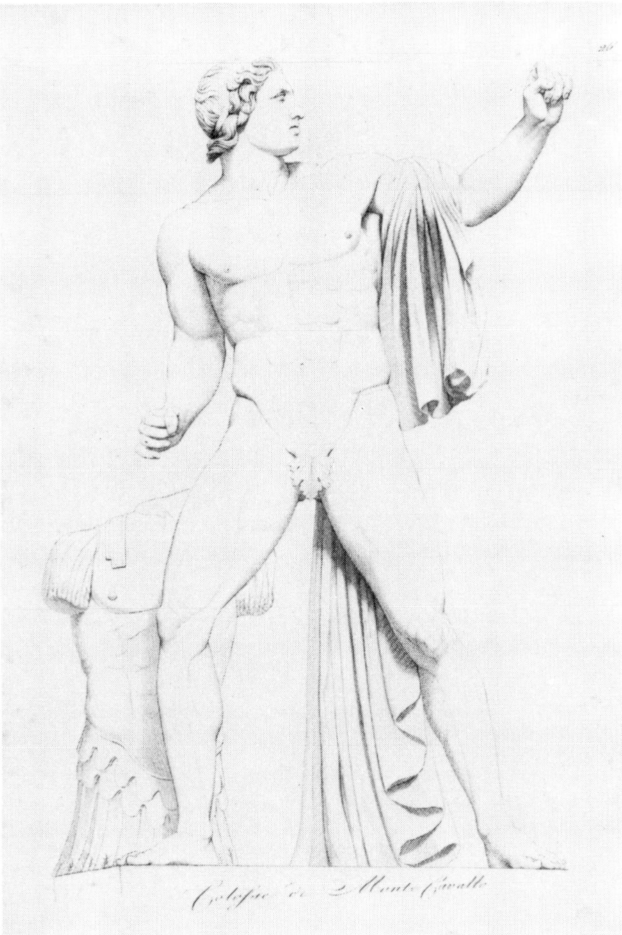

103 Giovanni Volpato and Raffaello Morghen: *Principi del Disegno*, 1786. Plate 26, *Dioscuro of Monte Cavallo.*

such as Winckelmann's *Monumenti Antichi Inediti* (1767). Flaxman could also have been encouraged by the stress on contour in the plates of the recently published *Principi del Disegno tratti dalle più eccelenti statue antichi* by Volpato and Morghen (1786), an important publication which Flaxman would have known, especially as its contents were so very much in accord with his own interests.[19] Although the plates in this book are slightly shaded and are not executed in pure outline (Plate 103), they lay a particular stress on contour in much the same way as Winckelmann had done in his writings.[20] Flaxman would also have known James Tassie's volumes of *Ancient and Modern Engraved Gems* (1791) in which all David Allan's engravings (except the frontispiece) are executed in outline.

Flaxman's outline engravings to the *Iliad* and *Odyssey* were the first important publications of literary illustrations devoted entirely to plates with virtually no text, depicted in a pure linear style. He had been preceded by one year by a more modest publication by the French artist Bénigne Gagneraux entitled *Dix-huit estampes au trait composées et gravées à Rome* (1792). But these line engravings were reproductions of his own classical subject paintings, not conceived as original illustrations, and their publication was a minor event without any of the contemporary impact of Flaxman's volumes.

The Homer volumes, together with the ones devoted to Aeschylus and Dante which Flaxman was to execute within the next few years, were in the vanguard of a new movement of literary illustration, to which the next important contribution was to be the publication in Rome in 1799 of *Les Argonautes selon Pindare, Orphée et Apollonius de Rhodes*, designed by Carstens and engraved by Koch. These twenty-four engravings are stylistically identical in their linearity to Flaxman's and were being prepared from 1792 onwards, the year in which Carstens arrived in Italy (Plate 104). But Carstens is not as economical in most of his compositions as Flaxman, often including more figures and using traditional perspectival space. Koch even claimed at the time that these plates were more 'painterly' than Flaxman's and that connoisseurs would therefore prefer them,[21] but he was to be proved wrong. Carstens's plates, like Gagneraux's, never achieved the same contemporary impact as Flaxman's. All three artists were in Rome at the same time and may well have known each other's work.[22]

The growing importance of outline engravings prompted George Cumberland to publish his *Thoughts on outline, sculpture, and the system that guided the ancient artists in composing their figures and groups* in 1796, appending to the text twenty-four of his own linear designs of 'classical subjects invented on the principles recommended in the essay' (Plate 105). Some of the engravings were executed by the author, others by Blake. In his essay Cumberland praised the 'inestimable value of chaste outline', the best line being one that is 'fine, firm, flowing and faint', of which the supreme examples, he claimed, were to be found in Raphael. Cumberland believed that a 'fine simple outline', without the addition of shading or colours, was capable on its own of possessing 'grace, action, expression, character and proportion'.

One would imagine from phrases such as these that Cumberland would have admired Flaxman's illustrations, but this is not the case. 'What then shall we say to our state of the arts in 1795', he asked, 'when professed artists, and professed dilletanti, have disco-

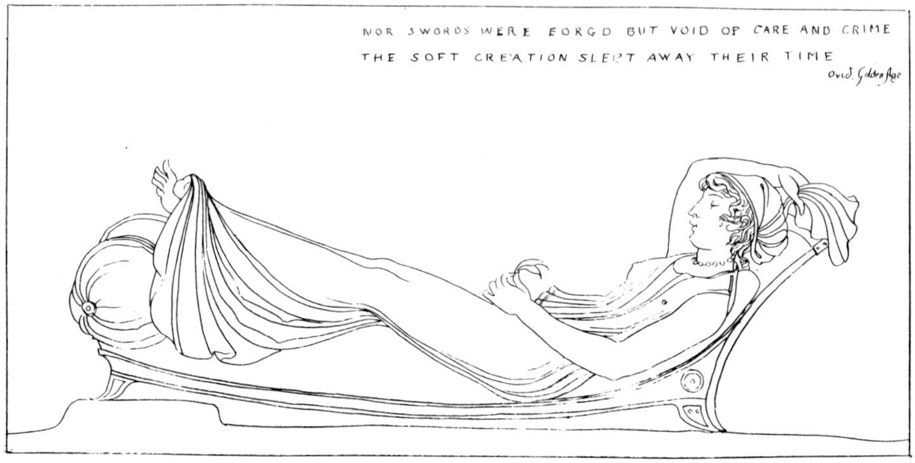

105 George Cumberland: *Thoughts on Outline*, 1796. Plate 6, Ovid, *Golden Age*.

vered so unmathematical an idea of form in general, as to publish works copied from the ancients, or invented in their style, with *outlines thick and thin alternately*, like the flourishes of a penman'. He continued by being more specific. 'In making this observation, I do not scruple to say, that I allude to two books lately published; the very tasteful Homer and Aeschylus by Mr. Flaxman; and the last volume of Sir William Hamilton's Grecian vases. This last volume . . . seems to have given the death's blow to all hope of ever seeing a faithful tracing of any outline design on copper-plate; . . . Mr. Tischbein has presented us with a heavy translation of these Greek vases, *finely flourished*, but materially unlike the originals, if proportion, character of heads, style of hair, or flow of drapery, were considered as worth preserving'. Unfortunately, Cumberland did not elaborate on Flaxman's outlines, but Cumberland's book is important because it reveals two different schools of thought within Neoclassicism on the subject of outline. True to his text, Cumberland's plates were executed with an unvarying thickness of line, comparable to the use of line on ancient Greek vases. Flaxman's plates on the other hand, as Cumberland rightly observed, were engraved with differing thicknesses which capture the variations of the original drawings, a style to which Cumberland took exception. He highlighted a significant difference in treatment between Flaxman's plates and Greek vases which other contemporaries overlooked. The vase painters (Plate 106) used a consistent thickness of line within a piece of drapery or a hairstyle, only changing the thickness from one part of the body to another. The drapery would all be in thin lines, whilst the hair would all be in thicker ones. Flaxman did not employ this technique, and neither did his engraver Piroli. They both preferred, whilst retaining the general linearity of a vase painter, to vary the thickness of lines of each piece of drapery or hairstyle.

Cumberland's adverse criticism of Flaxman's *Homer* and *Aeschylus* illustrations is far more perceptive than the looser comments by contemporaries who talked in generalities. Back in London, Flaxman found a few fellow artists hostile to his classical illustrations. Hoppner grumbled that they were 'all borrowed and purloined from a variety of things which he has seen. He has nothing original about him.'[23] Farington thought the designs were 'strictly formed on the Greek model, . . . each circumstance being copied from some authority'; and in the same diary entry the architect Robert Smirke is reported to have commented on 'a forced simplicity', which he justified as being 'very proper to such designs, when treated after the manner of antique designs'.[24] Such hostile comments, however, seem to have been unusual. Even Cumberland had been kinder, at least finding the volumes 'very tasteful'. William Cowper's comment when he received a copy of the *Odyssey*, that had been sent back from Rome to him by the Dowager Countess Spencer, is more typical: 'They are very fine, very much in the antique style.'[25]

On countless occasions, contemporaries referred in general terms to the 'antique style' of Flaxman's illustrations, unaware that yet another source lay behind them in addition to the arts of classical Greece and Rome. Hamilton stressed in his preface that Greek vase-painters 'borrowed from nature only', pointing to the source that Flaxman himself regarded as the ultimate one, not only for his *Homer* plates but for his other books as well. Later in life he met the American author Washington Allston, who after complimenting the artist on his classical and *Dante* illustrations, was told by the artist, 'I will now show you the sources of many

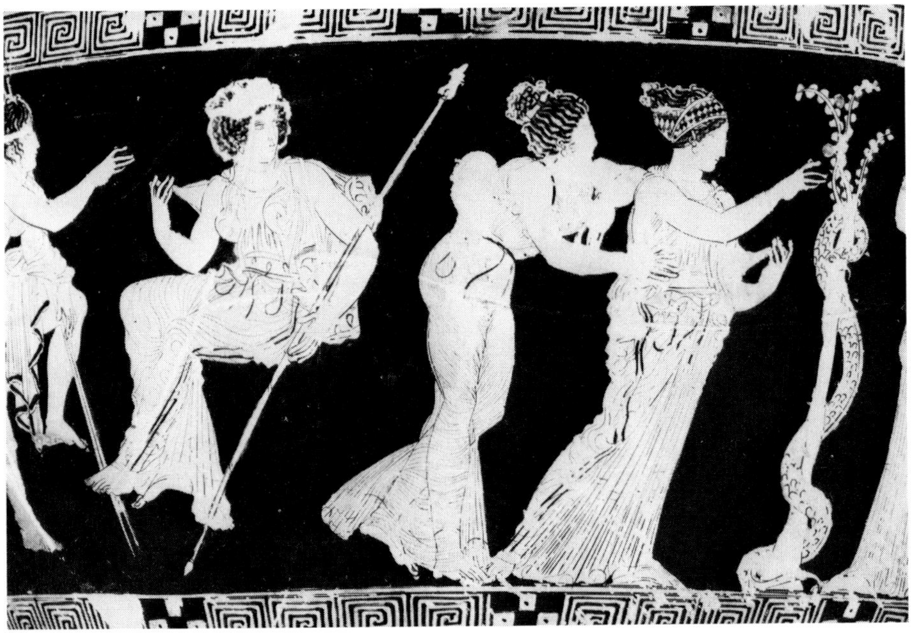

106 Meidias Painter: *Attic Red-Figure Hydria*, c. 410 BC. Detail.

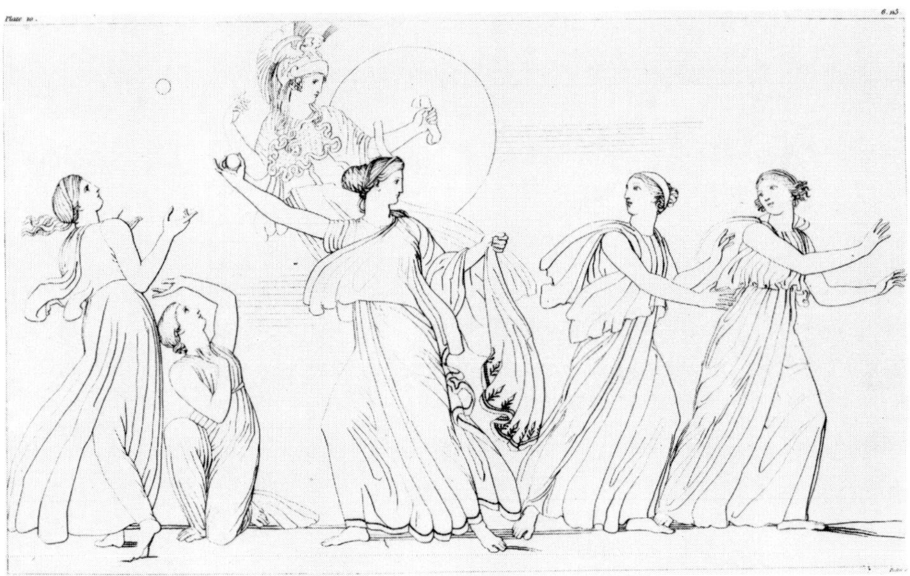

107 *Nausicaa throwing the Ball.* Engraving, 34·8 × 35·5 cms., after Flaxman by Thomas Piroli. *Odyssey*, 1805, Plate 10.

of them'. He proceeded to lay before Allston a large number of sketches made from nature showing unposed groups and attitudes.[26] When the plate of Penelope being surprised by her suitors was discussed above (Plate 92), a comparison was made with contemporary genre, and many more instances occur throughout the illustrations to substantiate Flaxman's claim that nature was an all-important source. When Hector meets Andromache, for example, he looks over her shoulder towards a nurse holding his son, in a very natural, everyday pose (Plate 87). When Nausicaa and her maidens play with a ball in the *Odyssey* (Plate 107), Flaxman has designed the main group with a vitality and naturalness paralleled in many of his sketches of children dancing or skipping (Plate 108), which he has then combined in the *Odyssey* plate with a Roman bas-relief of dancing bacchantes.

2 Aeschylus and Other Classical Authors

A few months after visiting Paris in 1802, Flaxman sent to Aubin-Louis Millin, the influential scholar and

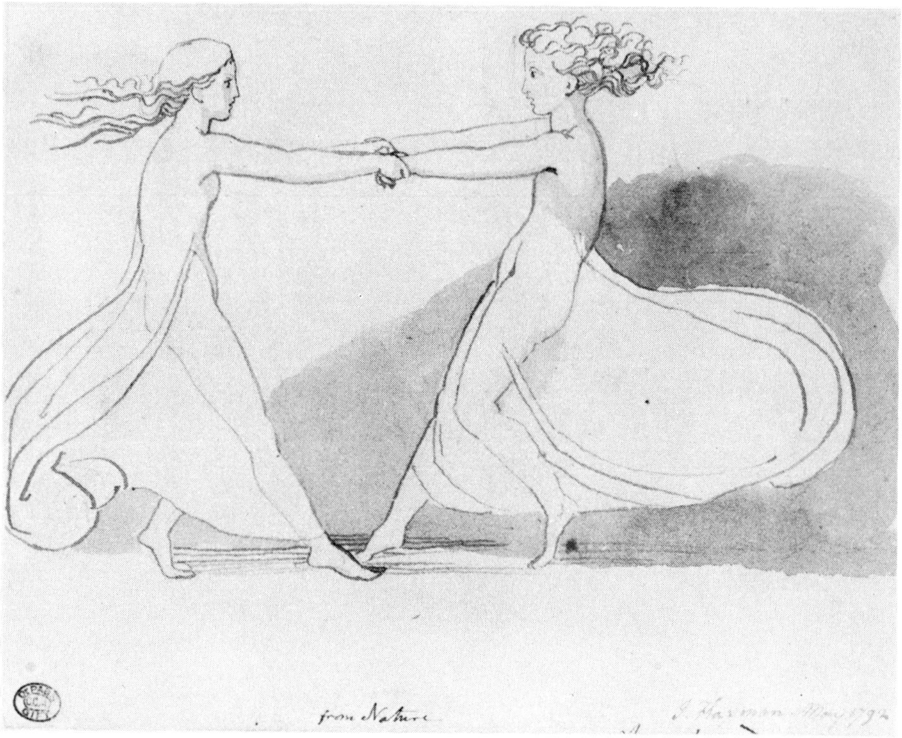

108 *Two Girls Dancing*. Pen and wash, 17 × 21·7 cms.

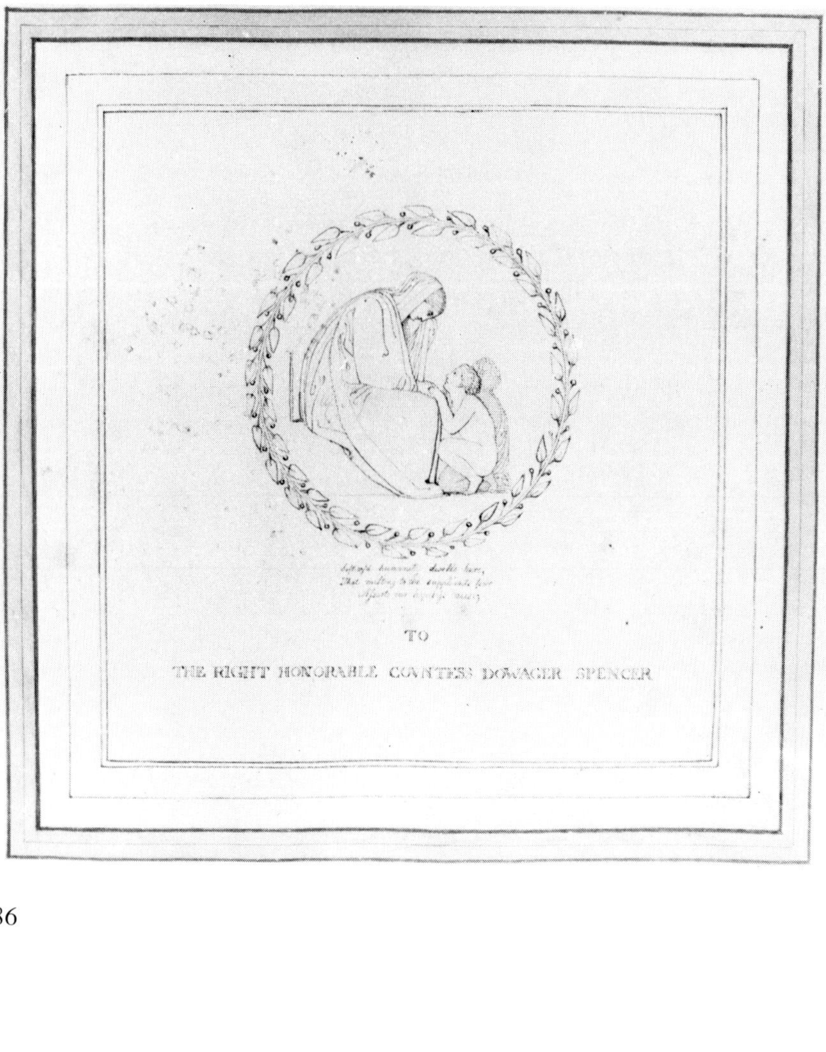

109 *Aeschylus: Dedication pages to Countess Sp*
Pen and ink, 29·7 × 47·6 cms.

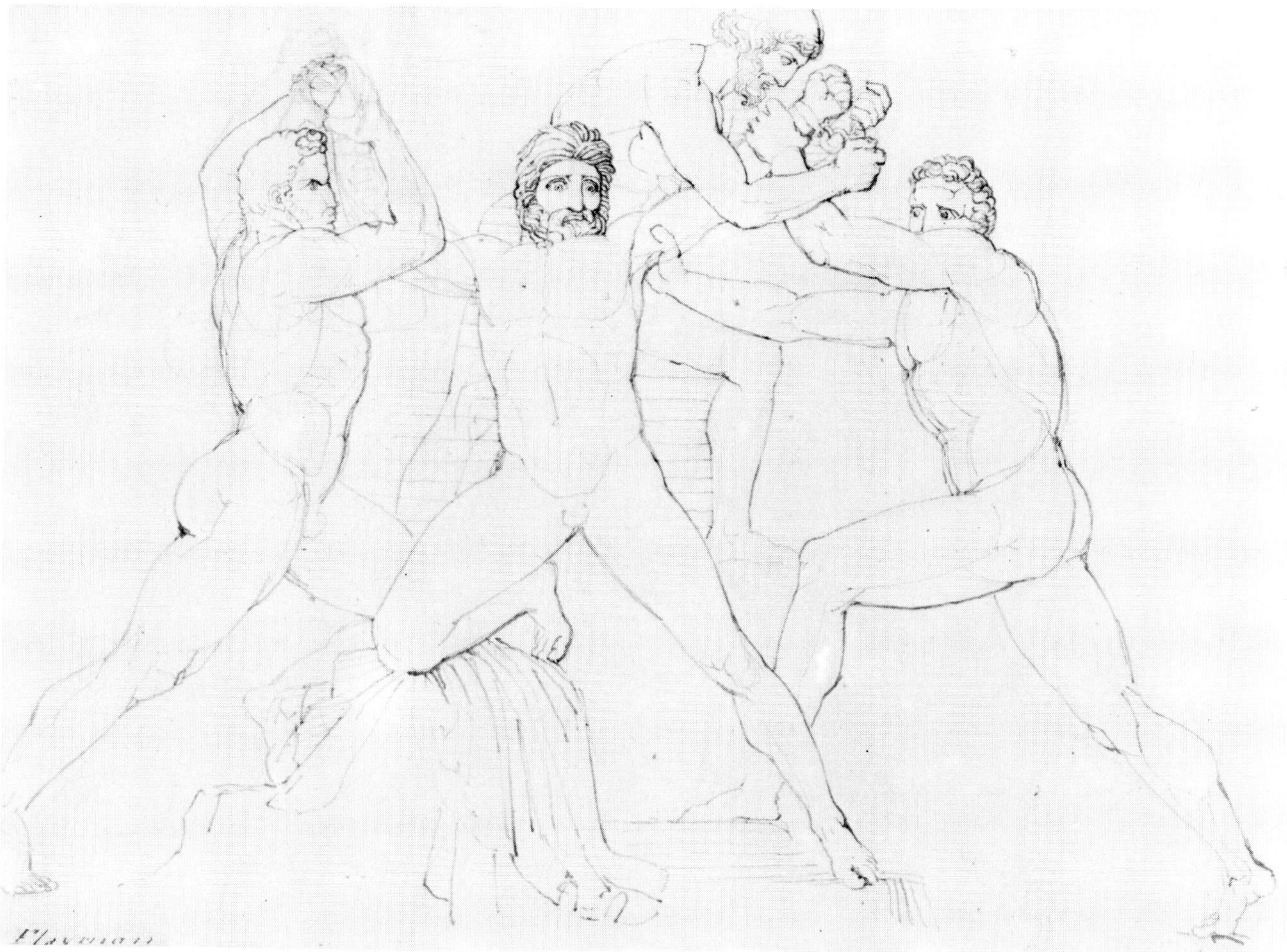

110 *Prometheus being chained to the Rock (Aeschylus).* Pen and ink and pencil, 23·6 × 33·2 cms.

curator of antiquities, a copy of his *Aeschylus* illustrations, and received a letter of thanks from the Frenchman which contained praise of the kind that by now was customary: 'dans cette belle composition se retrouve tout le génie des anciens'.[27] Flaxman had indeed drawn his *Aeschylus* illustrations in the same spirit as his *Homer*.

Like the *Iliad* and *Odyssey* designs, the thirty plates to Aeschylus were commissioned in Italy, by the dowager Countess Spencer, a cousin of Mrs. Hare-Naylor. Countess Spencer's own set of the original designs included a special dedication page, with a sentimentally tearful vignette (Plate 109). The volume was not published until shortly after Flaxman's return home, in January 1795, in both London and Rome. The editions were printed from two sets of plates that had both been engraved by Piroli, who was presumably the publisher of the Italian edition. Flaxman had returned to London with the other set of plates, and the English edition was mainly sold by his aunt Jane Matthews, although Flaxman himself marketed a few copies.[28] Unlike his other volumes, Flaxman retained the copyright of the *Aeschylus* and earned a modest income from subsequent sales. After his aunt died in 1800, Longman took over the publication about 1803, presumably at the time new editions of the *Iliad* and *Odyssey* were being planned under their imprint. Like the *Homer* series, the *Aeschylus* was to be reprinted many times. The original plates of the first London edition were to be used on fourteen more occasions up to 1828. Other editions appeared in the artist's lifetime in Hamburg (1802) and Paris (1803), and perhaps Rome in 1818. A posthumous edition was published in 1831, with the addition of five engravings.

Flaxman chose scenes from all seven of the surviving plays of Aeschylus, placing the emphasis on *Prometheus*, to which he devoted nearly a quarter of the plates. These varied from scenes of Prometheus enraged (Plate 110), whose fury is paralleled at the time in the

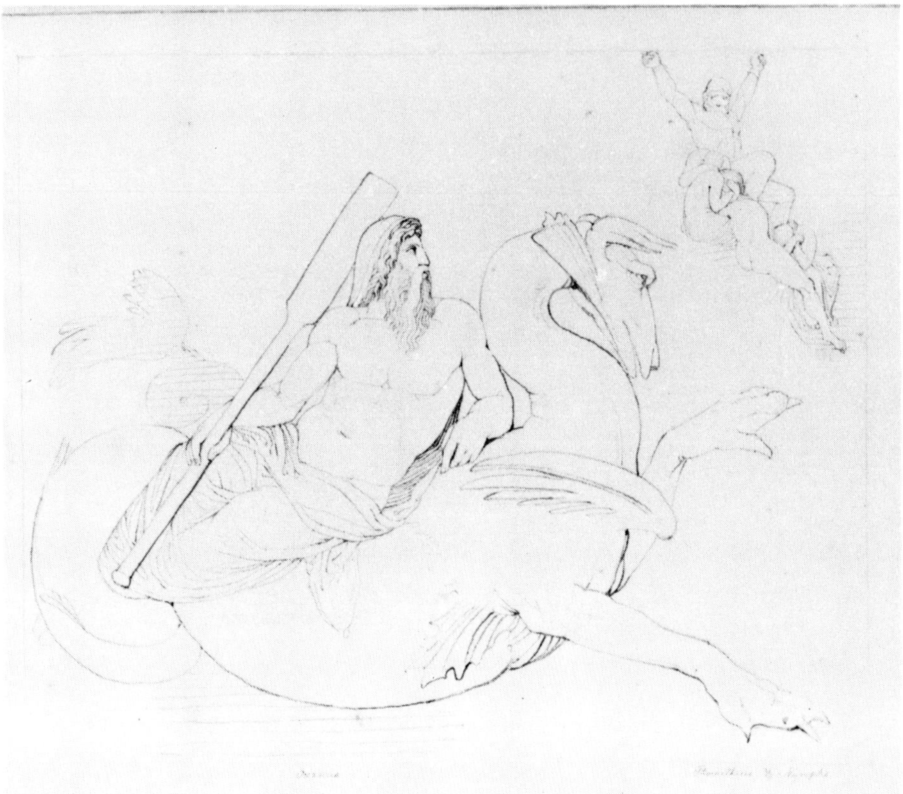

111 *The arrival of Oceanus (Aeschylus).* Pen and ink, 29·7 × 47·6 cms

marble of *Athamas (Plate 69),* to gentler scenes of conciliation. When Oceanus arrives on his winged beast to placate Prometheus, Flaxman designed a classical river god close in type to the famous large one in the courtyard of the Museo Capitolino, with Oceanus's legs neatly encircled by the animal's tail, reproduced here from Countess Spencer's set of drawings (Plate 111). The continuous sequence of curves formed by the beast's neck, belly and tail create a surface pattern which is both elegant and soothing in contrast to the deliberately jarring lines used in another plate that depicts the actual chaining. Schlegel greatly admired the *Aeschylus* illustrations, regarding them as Flaxman's best and particularly admiring this plate of Oceanus, which he said 'looks so marvellous that one does not ask if the poet's intention is being pursued, where in fact the animal is a four-footed bird'.[29]

Violent agitation and confrontation with the supernatural are skilfully handled in several plates devoted to *The Furies.* Dramatic movement and terror are created in the scene showing the appearance of the ghost of Clytemnestra (Plate 112). Equally successful is the illustration of the lines 'When, mantled in these sable-shaded stoles, / With blood-besprinkled feet we urge the chase, / Sinks darkling to the infernal shades'. These plates are amongst Flaxman's few emotionally charged scenes, and are as convincingly horrific as the one showing Ulysses with the ghosts in the *Odyssey* (Plate 95).

Amongst the *Choephorae* plates one shows Electra at the head of a procession of Trojan women carrying oblations (Plate 113); a drawing which in its simplicity and economy is a very poignant rendering of Aeschylus's lines. Its composition is clearly indebted to Roman bas-reliefs, in particular a first century BC one from the Ara Pacis Augustae in Rome, which had already influenced Benjamin West when painting a related theme of *Agrippina landing at Brundisium with the Ashes of Germanicus* (painted in 1786 and now in the Yale University Art Gallery).

In three illustrations to the *Suppliants* Flaxman tried to be as archaic as possible, attempting to create a historical past earlier than the fifth century BC. He had only a little firsthand archaeological evidence to use for his reconstructions, but sufficient to attempt deliberately archaising scenes. In two of the plates, one of which was added to the 1831 edition (Plate 114), Flaxman shows a knowledge of 6th century BC sculptures when drawing images of gods on their pedestals below which the chorus of the fifty daughters of

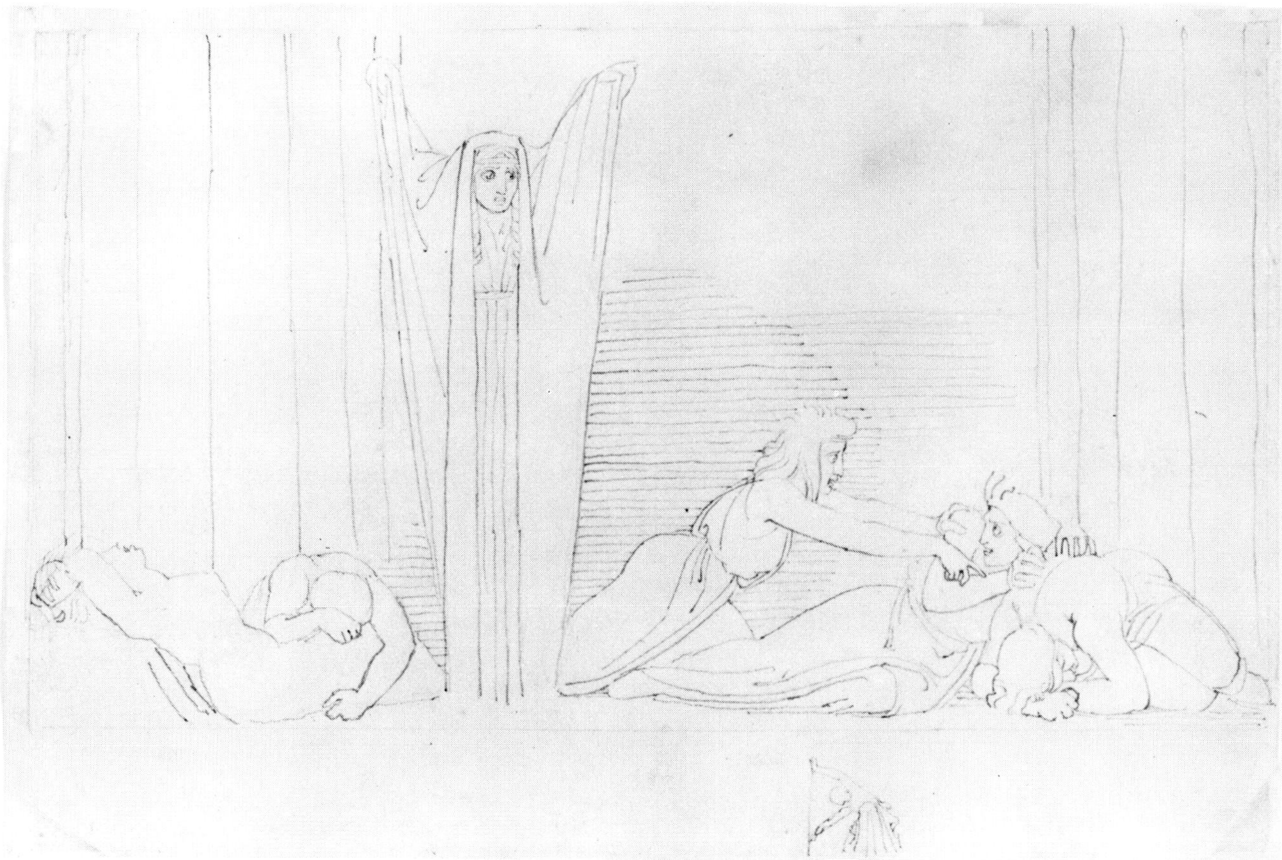

112 *The Ghost of Clytemnestra (Aeschylus).* Pen and ink, 21·7 × 34 cms.

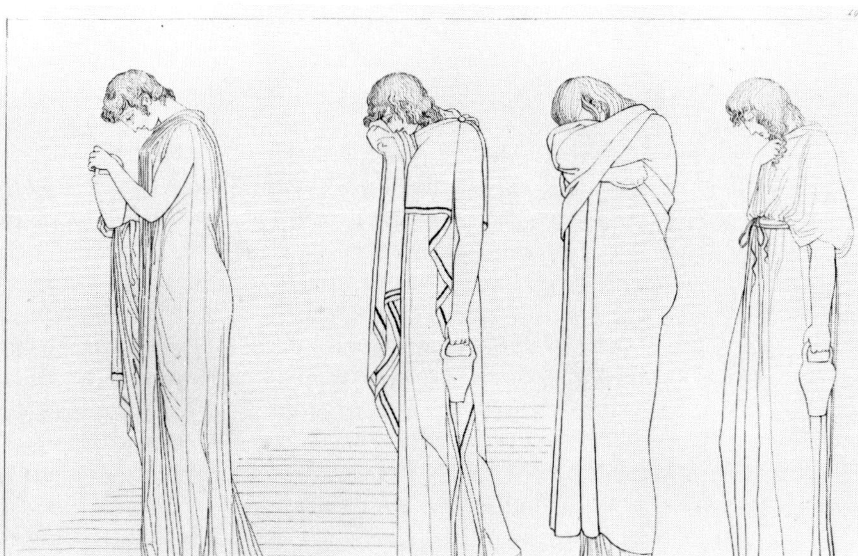

113 *Procession of Choephorae.* Engraving, 19·5 × 28·1 cms., after Flaxman by Thomas Piroli. *Aeschylus*, 1795, Plate 19.

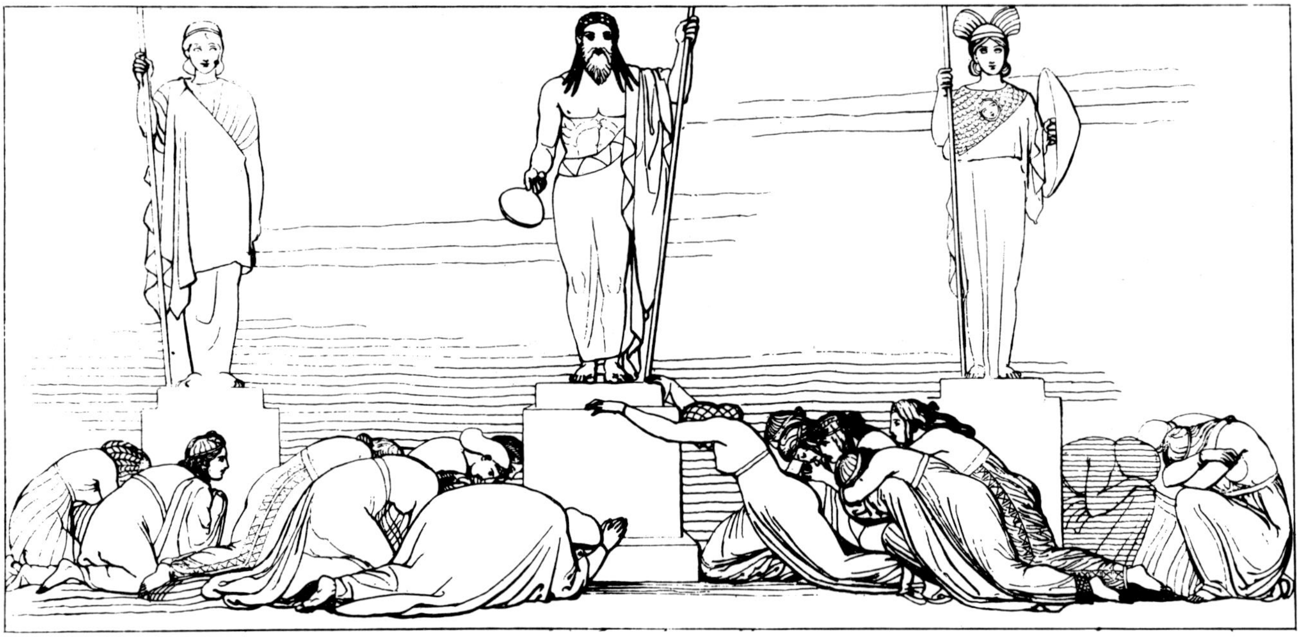

114 *Supplicants pray to the gods.* Engraving, 18 × 30 cms. after Flaxman, by Frank Howard. *Aeschylus*, 1831, Plate 12.

Danaus are pleading for protection. The third of this group of archaising drawings depicts Danaus, having come from the shore, instructing his daughters to remain within the safe vicinity of an altar. In the preliminary drawing this altar is ornamented with a deliberately crude Greek-key pattern and surmounted by two squat lions. These details were unfortunately altered for the engraving; the pattern was removed, and the lions became elegant sea horses. Flaxman's search for the primitive was therefore repressed and his contemporaries were not able to appreciate the full extent of his primitivism, especially as the plate with the frontal, archaic statues was only published posthumously. It is characteristic of Flaxman's caution that he should draw back from uncompromising statements of primitivism and wish to modify or even suppress them.

Flaxman published only one other set of designs. His fifth and last volume was devoted to Hesiod, and published much later, in 1817, without a patron; presumably he was now prosperous enough for this not to be a problem. He had been interested in Homer's contemporary from at least the time he had designed the *Apotheosis of Homer* plaque for Wedgwood, which incorporated a seated figure of a defeated Hesiod after their mythological poetic contest (Plates 27 and 28). Flaxman had even referred to the design in the early years as *Homer and Hesiod.* Hesiod then seems to remain in abeyance until 1805, when Flaxman exhibited at the Royal Academy a marble relief panel of *Mercury and Pandora* (Plate 235), a composition which was to be repeated exactly in one of the *Hesiod* plates. He has chosen the scene in which Pandora is being brought to earth on one of Mercury's shoulders, an incident which allowed Flaxman plenty of opportunity for a display of elegantly billowing drapery. Two years after exhibiting the marble, Flaxman was working on a series of Hesiod illustrations according to a report in the *Athenaeum*. But the set of drawings was only nearing completion seven years later, in 1814, a preparatory period longer than for his other books.[30] As he had no patron to hasten him, presumably the *Hesiod* scheme had to be continually put to one side to make way for other work. The thirty-six engravings, this time in a stipple technique producing a softer image on the page, were by William Blake, who was working on the plates from 1814 to 1816.[31] The contract with Longman was drawn up in the latter year, the costs of publication being born by Longman, and the profits shared equally between publisher and artist. Rather surprisingly, this was the first time Flaxman received proper royalties for one of his books, because, apart from the payment for the original drawings for his other books, he had received no additional income, except for a modest sum (as mentioned above) from the Aeschylus.

Only two hundred copies were printed, and by the time of his death one hundred and nine had been sold.[32] Hesiod's works were neither as popular nor as familiar as those of Homer and Aeschylus, but one would have imagined that sales would have been less sluggish, and might have been stimulated by the new Hesiod translation that Charles Abraham Eliot had published in 1812, and from which Flaxman quoted in the legends under his plates (using the second edition of 1815). But even Eliot had felt it necessary in his preface to justify his championing of Hesiod, saying that his poetry is not only of interest to the antiquary because it traces 'a picture of the rude arts and manners of the ancient Greeks', but his poetry also contains 'sublime philosophic allegories', 'romantic elegance' and 'daring grandeur'. It may well have been the *Hesiod* that William Bell Scott had in mind when in one of his attacks in the mid-century on the British public's lack of interest in high art, he claimed that 'even the designs of Flaxman . . . were a dead stock in the London market for years'.[33] The *Hesiod* illustrations were, however, not without their admirers, and there were one or two continental editions in the artist's lifetime, perhaps one in Rome in 1818, and another, definitely, in Paris in 1821. One German periodical that specialised in art news admired the *Hesiod* illustrations in 1823 because of their 'naïve grace and antique simplicity'.[34]

Grace is certainly the hallmark of many of the plates, especially the ones featuring Pandora, which are among the most charming and elegant of all Flaxman's illustrations (Plates 115 and 116), in which he consistently stressed Pandora's beauty at the expense of the mischief that she will shortly create, this altering the emphasis in Hesiod's lines. The prettiest plate shows her being dressed: 'Adored persuasion and the graces young, / Her slender limbs with golden jewels hung'. Hesiod's poetry also provided scope for violence, and Flaxman produced vigorous images of the Bronze and Iron Ages, which he contrasted with the calmer images of the Gold and Silver Ages. The last two compositions he was to repeat later in life on the sides of a silvergilt cup bought by George IV (Plate 269). The *Theogony* with the Titans and Saturn provided further energetic or horrific scenes contrasting those in the same poem in which the gentle movement of the waves predominate in illustrations of Venus and of the sea gods (Plates 117, 118 and 119).

Flaxman had been worried before publication about the reception of his designs. Towards the end of 1814 he was already confiding to a friend that 'if the critics determine to be like the text fitter for rustics than heroes, I shall think myself more fortunate than them, however they may be displeased with the work'.[35] At the same time he was telling Hayley that 'when I presume to step out of my house . . . the French artists and German critics intrude their speculations, "whether the Hesiod will be a second part of the Homer", "a second part (you will say) is always bad".[36] Inevitably comparisons can be made with the *Iliad* and *Odyssey*, but not to the detriment of the *Hesiod* series. It may have been because he was worried about a comparison with the 1790's, that he chose a different kind of engraving to achieve deliberately a different effect on the printed sheet (which is unfortunately largely lost in a photographic reproduction on a smaller scale).

Flaxman produced designs inspired by other classical authors, but these remained unpublished, including a small group from Sophocles (Plate 120). In 1805 he executed a set of drawings for Musaeus's *Hero and Leander*, which he sent to Hayley who had lent him a manuscript of his translation. Flaxman had 'looked over' the text earlier in the year 'with a view to the subjects for design in the story. I find some both beautiful, pathetic and such as may be perfectly decorous, which is an important matter, as neither the poet or the designer are in the heyday of life and therefore should be careful what they leave to posterity, and the *Hero and Leander* will always be more valued for beauty, nature, pathos and classical perfection, than for moral purity'.[37]

Flaxman did not leave a volume of engravings of *Hero and Leander* to posterity. His reputation was to rest on his *Homer*, *Aeschylus* and *Dante* volumes, and to a limited extent on his *Hesiod*, all authors which he would have seen as possessing the same characteristics as those he lists in the work of Musaeus, but without the exclusion of moral purity. The same descriptive words that Flaxman used in this letter could in fact be equally well applied to his own illustrations.

Such was Flaxman's reputation as an illustrator, that he was not only a seminal influence on other artists, but also through his work inspired the posthumous establishment in London of a School of Flaxman, or the Society for the Improvement of Historical Composition. In the pamphlet published to announce the programme of the new School, in 1829, it was hoped that members would meet once a month to discuss the outline compositions each of them had executed, the general aim being to improve the standard of composition amongst both painters and sculptors. The winning drawings of each month's composition for the first year were to be published in outline, with a dedication to the late John Flaxman.[38]

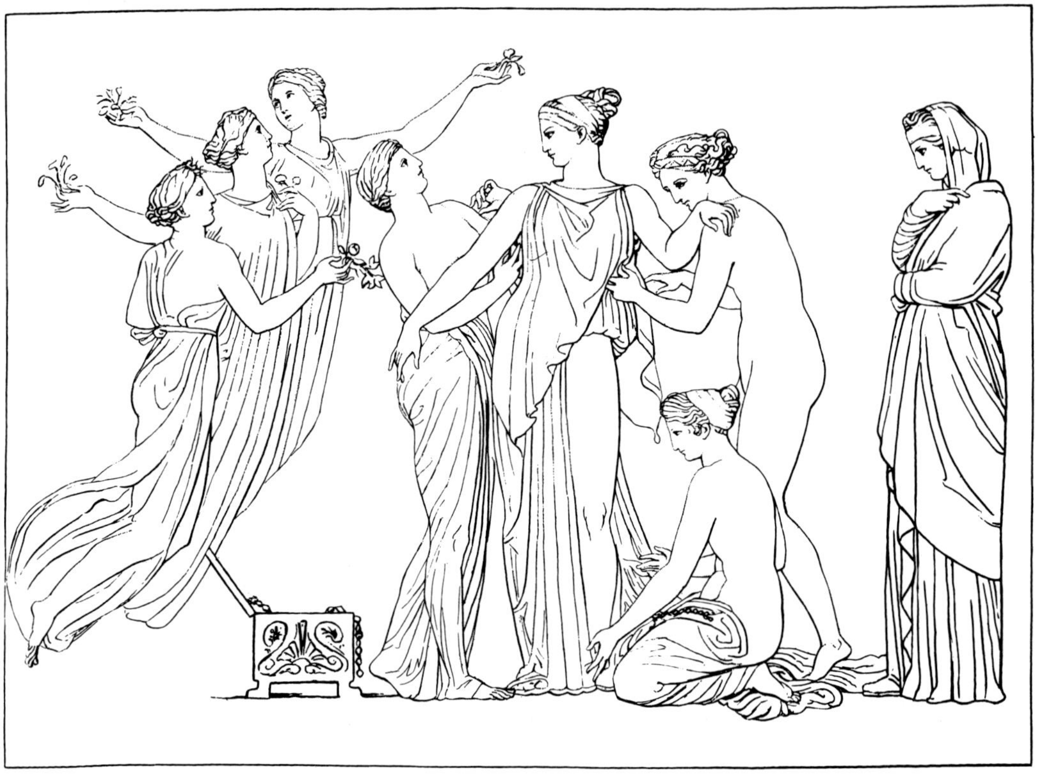

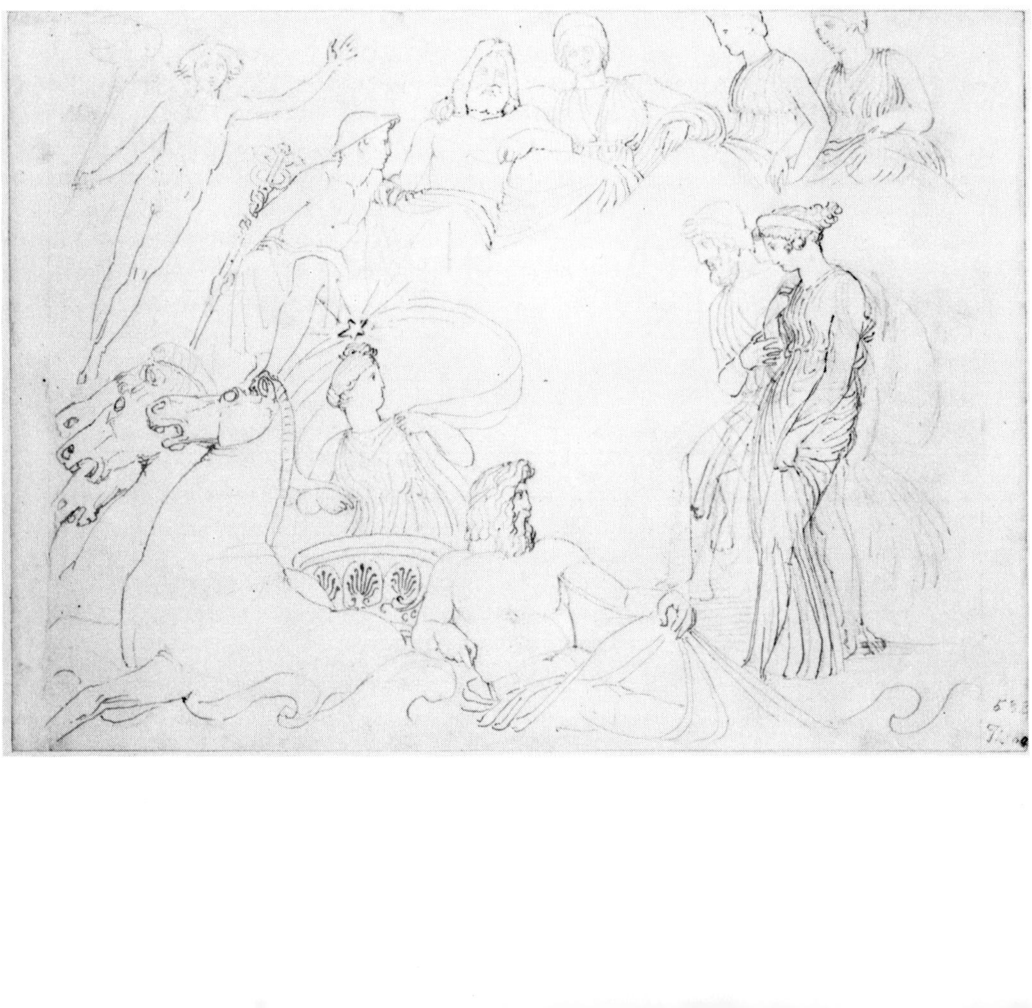

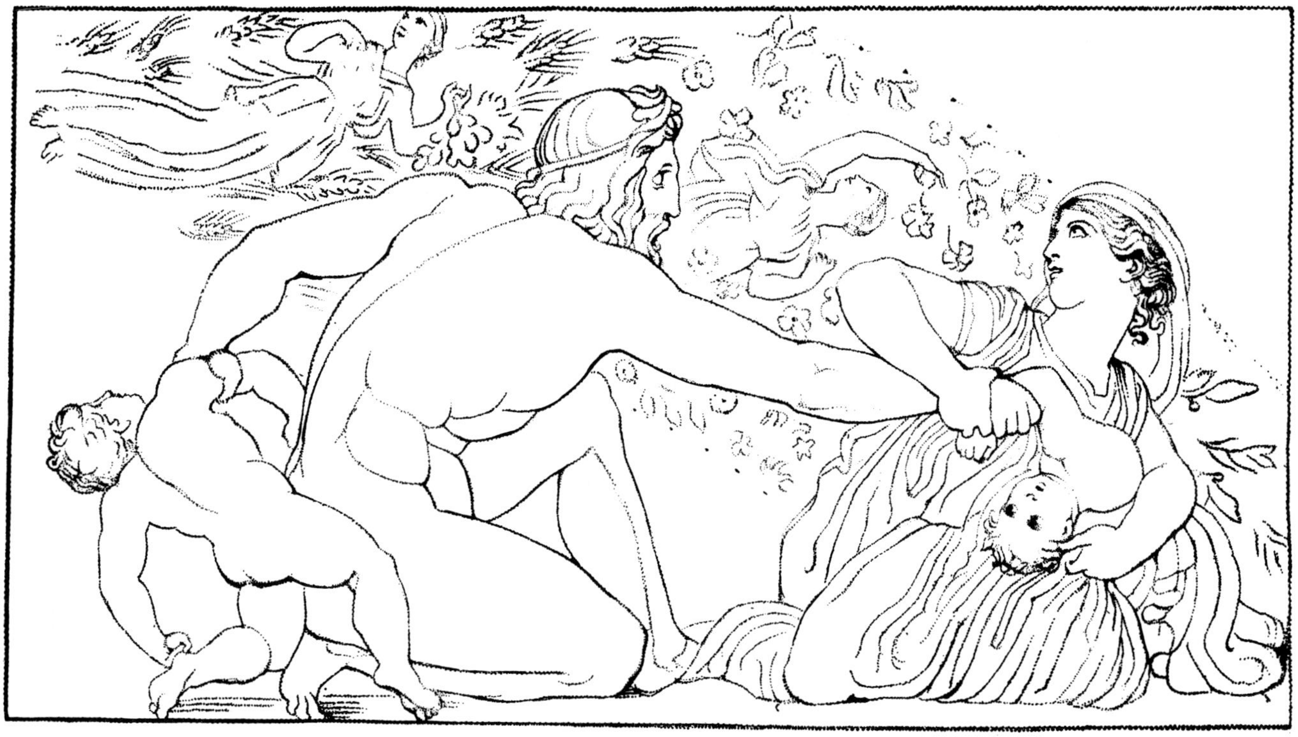

115 *Pandora attired.* Engraving, 20·2 × 27·9 cms. after Flaxman by William Blake. *Hesoid*, 1817, Plate 4.

116 *Pandora shown to the Gods (Hesiod)* Pen and ink and pencil, 19 × 26.4 cms.

117 *Saturn and his Children.* Engraving, 20·2 × 27·9 cms. after Flaxman by William Blake, *Hesoid*, 1817, Plate 31.

118 *Gods and Titans (Hesiod).* Pen and ink, 15 × 14·3 cms.

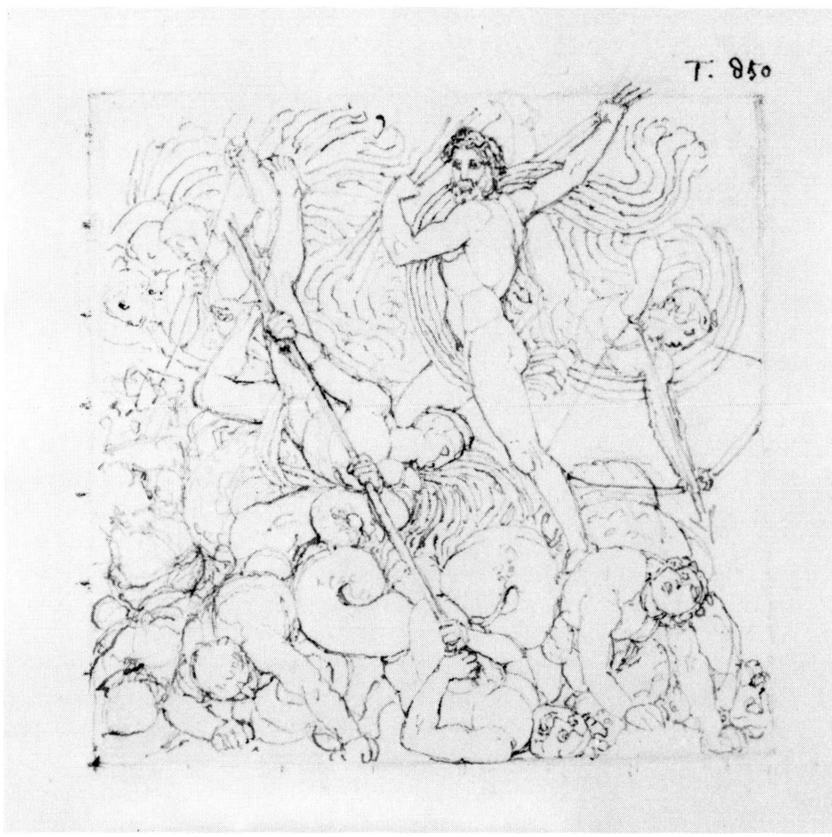

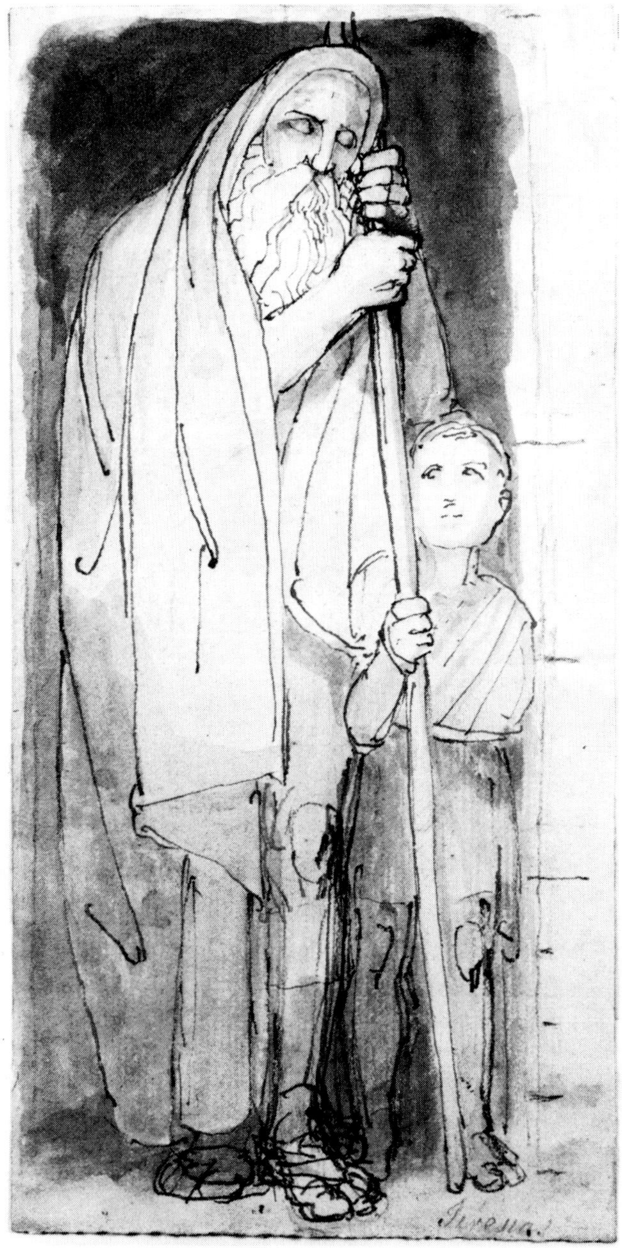

120 *The Blind Tiresias (Sophocles).* Pen and ink and wash, 19·7 × 9·8 cms.

3 The Divine Comedy and Modern Literature

Flaxman's name was so inseparable from his classical engravings that when someone suggested to Sir Walter Scott in 1804 that Flaxman should illustrate his 'Lay of the Last Minstrel', Scott was afraid that the artist was 'too classical to stoop to body forth my Gothic borderers' who might resemble 'the antique of Homer's heroes rather than the iron race of Salvator'.[39] Had Scott known Flaxman's *Dante* illustrations his reaction to the suggestion might have been different, because here was a text to which Flaxman responded in some of the illustrations with 'Gothic wildness', as Cunningham put it.[40]

At the same time as Flaxman was working on the sets of drawings for the *Iliad* and the *Odyssey*, he received a commission in 1792 from Thomas Hope for a set of a hundred and nine illustrations to the *Divine Comedy*. Although Hope's taste, reflected in much of his patronage, was essentially classical, he embraced a wide range of interests, stimulated by his extensive travels. As a well-read man he would have seen nothing inconsistent in a commission for a set of designs from Dante rather than from a classical author. As a man in the forefront of taste he may even have commissioned the *Dante* illustrations in a pioneering spirit.

The artist was to be paid a guinea for each drawing, and they were bound into one large, handsome volume with Neoclassical details in the tooling. Most of the *Dante* drawings reproduced here are from Hope's volume.[41] The series of engravings was intended for private circulation only, to be given to Hope's friends. He even refused to allow Flaxman to name any of his own friends to whom he would like to give copies of the engravings. This expensive kind of present was not unusual, and the idea could have been suggested to Hope by the lavish private publication of the first edition of the folios of Herculaneum antiquities, given away by Charles of Bourbon. The *Dante* illustrations, engraved by Piroli, were therefore published for the first time as a small private edition in 1793. Although a generous patron, Hope's initial plans were unduly selfish, and Flaxman's achievement would only have been known to a small circle, including the dowager Countess Spencer who was given a copy. But at least enough copies were in circulation for both Goethe and A. W. von Schlegel to have seen them by the time they wrote their enthusiastic assessments of Flaxman in 1799.

Probably because the illustrations had been pirated in a French edition in 1802, a public English one was issued at four guineas in London in 1807 by Longman, to whom Hope had sold Piroli's copper plates.[42] The same firm had already published the English editions of the *Iliad* and *Odyssey*, and had taken over the publication of the *Aeschylus*.[43] Unlike the 1790's classical illustrations, however, the *Divine Comedy* was not so frequently reprinted and re-engraved, and there seems to have been no German edition. Nevertheless, in spite of the fewer editions, the *Dante* volume was widely known.

Under each engraving Flaxman quoted in the legend lines both from the Italian text and from the English

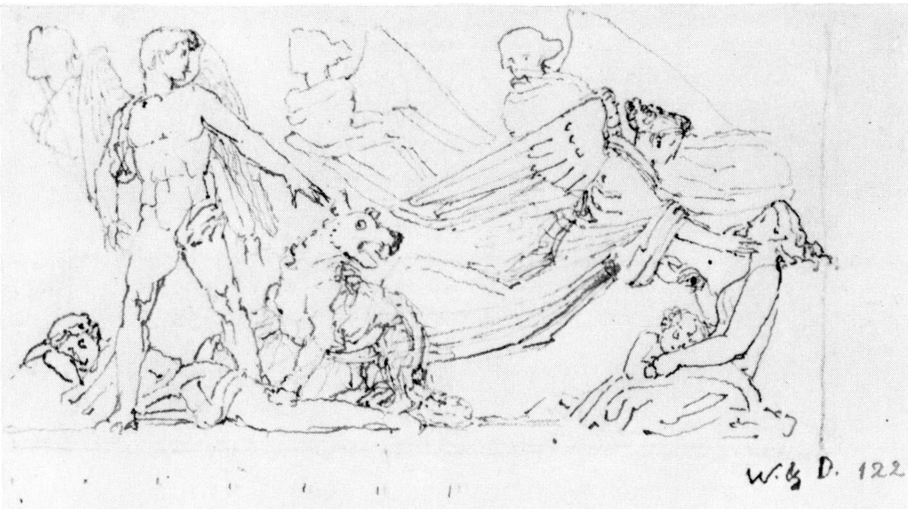

119 *Good Demons (Hesiod)*
Pen and ink and pencil,
22 × 18·5 cms.

translation of Henry Boyd, whose complete version of the *Divina Commedia* had been published in 1785.[44] The recent date of the translation reveals how tardily Dante had been accepted into the eighteenth-century canon of taste. As Boyd wrote in his introduction to the *Inferno*, which was dedicated to Lord Bristol, he had delayed his translation 'because the merit of his poem could not be tried by the reigning laws of which the author was ignorant, or which he did not choose to observe'. The changed assessments of Dante had begun in the 1750's when he was stoutly defended in Giuseppe Baretti's *Remarks on the Italian Language* and *Dissertation upon Italian Poetry* (both 1753). In 1781 two expositions of Dante's genius appeared; by Thomas Warton in the third volume of his *History of English Poetry* and by Hayley in his *Triumph of Temper*, and again in his *Essay on Epic Poetry* published in the following year. Dante's 'wild vision', as Hayley described it, was now to be appreciated in a period of early Romanticism: 'Sublimest fancy now directs his march / To opening worlds through that infernal arch'.[45]

Thomas Hope's commission reflected this new wave of appreciation, and resulted in the first extensive set of illustrations ever to be issued to the *Divina Commedia*. Amongst Flaxman's contemporaries and earlier eighteenth-century artists, an interest had been shown in Dante's imagery but not to such a sustained extent, and published illustrations were few. No illustrated edition of Dante had appeared between 1596 and 1757, when Antonio Zatta published his edition in Venice, illustrated by pupils of Sebastiano Ricci. Flaxman's volume would have been followed in Britain by Blake's project for Dante engravings, had the scheme not been interrupted by his death in 1827. Amongst Flaxman's contemporaries Fuseli had been his most important precursor, showing an interest in Dante as early as the 1770's during his Rome visit. Reynolds, rather unexpectedly, had been the first painter to exhibit a Dante subject at the Royal Academy, an *Ugolino* in 1773 (now at Knole). Flaxman therefore had virtually no precedents on which he could fall back, and thus produced his most consistently original series of illustrations.

Flaxman's use of precisely identifiable sources in the *Dante* plates are even less evident than in his classical illustrations, especially since in the *Dante* series he was also influenced by Trecento and Quattrocento art, which provided only general ideas and rarely specific motifs. Critics soon noticed these sources of Flaxman's style. Goethe in his essay of 1799 which was mainly devoted to the *Dante* illustrations, commented that Flaxman had 'a gift of adopting the innocence of the older Italian School', and A. W. von Schlegel in his essay of the same year noticed that Flaxman had absorbed principles from the fourteenth and fifteenth centuries.[46] Early Renaissance art influenced Flaxman's *Dante* plates in three different ways. Firstly the Last Judgment in both painting and sculpture provided him with a range of horrific expressions which he would not have found in antique art. Secondly, he was influenced by the simplified monumentality of draped figures in the work of such artists as Giotto and Masaccio. Thirdly he adopted Renaissance principles of harmony and symmetry, which are characteristics more prominent in the *Dante* illustrations than in any of his others.

Several versions of the *Last Judgment* appear amongst his Italian drawings, mostly rough sketches, including Nicola Pisano's figures of the damned on his Siena

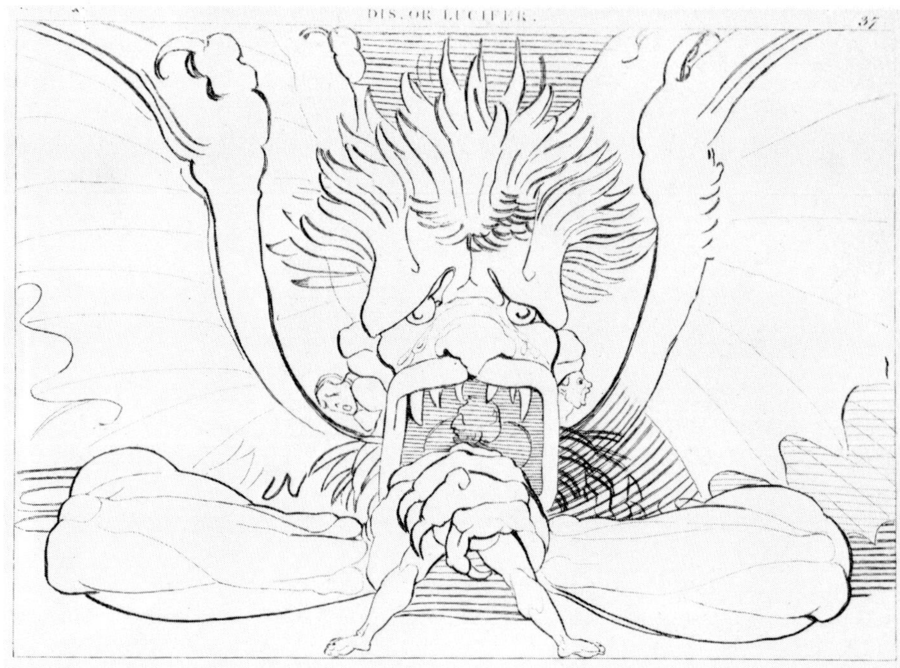

121 *Dis, or Lucifer.* Engraving, 16 × 20·5 cms. after Flaxman, by Thomas Piroli. *Divine Comedy*, 1793. Edition of 1807, Plate 37.

pulpit, the Trecento *Triumph of Death* in the Camposanto at Pisa (Plate 46), Maitani's *Last Judgment* on the facade of Orvieto cathedral (Plate 49), and the Signorelli frescoes inside (Plate 47), as well as Michelangelo's Sistine Chapel altar wall fresco. It has already been suggested in the previous chapter that it may have been because he was working on the *Dante* illustrations that he made some of these drawings.

Throughout the Dante illustrations Flaxman is often convincing when drawing human expression of agony, an important element in his art at the time since he was working simultaneously on the *Fury of Athamas* (Plate 69). Nearly a quarter of the *Dante* plates are necessarily concerned with anguish, from generalised fear to more specific pain under torture. The range runs from the third plate of the *Inferno* with the faces of the dead being ferried in Charon's boat, to the illustration in the *Paradiso* in which the sword of heaven is striking down the guilty. In his treatment of such subjects Flaxman has tried to be as varied as Dante himself.

The most powerful of these grotesque images, indeed the most awesome of all images in his art, is the one depicting the giant Dis or Lucifer in the last canto of the *Inferno* (Plate 121). He is shown standing buried up to his chest in ice, an enormous face flanked by two more looking sideways, framed by large wings as featherless as those of a bat. Each of his three mouths is devouring a sinner, at the sides Brutus and Cassius, whilst at the front Lucifer's long talons tear at the flesh of Judas Iscariot. Flaxman has meticulously included all the details supplied in Dante's long description, a literal rendering that is as gruesome as the lines themselves. Flaxman's image is schematic and bold, probably suggested by some Trecento source as in Plate 122. Other successfully rendered images of terror in the *Inferno* plates include the torture scene in the lake of pitch, and the attacks by fiery serpents (Plate 123), which contain echoes in the composition of the *Laocoon* (Plate 67). One of the most eerie of the *Inferno* plates is the forest of the Harpies (Plate 124).

The Dante illustrations are the only place in Flaxman's *oeuvre* where the subject-matter compelled him to use landscape settings. In the *Homer* illustrations he minimised landscape as much as possible, but with Dante this was not always feasible as he wished to translate the text faithfully. In the forest of the Harpies a human spirit is embedded in each tree, and the Harpies themselves appear perched on a branch. The half-human trees writhe in a convincingly supernatural way, and Dante seems to be truly amazed in Flaxman's design when he snaps a branch and hears one of the spirits speak. This is one of the best of Flaxman's landscape scenes in the *Dante* series.

The starkness of some of the *Dante* illustrations exceeds even that of the *Homer* plates. In the *Dante*, draped figures are represented by an outline that distils

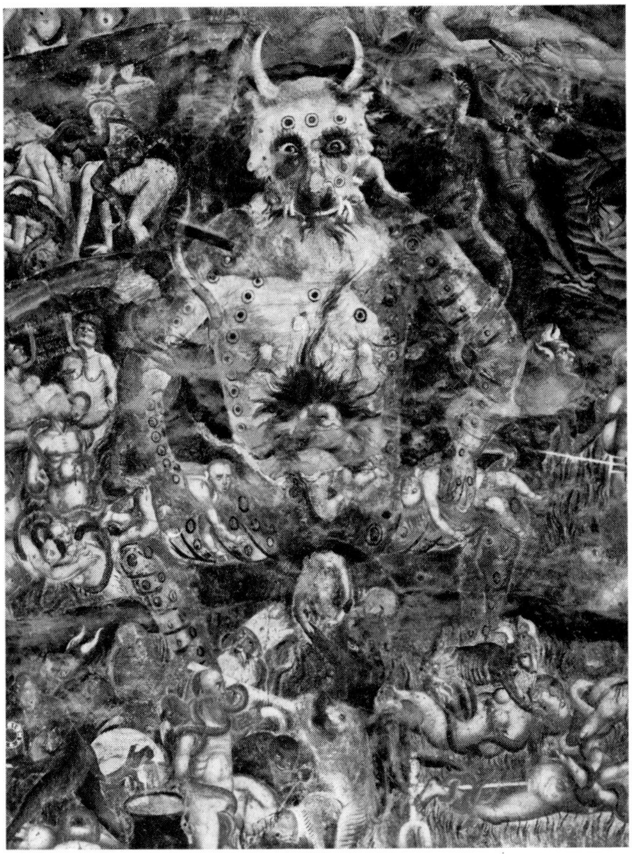

them into almost abstract shapes. This characteristic appears at the very beginning of the *Inferno*, where in the first two plates we are introduced to Dante, Virgil and Beatrice (Plate 125). One of the most striking examples of this extreme simplification occurs in the plate of the hypocrites in the *Inferno*, one of the illustrations that Goya copied (his copy is in the Biblioteca Nacional, Madrid). From the first rough sketch for this illustration, Flaxman decided to emphasise Dante's description of monk-like cowls drawn low over the eyes (Plate 126). He hides almost the whole face, and in the stooping postures captured in mere outline the poet's weeping, weary figures. In the final engraving, the hypocrites walk past the crucified Caiaphas instead of round him, and are mostly seen obliquely from behind, creating an even more inhuman scene than in the first sketch.

This near-abstract quality in Flaxman's figures was achieved almost entirely by his use of drapery. Draperies in the *Dante* illustrations derive partially from Flaxman's knowledge of medieval tomb figures in England, and partially from his more recent studies of the monumental robes in Trecento and Quattrocento frescoes by Giotto, Masaccio and other painters. An example of the English influence transposed into an Italian context can be seen in the plate in the *Purgatorio* showing the poets resting (Plate 127), in which the

122 Master of the Triumph of Death (? Francesco Traini): *Hell*: detail of Lucifer.

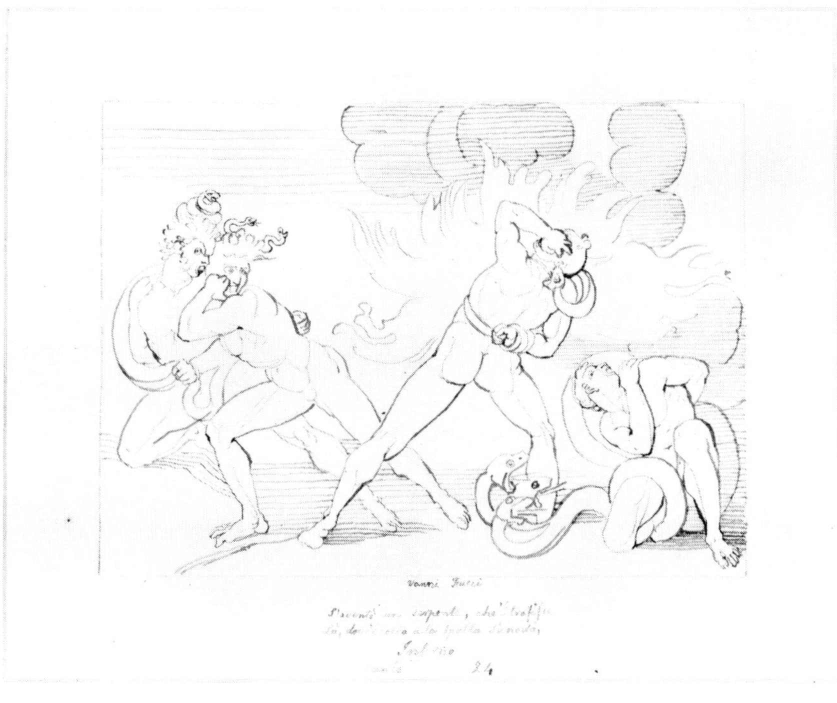

123 *The Fiery Serpents (Inferno)*. Pen and ink, 18 × 26 cms.

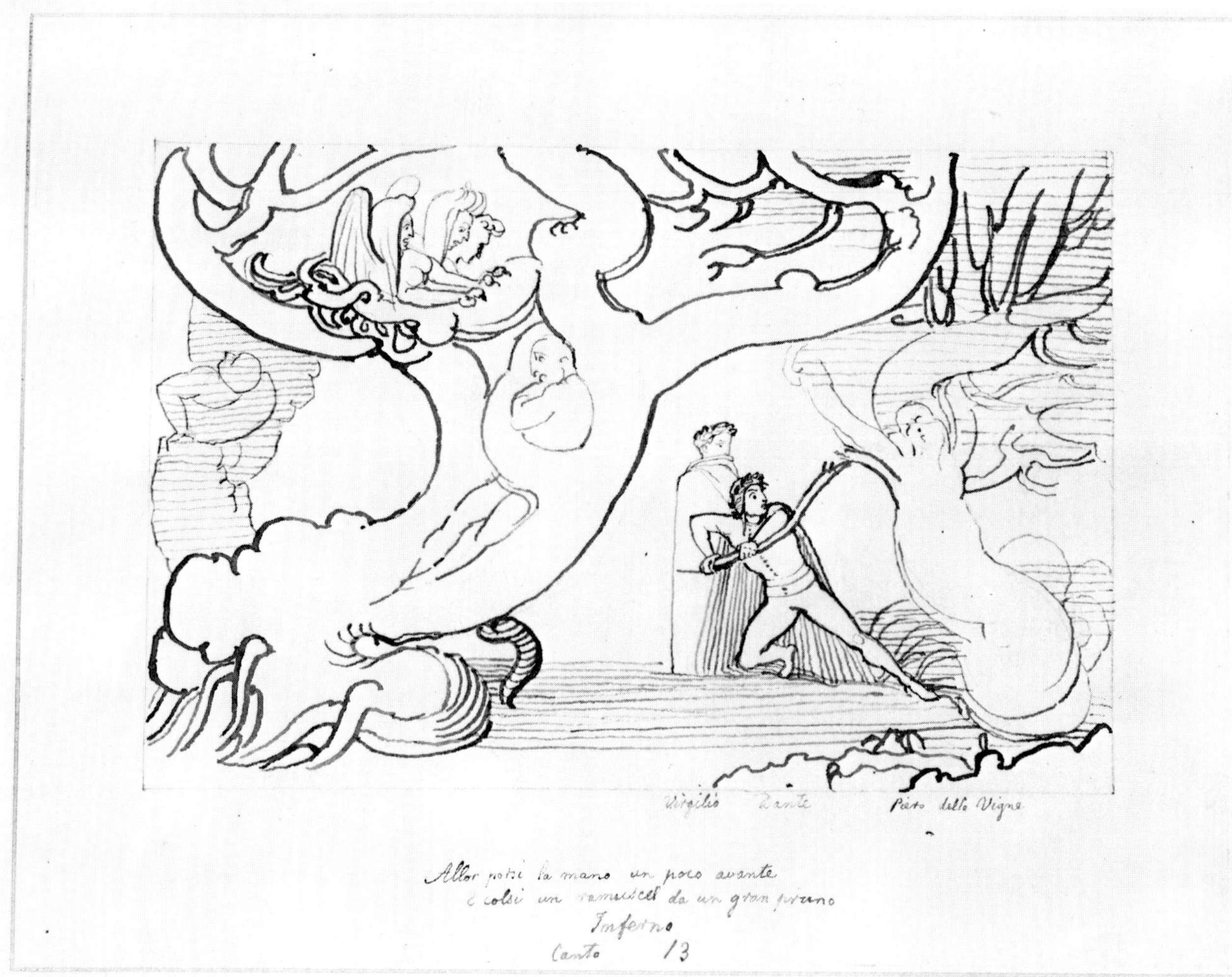

elongated, horizontal figures, especially that of Dante, are unmistakably derived from medieval sources.

Behind this influence however lay Flaxman's life studies of cloaked figures executed whilst he was in Italy. According to the artist's wife 'the common cloak of the lower classes of Italy suggested the drapery for Virgil and Dante' in the *Divine Comedy* illustrations.[47] Such studies were rapidly sketched on a small scale, using a minimum number of strokes to suggest the cloak, with often only one continuous line to record a featureless head. Flaxman was concerned with outlines, not with the material substance of either the cloak or the person. The drawings almost all look as if they had been rapidly sketched on the spot, in the street or church, since Flaxman always carried a sketchbook with him. In one church two men kneeling at prayer attracted his attention, but his sketch is not a study in

124 *The Forest of Harpies (Inferno).* Pen and ink, 18 × 26 cms.

125 *(facing above) Virgil and Beatrice meet (Inferno).* Pen and ink, 18 × 26 cms. Houghton Library, Harvard University (Photo Library).

126 *(facing below) The Hypocrites (Inferno).* Pen and ink and pencil, 19·2 × 13·7 cms.

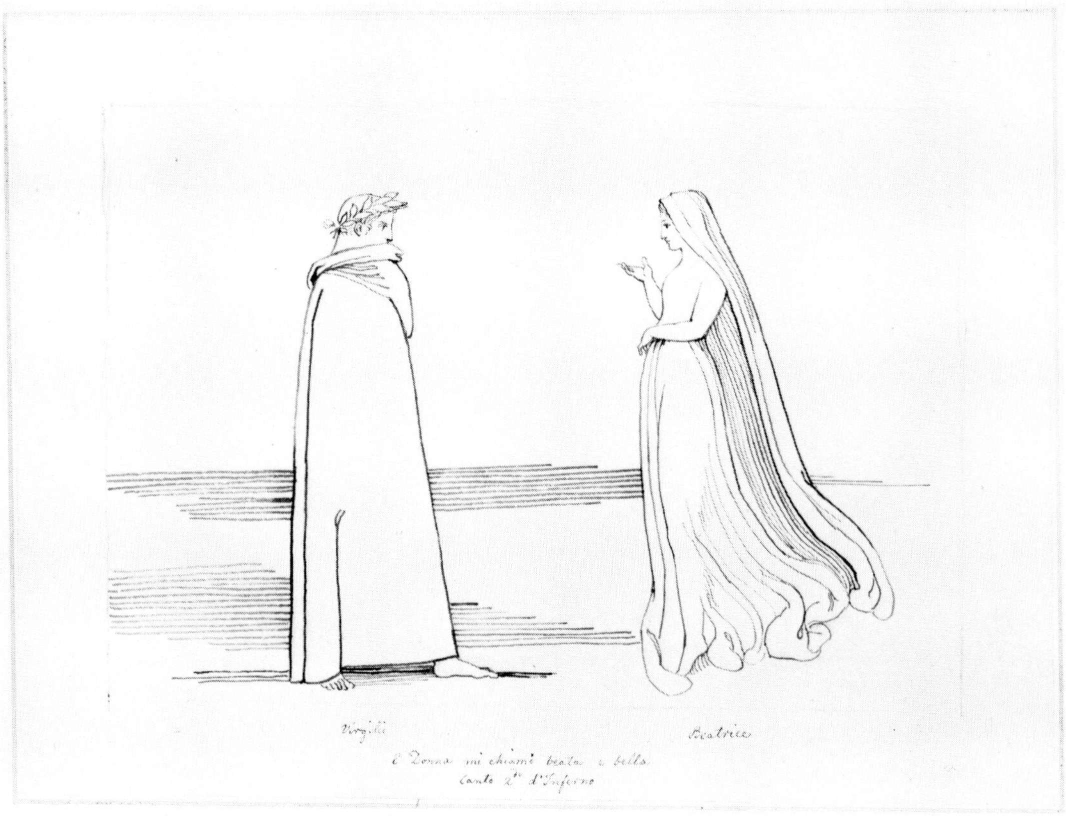
Virgilio
Beatrice
e Donna mi chiamò beata e bella
Canto 2do d'Inferno

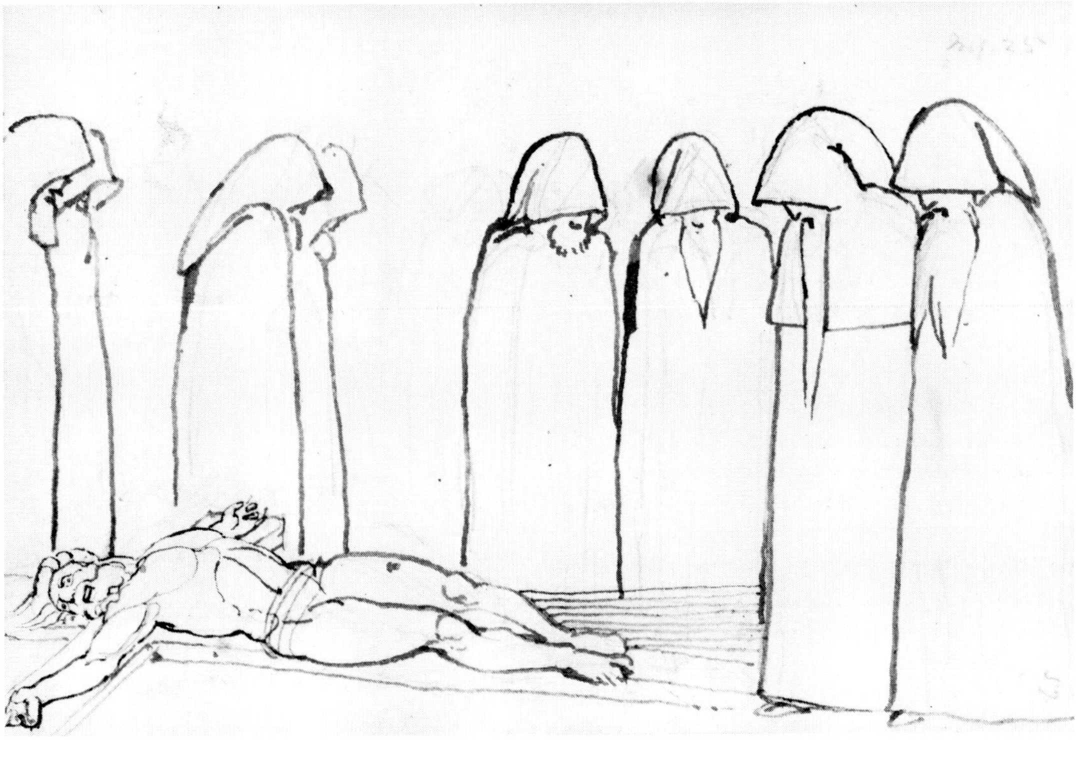

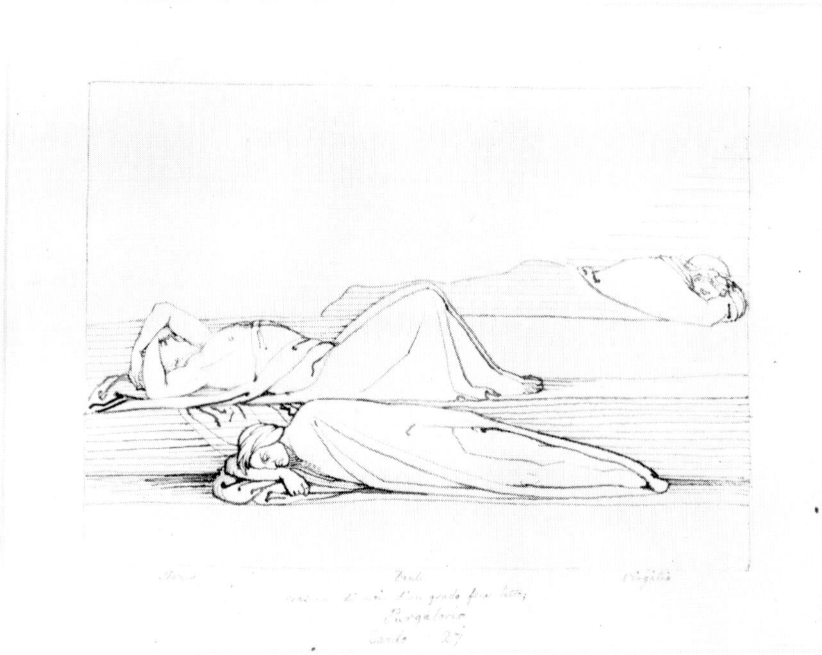

127 *The Poets Resting (Purgatorio).*
Pen and ink, 18 × 26 cms.

devotion but in drapery patterns. In another cloak study, a peasant is taking his siesta in the shade of a colonnade, again becoming a study in pattern rather than in characterisation (Plate 57). The economy with which these cloaked figures are rendered was further refined in the *Dante* plates. It is even possible that these outline cloak studies were made because of his work on Dante, where the subject-matter demanded cloaked figures.[48]

Symmetry is an important characteristic of some of the *Divine Comedy* compositions. Whereas amongst the *Homer* and *Aeschylus* illustrations only about half a dozen of the designs are symmetrically arranged around a central axis, nearly twenty of the *Dante* plates, mostly in the *Paradiso*, have been composed in this way. The lack of symmetry in the Greek designs shows the influence of bas-reliefs and vase paintings where symmetry was not a major consideration. But in the Dante plates these sources are hardly evident in the compositions, only more generally in their influence on the linear style. The more prominent use of symmetrical arrangements derived from Flaxman's studies of the period from the Trecento to the High Renaissance.

Flaxman's sketches of works of art from this period sometimes show a carefully balanced disposition of figures in the fresco or bas-relief, frequently selecting only a detail. Amongst the drawings already discussed which show this compositional symmetry are the apse mosaic of the *Death of the Virgin* by Cavallini in Santa

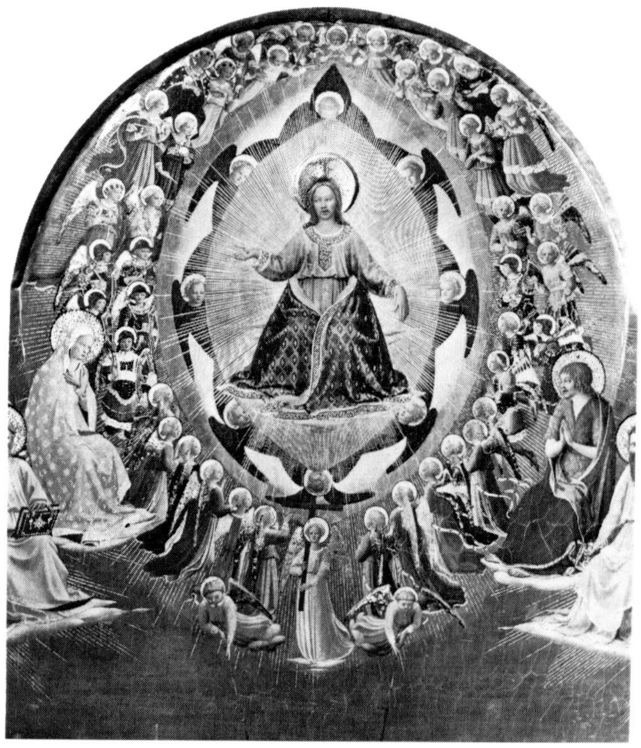

129 Fra Angelico: *Last Judgment:* detail.

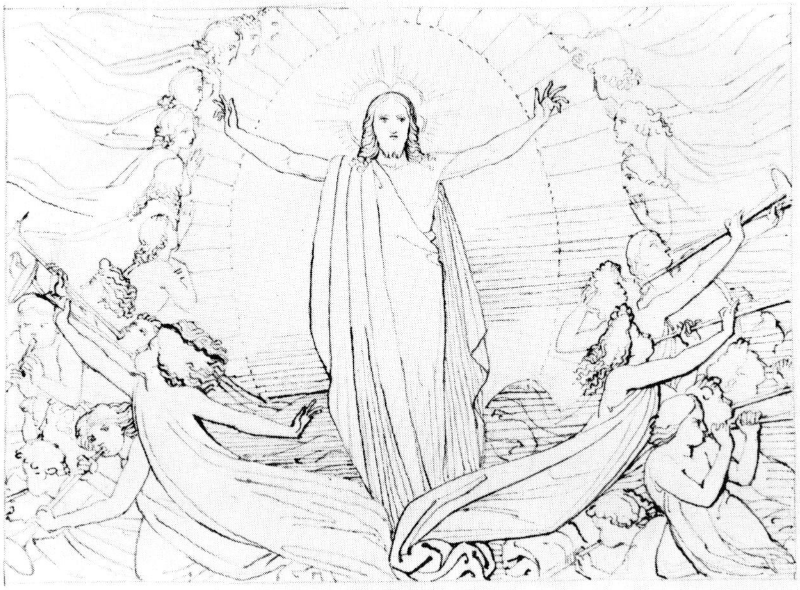

128 *The Triumph of Christ (Paradiso).* Pen and ink, 18 × 26 cms.

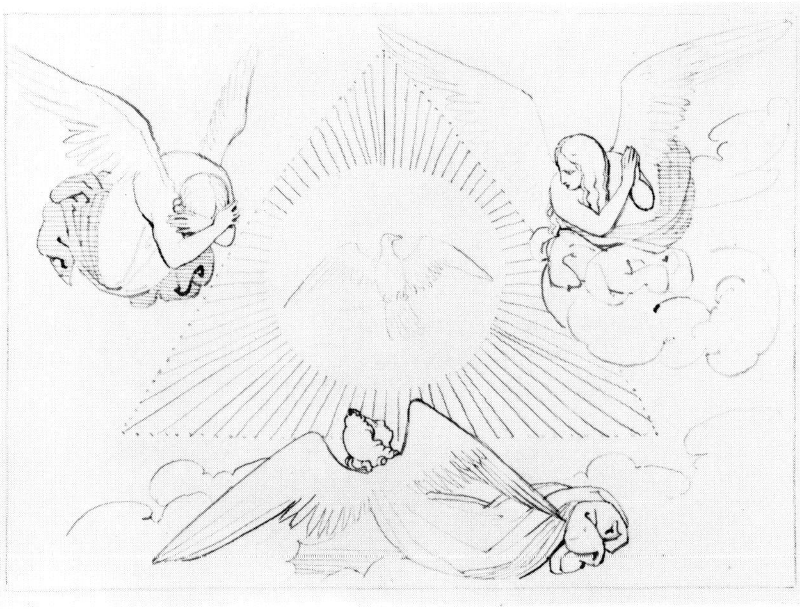

130 *The Adoration of the Trinity (Paradiso).* Pen and ink, 18 × 26 cms.

Maria in Trastevere in Rome, a detail from the fresco of the *Last Judgment* in the Camposanto in Pisa (Plate 46), and the *Transfiguration* from Bonanno's doors of the Duomo in Pisa. From the Quattrocento he drew the *Ascension* relief from Donatello's San Lorenzo pulpit, and several panels from Ghiberti's first Baptistry door, including the *Crucifixion*, Resurrection and *Ascension*. Amongst his diary entries also quoted earlier, is an enthusiastic comment on Raphael's *St. Cecilia*, which he particularly admired, for its 'simple and poetical composition' (Plate 41). The influence of such symmetrical compositions appears in a variety of the *Dante* plates, from the image of Dis (Plate 121) onwards. In the *Paradiso* a triumphant Christ appears in a centralised mandorla, reminiscent in its design of such works as the upper part of Fra Angelico's *Last Judgment* (Plates 128 and 129). For one of the *Paradiso* plates showing the adoration of the Trinity, Flaxman changed an originally asymmetrical design into a centrally-placed equilateral triangle with carefully disposed angels (Plate 130).

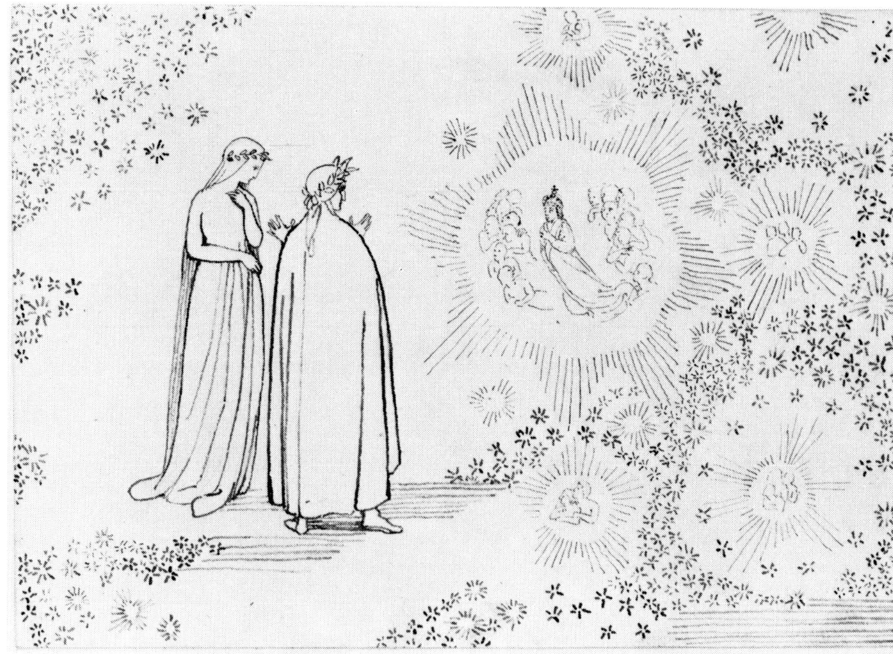

131 *Dante and Beatrice looking at the Empress Costanza (Paradiso).* Pen and ink, 13·5 × 19 cms.

The element of geometry introduced into some of the *Paradiso* plates is most successful in the last two examples just discussed: compare also Plate 131. In some of the other plates, however, in which the geometric element plays an important role, Flaxman's attempt to draw celestial imagery shows that it is an almost impossible task. In some illustrations stars and planets have been drawn almost with the precision of a treatise on astronomy, and are incongruously juxtaposed to an etherialised Dante and Beatrice or to a Crucifixion. These plates are as unsatisfactory as others in which disparate elements are combined, such as figures cut off below the waist to suggest the disappearance of the rest of the body in heavenly mist.

But these strictures do not apply to the plate of the beatific vision (Plate 132). Apart from the very faint dotted outline of God's head and shoulders in the centre, the design consists of a series of concentric circles, each composed of lines of varying thickness, radiating from the centre. Within the restrictions of black and white, Flaxman has very successfully visualised Dante's description of three circles of different hue symbolising God as Three in One. Such extreme geometric simplicity in Flaxman's art is rare. Were it not an attempt at a literal rendering of Dante's poetry, this design could be called totally abstract and linked with the geometric austerities of the architecture of Boullée. But such a link would be misleading.[49]

The beatific vision is the most serene use of geometry

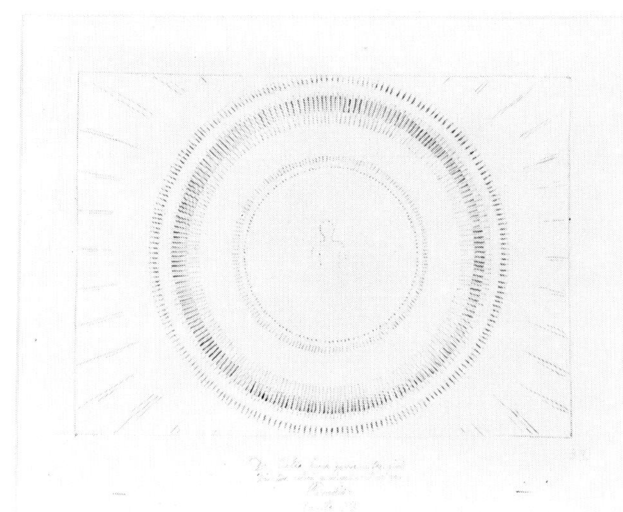

132 *The Beatific Vision (Paradiso).* Pen and ink, 18 × 26 cms.

in the *Dante* series, in marked contrast to the angularities of the background of the *Purgatorio* plate illustrating Lucifer hurtling through space like a thunderbolt (Plate 133). Turning the pages of the volume this is one of the plates that comes as a visual shock, as Flaxman no doubt intended. Apart from the earlier horrific image of Dis or Lucifer devouring his victims, no page prepares one for this startling phenomenon. The figures fall like those of the damned in a *Last Judgment*, against a

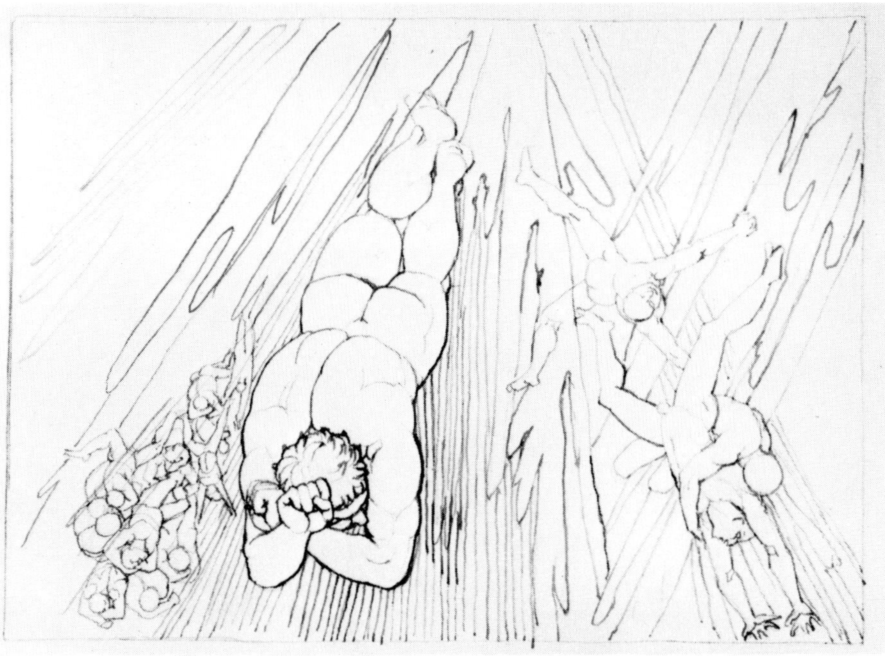

133 *Lucifer shooting down like a thunderbolt (Purgatorio).* Pen and ink, 18 × 26 cms.

background of jagged and discordant lightning flashes that brilliantly translate Dante's text.

A comparison of Flaxman's designs with Dante's lines shows a consistent attempt to translate the *Divine Comedy* as literally as possible into visual terms. All Flaxman's illustrations, whether to Dante or to other authors, are literal. His imagery is not transformed into a personal gloss on Dante, as Blake's illustrations were to be. Flaxman never used his chosen text as a springboard for Romantic subjectivity, even if some of the texts he illustrated—notably Dante—are themselves crucial sources for the Romantic movement. In the same way the image of mystical perfection mirrored in Flaxman's *Paradiso* should not be likened to the philosophy of Swedenborg, a misleading comparison made by an early commentator.[50] The mystical scenes are too concrete in their imagery to be Swedenborgian, and the compositional elements derive directly from Dante himself.

The type of angel that Flaxman evolved in his *Paradiso* plates was to influence subsequent designs for tombs when he returned home. Before going to Italy, he had used on the *Sarah Morley* monument (Plate 13) a rather angular angel with fluttering drapery, deriving from his familiarity with English late medieval sculpture. Under the impact of Italy and in particular the Quattrocento, Flaxman's angels were to be transformed. They now became rhythmically elegant beings, who in the *Paradiso* blow trumpets, and later on monuments will bear up to heaven the spirits of the dead.

In the Dante plates, the movement of the angels is frequently contained within an arc, with heads and legs flung backwards, and arms in a position of supplication or ecstasy. Flaxman sketched this kind of angel from the *Crucifixion* panel on Ghiberti's first Baptistry door (Mellon sketchbook), but there are many other examples of these types of Trecento and Quattrocento angels which Flaxman would have known (Plate 134). They reappear in the *Purgatorio* plates hovering as guardians over the Valley of the Princes, and occur often in the *Paradiso*, moving around the sun in one canto, in another adoring the Trinity (Plate 130), elsewhere forming part of the column of spirits ascending to Jupiter, encircling a triumphant Christ (Plate 128).

The newly developed gracefulness in Flaxman's *Paradiso* angels evolved at the same time as a more general elegance evident in many of his illustrations in the early 90's, in both Dante and the classical designs. The elegance was partially based on his use of drapery, and partially on a distortion of anatomy, in which he elongated the body from the waist downwards: this type of figure he frequently used for supernatural beings. The frequent appearance of angels in the *Paradiso* provided Flaxman with many opportunities for pattern-making with billowing draperies of extravagant length, sometimes rhythmically interlaced, creating a repetitive pattern. Angels weave their

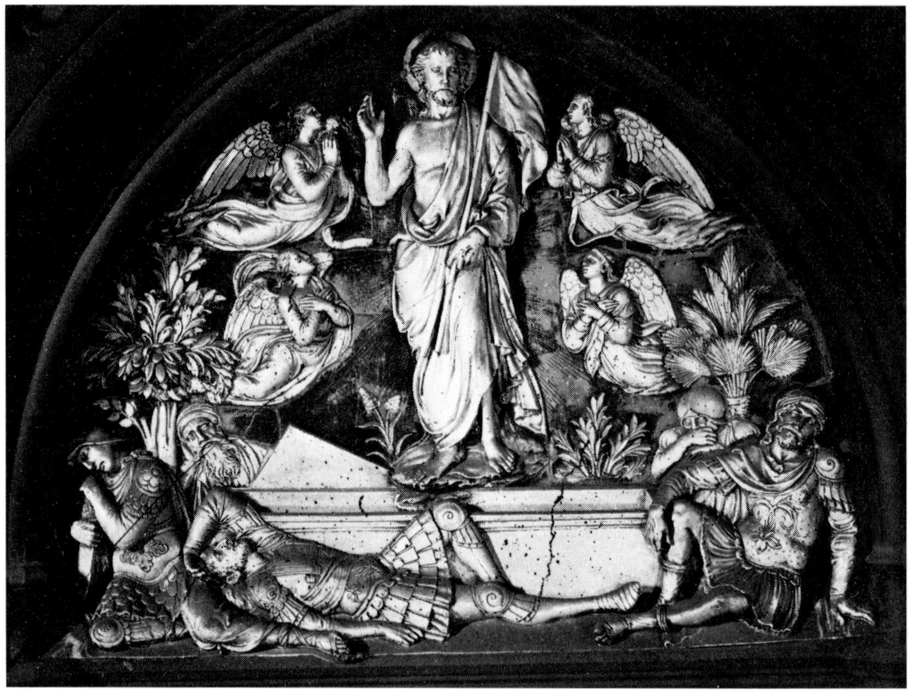

134 Luca della Robbia: *Resurrection.*

bodies across each other in a sweeping circular motion around the sun, they overlap their wings when joined in a celestial choir, or create a radiating pattern when celebrating the triumph of Christ (Plate 128).

In this engraving of the triumph, as in many others of the *Dante* series, Flaxman has imbued the design with an unmistakably Christian sentiment, a characteristic singled out for praise in A. W. von Schlegel's 1799 article. As Schlegel pointed out, Flaxman has not interpreted his angels as classical spirits or putti, but has opted instead for the Christian tradition, with long, flowing garments. This latter type of angel 'corresponds much better to strict church custom and to the pure delights of a Christian heaven. The angels can be regarded as heavenly choirboys at that eternal divine service and must therefore be clothed solemnly. The artist has given them that pious naivety with which they deliver their tidings in holy writings.'[51]

The Christian sentiment is particularly noticeable in the *Paradiso* plates, some of which in both composition and mood relate to later tombs. The figure of Christ in the plate of his triumph is very similar in sentiment to that of the *Redfearn* monument a few years later (Plate 179). The connection between angels in the Dante plates and later tombs has already been mentioned. A further link between these illustrations and his monuments can be seen in the theme of Christian sentiment combined with motherly love, which is the dominant characteristic of such an important tomb as the one to *Lady Fitzharris* (Plate 196), which has its forerunner in the *Paradiso* illustration of the birth of Cacciaguida (Plate 135). An apparition of the Virgin hovers at the end of the bed, whilst the baby Cacciaguida is being closely cuddled, in a pose relating to many of Flaxman's drawings of the theme of mother and child. Whilst based on nature, the composition of the *Dante* plate is at the same time characterised by an unmistakably contemporary sentiment, conceived within a Christian context.

On his return from Italy, Flaxman continued his association with Thomas Hope in a series of commissions, including a small bust of Dante. For other, unknown, clients about the same time he made busts of both Shakespeare and Milton.[52] The heads of the English poets however do not reflect an extensive interest in their writings on Flaxman's part, as scarcely any Shakespearean illustrations by him are known,[53] and only a few to Milton. Whilst in Italy, Hayley tried to encourage Flaxman to produce illustrations to Milton at a time he was writing a life of the poet, in the hope of persuading the publisher to include engravings.[54] Although Flaxman executed a few sketches, they were not published in Hayley's *Life*, and the only Miltonic designs by Flaxman that were to be published were three in Hayley's edition of Cowper's translation of the *Latin and Italian Poems* in 1808. These engravings,

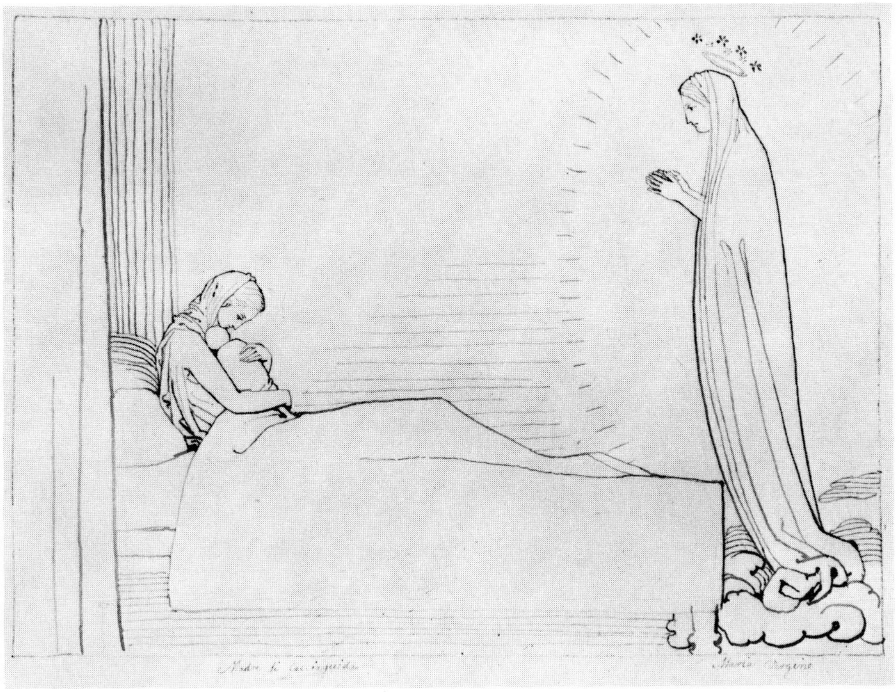

135 *The Birth of Cacciaguida (Paradiso).* Pen and ink, 18 × 26 cms.

136 *Satan fleeing from the Touch of Ithuriel's Spear (Paradise Lost).* Pen and ink and wash, 17 × 24 cms.

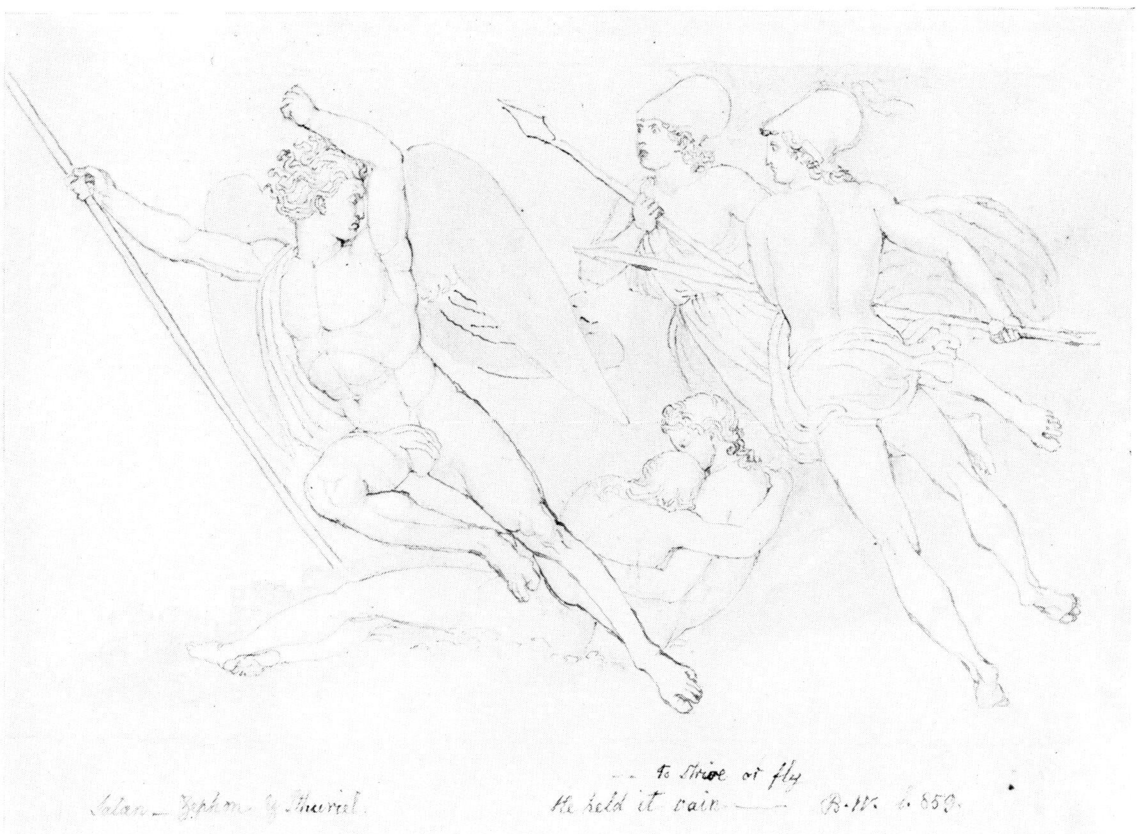

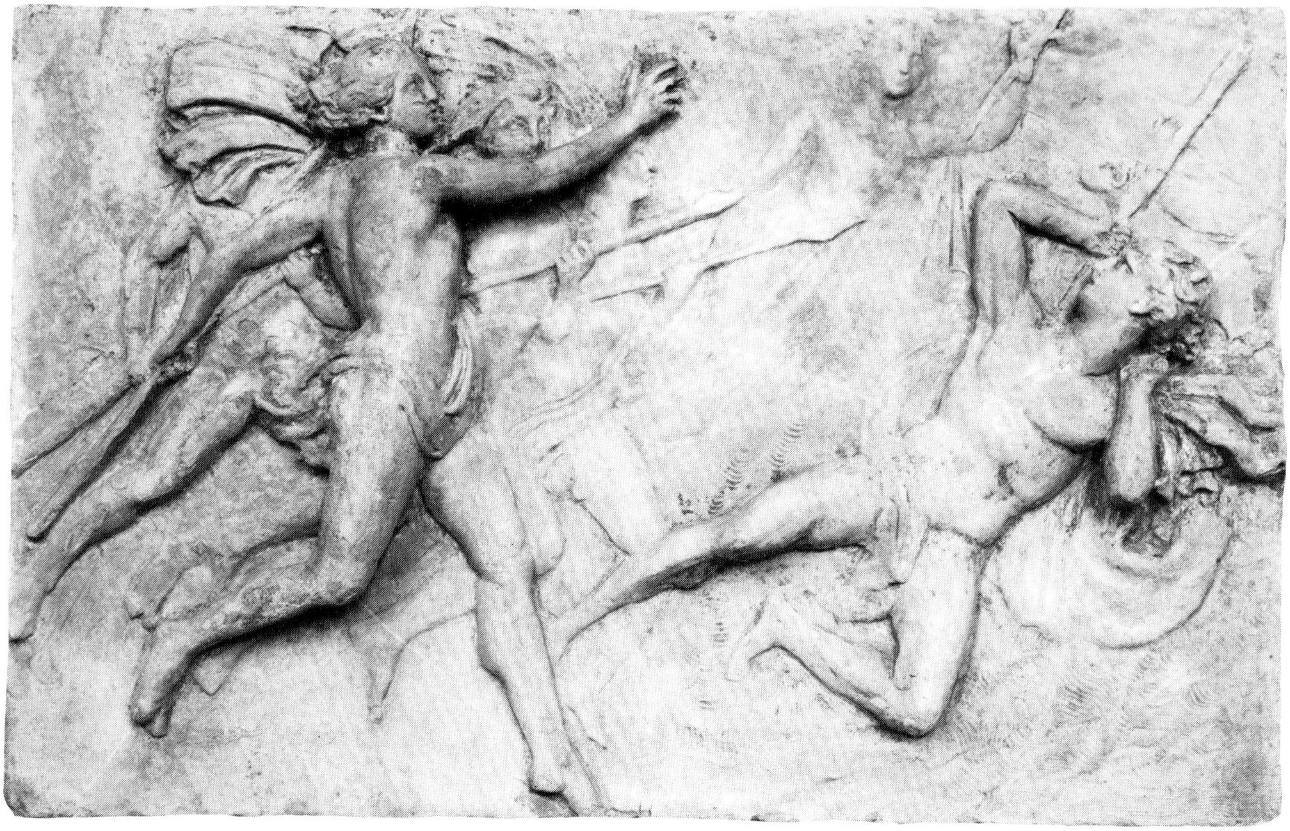

137 *Satan fleeing from the Touch of Ithuriel's Spear (Paradise Lost)*, c. 1826. Plaster, 29·8 × 46·9 cms.

together with the few scattered drawings, show that Flaxman translated Milton's lines into his customary linear style.[55] The design of Satan fleeing at the touch of Ithuriel's spear, reproduced in Plate 136, was to form the basis of a composition for a marble relief for which he received a commission in the last year of his life from the Duke of Bedford (Plate 137).[56] In a conversation in 1811 he explained why he had never undertaken a whole series of illustrations to Milton[57]. He said that he did not wish to compete with Henry Fuseli's designs, which had appeared both on a large scale in the oils of his ambitious Milton Gallery (1799–1800), and also in engravings, and that unlike Dante, Milton provided few figures for compositions. Flaxman nevertheless admired Milton's poetry, and had lamented that his old college, Christ's, Cambridge, contained no monument to him.[58]

Flaxman's illustrations to contemporary literature are very few in number. They include sketches to William Falconer's popular, long poem *The Shipwreck*, which had been first published in 1762, some sketches to Hayley's poem *The Triumph of Music*, and a series of twenty drawings in 1804 to Wieland's *Oberon*, which had been translated into English in 1798.[59] The last series, if ever intended for publication, may not have been engraved because Fuseli's *Oberon* illustrations, on which he was working at the same time, were published in the second English edition in the following year, 1805. Publishers at the time assumed that illustrations should accompany the full text, a combination of image and words that Flaxman disliked, as already mentioned. He preferred his illustrations to be published separately in their own right, and it was presumably for this reason that he reported in a letter in 1806 that 'I have refused to design for the works of several distinguished modern writers'.[60] Publishers might also have felt, like Sir Walter Scott and equally erroneously, that Flaxman was only capable of dealing with Greek subject-matter and could not adapt to more modern themes.

4 Religion and Morality: Christianity and Swedenborg

Towards the end of his life Flaxman was asked by

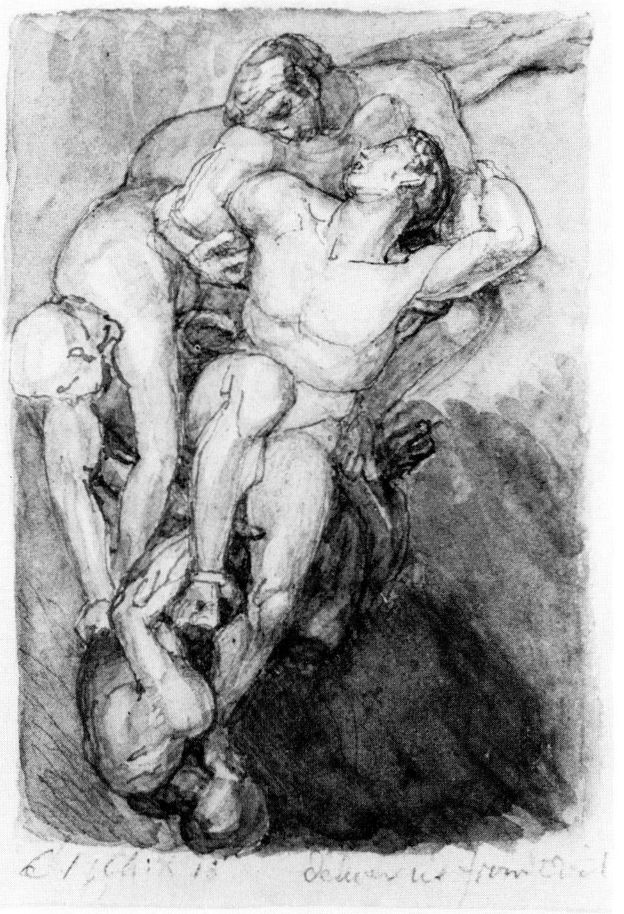

138 *Deliver us from Evil.*
Pen and ink and wash, 16·1 × 11·8 cms.

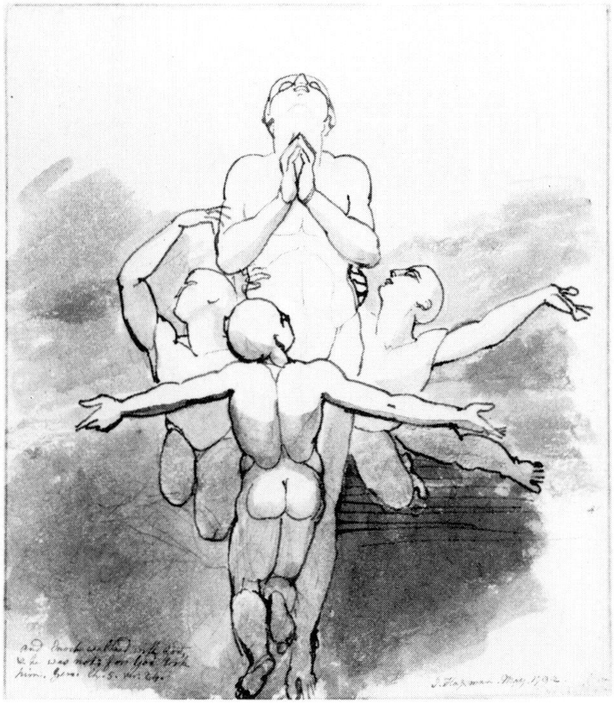

139 *Enoch raised to Heaven (Genesis),* 1792. Pen and ink and wash, 25·2 × 23 cms.

Cockerell 'why he had not illustrated sacred history', to which he replied that 'he had not been employed'.[61] In view of the success of his other illustrations, and his reputation for church monuments, it is puzzling why no patron or publisher in Flaxman's lifetime came forward to commission a set of religious illustrations. The lack of patronage may partially be explained by the general paucity of such illustrations at the time. Flaxman was reported in 1807 to be thinking of publishing his compositions to the Acts of Mercy, and to the Lord's Prayer (Plate 138) but the project did not materialise in his lifetime, and the two series were to be published posthumously.[62] Drawings to the apocryphal first *Book of Enoch* and other biblical scenes, and to the writings of Bunyan and Swedenborg seem to have been made with no publication in mind. His two illustrated poems, 'The Knight of the Blazing Cross' and 'The Casket', both moralising, Christian tales, also remained in manuscript, although a friend encouraged the publication of 'The Knight' on the grounds that Flaxman should not conceal 'from the world a work so eminently calculated to enlighten and improve it'.[63] Even in the Victorian period when Flaxman's reputation stood high, and his Christian sentiment was much admired, a report in 1865 that 'The Knight' was at last to be published proved to be incorrect.[64]

From the time before he went to Italy, Flaxman had been drawing religious scenes which were not related to reliefs on monuments, but conceived as illustrations in their own right (Plates 18 and 19). Only on rare occasions later in his career are reliefs illustrating New Testament scenes incorporated into his monuments (see Plate 183). Whilst in Rome, in spite of being very busy creating over two hundred commissioned illustrations, in addition to sculpture, he found time to continue his religious drawings, including designs from *Pilgrim's Progress.* These religious drawings were made for his own and his wife's enjoyment, as well as that of his friends.[65] In Rome his religious drawings showed an interest in the life of Enoch. He chose the incident in *Genesis* in which Enoch 'walked with God, and he was not, for God took him', transforming the text into a inspired transcendental vision (Plate 139). He was to return to this theme later in life after the first *Book of*

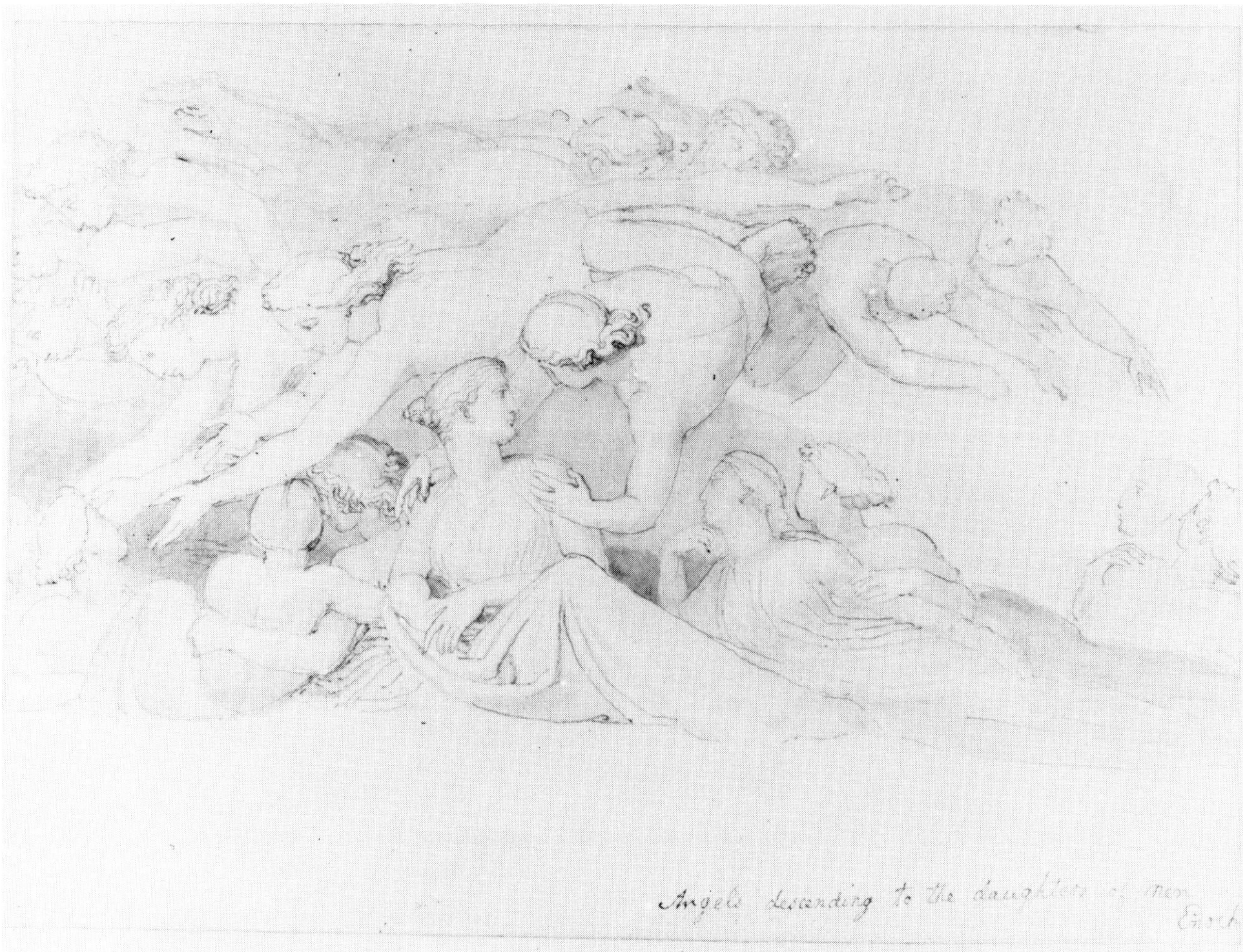

140 *Angels descending to the daughters of men (Book of Enoch).* c. 1821.
Pen and ink and wash, 16·5 × 23 cms.

Enoch had been translated into English for the first time in 1821, producing some particularly vigorous designs (Plate 140).

Over forty drawings for *The Pilgrim's Progress* have survived, ranging from rough sketches to carefully finished outlines that could have been cut without alteration on a copper plate (Plate 141) as well as other drawings which he completed with a wash. Some of the series was executed in Rome, and was continued later on Flaxman's return to London.[66] Flaxman was less successful in some of these designs than in his other religious drawings as occasionally they verge on the decorous and genteel, failing to capture the ruggedness of the original, simple allegory. Stylistically, Flaxman's illustrations are very similar to Stothard's, published as separate engravings without text between 1788 and 1791 whilst Flaxman was abroad, but he could have known them. Both artists ignored earlier publications, and turned some of their scenes into ones of contemporary domestic genre. Some of Flaxman's drawings show an intimate relationship between parent and child that is identical to that of his own sketches of everyday life in Rome and elsewhere; as genre scenes they have a delightful and charming innocence, but these are not characteristics demanded by Bunyan's text. Flaxman is closer to the spirit of the original allegory in scenes that include one of the giants (Plate 142).

Many isolated religious drawings survive inspired by subjects in the Old and New Testaments, as well as to the Apocrypha. Some relate stylistically to the tranquil scenes of parables, instruction, and death-beds that appear on a few of the bas-reliefs on his monuments. But the two drawings in Plates 143 and 144 have been

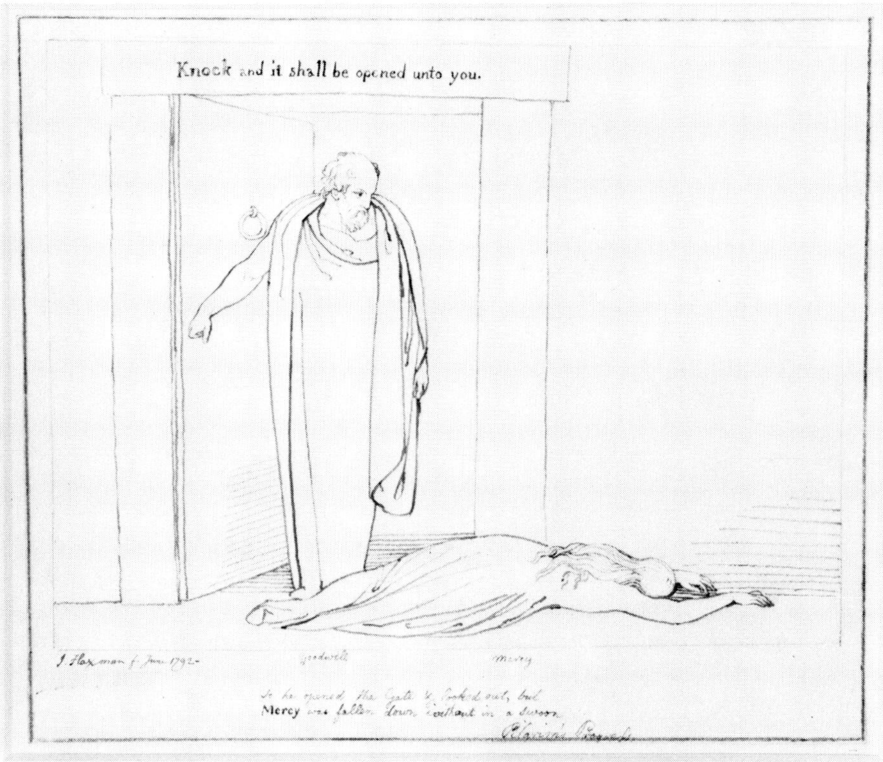

141 *Goodwill opens the Wicket Gate and finds Mercy fainted (Pilgrims Progress)*, 1792. Pen and ink, 20·2 × 24·2 cms.

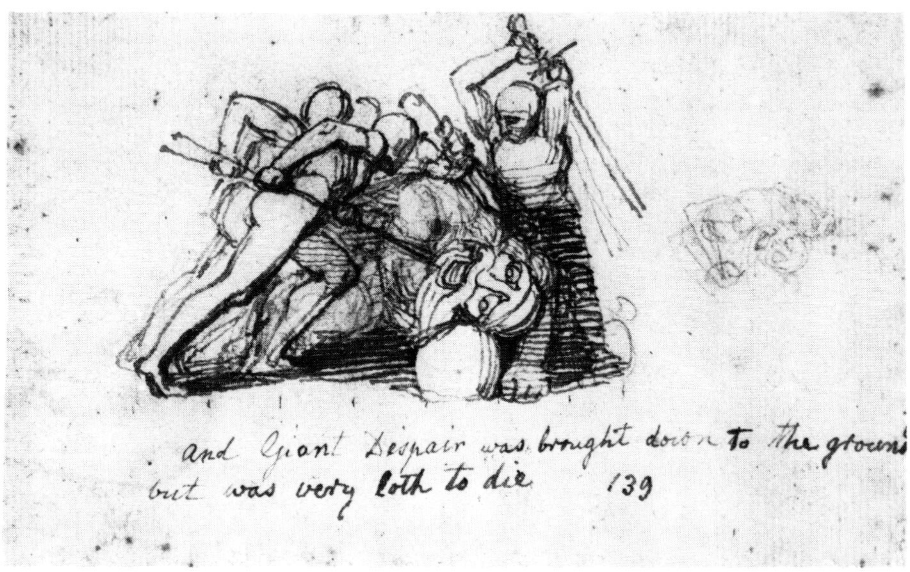

142 *The Death of Giant Despair (Pilgrim's Progress)*, c. 1792–95. Pen and ink and pencil, 10·8 × 16·5 cms.

chosen to illustrate a less familiar side to his religious illustrations, some of which have a vitality and dramatic movement comparable to the more energetic scenes in *Homer* and *Dante*. His drawing of the *Creation of the Heavens*, partly inspired by the scene of the same subject on the Sistine Chapel ceiling, is one of the most startling images in Flaxman's art, using Michelangelo's foreshortened figure of God which he has made simpler and more linear, counterbalancing an inward thrust by the outstretched arms of the angels, drawn parallel to the picture plane. The New Testament scene reproduced here illustrates the *Resurrection*, with an angel pushing

143 *The Creation of the Heavens*. Pen and ink and wash, 23·4 × 25·1 cms. See also page 240.

144 *The Resurrection*. Pen and ink and wash, 12·7 × 17·8 cms.

145 *The Knight grown strong in good deeds (The Knight of the Blazing Cross)*: detail, 1796. Pen and ink, 24·9 × 17·9 cms. (whole page)

146 *The Lord of Power defends the Righteous (The Knight of the Blazing Cross)*. 1796. Pen and ink, 24.9 × 17.9 cms.

147 *The Knight armed with power over storms and tempests (The Knight of the Blazing Cross)*: detail, 1796. Pen and ink, 24·9 × 17·9 cms.

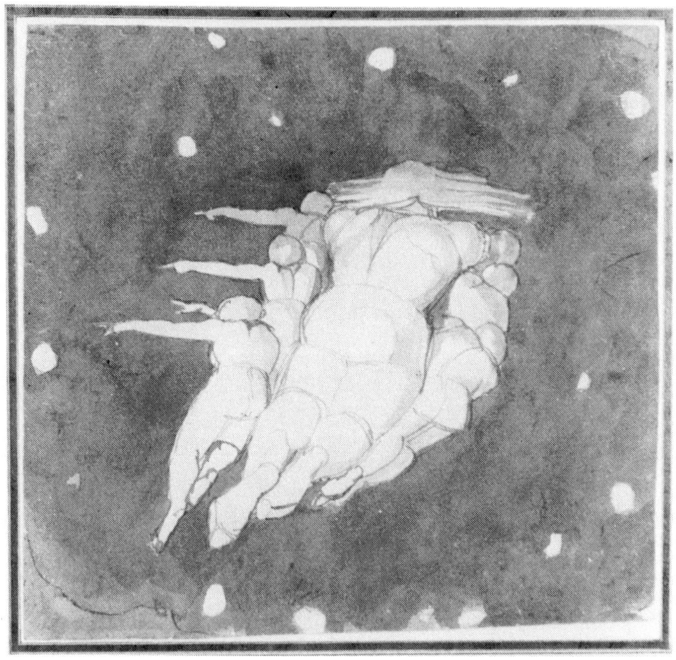

143

144

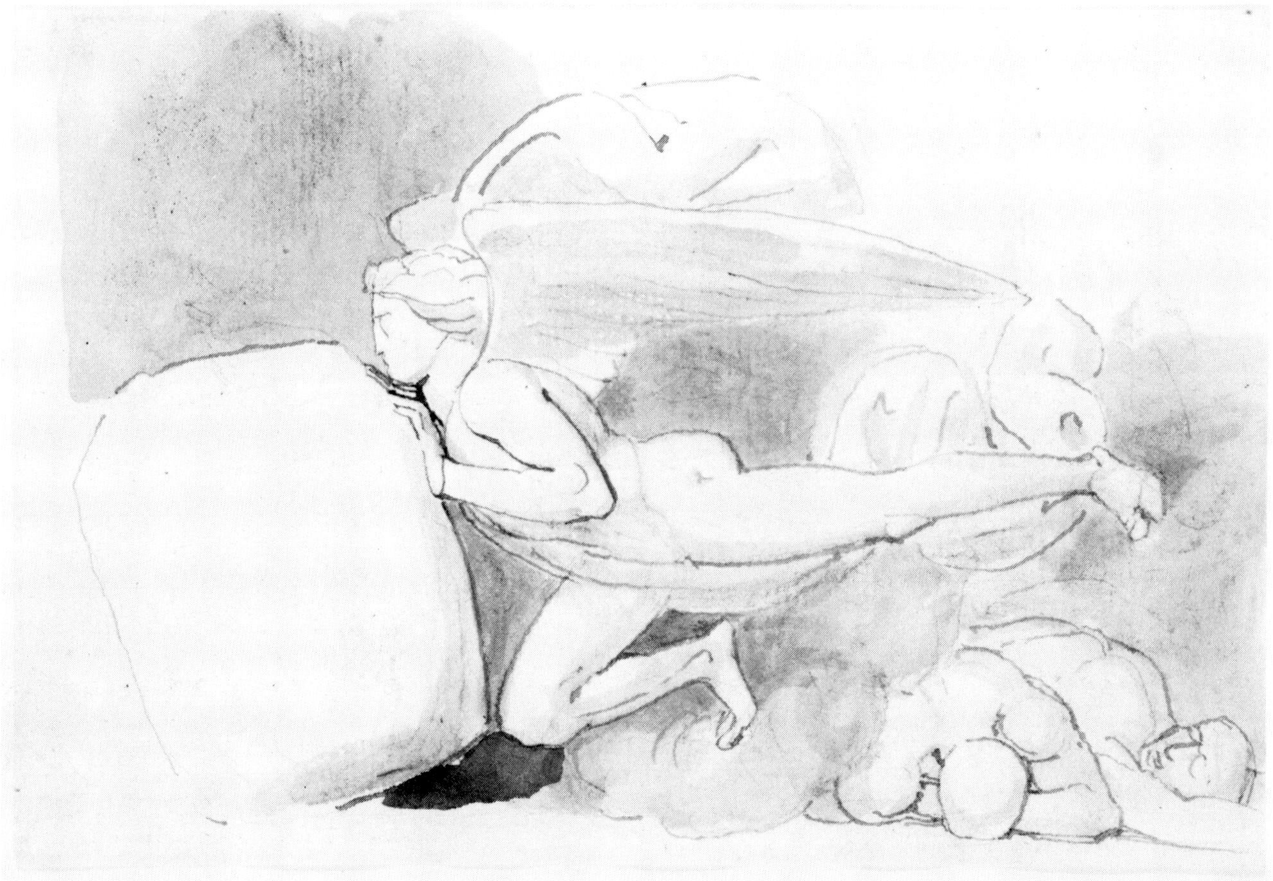

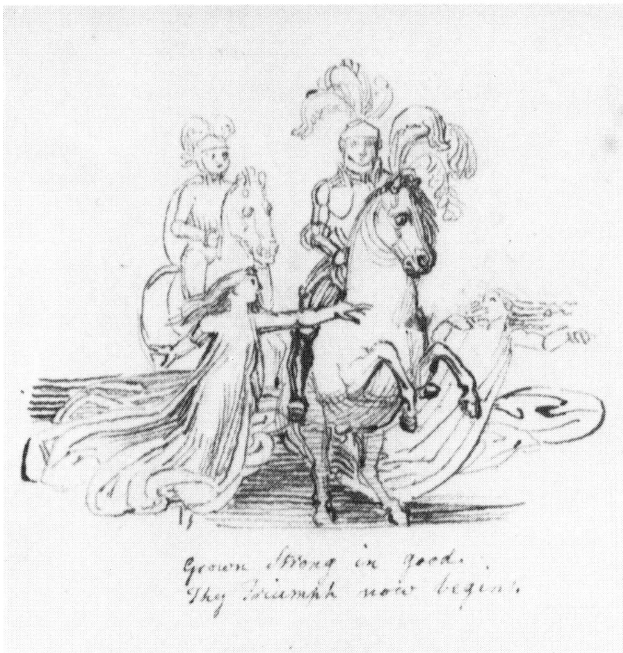

145

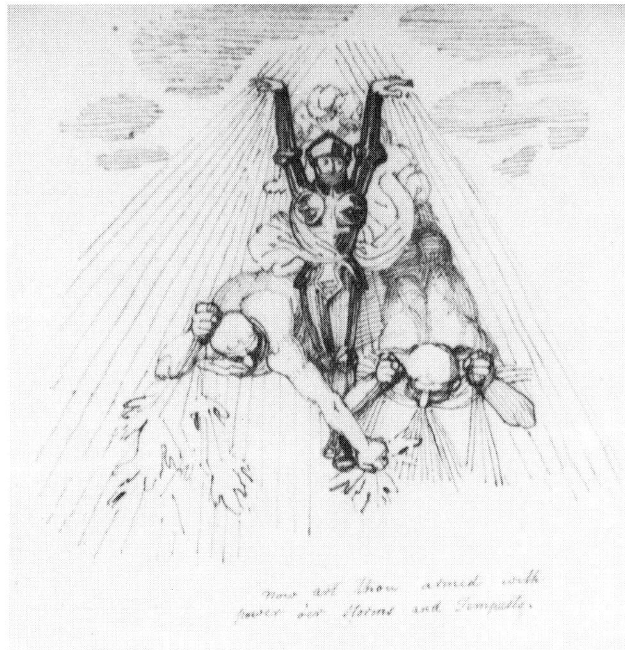

147

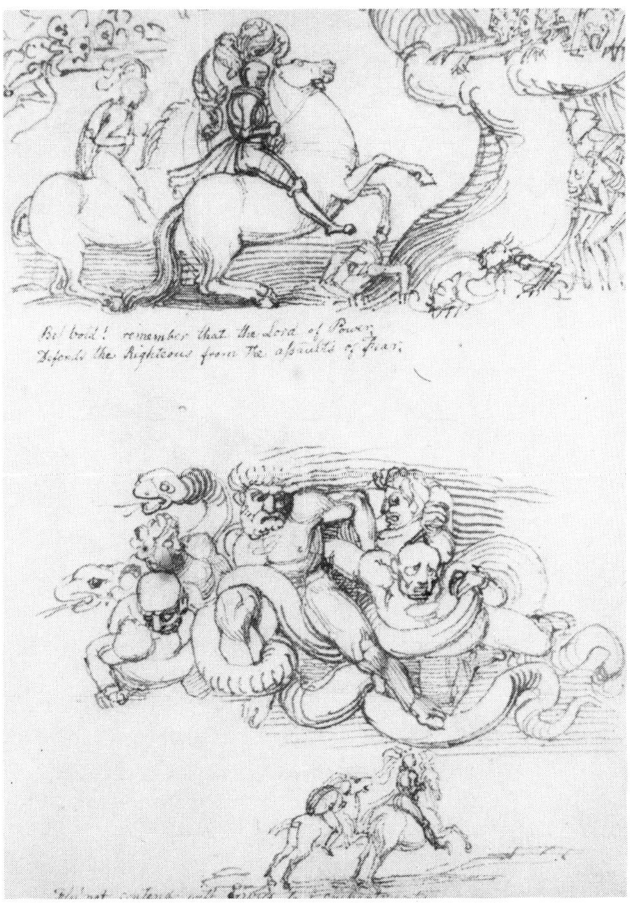

146

back the stone from the mouth of the tomb with an energy that far exceeds that of the more placid angels on his monuments. These drawings have a sense of thrust and movement for which Flaxman had little sculptural outlet in religious works.[67]

'The Knight of the Blazing Cross', a poem written and illustrated by Flaxman for his wife's birthday in 1796, shows how deeply indebted he was to Bunyan's kind of allegory. The dedication makes it clear that his wife suggested the project for an allegory of a knight errant who triumphs in 'the trails of virtue, the struggles and conquest of vice', attains to the spiritual world, returning to earth to become the associate of Faith, Hope and Charity, and ultimately dispenser of the Acts of Mercy. Unlike his other surviving poem 'The Casket', he tells the story of his Christian knight mainly through drawings with very little text. The knight, who is in effect an embodiment of Christ, sets out clad in armour with a magnificent plumed helmet and handsome charger, and the mood of the drawings varies from scenes of tranquillity when he is accompanied by female spirits, such as in Plate 145, to incidents of dramatic tension when he is fighting forces of evil (Plate 146), or, as in Plate 147, he is armed with the power to control storms and tempests. The drawings throughout the small volume are vigorously conceived, with a great deal of variety and interest. Most pages have two illustrations accompanied by text, a combination of image and words which he was later

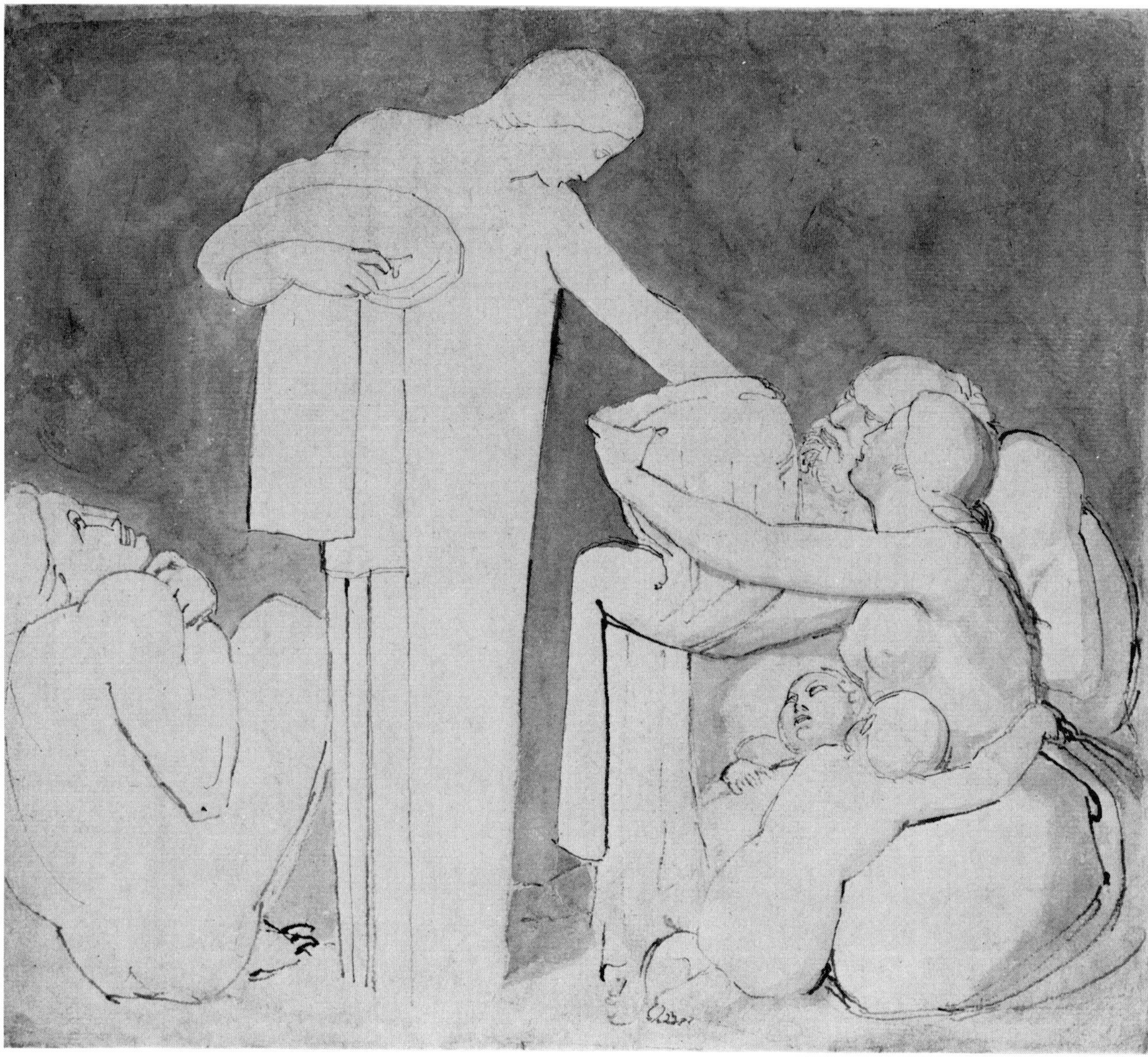

148 *Clothe the Naked (Acts of Mercy).* Pen and ink and wash, 26·4 × 29·9 cms.

to condemn. For a private work, however, he adopted principles different from those of his classical and Dante commissions.

The final drawings in 'The Knight' show the Acts of Mercy, which Flaxman was to rework as a separate series of illustrations, changing the medieval armour of the Knight into contemporary dress, and making the modelling simpler and more monumental, closer in spirit to Masaccio and Michelangelo. The revised series did not appear in his own lifetime however (Plates 148 and 149), except in the sculptural version of 'Instruct the Ignorant' that he used on the *Balme* monument (Plate 185). As he told one visitor to his studio in the last year of his life, he wanted his series of drawings of the Acts of Mercy to be 'regarded as attempts to confirm his faith and because of that he rejected my suggestion that he should etch them and have them published'.[68] Flaxman's other posthumous series of illustrations to *The Lord's Prayer* was partially a reworking of images carved on monuments, such as the panels to the *Baring Family* (see Plates 173, 177 and 178).

'The Casket', an illustrated poem which Flaxman wrote in 1812, is the only known surviving example of the light verse that he used to read to friends on winter

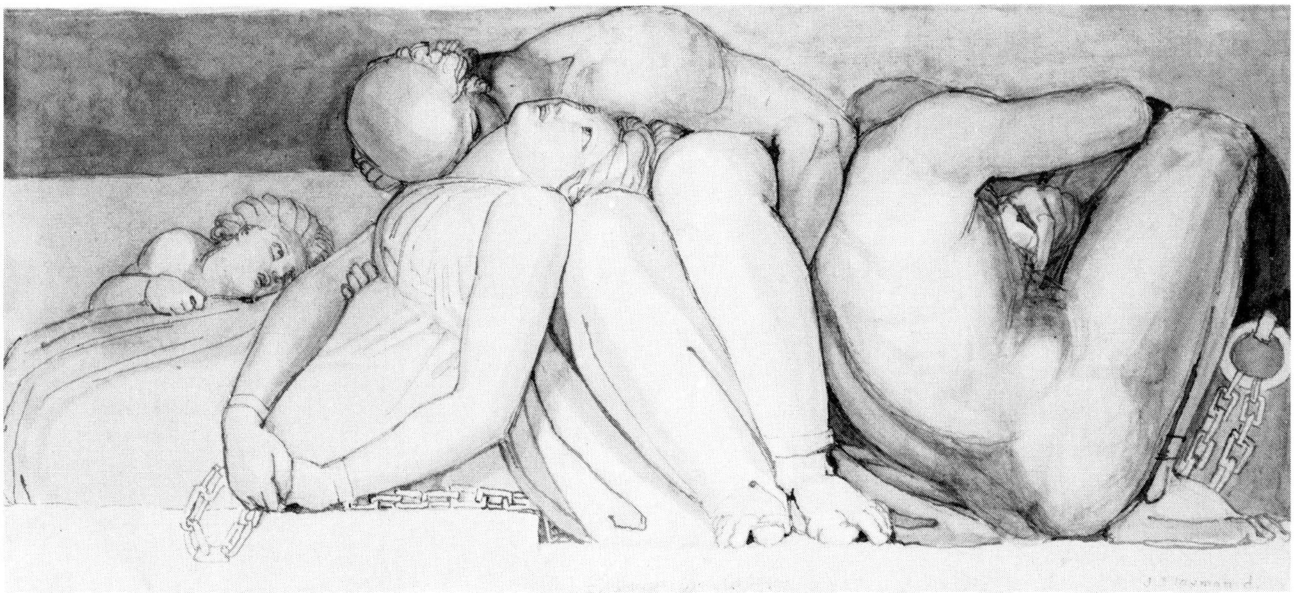

149 *Deliver the Captives (Acts of Mercy).*
Pen and ink and wash, 14·8 × 33 cms.

evenings (Plates 150, 152 and 153). The poem grew from a frivolous suggestion made by his wife and sister whilst discussing a small Chinese casket he had just bought and given to them.[69] The orientalism of the setting might also have been suggested by Southey's *Curse of Kehama*, which had been published only two years before, and which the poet believed Flaxman to be illustrating.[70] The lines of Flaxman's poem recount, in a light-hearted way, the travels of a casket brought from the orient, through Persia and the Mediterranean, until it finally reaches Britain. The casket had been made to contain the laws of morality, a counterpart to the box in the Pandora story in which he had already been interested in 1805 but the casket in the poem is to contain nothing evil (Plate 150). When a Chinese sorcerer tries to fill it with magic spells that would destroy both poetry and morality, the three daughters of Tien or Night banish him, and defend their casket from all attacks (Plate 151). Flaxman may have borrowed this part of his tale from Indian mythology, in which the Yakshis or daughters of Night are guardians of a secret treasure in the Himalayas.

Flaxman's verse, like that of 'The Knight', is crude, revealing only a modest literary talent, but interesting for its imagery and accompanying illustrations. Created for informal entertainment, it should be read in the spirit in which it was written, with its improbable juxtapositions of an exotic orient and the Lord Mayor's barge. One illustration suggests that Flaxman had been influenced by Persian or Moghul miniatures: Plate 150, which is set in Persia, shows a possible familiarity with miniatures depicting Krishna or a prince in love. It is known that Flaxman looked at Perisan and Moghul miniatures because he referred to them in his lectures, and also made copies of them in one of his sketchbooks (Plate 154).[71]

Flaxman started the poem by describing China and its people, and then introduced the princesses:

. . . Where dragon guarded arches rise
and tall Pagodas pierce the skies . . .
There sage Fo-hi and Con-foo-sze [Confucius]
Taught men just laws and policy
Settled the rank of Mandarins and Bonzes
  [Bhuddists]
with round well-buttoned hats upon their sconces
with a redundant swing of huge pig-tails
and long blue petticoats and longer nails—
The warrior tribe too a death doing race
with well shaped head and grinning face
Rustling in painted mail and leather bags
swords, pistols, bow-cases, arrows, Fally-wags
Gold and green spitting dragons
So that viewed at large
You'd take him for a garnished Twelfth cake
or a Lord Mayor's barge—. . .

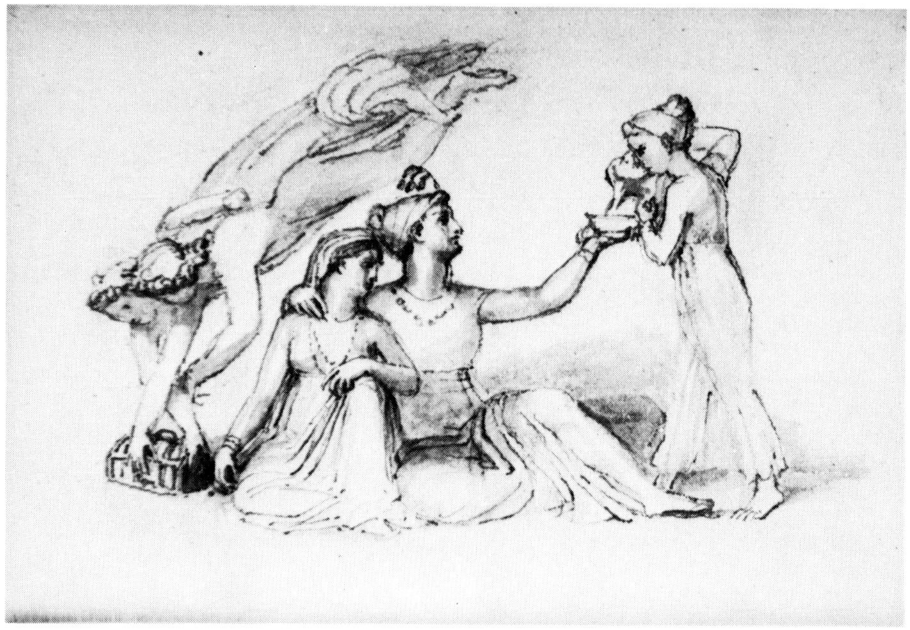

150 *Angels snatching the casket from Hafiz (The Casket),* 1812. Pen and ink and wash, 12 × 21 cms.

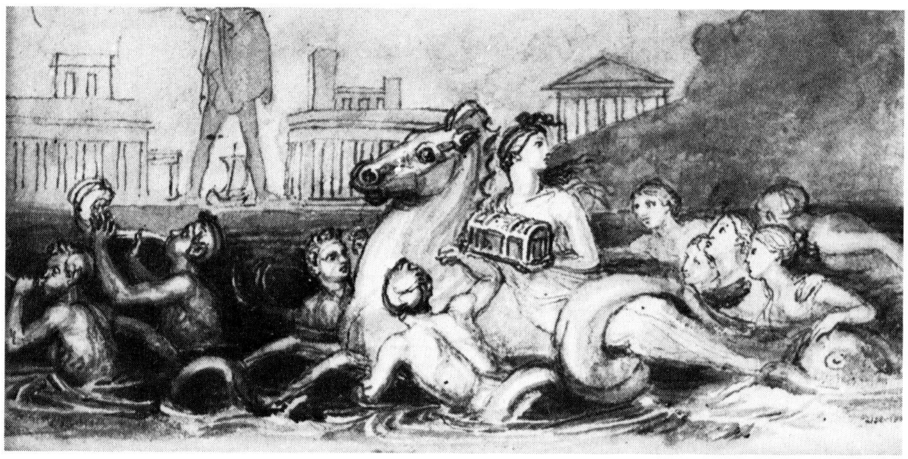

152 *The Casket being borne past the Colossus of Rhodes (The Casket).* 1812. Pen and ink and wash, 12 × 21 cms.

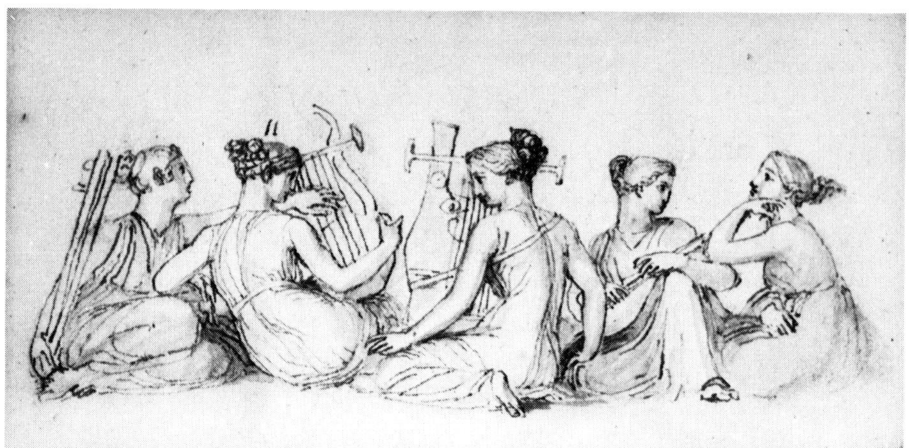

153 *Maidens playing music. (The Casket).* 1812. Pen and ink and wash, 12 × 21 cms.

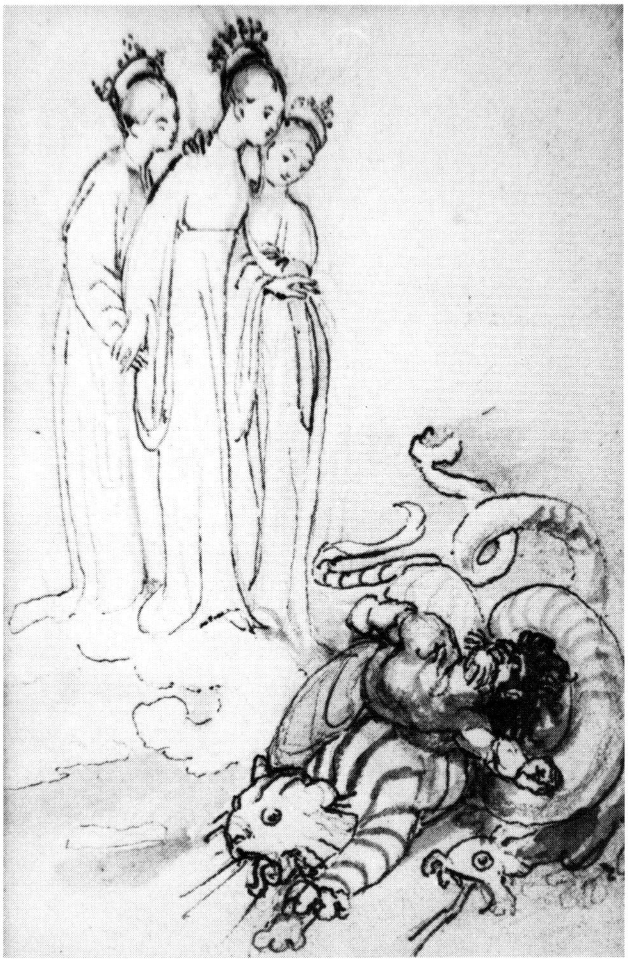

151 *The three daughters of Tien banish the magician Psi-Whong (The Casket)*, 1812. Pen and ink and wash, 12 × 21 cms.

In the mild beams of lunar light
varied with topaz radiance, amathystine bright
The angel daughters of Tien reclined
in rapturous delights refind
catch and impart the joys
of each celestial mind.
Ping-su, Lo-een and Sing-se, engaged to trace
each tender thought
In sisterly embrace . . . .

[Lo-een speaking]
Make me a casquet, grace it with your art
In it fair science shall her laws impart
In it shall virtue's moral law be given
sent down to man the best good gift from Heaven.
The sisters smile, assent and quickly prove
by prompt obedience, harmony of love,
Jasmin of hearts-ease gild the casket's sides
Gems were the flowers, and gems the plant divide
The handle golden dazzling to behold
With golden knobs in fillagrees of gold
Its wondrous lock was made by power divine
which opened only at the certain sign
That genius, Virtue made some offering there
Or gently pity there, let fall a tear—
Lo-een's bright eyes her silent joy expressed
Quick passed this thought within her glowing breast
'Tis mine to fill this chest with sacred lore',
When lo! Rude sounds disturb, ne'en heard before
Within that peaceful, pure abode.
Low muttering thunders and the louder gong
Announce the dread magician, fierce Psi-Whong
O'er his head roll with waving serpent spires
His glaring eye-balls dart blue-flashing fires
A grim fell tiger bears him through the air . . . .

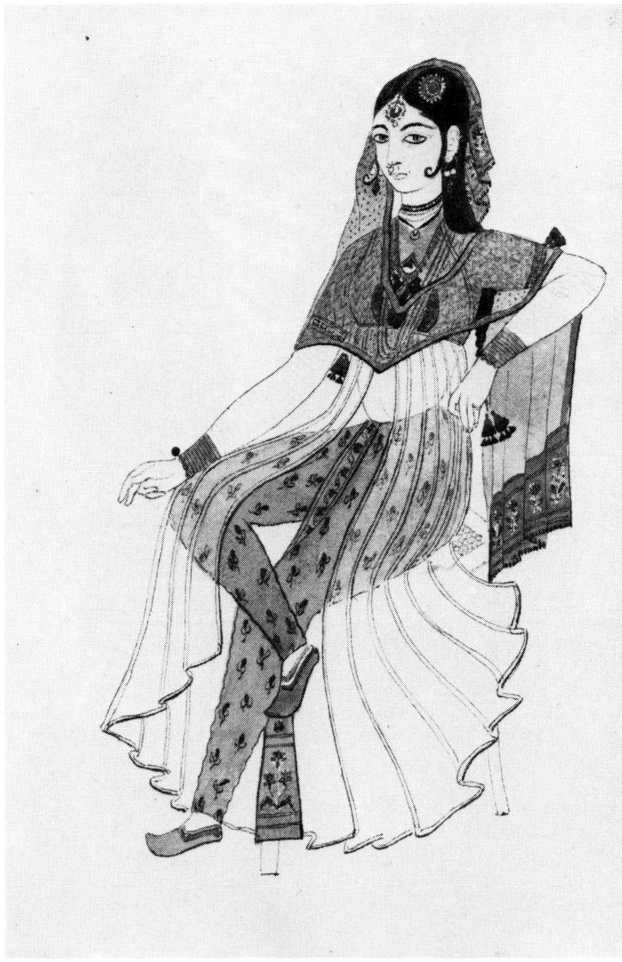

154 *Persian or Indian Lady seated, after a Persian or Moghul miniature.* Watercolour, 20·6 × 15·2 cms.

The illustrations discussed, together with his church monuments, are clearly the work of a Christian, belonging to the Church of England. A small group of drawings, together with one monument, provide visual evidence of Flaxman's sympathies with Swedenborgianism.

One of the mouthpieces of the sect, *The Intellectual Repository for the New Church*, praised most other journals in its obituary of Flaxman because they had mentioned that he was a Swedenborgian, but criticised an article in *The Times* that had claimed Flaxman had 'professed himself a member of the Established Church, and did not publicly associate with the congregation founded by Swedenborg, though he did not scruple to avow to his friends that he adopted, in general, the doctrines promulgated by that celebrated mystical theologian'.[72] *The Times* article was challenged a few days later, in the pages of the same newspaper, by the President of the Swedenborg Society, Charles Augustus Tulk, a friend of the Flaxmans. Tulk stated quite categorically that Flaxman's 'religious sentiments had for many years been framed entirely on the doctrines of Swedenborg'. Yet when a German critic wrote an account of his visit to Flaxman in 1826, he reported that 'none of his friends could say with certainty that he was a supporter of Swedenborg, but all spoke with great respect of his religious austerity and his great moral worth'.[73]

In 1784 Flaxman had joined the newly established Theosophical Society, founded to promote, translate and publish Swedenborg's writings, attending its meetings in the Middle Temple.[74] In the same year he already possessed some of Swedenborg's books, because he made a loan of some of them to Hayley.[75] From then until he went to Italy, there seems to be no evidence concerning Flaxman's further involvement with the new movement. Whilst he was abroad, the Society expanded rapidly, developing from reading circles into a more established religious organisation, and acquiring a growing number of sympathisers, including Blake. Shortly after Flaxman's return from Italy, one of the most active of the New Church ministers, Joseph Proud, established a chapel in Cross Street, Hatton Garden in 1797, where Flaxman was an active member of the committee for two years until Proud left in 1799 to establish a new chapel elsewhere in London.[76] A plain round font with simple mouldings, carved for the Cross Street chapel, has been traditionally ascribed to Flaxman.[77] But after the late 1790's the evidence suggests that although Flaxman continued to be sympathetic towards the aims of the New Church, he was not actively part of any congregation, a point which even the *Intellectual Repository* obituary admitted.

Apart from the New Church, another side to Swedenborgian activities was the establishment of a society in London in 1810 dedicated to the printing of Swedenborg's works. Flaxman subscribed every year to the new Swedenborg Society's funds from its foundation onwards, and was elected a member of the committee on three occasions, in 1811, 1815 and 1817, but he turned down the position in the first year on the grounds that he was too busy. At the annual meeting in 1816, the Society's *Report* records that in the course of proposing the health of the absent president, C. A. Tulk, Flaxman 'took occasion very forcibly and feelingly to expatiate upon the objects of the Society'.[78] Increasing illness in the last few years of his life prevented him from attending meetings, but he retained his interest in Swedenborgianism. Henry Crabb Robinson noted in his diary in 1823 that he had read to the Flaxmans parts of J. H. Jung-Stilling's works, but 'Flaxman thought his system very inferior to Swedenborg's. Flaxman declared his conviction that Swedenborg has given the true interpretation of the Old and New Testaments, and he believes in him as an inspired teacher. He says that till he read his explanations of the Scriptures, they were to him a painful mystery.'[79] A couple of years later Robinson recorded that Flaxman very much disapproved of Southey's mocking treatment of the New Church in his *Letters from England* (1808), since he 'cannot forgive derision on such a subject'.[80]

One of the most active Swedenborgians outside London was John Clowes in Manchester. Although a member of the Church of England as rector of the parish church of St. John, Clowes took a leading part in translating Swedenborg's writings from Latin into English, making them more accessible to a much wider public, and thus greatly aiding the expansion of the establishment of the New Church. To commemorate his fiftieth anniversary in the parish Flaxman was commissioned in 1818, through C. A. Tulk, to design a tablet for erection in St. John's (Plate 155). Flaxman already knew Clowes, who two years previously had been encouraging the publication of 'The Knight', and they had been together in 1817 when they examined Swedenborg's skull at Tulk's house, after it had been disinterred at the Swedish Church preparatory to being returned to his native country.[81] Flaxman would also have known at least some of Clowes's many publications; his main work *On Mediums* (1813) is referred to in a letter in the year after its publication.[82]

Many of Clowes's tracts show a concern for the

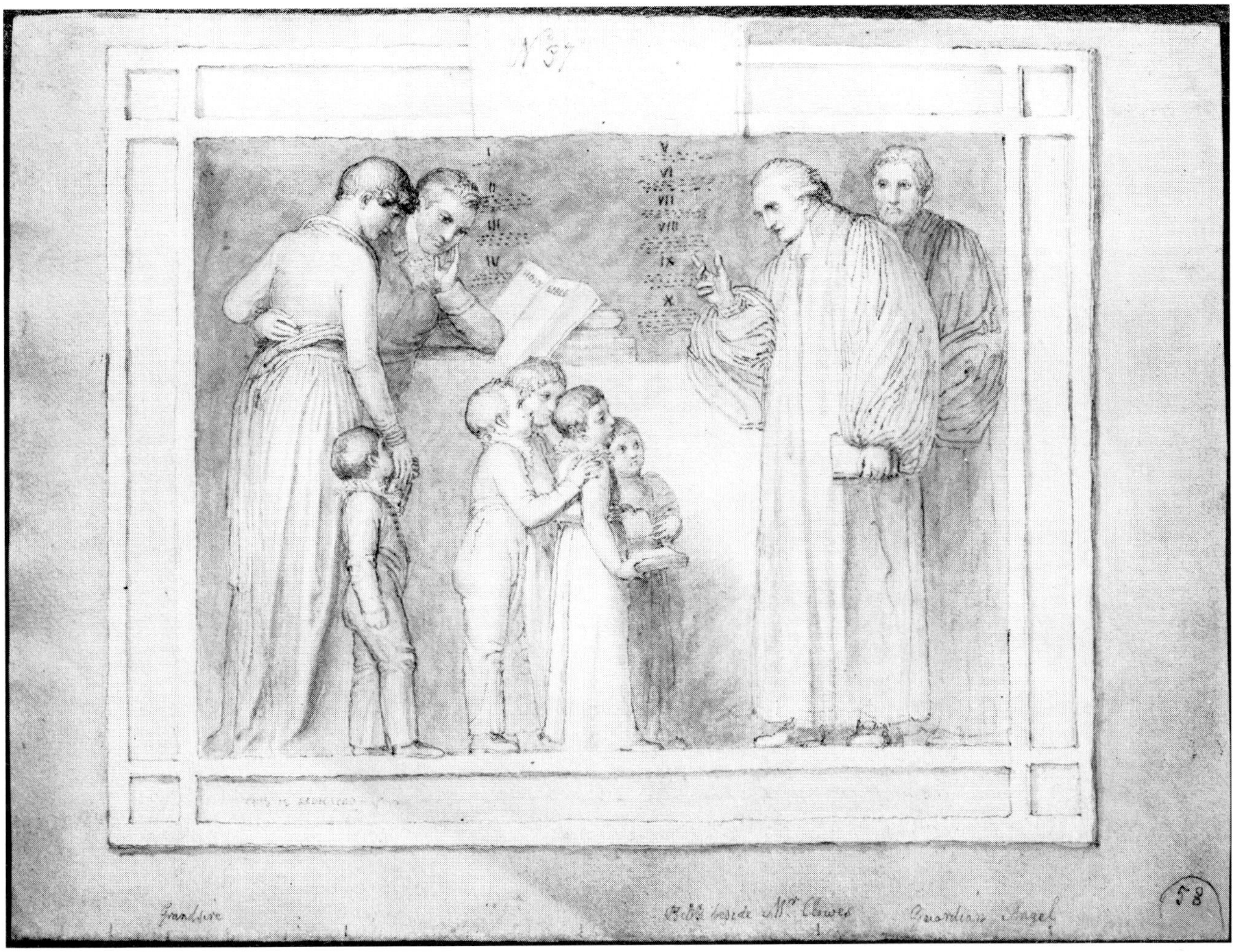

155 *John Clowes: monument: design*, 1818. Pen and ink, pencil and wash, 19 × 26·3 cms.

instruction of children, as he was a prominent campaigner for the establishment of Sunday Schools, as well as the author of pamphlets intended for children's own use. It was natural therefore that children should feature so prominently on Flaxman's relief.[83] Clowes is shown giving instruction on the Ten Commandments which are not only an essential part of the doctrine governing a Christian way of life, but also have a special place in Swedenborg's writings as rare examples of divine revelation to man. As recently as 1816 Clowes had devoted a series of twenty-four sermons to the Ten Commandments, spending most of his time on a Swedenborgian explanation of the double meanings of each, the 'natural' and the 'spiritual'. Behind Clowes himself appears a figure of a guardian angel, who might represent his own personal, Swedenborgian angel.[84] Clowes believed that angels were 'real, personified and organised forms of good, having frequently been seen as such by men like ourselves'.[85]

The difficulty of trying to relate Swedenborgian ideas to any other specific sculpture by Flaxman[86] can be demonstrated in the *Nelson* monument (Plate 220), as there is a New Church sermon on Nelson's death, delivered in York Street Chapel by Proud in 1806, and printed in that year. Amongst the fairly substantial body of Swedenborgian sermons that were published, this is the only one which because of its subject can be related to a particular monument by Flaxman. After talking in the customary New Church way about 'external' and 'internal' evil, resulting in crimes and wars, Proud told his congregation: 'Cultivate a true patriotic spirit; I do not call upon you in the trite and threadbare language to imitate the Spartan, the Greek, or the Roman; but be Christians, rally under the

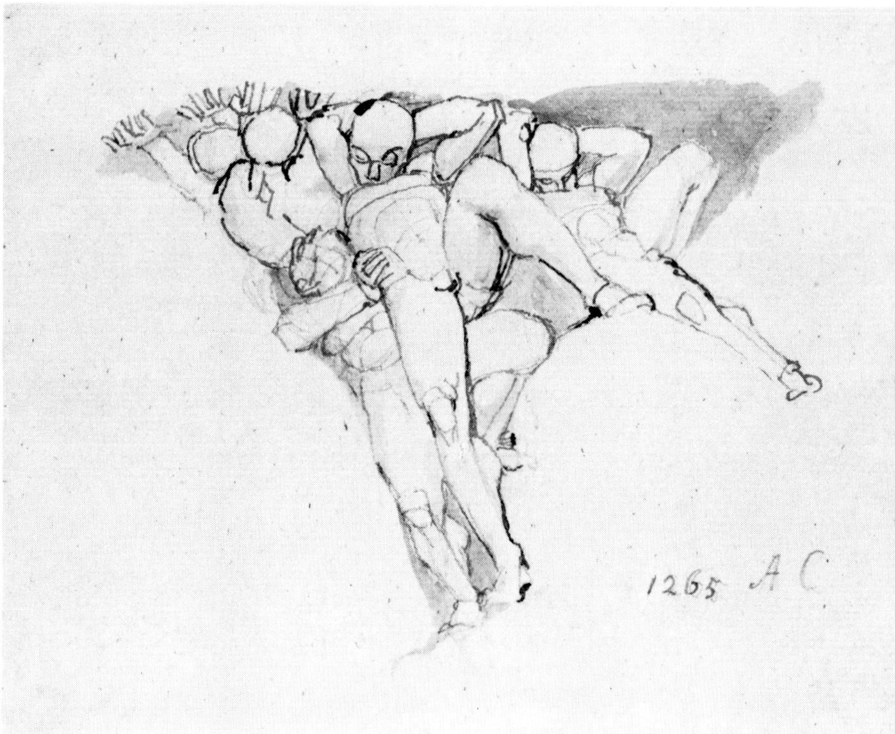

156 *Antediluvian Spirits pressing down upon my Head (Arcana Coelestia).* Pen and ink and wash, 13 × 14·9 cms.

standard of Jesus Christ, and you will excell them all'. Flaxman's monument shows a contrary point of view in which the Christian message is subservient, unusually for Flaxman, to a combination of images that are patriotic and moralistic, rendered in a style that is classical.

It has been claimed that his 'Knight' shows a Swedenborgian influence[87]. If one looks in New Church literature for possibly related material, it can be found in the collection of *Hymns and Spiritual Songs* which Proud edited for the use of New Church congregations. The ninety-first hymn is on the theme of victory over Satan, Death and Hell. This, taken together with other hymns, could be said to underly the theme of the 'Knight', especially as Swedenborgians believed in good and evil spirits attendant on man. But a more obvious source for the imagery of the 'Knight' lies further back in *Pilgrim's Progress*, as already mentioned, where the aggressive sense of evil—used by Flaxman—is contrary to Swedenborg's more passive idea. One could say, however, that Flaxman's familiarity with Swedenborgianism confirmed an interest in a theme already inspired by earlier Christian literature.

Flaxman executed a few drawings to Swedenborg's own writings, including passages from his major work, the *Arcana Coelestia*, as well as his *Christian Religion*[88]. Although Swedenborg's writings are mystical, and thus difficult to externalise in visual images, Flaxman succeeded in choosing passages in which a more concrete symbolism could be turned into pen and ink drawings. Perhaps some of these passages were singled out for his attention by C. A. Tulk, since a contemporary records that 'Flaxman felt so much interested in the writings as to make many drawings from them' after passages had been read out to him by Tulk.[89] The drawing reproduced in Plate 156 is typical of this series, illustrating the following passage from the *Arcana*, in which Swedenborg is elaborating on the first book of the Old Testament:[90] 'At a certain height above my head were some spirits, who flowed into my thoughts, and kept them as if bound, so that I was for some time in obscurity. They pressed down upon me with considerable force. The spirits around me, in like manner, were kept as it were bound by them, so that they could think of little but what thus flowed in; and this continued till they were excited to indignation. I was informed that these spirits were those who lived before the flood'.

5 Anatomy and Nature

The study of anatomy was a basic part of any student's

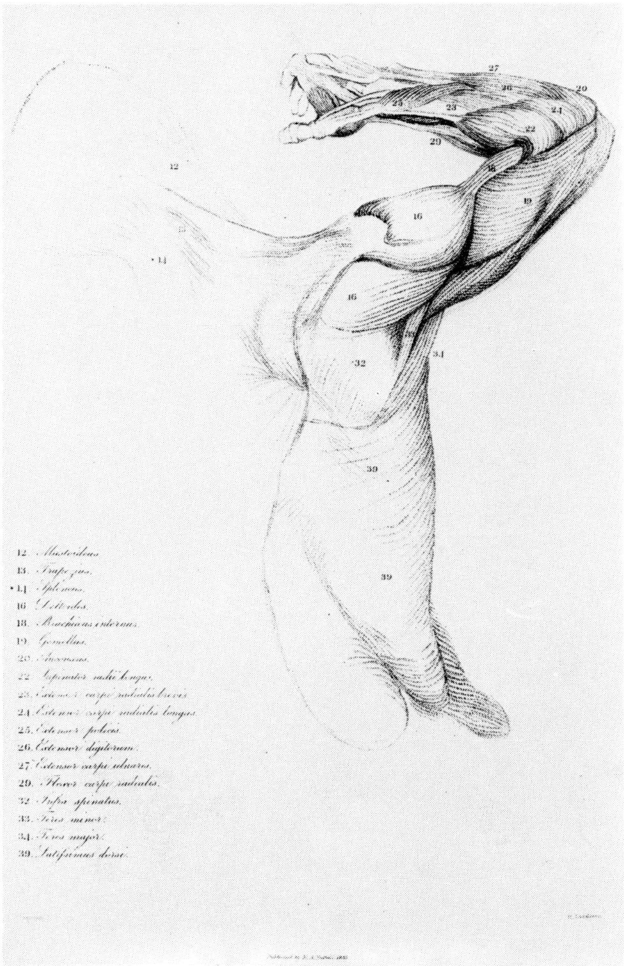

157 *Arm and Part of the Torso.* Engraving, 43·5 × 30·8 cms, after Flaxman by Henry Landseer. *Anatomical Studies*, 1833, Plate 12.

training and Flaxman throughout his life never relinquished these studies. He kept a human skeleton in his studio (it was eventually acquired by Soane), and his anatomical knowledge can be seen from the early self-portrait with one hand placed on a skull (Plate 6), to the posthumous publication by Henry Landseer of Flaxman's *Anatomical Studies of the Bones and Muscles for the Use of Artists* in 1833. As a student at the Royal Academy Flaxman would have benefited from the teaching of William Hunter. In Flaxman's own day as a Professor, the chair of anatomy was held by the equally distinguished anatomist Sir Anthony Carlisle. In addition to these experts Flaxman was in correspondence, before he had visited Scotland, with the third of the famous generation of Edinburgh anatomists, all of whom were called Alexander Monro. Flaxman sent him a present in 1812 of what purported to be Raphael's skull, received in 1813 letters of introduction from him to Sir Walter Scott and the Earl of Buchan, for use during his Scottish tour, and carved his grandfather's bust (in the Upper Library, Old College, Edinburgh University).[91] Flaxman owned the third Alexander Monro's *Outlines of the Anatomy of the Human Body* (1813), the influential and widely used *Anatomy of Expression in Painting* (1806) by Sir Charles Bell, as well as other anatomical books including Stubbs's *Anatomy of the Horse* (1766).[92]

Apart from Flaxman's anatomical drawings, many of which are contained in three of his sketchbooks in the Fitzwilliam Museum, the main body of such drawings are those used as the basis for the posthumous engravings in the *Anatomical Studies*. The preface, by William Robertson, justified the publication on the grounds that existing anatomical treatises were not only too costly, but also too specialised for the requirements of an artist. Flaxman's drawings of both myological and skeletal studies, at the modest price of £1.4s., must therefore have been invaluable. Although some of the drawings are of the kind one expects to find in any anatomical treatise, such as frontal images clearly analysed, others are drawn from oblique angles that would be of use only to an artist. Poses of parts of the body are often those of an artist's model in a life class, stripped of clothes and flesh. Even some of the drawings of skeletons are taken from oblique angles. That the drawings of skeletons have been taken from actual examples is clearly shown in one plate in which an imperfect specimen with a defective spine has been drawn, whereas a textbook would have chosen a flawless example. All the drawings are accurate and clear, with no obscuring shading, and are excellent of their kind. The drawing reproduced in Plate 157, depicting a bent arm, is a good example of Flaxman's use of oblique angles to provide more information on the working of the muscles in action than a straightforward anatomical illustration would normally do.

Assessments of Flaxman's art shortly after his death stressed his great debt to the art of classical antiquity, and some perceptive early writers spotted his debt to medieval art, but one other major source was sometimes overlooked, namely that of nature itself.

In some of Flaxman's illustrations and tombs the sources for the pose of a Penelope, or a figure of Resignation, or a reclining tomb figure (Plates 93, 174, 211) can be found in intimate contemporary poses of women sewing, relaxing whilst reading, quietly sitting looking out of a window, and other genre scenes of everyday life. Flaxman's studies of children, and the theme of the mother and child, are crucial for the

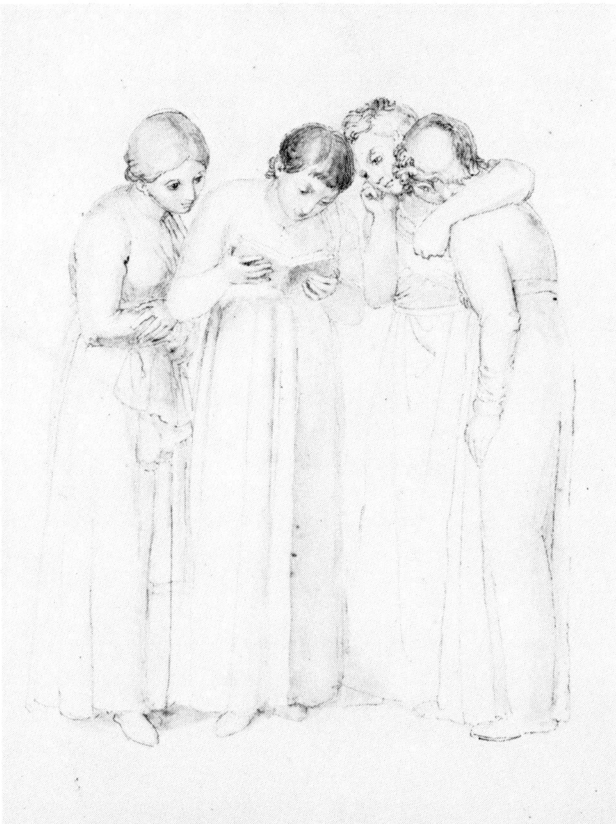

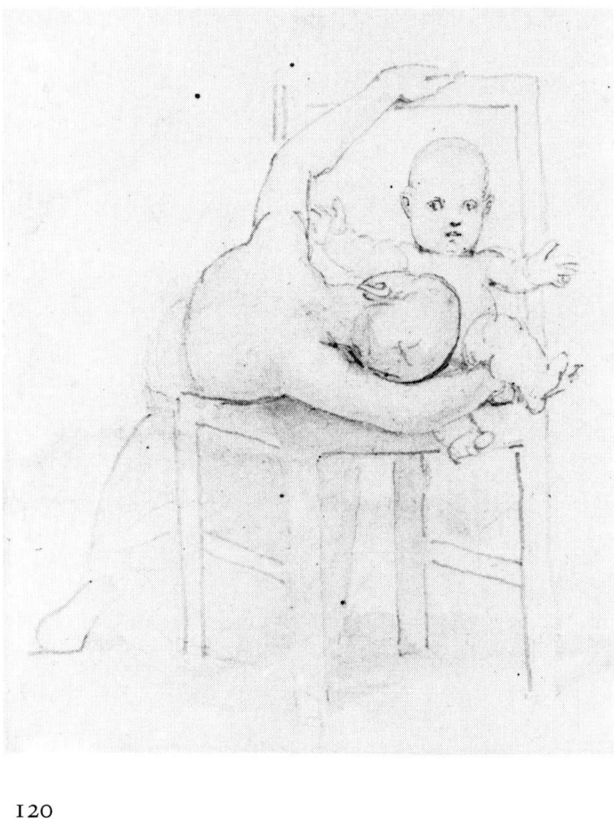

understanding of such monuments as the one to *Lady Fitzharris* (Plates 196 and 197). Some of these sources have already been discussed in this chapter, whilst those relating to tombs will be considered in Chapter VI. There is no need to go back continually to examples in earlier art to find Flaxman's sources; he was just as likely to take his poses from the everyday world. Such a source is evident not only from his own drawings, but also from diary entries and other contemporary comments.

Whilst in Italy, Flaxman had sent home some practical advice for his sister to follow when drawing, stressing the importance of observing nature. The passage has already been quoted at length, but it is worth repeating here one part, as it so obviously described his own practice. His sister was told 'that when she makes a drawing she may get some of her friends to sit for each of the figures, never to produce anything without studying nature in this manner'.[93] Surrounded as he was when he wrote the letter by the art of the past, and above all by classical antiquity, he nevertheless stressed the paramount importance of nature, as any other artist would have done.

Some of Flaxman's drawings of figure compositions are inscribed 'from Nature', and cannot usually be connected directly with any particular tomb or illustration. A few of these drawings are rough sketches, others are carefully finished with a shaded wash, like the delightfully intimate group of four girls reading in Plate 158. Flaxman loved to draw children of all ages, either grouped or singly, and in some of his sketches he captured them in the most playful of moods like the domestic romp that is portrayed in Plate 159, or drew children whilst dancing or skipping (Plate 108). Sometimes in his drawings he puts together on one sheet different kinds of groups of children and adults. In the British Museum for example, there is a sheet of such groups labelled 'Youthful gaiety', 'Divided attention', 'Maternal care' and 'Concern'. Such a variety of poses and emotions would form part of an enquiring and expanding dossier on the life around him, to which Flaxman could turn for reference for later compositional ideas.

Flaxman also attached great importance to studies of drapery. He devoted a whole lecture to the subject at the Royal Academy, and what he told his students,

158 (*above left*) *Four Girls Reading*. Pen and ink and wash, 35·2 × 26 cms.

159 (*left*) *Domestic Scene*. Pen and ink and wash, 16 × 11·3 cms.

together with his many drawings, show an interest not only in the draperies of ancient sculptures and later works of art, but also in modern dress and cloaks. Most of the drapery drawings belong to the period when Flaxman was in Italy, and have already been discussed. If put together with other, not easily datable, drawings they show a wide range of interests in drapery from peasant cloaks to large skirts, and even to laundry blowing on the washing line (Plate 160).

Flaxman also occasionally drew plants and animals, including not only lions (which would eventually be useful allegorically) but also horses, cows and cats. His plant drawings include two sheets of leaves of an artichoke plant: these he gave to Soane (Plate 161). Flaxman's interest in botany was put to good use in the banana trees that appear on the relief of the monument to Sir William Jones (Plate 162). Apart from studying nature at first hand, Flaxman also had a good collection of casts of foliage and flowers in his studio, which unfortunately disappeared after his death.[94]

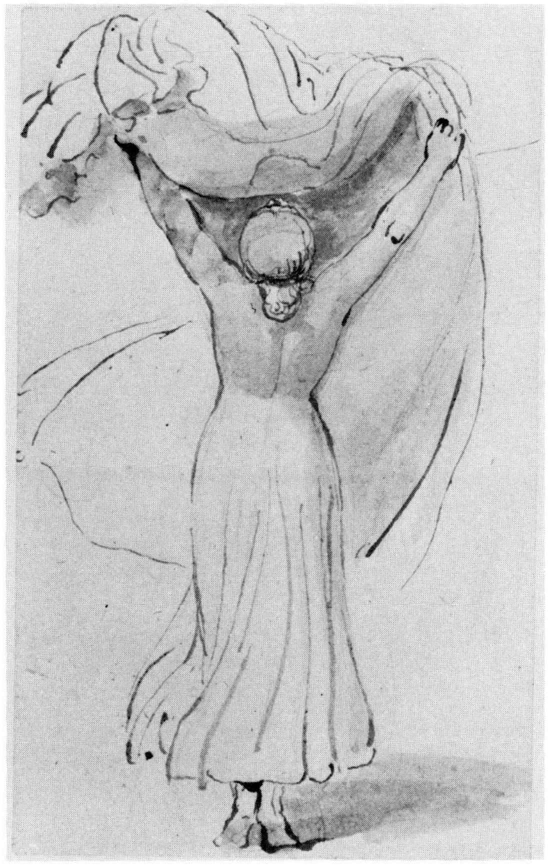

160 *Woman with Washing on a Line.* Pen and ink and wash, 20·4 × 13 cms.

161 *Artichoke Plant Leaves.* Pencil, 23·3 × 40·6 cms.

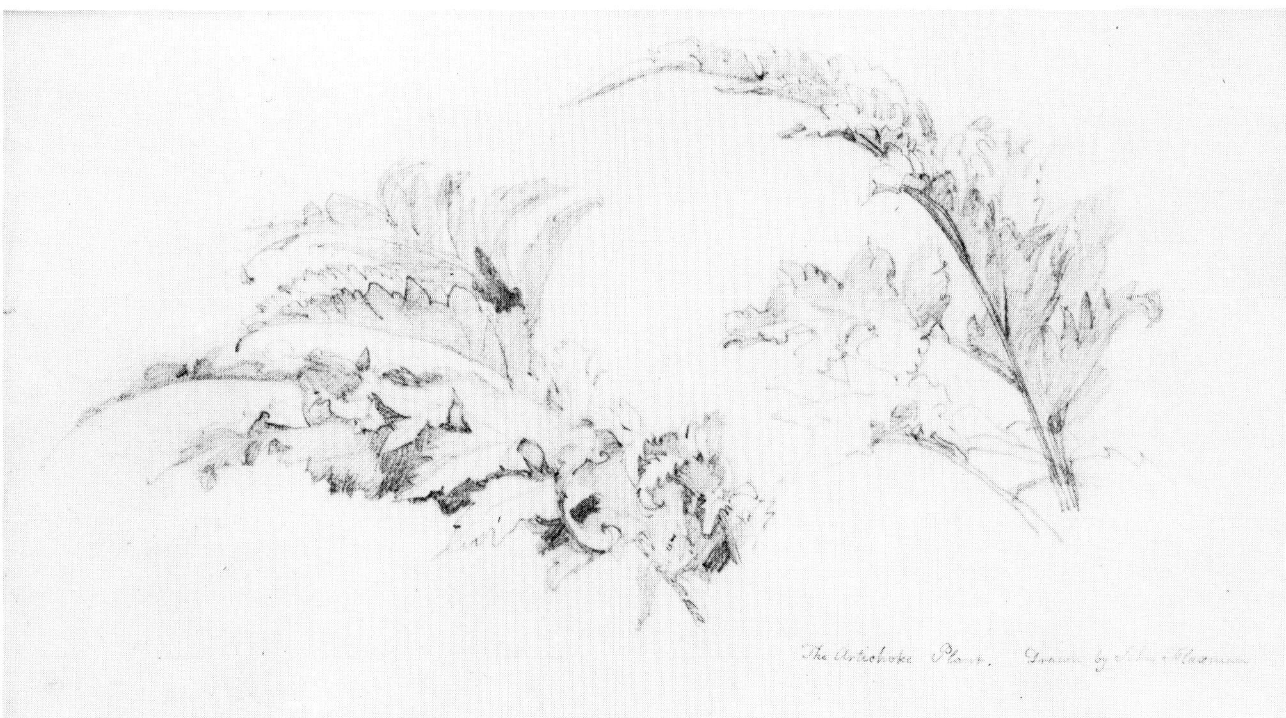

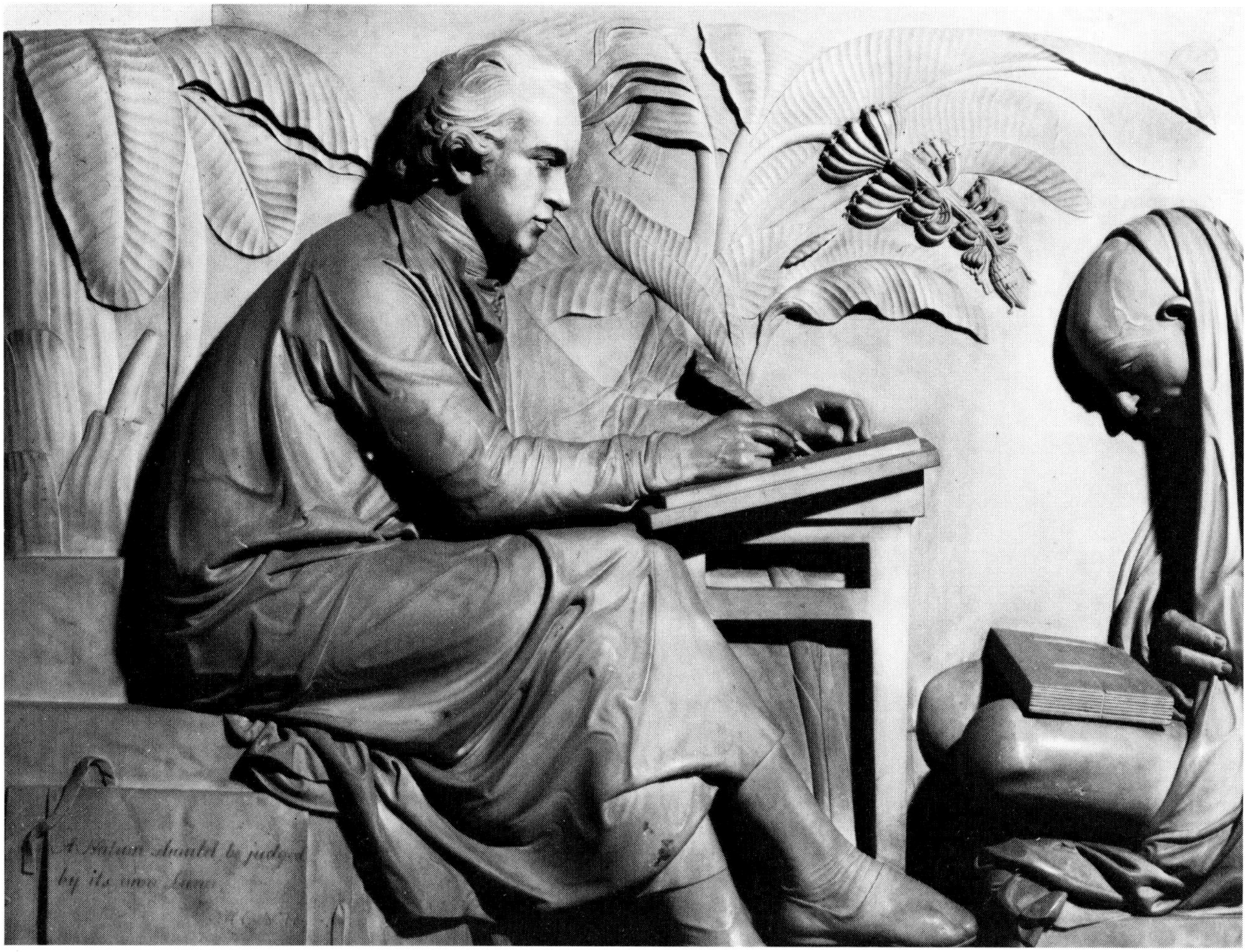

162 *Sir William Jones: monument: detail of Banana tree*, 1796. University College Chapel, Oxford

The anatomical, life, drapery and other drawings taken from subjects in the world around him, show how fundamental nature was to Flaxman in the creative process. He stressed its importance whenever he had the opportunity: 'although principles may be laid down from works of art', he wrote once, 'practice can only be acquired by a diligent imitation of nature.'[95] When Holman Hunt was explaining the aims of the Pre-Raphaelites as 'simply fuller Nature', he included Flaxman amongst earlier artists who 'are always most able in those works in which their own direct reading of Nature overpowers their obedience to previous example'.[96]

CHAPTER VI

Sculptor of Tombs: after 1794

George Cruikshank caricatured the Antiquarian Society in 1812, placing Flaxman in one corner of the print expounding from an open Bible (Plate 163). When Fuseli set out to hear Flaxman's first lecture at the Royal Academy, he is reported to have said rather scathingly that he was going to 'sermon the first by the Reverend John Flaxman'.[1] These two satirical references to the dominant role of religion in Flaxman's life are clear indications of how important this aspect of his art was in the eyes of contemporaries, and many monuments in cathedrals and churches are still reminders of the extent of the business in funerary works run from his studio. Tombs were to occupy most of Flaxman's time from 1794 onwards. He kept himself regularly in the public eye as a designer of tombs by often showing models or completed sculptures for monuments amongst his works at Royal Academy exhibitions, and there were still commissions to be fulfilled at the time of his death which had to be completed by studio assistants. His reputation as a designer of monuments had been firmly established on his return from Italy by his *Mansfield* tomb, even before its erection in Westminster Abbey in 1801 (Plate 76). He had chosen the model for this monument as his sole contribution to the Royal Academy exhibition in 1796, and in a letter written at the time his wife records how important the choice was to be because it 'has brought several amateurs to see him, among the rest Lord Lansdowne and Durham's noble Bishop who wishes on his return to town to become more acquainted with my hero'.[2]

Towards the end of his stay in Italy, Flaxman explained in a letter that all his outline engravings were intended to show 'how any story may be represented in a series of compositions on principles of the ancients, of which as soon as I return to England I intend to give specimens in sculpture of different kinds, in groups of bas-reliefs, suited to all purposes of sacred and civil architecture'.[3] He little knew at the time that he was to receive few civil commissions, and that even in sacred works he was to have little opportunity to show relief panels carved in a style equivalent to that of his illustrations. Flaxman was perhaps forgetting that contemporaries scarcely knew his secular commissions executed in Italy, important though they were in his own eyes. The *Fury of Athamas* was first captured by the French troops, and even when it finally arrived in England it disappeared into the privacy of a country-house, and was never engraved. His *Hercules and Hebe* was never finished. His *Cephalus and Aurora* was also bought for a private collection, but at least it was put in a London house regularly open to visitors, and was to feature as part of an engraving in Hope's *Household*

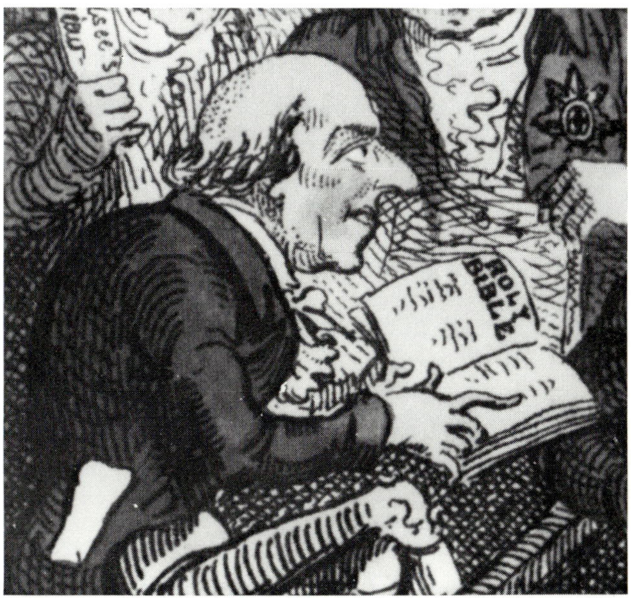

163 George Cruikshank: *The Antiquarian Society*, 1812. Etching, detail showing John Flaxman.

Furniture in 1807. The great admiration in which the two patrons of the *Athamas* and *Cephalus and Aurora* held Flaxman did not lead to a flood of similar commissions from other clients. Instead, Flaxman was to emerge as a major designer of funerary monuments at the turn of the eighteenth century, creating essentially Christian rather than pagan works in an age of Neoclassicism. Foreign visitors to his studio in the 1820's recorded with surprise how important monuments had become for Flaxman, since abroad he was known almost exclusively through his illustrations to classical authors and to Dante. 'In his workshop', wrote A.W. von Schlegel, 'I found him occupied with great works of sculpture, especially tombs . . . . These special commissions, and also perhaps the pious bent of his disposition, distanced him in later life from mythological subjects, the real field of the sculptor.'[4]

In the last year of his life Flaxman was visited by another German critic who recorded in detail their conversation, providing a particularly valuable record of the sculptor's views, especially on the subject of Christianity and of monuments. Flaxman did not usually talk with such frankness according to C. R. Cockerell, so it is fortunate that much of the conversation was written down.[5] The visitor told Flaxman 'You still love antique art, as at the time when you made your sketches for Homer and Aeschylus. I thought the poetry of the Greek world was the principal area for your artistic activity and was thus surprised when I saw just how sincerely you grasp Christian subjects, and how frequently you occupy yourself with them'. Later in the interview, to clarify this misunderstanding with 'an earnestness which seemed to come from inner motivation', Flaxman said 'The purpose of my lectures at the Academy was to demonstrate that art can perform greater things in the sphere of Christianity than in that of paganism, for Christian ideas are more noble than pagan, and the best that the art of the Greeks and Romans has produced is also contained in Christian ideas, for example the battle of the giants, which is admirably depicted by the Apocalypse.' This aim is not, in fact, so clearly evident in the published lectures themselves where it has become buried under facts and examples, and it is interesting to hear Flaxman expressing his intentions with such clarity in the course of the interview. He went on to tell his visitor 'The most noble feature of Greek art arose from remembering the idea of a single God and the fall of the human race, which had been left over from paganism and was only clarified again through Christ; the truth, grace and physical beauty of nature can be applied just as well to Christian subjects as to pagan ones, and I maintain that in the Old and New Testaments more favourable subjects for art can be found than in pagan mythology.' After a digression Flaxman resumed the discussion by saying 'In my opinion art and science are given to man to lead him from destruction and wickedness (into which the world plunged before and after the appearance of Christianity) towards improvement, to reveal to him a feeling for what is noble and to keep alive his higher destiny.' He went on to say that the highest motive of an artist 'must always be love of excellence, the striving for excellence and all opposition is punished by disappearing and being forgotten about. The artist who panders to the depravity, ruin and superficiality of his fellows is sooner or later despised, his works do not last, and he cannot be happy in his own life. That the golden age of Greek art was not one of depravity is revealed to us by the high-minded ideas of Plato, thoughts which were expressed not only in his writings, but which were widespread among a great number of educated minds.'

Flaxman's high ideals, based on both classical art and Christian belief, found expression in one of the most extensive ranges of religious works executed by any European artist in Flaxman's lifetime. The main outlet of this expression was in monuments, paralleled by the lesser number of his religious illustrations. In designing tombs, Flaxman was fusing different trends current in the late eighteenth century. His forms were often borrowed in part from the architecture and sculpture of classical antiquity which meant using secular sources, the more pagan side of the Enlightenment. The frequent references back to a classical or to a medieval past Flaxman also shared with many of his contemporaries in an area which is sometimes described as early Romanticism. In addition, his tombs embody a contemporary vogue for melancholy and Christian sentiment, further aspects of taste which can be called early Romantic.

The Christian ideals which inspired Flaxman's sculptures and drawings were those current from the middle of the eighteenth century, and the contemporary attitude to death is particularly relevant to the designs of Flaxman's tombs. Death was no longer a fearful or macabre occasion to be commemorated with a range of imagery that included skeletons. These had almost entirely disappeared from tombs in Flaxman's day (Plate 164). Death had become an acceptable and almost beautiful event demanding a pious and innocent response, which was imbued with a gentle melancholy and sentimental charm. The melancholy was neither deep nor pessimistic nor inspired by religious terror (which the eighteenth century called 'black' melan-

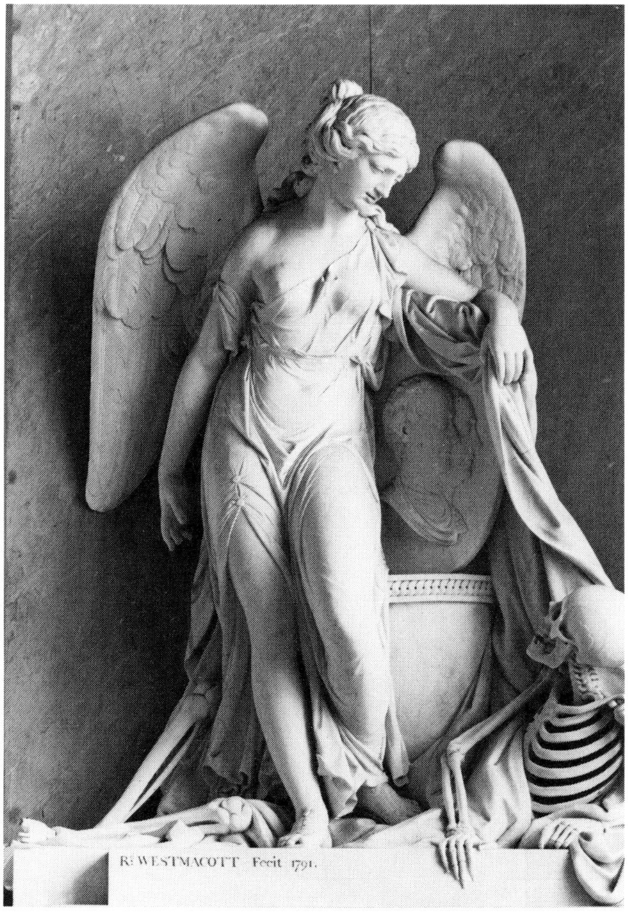

164 Richard Westmacott the elder: *James Lenox Dutton: monument: detail.* 1791.
St. Mary Magdalene, Sherborne, Gloucestershire.

choly). Rather, death inspired 'sweet' or 'white' melancholy, of which there are countless examples in contemporary literature. Parallel to the secularism and the immorality of the time was an equally strong trend of religious piety, which was sincere and without affectation, producing much devotional writing in the form of poetry, prose and prayers by such authors as Samuel Johnson. The *Olney Hymns*, frequently reprinted from 1779 onwards, and to which William Cowper contributed some of the finest devotional verse of the period, were widely read examples of a growing evangelicalism. In a hymn by Cowper devoted to mourning one reads:

'The favour'd souls who know
What glories shine in Him,
Pant for his presence, as the roe
Pants for the living stream'. . . .

The cult of melancholy in poetry was dominated by Gray's famous masterpiece of the *Elegy written in a Country Churchyard* (1751), which was to influence the increasing number of meditations on the brevity of mortal life and on death. A similar mood lies behind the widely read *Complaint, or night-thoughts* of Edward Young (1742):

'Why start at death! Where is he? Death arrived,
Is past; not come, or gone, he's never here.
Ere hope, sensation fails; black-boding man
Receives, not suffers, death's tremendous blow.
The knell, the shroud, the mattock, and the grave;
The deep damp vault, the darkness and the worm;
These are the bugbears of a winter's eve,
The terrors of the living, not the dead.'

Such Romantic melancholy is continued, for example, in the sonnets that Sir Brooke Boothby wrote at the end of the century in grieving commemoration of his daughter Penelope, in which one poem starts:

'Yes, there's a charm in grief; the heart-drawn tears,
That down my breast so oft in silence flow,
I would not for the warmest joys forego,
When hope's bright beam the youthful bosom cheers. . . .'[6]

Christianity had become sentimentalised by the time Flaxman was designing his monuments, and he was as much a man of feeling in stone as Young or Boothby in their verses.[7]

1 Life everlasting

An afflicted mother comforted by an angel was the title Flaxman used for the model of his monument to *Mary Lushington* when he exhibited it at the Royal Academy in 1800 (Plate 165). The composition, like its title, is unmistakably Christian in theme. A winged angel is consoling a grieving mother lying prostrate across the lid of a sarcophagus by drawing her attention to the inscription on the arch above: 'Blessed are they that mourn for they shall be comforted'. Most of Flaxman's monuments, as one might expect, carry mottoes largely derived from the New Testament, combined with often lengthy inscriptions. William Hayley provided the words for the *Mary Lushington* slab, in which he lay stress on the grief at the loss of an eldest daughter aged twenty-five. But it was a grief that could be surmounted as a result of Christian belief:

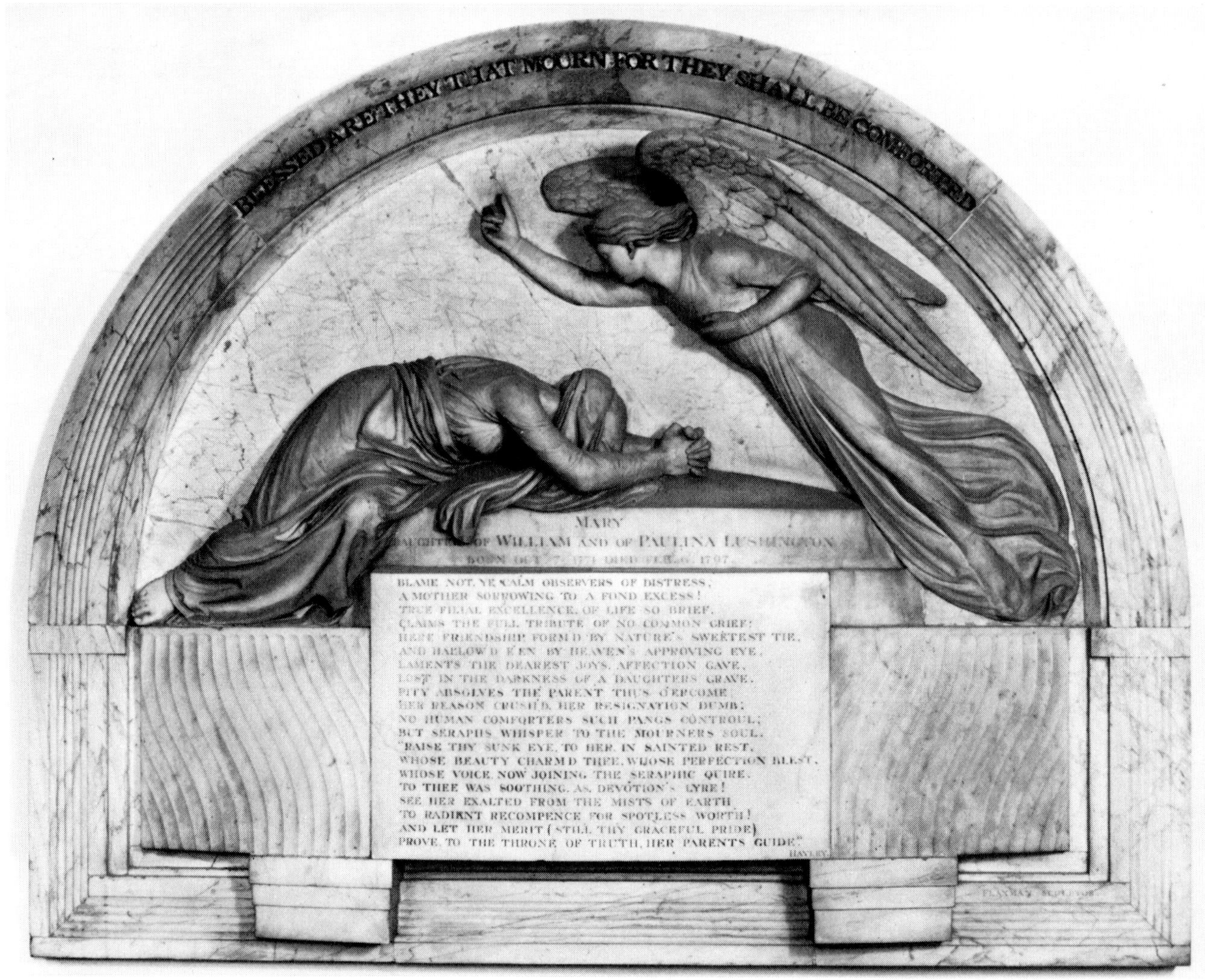

165 *Mrs. Mary Blackshaw (Mary Lushington): monument,* 1798–99.
St. Mary, Lewisham, Kent

'. . . Pity absolves the parent thus o'ercome;
Her reason crush'd, her resignation dumb.
No human comforters such pangs controul;
But seraphs whisper to the mourner's soul:
"Raise thy sunk eye to her in sainted rest,
Whose beauty charm's thee, whose perfection
blest . . ." '

The imagery and the words both draw attention to a transcendental God, with a clear indication of a Christian salvation. In some of his other monuments Flaxman even shows the spirit of the deceased rising to heaven, or illustrating passages from the New Testament which demonstrate the belief in a resurrection. Such profoundly Christian works justify one Victorian critic's assessment of Flaxman as the 'Fra Angelico of sculpture'.[8]

The theme and the style of the *Mary Lushington* monument are both clear indications of future tombs, even if on this occasion the various stylistic elements of the design remain disparate, failing to fuse into a harmonious whole. Flaxman has combined antique sarcophagus and drapery forms with an angel whose anatomy is essentially medieval in its disproportionate elongation. These elements were already evident in his style before going to Italy; to them he has now added a certain elegance, especially in the angel, deriving from the Quattrocento. Similar elegant angels had already made their appearance amongst his illustrations to Dante (Plates 128 and 130), and this new form will from now onwards predominate in his tomb designs. Another lesson learnt from his Italian visit is evident in the pose of the mother, which is reminiscent of that of the *St. Cecilia* by Maderno in Santa Cecilia in Trastevere in Rome, a work sculpted in a century from which Flaxman usually derived little inspiration, save when the works, like Maderno's, are restrained. The added poignancy of a grief that is hidden—a device familiar from ancient Greek tragedy onwards—was to be used on some of Flaxman's subsequent monuments.[9]

Flaxman re-used the basic layout of the composition of the *Mary Lushington* monument a few years later, refining its imperfections into a more rhythmical design, when commemorating *Isaac Hawkins Browne* the elder, in his old college, Trinity, Cambridge (Plate 166). This rather belated monument (since Browne had died in 1760) was exhibited in its marble version at the Royal Academy in 1805 with the title of *Angels strewing flowers on the Tomb of a deceased Poet.* Hawkins Browne was a poet whose books Flaxman would undoubtedly have found sympathetic since they contained lines which aptly describe his own approach to art. Just as Shaftesbury was an important source at the end of the century for the link Neoclassicists made between art and morality, so he was also an influence on Browne's *Design and Beauty* (1734). This poem contains lines very appropriate to the art of the period around 1800 when Browne wrote that 'the true sublime attains / The noblest purpose by the simplest means', and on the following page argued that 'Alike in art simplicity bestows / An awful stillness and sublime repose; / Great without pomp.'

At the same time as he was working on the *Mary Lushington* monument, Flaxman was treating a similar theme for another tomb on a vertical panel. As the figures on the monument to *Agnes Cromwell* (Plate 167) are not restricted to the confines of an earthbound semi-circle, Flaxman is much more successful in suggesting a transcendentalism in keeping with the religious beliefs he is commemorating. He was to use this vertical format on many subsequent tombs. He was also from now onwards to often use this type of angel without wings. When he carved them in this form on the *Isaac Hawkins Browne* monument a Cambridge don was to object because he presumably thought that wingless ethereal beings might be mistaken for pagan spirits rather than Christian angels,[10] but Flaxman successfully imbued these beings of classical origin with an unmistakably Christian, and contemporary, sentiment.

Agnes Cromwell was the daughter of a naval captain and had died at the age of eighteen. Her youthful figure

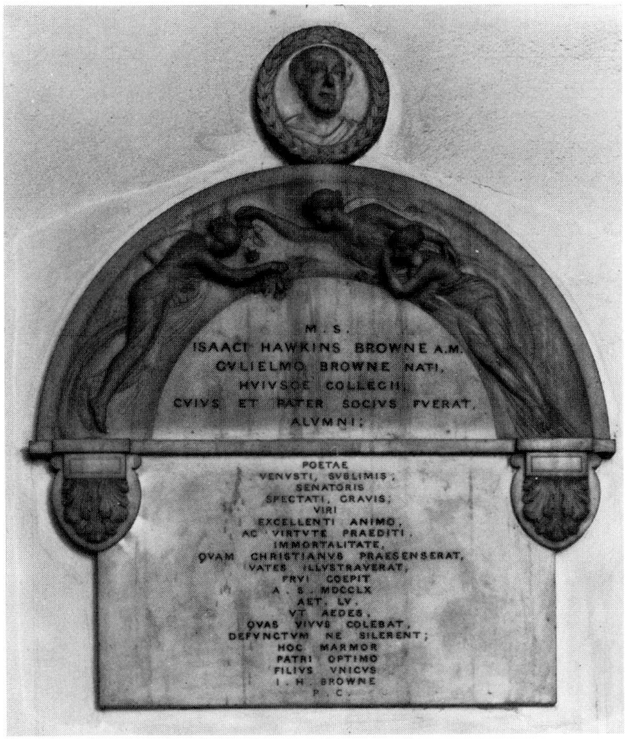

166 *Isaac Hawkins Browne: monument.* 1805. Trinity College Chapel, Cambridge.

is being born heavenwards by three angels, her hands clasped in prayer, gazing up in the direction of the inscription on the pediment, 'Come thou blessed'. The elegantly curving group of four figures amply fills the space of the stele without overcrowding it. The carving ranges from very low to high relief, creating a subtle balance between linearity and chiaroscuro, and thus giving the surface of the marble both variety and vitality. Flaxman has expressed pathos and devotion through one of the most graceful and delicate of all his compositions. He has fused the classicism of the stele and of the draperies with his new-found Quattrocento elegance, using as the basis for his composition the well established formula of an apotheosis (Plate 168). He also brought to the design on the *Cromwell* monument his experience in working on the *Homer* illustrations. There the fusion of figures into a continuously curving movement had been successfully exploited in the plate showing Thetis ordering the Nereids to descend into the sea (Plate 169).[11]

This small scale monument was to become one of Flaxman's most influential works, with many subsequent imitations by other sculptors. It was well known at the time not only from the exhibition of the marble relief itself at the Royal Academy in 1800 and

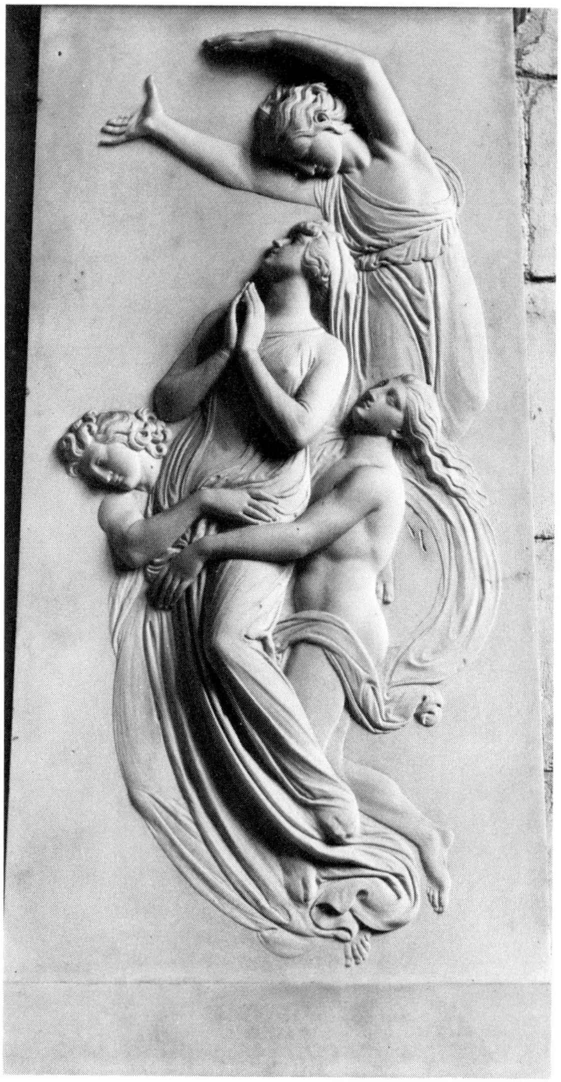

167 *Miss Agnes Cromwell: monument*, 1798–1800.

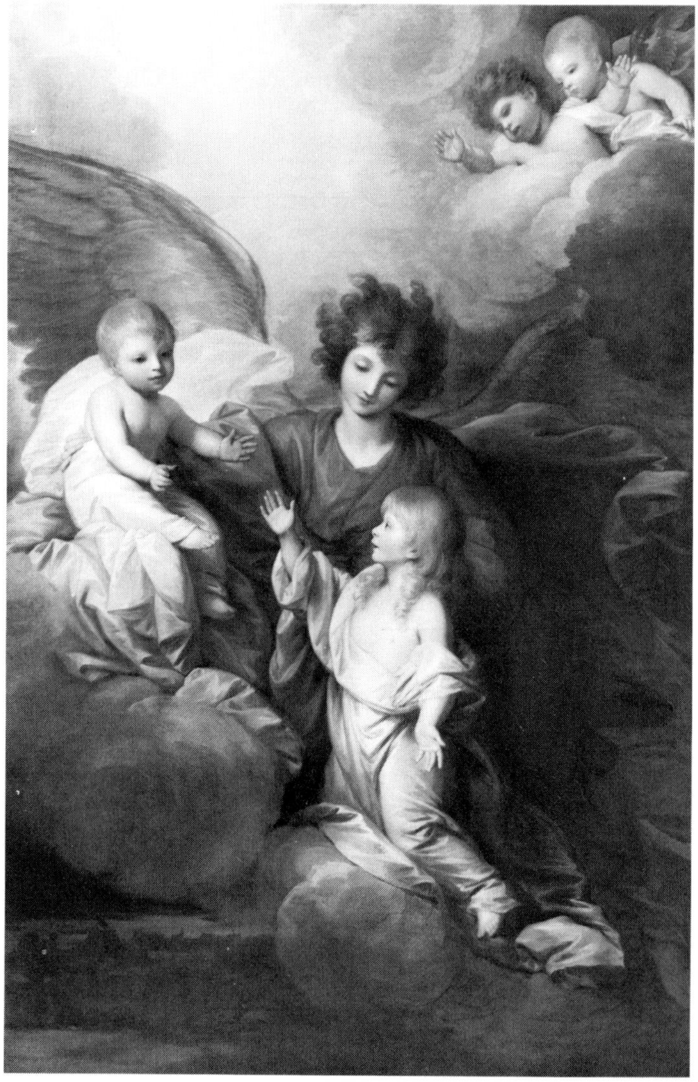

168 Benjamin West: *The Apotheosis of Prince Octavius*, 1783.

the small bas-relief he had shown there three years previously with the title *Come thou beloved*, but also from the plaster models which could have been seen in his studio, as well as the engraving that appeared in James Dallaway's account of Chichester Cathedral which was based on a drawing which Flaxman had provided.[12]

Chichester Cathedral already contained two of Flaxman's monuments when he received the *Cromwell* commission: to *William Collins* (Plate 75) and to *Jane Smith* (1796). He had therefore written to Hayley with great pleasure in the summer of 1798 to tell him that 'I am going to make another little monument for Chichester Cathedral price £50.'[13] The *Collins* and the *Cromwell* monuments were to remain, according to the sculptor's sister-in-law, his favourite works.[14] The *Cromwell* monument was the kind of work by Flaxman that would have inspired some of the perceptive comments made by Lawrence in 1826 when he so aptly pinpointed the best and most original aspects of Flaxman's designs for tombs: 'not even in Raphael have the gentler feelings and sorrows of human nature been traced with more human pathos'.[15]

Flaxman re-used the design for the Cromwell monument on several occasions, thus demonstrating its popularity.[16] He also re-worked the theme of the resurrection, retaining the basic idea of rising figures, as in his monument to *Elizabeth Knight*, using for this commission the biblical text 'Then shall the good be received into life everlasting' (Plate 170),[17] in which

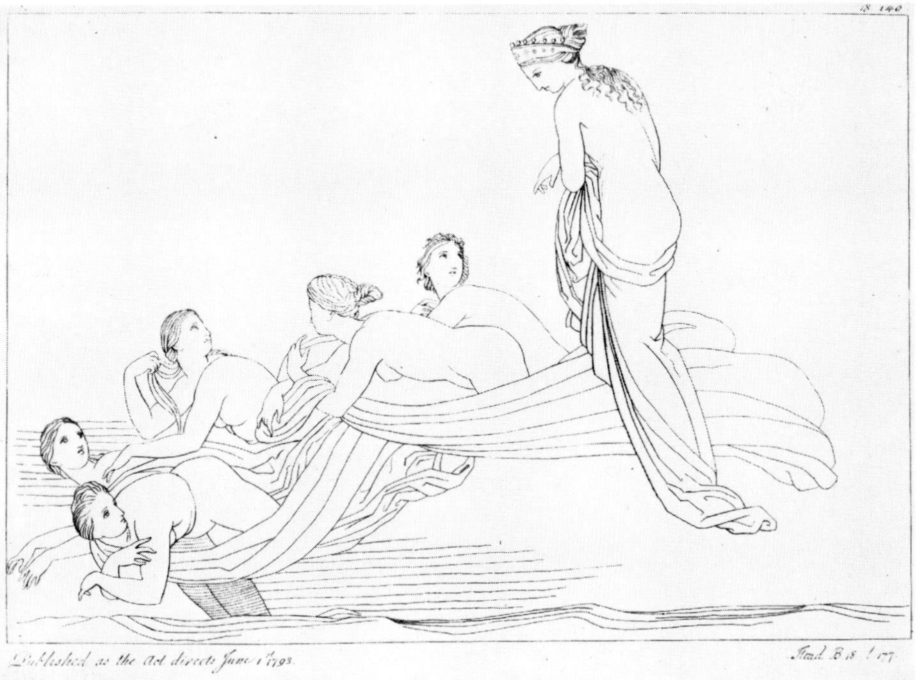

169 *Thetis ordering the Nereids to descend into the Sea.* Engraving, 18·2 × 25·2 cms. after Flaxman by Thomas Piroli. *Iliad*, 1793, Plate 23.

the white marble figures are placed against a grained, darker marble background, a colour contrast which Flaxman rarely exploited. In the design for the monument to *Mary Lady Rendlesham*, the image of the spirit of the deceased being carried up to heaven by an angel appears on a low relief panel mounted above two mourners carved almost in the round (Plate 171), also an unusual tomb for Flaxman since he rarely combined a relief with freestanding figures in this way, producing a strikingly different arrangement from usual.

The theme of Flaxman's most elaborate, privately commissioned monument can also be related to this group of tombs. In 1806 Sir Francis Baring, a wealthy London merchant, Director and Chairman of the East India Company and a Member of Parliament, ordered a monument to commemorate his wife who had died two years previously. Sir Francis himself died in 1810 before the monument was completed, and by the time it was erected in the family church of St. Mary, in the village of Micheldever in Hampshire, the monument commemorated not only Sir Francis and Lady Baring, but also two grand-daughters. Even more epitaphs were to be added later in the course of the nineteenth century. The final cost, partially met by Sir Francis, and partially by his son Sir Thomas, amounted to the handsome sum of £1,387.

The design of the *Baring* monument is unique in Flaxman's *oeuvre* in that it consists of three separate wall panels, originally set between the arches of the Gothic Revival chancel. Unfortunately the late nineteenth century remodelling of the chancel led to the removal of these divisions, so that the panels are now all mounted, rather uncomfortably, on one continuous plain wall.

George Dance's design for the chancel, as originally built, of which a detail is reproduced in Plate 172, gives a clear idea of the setting for the panels, with the first one *in situ*. In keeping with Dance's architecture, Flaxman's panel is surmounted by a late medieval canopy, with quatrefoil tracery on the plinth (Plate 173). As the drawing in 1806 only shows one panel, the central one in the final arrangement, it seems that the monument started as a relatively modest concept but was probably elaborated into its multiple form before Sir Francis died, since Flaxman exhibited reliefs relating to all three parts of the monument at the Royal Academy in 1809.

Each panel illustrates a part of the Lord's Prayer. The central design, showing a female figure symbolising Resignation, seated facing the direction of the altar, illustrates the text 'Thy will be done'.[18] Already in 1801, before receiving the commission from Sir Francis Baring, Flaxman had shown a panel at the Royal Academy with this title. The figure of Resignation is

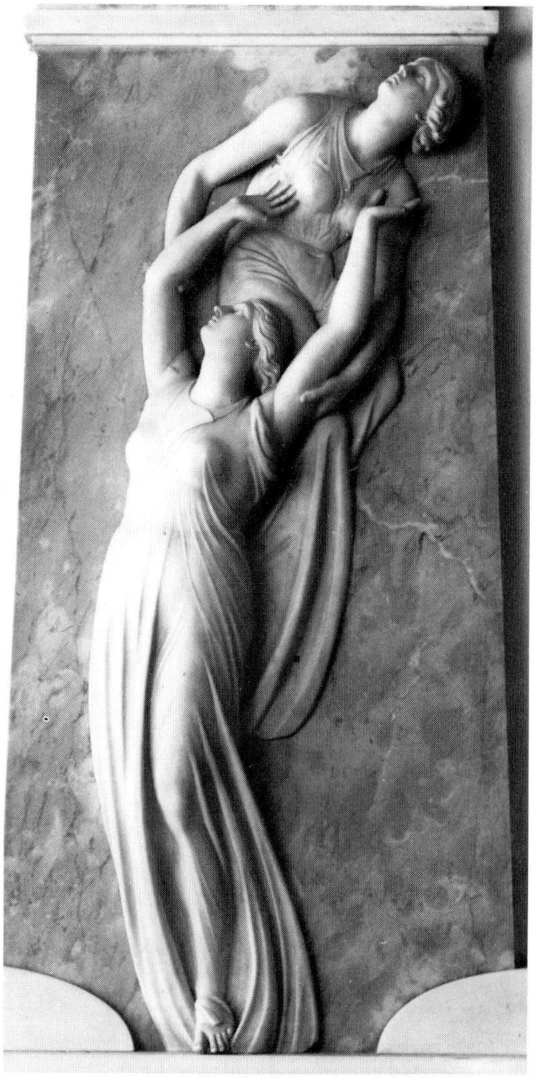

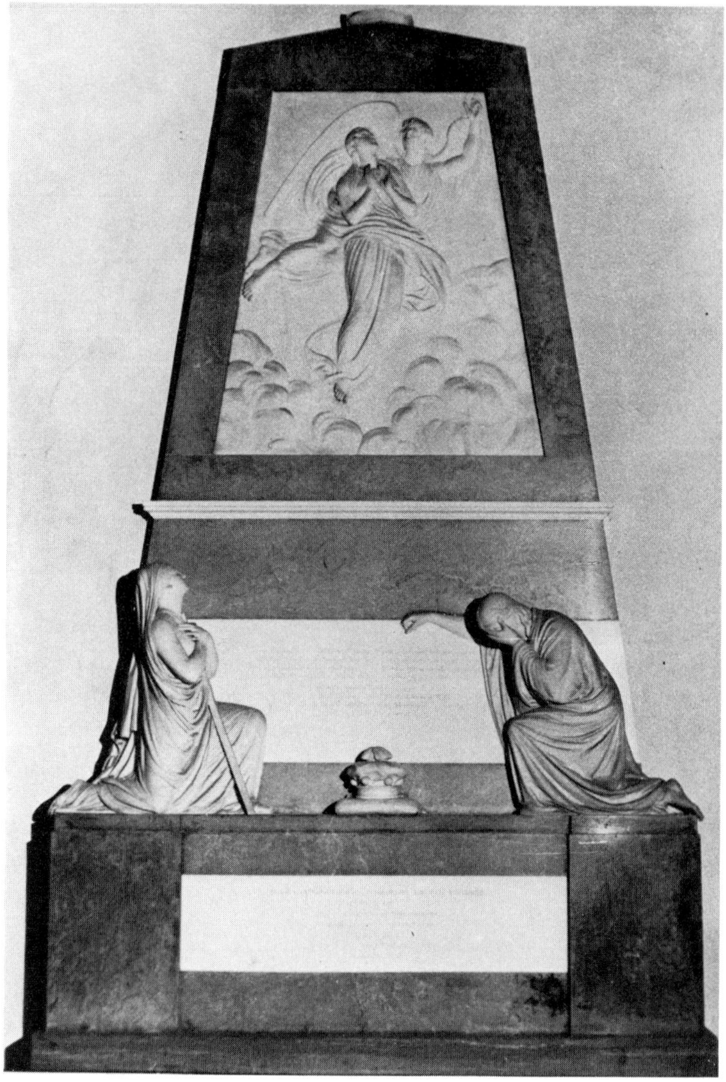

characterised by the same piety as that found in Cowper's hymn entitled 'Submission' which is amongst his contributions to the *Olney Hymns*, expressing a devotional Christianity that Flaxman would have shared:

'O Lord, my best desire fulfill,
And help me to resign
Life, health, and comfort to thy will,
And make thy pleasure mine.

Why should I shrink at thy command,
Whose love forbids my fears?
Or tremble at the gracious hand
That wipes away my tears? . . .'

Flaxman's personification of Resignation is also in harmony with the increasing tendency in English religious poetry from the mid-eighteenth century onwards to compose sentimental Christian verses to a pantheon of such abstractions, including amongst other figures Charity, Innocence and Truth.[19] For the monument, Flaxman seems to have used studies from nature of a lady seated at a window or by a fireside, which he has imbued with an appropriate Christian sentiment, changing the costume from a contemporary one into that of a timeless allegory (Plate 174). There is also a hint, suggested earlier when discussing Flaxman's Italian visit, of the donor's wife from Masaccio's *Trinità* (Plate 175).

In a group of his monuments, separate from the *Baring* Resignation, Flaxman employs an isolated,

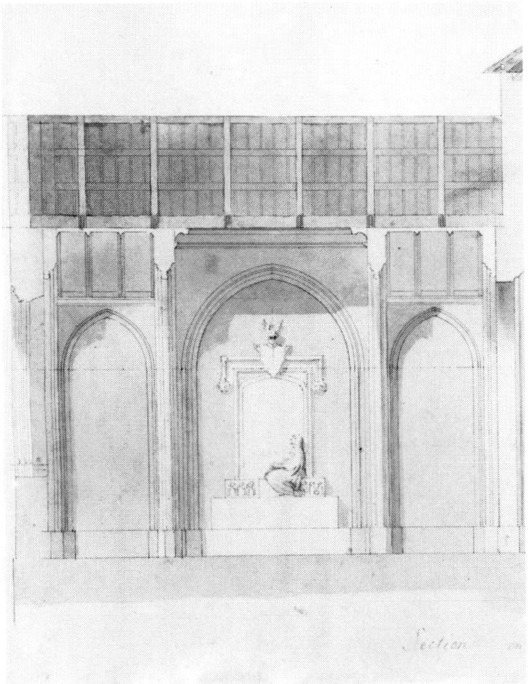

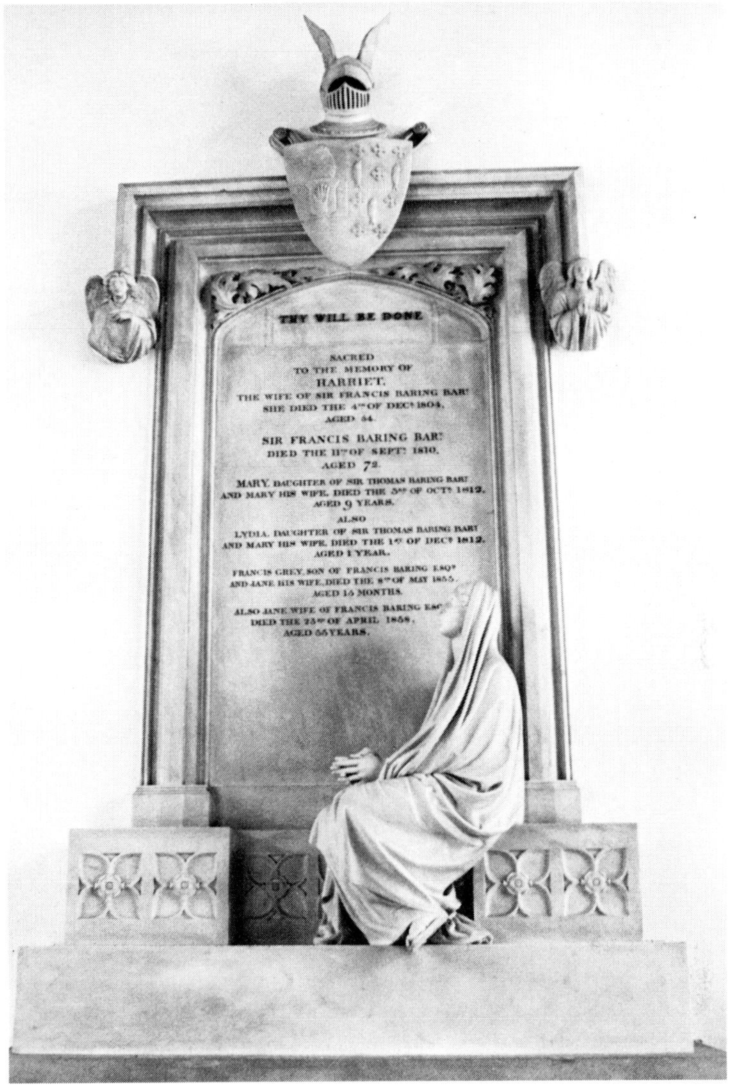

170 (far left) *Elizabeth Knight: monument*, 1806–9.
All Saints, Milton, Cambridgeshire.

171 *(left) Mary, Lady Rendlesham: monument*, 1814.
St. Gregory, Rendlesham, Suffolk.

172 *(above)* George Dance: *Design for Micheldever Church*, 1806
Detail of chancel.

173 *(right) Baring Family: monument.*
Central panel: *Thy will be done*, 1806.
St. Mary, Micheldever, Hampshire.

mourning or contemplative figure, seated, sometimes with an open Bible on their lap. These figures tend to be more strictly classical than the *Baring* one, and only the expression of piety and the accompanying clue such as a Bible make it clear that this is a Christian and not a pagan monument. A good example of this type is the monument to *William Miles* (Plate 176). A draped female figure is seated at the foot of a broken column, with its Corinthian capital lying at her feet, symbolising the passage at which the Bible is open, the well known lines from *Ecclesiastes*: 'Then shall the dust return to the earth as it was: and the spirit shall return unto God who gave it'. The original version of the design cost William Miles's son 400 guineas, but this pattern was available to other clients at prices ranging from £100 to £200, being shipped as far afield as Barbados and Madras, as well as being used on several occasions in English parish churches.[20] The fact that he executed this design for the monument erected to one of his important Italian-period patrons, Mrs. Georgina Hare-Naylor who had commissioned the *Homer* illustrations (1810, in St. Mary's, Twyford, Hampshire), suggests that the sculptor regarded this well-tried formula as one of his best.

The composition of the two side panels of the *Baring* monument is different in character from these isolated figures (Plates 177 and 178). The left relief depicts 'For Thine is the kingdom', and the right 'Deliver us from evil'. In both a centrally placed figure, in one case male, in the other female, is rising upwards with the aid of attendant angels, who on this occasion are winged. The turbulent activity of the panels, especially in the one depicting the fight against the evil forces of the serpent

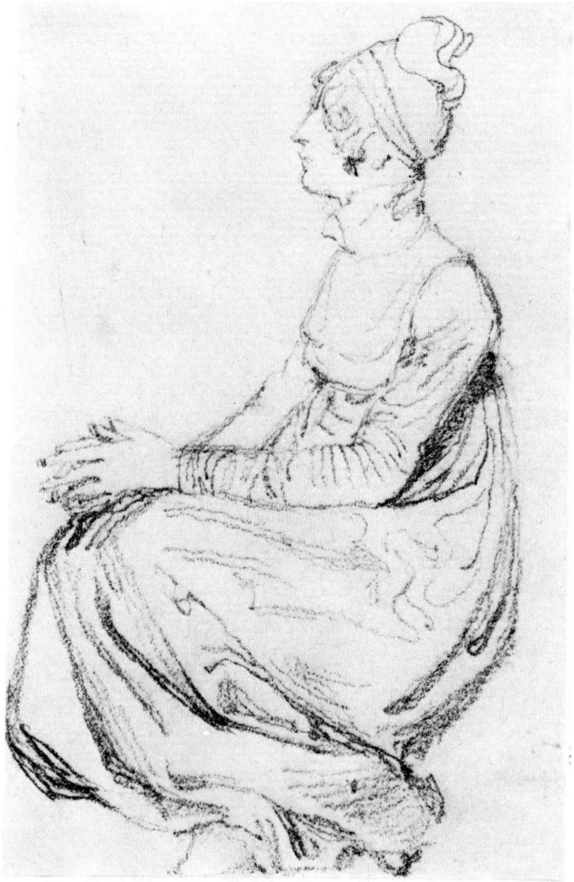

174 *Lady Seated with Hands clasped.*
Pencil, 13 × 8·6 cms.

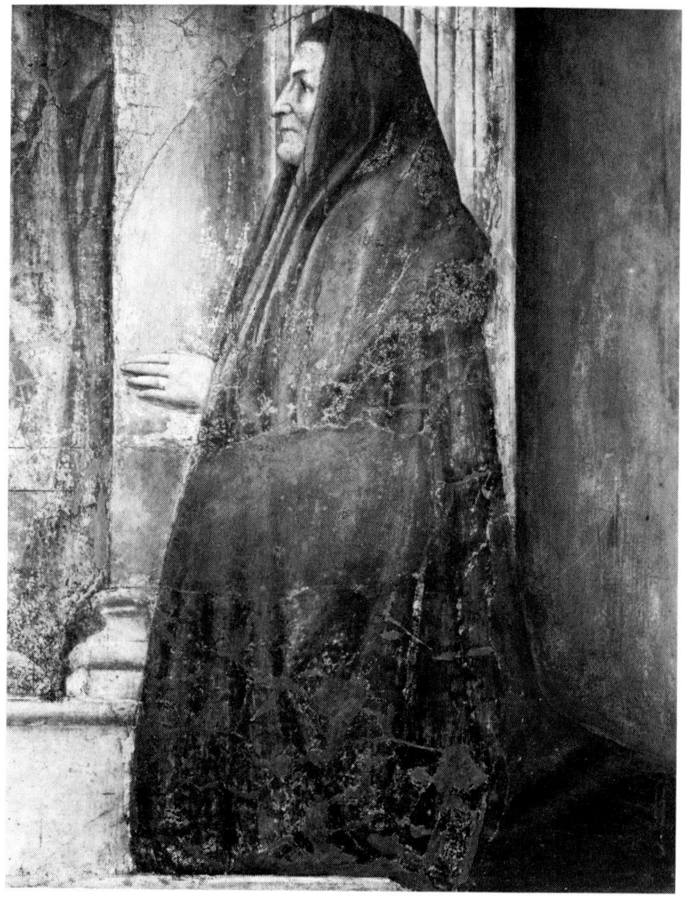

175 Masaccio: *Trinità*: detail of donor's wife.

and demons, contrasts markedly with the tranquillity of the larger central relief. These side panels belong to a small group of Flaxman's sculptural reliefs in which on rare occasions only he illustrated specific verses or stories in the New Testament. His imagery when relating to Biblical texts was usually more generalised, as in the other monuments discussed so far. The rarity of such imagery was probably one of the reasons why John Britton chose the *Baring* monument (together with the equally unusual *Mansfield* monument) for inclusion in his *Fine Arts of the English School*, published in 1812. The text that accompanied the engraving of the panel 'For Thine is the Kingdom' praised it highly because 'like the mid-day sun shining on a waste [he] can confer pleasure on a representation of the simplest objects', thus drawing attention to a neglected and under-patronised aspect of British sculpture at the time.[21] Perhaps Flaxman hoped for more commissions of this kind by exhibiting models and reliefs of such themes on several occasions at the Royal Academy. Versions of *Deliver us from Evil*, for example, were shown there as early as 1805, before he had received the *Baring* commission, just as *Thy will be done* had appeared in those rooms as early as 1801. But the widespread familiarity which potential clients must have had with the imagery used on the *Baring* monument led to a very few commissions for other illustrations of passages from the New Testament.

Amongst this group of works in which Flaxman employed a more didactic use of Christian imagery is a small monument commissioned for an outdoor setting in a churchyard, but subsequently moved within the church, the slab commemorating the *Children of Francis Redfearn* at the newly built Gothic Revival church of St. Cuthbert, Edinburgh (Plates 179 and 180). The mandorla that Flaxman has used is an ideal shape for a small-scale monument with a restricted area of carving.[22] The centralised figure of Christ, flanked by the

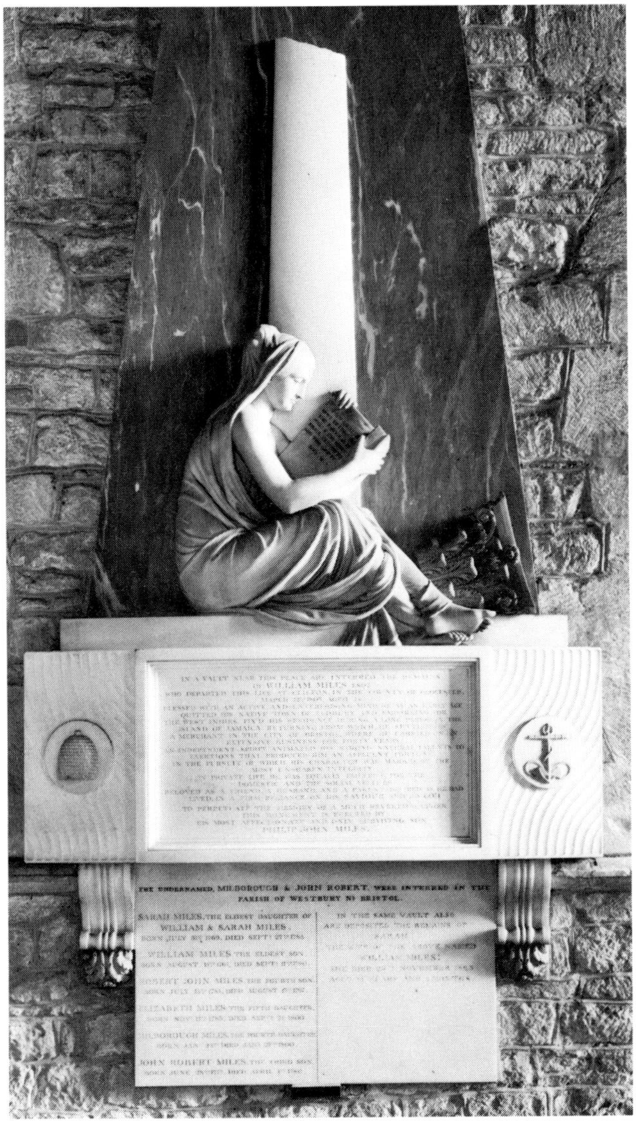

176 *William Miles: monument*, 1803.
St. Michael, Ledbury, Herefordshire.

Redfearn children, is more hieratic in its frontality than is usual for Flaxman, but the formality of the arrangement is offset by Christ's gentle features, and by the playfulness of the infants.[23] The composition illustrates the text, inscribed above, 'Suffer the little children to come unto me, and forbid them not, for of such is the Kingdom of God'.

Other texts that Flaxman illustrated included 'I am the Resurrection and the Life. He that believeth on Me,

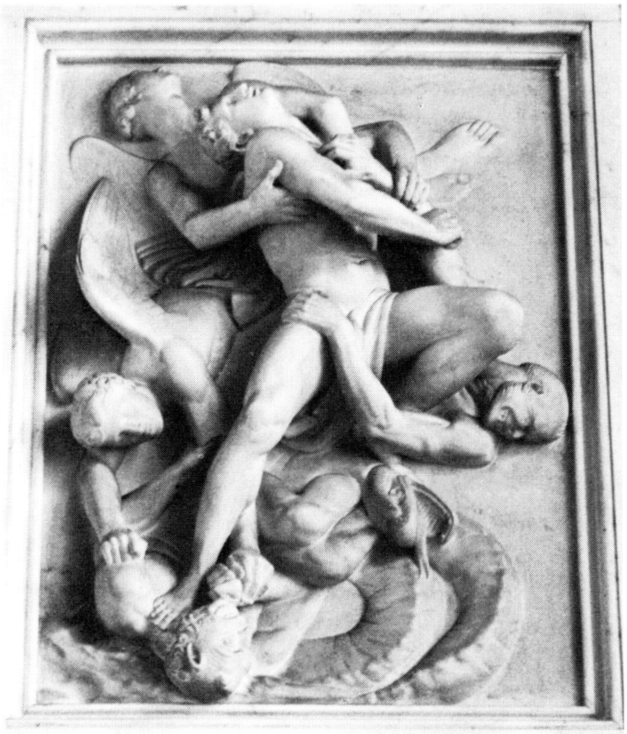

177 *Baring Family: monument.*
Right panel: *Deliver us from evil*, c. 1809–10.
St. Mary, Micheldever, Hampshire.

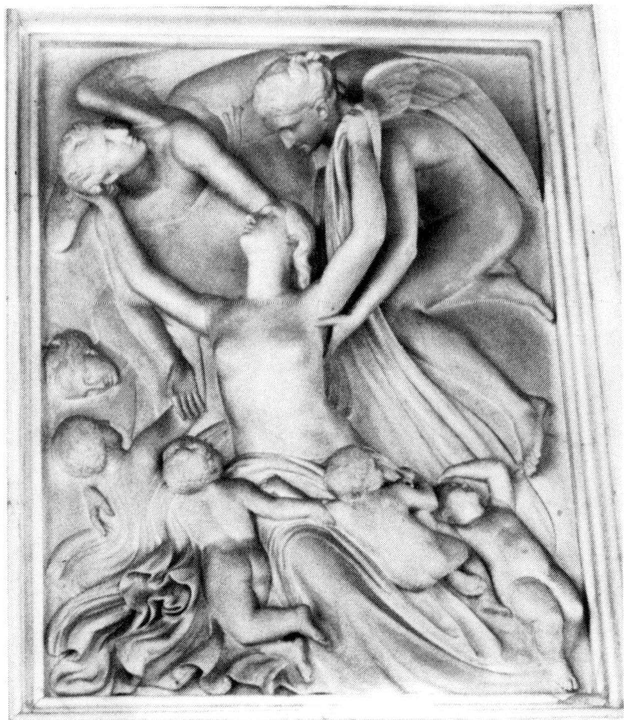

178 *Baring Family: monument.*
Left panel: *For Thine is the Kingdom*, c. 1809–10.
St. Mary, Micheldever, Hampshire.

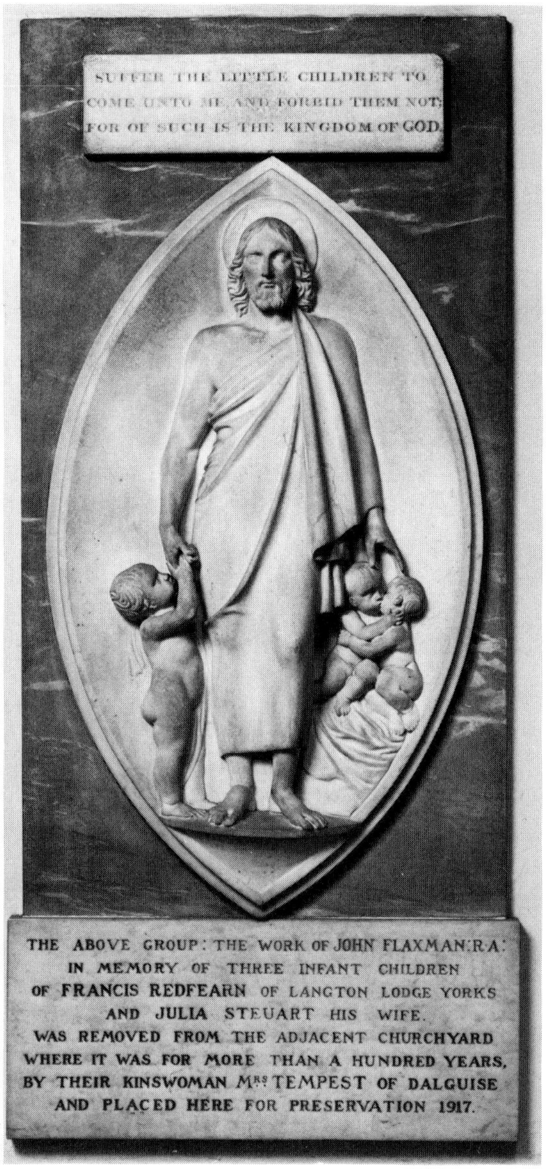

179 *Three children of Francis Redfearn: monument,* 1803–4. St. Cuthbert, Edinburgh.

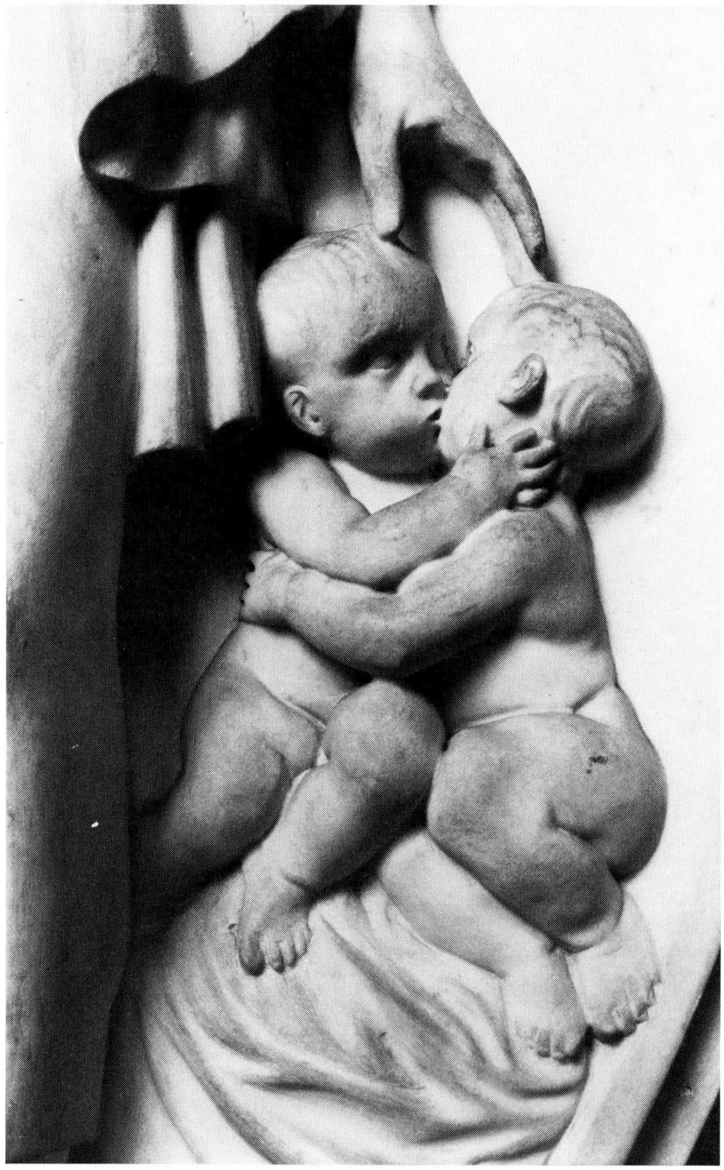

180 *Three children of Francis Redfearn: monument: detail.*

though he were dead, yet shall he live', a text which appears above a relief panel of Religion comforting a mourner (Plate 181), drawn for a monument in Brecon Cathedral in 1813, to *William and Thomas James* and again three years later on the memorial to *Eliza Caswall* (in St. Catherine's, Sacombe, Hertfordshire). On rare occasions a parable or miracle was chosen. A panel illustrating the good Samaritan forms the *William Bosanquet* monument (erected in 1814 at St. Mary the Virgin, Leyton, Essex) (Plate 182) and the scene of the raising of Jairus's daughter constitutes the entire imagery on the memorial to *Emily Mawbey*, who had died at the age of twenty (Plate 183). Shortly after his return from Italy Flaxman had exhibited at the Royal Academy in 1797 a model entitled the *Raising of Jairus's Daughter* which is not connected with any known monument of that time. Presumably executed as a speculative piece, its character was noted by Cunningham as 'perfect innocence and serene loveliness'.[24] Flaxman seems to have kept the work in his studio and used it much later in 1822 as the basis for the *Mawbey* commission. The oblong panel, carved in low relief, is

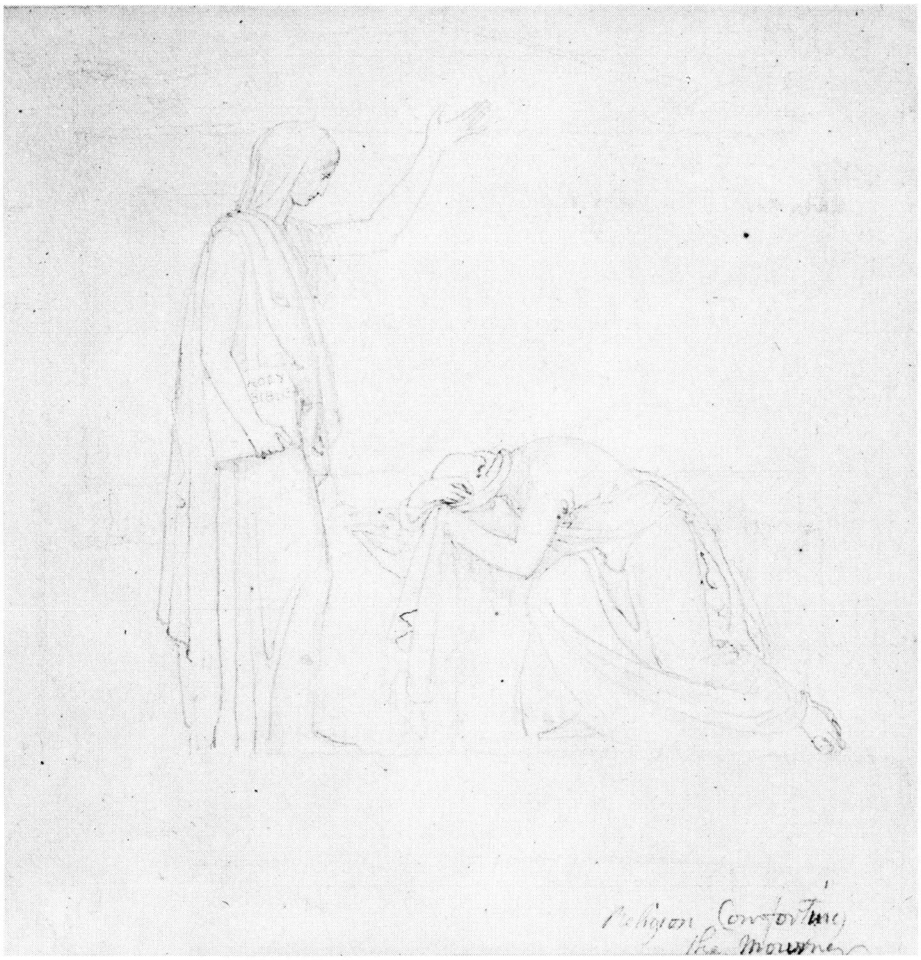

181 *Religion comforting the Mourner*, c. 1813.
Pen and ink and pencil,
20·2 × 19·8 cms.

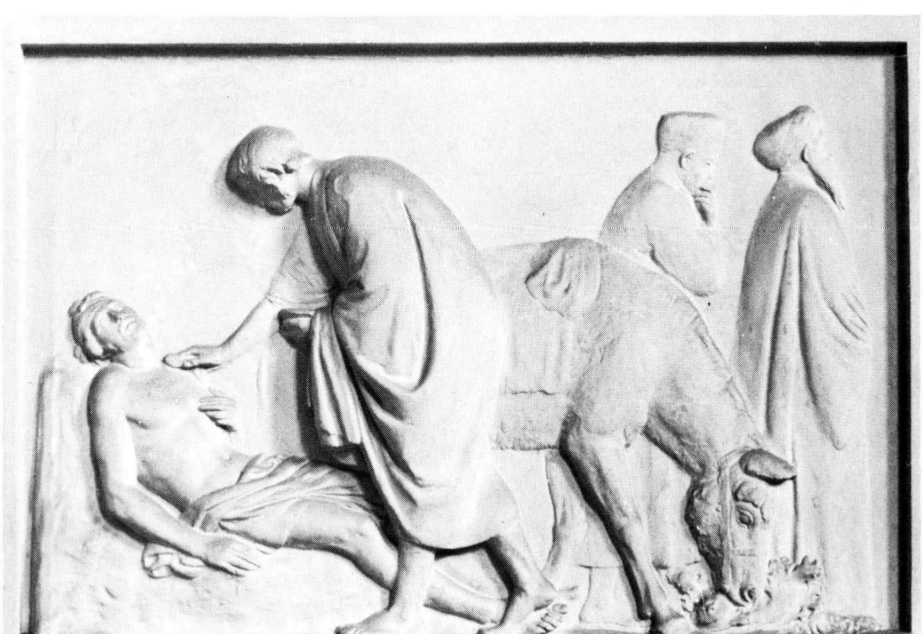

182 *William Bosanquet: monument: model.* 1813–15.
Plaster, 66 × 101·6 cms.

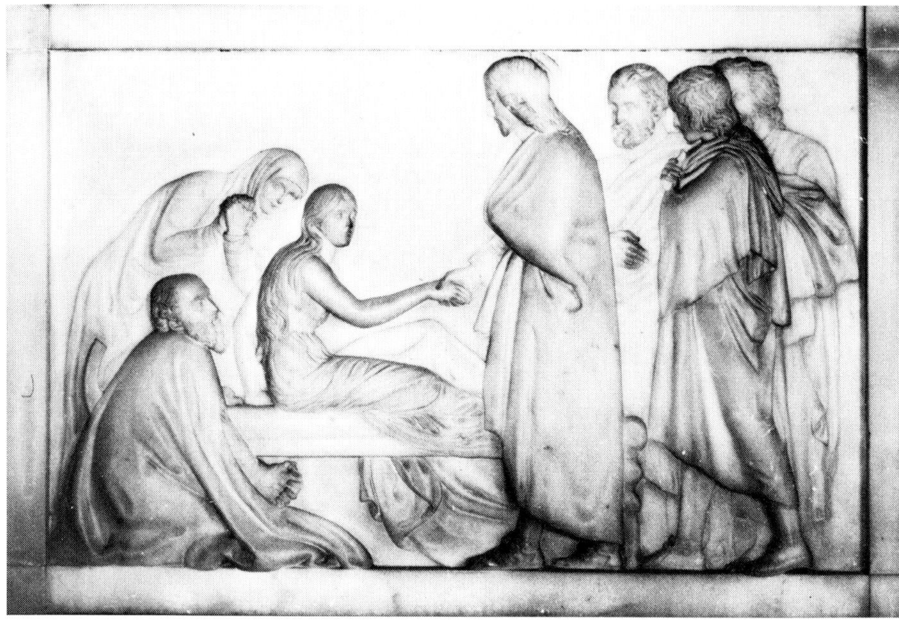

183 *Emily Mawbey: monument*, 1822–23.
St. Peter, Chertsey, Surrey.

one of the few occasions in Flaxman's *oeuvre* in which he treated a Christian theme in marble in much the same way as he had organised his imagery for the engraver of Homer and his other illustrations. As in these other works, Flaxman has pared the story down to its basic essentials, eliminating unnecessary details as well as removing any suggestion of background. Like the *Bosanquet* panel, the emphasis is on linearity and on simplicity in the treatment of the subject, which has been placed in a restrained architectural framework. In works of this kind, Flaxman's imagery is essentially pictorial rather than sculptural, belonging to a tradition of religious art that includes such works as Poussin's *Sacraments*, which Flaxman could well have known. The Christian message of such a panel provides ample support for Flaxman's conviction that Christian imagery was 'more interesting and instructive' than the 'trifling ornaments and far-fetched allegories generally used'.[25]

2 Charity and instruction

The eighteenth century was the golden age of philanthropy, and Flaxman's monument to *Thomas Yarborough and his Family* executed between 1803 and 1806 is a fine record of this aspect of contemporary life (Plate 184). The relief panel shows the two youngest daughters of the family, under whose will the memorial was commissioned, distributing alms to the poor, illustrating the daughters' lifetime generosity to charities. Their pious acts are emphasised by the inscription above the panel, 'Blessed are they that consider the poor'. By using the simple device of a plinth, Flaxman has clearly demarcated the givers from the receivers, drawn attention to the daughters themselves, and made the poor unmistakably submissive by putting them in a lower position in the composition. Within such formality, Flaxman has treated his figures almost as if they formed part of a genre scene, and at the same time represented the three ages of man. The hands at the focal point of the composition with the fingers curled ready to receive the coins, together with the head of this central beggar-woman, are amongst the many beautifully observed examples of naturalism on this relief. The baby peeping over the shoulder of the same woman, the attentive little dog, and the light grace with which one sister has placed an arm around the shoulder of the other, help to make the *Yarborough* monument one of Flaxman's finest works. The reasonable sum of money available for this monument, £500, had made it possible for the sculptor to take a great deal of care over a theme which he obviously found sympathetic. According to Cunningham, Flaxman himself regarded this monument as one of his 'most effective compositions'.[26]

The basic composition of the design of the *Yarborough* relief can be found amongst the Acts of Mercy—the one of feeding the hungry—which Flaxman illustrated at the end of his poem of 'The Knight of the Blazing Cross', a series of drawings which he then

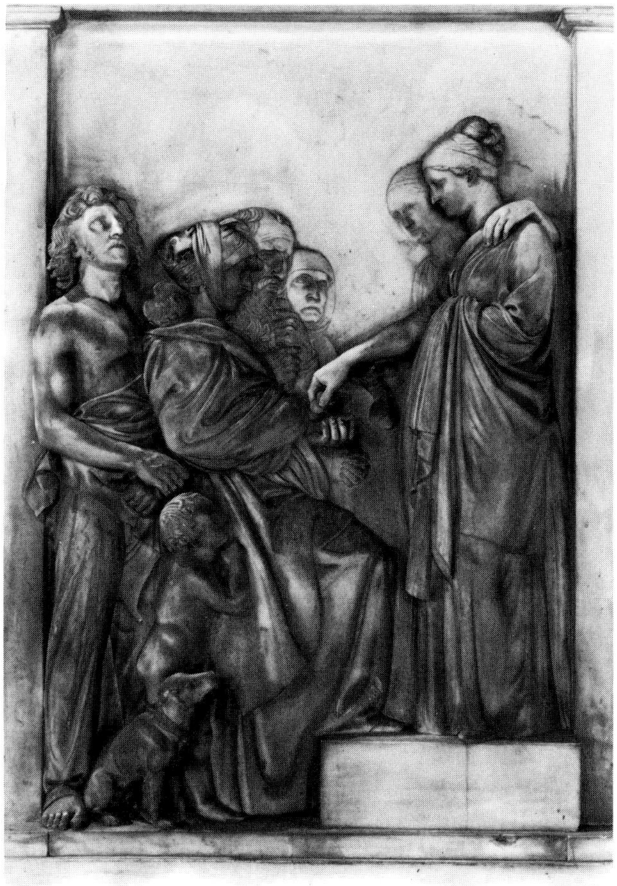

184 *Thomas Yarborough and his Family: monument*, 1803–6. Detail.
St. Mary Magdalene, Campsall, Yorkshire.

re-worked with a view to a possible separate publication.[27] Other acts of piety appear on Flaxman's monuments, in the form used in 'The Knight' or as a personification, such as the figure of Charity.

Flaxman regarded his monument to a teacher, *Abraham Balme*, as another of his 'most affective compositions' (Plate 185). It originated in the drawing in 'The Knight' illustrating the lines: 'Instruct the ignorant in heavenly things, / And arm the untaught mind, / Against the assaults of evil'. The grouping and the pose of Balme himself also echo the left half of a rough sketch that Flaxman had made when in Italy of the panel of *Christ amongst the doctors* on Ghiberti's first Baptistry doors (Plate 186). Balme himself had lived to the age of ninety and is shown on the relief panel as a venerable old man. In a simple illustration of a lifetime of teaching, Flaxman shows the deceased in a Roman toga and sandals flanked by a boy and girl in contemporary clothes.

The problem of how to dress a teacher, whether to put him back into a classical past or whether to portray him as his pupils knew him, was a dilemma which Flaxman had to resolve when he received a commission from a group of Wykehamists in London in 1800 for a memorial to their late headmaster at Winchester College, the Reverend Dr. Joseph Warton (Plate 187). An early life of the headmaster says that the Wykehamists wished 'to perpetuate their gratitude and love and to hand down to posterity both the lineaments and fame of their revered, their inimitable instructor'.[28] One member of the committee in a letter to a nephew stressed Warton's 'very instrumental' role whilst at Winchester in instructing his pupils in 'true classical taste', and the prominence of Homer's portrait on the monument is probably a reminder of this aspect of the deceased's teaching. Aristotle is almost certainly included as the author of the *Poetics*, which laid the foundation for subsequent literary criticism. Thematically, therefore, the monument incorporates references to all three of Warton's roles as teacher, critic and poet. His skill in holding the attention of young pupils on religious subjects, whether reading a service or giving a discourse, was well known, but the monument omits any reference to Warton's Christian beliefs, either in the imagery or in the Latin inscription.

In designing the monument Flaxman had to resolve the problem of which of Warton's activities, as a schoolmaster, as a critic or as a poet, he should stress. The first designs which he drew for the committee's consideration were entirely classical in both theme and style, although there were no known classical precedents for relief panels depicting masters and pupils (Plate 188). Flaxman has not even borrowed any compositional ideas from the Trecento monuments to professors at Bologna University which are the earliest important examples of tomb designs showing master and pupils. In his Warton monument the original idea of a seated figure instructing four boys remains the principal part of the composition in the final marble, but the togas and bare feet have been replaced by contemporary dress. The pedimental masks of Electra and Antigone disappear, but the lyre is enlarged to become a dominant element rising above the monument, presumably to stress Warton's reputation as a poet. In the final monument, the background herm heads are rearranged, and identified as those of Aristotle and Homer. The detached wall medallions are removed and placed on the side of the monument itself, and the detached incense burners disappear. These last alter-

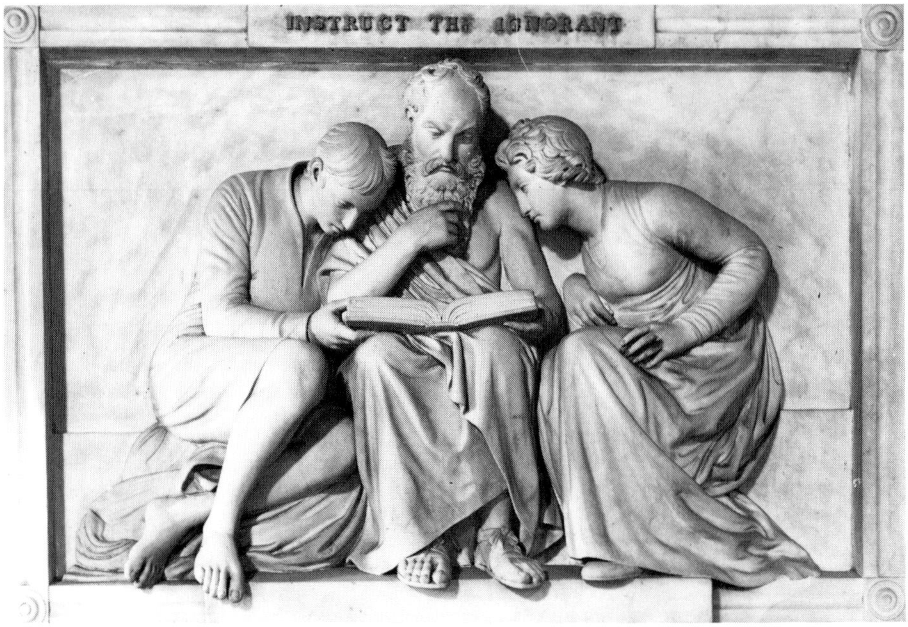

185 *Abraham Balme: monument*, 1809–12.
Bradford Cathedral.

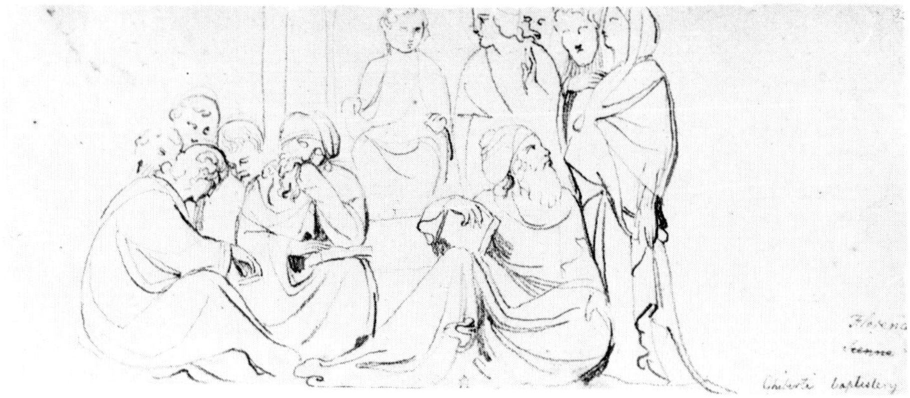

186 *Christ among the Doctors, after Ghiberti, Baptistry, Florence.*
Pencil, 15·2 × 36·2 cms.

ations indicate the major change that took place in the shape of the monument. Originally intended to be sited against an aisle wall in Winchester Cathedral, and therefore conceived as a stele, the committee moved the site to a freestanding one above the step on the south side, a change of which the sculptor approved when brought down to Winchester to see the setting.[29]

The charming and intimate genre group of four attentive boys, as if drawn from life, are probably portraits of the children of Flaxman's patroness Mrs. Hare-Naylor. She knew the sculptor well, and had Winchester connections herself (being a daughter of an ex-prebendary of the cathedral): it is possible that Flaxman wished to pay her a compliment by including her four sons, whose governess was Flaxman's sister, on the monument. As Flaxman's group of children on the monument to *Lady Fitzharris*, to be discussed shortly, is certainly based on life studies, there is every possibility that they are on the *Warton* monument as well.[30]

Flaxman also executed several monuments of preachers and missionaries instructing their congregations or the young. These included one of the Reverend John Clowes in Manchester (Plate 155), which has already been discussed in the previous chapter, and another to the Reverend Christian William Gericke, who had died as a missionary in India in 1803 (Plate 189). The marble made in about 1810 was sent to Madras, where it joined an increasing number of monuments to the British who had died in the sub-continent, in St. Mary's

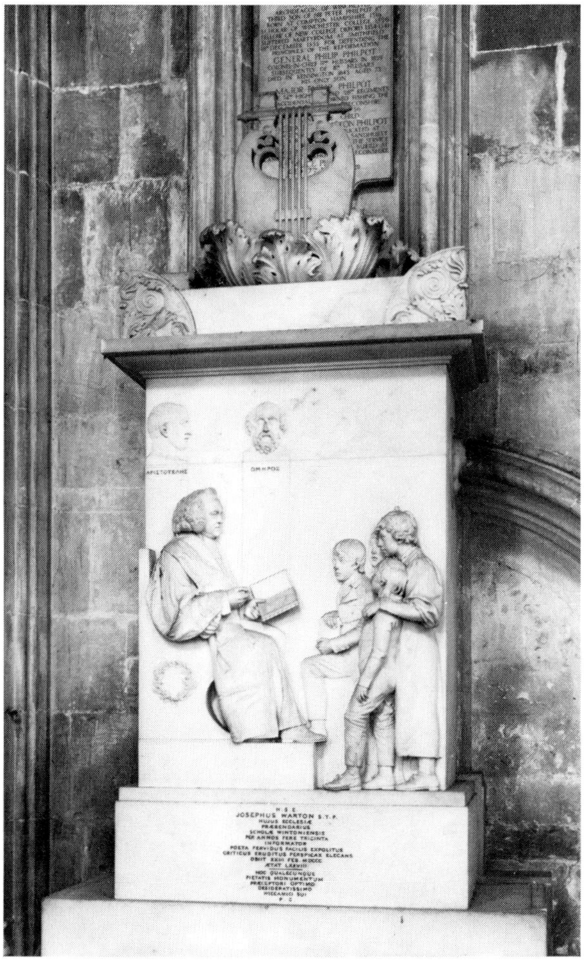

187 *Reverend Dr. Joseph Warton: monument,* 1800–4.
Winchester Cathedral.

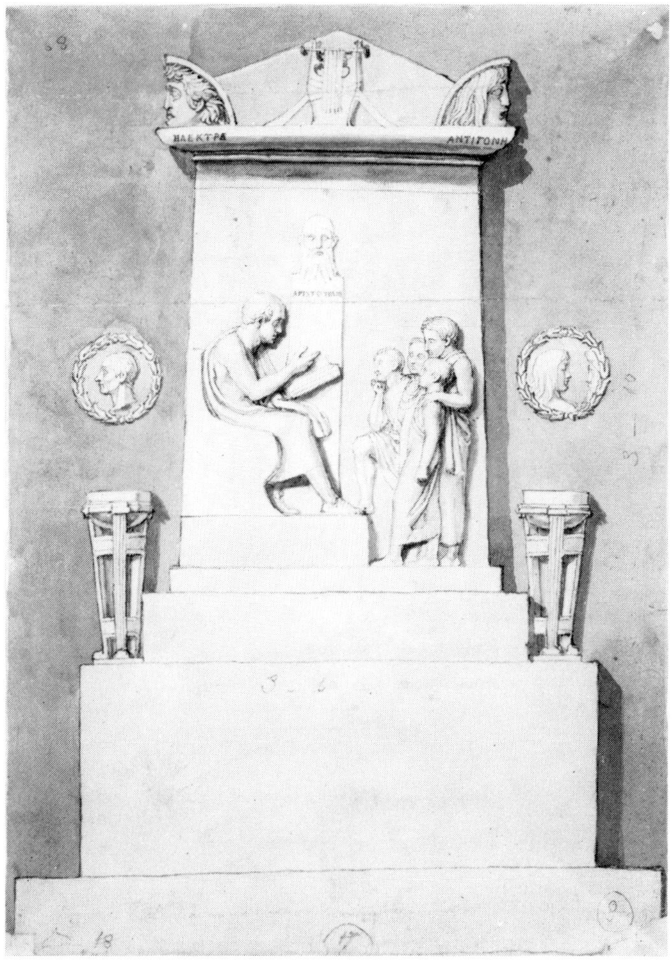

188 *Reverend Dr. Joseph Warton: monument: design.*
Pen and ink and wash, 29·4 × 21·4 cms.

church in Fort St. George. Gericke is shown preaching, with one hand holding a Bible and the other pointing to the inscription 'Believe in the Lord Jesus Christ', whilst a group of children cling to his surplice and an attentive adult Indian leans on his staff.[31]

Flaxman's tomb to *Sir William Jones* at University College, Oxford, is a major monument in this group illustrating the activities of the deceased (Plate 190). Flaxman has concentrated on the role of the famous orientalist as a scholar, stressing in the main panel one aspect of his activities, the accumulation of information for his important *Digest of Hindu and Mohammedan Laws.* Prominence is also given to law in the inscription beneath the group, and in the writing on the folder propped against Jones's seat: 'A nation should be judged by its own laws', a quotation from the Laws of Manu, the Hindu system of duties which Jones had translated. The magnificent banana tree in the background (Plate 162) may have been included not only as an attractive element in the composition suggesting an exotic setting, but also as a reminder of Jones's botanical interests. Above the inscription, the carving of a lyre and an Indian vina illustrate Jones's knowledge of oriental music; he had for example written a long aritcle on 'The Musical Modes of the Hindus' in the *Researches* published by the Asiatick Society of Calcutta, of which he was the President. Other articles which Jones published in the same periodical included a long examination of 'The Gods of Greece, Italy and India'.[32] Flaxman has therefore managed in his design not only to suggest Jones's involvement with the relationship of European and Eastern civilisations, but also the three areas of interest in Jones's life in India: law, music and botany.

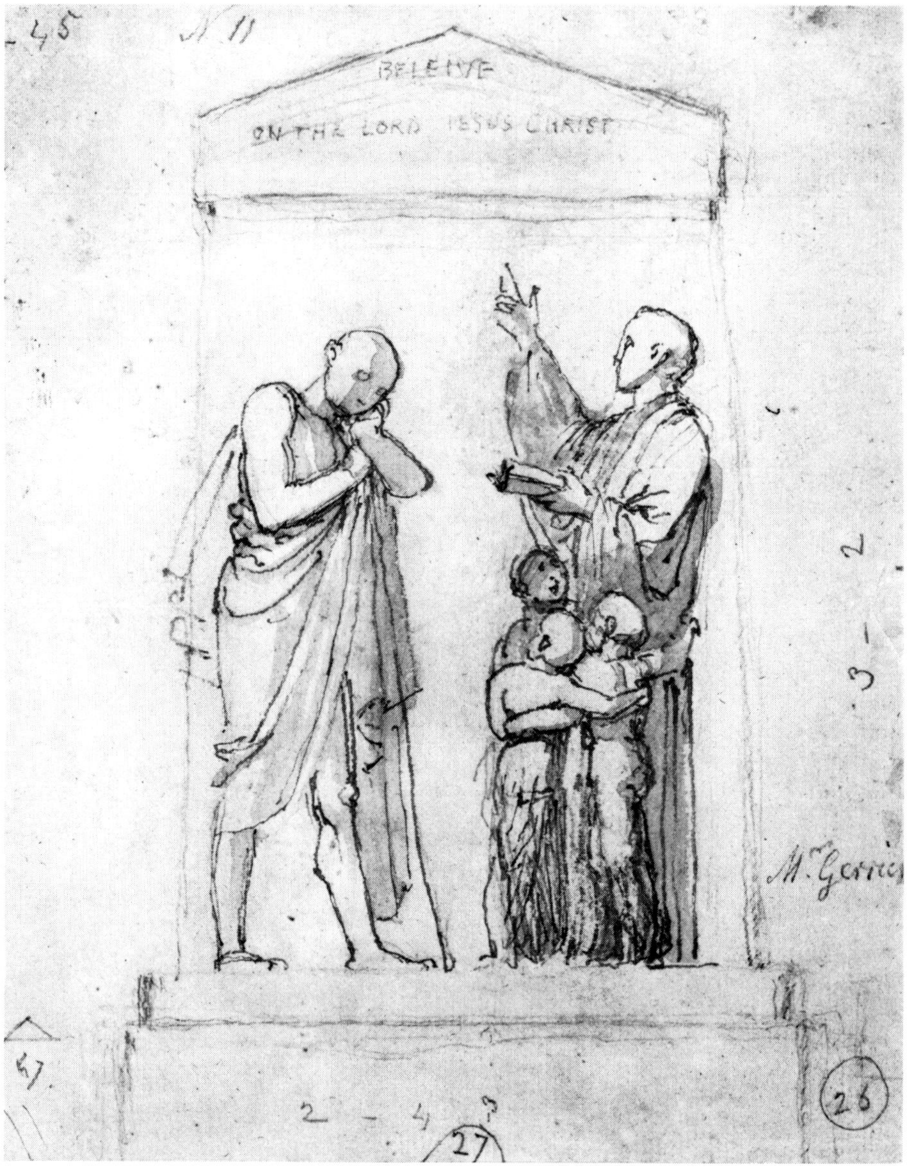

189 *Reverend Christian William Gericke: monument: design,* 1809–12.
Pen and ink, pencil and wash, 20·3 × 16·2 cms.

The *Jones* monument, commissioned by Sir William's widow in 1796, was originally intended for Calcutta, but as another one had been erected there she donated it to his old college, where it occupies the most prominent site in the ante-chapel. For this large work the sculptor received £500, lavishing what seems to have been a great deal of care and attention on the monument. Several drawings show that he made life studies as the basis for the figures of the Indians (Plate 191), resulting in another successful genre group in the main panel, which is finely chiselled. The architectural forms chosen for the design are unusually complex for one of Flaxman's monuments, and have been assembled into a strikingly original composition. Even before Flaxman had received the commission, William Hayley was assuming he would be asked. Hayley had published *An Elegy on the Death of Sir William Jones* in 1795, in which he was already writing:

'Flaxman! thy energy of thought benign,
Thy feelings tender as the mournful dove,
Teach stone to breathe those charms of chaste design,
That best may soothe the pangs of widow'd love.'

The finished monument was indeed to be tender in feeling and chaste in design.

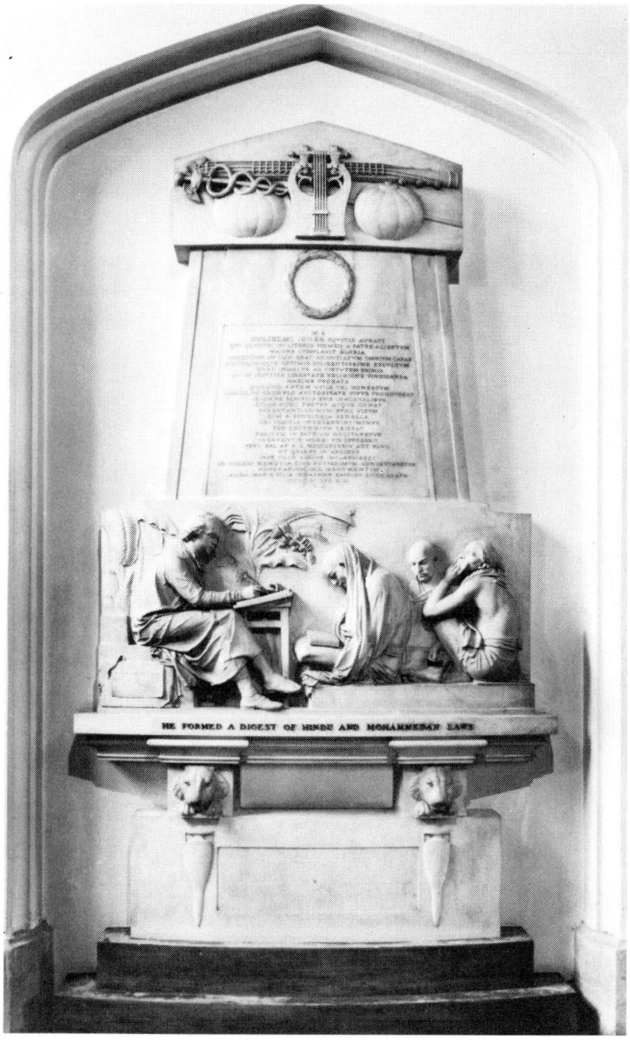

190 *Sir William Jones: monument*, 1796.
University College Chapel, Oxford.

On some of Flaxman's monuments Christian virtues are not demonstrated in illustrative panels, but as statues personifying the virtues, either used singly, or very often as a pair chosen from Faith, Hope and Charity, the two figures flanking an inscription panel. This pattern was a very popular one for which Flaxman received many commissions. The statues are clad in either classical or modern dress, and could be inserted into either classical or Gothic frameworks without any change being made to the figures themselves (Plates 192 and 193). The monument to *Ann Lady Clarke* is one of Flaxman's most austere with only a few stark elements of the Greek Revival. Whereas the monument to *Mrs. Mary Arbuthnot* is one of the artist's few Gothic Revival works, with a Perpendicular framework, presumably chosen deliberately to echo the Gothic Revival style church in which it was housed. It was apparently the first monument to be mounted in the church and thus set a precedent for all subsequent monuments in the building, which are entirely in Gothic Revival styles.

Flaxman removed as much allegory as possible from the designs of his monuments, preferring a simplicity of statement. Many of his monuments are stripped to a basic message of the comforts of religion without the adventitious aid of clouds, cupids and other celestial decorations. At the turn of the century Flaxman was taking a leading part in the reduction of allegory associated with church monuments, a cleansing process which had been started, but only tentatively, by Thomas Banks.

Many churches provide ample illustration of the difference between Flaxman's approach and that of earlier generations, or older contemporaries. One of the best examples is in the church of St. Mary the Virgin at Great Brington in Northamptonshire, used by the Spencer family. Here on the death of John, Earl Spencer in 1783 a memorial by Nollekens was erected, showing a classically inspired, partially draped female figure floating on a cloud, with a cornucopia overflowing at her feet with natural produce and worldly wealth. For the same church Flaxman was to design the memorial to his ex-patroness *Georgina, Countess Spencer*. A simple, rectangular inscription panel is flanked by figures of Faith and Charity (Plate 194). This latter virtue was important in Flaxman's memorial imagery as it related to a favourite theme of the affections of a mother for her children. Flaxman's figures of Charity are usually imbued with the same intimacy and treated with the same naturalism as one finds in his genre groups. When Flaxman exhibited his Charity for the *Spencer* monument at the Royal Academy in 1819 he entitled it *Family Affection*, an appropriate title for the whole series of such statues and their related drawings (Plate 195). They show the tenderness and love of a family group expressed with a delicate restraint and sentiment that unmistakably belongs to the end of the eighteenth and the early nineteenth centuries. When the *Spencer* monument had been erected the *Gentleman's Magazine*, which occasionally reported on Flaxman's activities, praised it highly as a 'beautiful' work.[33] Flaxman's choice of a Charity, together with a Faith, for the monument to an important patroness provides a significant contemporary indication of how Flaxman's various designs were evaluated; his formula of paired virtues was frequently commissioned.

The finest expression of family affection in Flaxman's sculptures is the monument to *Lady Fitz-*

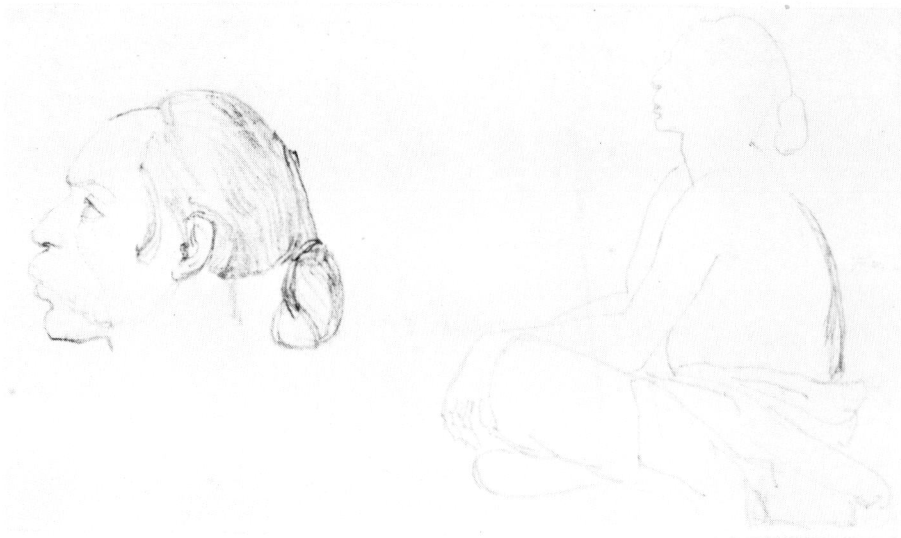

191 *A Hindu: Studies for Sir William Jones monument,* 1796.
Pencil, 11·5 × 19·7 cms.

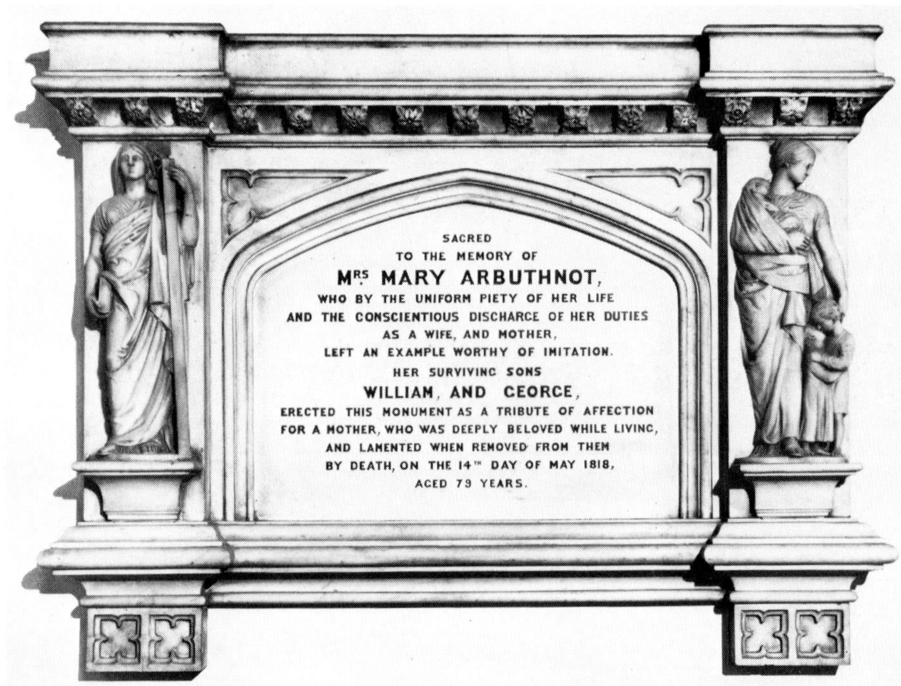

193 *Mrs. Mary Arbuthnot: monument,* 1822–23.
St. John, Edinburgh.

harris, a group of figures just over half lifesize sited near the altar in Christchurch Priory, Hampshire (Plates 196 and 197). Harriet Susan, Viscountess Fitzharris had died in 1815, and in the following year Flaxman started work on the monument. The design originated as a relief panel showing the seated mother together with her three sons, the youngest on her lap. From these modest beginnings the composition evolved into a freestanding group, designed to be seen fully

192 *Ann Lady Clarke: monument,* 1800–2 Tewkesbury Abbey

194 *Georgina, Countess Spencer, monument.* 1816–19.
St. Mary's, Great Brington, Northamptonshire.

195 *Family Affection or Charity.*
Pen and ink and wash, 17·2 × 12 cms.

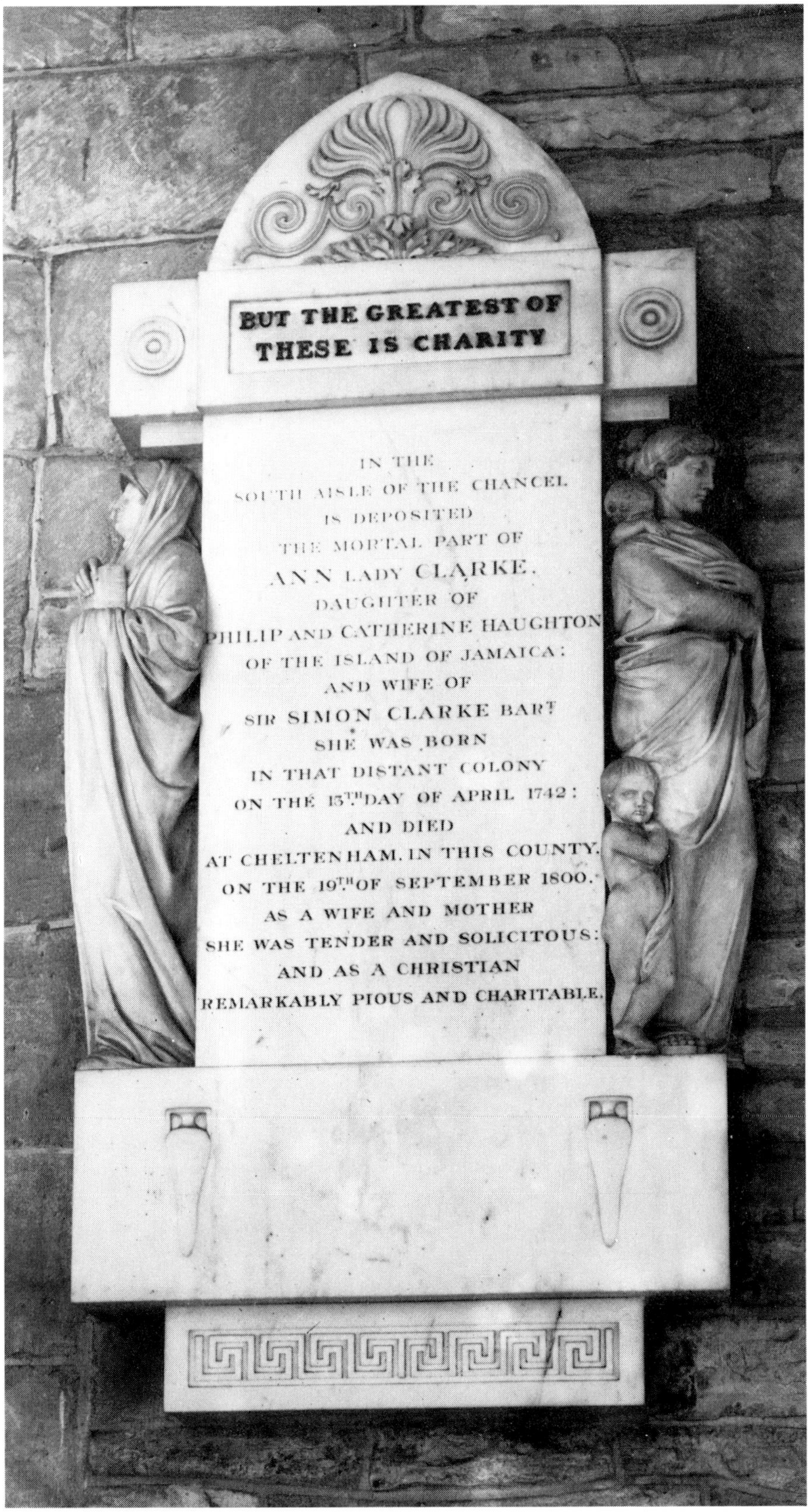
BUT THE GREATEST OF
THESE IS CHARITY
IN THE
SOUTH AISLE OF THE CHANCEL
IS DEPOSITED
THE MORTAL PART OF
ANN LADY CLARKE.
DAUGHTER OF
PHILIP AND CATHERINE HAUGHTON
OF THE ISLAND OF JAMAICA:
AND WIFE OF
SIR SIMON CLARKE BART
SHE WAS BORN
IN THAT DISTANT COLONY
ON THE 13TH DAY OF APRIL 1742:
AND DIED
AT CHELTENHAM. IN THIS COUNTY.
ON THE 19TH OF SEPTEMBER 1800.
AS A WIFE AND MOTHER
SHE WAS TENDER AND SOLICITOUS:
AND AS A CHRISTIAN
REMARKABLY PIOUS AND CHARITABLE.

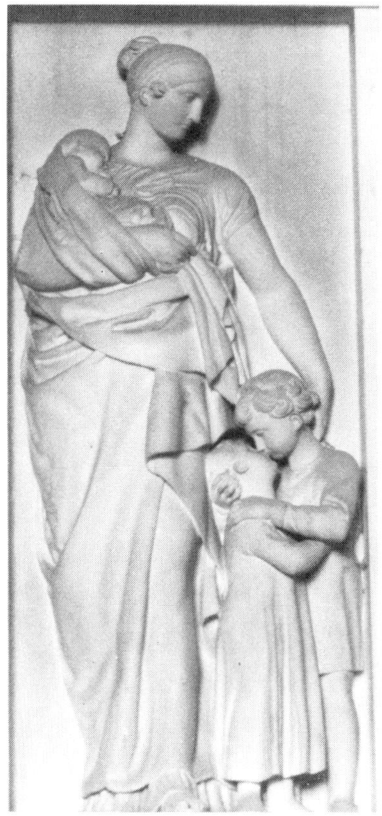

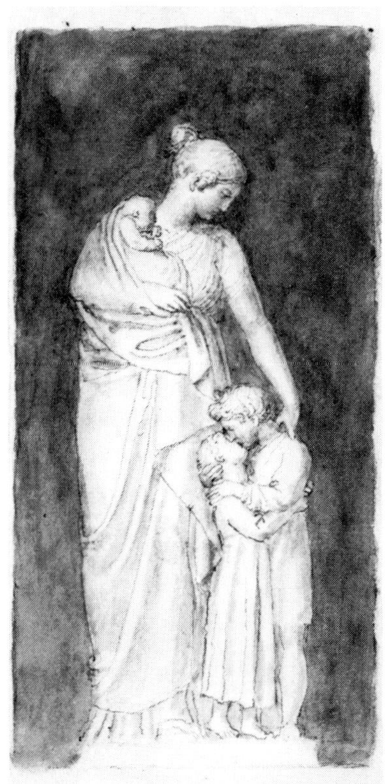

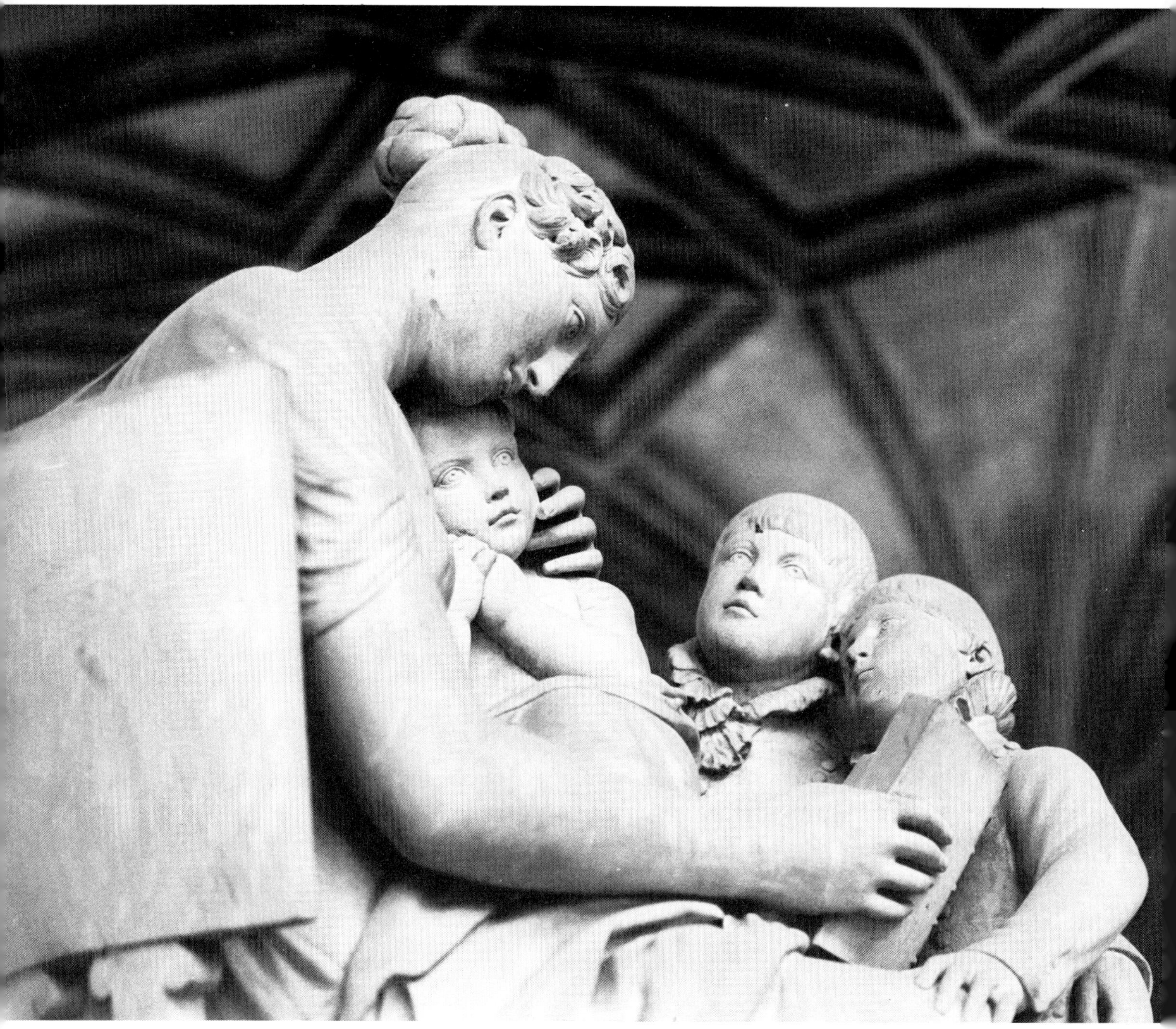

197 *Harriet Susan, Viscountess Fitzharris: monument*, 1816–17.
Detail.
Christchurch Priory, Hampshire.

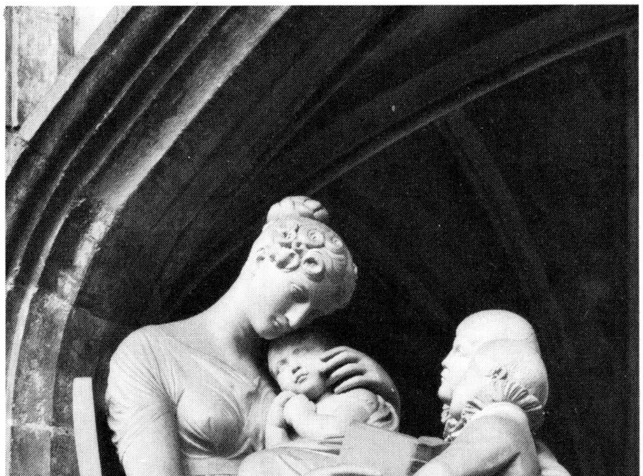

196 *Harriet Susan, Viscountess Fitzharris: monument*, 1816–17. Christchurch Priory, Hampshire.

in the round, so that the composition still looks interesting whilst one walks up the side steps of the chancel approaching the monument from behind.[34] Freestanding monuments were becoming rare by the turn of the eighteenth century partially for the practical reason that churches were becoming so full there was little room left for them. Such a commission (apart from the earlier ones for the *Mansfield* monument and—a different category—the Napoleonic memorials) was therefore a rare event in Flaxman's career.

The theme of maternal affection was dear to Flaxman's heart, and he decided at an early stage to make all the portraits of the boys as natural as possible by drawing all of them from life into one of this sketchbooks (Plate 198). The second son Edward, in the drawing reproduced here, is standing in a pose close to that used on the final monument, with his left arm extended as it is intended to rest on his mother's knee. For the final grouping Flaxman may have used his friend Mrs. Charles Augustus Tulk and her children. Certainly drawings he made of her in the same year are remarkably close both in mood and in the general, if not in the detailed, arrangement (Plate 199). The close intimacy of a mother with her baby had been expressed with delicate charm in the birth of Cacciaguida amongst the Dante illustrations (Plate 135).

Maternal affection was an important theme in late eighteenth and early nineteenth century art, especially painting, and many examples could be cited, including Romney's fine oil portrait of *Mrs. Carwardine and Child* (1775; in Lord Hillingdon's collection), a work which Flaxman could well have known. Closer in sentiment and nearer in date is Richard Cosway's *Affection* included in the engravings after his works published with the title *Drawing Book of Figures* in 1802 (Plate 200). The stress that Flaxman placed in his lectures on the maternal groups of Michelangelo (Plate 201), Raphael and Correggio suggests that he saw a Renaissance origin for this important theme.[35] In his own day, the increasing importance of affection in art can undoubtedly be related to the changing attitude towards children throughout the course of the eighteenth century, when children were becoming less repressed and educational ideas were being liberalised.[36] In literature, domestic pathos and childhood innocence became major topics, seen for example in the *Vicar of Wakefield* and the early poetry of Blake.

The Romantic naturalism of Flaxman's group in the *Fitzharris* monument shows the mother reading to her children from the Bible, fondly holding the youngest on her lap, whilst the two older boys stand listening attentively, in a closely knit group. The composition illustrates that part of the long, prose inscription on the pedestal which says of Lady Fitzharris that 'the care and education of her children were her darling objects, on them she equally bestowed the vigilant fondness of a mother and the successful efforts of a well cultivated mind.' Simple, human emotions are being expressed by entirely contemporary images, without any references to a classical vocabulary either in style or subject. The theme of mother and child does not feature in classical art. In its natural treatment of the theme of motherly affection, the *Fitzharris* monument was to become the precursor of similar tombs by younger sculptors, notably Chantrey. The intimacy of the relationship

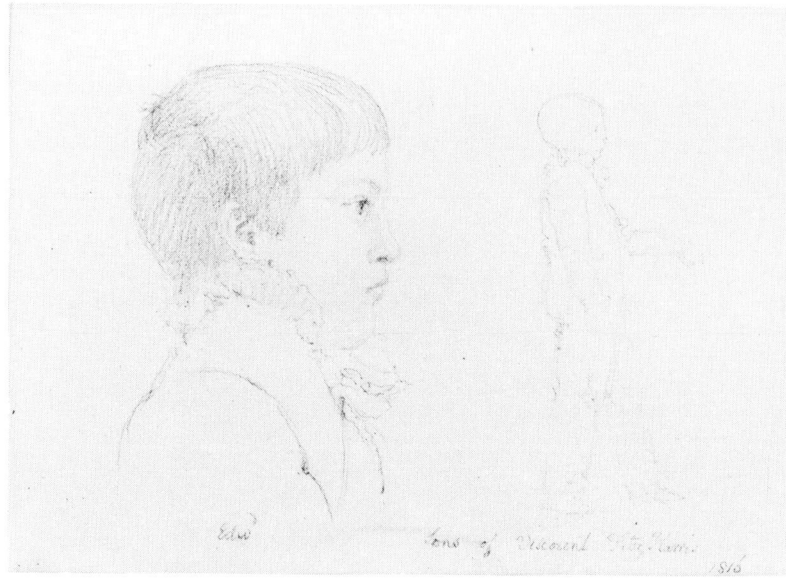

198 *Edward, a son of Viscountess Fitzharris,* 1816.
Pencil, 16·2 × 23·2 cms.

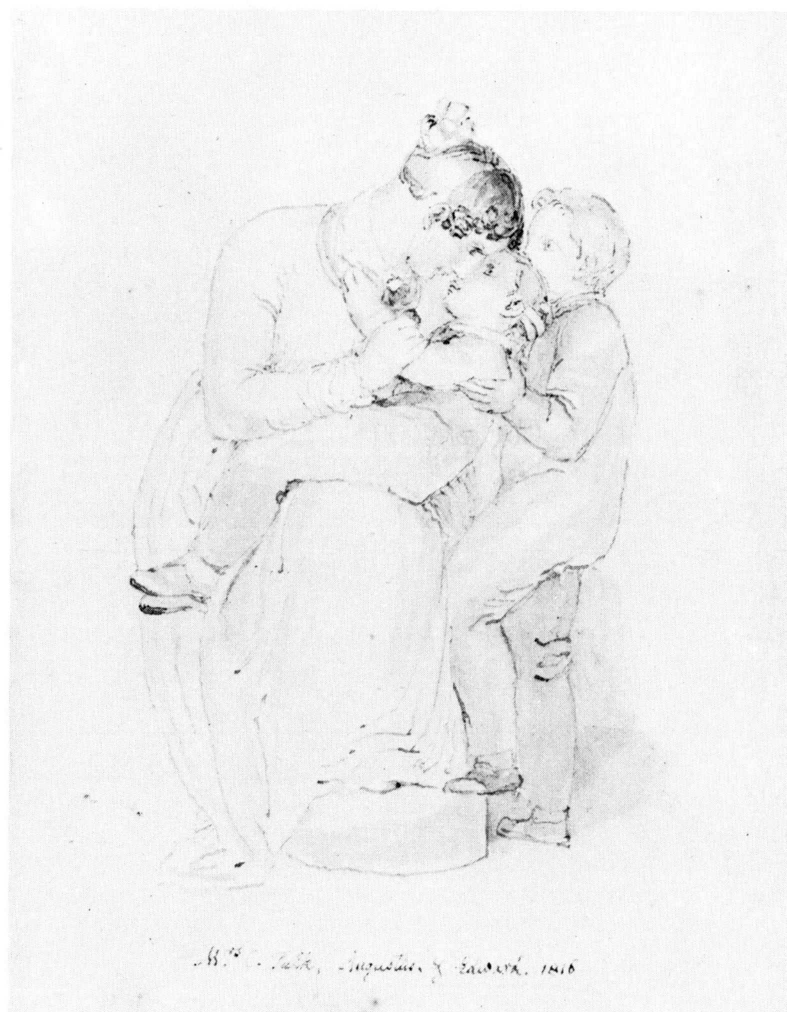

199 *Mrs. Charles Augustus Tulk, with her sons Augustus and Edward,* 1816.
Pen and ink and wash, 15·8 × 11·6 cms.

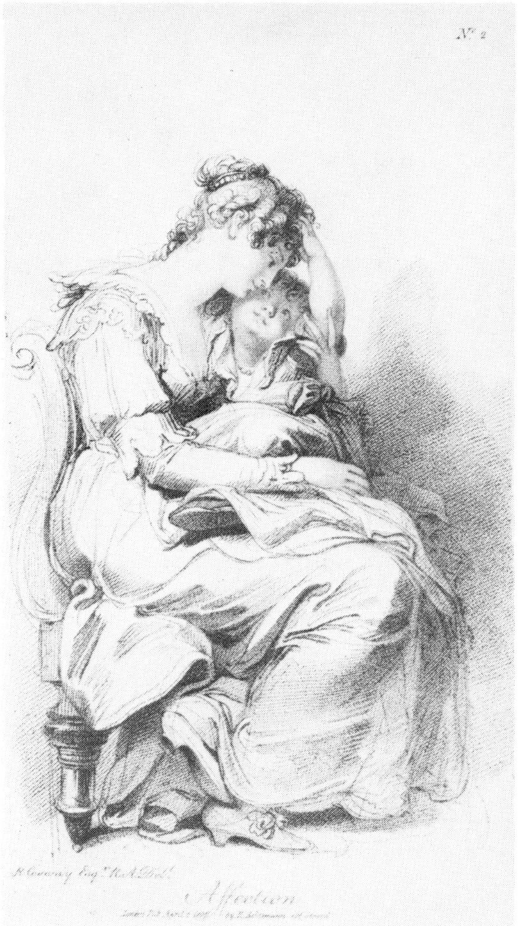

200 Richard Cosway: *Affection*. Engraving from *Drawing Book of Figures*, 1802, Plate 2.

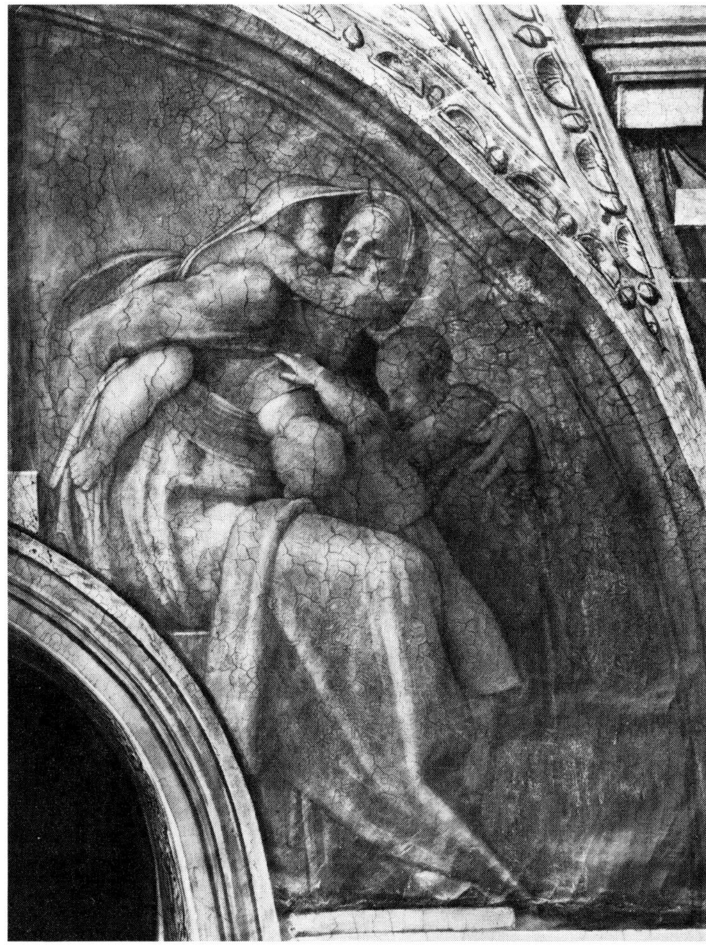

201 Michelangelo: *Joram with three of her children.*

expressed on the monument was unusual in the context of British sculpture at the turn of the century, with the possible exception of Banks, and found no parallel on the Continent at the time. With good reason, therefore, Lawrence in his 1826 discourse specifically mentioned in his assessment of Flaxman's work the 'inimitable groups of childhood and maternal affection'.[37]

3 Domestic affliction

'She may not often have an opportunity to hear a man speak upon his death-bed', says a character in one of Fanny Burney's novels, summoning a young niece to his bedside in the belief that his own end was close at hand.[38] She thus draws attention to an important aspect of devotional instruction in the second half of the eighteenth century, which can be found for example in the popular evangelical writings of Henry Venn entitled *The Complete Duty of Man*, first published in 1763 and frequently reprinted. He devoted a chapter to methods of instructing children, in which parents are told that the young would find it a 'great benefit' to learn at an early age about death and sickness, and that whenever a friend, neighbour or servant dies the occasion should be used for a lesson of God's will. Such a death-bed scene had been imagined by James Hervey in his widely read *Meditations among the Tombs*, first published in 1748 and often reprinted: 'The soul, just going to abandon the tottering clay, collects all her force, and exerts her last efforts. The good man raises himself on his pillow; extends a kind hand to his servants, which is bathed in tears; takes an affecting farewell of his friends; clasps his wife in a feeble embrace; kisses the dear pledges of their mutual love; and then pours all that remains of life and of strength, in the following words, "I die, my dear children: but God, the everlasting God, will be with you. Though you lose an earthly parent, you have a Father in Heaven, who

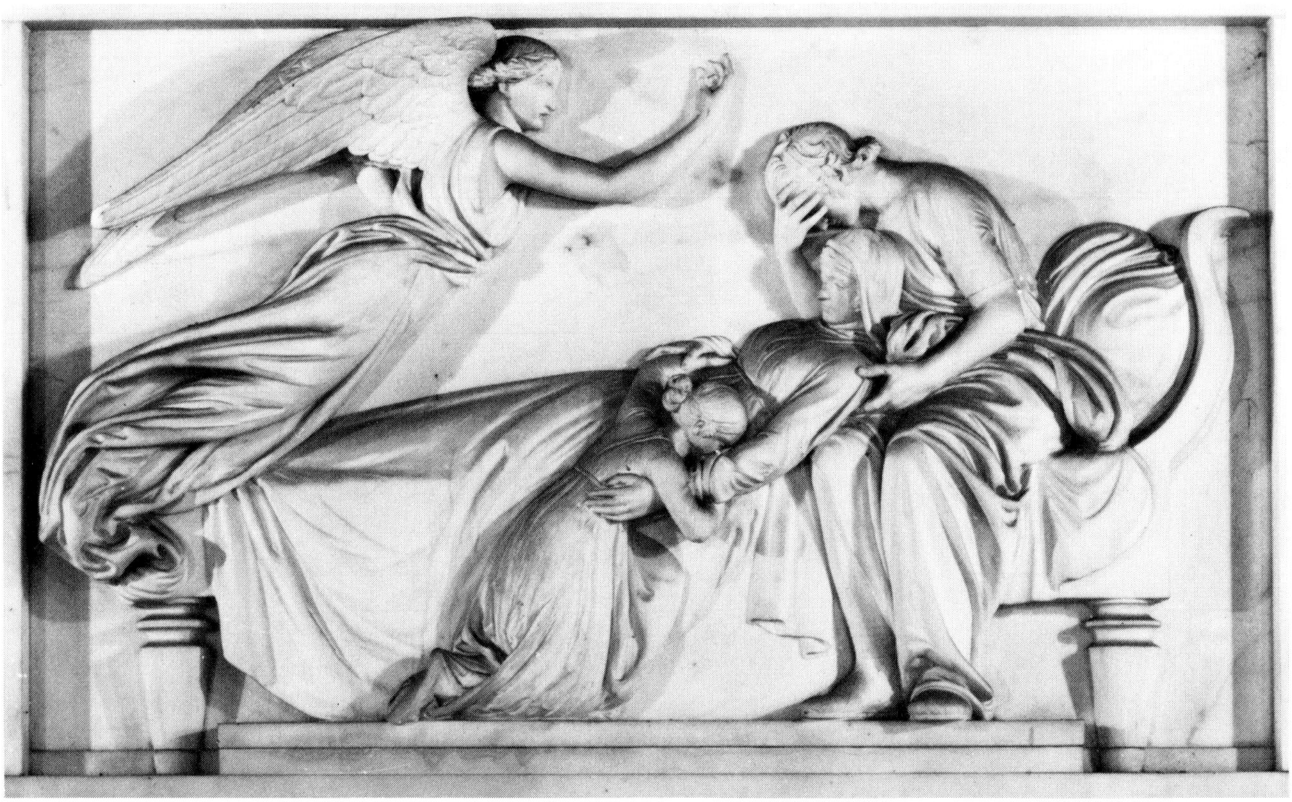

202 *Julia Annabella, Lady Shuckburgh-Evelyn: monument*, 1798–c.1802.
St. John Baptist, Upper Shuckburgh, Warwickshire.

lives for evermore. Nothing, nothing but an unbelieving heart, and irreligious life, can ever separate you, from the regards of His providence, from the endearments of His love".'[39]

The devotional sentiment and religious melancholy of such a passage in one of the best known of all the prose and verse meditations on death in the latter half of the eighteenth century, and which had a profound influence on later works such as Young's *Night Thoughts*, would not have been unknown to Flaxman.[40] The sentiment and melancholy of such passages are identical to those expressed in Flaxman's monuments showing death-bed scenes.

One such scene may have derived inspiration for its composition from a Roman sarcophagus. In 1798 he received a commission from the widower for a monument to *Julia Annabella, Lady Shuckburgh-Evelyn* for erection in the family's local church in Warwickshire (Plate 202). She is shown lying on her death-bed mourned by her husband and only daughter, whilst an angel hovers above pointing heavenwards. The classical prototype behind such a grouping can be found on the *Meleager* sarcophagus in the Albani collection, which Flaxman could easily have known, especially as it was familiar in engravings from as early as Bartoli's *Admiranda* (Plate 203). A similar source could lie behind Banks's *Mrs. Petrie* monument executed only three years earlier (Plate 204). There is, however, an important difference between the two sculptors in their interpretations of their death-bed scenes. The older artist has been uncompromisingly Neoclassical in his use of antique imagery, only introducing a cross to suggest a Christian context.[41] But in spite of his use of a classical formula, Flaxman's scene is a contemporary one, treated naturalistically, with a compromise in the dress between modern and classical. A marble panel which may have been for this monument was exhibited by Flaxman at the Royal Academy in 1802 with the title of *Domestic Affliction*, a title which aptly characterises both this and other death-bed scenes by him. They all illustrate mortal grief on earth, seemingly inconsolable, but at the same time there is a Christian promise—either in the imagery or the inscription—of an afterlife, achieving a delicate balance between the real world and that beyond the grave. The scene of death has become, in works like the *Shuckburgh-Evelyn* monument, a

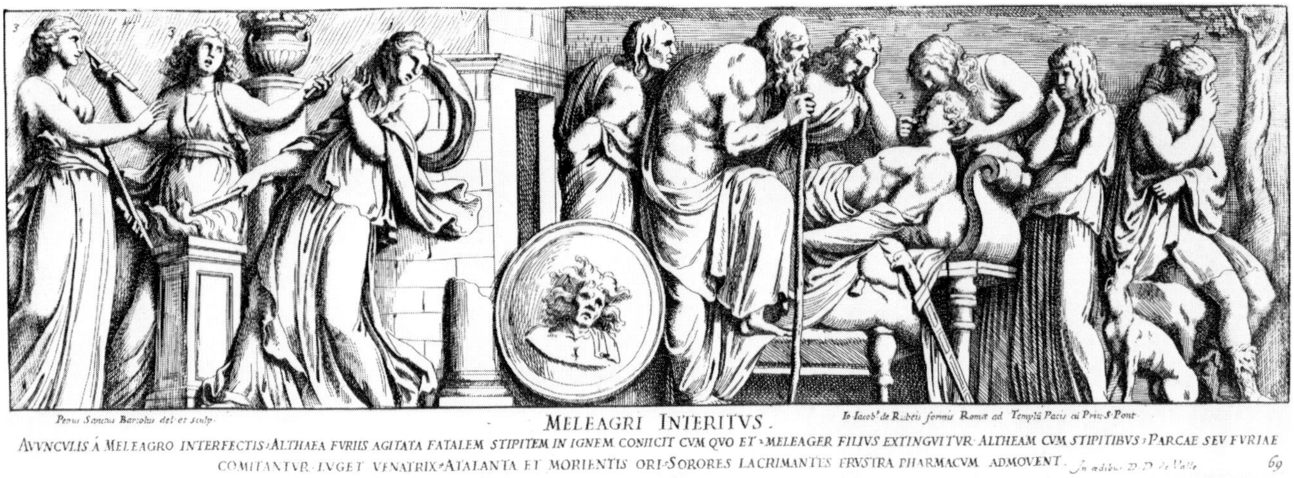

203 Pietro Santi Bartoli: *Admiranda Romanorum Antiquitatum*, 1693 edition. Plate 69, *Death of Meleager*.

204 Thomas Banks: *Mrs. Margaret Petrie: monument*, 1795. St. Mary, Lewisham, Kent.

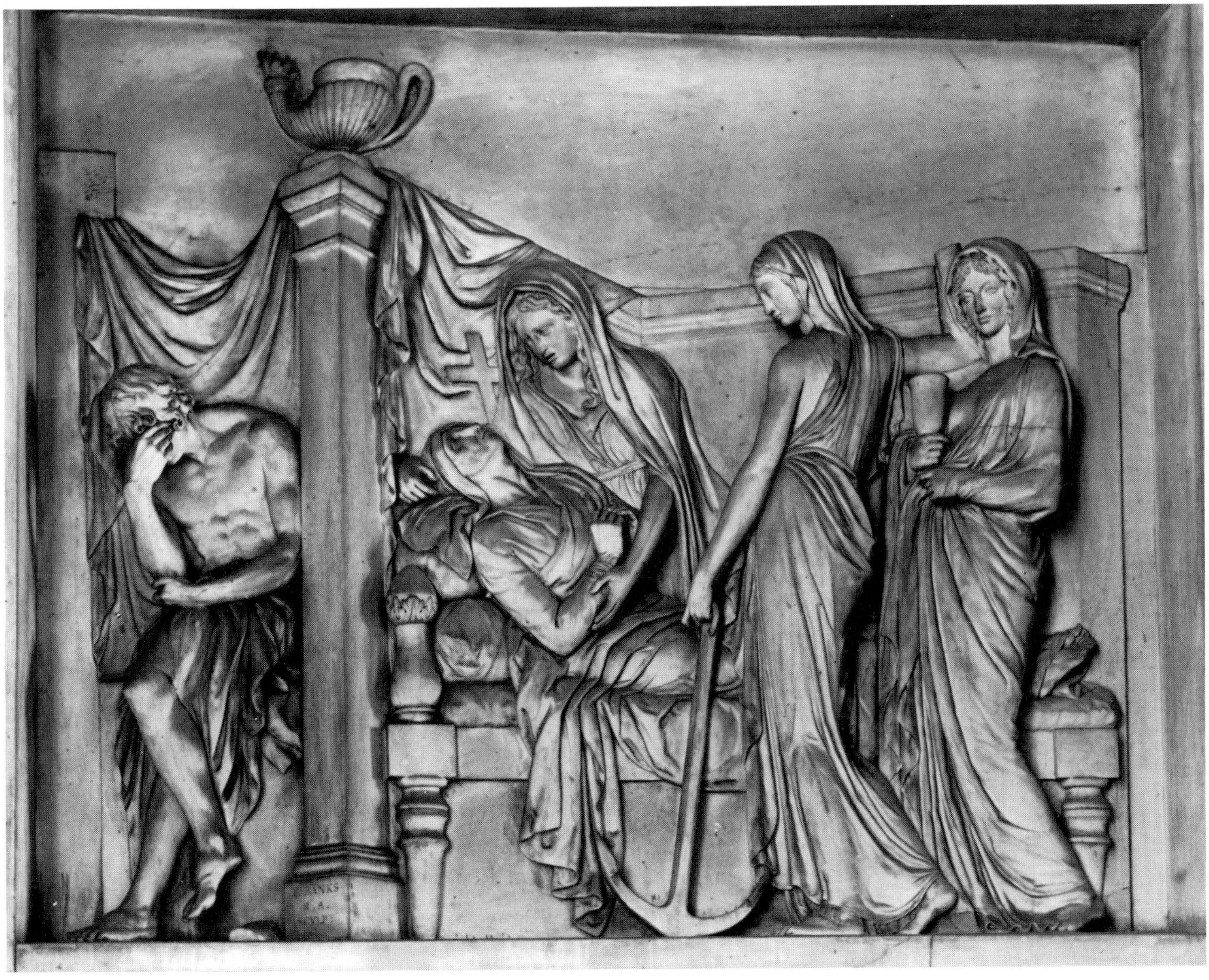

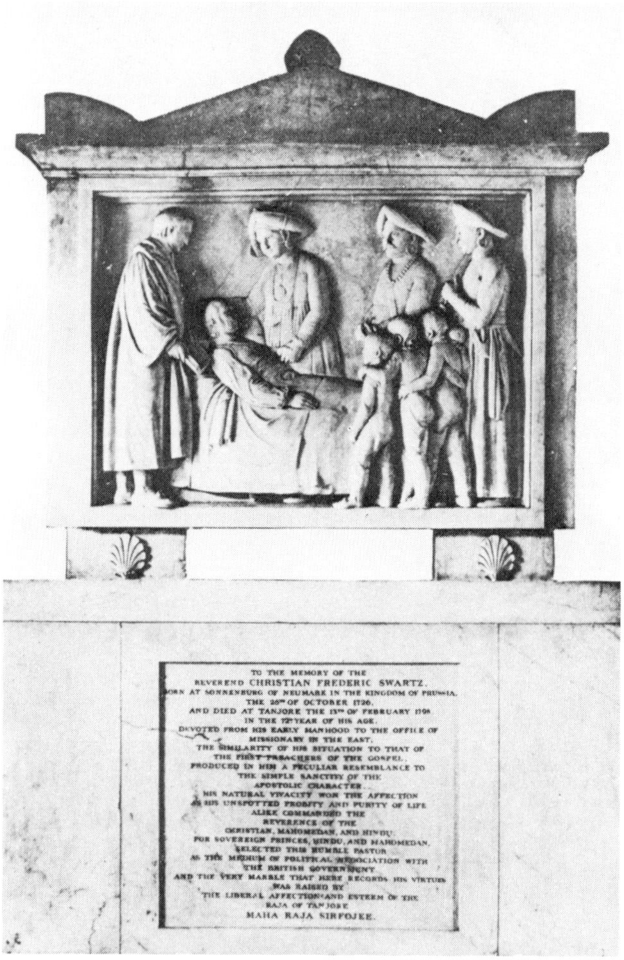

205 *Reverend Christian Frederick Schwartz: monument*, 1805.
Church in Little Fort, Tanjore, India.

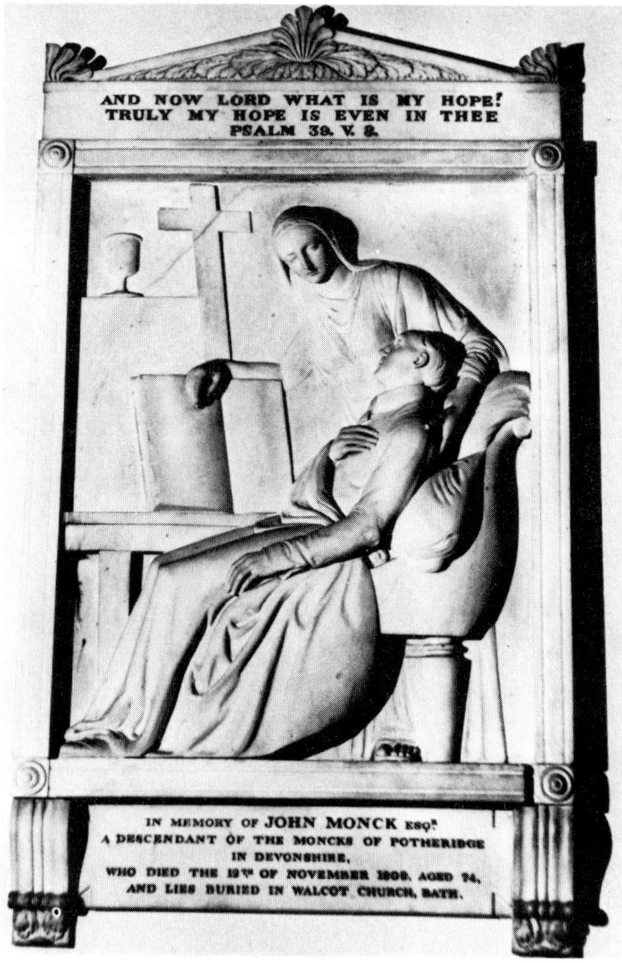

206 *John Monck: monument.* Died 1809.
St. Mary the Virgin, Reading, Berkshire.

contemporary and domestic event with the participants usually in modern dress, expressing emotions which are restrained. They are images of contemplative piety. This treatment of the death-bed theme almost as a realistic genre scene characterises other monuments by Flaxman, ranging from one to *Mrs. Charlotte Nicholas*, commissioned in 1800 (in Holy Cross, Ashton Keynes, Wiltshire) to later works such as the memorial to *Mrs. Mary Ann Bosanquet* of 1820 (in St. Teilo, Llantilio Crossenny, Monmouth).

The naturalism of the dying figure propped up on pillows, surrounded by relatives or friends, was a composition used by Flaxman for one of the most attractive of his tombs to be shipped overseas, that of the missionary *Reverend Christian Frederick Schwartz* in the church of the Little Fort at Tanjore, in southern India (Plate 205). He had been a missionary in Tanjore, where he had also taken an active part in the city's government, negotiating on its behalf with the British authorities, a dual role reflected in the choice of mourning figures. These include the Raja of Tanjore whom he had tutored but had not converted to Christianity, and whose portrait Flaxman was shortly to execute (see Plate 250).[42] He stands behind the bed with two of his servants, together with Schwartz's fellow missionary, Gericke (whose own monument has been discussed). In the foreground are four boys from the missionary school. As on the *Jones* monument of only a few years before, Flaxman has successfully represented two civilisations side by side, observed with a careful attention to detail. The Raja had written to the Society for the Promotion of Christian Knowledge in 1801 requesting they commission a monument, and they apparently chose Flaxman. When the monument arrived in India, the Raja was reluctant to allow it to go at once into the church, and kept it for a while in the

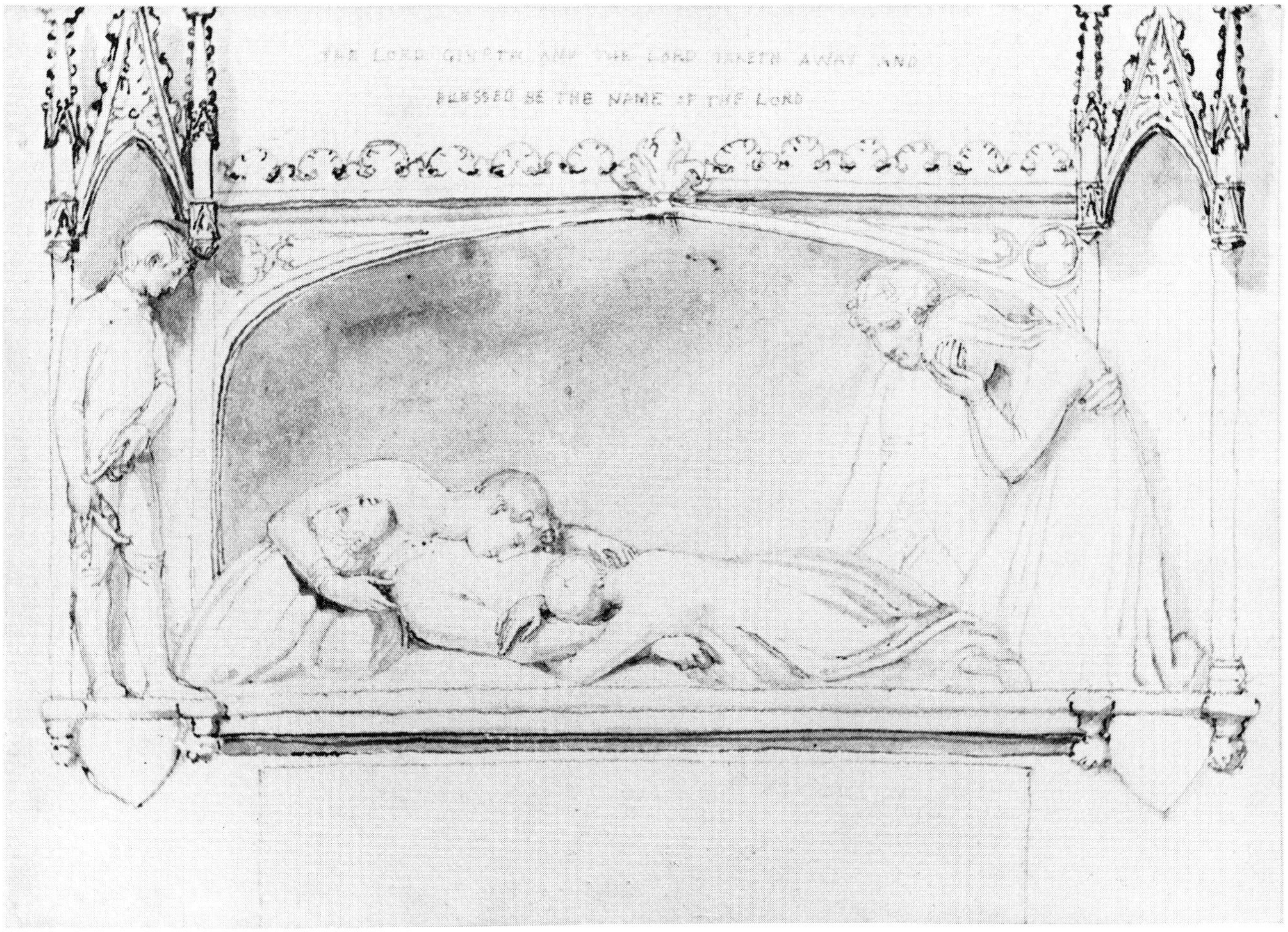

207 *Matthew Quantock: monument: design*, 1813–14.
Pen and ink and wash, 18·8 × 26·6 cms.

principal room of his palace amongst the portraits of his ancestors.[43]

Sometimes the death-bed scene would be treated in a more allegorical manner. On the relief panel showing the dying figure of *John Monck* (Plate 206) family and friends have been omitted, and instead only a standing figure of Religion is providing solace, her arm leaning on a large open Bible, with a cross in the background. The aged man has turned towards her, and seems to be uttering the words from the Psalm that are inscribed above the monument, 'And now Lord what is my hope?' The composition has the same poignant intimacy as other death-bed scenes, not on this occasion between husband and wife but between a mortal and a spiritual figure.

Amongst Flaxman's drawings is one which shows him trying to organise one of his death-bed scenes within the complex framework of a Gothic Revival arch flanked by two niches (Plate 207). Matthew Quantock had drowned whilst skating at the age of thirty and in the preliminary idea for the tomb Flaxman laid out the dead body so that it almost filled the whole width of the central part of the composition, showing a heavy indebtedness to medieval tomb figures. Flaxman surrounded Matthew with his parents, sisters and brother, who stands on the left holding some skates; these additional figures are so organised as to break across the framework in a manner not found in medieval monuments, and the architecture became background scenery to a contemporary genre event. This attractive and original design was not however the one finally executed. Perhaps the clients found it too expensive with six figures, or too unconventional in its design. The marble that was erected in Chichester Cathedral (Plate 208) is still a Gothic Revival work, but the children have been removed leaving only the

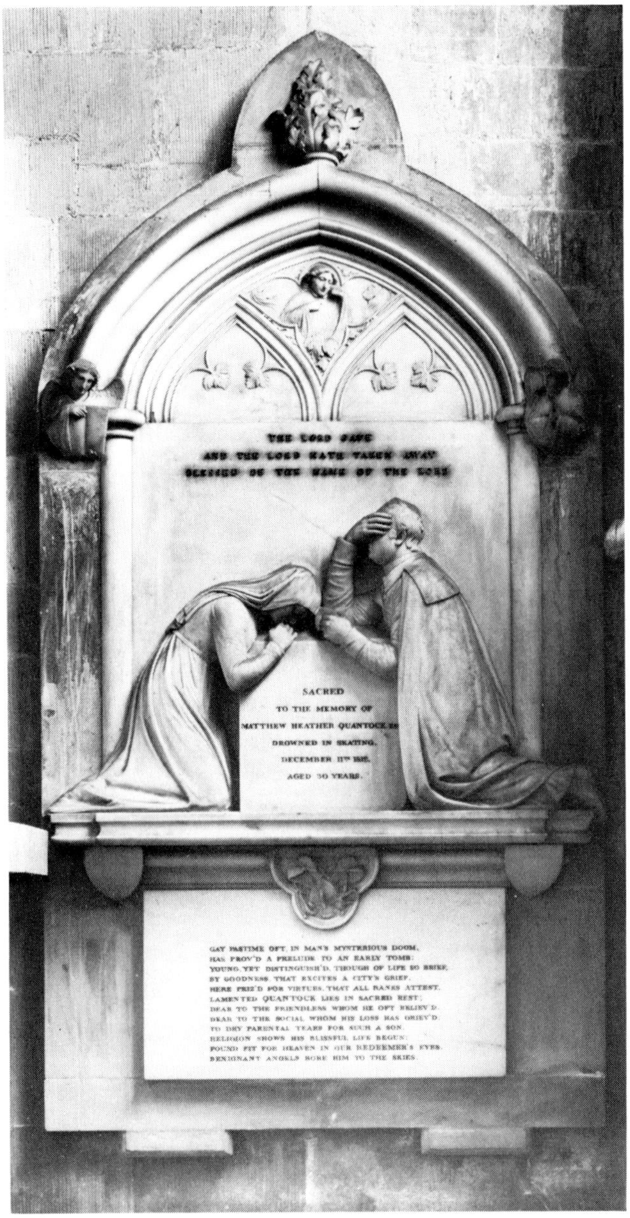

208 *Matthew Quantock: monument*, 1813–14.
Chichester Cathedral.

parents to mourn, the reference to skating appears only in the inscription, and the narrative genre element has disappeared. The result, when compared with the original idea, is dull.

The disposition of Matthew Quantock's body in the preliminary drawing belongs to a group of Flaxman's deathbeds in which a single prostrate figure, leaning on pillows, is framed by a Gothic arch. The effigy is shown in contemporary dress, but the pose itself ultimately derives from Etruscan sarcophagi lids, and from more recent sculptures such as Arnolfo di Cambio's *Madonna della Natività* (Plate 210). The example reproduced here of *Mrs. Sarah Udny* (Plate 209) is typical of this type of monument which although having historical precedents behind it, is a contemporary work both in dress and in treatment. The sculptor has allowed the figures to go beyond the confines of the framework, deriving the details of the pose from naturalistic studies made of family or friends lying meditating whilst reading (Plate 211).

For the monument to the Irish poetess *Mrs. Mary Tighe* (Plate 212), designed for an open air setting in the churchyard of her home parish, Flaxman placed her on a mattress, eternally asleep, an idea which Thomas Banks had used with great success for his *Penelope Boothby* monument of 1793 (in St. Oswald's Ashbourne, Derbyshire). Mary Tighe's contemporary fame rested on the volume which contained her longest, sentimental poem, *Psyche*, and the inclusion of the statuette at her head is an obvious allusion to this work. Flaxman kept the model for the monument in his drawing room, where it was seen by a visitor in 1824, who commented that 'it seems to be a favourite with the artist'. The visitor admired the 'beautifully composed' lines of the figure and the draperies, and noted that 'near the head sits a fairy-like Psyche in a mournful attitude'.[44]

Mary Tighe's poem had been printed in only a small the edition in 1795, but re-issued posthumously in 1811, the year after her death, rapidly being reprinted several times. The reasons for the immense popularity of the poem at the time, which caught the young Keats's imagination, can be seen in phrases used by contemporary critics when they speak of the 'elegance of design', 'feelings of the purest passions', and a 'fine purity of innocence';[45] phrases which are equally applicable to the monument itself. Flaxman must have regarded this as yet another sympathetic commission, and would have found in her verses lines with which he would no doubt have felt in accord because of their Romantic, melancholy sentiment:

> . . .'Most sweet would to my soul the hope appear,
> That sorrow in my verse a charm might find.'. . .

Sorrow and charm are combined by Flaxman in yet another series of monuments in which a mourner, usually female, in antique dress, leans over an urn and hides her face in her hands. This pattern was derived from classical prototypes of such weeping figures as those of Andromache or Agrippina. This was the least original of Flaxman's patterns, having become by the

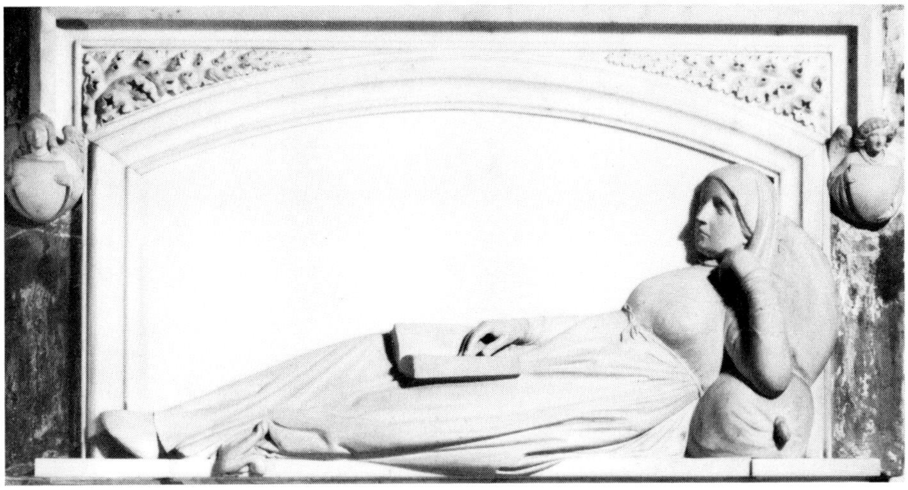

209 *Sarah Udny: monument*, 1812.
Chichester Cathedral.

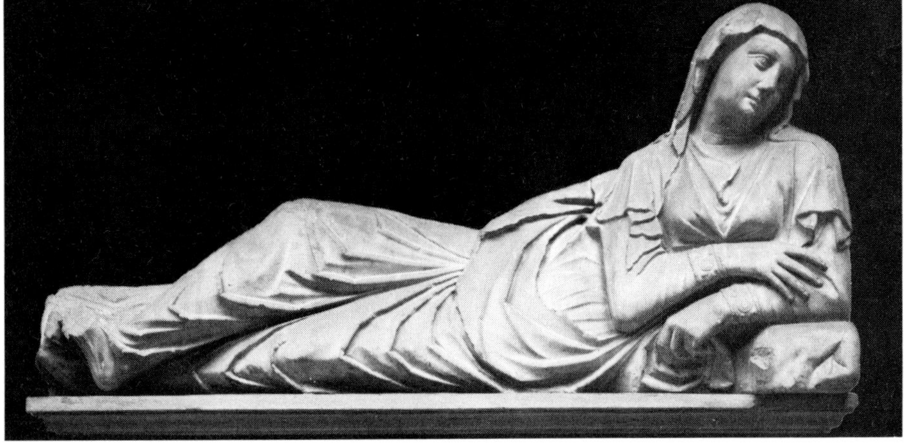

210 Arnolfo di Cambio: *Madonna della Natività.*

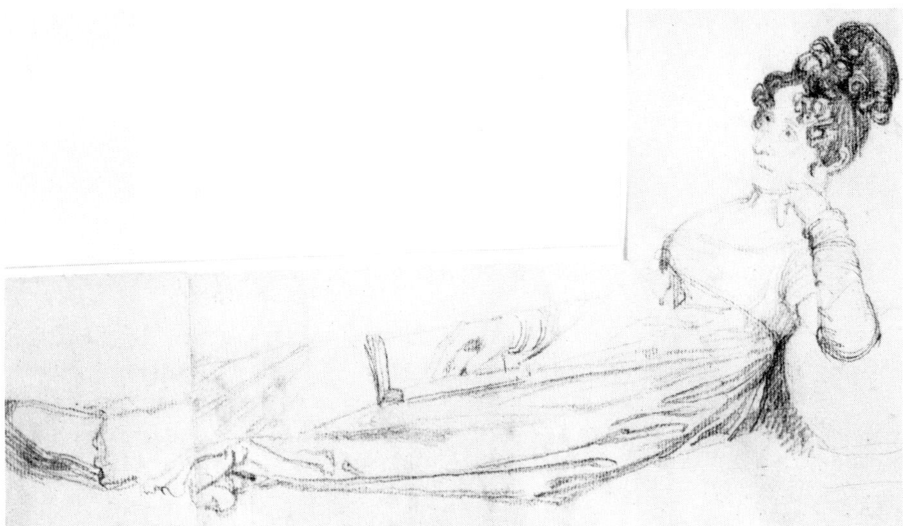

211 *Lady reclining with a Book.*
Pencil, 18 × 33 cms.

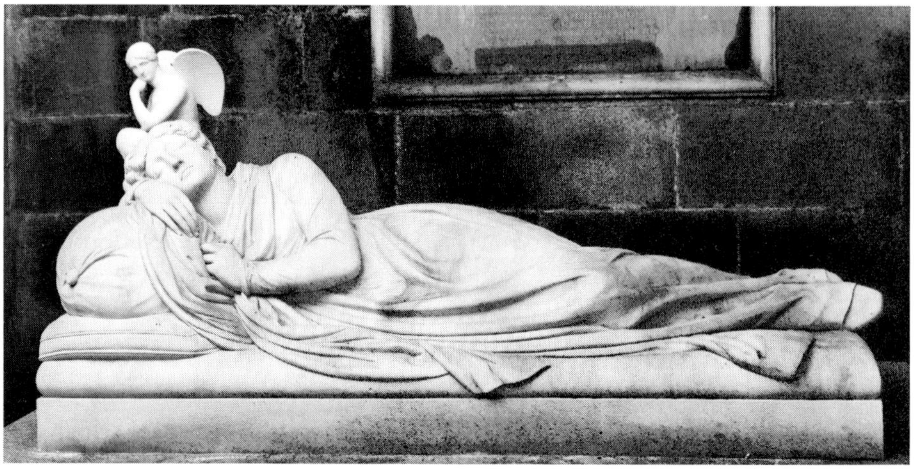

212 *Mrs. Mary Tighe: monument*, 1814–15.
Parish Churchyard, Inistioge, County Kilkenny.

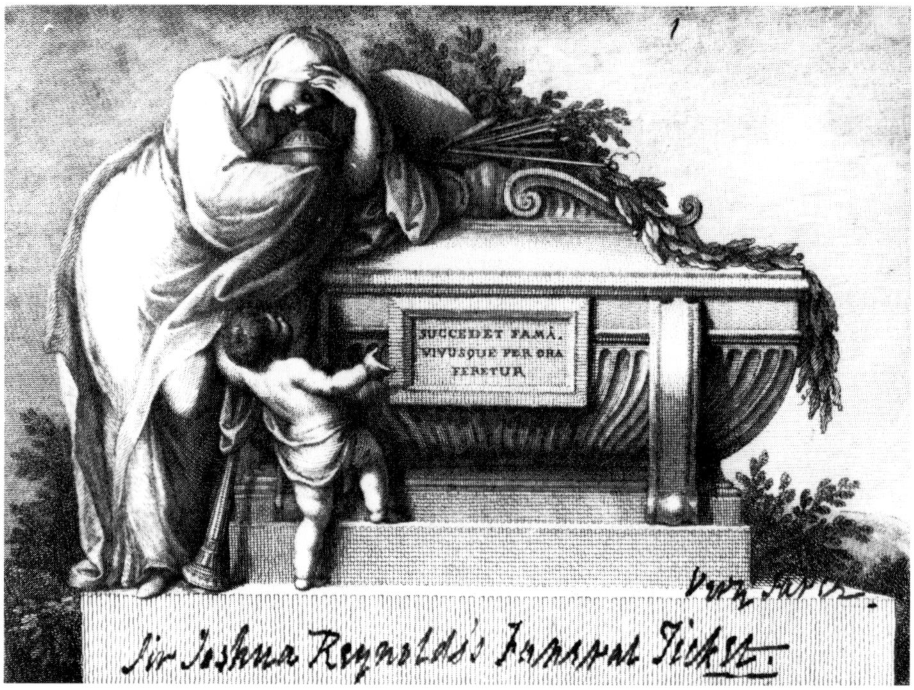

213 Edward Francis Burney: *Sir Joshua Reynolds's Funeral Ticket.*
Engraving by Francesco Bartolozzi, 1792.

turn of the century not only a common form of church monument, but also the composition generally used on mourning jewellery and funeral cards (Plate 213), where the imagery is also often combined with a weeping willow. Flaxman's tombs using this design are the closest in his oeuvre to classical prototypes, since many Roman tombs of this kind had survived, and in addition many engravings were available in the archaeological literature. The weeping, single figure makes a frequent appearance not only on Flaxman's monuments, but also on those of many of his contemporaries both in Britain and on the Continent. The image was entirely pagan, and as a group in Flaxman's *oeuvre* forms the least overtly Christian series of monuments that he executed amongst the patterns frequently chosen by clients. The sentiment expressed is one of generalised piety. Only the occasional use of a Biblical text acts as a reminder that these are Christian monuments not pagan ornaments perhaps sited in some 'picturesque' garden layout. By putting to one side any Christian characterisation, which is such an essential and often original element in many of Flaxman's other monuments, he is conforming more to contemporary, secularised taste, in which religious belief is more

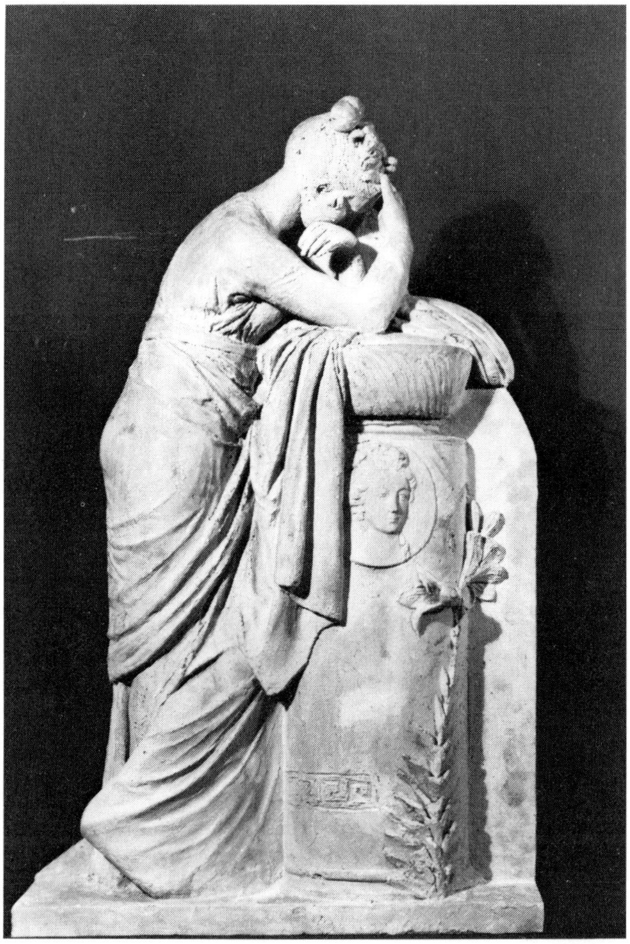

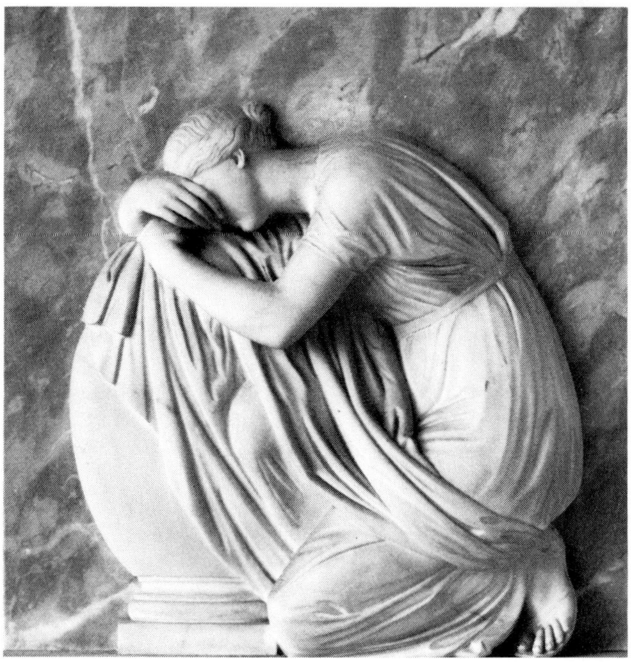

generalised and not specifically Christian.

At their best these monuments are attractive and elegant exercises in the Neoclassical idiom, with a variation between a standing or a kneeling figure (Plates 214 and 215), or occasionally a seated one. For the final marble of the monument to the *Honorable Barbara Lowther*, commissioned by her sister the Duchess of Bolton at a cost of 220 guineas for St. Mary Magdalene, Richmond, Surrey, Flaxman added an inscription tablet below and flanking pilasters, and set the whole composition against a background slab of grey marble. The design epitomises the 'gentle manners' and 'refined taste' of the deceased to which the inscription refers.

For the last decade of his career, however, this type of monument became increasingly stereotyped, sometimes even clumsy in execution, showing a lack of interest on the sculptor's part in a formula that was requested too often. Flaxman often exhibited the model or finished marble for other types of monuments at the Royal Academy, but from this group he seems not to have exhibited designs in this way, suggesting that the sculptor did not regard them as sufficiently original.

4 Fit for a hero

The most active period of Flaxman's career coincided with the Napoleonic Wars, and as one of the principal sculptors of the time he naturally received commissions to commemorate some of the heroes who had fought on land and at sea. Flaxman's tombs of this kind are usually pagan and humanistic images, sometimes presented with funerary pomp, unlike the majority of his other tombs which stress Christian virtues and include Biblical texts. Despite the patriotic secularism of his war monuments, however, some of them nevertheless include the familiar elements of sentimental piety.

Flaxman's preliminary drawings for the large free-standing monument to *Admiral Earl Howe* in St. Paul's Cathedral, commissioned in 1803, show that for this major work he suggested at an early stage that Howe's considerable naval achievements should be expressed in terms of imperial Roman splendour (Plate 216).[46] A pile of trophies, helmets and a laurel wreath, together

214 *(above left) Honourable Barbara Lowther: monument: model,* 1805–7.
Plaster, 116·2 cms. high.

215 *(below left) Caroline Elwes: monument.* Died 1812.
St. Andrew, Great Billing, Northamptonshire.

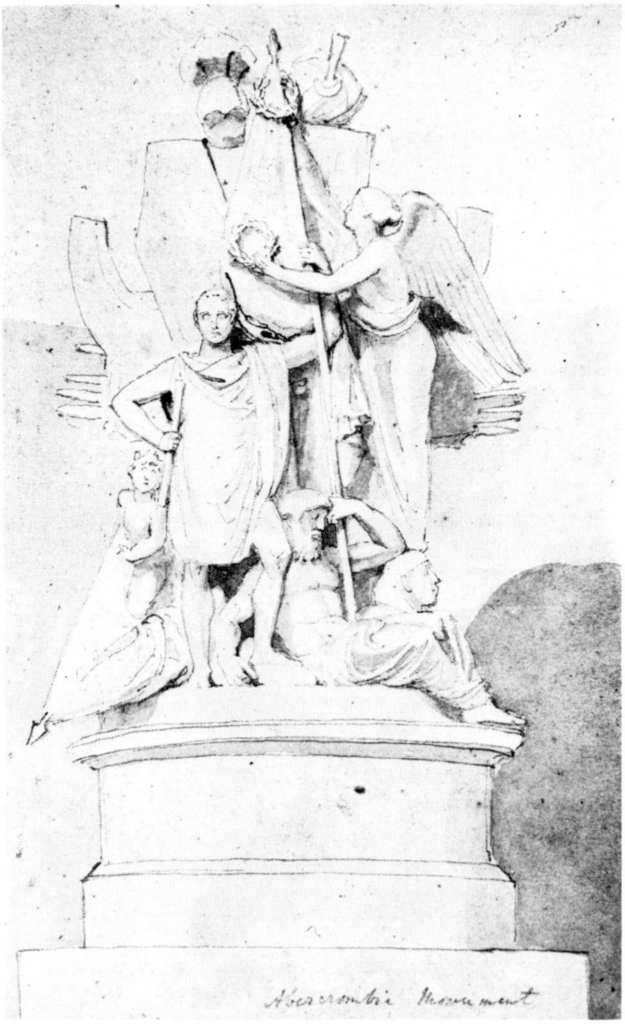

216 *Admiral Richard, Earl Howe: monument: design*, c. 1803. Pen and ink and wash, 23·4 × 14·9 cms.

with the hull of an antique Roman galley, form the background to the admiral who is wearing a toga and about to be crowned by a winged Victory. The monument in this form would have included neither British nor contemporary references in its imagery. This totally antique concept, assembled however into a composition which an ancient Roman would find unfamiliar, was altered by the stage of the final marble, presumably because of its lack of specific patriotism (Plate 217). The outline form of the monument has been changed into a more broadly based pyramid. The prow of the galley has become that of the *Queen Charlotte*, behind a lifesize seated Britannia. On a lower level Howe stands dressed in contemporary naval uniform and boat-cloak. A British lion has been introduced on the right: Victory, no longer crowning the hero, is placed on the left together with Fame reading the inscription (Plate 218), which commemorates Howe's two main victories: the relief of Gibraltar in 1782 and the defeat of the French fleet on the famous 'Glorious First of June' in 1794.

A pyramidal composition incorporating several lifesize figures had already been used by Flaxman for his freestanding *Mansfield* monument in Westminster Abbey (Plate 76). He had been at that time influenced by the seventeenth-century papal tombs in St. Peter's, both in the overall design and in the combination of contemporary and allegorical figures. This influence is still evident in the *Howe* monument, omitting—as he had done on the *Mansfield*—any reference in the imagery to an afterlife. Flaxman has stressed the worldly and the pagan. But his combination of realism and allegory is not entirely successful, and the composition remains a series of disunited elements that fail to blend into a harmonious whole. The image of the admiral himself is also rather wooden. As the lighting in the cathedral was different from that of his own studio, Flaxman had left the marble unfinished when it was

218 *Admiral Richard, Earl Howe: monument: detail*, 1803–11. St. Paul's Cathedral.

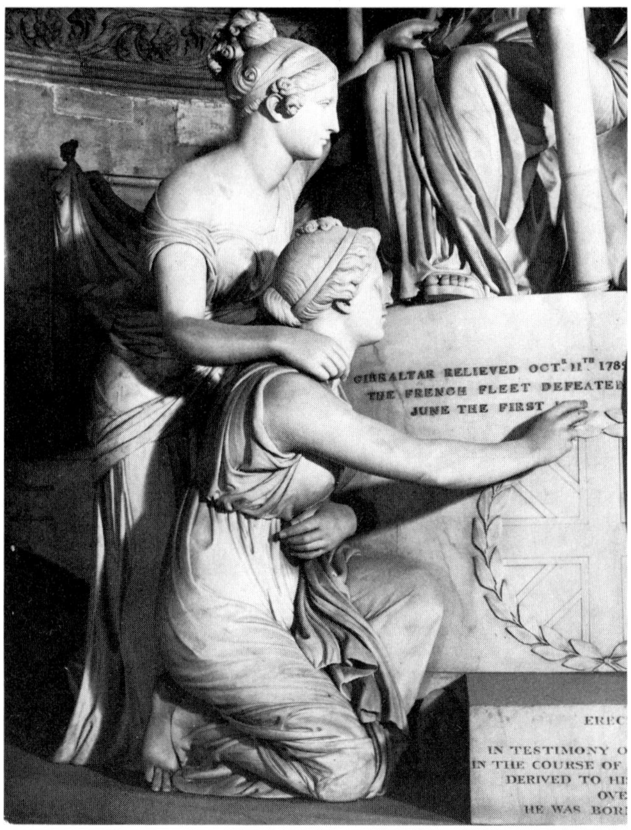

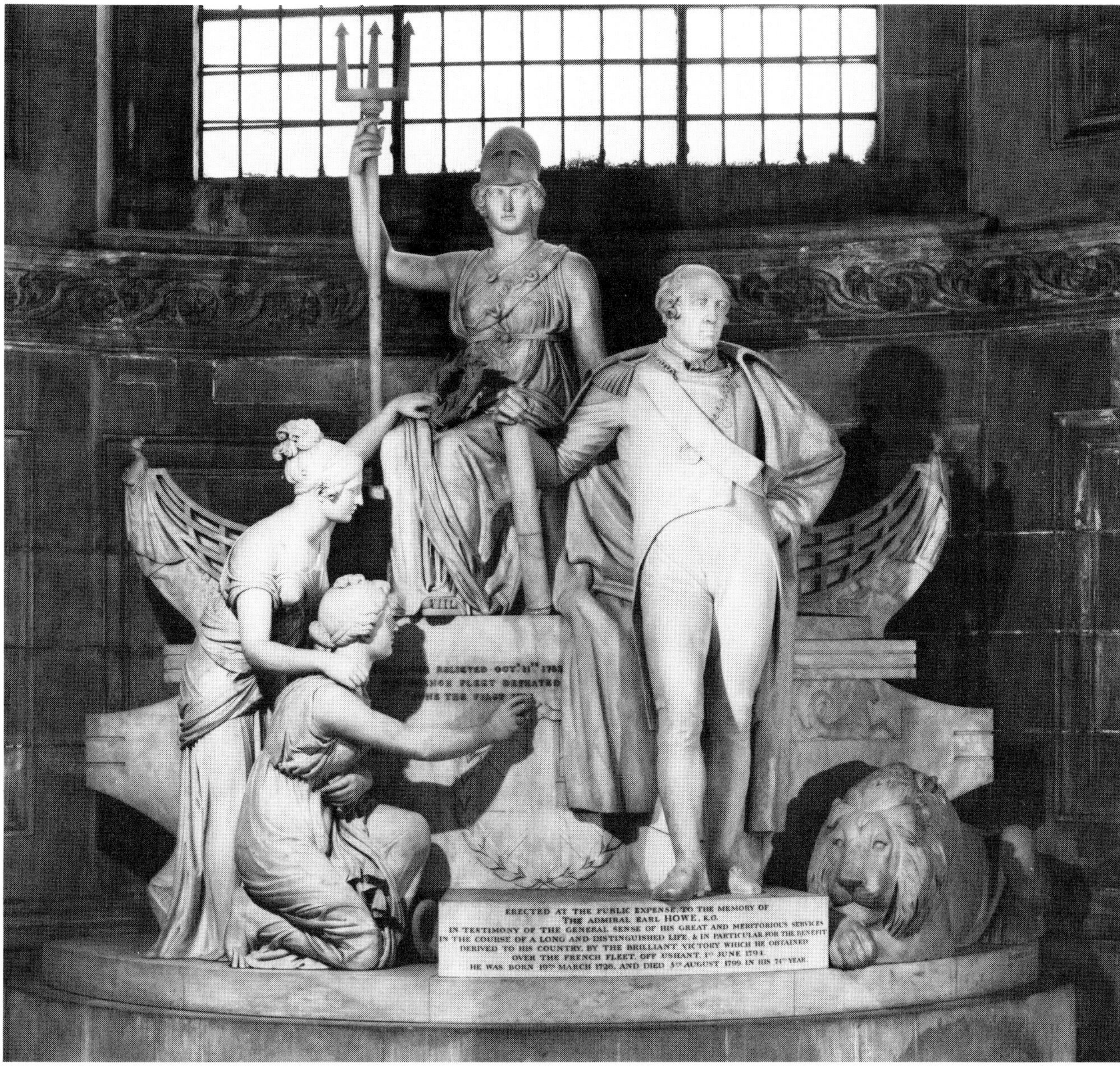

217 *Admiral Richard, Earl Howe: monument*, 1803–11. St. Paul's Cathedral.

transported to its site, so that the carving could be finished *in situ*.[47] The most successful part is the group in which, as Flaxman described them, 'Victory (without wings) leans, like a sister, on the shoulder of Fame, beholding with delight the record of her heroes' deeds'.[48] This 'delight' has been rendered in a pair of graceful, Neoclassical young ladies, correct in their antique dress and hairstyle but imbued with a familiar turn-of-the century charm.

In spite of these strictures however, Flaxman was more successful in visual terms in rising to the demands of such a commission than his contemporary rivals. Four sculptors had been commissioned by the Treasury's Committee of National Monuments or 'Committee of Taste' as it was to become known, established in 1802, to produce a series of memorials to heroes of the Napoleonic Wars. These were to be sited in St. Paul's Cathedral, which had hitherto been kept clear of monuments. Howe, together with General Sir Ralph Abercromby as commander-in-chief, were each to be commemorated with the most costly monuments at 6,000 guineas apiece. The young Richard West-

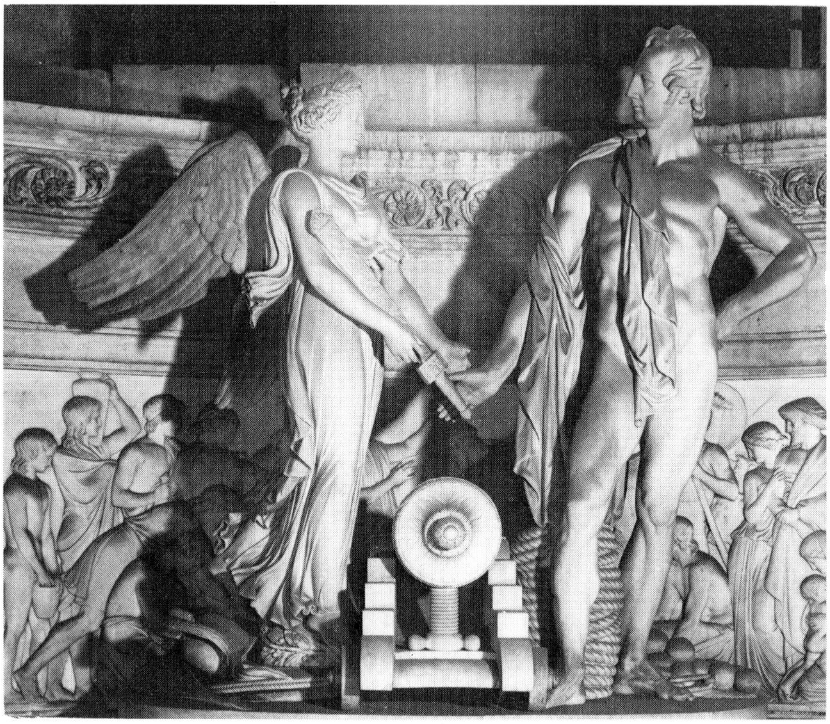

219 Thomas Banks: *Captain Richard Rundle Burgess: monument: detail.* 1802. St. Paul's Cathedral.

macott, whose sojourn in Italy had slightly overlapped with Flaxman's and who was to be a serious rival over the Napoleonic monumental commissions, received the one to Abercromby. He produced a narrative group of the General falling off his rearing horse into the arms of an officer, an uncomfortable piece of realism that looks incongruous in its setting. The other two commissions, each worth 4,000 guineas, went in one case to the elderly Banks for a memorial to Captain Westcott, who appears as a classical hero in a chiton in the arms of a winged Victory. The other commission went to the rather mediocre sculptor Rossi for a joint monument to Captains Mosse and Riou, who had both been killed at the battle of Copenhagen in 1801.

The new committee of 1802 superseded the one which had been set up in 1796 when it was realised that all the memorials that would be necessary in the wars could not be accommodated in the already overcrowded space of Westminster Abbey. Only Wren's tomb existed in St. Paul's and its clear aisles and crossing were obvious sites for the new monuments to Napoleonic War heroes. In this earlier period only two had been commissioned for the cathedral, both of which were artistic failures (Plate 219). Banks had carved Captain Burgess (killed at the battle of Camperdown) almost completely naked as he received a sword from a classical Victory poised on a modern cannon, whilst Rossi had shown Captain Faulknor dressed only in a classical chiton as he collapses into Neptune's arms. The members of this committee dispensing public funds had been elected by the Royal Academy. Richard Payne Knight's anti-Adacemy lobby not only led to the establishment of the new committee, but also to the exclusion of the Academy from it. The men responsible for commissioning the *Howe* monument included Charles Townley, Sir George Beaumont, and Henry Bankes (who was an M.P. and a Trustee of the British Museum) working under the Paymaster as chairman, Charles Long (later Lord Farnborough). By the time the *Nelson* monument was commissioned Thomas Hope had joined the committee, as well as Flaxman's future patron Lord Egremont.

By the time of Nelson's death, St. Paul's Cathedral was already becoming occupied by large Napoleonic War memorials, or would shortly be so when the works arrived from various studios. A writer in the *Monthly Magazine* in 1806 was perhaps justifiably disconcerted by such grandiose developments, saying that 'if we erect such stately monuments to captains and subaltern generals, who, gallant men though they be, fill no assignable space in the eye of Fame, what mausoleum, what pyramid, shall we raise to the memory of the immortal Nelson!'[49] The writer would have found the answer erected in the cathedral in 1818, a further commission for Flaxman (Plates 220 to 222).

Commissioned in 1807, Flaxman's *Nelson* monu-

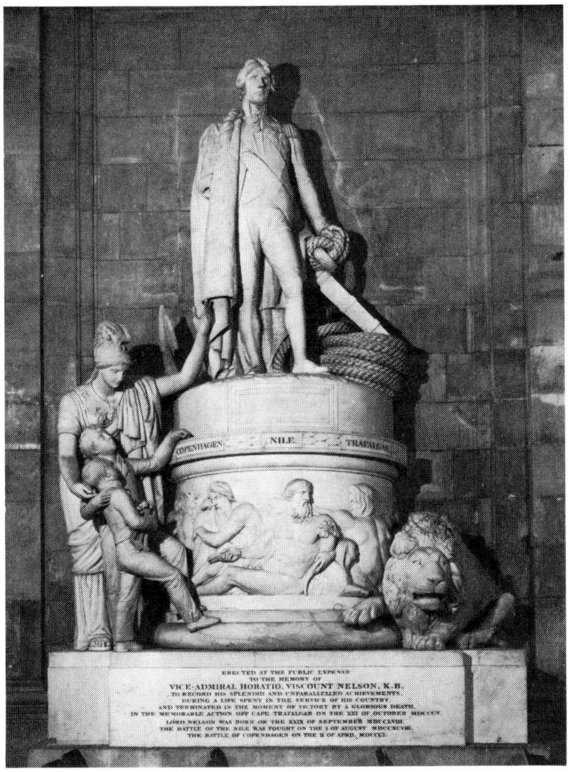

220 *Vice-Admiral Horatio, Viscount Nelson: monument,* 1807–18.
St. Paul's Cathedral.

221 *Vice-Admiral Horatio, Viscount Nelson: monument: detail with Minerva and midshipmen.*

222 *Vice-Admiral Horatio, Viscount Nelson: monument: detail with head of Nelson.*

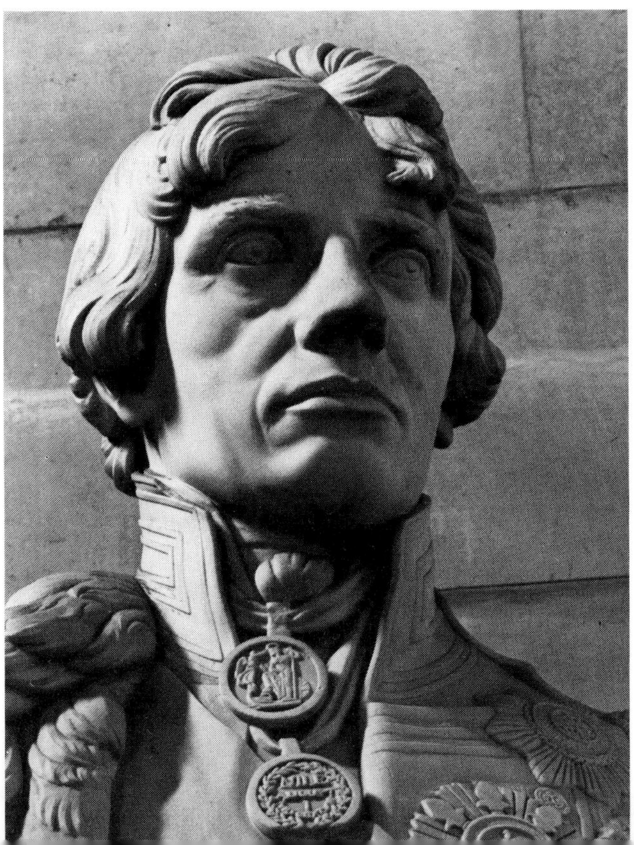

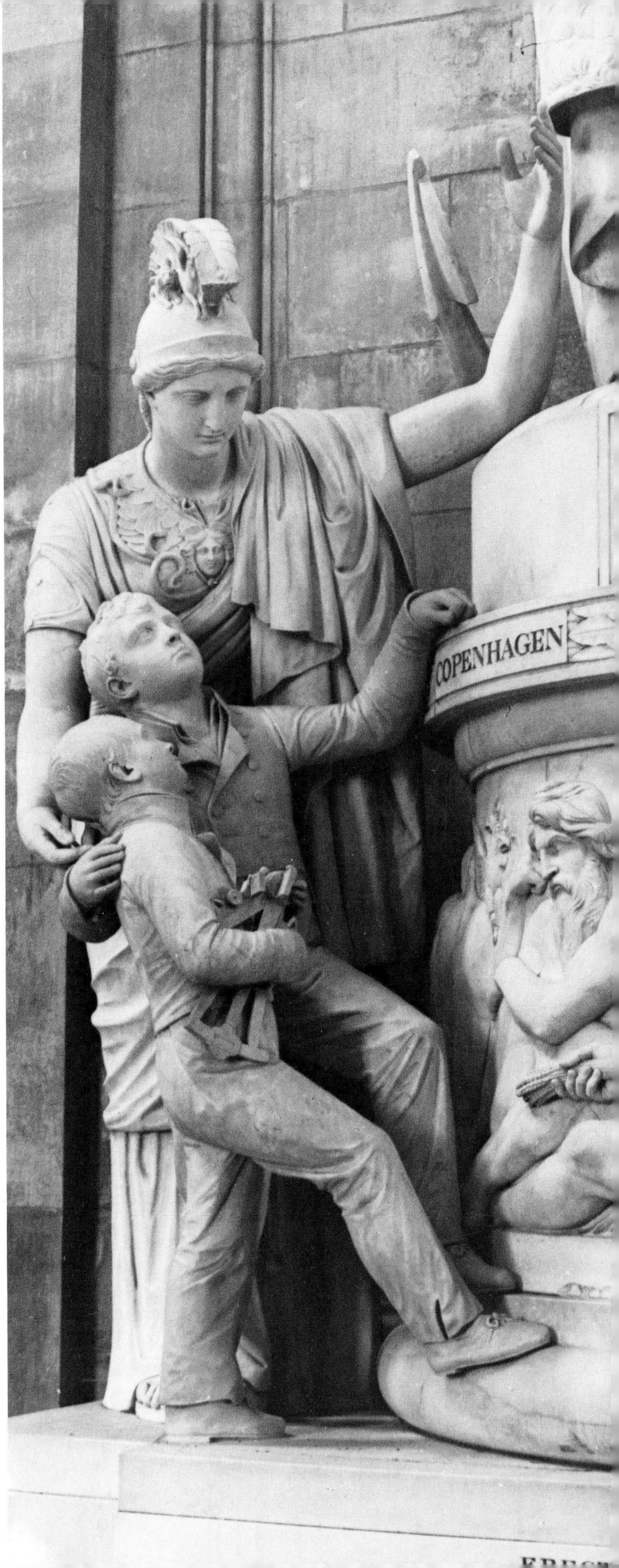

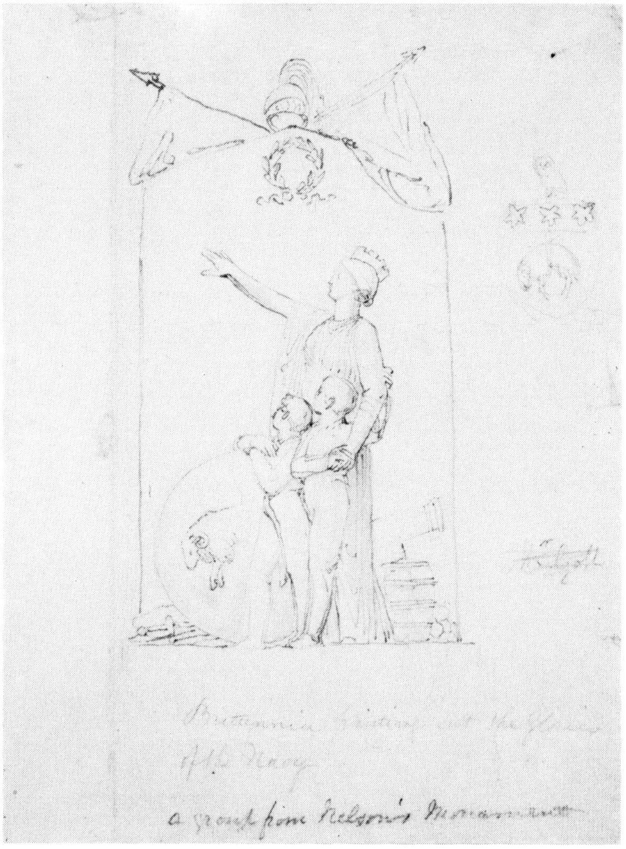

223 *Vice-Admiral Horatio, Viscount Nelson: monument: design.* c. 1807. Pen and ink and wash, 24 × 18·6 cms.

ment is a much more successful work than his earlier *Howe*. Nelson, rather than Britannia, is now placed at the apex of the pyramid, standing beside an anchor and a coiled rope. Minerva stands below, drawing the attention of two midshipmen to the hero. The nautical references are continued in the classical river gods carved in relief on the pedestal, which is inscribed with the names of Nelson's three main victories at Copenhagen, the Nile and Trafalgar. The composition is completed by the usual lion. Nelson's funeral car and coffin, which had been seen by thousands on its way from Greenwich to St. Paul's, had also combined classical allegory with contemporary realism. The car had been carved with the prow and stern of the *Victory*; symbolic palm trees supported a classical canopy over the coffin. The drapes were embroidered with the names of Nelson's main battles, and the emblems on the outer coffin included the British lion, Britannia, Neptune, the Sphinx, an eagle, crocodile, sea-horse and dolphin. Although Flaxman was using an accepted mixture of allegory and realism, his design for the monument echoes some of the elements of the 1806 procession.

In the *Howe* monument Britannia had occupied a very prominent place in the design, clutching a rather dominating trident. In the *Nelson* Britannia has given way to a Minerva. These two allegorical figures were regarded as alternatives on war monuments. On the *Nelson*, Minerva is placed behind the midshipmen in their contemporary dress, she performs a less stridently didactic and patriotic role. Indeed her role is almost a motherly one, as she bends down with one arm stretched round them, so that this group has affinities with the naturalistic genre scenes on Flaxman's other tombs of the same period depicting a teacher or minister with his pupils. Before he had completed the *Nelson* monument he was to work on the *Fitzharris* commission, using a composition that might have grown out of the group of Minerva with the midshipmen. Preliminary drawings for the *Nelson* monument (in the British Museum and York City Art Gallery) emphasise the motherliness of this group, suggesting that from the early stages of the design Flaxman intended to stress this element on the memorial (Plate 223). In doing so he was not only employing a favourite theme of the mother and child, but he might also have been influenced by one of the many eulogistic poems published on Nelson's death. One such poem[50] concluded with the lines:

'. . . when autumn brings the shadowy year,
Thy circled urn shall drink her warmest tear:
The mother there shall lead her child to con
The deeds engraven on thy sculptur'd stone!
The boy shall turn a hero from the pile,
And rise the future Nelson of the isle!'

The maternal aspect of this group was the most significant part of the *Nelson* monument to strike a German critic a few years later when he saw it for the first time: 'Full of inner motherly love and also respect for the hero, this tall woman seems to lead the boys, and this double feeling is expressed as much in her face as in her very noble bearing. This single figure was sufficient for me to acknowledge the respected artist, whose mind and soul strike through the most difficult and reluctant material and captivate the observer'.[51]

The figure of the admiral himself on the monument appears at first sight to be realistic, especially as Nelson is shown in contemporary uniform. Flaxman would doubtless have agreed with Southey's criticism made in 1807 about earlier Napoleonic monuments, when he had written (in a book which Flaxman knew): 'The artists know not what to do with their villainous costume, and, to avoid uniforms in marble, make their unhappy statues half naked'.[52] Flaxman's *Nelson* stands alone, as if still in command, without any allegorical clutter surrounding him, unlike Benjamin West's design for the pediment at Greenwich Hospital (1810–12), where the half naked Nelson is dying in the lap of Britannia or, worse still, the projected monument by Canova. C. R. Cockerell expressed alarm that the Italian might be commissioned rather than Flaxman. 'May our sense and taste defend us from his [Canova's] monument to Lord Nelson,' he wrote. 'The four quarters of the globe with elephant's heads and American feathers, the hackneyed plan of a square upon a round, the bas-reliefs representing a dead Roman borne from a galley to Britannia in the dress of a theatrical priestess. What is the English tar to say when he sees his beloved Nelson in a Roman petticoat, why, will he say, are British sailors to imitate a Roman dress, are we not as original, as great a people as ever ruled the waves and influenced the world!'[53] Flaxman would have shared his friend's patriotism expressed in this form, and he created a contemporary, naturalistic image which any British tar would recognise.

Flaxman has, nevertheless, to some extent idealised his figure. Nelson's blind eye is not evident, and the sculptor has so arranged the folds of the cloak that one is not aware that Nelson had lost an arm. When a limited competition was held for a *Nelson* monument in Birmingham, Westmacott made no attempt in his design to conceal the empty sleeve, and tucked it into Nelson's sash, making it a prominent feature.[54] Even before he received the commission for the St. Paul's monument, Flaxman was already giving some thought to Nelson's defects, writing in a letter that 'although Lord Nelson had nearly or quite lost the sight of one eye, that was no apparent defect in his face, and in the execution of a statue the loss of his arm might be so indicated yet obscured that it would not injure the general effect of the work, or he might be represented as you observe in his perfect figure'.[55]

Nelson's triumphant achievement had captured contemporary imagination much more so than Howe's. The *Nelson* monument is not only better because Flaxman had learnt from his earlier mistakes, but also presumably because he was in sympathy with the deeds of the man he was recording, whom he had even met. After hearing the news of Trafalgar he had written to Hayley telling him, that 'we, with all our countrymen deplore the loss of gallant Nelson. I thank you for the wish that I may execute his monument; he certainly expressed the wish that I should the morning we met him at Sir William Hamilton's.'[56] A fortnight later he was working on a marble bust of Nelson 'for one of his friends, which I think will be a striking likeness'.[57] Flaxman would have agreed with West that an important contemporary event should 'excite awe and veneration', and that Nelson should not be represented as he actually died 'in the gloomy hold of a ship like a sick man in a prison hole'.[58] Flaxman did not go so far as to create either an *Apotheosis* or a complex allegorical scene like West,[59] but created a glorification of a different kind, still alive, proudly in command, his deeds exciting awe and inspiration in the eyes of the next generation, represented by the midshipmen.

The *Nelson* and *Howe* monuments were Flaxman's grandest Napoleonic works; his only other large memorial was the one to *Captain James Montagu* in Westminster Abbey, which had been commissioned by the Treasury in 1798 for 3,500 guineas, independently of the Royal Academy's committee. Commissions for a series of monuments to war heroes had been considered by Parliament that year, resulting in requests for designs from five sculptors, amongst them Flaxman. At the time he was apprehensive about being awarded any of the commissions, but nonetheless submitted three models.[60] His pessimism disappeared with the contract for the monument to *Montagu*, who had served under Howe at the battle of Ushant at which he had been killed. The main part of the monument consists of the usual repertoire of a contemporary officer with a Victory and lion, together with mourning figures. The most interesting part of the monument is the relief on the pedestal (Plate 224), which is unusual in design for Flaxman's monuments since it is a well-observed, realistic illustration of the sea battle at which Montagu had been killed in 1794. Normally Flaxman represented the activities of his hero on land or sea symbolically. The rarity of such a panel as this one in Flaxman's oeuvre is perhaps explained by the fact that he normally held the belief that such battle scenes, at least those on ancient Roman columns, were nothing more than mere 'paragraphs of military gazettes'.[61]

Other Napoleonic War memorials by Flaxman were on a smaller scale. Outside London, less money was available for grand commissions. When Flaxman was chosen to execute the joint monument to *Captains James Walker and Richard Beckett*, who had both fallen in the battle of Talavera in 1809, a fee of £700 had been raised by public subscription in Leeds. This was the town where the two men had been born, and it was intended that the monument should be sited in the local parish church of St. Peter (Plate 225). The money had been raised and the commission placed within a year of the

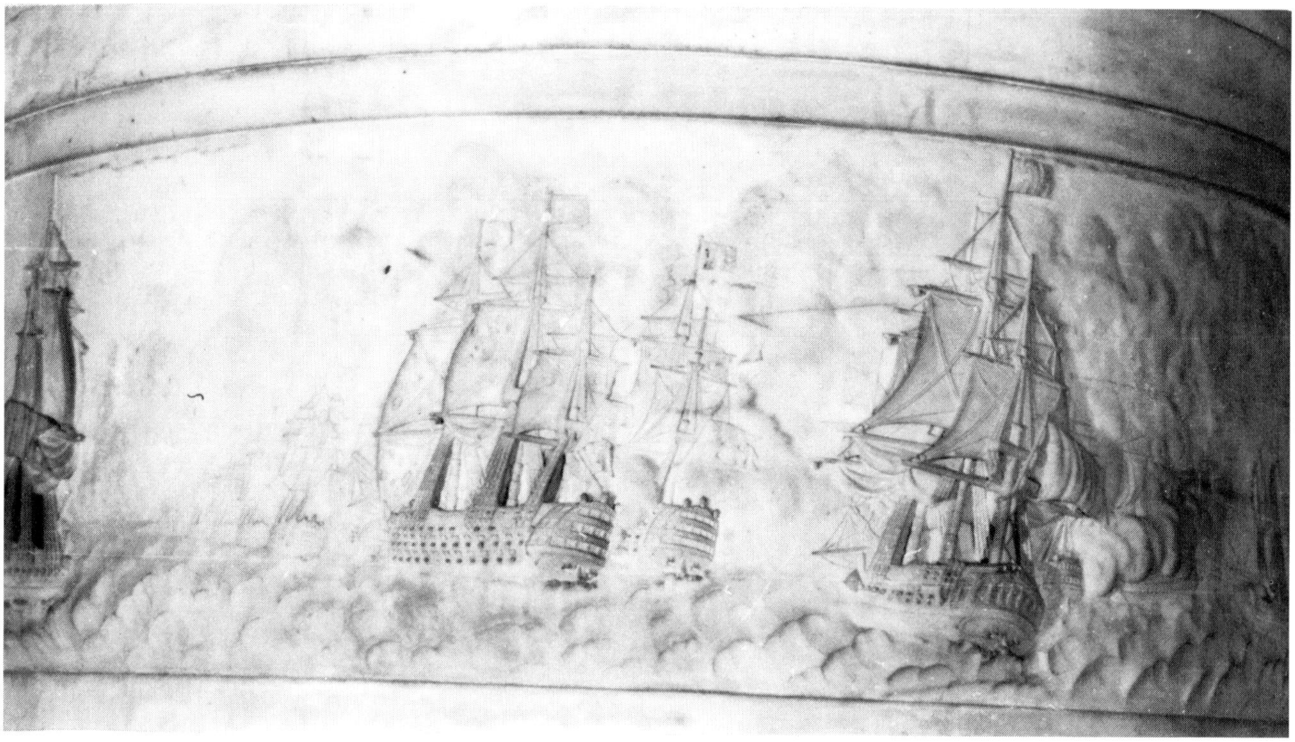

224 *Captain James Montagu: monument*, 1798–1804.
Detail: *The Glorious First of June, the Battle of Ushant, 1794.*
Westminster Abbey.

mens' death, showing a fervent patriotic spirit backed up by adequate, if not lavish, industrialists' cash. The images of the two men do not feature on the monument; perhaps none were available for Flaxman to use. Instead, a single figure of a winged Victory, melancholy not triumphant, sits upon a cannon leaning against three standards, one of which is inscribed with the name of the fatal battle in the Peninsular campaign. The upper space of the background slab is filled with the curve of a palm tree, and on the base the usual lion, but this time in relief. The mood of the monument is poignant, recording patriotic devotion. A neatly organised design, it shows the sculptor's skill in responding with a new composition to yet another war memorial, on a more modest scale of nearly nine and a half feet high. In the year of Flaxman's death, the assessment of Flaxman's works that appeared in the *Gentleman's Magazine* singled out this monument for special attention, praising it as a 'beautiful cenotaph'.[62]

Britannia or Minerva feature on many war memorials by both Flaxman and his contemporaries, often together with a lion, forming the most common allegorical imagery. Amongst other monuments by Flaxman using these figures is a smaller work in St. Paul's Cathedral to *Captain Willett Miller*, who had taken part in the Nile campaign and been killed in 1799 (Plate 226). Minerva is shown helping a winged Victory hang a medallion of the deceased man on to the palm tree. Sometimes on other monuments Britannia appears in a more didactic role comparable to that of the Minerva on the *Nelson* monument, as for example on the one to *Charles, 1st Marquis Cornwallis*, Governor-General of Bengal and Commander-in-Chief in India made between 1807 and 1813, formerly in St. George's, Penang but destroyed in the 1939–45 war. On that monument, Britannia shows a medallion of the deceased to an Indian boy, whilst an Indian woman mourns beside a palm tree.

Some heroes, however, were commemorated without any naval or military pomp or allegory. Admiral Sir Charles Thompson had been second-in-command at the battle of Cape St. Vincent in 1797, and had died two years later. But the imagery on his memorial (Plate 227) in the parish church of Holy Trinity at Fareham in Hampshire is modest in comparison to Captain Miller's, who had taken part in the same battle. Admiral Thompson is remembered by an inscription tablet flanked by two young naval officers, one holding

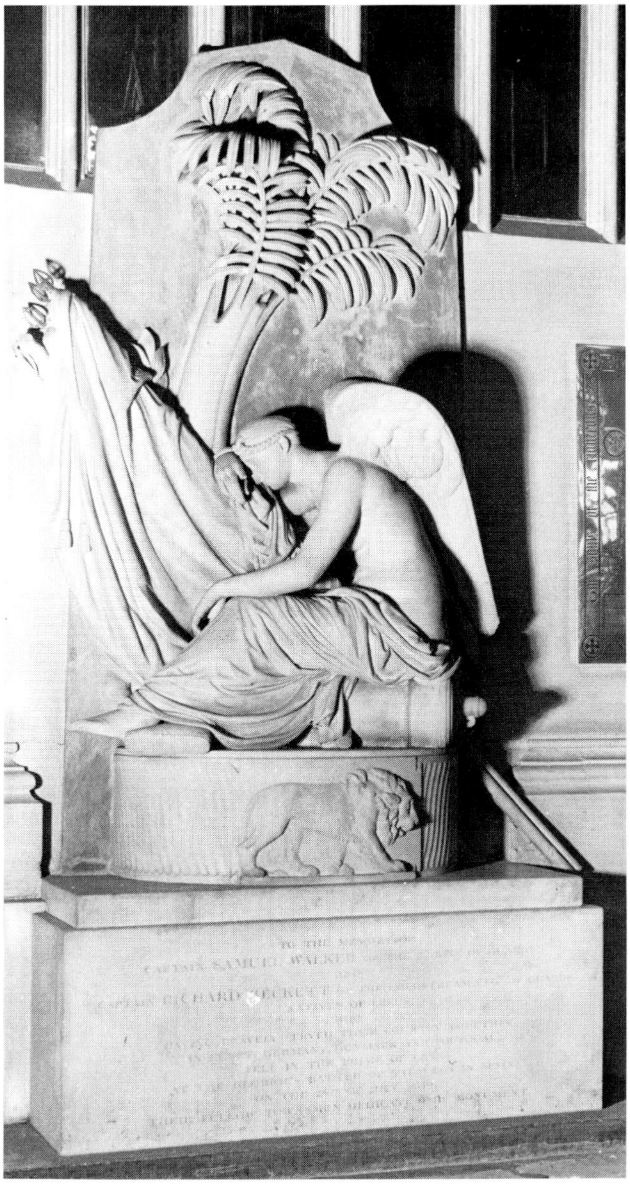

225 *Captains James Walker and Richard Beckett: monument,* 1810–12.
St. Peter, Leeds, Yorkshire.

a sextant, and the other a line and plummet. There is no reference to war even on the pediment, which is surmounted by a globe as a record of his interest in astronomy.

Flaxman's most ambitious project for a Napoleonic memorial would have been sited not in a church but in the open air, on the top of Greenwich Hill. A public subscription, under the patronage of the Duke of Clarence, was opened in 1799 for the erection of a column to commemorate recent naval victories. Artists were invited to send ideas and models in to the committee, and surviving designs by such architects as Jeffry Wyatt and C. H. Tatham show that they conformed to the committee's request for a column, Tatham producing some particularly interesting suggestions, which he eventually published (Plate 228).[63] Flaxman, however, disapproved of the idea of a column, and countered with ideas for either a triumphal arch or a gigantic statue. The triumphal arch seems to have gone no further than the drawing stage, which shows that Flaxman planned an enormous one, dwarfing carriages and people below, and surmounted by a seated statue of Britannia (Plate 229).[64] Flaxman's scheme for a colossal statue of Britannia on the other hand, was not only modelled and exhibited at the Royal Academy in 1801 (now in the Soane Museum), but also justified in a pamphlet which the artist wrote and illustrated, with his designs engraved by William Blake (Plate 230).

It was the only occasion in Flaxman's career when he justified a project in this way, hoping to win a competition. When still in its manuscript form, Flaxman had read his pamphlet to Lord Spencer who approved of it, and had asked for a copy of it to show to Pitt. Farington then claims that he encouraged Flaxman to print it.[65] Up to then Flaxman had rarely put pen to paper on the subject of his own art and that of classical antiquity, and his pamphlet of 1799 was his first noteworthy publication. Flaxman's statue would have been two hundred and thirty feet high, and he justified his proposal by citing antique precedents. He surveyed the famous public monuments of antiquity advocating that the committee should follow ancient forms not of the column and obelisk, but of the public statue, an idea that had first been suggested to him by George Dance. As Flaxman asserted: 'How much more sentiment and interest there is in a fine human figure than can possibly be produced in the choicest piece of architecture, and especially when that figure represents the protecting power or genius of the country'. Flaxman aspired to achieve the magnitude, no less, of the Colossus of Rhodes. He might be excused such an excessive grandeur on the grounds of a patriotic desire to make the monument worthy of the achievements of the men it would have commemorated. But as a hostile pamphlet attacking his project pointed out, the scale would have been overpowering for the Hospital below.[66] Flaxman's scheme was an obvious target for attack. He was accused by one critic of not being content with only 'cutting marble into men; he wishes to hew Greenwich Hill into a woman large enough to graze a couple of goats in her lap', and another wag claimed,

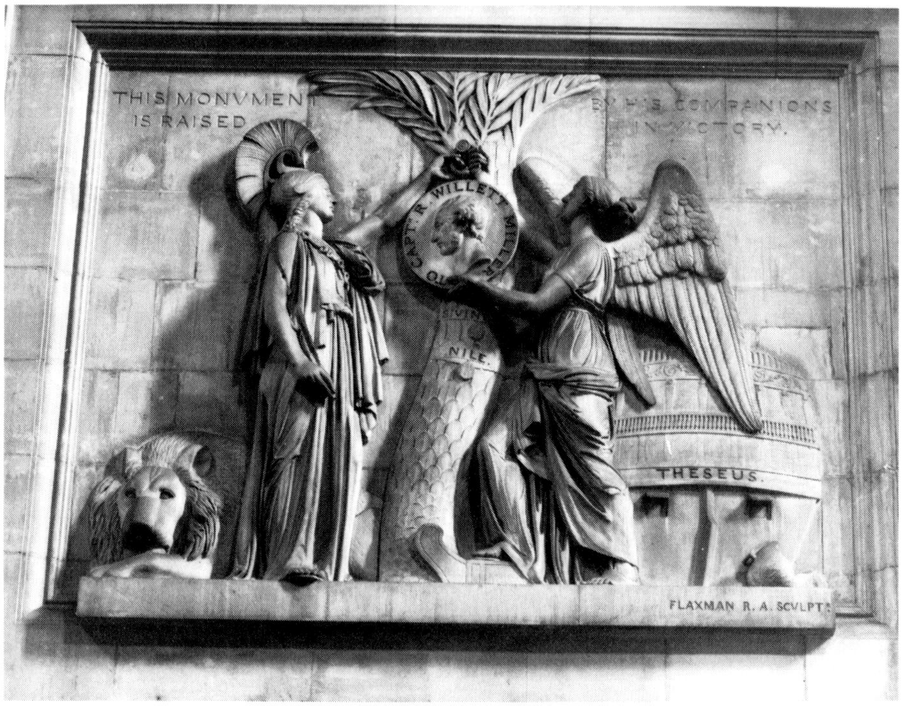

226 *Captain Willet Miller: monument.* Died 1799.
St. Paul's Cathedral.

227 *Admiral Sir Charles Thompson, Bart.: monument: design*, 1801–2.
Pen and ink, wash and pencil, 25·3–18·8 cms.

228 Charles Henry Tatham: *Design for a National Monument.*
Plate III from his *Three Designs*, 1802.

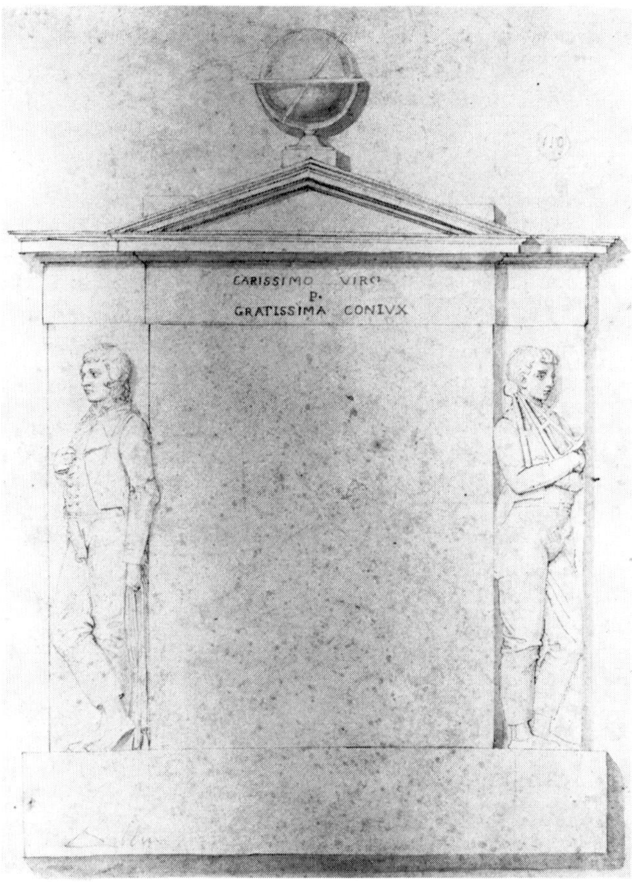

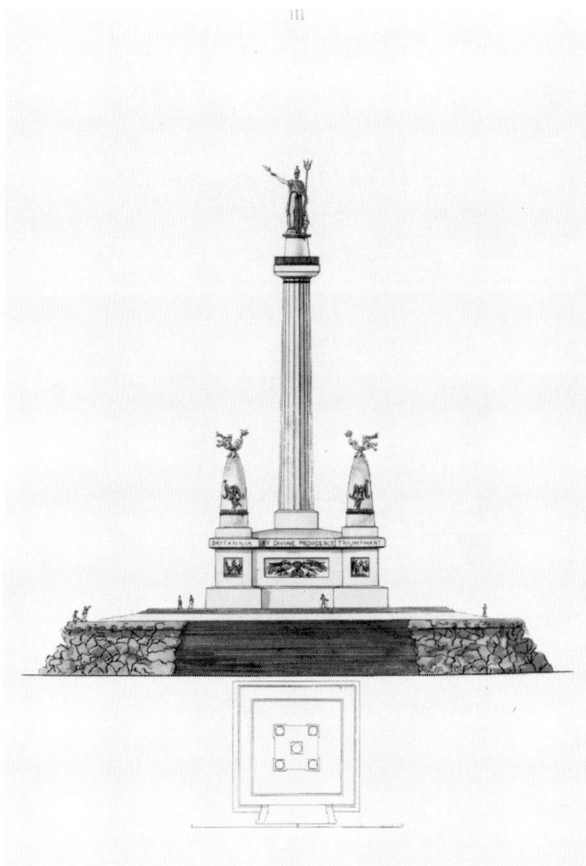

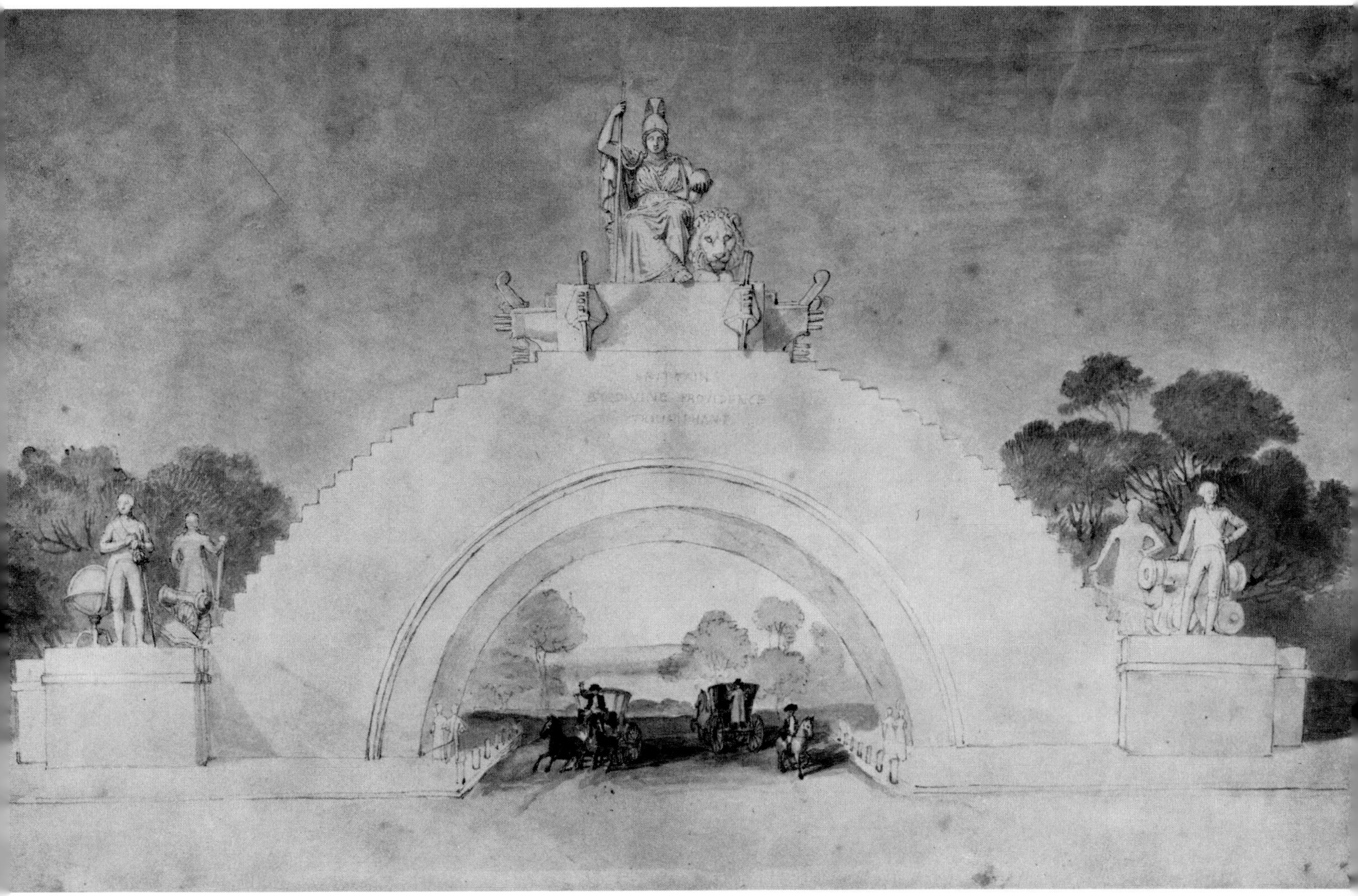

229 *Triumphal Arch surmounted by Britannia*, 1799.
Pen and ink, and pencil, 30 × 48·2 cms.

'There is to be a show at Greenwich of *little* Flaxman and *big* Britannia'.[67]

The critics need not have worried, as the project was quietly dropped, possibly because the committee did not find a suitable design, or there was not enough money available, or they could not agree on a site. The whole project, on the other hand, may merely have suffered from lethargy on the committee's part. A few years later Haydon was even to imagine a colossal Britannia sited on the cliffs of Dover permanently looking across to France.[68]

Britain was left without any general memorial to the heroes of the Napoleonic Wars, except for the later, and unfinished, recreation of the Parthenon on the top of Calton Hill in Edinburgh, which was intended as a national monument. Otherwise no general war memorials were to be erected in the British Isles for the rest of the century, not even for the Crimean War; in fact none were to be erected until those commemorating the dead of the 1914–18 war. In this respect Britain was unlike contemporary France and Prussia, both countries commemorating their war dead in the course of the nineteenth century, in such monuments as the Arc de Triomphe in Paris. For Flaxman himself, such colossal figures were to remain merely on sheets of paper, fantastic visions like the giant statue of the four metals in his illustration to the *Inferno*, or his later recreation of the Colossus of Rhodes in the background of one of his drawings for his own poem 'The Casket' (Plate 153).

5 Minimal costs

Some of Flaxman's monuments are small in scale and

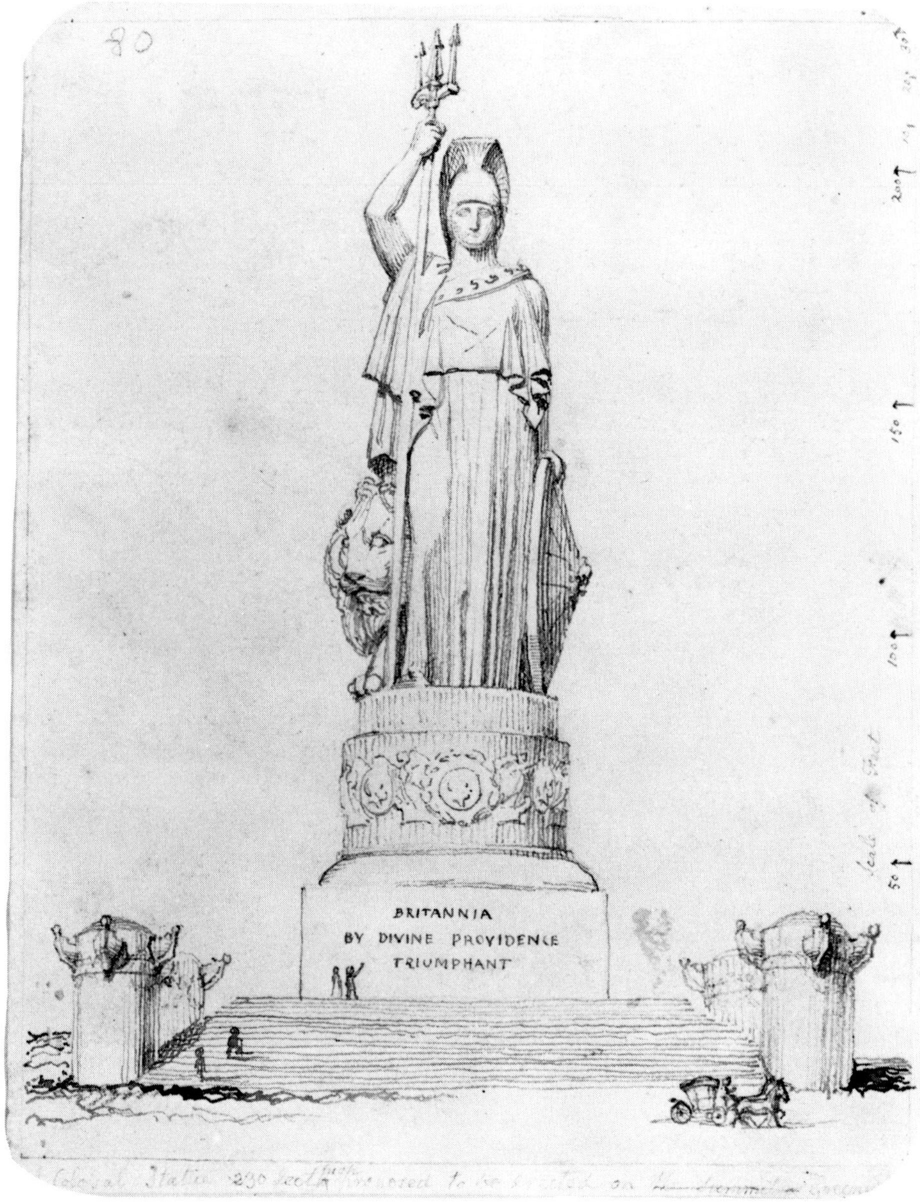

230 *Colossal Statue of Britannia for Greenwich Hill*, 1799.
Pencil, pen and ink, 19 × 15·2 cms.

simple in their use of motifs, consisting of no more than one or two items chosen from the funerary repertoire of an urn, a lamp, a sarcophagus, a flag or a Bible, without the addition of any figures. So basic are these monuments that unless they are either signed or documented, they would usually pass unnoticed as the work of Flaxman. Most were probably carved entirely by his assistants, using only a rough drawing sketched by Flaxman. These more pedestrian works were presumably often commissioned because the client had little money to spend, but sometimes it might reflect a sense of humility on the part of the client whose religious beliefs would decry more elaborate tokens of burial, even if he could afford them.

On occasions a memorial might be pared down to only a coat of arms on an inscription tablet, like the one erected in his own church by the Rector of St. George's, West Grinstead, Sussex, in memory of his wife, *Mrs. Elizabeth Woodward* (1799). A garlanded urn surmounting an inscription tablet ornamented with scrolls and palmettes is all that commemorates the *Honorable Mrs. Anne Brudenell* in St. George's Chapel at Windsor (1804). Admiral Sir Charles Cotton, who died in 1812 and had been Commander-in-Chief of the Channel

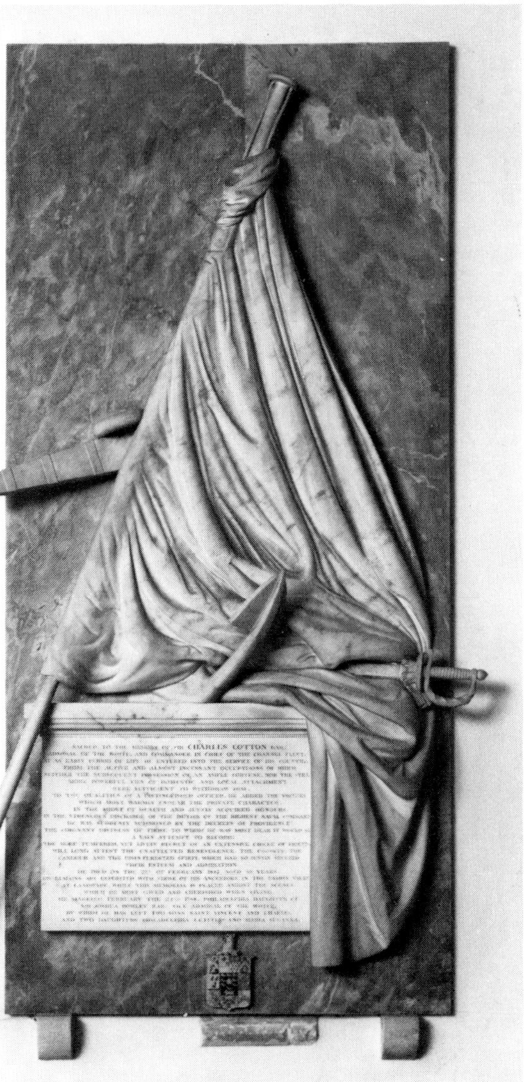

231 *Admiral Sir Charles Cotton: monument.* Died 1812. St. Mary Magdalen, Madingley, Cambridgeshire.

Fleet, is not commemorated in the church of St. Mary Magdalene at Madingley, near Cambridge, with any naval pomp or allegorical seagods. His memorial consists only of a standard draped across a slab, almost concealing an anchor and sword (Plate 231).

The death of the poet William Cowper in 1800 was to be commemorated two years later by one of Flaxman's simplest designs, erected in the parish church of St. Nicholas at East Dereham, Norfolk, where Cowper had gone to live with Mrs. Mary Unwin only five years before his death. The memorial consists of only an inscribed slab surmounted by a palm branch and two volumes, a large Bible against which leans, symbolically smaller, a copy of Cowper's own widely acclaimed *Task*. For the last volume of Cowper's works to be edited by Hayley, Blake engraved a frontispiece showing the monument *in situ* (Plate 232). Simple though the design is, Flaxman seems to have taken into account the shape of the Gothic window above, which is echoed in the curve of the palm on the monument, so that without using actual Gothic Revival forms Flaxman has managed to relate the monument most effectively to its setting.

Cowper himself would no doubt have approved of the starkness of the monument, which is a perfect reflection of the poet's characteristic modesty and strict Evangelicalism. As one of the principal Christian poets in the second half of the eighteenth century, and one of the best known cases of religious melancholy, he had frequently stressed the need for atonement in his contribution to the *Olney Hymns* and had often attacked worldly materialism in his *Task*. Only forty-five guineas had been available to meet the costs of the monument which, fortunately for the poet, had prevented the erection of a more elaborate memorial. Cowper's friend Lady Hesketh, as well as Hayley, had made a variety of suggestions for a design, the most inappropriate one being Hayley's for an embracing couple of figures of Poetry and Religion (rather like Love and Pity on the *Collins* monument), who would have been accompanied by a medallion portrait, a Bible and a scroll, as well as an inscription tablet large enough to accommodate an epitaph fourteen verses in length.[69] Hayley eventually produced a much shorter epitaph which pleased the sculptor, since it combines references to 'exertions according to God's providence for the benefit of mankind, with the appointed consequent blessedness of exaltation to the heavenly company of saints and holy ministers'.[70]

6 Business arrangements

Work on monuments kept Flaxman's studio busy. A letter written by the sculptor's wife to one of their friends in 1810 gives an unusually detailed account of work on hand.[71] She reported that the *Howe* monument was 'nearly completed', the *Nelson* was 'advancing slowly', and the ones to *Lord Cornwallis* and to *Josiah Webbe* (chief secretary of the Madras government) were to be shipped out east next year (the latter destined for St. Mary's, Fort St. George, Madras). She also mentioned the *Walter Long* monument for Salisbury Cathedral as a 'pretty little Gothic thing', as well as 'an interesting figure mourning the loss of two young men who died for their country's cause for Leeds', refering to the *Walker and Beckett* monument. The statue of *Reynolds* for St. Paul's was also being worked

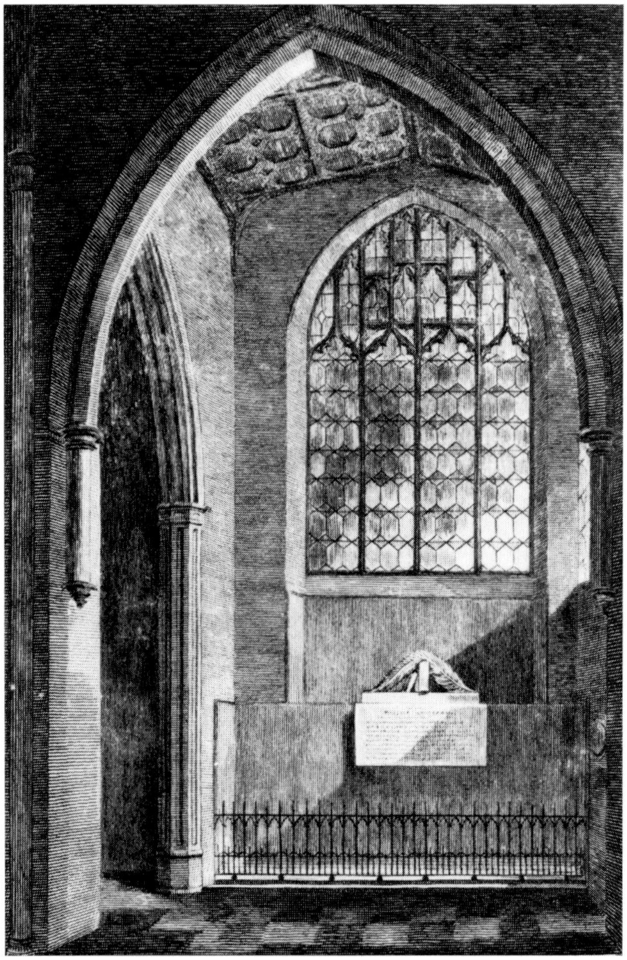

232 *William Cowper: monument*, 1802.
Drawing by Francis Stone, engraved by William Blake. Frontispiece to William Hayley, *Cowper*, Volume III, 1804.

on, and that of *Pitt* for Glasgow was on the 'eve of its journey northwards'. In addition, she mentioned 'a few others' without specifying them. The same letter also records work on the frieze for Covent Garden Theatre. In addition to all these sculptures, 'our evenings are spent in making designs for the Shield of Achilles, for a royal salver, and our odd moments are engaged in making out sketches from nature'.[72]

Monuments left the studio carefully packed in wooden crates for transport inland by carriage, or occasionally by the new canal system.[73] If going abroad, the crates were delivered to the docks, and the necessary customs dues paid. On arrival at its destination, if in England, the monument would often be erected, providing it was not an economical tablet, by masons despatched from London for the purpose, even if the church was as far away as Herefordshire (which could take up to 13 days of a mason's time, as for the erection of the *Miles* monument (Plate 176).[74] Flaxman did not send masons as far away as Edinburgh as this was impractical. In a letter of 1823 to his Edinburgh contact, Flaxman shows how meticulous the sculptor was about the erection of his monuments. 'Enclosed is the receipt for the two cases containing the monument for Mrs. Arbuthnot' (Plate 193), he wrote, 'accompanied by the requisites for affixing it against the wall of the chapel, that is to say the copper cramps, for which holes are cut in the marble, and a small model of the whole monument to prevent the possibility of any mistake in affixing the parts—as I know there are masons of great ability in Edinburgh, I will beg the favour that one of tried skill may be employed to set it up who will be careful not to damage the work'.[75]

Some monuments involved Flaxman in high costs as well as the expenditure of much time. In connection with the monument to *Sir William Jones* in University College chapel, Flaxman went specially to Oxford for six days to supervise its erection, which took three weeks altogether. He had to pay the coach fares from London as well as the board in Oxford for the two masons who undertook the work, in addition to his own expenses, plus materials and packing, which amounted to nearly £103, excluding the cost of the marble itself. The replacement of the top panel, with which for some unknown reason Flaxman was dissatisfied, cost the sculptor £20. All these costs had to be met out of the £500 that was paid for the commission.[76] Although some contracts specified that expenses were to be additional to the fee, this was not always the case.

The cost of the majority of tombs was borne by descendants and relatives of the deceased, who in most instances did not, or could not, lavish large sums on memorials. The £2,500 spent on the *Mansfield* monument was unusual because of a legacy from a grateful client. Apart from this example, the most expensive, privately paid, monument, was the *Baring* one, which cost nearly £1,400 between 1806 and 1813. An average price for the larger monuments of more affluent clients was nearer £500, such as the *Yarborough* monument. The £200 price range included monuments as important as the one to *Lady Fitzharris*. One of Flaxman's own favourite tombs, that to *Abraham Balme*, was cheaper in price at £105. Against such prices the figure of £6,300, out of which all expenses had to be met, for each of the *Howe* and *Nelson* monuments, seems lavish, and a just recognition in financial terms of Flaxman's achievement. Never a financially greedy man, he was apt to undervalue his monetary worth, and therefore lived a comfortable and modest life without any obvious signs of affluence.

CHAPTER VII

Sculpture: Secular Commissions

When Flaxman was elected a full Royal Academician in 1800[1] he presented as his Diploma piece a marble relief of *Apollo and Marpessa* (Plate 233), a choice that suggests that Flaxman may have regarded a classical subject as more important than a religious one, especially as a few years later there are hints that Flaxman was hoping to receive more secular commissions. He was not to know in 1800, however, that monuments were going to take the dominant place in his studio, and remain his main source of income. In view of his subsequent career, remarks made five years later in his address on the death of Thomas Banks are strange, unless interpreted in the light of Flaxman's own hidden hopes. Describing the state of sculpture in early eighteenth-century England, he told fellow Academicians that it had been 'reduced to the narrow limits of monument-making, and by these means degraded to a sort of trade'. As this was a formal address, presumably carefully prepared, Flaxman's turn of phrase must have been deliberately chosen. Flaxman's attitude towards the relevant importance of church monuments and secular commissions is also mentioned, in the same year, in a letter that his wife wrote to Hayley. She grumbled that early July was a very busy time of year, when 'the great folks on leaving town come to see the state of their works, others to leave their orders, others settling inscriptions and others their accounts'. She only wished Flaxman could escape this drudgery to 'a cottage with plenty of ground for his working studies, and where he may employ his talents as he best likes, not cramped by the obstinate will or foolish whim of anyone, but let the world see the inward man. I think he would yet surprise them all—we should see the bold conception of a Phidias united to the high finished graces of a Praxiteles'.[2] This 'inward man', of which Mrs. Flaxman spoke so passionately, could only be revealed by refusing commissions, the majority of which were for tombs.

The preliminary drawings of the theme of Apollo and Marpessa, rarely illustrated in classical art, include the figure of Idas in a chariot in which he had carried off his lover Marpessa (Plate 234). Flaxman chose the moment when Apollo has caught up with them, successfully taking away Marpessa whom he had already been wooing. Flaxman established a tension between the three figures as Idas and Apollo each strive for Marpessa's love. In the marble, however, Flaxman has removed this tension, and Apollo is wooing Marpessa without a hint of the struggle of mortal against immortal. Although knowing the detailed version of the story in Apollodorus,[3] Flaxman has turned the relief into a more timeless image of youthful love, which

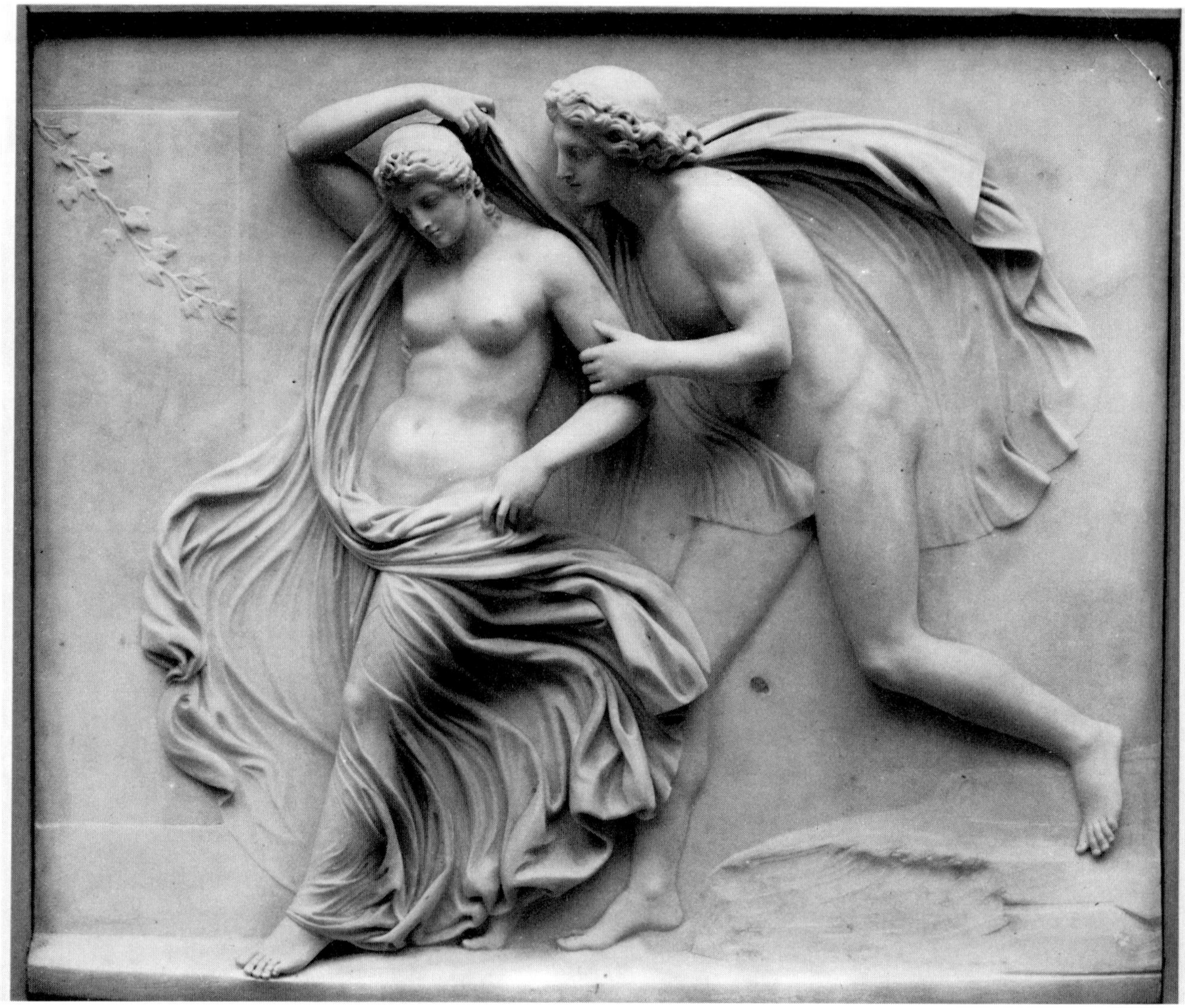

233 *Apollo and Marpessa*, 1790–c. 1794.
Marble, 49·8 × 54 cms.

happens to be in classical dress. The style of the drawings is identical with that of the classical illustrations of the 1790s, and the dark wash of the background is a continuing reminder of Flaxman's love of Greek vase painting. The drawings suggest that he had been looking again at the Meidias Vase (Plate 31), from which he already had taken his Wedgwood composition of *Hercules in the Garden of the Hesperides*. This time he seems to have been looking at the story of Castor and Pollux carrying off the daughters of Leukippos, which he has reversed. The swirling draperies of Flaxman's relief are also classical in origin, but the charm and sentiment expressed by the two figures is unmistakably contemporary. As it was his Diploma piece, he presumably carved the panel entirely himself, which is sensitively cut and delicately finished, and in unusually high relief for Flaxman.

The success of this panel must have encouraged Flaxman a few years later to execute another classical subject as a small relief, choosing the equally attractive story of Mercury bringing Pandora down to earth (Plate 235). When exhibited at the Royal Academy in 1805, Flaxman's wife said that he had chosen the subject 'from his favourite Hesiod', and described the panel as 'in the true Athenian style, simple, elegant and grand'.[4] Flaxman must have liked this very elegant design since he was to re-use the identical composition in one of his *Hesiod* illustrations a few years later.

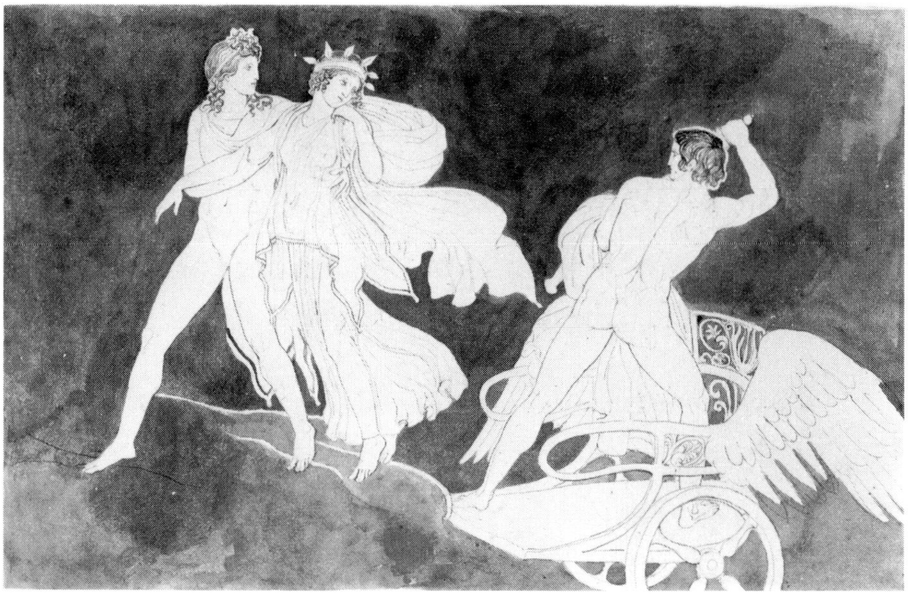

234 *Apollo carrying off Marpessa from Idas.*
Pen and ink and wash,
25·7 × 41 cms.

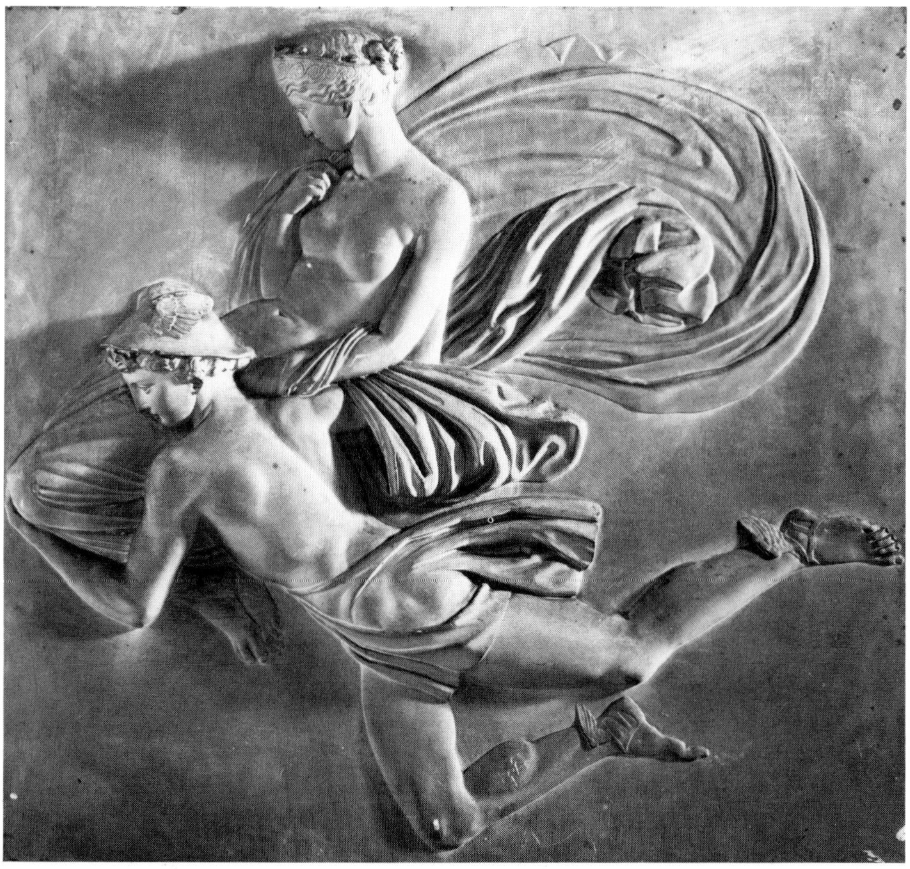

235 *Mercury bearing Pandora to Earth*, c. 1805.
Plaster, 72 × 80 cms.

Sometimes Flaxman was commissioned to execute architectural sculptures, as well as the occasional fireplace, and thus became involved in the work of some of the leading Neoclassical architects of his day, including Holland, Smirke, C. R. Cockerell and Nash. The first of Flaxman's designs to be used in an architectural context, were not initially created for their setting. The reliefs that ornament the exterior of the Rotunda at Ickworth House, which are largely taken from Flaxman's *Homer* illustrations, were mostly executed by the Carabelli brothers in 1800 and 1803 (Plate 236). The Ickworth reliefs are a very successful transposition of the engravings into another medium, a pleasant idea presumably suggested by the patron, the Earl-Bishop of Bristol, who intended to place the *Fury of Athamas* inside his new house.

The work at Ickworth coincided with the commission at Woburn Abbey for a pediment for a Temple of Liberty, Agriculture and Commerce designed by Henry Holland for Francis Russell, fifth Duke of Bedford, who laid the foundation stone shortly before he died in 1802 (Plate 237). The Temple still forms one end of the Sculpture Gallery, facing at the other end of the room the one dedicated to the Graces designed by Wyattville, which displays Canova's famous group. The Temple of Liberty houses a Nollekens bust of Charles James Fox, and around the walls are busts of his most intimate Whig friends. An inscription refers to the Napoleonic Wars, from which it is clear that the project was inspired by the Peace of Amiens, as well as being a more general celebration of liberty, peace and plenty as illustrated by Flaxman's allegorical figures. The style and composition of Flaxman's pediment are well adapted to this gem of Greek Revival architecture, which is based on an Ionic temple reproduced in Stuart and Revett's *Antiquities of Athens*. The Sculpture Gallery at Woburn is an important example of Neoclassical taste in the first two decades of the nineteenth century, representing not only the commissions of the fifth Duke, but also the expansion of the antique and modern collections by the sixth Duke, who added works by Chantrey, Westmacott, Thorvaldsen and Canova. The sixth Duke in fact wanted to add another work by Flaxman to the collection, commissioning in the last year of the sculptor's life a marble relief of the *Flight of Satan from Paradise*, but Flaxman did not live long enough to fulfil the commission.[5] (Plate 137).

A few years after the Woburn pediment Flaxman was commissioned in 1809 to create a more ambitious series of architectural sculptures: the friezes for the facade of Smirke's rebuilding of Covent Garden Theatre after a recent disastrous fire (Plates 238 and 239).

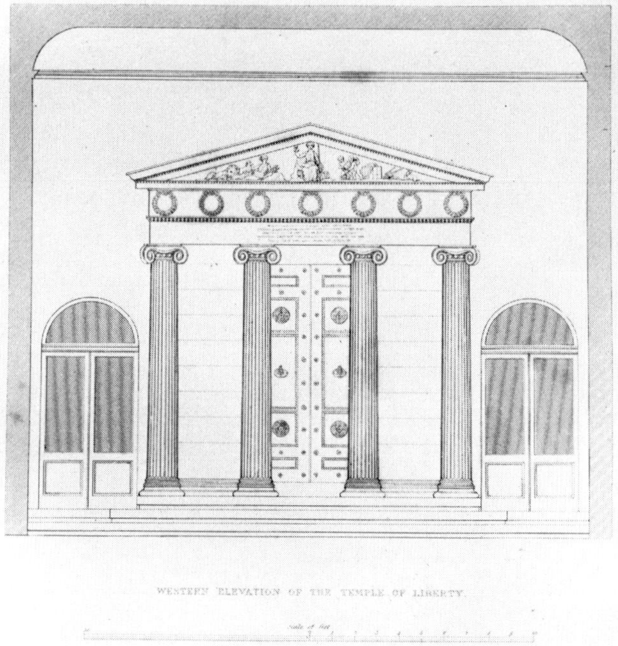

237 *Temple of Liberty, Woburn Abbey*, 1802–3.
Engraving from Henry Corbould and Henry Moses, *Woburn Abbey Marbles*, 1822, Plate 37.

Flaxman also supplied a large statue of *Comedy* a couple of years later.[6] For the wall to the right of the portico Flaxman designed a long frieze on the theme of *Ancient Drama*, and to the left, *Modern Drama*. He produced drawings for both and a model for the former. The model for the latter, however, was executed by Smirke's protégé, Rossi, who was Flaxman's junior by only a few years. Rossi also cut the stone of both friezes, and although he executed his task faithfully, he must have undertaken this work reluctantly. Rossi had already started to establish himself as a sculptor, albeit a minor one, and he grumbled to the inveterate gossip Farington that it was taking him off other work (a monument in St. Paul's), and 'he spoke of the little power Flaxman has in working upon marble or stone. His power is confined to designing and modelling'.[7]

Unfortunately the theatre was again badly damaged by fire in 1856, and after the rebuilding by E. M. Barry Flaxman's friezes were cut and arranged in the wrong order (as one sees them today on the renamed Royal Opera House). However, contemporary drawings and an engraving, as well as four plasters in the Victoria and Albert Museum, clearly show how the friezes looked in their original setting.[8] *Ancient Drama* is divided into comedy and tragedy, with the seated figures of Aristophanes, Menander and Aeschylus in the centre. The

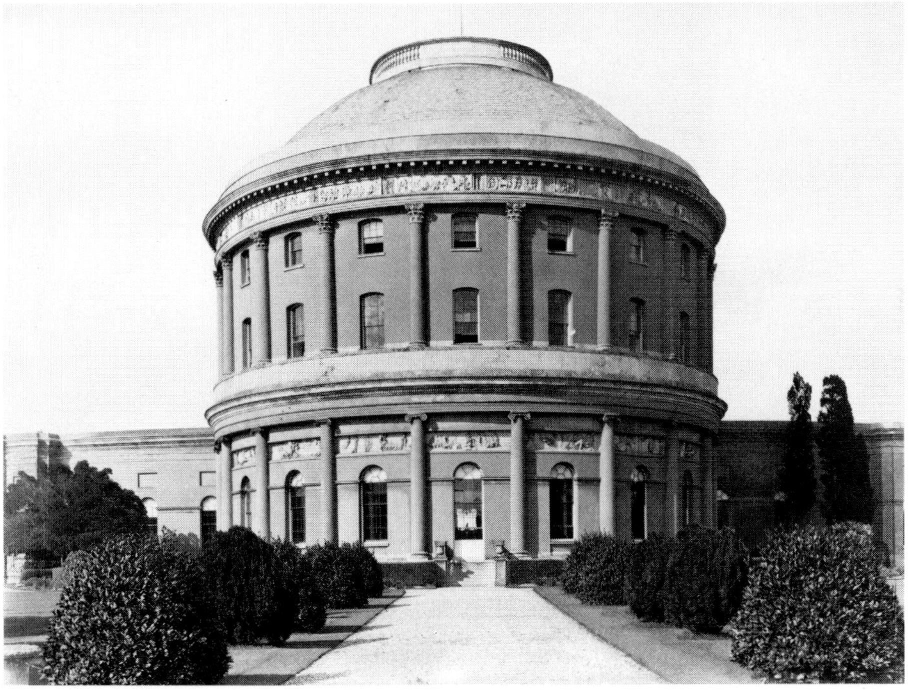

236 Carabelli Brothers: *Reliefs*, mostly after Flaxman's *Homer*, 1800–3. Rotunda, Ickworth House, Suffolk.

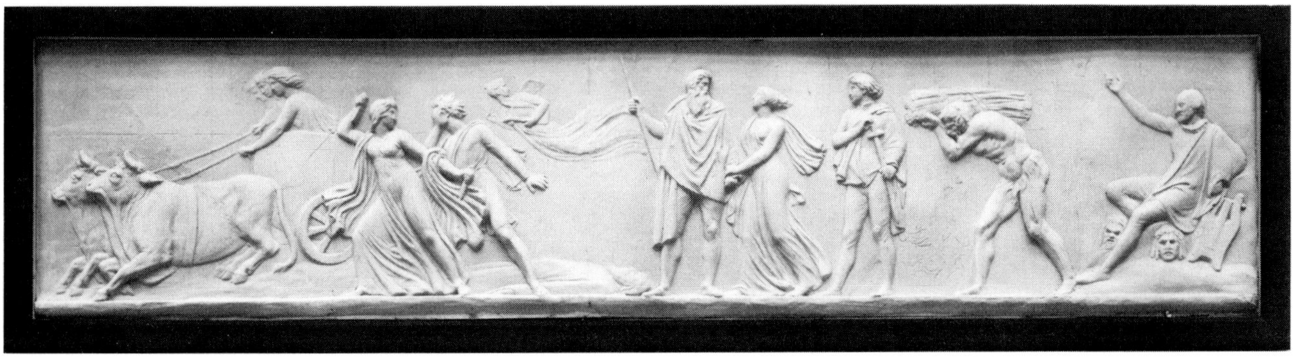

238 *Covent Garden Theatre Frieze: Modern Drama, left section*, 1809. Plaster, modelled after Flaxman by John Charles Rossi, 39·1 × 174 cms.

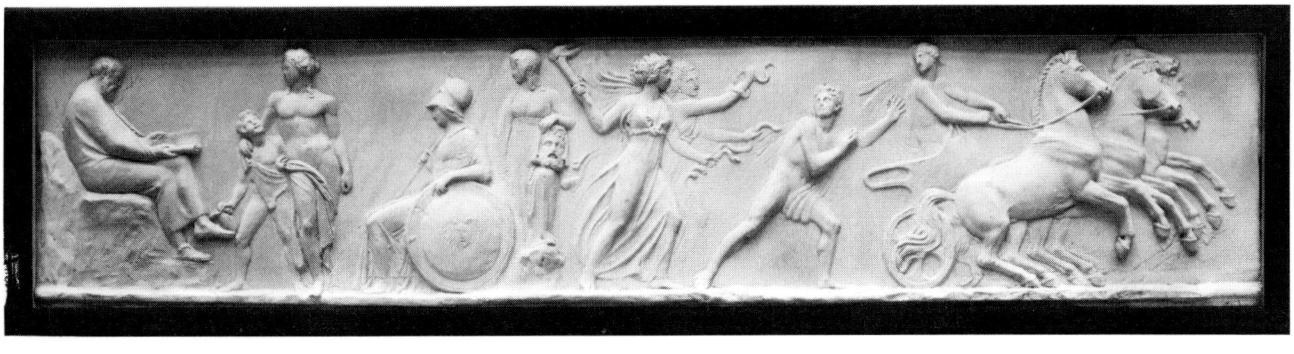

239 *Covent Garden Theatre Frieze: Ancient Drama, right section*, 1809. Plaster, 39·1 × 180·8 cms.

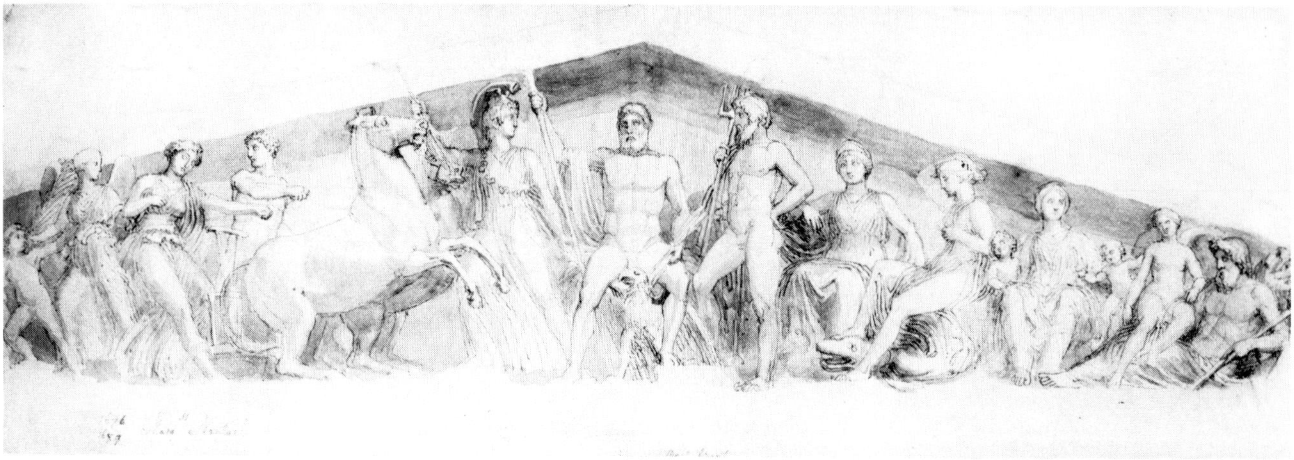

240 *West Pediment of the Parthenon: reconstruction*, c. 1802. Pen and ink, wash and pencil, 24·8 × 72·4 cms.

movement along the frieze is provided by such figures as the Muses, the winged horse of Pegasus symbolising immortality, and (in the centre of Plate 238) Orestes fleeing from the Furies in the direction of Apollo's chariot. *Modern Drama* is arranged in a similar way, with seated figures of Shakespeare and Milton in the centre, on either side of whom are scenes from *Comus* and (in Plate 239) from *Macbeth* and *The Tempest*. On the left of the illustration can be seen Hecate's oxen-drawn chariot about to descend to the Underworld. Like the frieze from the Parthenon, the possible monotony of figures the length of a long relief has been avoided by a variety of poses, and by the maintenance of a careful balance between lively and quieter scenes.

By the time Flaxman received the Covent Garden commission he was familiar with Lord Elgin's collection, which had been available for study in the grounds of Lord Elgin's London house in Park Lane since 1807. Flaxman had already seen plaster casts of the Parthenon marbles when in Paris in 1802, he would have known the engravings that had appeared in Stuart and Revett's *Antiquities of Athens*, but the sight of the actual marbles themselves naturally had a much greater impact than such substitute versions. At some stage, perhaps when in Paris in 1802, or later when advising Lord Elgin, he drew a restoration of the sculptural group in the west pediment of the Parthenon (Plate 240).[9] It is not surprising that when Flaxman came to design his first and, as it was to turn out, his only long frieze of continuous incidents he should have been influenced by the Elgin Marbles. Flaxman had been involved with them at an early stage; already in 1807 his advice was being sought on their restoration, and he had helped in the arrangement of the display by fitting together some of the disconnected pieces.[10]

The Muses on the Covent Garden friezes might derive from the Elgin Marbles, but a much more obvious link is provided by the horses drawing Apollo's chariot (on the right of Plate 238), which are closely related in style to the magnificently lively animals on the Parthenon frieze (Plate 241). Flaxman very rarely sculpted animals, and his horses in illustrations to Homer are more stereotyped and less vital than those modelled in 1809. The Parthenon horses were to receive special attention in Flaxman's fourth lecture at the Royal Academy, in which he refered to 'the most precious examples of Grecian power in the sculpture of animals', the horses seem 'to live and move, to roll their eyes, to gallop, prance and curvet. . . . The beholder is charmed with the deer-like lightness and elegance of their make'.

Flaxman seems to have responded more quickly as an artist to the Elgin Marbles than other contemporary sculptors and painters, and he may be the first artist to have produced works clearly showing their influence. Flaxman's innate classicism, which was showing an increasing tendency to veer in the direction of naturalism, would have found confirmation and encouragement in these Greek sculptures. It is possibly because the classicism of other artists was developing in a different direction, that they were slower to show any response to the Elgin Marbles in their own work. Haydon extolled their virtues but to little apparent effect in his own art, and West claimed at the parliamentary enquiry into the purchase of the marbles that he had learnt much from them, somewhat unconvincingly citing two of his own recent large and pretentious canvases as evidence.[11]

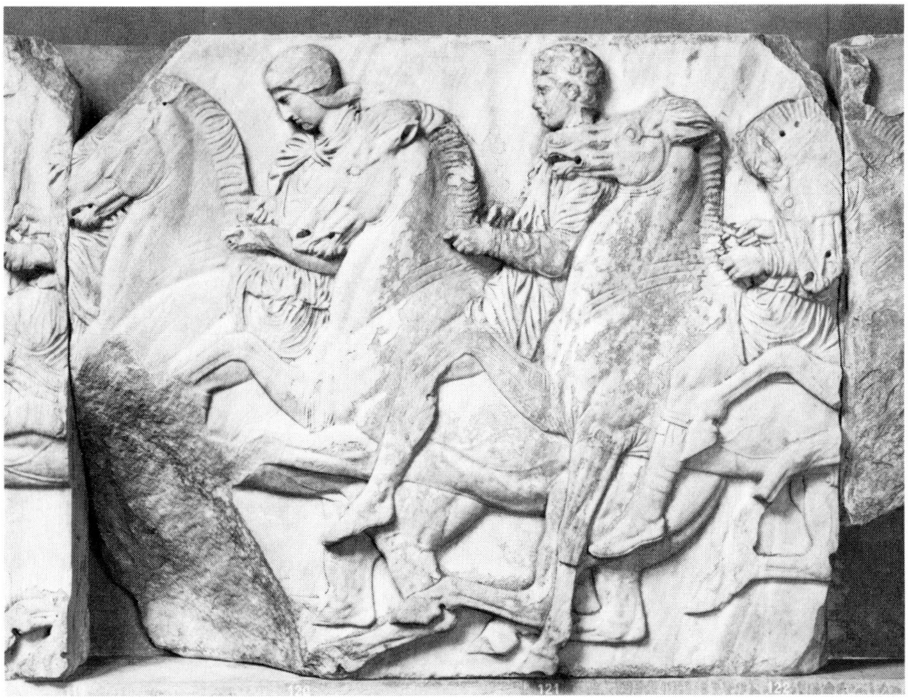

241 Frieze of the Parthenon: *Panathenaic Procession with Horsemen*, or *Procession of Marathon Heroes*, c. 440–438 B.C. Detail.

The controversy that raged over the Elgin Marbles, their aesthetic merit and their financial value, once they arrived in London, stimulated lively and at times acrimonious, discussion, particularly on the differences between Greek and Roman art. The climax of the controversy can be read in the submission presented to the House of Commons select committee set up to consider the government's purchase. Richard Payne Knight was surprisingly hostile to the Elgin Marbles, claiming they were as recent as the time of Hadrian. He was opposed by West, Lawrence, Chantrey and other artists, as well as by Flaxman whose evidence was described by one contemporary as 'very ingenious'.[12] Like other artists submitting evidence, Flaxman failed to draw clear distinctions between Greek and Roman art even at this late date. He agreed that in general the marbles were 'the finest works of art I have seen', thought them undoubtedly the work of Phidias and his assistants and said they were 'superior to any of the works of antiquity', but then made exceptions of the *Laocoon* and *Toro Farnese*. He thought the Elgin *Theseus* superior to the *Torso Belvedere*, but as the *Theseus* was badly weathered he preferred the *Apollo Belvedere*, in spite of it being a copy, because the *Apollo* was more ideal. Diffuse though Flaxman's opinions may have been, they carried great weight in favour of the government's purchase.

Flaxman's advice was also sought in connection with other collections of ancient sculptures in both Oxford and Cambridge. A scheme to display the Arundel Marbles in the Radcliffe Camera in Oxford was going to be supervised by Flaxman. The building would have been a fine setting for the collection, especially as Piranesi's candelabra were already there. The project, however, was not realised; the Arundel Marbles were displayed in the Schools and remained there until late in the century[13]. In Cambridge, Flaxman gave advice to the Reverend Edward Daniel Clarke, a mineralogist and don, who had travelled widely in the Near East, and had brought back from Greece and elsewhere in the Mediterranean a group of Greek marbles which he presented to the University. When he published a catalogue of the collection, Clarke included three drawings by Flaxman, two of which were proposed restorations, sensitive in treatment, by the sculptor to an important statue of Ceres found at Eleusis (Plate 251).[14]

Flaxman had to wait until the last year of his life for his biggest architectural commission. This would have formed part of John Nash's enlargement of Buckingham House into a palace for George IV, and if executed would have been the largest single commission in the whole of Flaxman's career. The magnitude of the architect's requirements reflected the King's megalomaniac rebuilding programme which was getting increasingly out-of-hand. At the time of his death none of Flaxman's ideas had been realised, as they seem not to have been pushed beyond the stage of rough drawings. Had he left more detailed drawings or models, assistants could presumably have carried out Flaxman's intentions.

Flaxman's Buckingham House commission encompassed three pediments, two friezes, at least fifteen statues and an arch, as well as various chimneypieces. Precise details of all the parts of the commission have not survived, and not all the titles of the pieces of statuary are known. It is not clear if the arch is an early stage of the Marble Arch, which was to be the original gateway into the new palace forecourt (before it was removed later in the century to its present site at Hyde Park Corner). The pediments and friezes by Flaxman were almost certainly intended for the public side of the palace, that is the central block and two wings around an open forecourt facing Pall Mall. Drawings survive for the three pedimental groups (Plate 243), *Britannia Triumphant* in the centre, flanked by *The Muses* and *The Sciences*. The friezes were to be devoted to *Magna Carta* and *Naval Victories*.[15] The iconography of Flaxman's sculptures, presumably discussed with both patron and architect, was to be retained, with modifications, in the sculptures that were eventually executed by other artists and which are still on the Palace facades. It is much to be regretted, as Flaxman's architectural sculptures are so rare, that he did not live to fulfil any part of this lavish commission.

Flaxman's account-books list a variety of other secular commissions and jobs in which he and his studio workmen were involved, ranging from such tasks as the supervision of the removal of Canova's colossal statue of *Napoleon* from Richmond to Apsley House, to the restoration of plaster-work in a London house.[16] Flaxman also executed chimneypieces for such patrons as Thomas Hope, Samuel Rogers and Sir Thomas Baring. Most of these minor commissions have either disappeared or are difficult to identify, but the example at Grange Park is presumably typical. Cockerell commissioned the chimneypiece for Sir Thomas's new house, but he only managed to extract from the sculptor a design he had first executed whilst in Italy of a *Grecian Feast* (Plate 244). For this thirty-year-old design Flaxman charged £150. Thomas Hope had once paid as much as £200 for a chimneypiece from Flaxman.[17]

Menial tasks were useful in producing a little more occasional income, as well as a means of obliging friends and patrons, but such work formed a minor part of Flaxman's activities. Other small commissions included a pair of statuettes of *Cupid* and *Psyche* for Samuel Rogers in 1824, and another pair of *Raphael* (Plate 245) and *Michelangelo* a couple of years later for Sir Thomas Lawrence.[18] These four sculptures are pleasant little

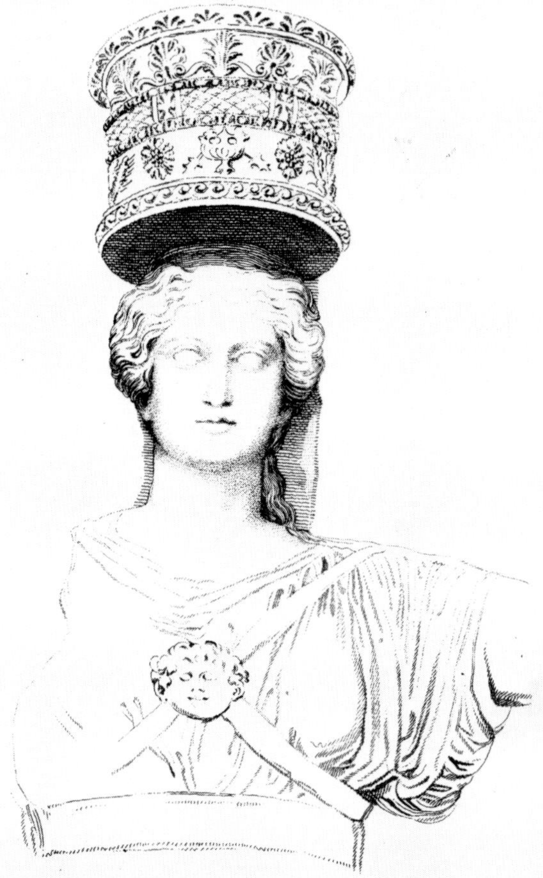

242 *Ceres from Eleusis: Proposed Restoration.* Engraving after Flaxman by P. W. Tomkins.
Frontispiece to E. D. Clarke, *Greek Marbles*, 1809.

works, modest both in scale and intention. But Flaxman might well have imagined that after the *Fury of Athamas* and the *Cephalus and Aurora* commissions for more large freestanding works would follow, especially as the latter group received wide publicity through the engraving in Hope's book on his own house. However, Flaxman was to receive only two commissions for further freestanding figures (apart from Covent Garden and Buckingham House). Both came from the same patron, the third Earl of Egremont.

Petworth House already contained a rich and varied collection of antique sculptures, which had been assembled in the middle of the previous century by the third Earl's father. After he inherited this collection, together with a distinguished group of paintings, the third Earl inaugurated at Petworth an era of enlightened patronage of contemporary art. One of the most constant

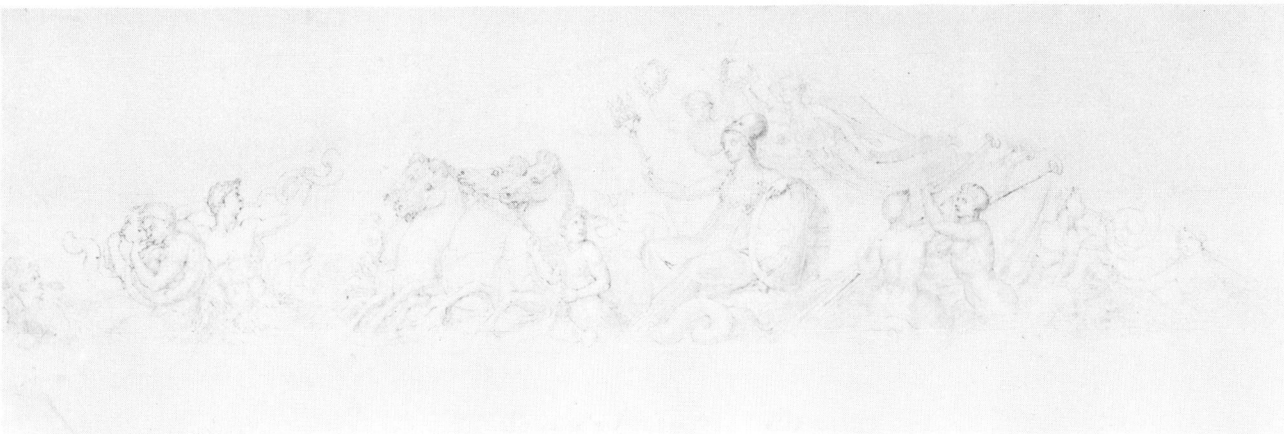

243a *Britannia Triumphant: Pediment for Buckingham Palace*, 1826.
Pencil, 15·7 × 47 cms.

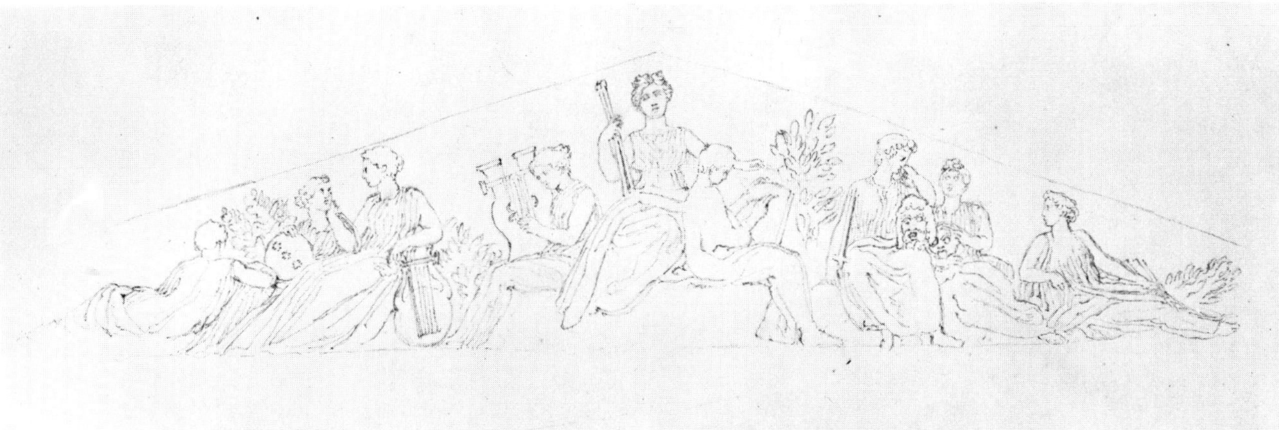

243b *The Muses: Pediment for Buckingham Palace: design*. 1826.
Pencil, 16·8 × 43 cms.

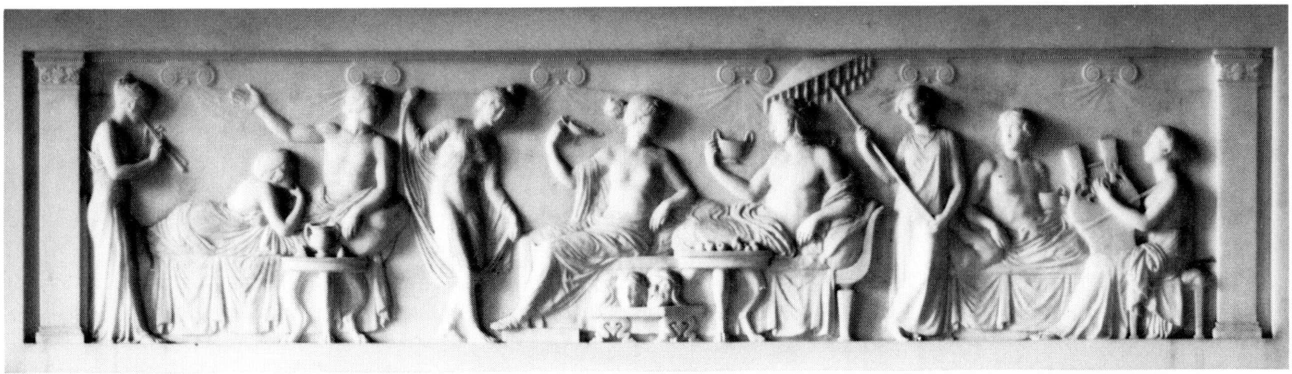

244 *Grecian Feast*, 1823–24. Marble fireplace relief.
Grange Park, Hampshire.

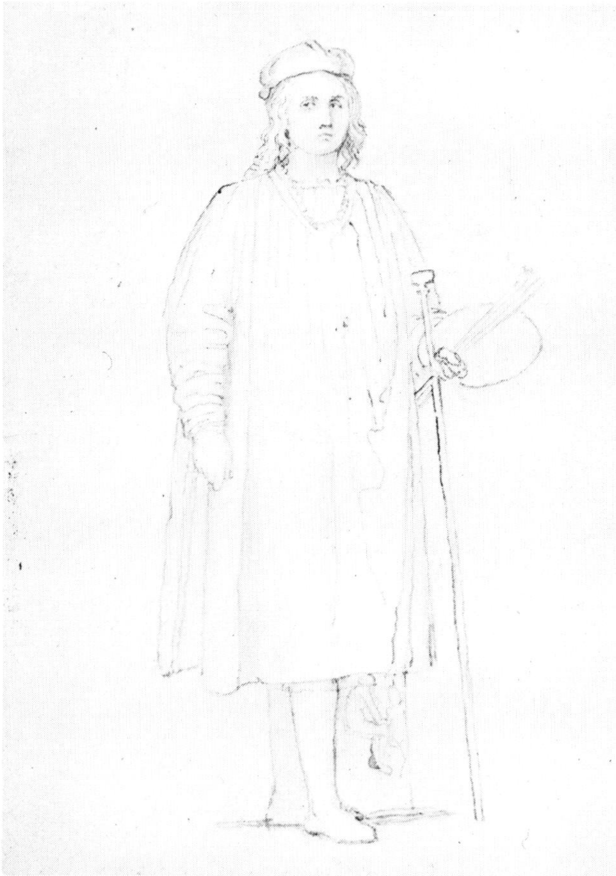

245 *Raphael: design for statuette*, 1826.
Pen and ink and wash, 16·3 × 11·6 cms.

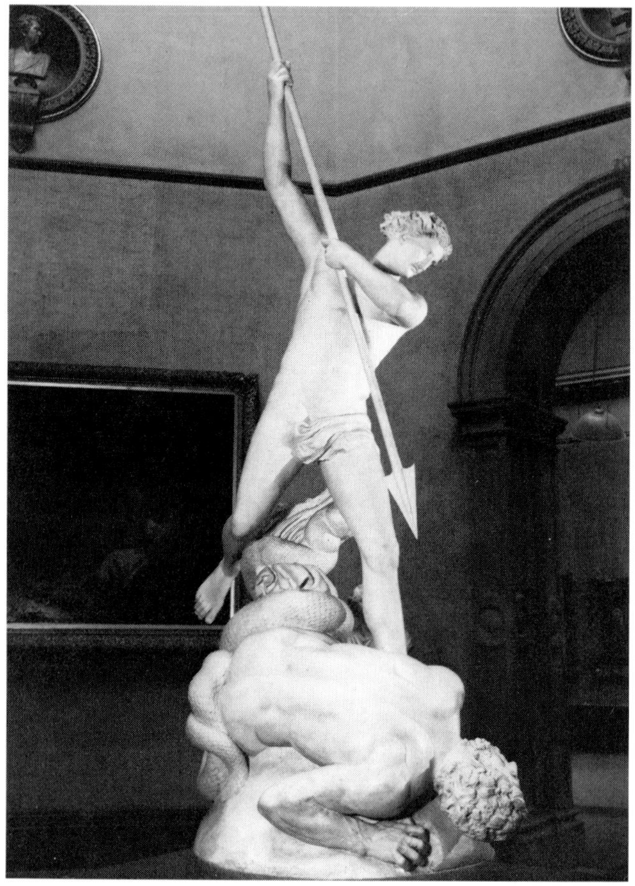

246 *St. Michael overcoming Satan*, 1819–24.
Plaster, 335·3 cms. high.

visitors was Turner, who in some of his watercolour sketches executed in the house recorded the light falling on Flaxman's large *St. Michael overcoming Satan*, a dominant feature in the North Gallery (Plate 247). This part of the house had been created by the third Earl to house his expanding modern collection, as well as some of his father's classical pieces. Flaxman's *St. Michael* (Plate 246) together with the other commission for a *Pastoral Apollo* (Plate 248), were housed in the company of works by many of the artist's friends and contemporaries, including Fuseli, Blake and Romney among the painters, and Westmacott and Rossi among the sculptors. The North Gallery at Petworth remains one of the most important, and untouched, examples of the taste of a discerning collector in the eighteenth and early nineteenth centuries.

Both the *St. Michael* and the *Apollo* were completed in 1824, and by the time the final payments for them had been made, they cost a total of £3,571, the largest sum that Flaxman received for secular commissions from one patron.[19] Contemporaries regarded them as important works, especially the *St. Michael*. Flaxman allowed the *Apollo* to mature over a long period, having received the commission in 1813, showing what must have been the model for it at the Royal Academy the following year, and exhibiting the final marble as late as 1824. The *St. Michael* was completed more quickly; commissioned in 1819, a model was exhibited at the Royal Academy in 1822, and the final marble completed only two years later.[20]

Flaxman's *Apollo* unfortunately does not measure up to the importance and rarity of Egremont's commission, as it is a languid and effeminate version of many classical images of the god, possibly influenced by the Kassel *Apollo* which Flaxman could have seen on his way back from Italy, but also reflecting the rather sentimentalised rendering of the Vatican *Apollo Sauroktonos* that appeared in contemporary engravings, such as the plate in Winckelmann's *Monumenti Antichi Inediti* (Plate 249). There was such a strong tradition for images

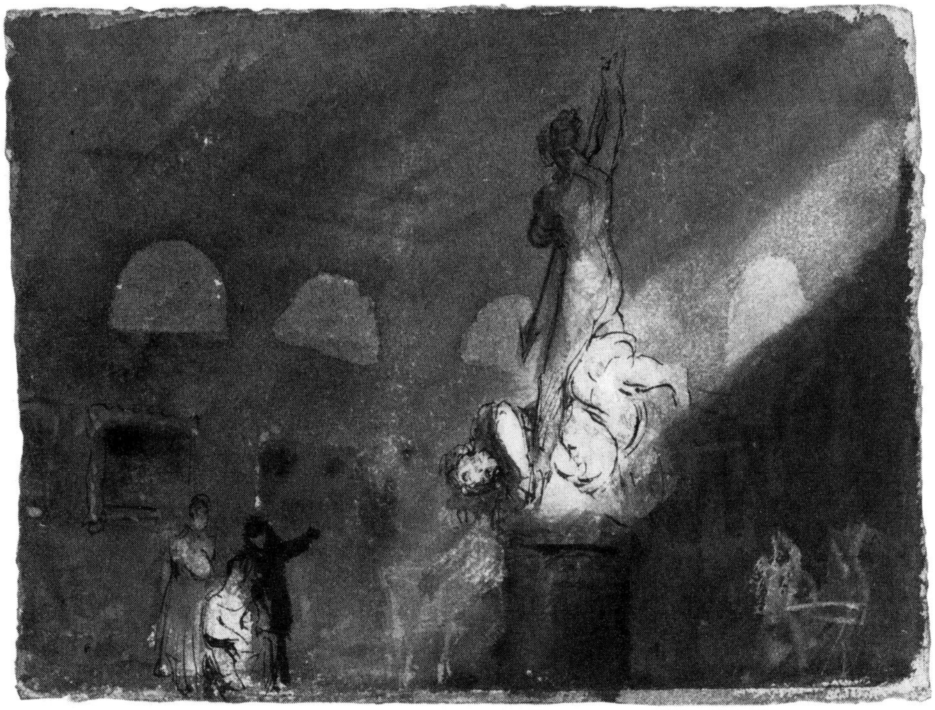

247 J. M. W. Turner: *Petworth: The Gallery, with Flaxman's St. Michael*, ?1828. Watercolour and bodycolour, with pen and ink, 14·2 × 18·9 cms.

248 *Pastoral Apollo*, 1813–24. Marble, 83·5 cms. high.

249 J. J. Winckelmann: *Monumenti Antichi Inediti*, 1767. Volume I, Plate 40, *Apollo Sauroktonos*.

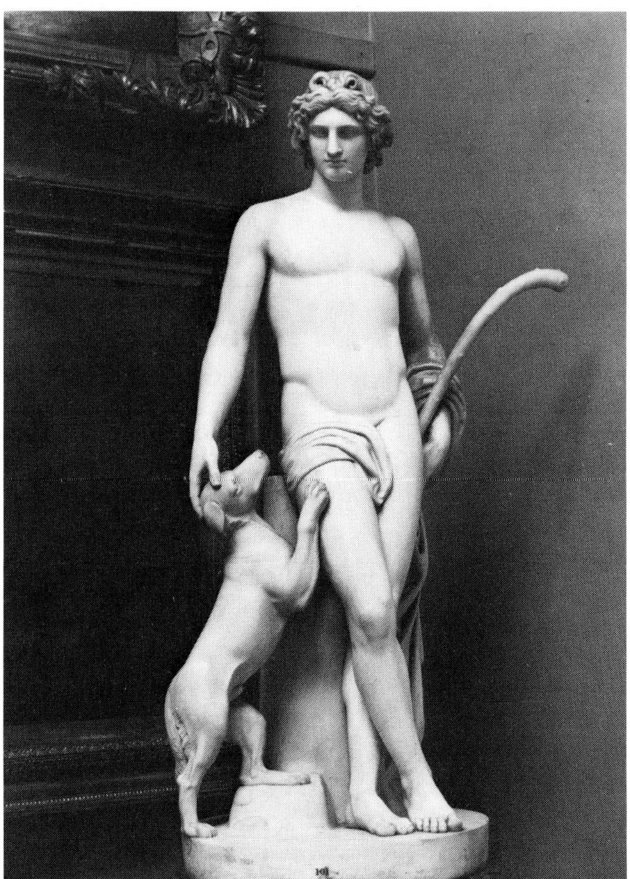

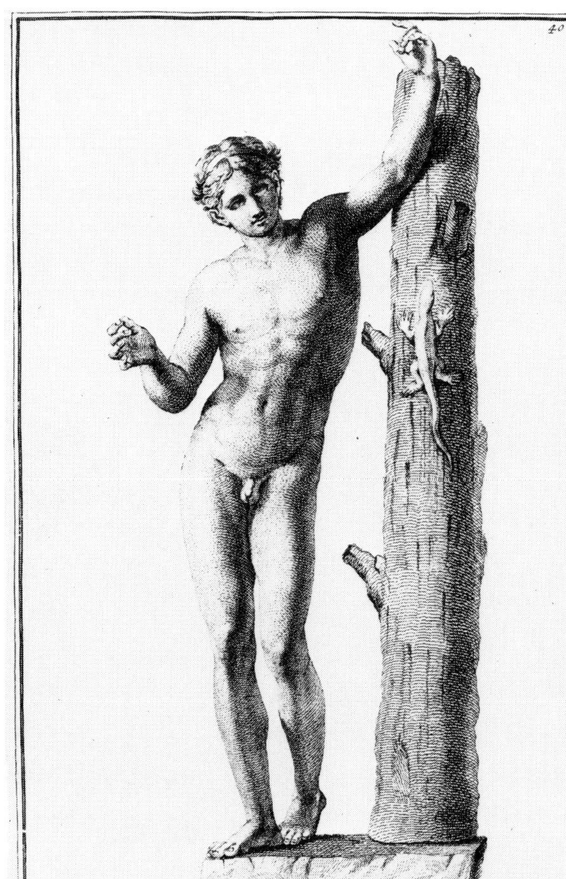

of a standing Apollo in classical sculpture and gems, that Flaxman seems to have been inhibited from producing a powerful image of his own. Perhaps the unusually long period during which Flaxman worked on the *Apollo* was a reflection of the difficulties he encountered in producing a satisfactory piece. The tedium of the marble is further impaired by the insensitive carving, which looks largely like studio work. The firm grasp of naturalism in the anatomy of Apollo's hands and feet, and in the dog, are amongst the statue's better features, together with some attempt to break away from a pastiche of the past by introducing an element of contemporary sentiment in the action of fondling the dog.

In his life of Flaxman, Cunningham was particularly enthusiastic about the *St. Michael* which he claimed was a work of 'the highest merit, the conception is epic, the grouping grand, and the action godlike'. Cunningham then continued in a didactic vein: 'Artists, who hope they are historical or poetic, would do well to look at the divine composure of this group, all is elevated, there is nothing low, there is much to excite awe, and nothing to disgust'.

It was unusual for Flaxman to execute a sculpture intended to be viewed fully in the round, and he rose to the occasion with a composition that showed he had forgotten none of the lessons learnt when copying sculptures by Cellini and Giambologna into his Italian sketchbooks (Plates 64 and 72). Then he had drawn Cellini's *Perseus and Medusa* and Giambologna's *Rape of the Sabines* from several different viewpoints, including even a plan of the Cellini to show its complexity of angles. Also like these two sixteenth century groups, Flaxman has chosen a theme of violence in his *St. Michael*, which is also rendered in an upward, twisting movement of bodies. Whilst in Italy he had also drawn some of the ancient Roman statues from more than one position. But all this information was not immediately put to use in his own sculptures, which were conceived essentially from a single viewpoint. Even a freestanding group such as the *Fury of Athamas* only makes its impact from the front; none of the emotional intensity is apparent from behind. *Cephalus and Aurora* and *Hercules and Hebe* were intended to be seen at their best from a frontal viewpoint. These earlier groups show that Flaxman was strongly influenced by the belief then current in archaeological writings, including those of Winckelmann, that the ancients designed their sculpture usually to be seen from a single, frontal viewpoint.

The nearest parallel to the *St. Michael* in Flaxman's work is one of the illustrations in his *Hesiod* showing the battle of the gods and titans, in which fallen figures, twisting tails and poised weapons could be said to foreshadow the *St. Michael* (Plate 118). The sculpture is vigorous, with a lively contrast between the youthful and graceful St. Michael and muscular, Michelangelesque Satan. The figure of St. Michael is another echo of a classical Apollo, but his vitality carries more conviction than the Apollo in the other Egremont commission. The two groups may have been conceived as a contrasting pair of the active and the passive; but whereas Flaxman was usually successful with passive roles, he has on this occasion only succeeded with the active.

Contemporary and near-contemporary discussions of Flaxman's work frequently singled out the *St. Michael* as one of the sculptor's outstanding achievements. Lawrence, in his funeral oration on Flaxman at the Royal Academy, in a perhaps over-generous moment, was to say that: 'In piety the minds of Michelangelo and Flaxman were congenial. I dare not assert their equality in art. The group of *St. Michael and the Fallen Angel* is a near approach to the greatness of the former'.[21] The group remained popular into the Victorian period, and was selected by the Art Union of London in 1843 as the first sculpture they issued to their subscribers in a small bronze reduction.

CHAPTER VIII

Portraits

250 *Raja Sarfogi (Sarabhoji)*, 1803–5. Marble, lifesize.

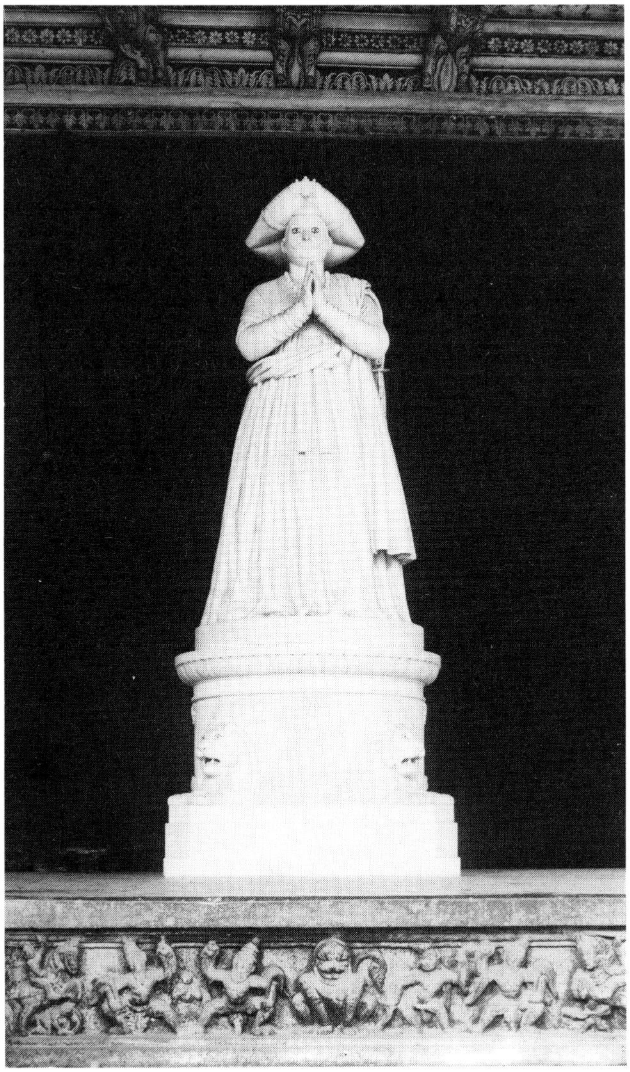

Flaxman's portraits are a less familiar aspect of his work, which some of his obituary notices even overlooked.[1] A few of his portrait statues and busts were commissioned as alternatives to monuments in churches and cathedrals, and others were erected in places such as public squares, a town hall, a library and an Indian palace.

A portrait in the form of a lifesize, standing statue in marble was a rare type in British sculpture. As there was little demand for works on this scale, Flaxman, like other artists, received few commissions for such statues. His contributions to this genre, however, show Flaxman's ability to adapt to any kind of commission, and this group of sculptures—all in contemporary dress—form an interesting, if minor, aspect of his *oeuvre*.

One of the earliest commissions for a lifesize statue, costing £1,200,[2] came from India in 1803, from a client who wished to erect an image of himself during his own lifetime in his palace. Raja Sarfogi (Sarabhoji) of Tanjore never visited England, and presumably selected Flaxman because he liked his monument to the Reverend Christian Frederick Schwartz (Plate 205). Flaxman must have been sent an Indian miniature so that the features, as well as the unusual hat and dress, would be correct (Plate 259); the miniature had presumably also been used for the monument. Flaxman carved the figure of the Raja with his hands clasped in a gesture of reverence creating an imposing image when erected on its high pedestal in a private hall of the palace.

When the younger Pitt died in 1806, many cities and public bodies throughout Britain wished to commemorate a politician who had been as popular as Nelson in the war against Napoleon. In 1808 the city authorities of Glasgow turned to Flaxman for their celebratory statue, willing to spend the sum of £1,300. The statue was completed in 1812, and was originally sited in the old Town Hall (Plate 251). A few years earlier, in 1807, when the Senate of Cambridge University had been considering possible sculptors for their statue of Pitt, Flaxman's name had been amongst those considered together with Canova, Nollekens, Bacon, Garrard and Westmacott. But in spite of Flaxman's merits being canvassed by William Gell and E. D. Clarke, the commission had gone to Nollekens.[3] Flaxman had also failed to win another Pitt commission for the monument to be erected in Westminster Abbey, which had gone in 1807 to Westmacott. However, the model that Flaxman made for this projected monument (now in the Soane Museum) was to be used as the basis for the composition of the Glasgow statue. In both statues Pitt stands with one arm raised as if making a

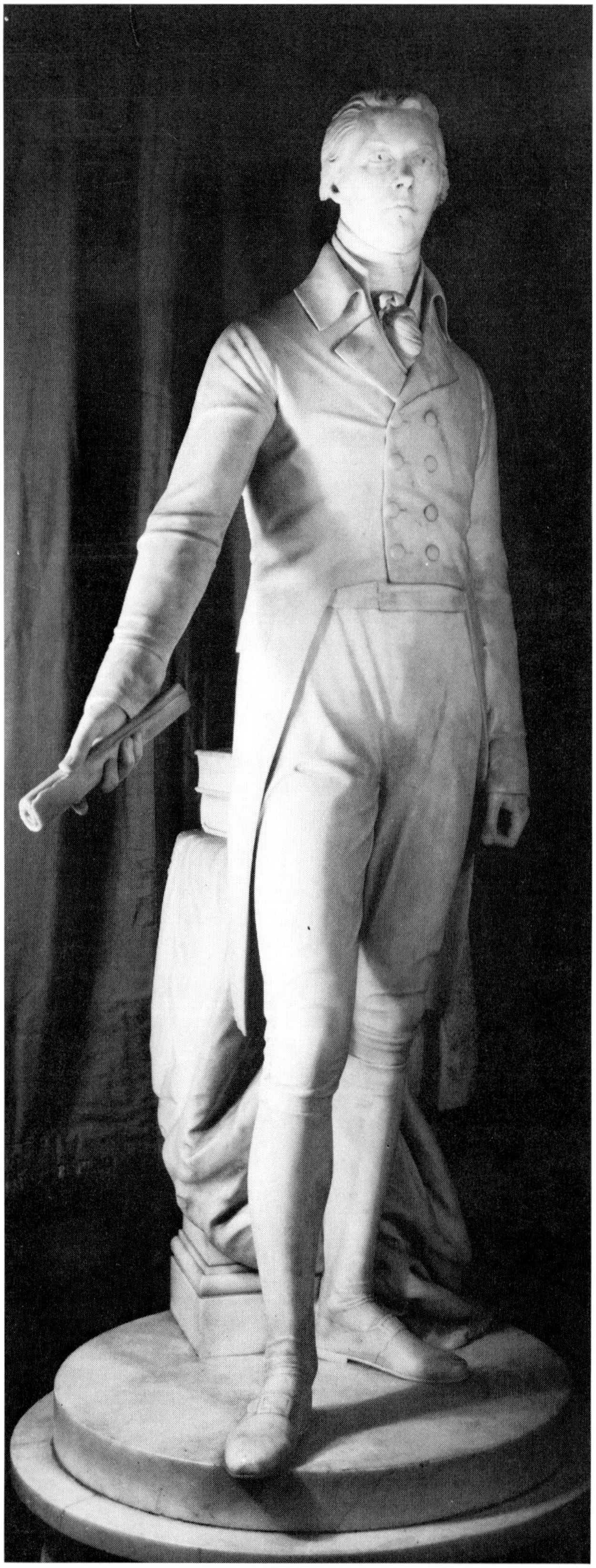

251 *William Pitt*, 1808–12.
Marble 281·75 cms. high.

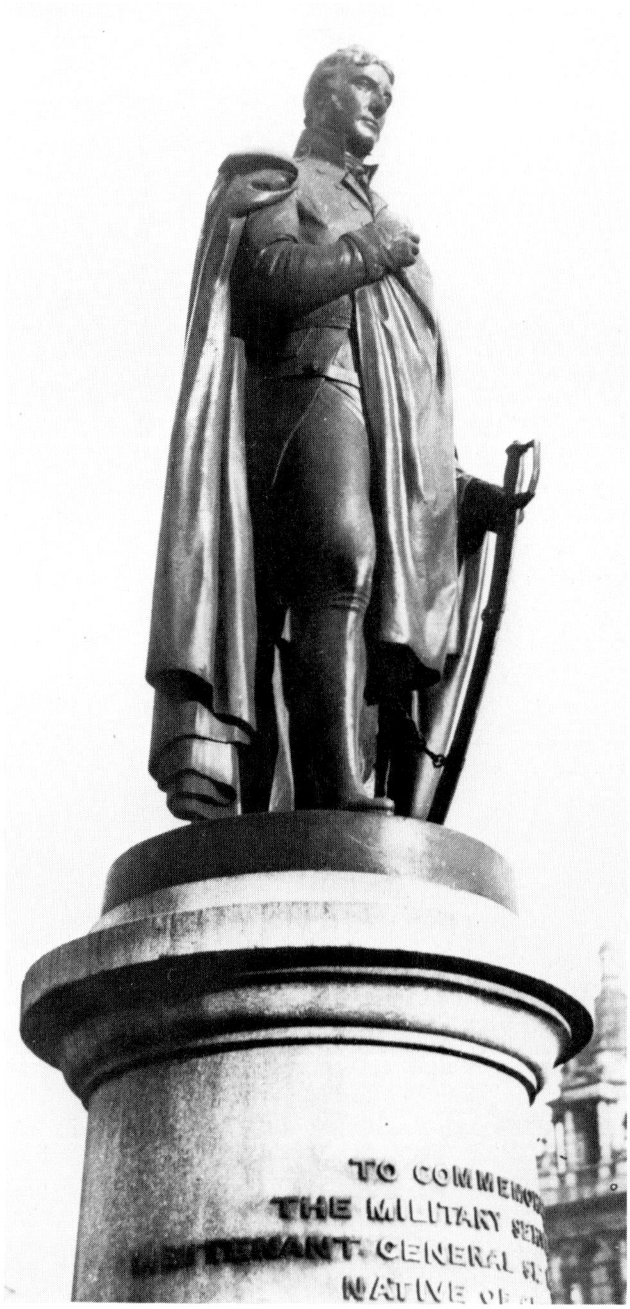

252 *Sir John Moore*, 1810–18.
Bronze, lifesize.

speech in the House of Commons, but this does not give the statue any sense of vitality and it must unfortunately rank amongst Flaxman's weaker pieces.

A decade later Glasgow was again to approach Flaxman for a statue to commemorate a Napoleonic figure, the locally-born General Sir John Moore, who had played such an important part in the campaigns, especially in the Spanish Peninsula (Plate 252). The minute-book of the subscribers' committee for the Moore statue not only reveals a conflict of opinion about whom should be approached to execute the work but it also records the detailed specifications that the sculptor was expected to take into account.[4] The kind of arguments that took place were—and still are—very typical of such committees, and the meticulous requirements would presumably be regarded by the artist as a tiresome but not unusual part of such a public commission. When the committee started its deliberations, it showed a preference for Flaxman, but acceded to a request from Sir John Moore's brother that Nollekens should be chosen instead. He told the committee in a letter that 'the reputation of Mr. Flaxman is great, but perhaps you are not quite aware for what species of excellence he is chiefly distinguished. I understand his reputation is for compositions of a different kind from that which you have decided upon. The sculptor who has been considered as the superior for carving portraits is unquestionably Mr. Nollekens'. Nollekens, however, turned the commission down because he was too old, and could not complete the task within the required two years. Sir John Moore's brother then made scathing remarks about Flaxman, and countered with the suggestion of Rossi, whose model for the composition for the Moore monument in St. Paul's he had just seen and thought the best amongst nine others, at the British Institution. (That commission was eventually to go to Bacon.) In the end, however, the Glasgow committee asked the artist they had chosen in the first place, and Flaxman agreed to undertake it in the summer of 1810. The committee had raised the handsome sum of £3,600, of which £400 was to be kept for a railing and sundry expenses and the remainder was to be paid to the sculptor, out of which he had to meet costs of materials, labour and transport. 'We wish the statue', decreed the committee, 'as much colossal as the funds will permit'. They certainly intended to get value for money, and so that the statue should be as they envisaged, they laid down certain stipulations. Flaxman was told that the face must be a good likeness and therefore he should use as a model Lawrence's oil painting (now in the National Portrait Gallery, London). Exaggeration in the pose was to be avoided. It must be 'such a statue as the ancients would have erected to a warrior'. He was however to wear contemporary dress, the minutiae of which were to be simplified but to leave no doubt as to Moore's profession. Trophies and other ornaments were to be avoided. The committee at least allowed Flaxman to decide whether the figure should be in repose, or commanding, or receiving his fatal wound. Given so many restrictions, Flaxman wisely chose a moment of repose. The statue, however, took many years to complete, not just two, and was only ready for transportation north in the summer of 1818. When it arrived, it was mounted in George Square, on a granite column, as requested by the committee, where it has remained to this day.[5]

Other statues of men of action and politicians include two more men whose lives were associated with India. The East India Company in 1820 commissioned a statue of *Warren Hastings*, at a cost of £1,000. Much earlier in his career in 1784 Flaxman had modelled a portrait of Hastings for a Wedgwood medallion, possibly using a Nollekens bust for the features. Only a year later Hastings had returned from India to England, and the conspiracy of charges against him was to begin. But by 1820 the great and controversial governor-general had been dead for two years, and the Company that had saved him from financial ruin by granting him a pension, now wished to commemorate Hastings in a suitable manner. They chose Flaxman to execute a lifesize statue for the London offices (now in the India Office, London), a commission that made amends for Flaxman having failed to get the one for the Hastings monument in Westminster Abbey, which had gone to Bacon. A few years later in 1826 on the death of the Marquess of Hastings, who had been governor-general and commander-in-chief in Bengal, the British inhabitants of Calcutta subscribed towards a commemorative statue, choosing Flaxman as the sculptor. The marble was finally completed by Flaxman's brother-in-law, Thomas Denman, who had been working for many years in Flaxman's studio, and sent out to Calcutta (it is now in the collection of the Victoria Memorial there).[6]

When sculptors were being chosen to execute four statues of 'benefactors of the English people' to be placed in the crossing of St. Paul's Cathedral, three commissions went to the elder Bacon, and one to Flaxman for Sir Joshua Reynolds (1803–13) (Plate 253). By then the other statues to John Howard of prison reform fame (Plate 254), Dr. Samuel Johnson and the orientalist Sir William Jones had been executed. Johnson and Howard were both clad as Roman heroes,

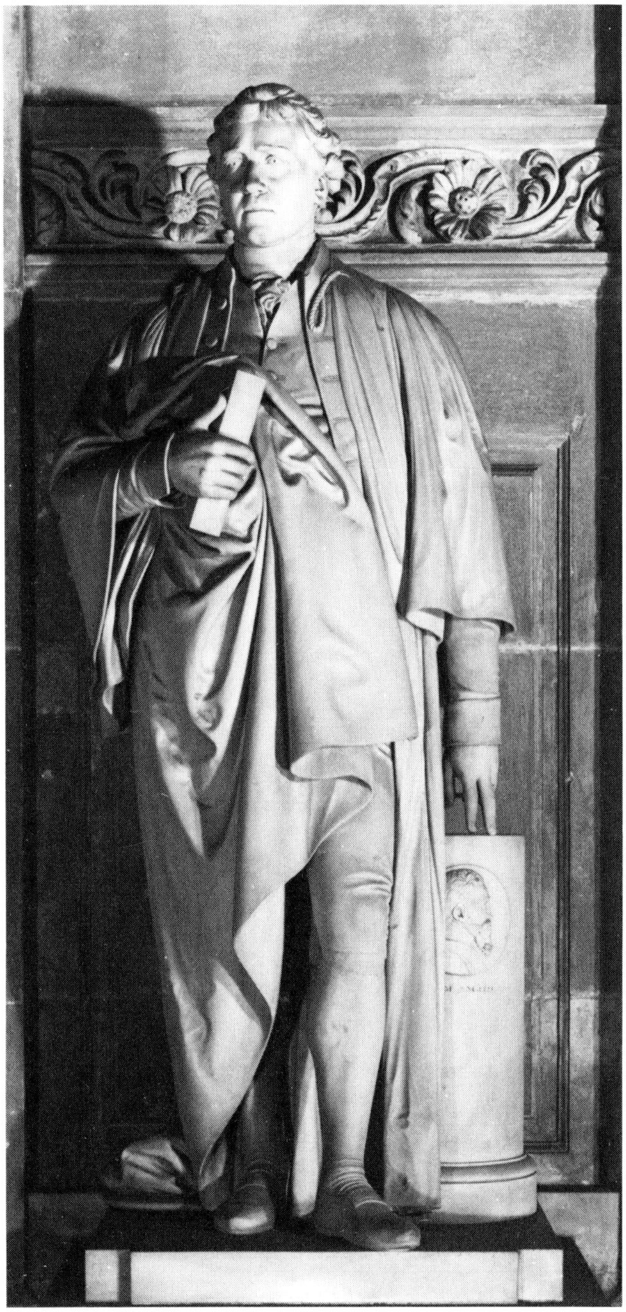

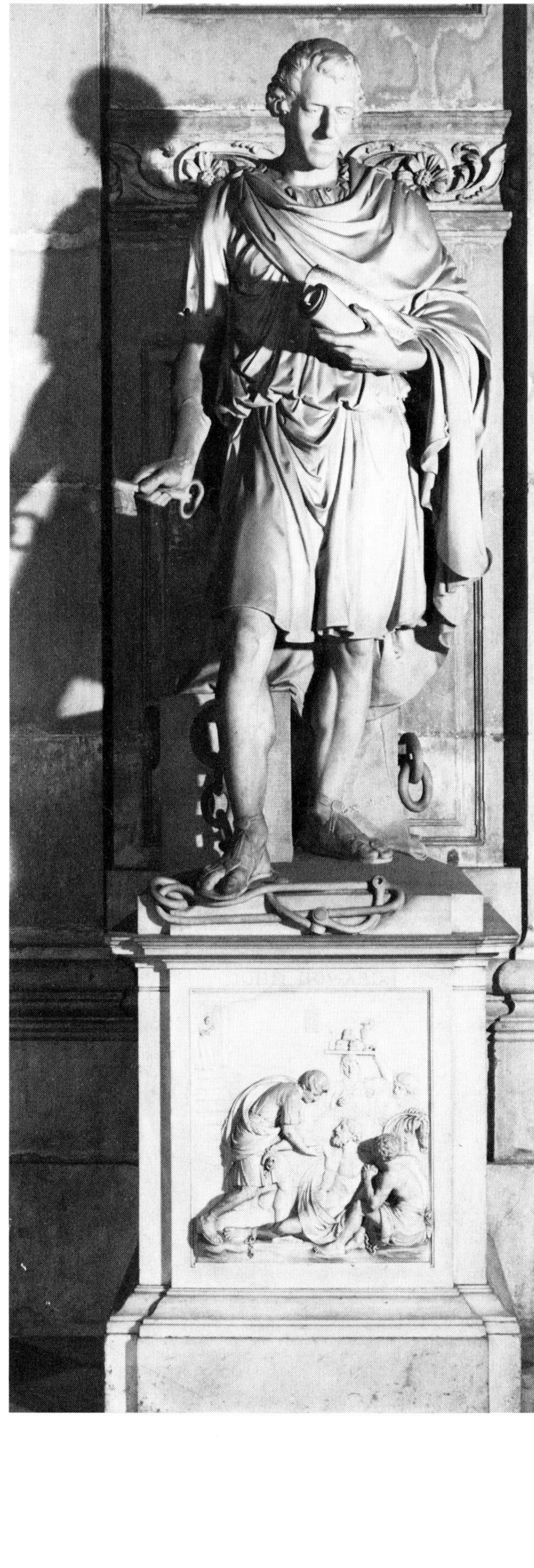

253 *Sir Joshua Reynolds*, 1803–13.
Marble, lifesize.
St. Paul's Cathedral.

254 John Bacon the elder: *John Howard*. 1795.

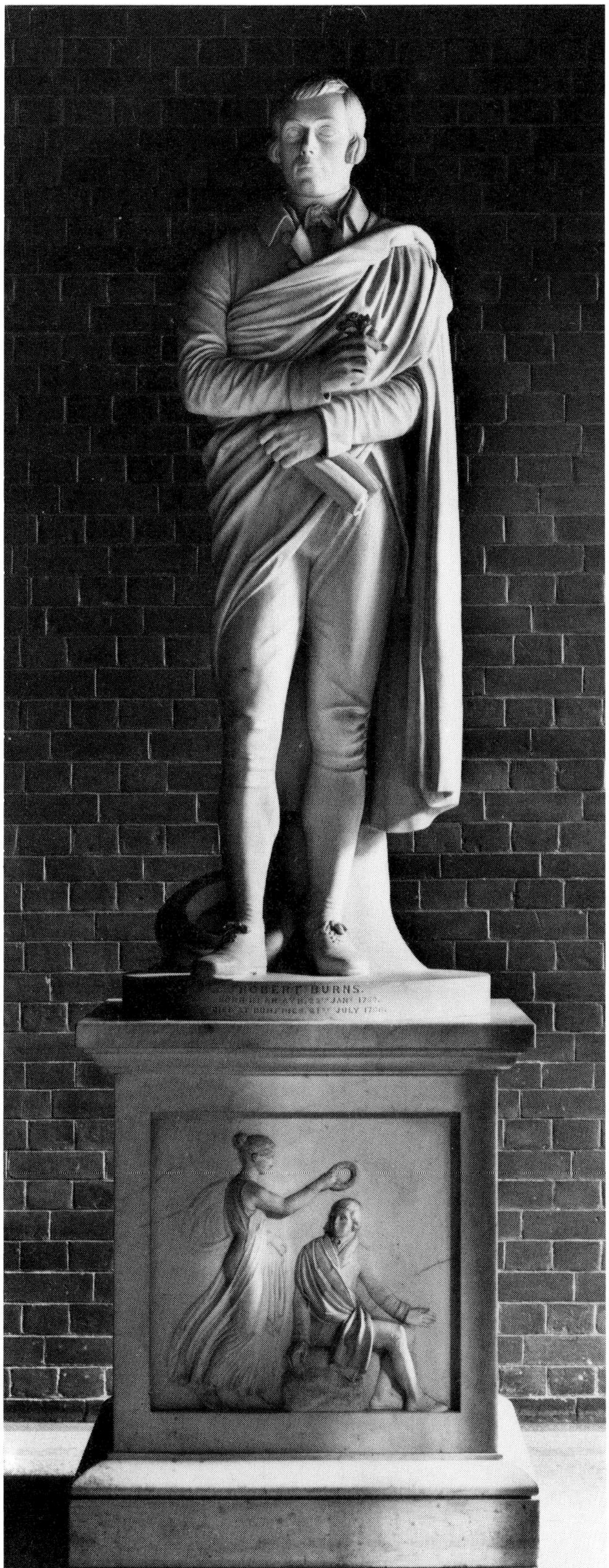

Flaxman dressed his Reynolds in a contemporary manner. As Flaxman had known Reynolds, his image of him carries more conviction and has a greater robustness than either of the Hastings statues, and has a more commanding presence in the St. Paul's crossing than any of the other three statues by Bacon. Flaxman was probably well satisfied with the result himself, since he exhibited a small model of the *Reynolds* at the Royal Academy in 1807. The statue in St. Paul's was one of the few sculptures by Flaxman mentioned in Ludwig Schorn's article on him; Schorn had seen the *Reynolds* when visiting London, and wrote a very sympathetic description of it, praising in particular its 'noble bearing'.[7]

Another example of a lifesize statue commissioned for an ecclesiastical setting, can be seen in the newly-built Gothic Revival cathedral of St. Andrew's in Aberdeen, of which Bishop John Skinner laid the foundations in 1816, the year of his death. He had been very active in the cause of the Episcopal Church in Scotland, and the new cathedral represented the culmination of his work. He is commemorated in Flaxman's statue, placed at the end of one of the aisles, wearing his vestments and holding an open Bible. Flaxman has not, however, included any Gothic Revival motifs on the pedestal, and the statue itself is a straightforward and rather mediocre portrait.

Flaxman was more successful with another and more important Scottish commission, his statue of *Robert Burns* (1822–26) whose poetry the sculptor, like many of his contemporaries, much admired (Plate 255). Flaxman's main Edinburgh contact was the poet's publisher, George Thomson. At about the same time Thomson was instrumental in procuring for Thomas Stothard the commission for the decoration of the dome of the new Advocates Library in Edinburgh with the subject of the *Scottish Parnassus*, which includes Burns amongst its numerous figures. Thomson also hoped that Flaxman might receive the commission for an equestrian statue to George IV which was going to be erected as a result of a public subscription in Edinburgh.[8] But Flaxman was not to receive this equestrian commission, and his main work in Edinburgh was to remain the statue of *Burns*, also paid for by a public subscription, and destined for a site in the University's library. Flaxman never met Burns, and used one of Alexander Nasmyth's portraits for the features, but unlike the painter he has shown Burns wearing the plaid. Flaxman's image is therefore at once

255 *Robert Burns*, 1822–26.
Marble, 292·4 cms. high (including plinth).

more Scottish and also more classical, as the draping of the plaid is close to that of the toga. The ambiguity is probably intentional because the pedestal, which Flaxman usually left plain, has been carved in low relief with a classical Muse crowning the poet seated out-of-doors, again wearing the plaid. In the statue itself, Flaxman makes a direct reference to one of the poet's odes by portraying him with a mountain daisy in one hand. Flaxman found the *Burns* commission a very sympathetic one, as he explained in a letter to Thomson: 'A few years will probably end my course. I have lost my excellent wife. I have no children to provide for. I have no longer any object to accumulate money. The poems of Burns from their first appearance here were a source of gratification and delight in my family, and I know not how I could better close the labours of my life than by contributing a work in which I see his friends so greatly interested, and which I anxiously wish should be creditable to all concerned'. When there was some doubt as to whether enough money could be raised to meet the expense of the commission, Flaxman generously offered to execute it 'without any view to remuneration'.[9]

In addition to portrait statues, Flaxman also executed a few busts. When Thomas Hope arranged the works of art in the suite of rooms on the first floor of his London house, a floor which was conceived as a museum rather than as living quarters, he devised a modest joke for the Dining Room mantelpiece. On either side of a bust of his brother Henry Philip, who was also an antiquarian, he placed two large heads of horses, because the Greek word for 'Philip' means 'horse-lover'. The bust itself is a particularly interesting work by Flaxman (Plate 256),[10] which he exhibited at the Royal Academy in 1802. This was unusual for Flaxman since he generally exhibited classical pieces or works relating to monuments and did not normally draw attention to his portraits. The *Reynolds* was to be another exception, but he only exhibited a model of it.

The portrait of Henry Philip Hope is stylistically important because of the deliberately austere manner in which Flaxman has conceived it. Thomas Hope explained the style in his *Household Furniture* in some detail, in a passage to be quoted below, that suggests that he realised that the novelty of the form needed some justification. Flaxman has chosen the uncompromising form of the herm, in which the head is carved frontally, square with the block of marble, rather than the later Roman imperial type of bust, in which the head can be set at an angle to the torso; a type much favoured by Nollekens and earlier sculptors such as Roubiliac. Rossi used the herm for his bust of the architect George Dance in the same year, and Thorvaldsen used it several times, choosing the herm for his *Self-Portrait* of 1810 (Kunstakademiet, Copenhagen). Its rarity amongst Neoclassical sculptural busts, however, suggests that patrons found this manifestation of the classical revival too puritanical. In portraiture, the herm is the most archaic of forms, and its austerity must have appealed to Thomas Hope's Greek Revival tastes, as well as to Flaxman's love of simplicity. Flaxman also chose the herm for his posthumous bust of the famous surgeon and anatomist, John Hunter, commissioned by the Royal College of Surgeons in 1800 and completed in 1805 (and still in the College's collection). The forerunners to these lifesize white marble portraits in Flaxman's own *oeuvre* are three very small plasters which he had executed soon after his return from Italy, depicting his father and two friends, William Hayley and the painter Henry Howard (all on the Breakfast Parlour mantelpiece in the Soane Museum).[11] Earlier examples of the herm in other sculptor's works are rare,

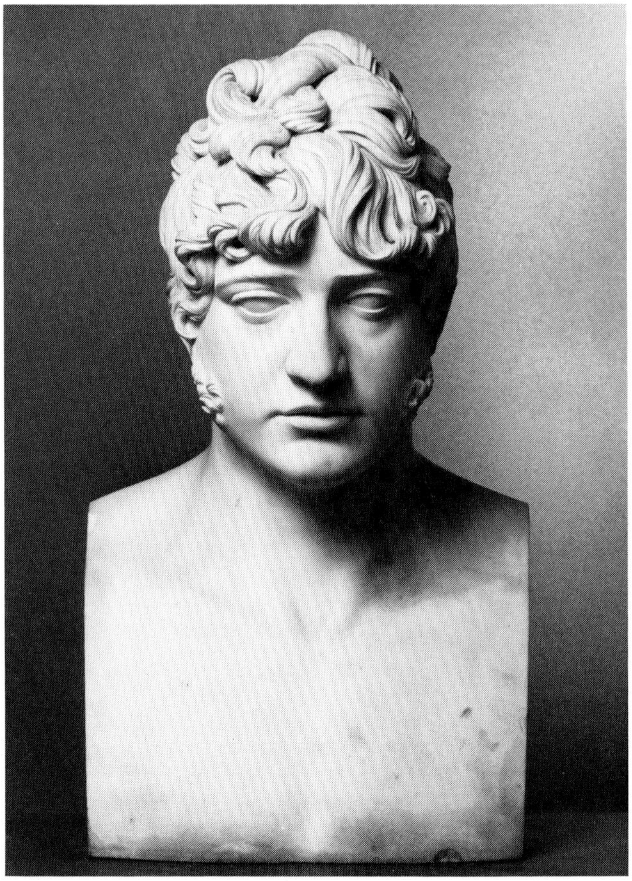

256 *Henry Philip Hope*, 1802.
Marble, 54·2 cms. high.

but they include, appropriately, the bust of the antiquarian and history-painter, Gavin Hamilton, who late in life (1784) sat to Christopher Hewetson in Rome, a bust which Flaxman could have later seen in the collection of Sir William Hamilton in Naples.[12]

Flaxman therefore, having experimented satisfactorily on a modest scale with the three busts of family and friends in the later 90's, presumably felt confident to launch into a bigger scale with *Henry Philip Hope*. The aesthetic was explained by Thomas Hope in the notes that accompany the illustration of the chimneypiece and is worth quoting at length: 'In a production of the pencil, which can only exhibit a face in a single aspect, if the most striking or most favourable view of that face be not a direct front view, there may, in the eligibility of bringing the features more in profile, be a very good reason for turning the head somewhat over the shoulder. Nay, even in a work of the chisel, if it be an entire statue, the peculiar attitude or action of the body may present a sufficient motive for giving such a turn to the head. But if a mere bust, which we may easily view in every possible aspect, by ourselves moving round it, in place of being allowed to leave this task entirely to the beholder, be made itself to turn its face away from our sight, though it have not a body, to account for this less easy and less usual position of the head, the portrait loses all claim to naturalness and truth; it forfeits the appearance of dignified simplicity, which is so essential and so fascinating, for an air of inane and pompous affectation; and it moreover, from the different direction given to the face and to the chest, can seldom be so situated as not to look ill placed and awkward. I shall beg to add that the Grecian method of cutting the chest square, and placing its whole mass immediately on a herm or other solid support, seems much preferable to the more prevailing Roman fashion of rounding off that chest, and balancing its centre only on a slender and tottering pivot'.

Thomas Hope would therefore presumably have disapproved of Flaxman's bust of *General Pasquale de Paoli* which forms part of his monument in Westminster Abbey, and which the sculptor had shown at the Royal Academy in 1798. Flaxman used a 'tottering pivot' to support the bust, which shows a modest skill in this type of portraiture, but not as successful as Nollekens or Chantrey. Flaxman was not unshakeably dedicated to the herm at the time he was executing the *Hope* and *Hunter* portraits, because he used the Roman imperial bust for the portrait of *Josiah Wedgwood* which forms the principal part of his monument in Stoke-on-Trent parish church (1803), and also for the portrait of another industrialist for whom he had worked, Matthew Boulton, on his tomb in Handsworth parish church, Birmingham (Plate 257).[13]

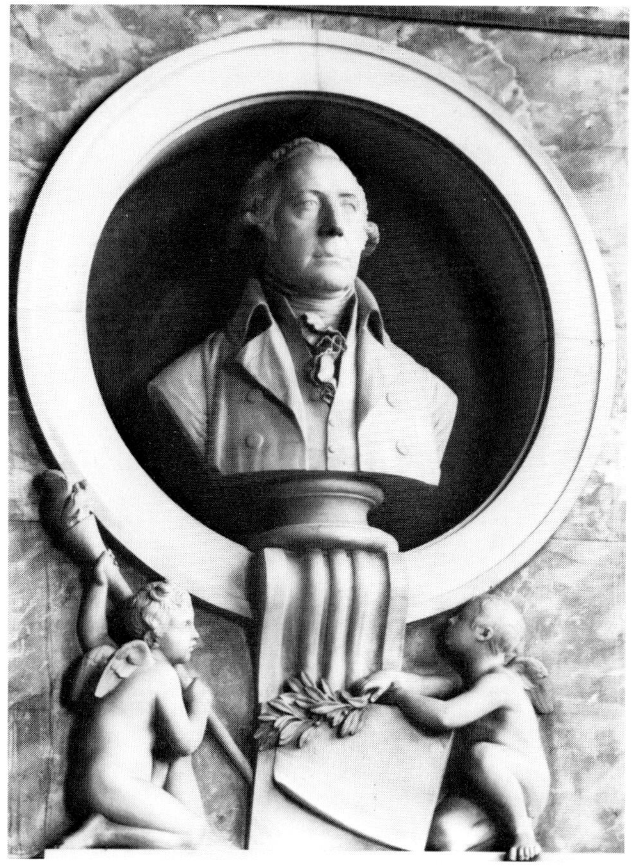

257 *Matthew Boulton: monument: detail,* 1810–13. St. Mary, Handsworth, Birmingham.

In his many portrait drawings of family, friends and acquaintances, Flaxman's classical references and search for primitive simplicity gave way to an intimacy and spontaneity that is closely akin to the contemporary tradition of portrait drawing. The sitter's features and other details are shaded and outlines are softened. One might expect his portraits to relate stylistically to his other works, and therefore to parallel perhaps the portrait drawings of Ingres, but this is not the case. Flaxman had already shown some skill in such drawings before he went to Italy, as well as gaining valuable experience whilst preparing designs for Wedgwood's jasper medallions. Nearly all the portrait drawings that have survived belong to the period after Flaxman's return from abroad and are usually of the sitter's head and shoulders, but occasionally they show more of the figure, up to full-length.

A large group of portrait drawings is contained in a volume mostly compiled in 1804, perhaps as a present

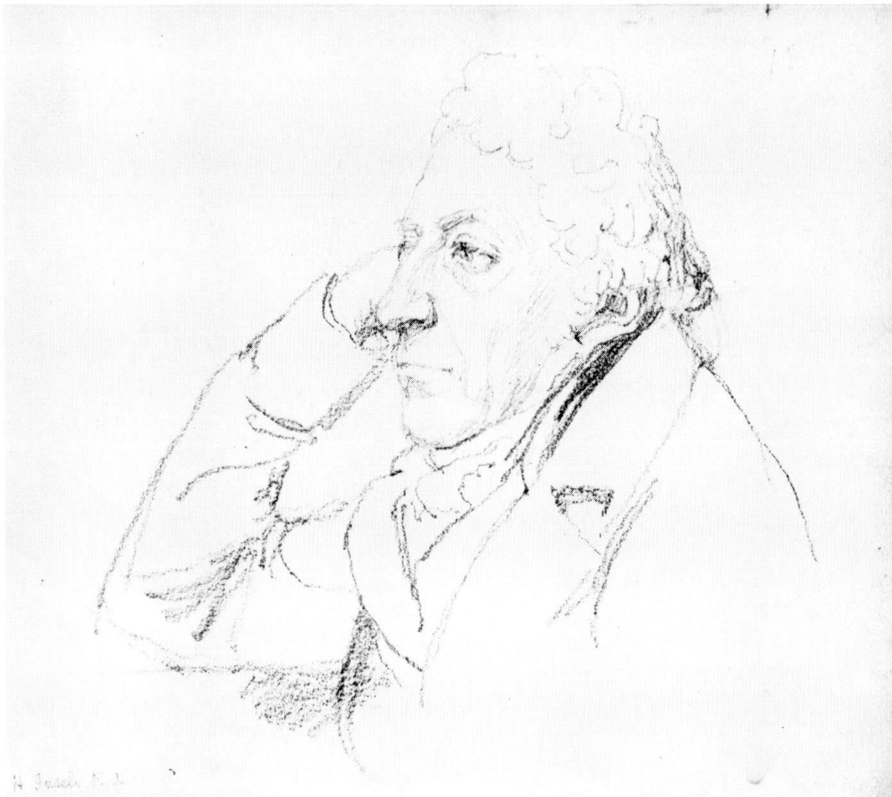

258 *Henry Fuseli*, c. 1804.
Pencil, 18·4 × 22·2 cms.

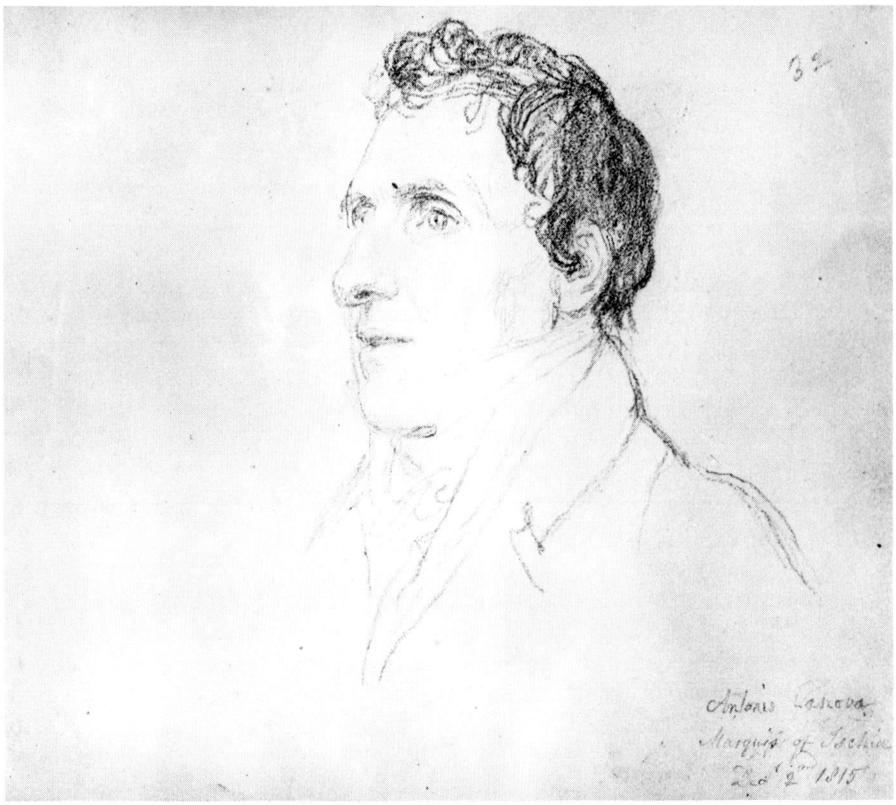

259 *Antonio Canova*, 1815.
Pencil, 18·4 × 22·2 cms.

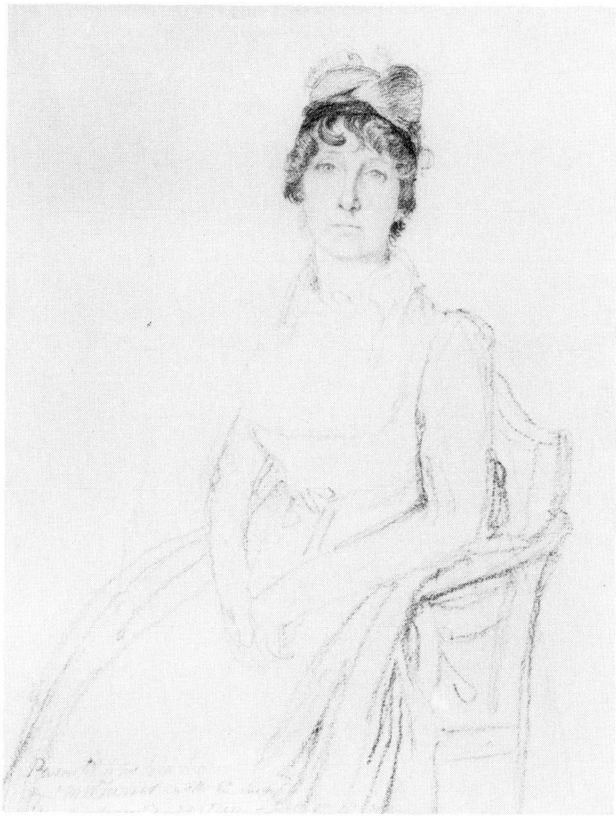

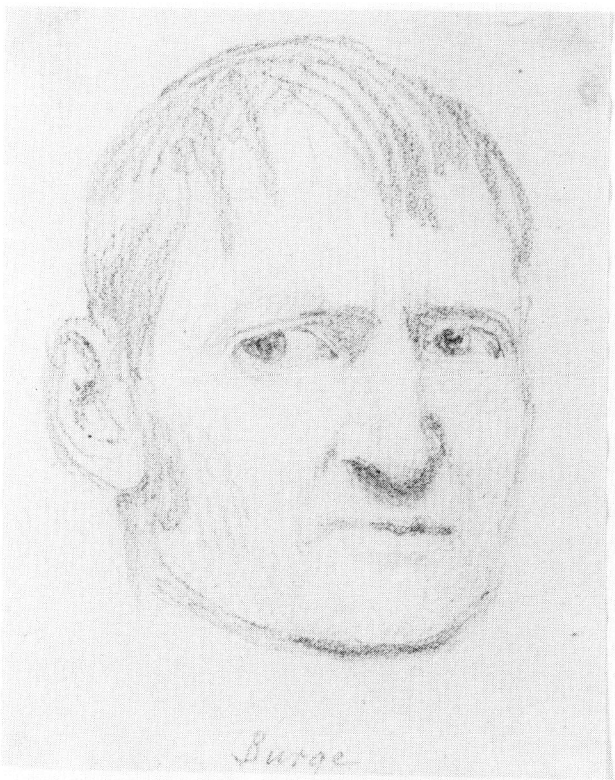

for his wife as a permanent record of their circle of friends at the time (it is now in the Fitzwilliam Museum, Cambridge). As one might expect, many artists feature in the volume, including the elderly Thomas Banks (who was to die the following year), William Blake, Henry Fuseli (Plate 258), Benjamin West and Thomas Daniell, together with the engravers Robert Cromek and James Parker, as well as other acquaintances.[14] Later, in 1815, Flaxman added to the volume a head of Canova, drawn when he was visiting London (Plate 259). Other drawings in the volume include a group of figures seated around a table, and a caricature.

Portrait drawings by Flaxman are scattered throughout other collections. Soane acquired a roughly drawn profile of the French architect Charles Percier, which Flaxman had drawn whilst in Paris in 1802. Turner owned a very attractive three-quarter length portrait of Mrs. Soane, which he later gave to the architect in 1830 (Plate 260). Flaxman also drew his wife, sister-in-law, and elderly father (Plate 4), as well as a fine head of his marble polisher John Burge (Plate 261).

The portrait drawings were amongst the private part of his art, not usually preparatory to any sculpture or connected with any project, and were not intended for exhibition or engraving. Like any artist who is interested in people and nature, Flaxman's drawings record a boundless concern with the world around him.

260 *(above left) Mrs. John Soane.*
Pencil, 29·2 × 22·8 cms.

261 *(left) John Burge.*
Pencil, 10·8 × 8·9 cms.

CHAPTER IX

Royal Plate and Other Metalwork

Opulence, reflecting the extravagant taste of the Prince Regent, characterises some of Flaxman's designs for silverware executed for the large and prosperous firm of royal goldsmiths, Rundell, Bridge and Rundell. Flaxman responded with enthusiasm to a series of costly commissions for decorations appropriate for banquets, and for once in his career suppressed an innate sense of restraint. In his smaller metalwork pieces, however, for royal and other clients, Flaxman's designs have stylistically more in common in their decoration with his own book illustrations.

Flaxman's larger pieces reflect the intricate and more massive taste in silver and gilt plate that had been developing from the 1790's onwards, which in its more ornate examples combined a love of realistic genre detail with the elaboration of classical marble vases from the late Roman Empire. The taste was paralleled in garden ornaments by the great popularity of the *Borghese* and *Medici Vases*, from the latter part of the eighteenth century right through the reign of George IV. Flaxman's plate would not have looked out of place amongst the pages of the key series of Regency designs published by the architect Charles Heathcote Tatham in 1806, *Designs for Ornamental Plate*. Flaxman's larger examples of plate show that he would have agreed with Tatham's comments in his preface that 'massiveness [is] the principal characteristic of good plate', whereas until recently 'light and insignificant forms have prevailed, to the utter exclusion of all good ornament whatever'. Tatham also argued in his preface that the only basis for modern design was a familiarity with antique forms, another point with which Flaxman would certainly have concurred.

Flaxman had already had ample experience in designing objects which were to be executed by other men under factory and workshop conditions when he had worked earlier in his career for Wedgwood. It was a natural extension of his interests in the applied arts to include plate, especially as in many respects the pieces are sculptures on a smaller scale.

Two years before Flaxman started work on Nelson's monument for St. Paul's Cathedral, he was commissioned to design a silver vase to commemorate the Battle of Trafalgar. The commission came from Lloyd's Patriotic Fund, which had been established by the famous London underwriters and had raised large sums of money after each naval victory. The vase (Plate 262) was for presentation either to admirals and captains who had taken part in the battle of Trafalgar, or to their widows. Between 1805 and 1809 as many as sixty-six of these vases were made for Rundell's. Like the Nile Cup that had been presented to Nelson himself

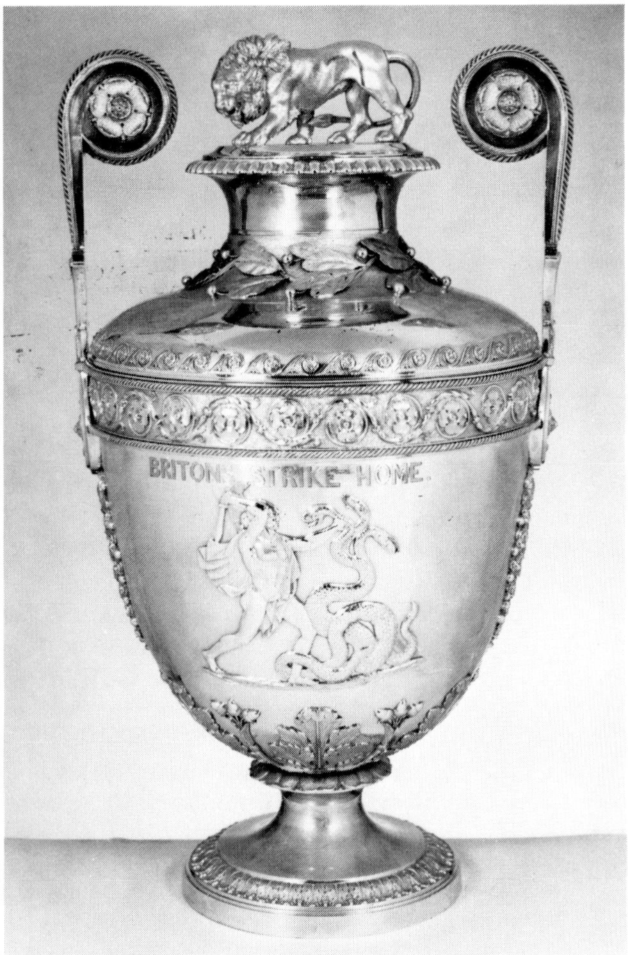

262 *Trafalgar Vase*, 1805–6. Silver 43·2 cms. high. Executed after Flaxman by Benjamin Smith and Digby Scott for Rundell, Bridge and Rundell.

(1799–1800, in the National Maritime Museum, London), which had been made and also probably designed by Paul Storr, Flaxman in his Trafalgar Vase used both a classical shape and detailing, with only a few allegorical motifs and lettering to indicate the contemporary event being commemorated. Flaxman's volute *krater* is surmounted by a lion, on one side of the vase is a low relief of a seated Britannia holding a small winged Victory, together with the words—in disproportionate lettering—'Britannia Triumphant'; on the other side Hercules is fighting with the Hydra. The design is a competent exercise in the new heavier Neoclassical style, but not one of Flaxman's more inspired pieces of plate. The Vase did however forge a firm link between Flaxman and Rundell's that was to last to the end of Flaxman's life. The widespread distribution of the Trafalgar Vases, the most mass-produced of the more expensive souvenirs of the Napoleonic Wars, helped to establish Flaxman's reputation in the field of metalwork, and presumably encouraged the Prince Regent in 1809 to give Flaxman one of his most lavish commissions.

The Prince Regent was to spend the handsome sum of just over £4,000[1] on two silvergilt candelabra, designed by Flaxman, and made for Rundell's by Paul Storr, who by now had become the firm's principal silversmith, from 1807 to 1819 (Plates 263, 264 and 265). The candelabra form part of the Grand Service of royal plate, and were later described by the makers as 'very superb', reflecting their justifiable pride not only in the design but also in the high quality of the craftsmanship.[2] For splendour they are only equalled in Flaxman's designs for plate by his four gilt ice-pails, executed much later by John Bridge in the year of Flaxman's death, also to form part of the Grand Service (Plate 266). Each consists of three weighty tritons riding on the waves, supporting a vase surmounted by Venus rising from a shell, an elaborate design that reflects contemporary interest in Continental sixteenth century plate, and which can also be paralleled stylistically by the Parisian work of Odiot.

On the bases of the candelabra sit three piping fauns which are more reminiscent of sixteenth-century sources in Riccio than of classical antiquity itself. Around the upper tier on one candelabrum is the story of the three Graces gathering the golden apples of the Hesperides, and on the other Mercury is presenting Bacchus to the nymphs: two of the most popular tales from classical mythology. Flaxman has skilfully combined Roman architectural decorations with naturalistic detail, providing a variety of intricate forms that prevents these massive candelabra from becoming overpowering. Each design is conceived as a series of elegant curves, leading the eye upwards, either to the serpent curling round the stem or to Mercury hovering amongst the grape vines. Earlier in his career, in 1785, Flaxman had used the subject of the apples of the Hesperides on a Wedgwood piece, choosing the moment in the story when Hercules is about to fulfil one of his labours (Plate 30), and using an engraving of a design on a vase in Sir William Hamilton's collection (Plate 32). Twenty-five years later, Flaxman retained the central position of the tree encircled by the guardian serpent, and flanked by the three daughters of Erebus and Night. The stress on linearity, however, has now disappeared and been replaced by a graceful realism modelled fully in the round. On the Bacchus candelabrum this naturalism has become playful and akin to Flaxman's studies of domestic genre, including the

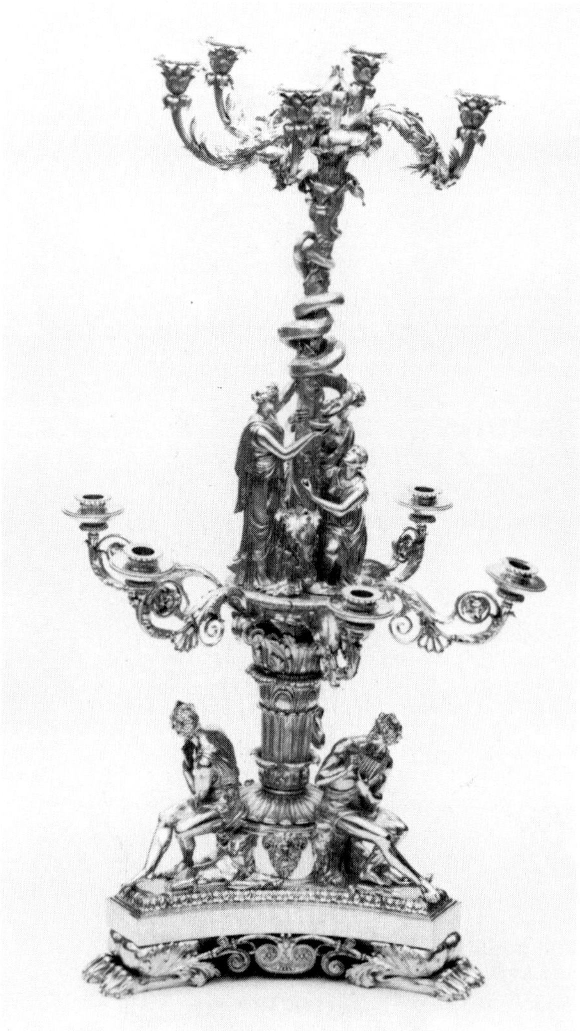

263 *Candelabrum: Three Graces gathering the Apples of the Hesperides*, 1809.
Silvergilt, 127 cms. high.
Executed after Flaxman by Paul Storr.

theme of the mother and child; although a classical incident it is treated almost as if it were a contemporary scene, a transformation that is not found on the earlier Wedgwood plaque.

The Prince Regent's acquisitions of pieces of Flaxman's plate continued shortly afterwards in 1812 when he received from his mother, Queen Charlotte, the present of a Theocritus Cup (Plates 267 and 268). This piece, illustrating scenes from the Greek poet's first *Idyll*, was a popular one since at least three others were made for a Winchester headmaster, a Liverpool alderman and for the Prince Regent to give to the Bishop of Winchester.[3] When Soane acquired a plaster model for one of the panels he incorporated it into the decoration of his chimneypiece in the Breakfast Parlour of his house in Lincoln's Inn Fields, London. In the Theocritus Cup Flaxman was recreating an imaginary work of art described in detail in Greek literature. He did not follow Theocritus slavishly, however, since the silver cup the poet described is a flatter, more open *kylix* with the decoration on the inner surface, whereas Flaxman chose a *calyx krater* and placed the decoration around the outer surface. The incidents illustrated on both sides of Flaxman's cup follow the lines of Theocritus fairly closely, and are executed in a linear, low relief stylistically close to his engravings. As in his illustrations, Flaxman has pared down his story to its basic essentials. He has incorporated three incidents, united with continuous trails of vines on one side, changing into ivy on the other, and continuing the stems down into the handles, which as a result are not Greek. On one side of the cup stands a woman, described by Theocritus as 'such a thing as the gods might fashion', who is flanked by young men contending for her love, 'yet these things touch not her heart'. On the other side of the cup an elderly fisherman is pulling in his net, whilst nearby a little boy is sitting supposedly guarding the grapes from thieving foxes, but he is too intent on making a cricket-cage, and fails to notice that a fox is about to steal his food. The cup, which Theocritus described as 'a marvel that will strike thy heart with amaze', is being given in the poem to a goatherd in order to encourage him to sing. Flaxman found a sympathetic text to which he responded with an imaginative design, suffused with classical knowledge yet without specific borrowings, and incorporating—as on the candelabra—naturalism and delightful genre detail. The treatment of the landscape background is the nearest that Flaxman ever comes to the kind of relief on Ghiberti's second bronze Baptistry doors, which—in theory—Flaxman disliked because of the elaborate backgrounds in the panels.[4]

Later, in 1826, Flaxman was to design for Rundell's another Greek-inspired vase (Plate 269). This time he took his theme from Hesiod, translating two of his own engravings very successfully into low relief decorations, the panel of the Silver Age being executed in white silver, and that of the Golden Age in gilt. The clean-cut outlines of the two-handled *skyphos* have been left austerely plain, and the only engraved decoration is mostly based on the more geometric and less florid form of the Greek honeysuckle pattern. Although only a small vase, it sums up beautifully on a miniature scale the essential characteristics of the Greek Revival.[5]

In 1817, the year in which Flaxman designed a cup mounted on a tripod for presentation to John Kemble on his retirement from the stage, and which was also

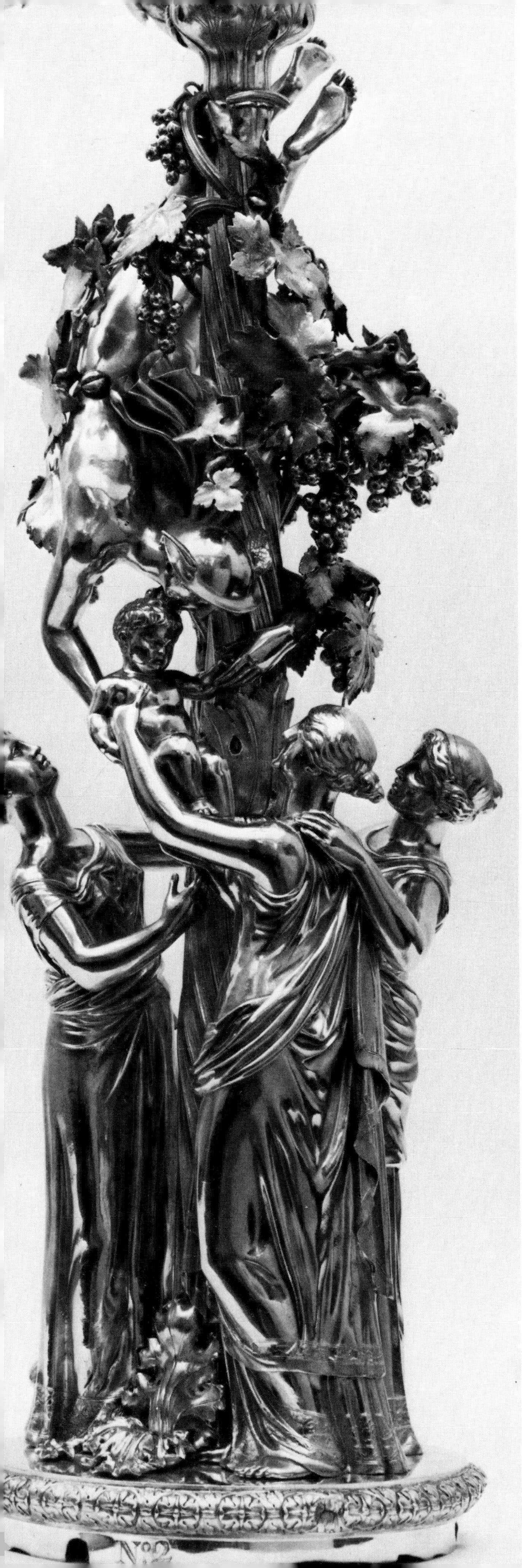

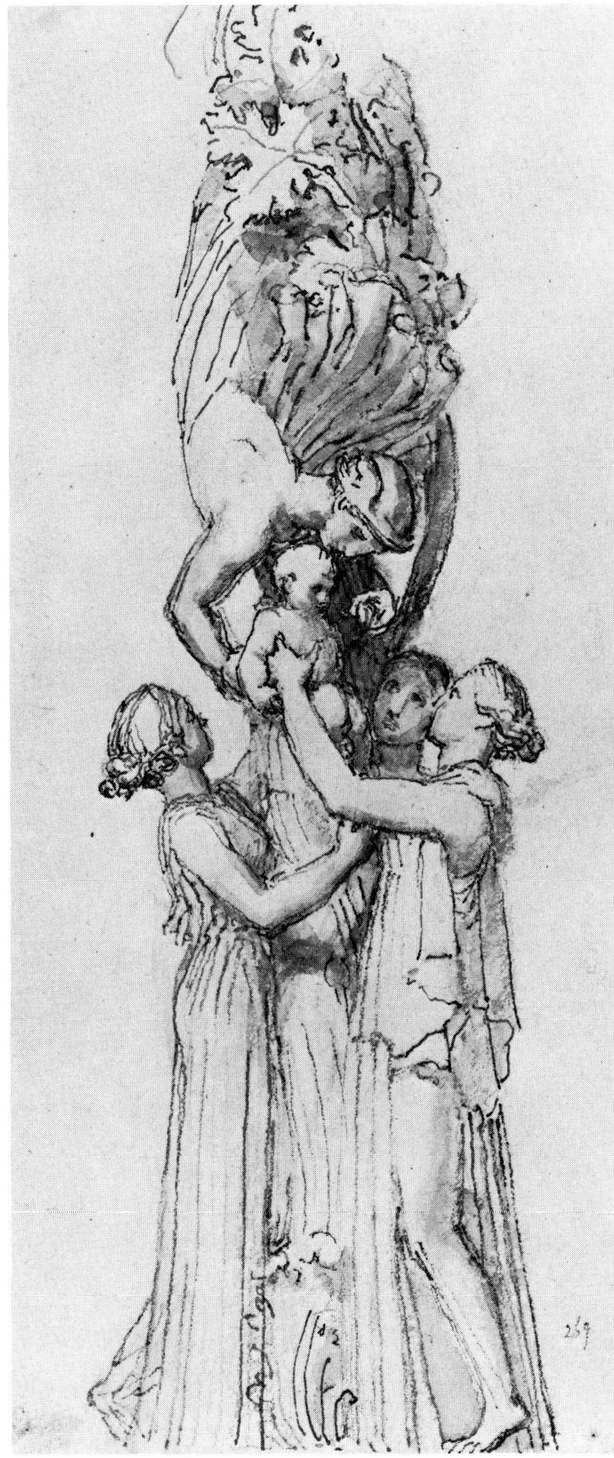

264 *Candelabrum: Mercury presenting Bacchus to the Nymphs: detail*, 1809.
Pair to Plate 263.

265 *Candelabrum: Mercury presenting Bacchus to the Nymphs: design.*
Pen, wash and pencil, 24·6 × 10·6 cms.

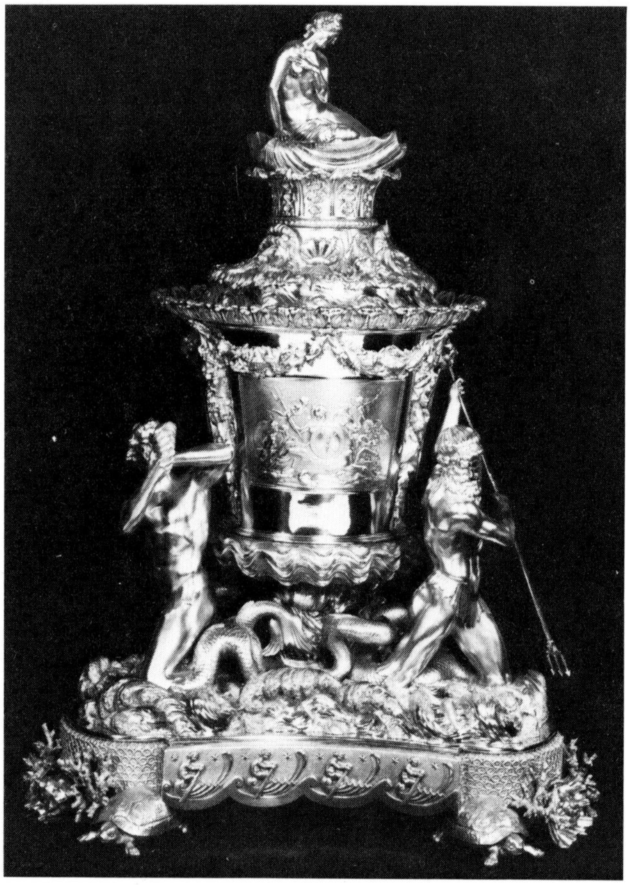

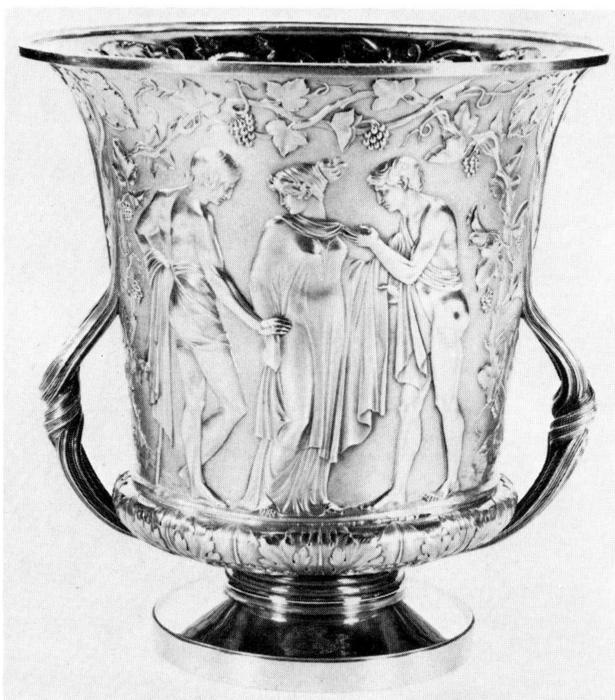

made for Rundell's, Flaxman committed himself more fully to the firm, apparently becoming its chief modeller for the rest of his life.[6] The elder William Theed had held this post until his death in 1817, and had added Flaxman's former pupil E. H. Baily to the firm's staff a couple of years previously. Baily was kept busy working for Rundell's, modelling the Kemble Vase from Flaxman's drawings, and making innumerable designs which survive in a volume labelled 'Designs for Plate by John Flaxman', but which have now been convincingly attributed mostly to Baily, who in some instances had been inspired by ideas of his former master.[7] Designs by Thomas Stothard as well As William Theed are in the same volume, and show, together with actual examples by or attributed to these fellow artists, that Flaxman shared with them the same basic ideas on silver design.

Flaxman's major work for Rundell's at the beginning of the 1820's was the *Shield of Achilles*, his other recreation of a literary description of an imaginary work of art (Plate 270). The idea for the shield originated in 1810, but the final model was not completed until 1818, by which date Rundell's had paid Flaxman six hundred guineas for twenty-four drawings and five models, including the final one.[8] The shield was eventually made in silvergilt for the first time in 1821, when it was acquired for 2,000 guineas by George IV, who had succeeded to the throne the previous year. Presumably in an ebullient mood, he wished to celebrate the event by expanding the collection of royal plate still further. The *Shield of Achilles* was displayed prominently at the coronation banquet in July 1821. The royal collection already possessed a large sideboard dish illustrating the theme of the *Triumph of Bacchus and Ariadne*, which had been designed by Stothard, and also made for Rundell's, in 1814 (Plate 271). The composition of this dish and the shield are in some respects similar, and it is possible that Flaxman influenced his fellow artist. The similarities may however have been prescribed in the commisions. Both works have a central motif of a chariot flanked by several figures, but

266 *(above left) Ice Pail*, 1827.
Silvergilt, 57·8 cms. high.
Executed after Flaxman by John Bridge.

267 *(left) Theocritus Cup: Two Youths contending for a Maiden's favour*, 1812.
Silvergilt, 23·5 cms. high.
Executed after Flaxman by Paul Storr.

268 *(right) Theocritus Cup: Fisherman and Boy.*
Reverse side of Cup in Plate 267.

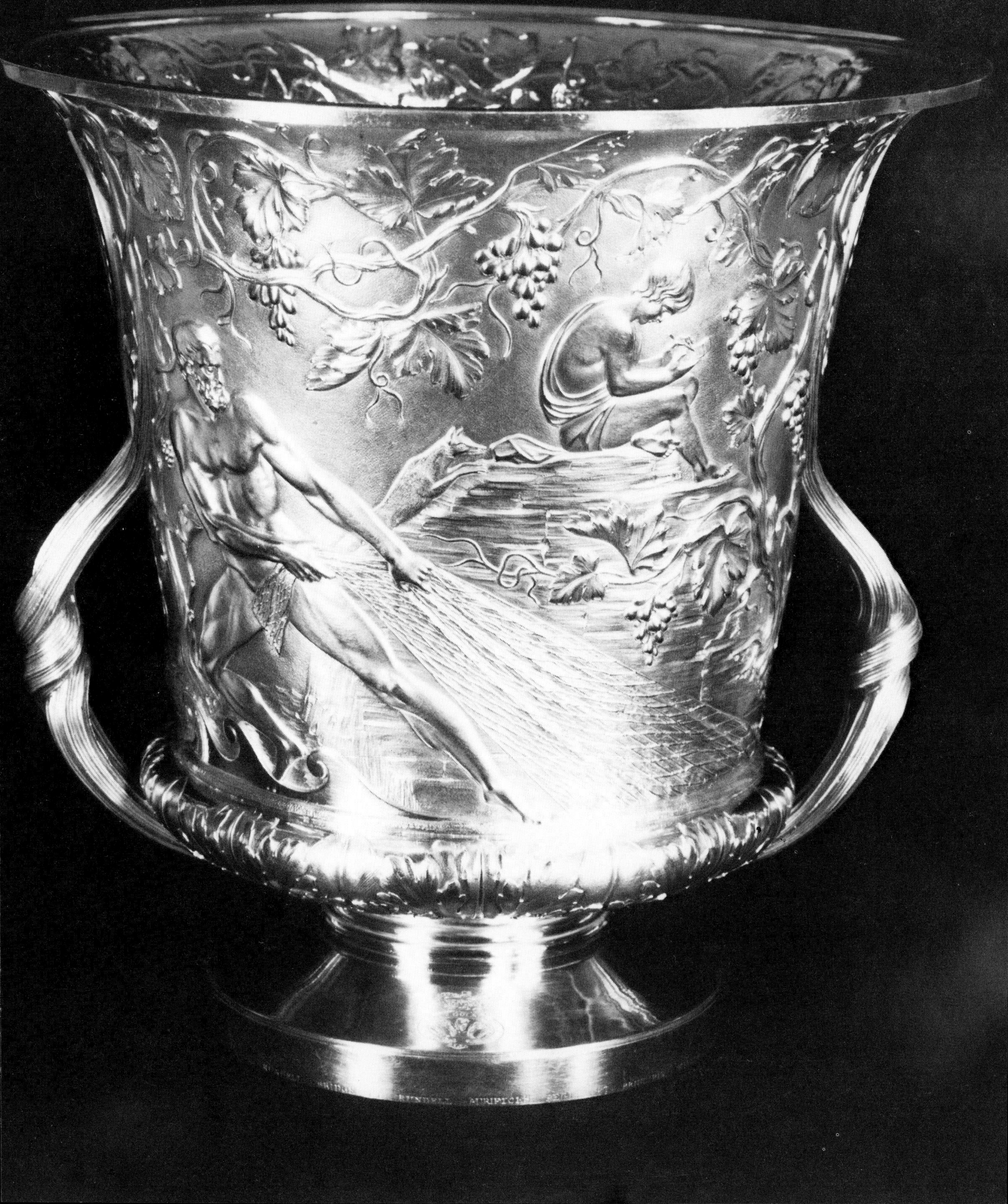

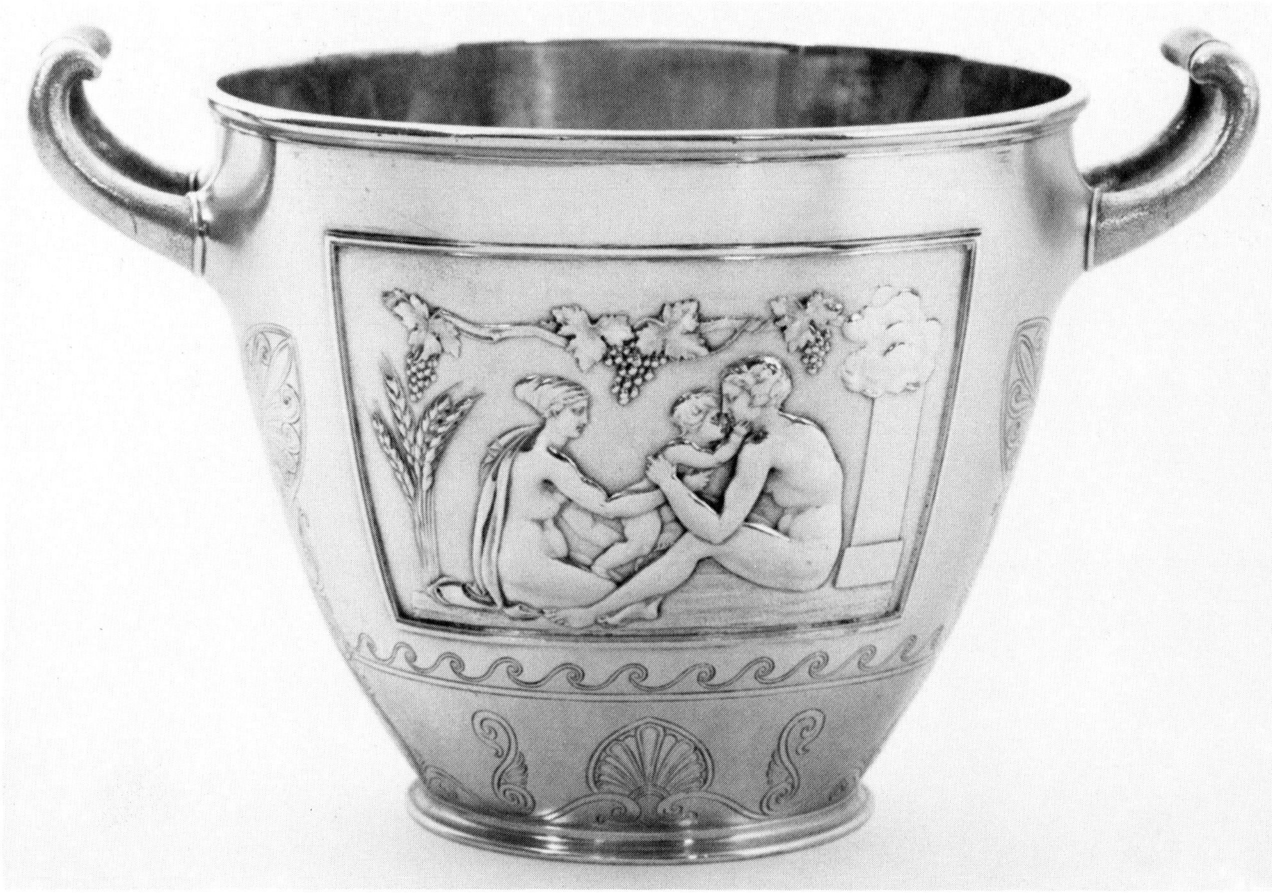

269 *Two-handled Vase: gold and silver ages,* 1826. Parcel gilt and silver, 14·6 cms. high. Executed after John Flaxman by John Bridge.

whereas Flaxman's represent constellations, Stothard's are putti; Flaxman's chariot is pulled by horses, Stothard's by centaurs. The *Shield of Achilles*, almost certainly influenced another design for plate by Stothard, namely the shield presented to the Duke of Wellington in 1822 by the merchants and bankers of the City of London, which also has battle scenes around its perimeter (in the Wellington Museum, Apsley House, London). Flaxman's *Shield of Achilles* also helped to set the pattern for a series of shields and sideboard dishes throughout the Victorian period, when it became fashionable to display collections of massive pieces of silver.

Flaxman's shield was highly praised at the time, and in succeeding decades. Rundell's themselves described it in their catalogue of the royal plate as 'this masterpiece of modern art', and Cunningham's biography records that Flaxman was 'justly proud' of this 'magnificent' piece, which was 'considered by many as one of the artist's most successful works'. Other silver versions were made for the Duke of York (now in the Huntington Art Gallery, San Marino), the Duke of Northumberland and the Earl of Lonsdale, making this group one of the most costly series of works that Rundell's undertook in Flaxman's lifetime in terms of the large number of hours employed by the silver chasers, together with the weight of the silver, each shield containing over six hundred ounces.

As a classical scholar, Flaxman went to the Greek text of Book XVIII of the *Iliad* for his source, not to Pope's translation.[9] It was presumably because he was working from the original text that Philip Rundell, who was not himself a classical scholar (and whose behaviour was very ill-mannered), was rather bored with Flaxman's regular evening visits to read and expound on the *Iliad* at the time he was working on the Shield. Rundell therefore left the discussion of the text with the artist and the final formulation of the design to his nephews, who were more educated.[10]

Homer provides a vivid description of the shield

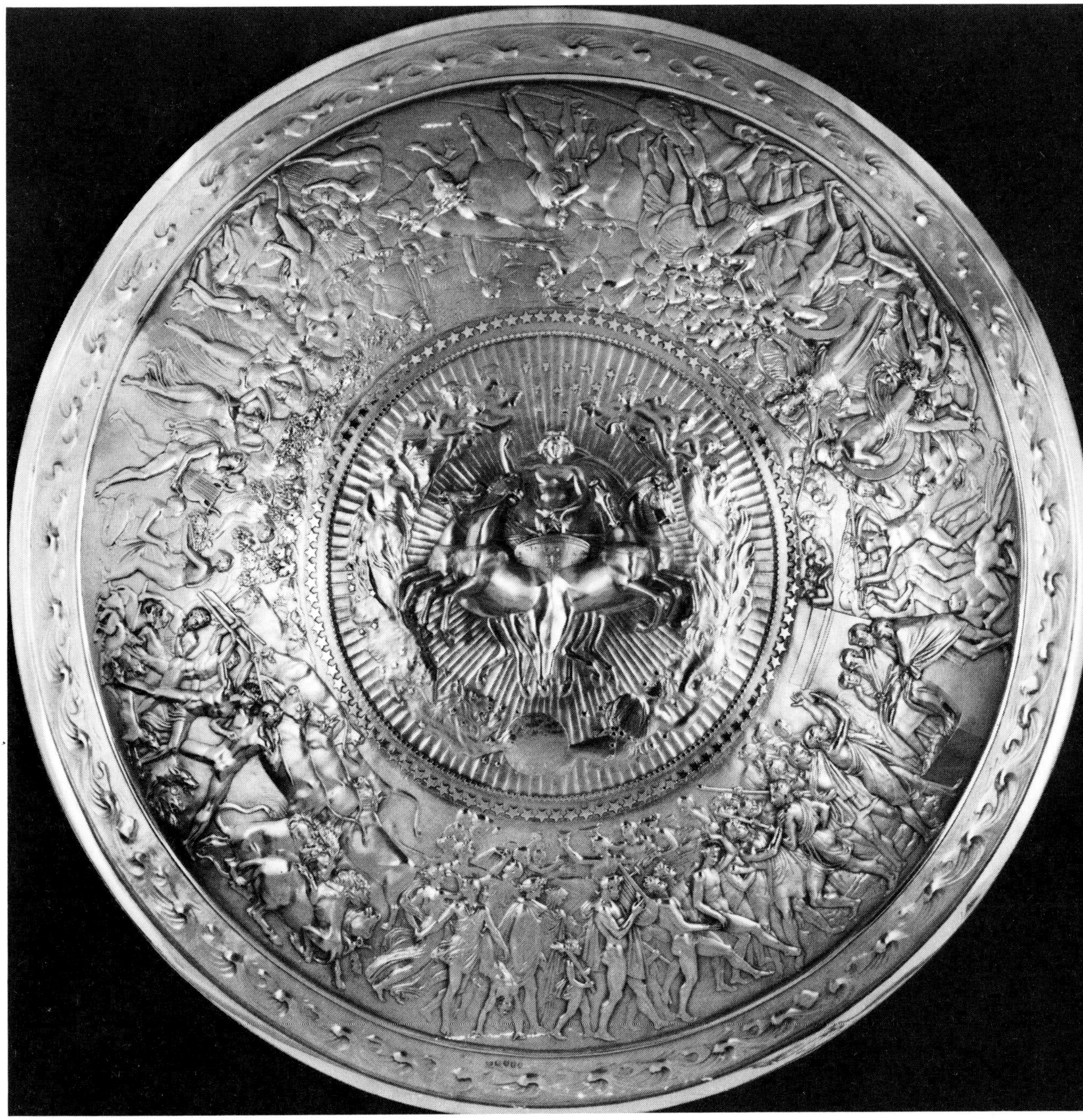

270 *Achilles Shield*, 1821. Silvergilt, 94 cms. diameter. Executed after Flaxman by Philip Rundell.

specially made for Achilles by Hephaestus, who from his cauldron of bronze, tin, gold and silver forged a truly resplendent piece of armour, the most famous in classical literature. Flaxman followed the description closely, even to the extent of making the shield lifesize. When the shield had appeared in his illustration in the *Iliad* (Plate 272), together with the other specially forged pieces of armour brought down to earth by Thetis, Flaxman had contented himself with a mere suggestion of its rich detailing, the only clear motif being the outer rim with its pattern of waves. Benjamin West in his oil paintings of the same subject, one of which was commissioned by Thomas Hope, also evaded the problems of painting Homer's description

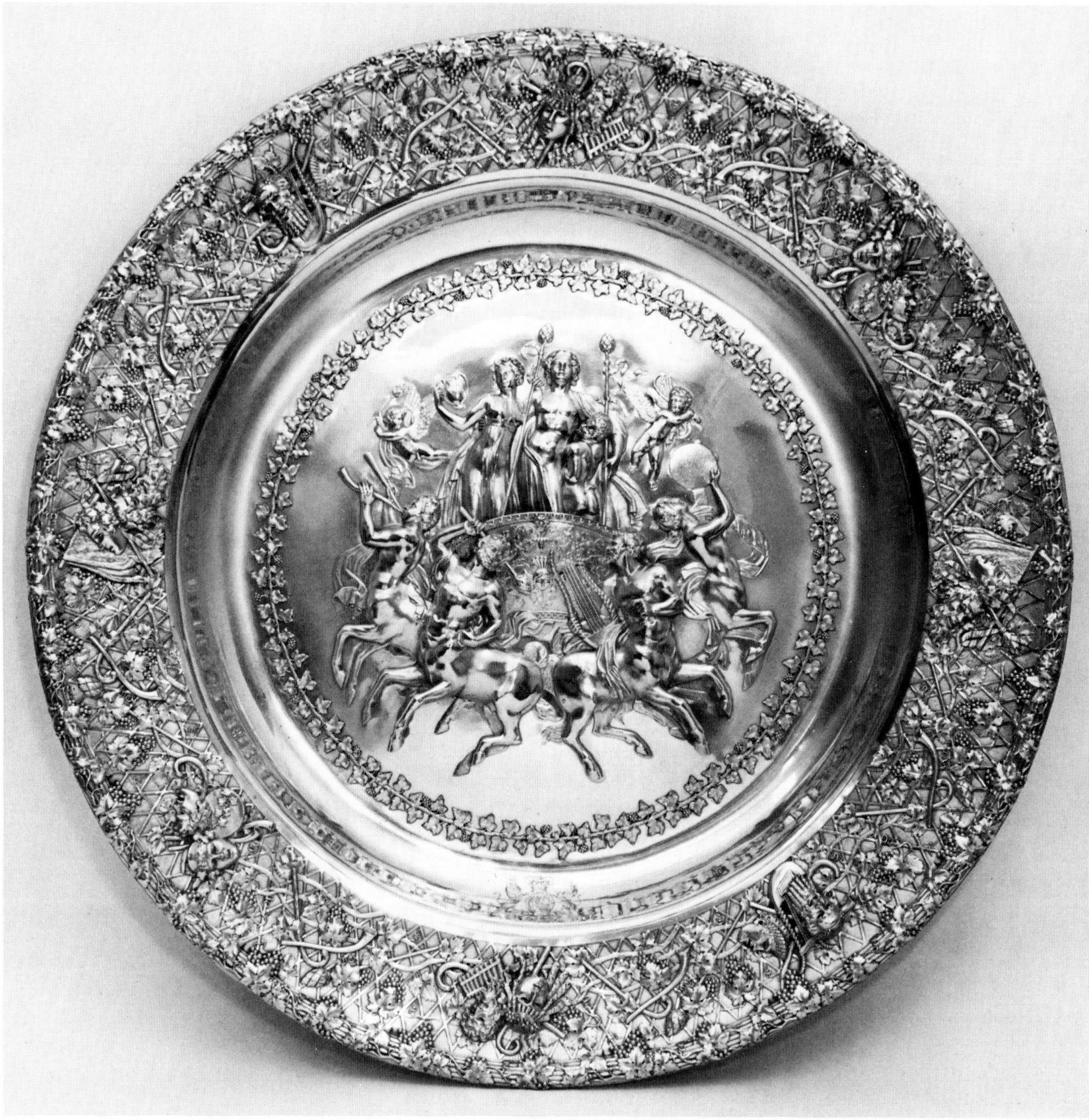

271 Thomas Stothard: *Triumph of Bacchus and Ariadne: Sideboard dish.* 1814. Silvergilt, 79 cms. diameter. Executed by Paul Storr.

in detail, perhaps following the sculptor's example (dated 1804–5; now in the New Britain Museum of American Art, Connecticut; and private collection). From 1810 onwards Flaxman must have regarded the recreation of the shield in three dimensions as a considerable challenge. It was unusual for Flaxman to devote such an extended period to one project, and it must therefore have meant a great deal to him. Not only must he have been aware of the great demands he would eventually make on craftsmen in order to realise his ideas, but in designing it he was confronted with a complex series of images which in the lines of the *Iliad* add up to a picture of the whole universe, both in the heavens and life on earth.

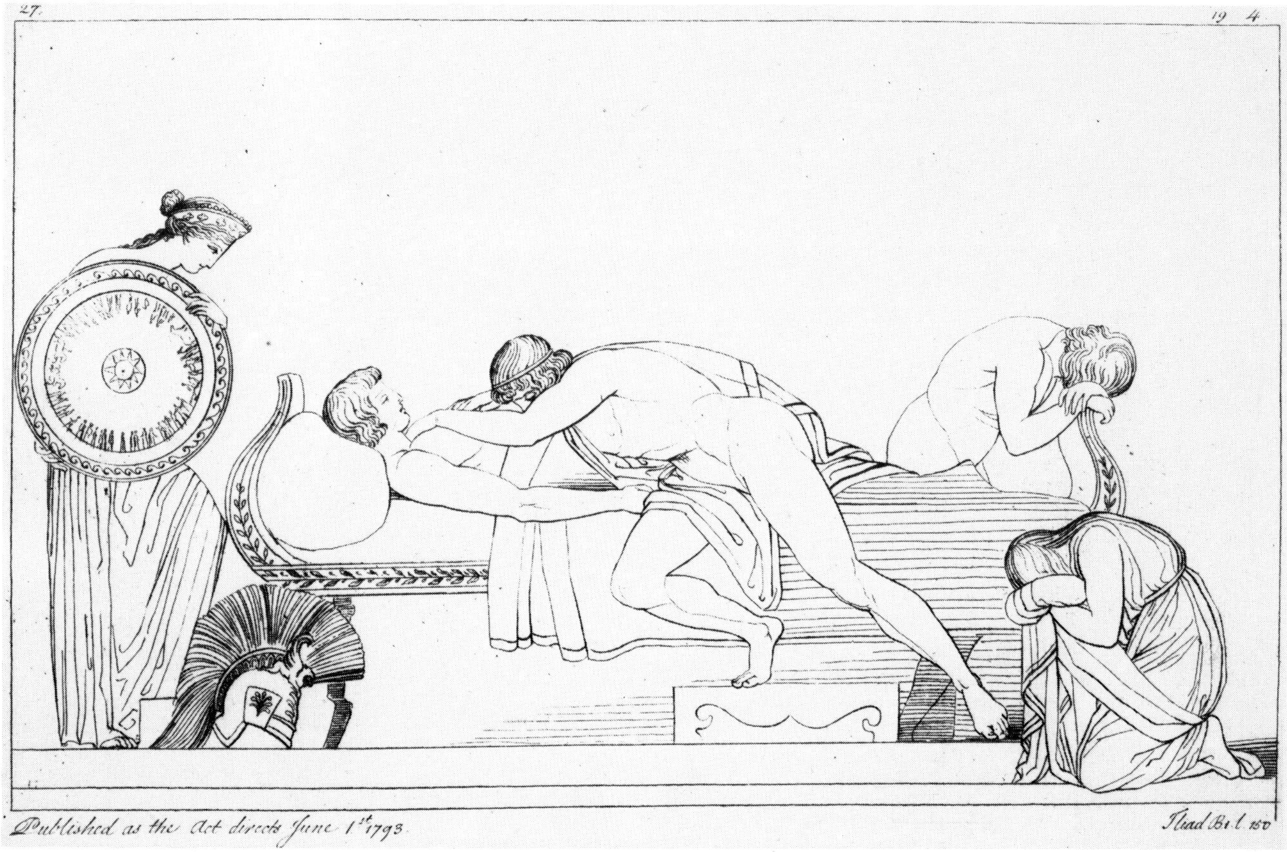

272 *Thetis bringing the Armour to Achilles.* Engraving, 19·1 × 28·8 cms. after Flaxman by Thomas Piroli. *Iliad*, 1793, Plate 27.

Homer's shield has three basic themes, one celestial, and two terrestial, one of which is peaceful and the other warlike. Homer's description is meticulous, but he does not specify the actual layout of the composition. Only at the end of the description is there a specific reference to one part of the shield, namely the rim, which was ornamented with 'the mighty stream of ocean'. Homer starts his description with the celestial theme, which Flaxman has logically placed in the centre of the design, as Pope and other commentators had suggested. The sun, in the form of Apollo in his chariot, is surrounded by various constellations and a full moon. The remaining, and longer, part of Homer's description is interpreted by Flaxman as a continuous story revolving around the central motif, a general layout he had used in his *Iliad* illustration. He thus rejected Pope and other commentators who believed that the circumference was divided into separate compartments. As a result, Flaxman's design is rhythmical and unified, with subtle changes of direction demarcating the various scenes. It could even be based on a firsthand knowledge of classical silver, in which relief decoration on vases, cups and bowls was often treated as a continuous sequence of figures, similar to those on pottery and relief sculpture. The classicism of Flaxman's shield is, however, not derived entirely from the antique since the treatment of some of the scenes has more in common with the art of the Quattrocento. Ghiberti's second bronze Baptistry doors could have influenced the scene of reaping, for instance, and the dancing figures in the wedding procession are more reminiscent of the Donatello and Luca della Robbia *cantorie* than of the common source in classical sarcophagi.

Homer's first scenes are set in cities, starting with a wedding procession, banquet and dancing, with some of the men drawn away from the events because of a case of litigation which is being argued. All these incidents appear at the bottom part of Flaxman's shield. Moving further up the right side, one comes to the other city which is being besieged, from which some of the inhabitants are secretly leaving to prepare for an ambush led by Pallas Athene and Ares (Plates 273 and 274). At the top of the shield (upsidedown in Plate 270) is a field being ploughed, leading, as one comes down the left side, into a

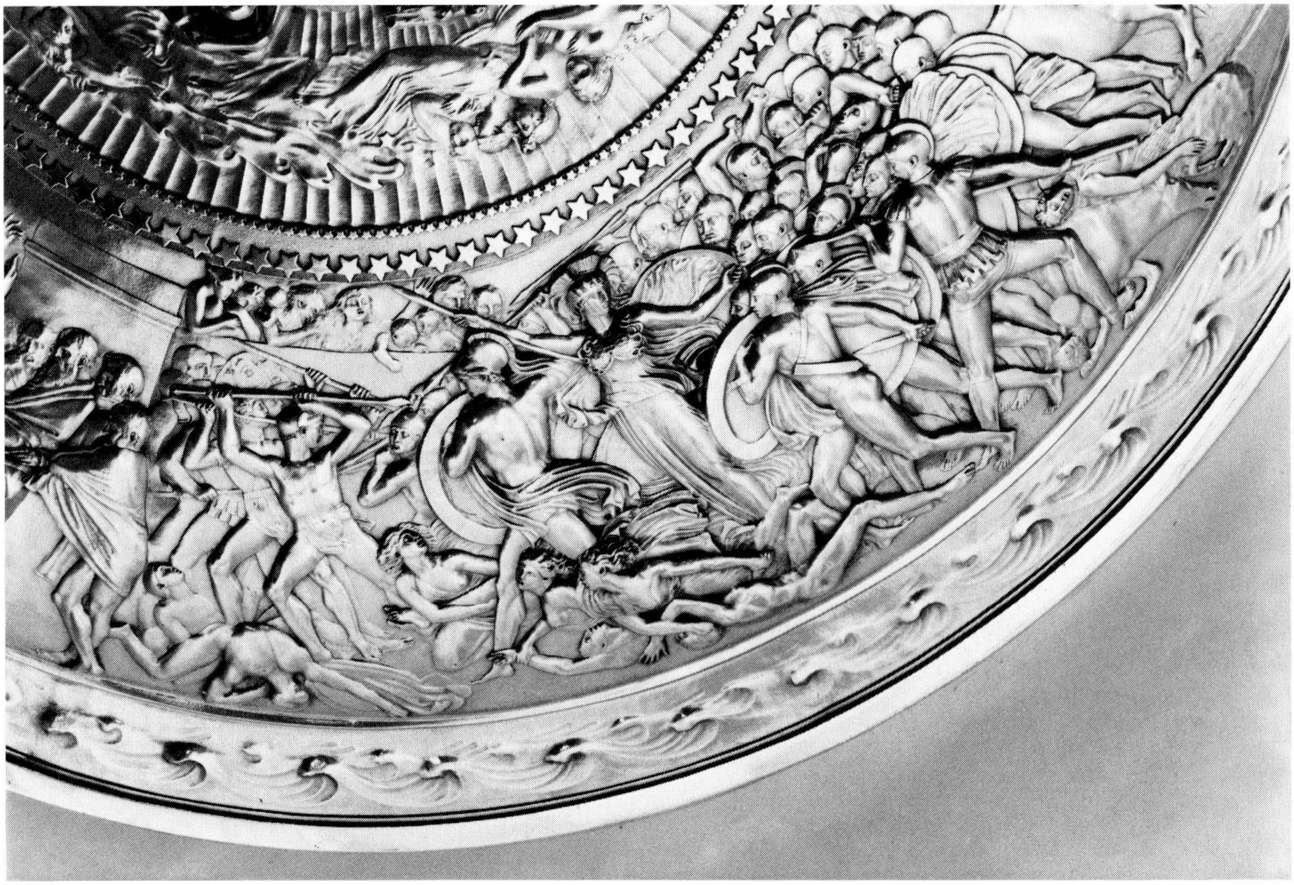

273 *Achilles Shield: detail: Seige, Ambuscade and Military Engagement.* Detail of Plate 270.

274 *Achilles Shield: Seige, Ambuscade and Military Engagement: design.* Pen, wash and pencil, 22·7 × 38·7 cms.

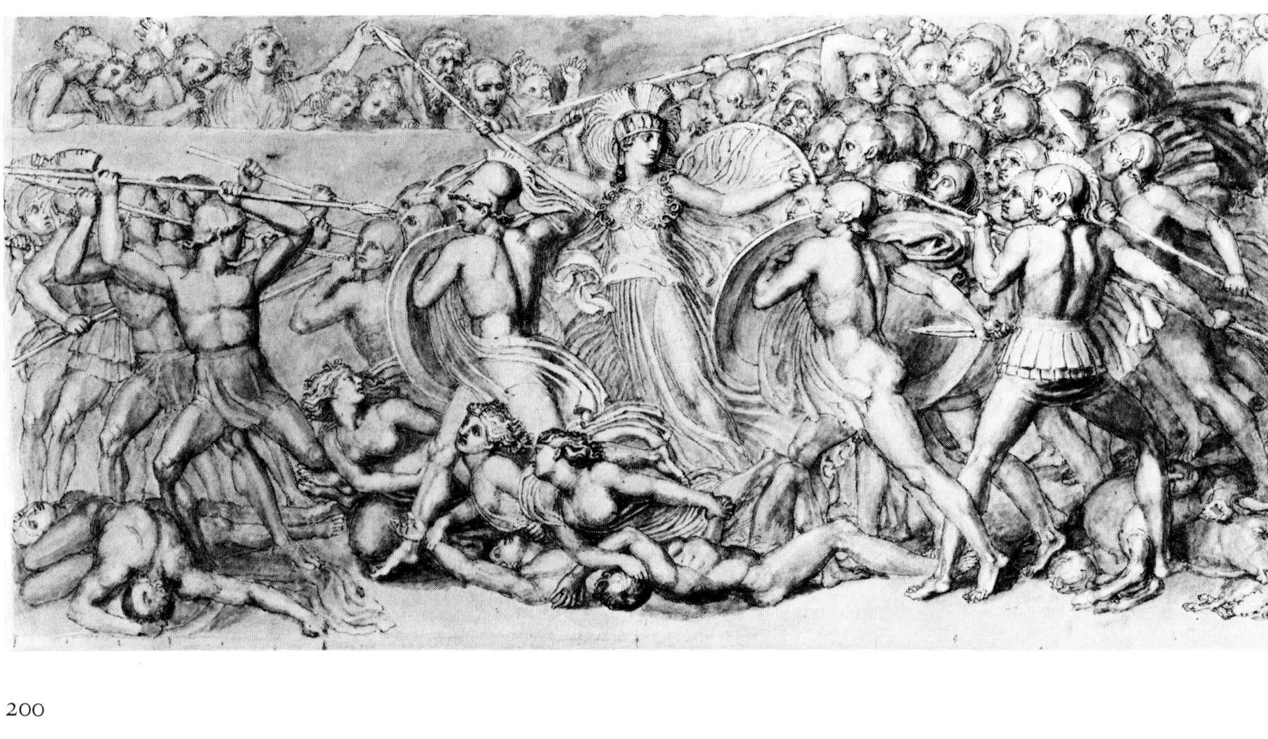

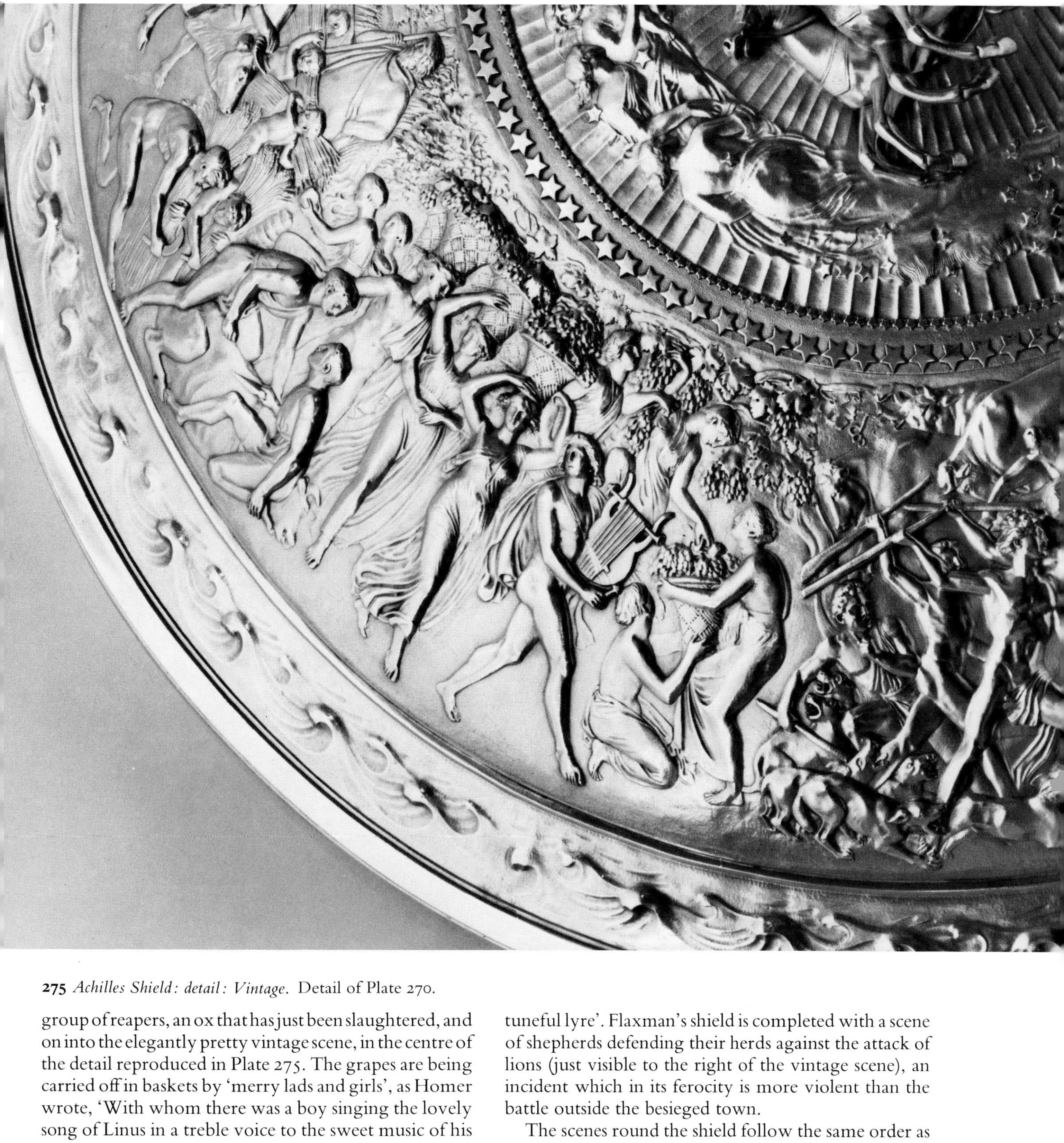

275 *Achilles Shield: detail: Vintage.* Detail of Plate 270.

group of reapers, an ox that has just been slaughtered, and on into the elegantly pretty vintage scene, in the centre of the detail reproduced in Plate 275. The grapes are being carried off in baskets by 'merry lads and girls', as Homer wrote, 'With whom there was a boy singing the lovely song of Linus in a treble voice to the sweet music of his tuneful lyre'. Flaxman's shield is completed with a scene of shepherds defending their herds against the attack of lions (just visible to the right of the vintage scene), an incident which in its ferocity is more violent than the battle outside the besieged town.

The scenes round the shield follow the same order as

those in Homer, and include all the incidental details that he mentions. The only disparity between the text and the work of art is that Homer envisaged his shield as coloured, using different metals and enamels. The vintage scene in Homer, for example, is wrought in gold, the grapes are black, the supporting poles are in silver, and the scene is surrounded by a ditch of blue enamel. Not only would the recreation of Homer's colours have demanded incredibly skilled virtuosity by modern craftsmen, adding to an already high cost, but such colouring would have been contrary to the Neoclassical idiom and its dislike of elaborately coloured sculptures and decorative objects.

Flaxman's love of Gothic art found an outlet among his designs for Rundell's in his *National Cup* (Plate 276), which reflects a growing antiquarianism amongst silversmiths and such prominent collectors as William Beckford and the Prince Regent from about 1815 onwards. Gothic as well as sixteenth-century forms were being revived, from the beauties of medieval chalices to the splendours of works then attributed to Cellini. Silversmiths realised that here was a wealth of ornament from which they could borrow even richer and more varied than that of classical antiquity, and this multiplicity of styles in metalwork was to last for the rest of the century. Rundell's bought in 1822 a magnificent nautilus cup and cover attributed by Flaxman and other connoisseurs to Cellini, which the firm sold to George IV (still in the Royal Collection, it is now identified as from late sixteenth-century Nuremberg). In the same period, 1823, Rundell's made a standing gilt cup and cover, ornamented with an intricate late Gothic arcading, and set with diamonds and sapphires.[11] This piece too was acquired by George IV, who also bought Flaxman's *National Cup* (made 1824, designed 1819).[12] Rundell's were in the forefront of the antiquarian revival of plate set with jewels, and the *National Cup* is an elaborate example of this trend, incorporating diamonds, emeralds, amethysts, rubies and turquoises as part of a cup of Gothic shape, ornamented with fourteenth-century architectural motifs, with niches containing figures all surmounted by a vigorous St. George slaying the dragon.

Flaxman's work for Rundell's was very varied,

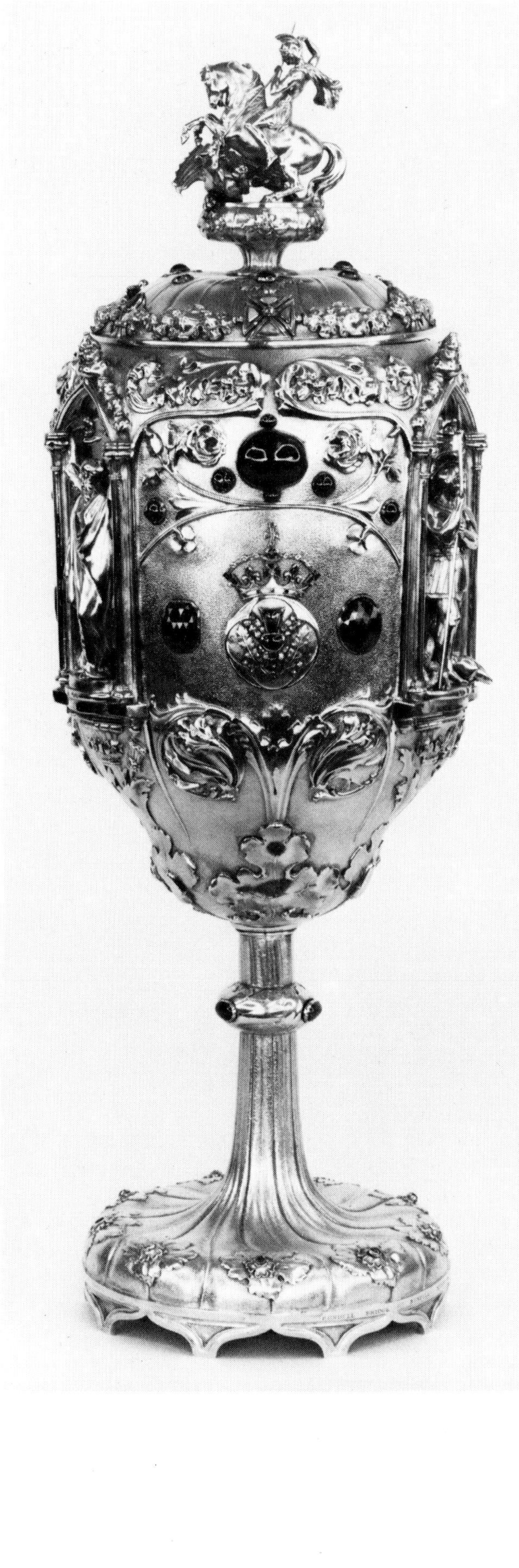

276 *National Cup*, 1824.
Silvergilt and jewels, 48·2 cms. high.
Executed after Flaxman by John Bridge.

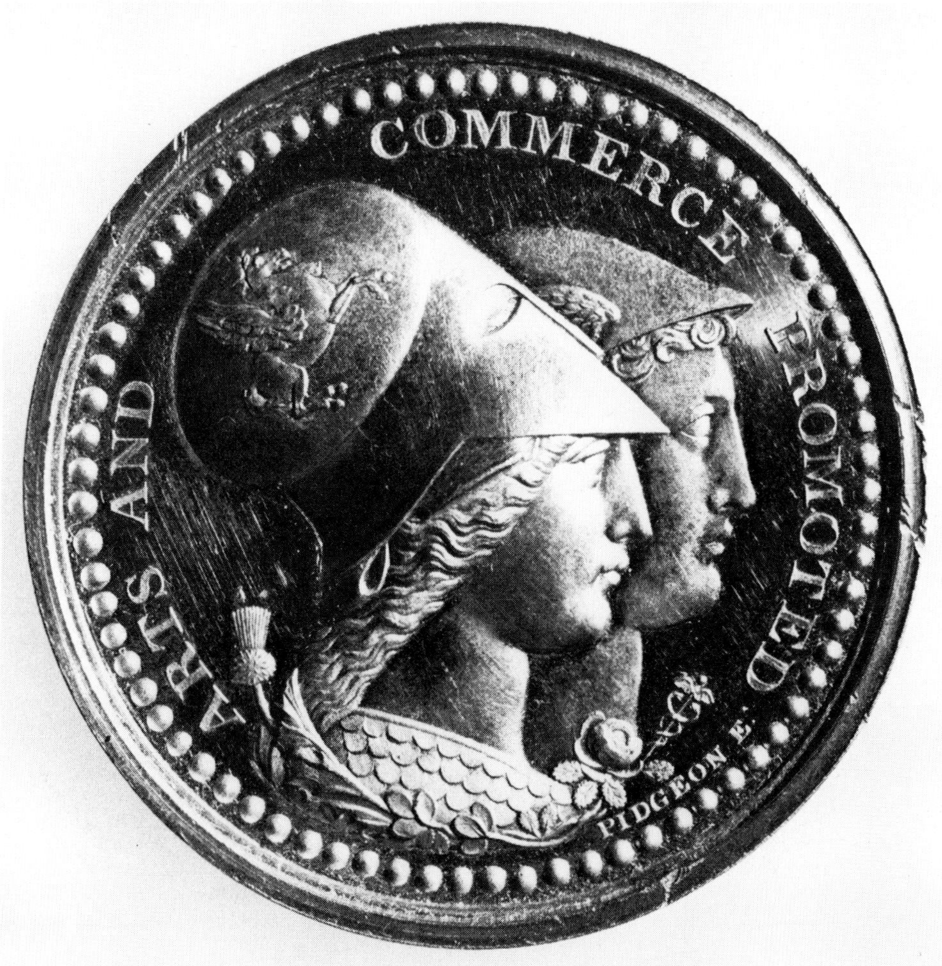

277 *Royal Society of Arts Gold Medal: Minerva and Mercury*, 1805.
Gold, 4·3 cms. diameter.
Dies cut after Flaxman by G. F. Pidgeon, struck at Soho Mint.

ranging from some of the grandest commissions that the firm ever executed to simpler vases and jugs. In the last decade of his life, Flaxman had a considerable influence on the firm's design policy.

Rundell's was the main firm for which Flaxman designed after 1800, but he also continued his father's association with Matthew Boulton, on a modest scale. On a few occasions Flaxman produced designs for commemorative and other medals for the Soho Mint in Birmingham. He designed the medal that the Earl of St. Vincent gave in 1800 to the sailors of his flagship who had remained loyal after a mutiny three years previously. Flaxman supplied the drawings and models, and the die was cut by Conrad Heinrich Küchler. One side of the medal depicts the head of the earl, and the verso shows a naval officer shaking hands with a bluejacket.[13] In 1803 Flaxman designed a commemorative medal for the fifth Duke of Bedford, who had commissioned the Temple of Liberty pediment from Flaxman. From the Royal Society of Arts in 1805, Flaxman received a commission to design their Gold Medal, which remained in use as the Society's main honorary award until 1820. The reverse was left plain, except for a laurel wreath, so that it could be engraved with the recipient's name, date and the reason for the award. The front (Plate 277) made obvious reference back to classical coinage and cameos. On this occasion the dies were cut for the Soho Mint by G. F. Pidgeon.[14] Flaxman's involvement throughout his career with both art and commerce is appropriately symbolised in the Society of Arts' commission.

Later, in 1836, when the House of Commons was collecting evidence on the fine arts and their connection with manufacturers, Flaxman's work was frequently cited in the evidence given to the committee. His metalwork was mentioned more frequently than any other aspect of his art.[15]

CHAPTER X

Professor of Sculpture

Flaxman's appointment as the Royal Academy's first Professor of Sculpture in 1810, at an annual stipend of £60, marked the climax of his official recognition. He was never knighted, and was not to receive any other formal acknowledgement of his achievement apart from his election to the Accademia di San Luca in Rome in 1816. His post at the Royal Academy, which he held until his death, entailed giving six lectures a year. Though he spoke with a weak voice, he delivered his lectures with clarity and was audible to a large audience, illustrating his points with drawings. His unimposing stature was counteracted, for one diarist at least, by the sculptor's animated face.[1]

Flaxman's lectures are of interest as a pioneer attempt by a British sculptor to speak extensively about his art. In the Academy itself his only precursor had been Reynolds, who devoted his tenth discourse in 1780 to sculpture, in which he perpetuated the academic canon that sculpture was a lower order of creativity than painting. On the Continent, the closest parallel was to be found in the writings of Falconet, one of whose books, *Réflexions sur la sculpture*, had appeared in English in 1777. Another equivalent publication, although not by an artist, was Count Cicognara's *Storia della Scultura*, which was being published at the same time as Flaxman was delivering his lectures, and which examined a wide range of works from antique to Trecento, Renaissance and more modern. Flaxman also attempted to survey the past and present state of the art of sculpture both in Britain and abroad; as the first occupant of the chair he seems to have felt obliged to set sculpture within a broad historical framework. The result was the only large corpus of Flaxman's ideas to be published,[2] and one of the few extensive literary works by any practising artist during the Neoclassical period. As his sister wrote to John Murray at the time the manuscript was being prepared for publication: 'This work will be the first of the kind, and that is a vast advantage, independent of its excellence.'[3]

The livelier lectures are those in which Flaxman's views are not buried under the weight of existing antiquarian and other literature. His best and most personal discourses are the first, devoted to English sculpture, and the last on the post-medieval period, mainly on the Continent which he treated with some frankness. Isolated passages scattered throughout other lectures on a variety of topics are also expressions of personal opinions. His addresses on the deaths of Banks and of Canova provided further opportunities for original or idiosyncratic assessments of seventeenth century and more modern sculpture.

It might have been expected that Flaxman's first

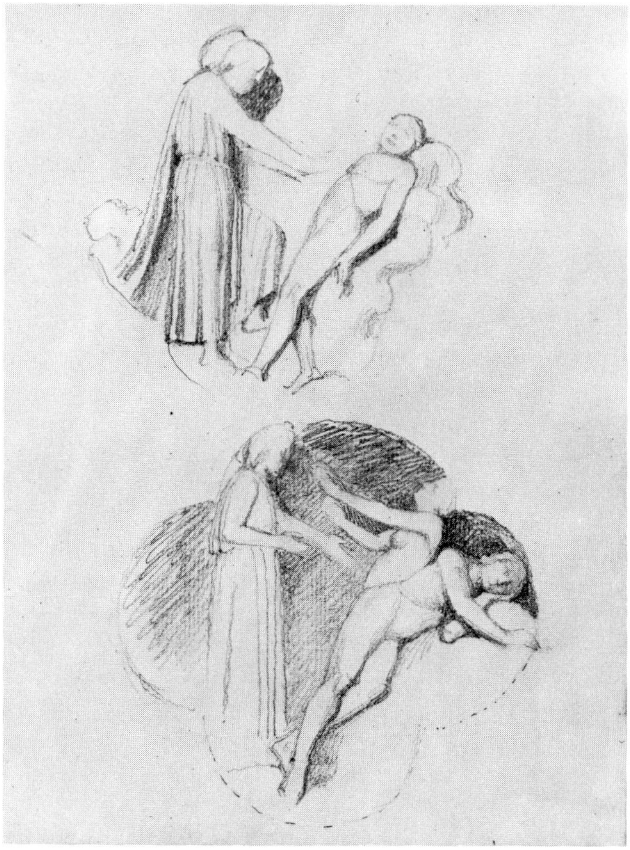

278 *Creation of Adam and Eve, after reliefs on Wells Cathedral,* c. 1812–13.
Pencil, 26·4 × 20·8 cms.

lecture would have been on the antique. But by choosing English sculpture he showed his deep feeling for the art in his own country that had been developing since the 1780's. His sketchbooks also show this continuing interest in English sculpture for he made two extensive tours, in 1812 and 1813, spending much of his time looking at medieval architecture and sculpture.[4] When he delivered his first lecture in 1811 the Napoleonic Wars were still raging, so that foreign travel for young artists had for the most part been curtailed, and more attention was being devoted generally to the history of the arts on the British side of the Channel. To the increasing bulk of British antiquarian literature, there was now to be added from 1807 onwards John Britton's *Architectural Antiquities* which was to play such an important role in arousing interest in a British rather than in a classical past.

Flaxman's discussion of the Romano-British period showed that he had firsthand knowledge of a few works, even if his comments were fairly cursory and derived largely from John Speed's *History of Great Britain* (1611). Saxon sculpture he found very disagreeable because whether it aimed at representing 'the human or brutal figure, [it] is frequently both horrible and burlesque'. He was to expand this point in a later lecture when discussing Continental 'painting and sculpture under the Goths and Lombards, [which] instead of exalting the intellect by the contemplation of beauty, heroic and divine, burlesqued the human figure by such clumsy and absurd forms, as could scarcely be supposed to be intended for man'.[5] Even with his interest in early or primitive civilisations, Flaxman could not appreciate the vigorous qualities of Romanesque imagery. It was not until he reached the mid-thirteenth century that Flaxman found English works which he was able to praise.

By the time he came to discuss the sculpture on the west facade of Wells Cathedral in his first lecture, Flaxman's personal enthusiasm overcame a somewhat dutiful chronology. Whilst preparing his lectures, he seems to have started to compile a list of 'magnificent works of sculpture still remaining', and had begun the list with Wells.[6] He particularly admired the treatment of subject-matter there, saying in his lecture that it was 'magnificent and varied' as well as 'useful', depicting the Creation, the Flood, important acts of the Patriarchs and the Last Judgment. The scene of the Creation of Eve in Flaxman's drawing reproduced in Plate 278 was later to be used as an illustration in the published version of the *Lectures*. But even in a thirteenth-century facade that Flaxman admired so much, he was also able to find faults: 'This work is necessarily ill drawn, and deficient in principle, and much of the sculpture is rude and severe: yet, in parts, there is a beautiful simplicity, an irresistible sentiment, and sometimes a grace, excelling more modern productions.'

On his tours he made a point of seeing the three surviving stone crosses that Edward I had raised in the 1290's to the memory of Queen Eleanor at Waltham, Geddington and Northampton (Plate 279). He praised them highly in his lecture: 'the statues have considerable simplicity and delicacy; they partake of the character and grace particularly cultivated in the school of Pisano' (Flaxman even wondered whether some Nicola Pisano pupil could not have executed the elegant figures on these crosses).

As Flaxman proceeded through the Middle Ages he became increasingly enthusiastic. The period of prosperity during Edward III's reign made possible the 'richness, novelty and beauty' of York and Gloucester Cathedrals, as well as the 'intricate and diversified' figures on window mullions, like the ones at Dorchester in Oxfordshire. When discussing the late thirteenth

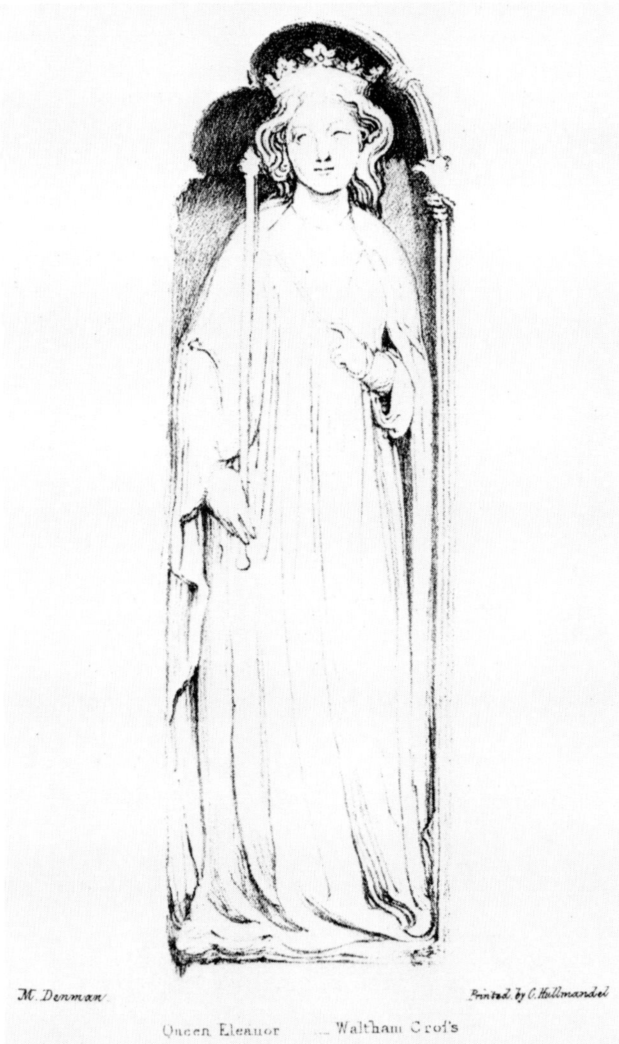

279 *Queen Eleanor, Waltham Cross.*
Drawing after Flaxman by Maria Denman. Lithograph from Flaxman, *Lectures*, 1829, Plate 5.

and fourteenth centuries Flaxman analysed in detail a variety of sculptures, mostly tombs, which he greatly admired. These sculptures ranged from minor works such as the statues of Henry VI and Archbishop Chichele over the entrance gates to All Souls' College in Oxford (the former praised for its 'purity', 'delicacy' and 'grace'), to elaborate monuments in Westminster Abbey.

In the Abbey he singled out for special attention the monuments to Edmund Crouchback, Earl of Lancaster and to Aymer de Valence, Earl of Pembroke, two of the most important medieval monuments there. Flaxman was following in the steps of Gough, who had already said that in the *Lancaster* monument 'I know not which most to admire' (Plate 280).[7] These two monuments elicited high praise from Flaxman, together with a choice of adjectives that throws light on his own sculptures: 'The loftiness of the work, the number of arches and pinnacles, the lightness of the spires, the richness and profusion of foliage and crockets, the solemn repose of the principal statue, representing the deceased in his last prayer for mercy to the Throne of Grace, the delicacy of thought in the group of angels bearing the soul, and the tender sentiment of concern variously expressed in the relations, ranged in order round the basement, forcibly arrest the attention, and carry the thought not only to other ages, but other states of existence'. The way in which Flaxman described these tombs shows how much he valued their Christian content, expressed above all through 'tender sentiment', a phrase which is unmistakably contemporary and applicable to his own monuments. An equally lyrical description of the *Pembroke* monument was going to appear a few years later in Edward Blore's *Monumental Remains* (1826).

In describing another tomb Flaxman's enthusiasm ran away with him, leading to exaggerated praise at the expense of Italian Renaissance works of the same period. The fifteenth century monument to Richard Beauchamp, Earl of Warwick (in St. Mary's, Warwick) was not excelled, according to Flaxman, even by Ghiberti and Donatello; he found the figures 'so natural and graceful, the architecture so rich and delicate'.

The outstanding medieval building for Flaxman was Henry VII's Chapel in Westminster Abbey. In discussing it however, he clearly preferred late medieval figures to those on Torrigiano's tomb, where the figures 'have a better proportion and drawing in the naked than those of the chapel; but the figures of the chapel are very superior in natural simplicity and grandeur of character and drapery'.

Flaxman continued his lecture with the customary lament for the ravages of the Reformation and the Civil War, which he said had led to the decline of native sculpture, necessitating the employment of such foreign-born artists as Cibber and Scheemakers. From this period of the 'abasement of native art' he cited only two works by native-born sculptors, John and Matthias Christmas, and Nicholas Stone. The Christmases' *Sir William and Lady Pitt* monument (Stratfield Saye, Hampshire) is a curious seventeenth century example to have chosen as it is somewhat inept. He presumably had seen it a few years before at the time he was designing a monument to *Lord Rivers* in the same church. Stone however is represented by his fine monument to *Francis Holles* in Westminster Abbey, which Flaxman

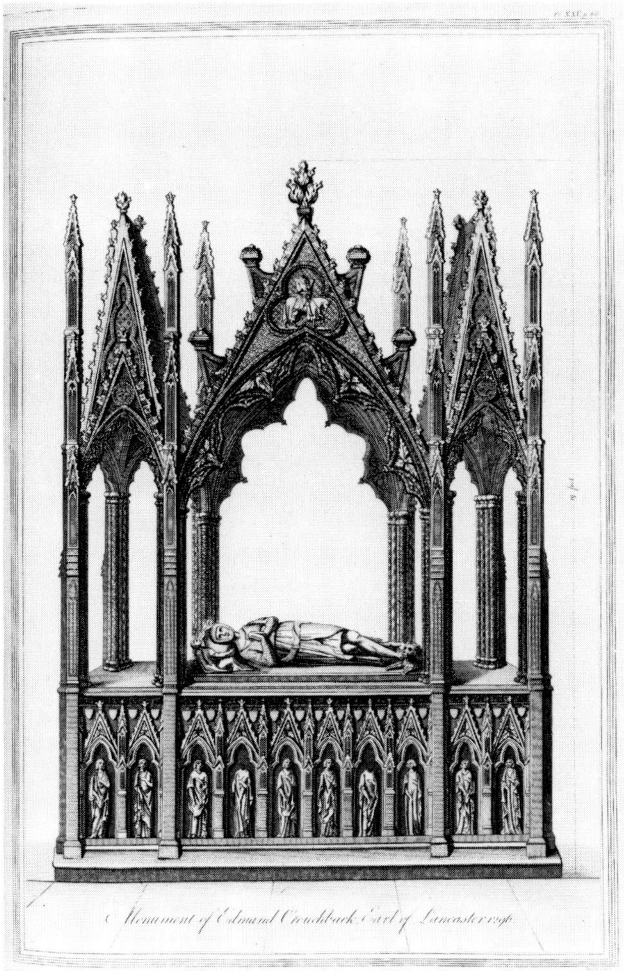

280 Richard Gough: *Sepulchral Monuments of Great Britain*, 1786–96. Volume I, plate 25, *Monument to Edward Crouchback, Earl of Lancaster.*

rightly praised for 'a grandeur of conception by no means common at that time'.

Flaxman concluded his first lecture on a stirring patriotic note. Against a background of war, he had been expounding for an hour on the glories of his own country's sculptural achievements, which from the thirteenth to the fifteenth centuries he regarded as comparable to the best achievements in Italy at the same time. Only with Thomas Banks had the British school of sculpture again become eminent. As one listener recorded in his diary, the audience had much appreciated this 'John-Bullism', and 'in one or two instances the lecture was applauded'.[8]

In this lecture Flaxman had restricted himself to sculptures on buildings and monuments, and had not extended his range to figures on smaller works such as reliquaries and croziers. As a sculptor who was actively involved at the time he was preparing the lectures in designing for the decorative arts, the exclusion of an important field of medieval decorative sculpture is surprising. He does not follow the example of John Carter's *Specimens of Ancient Sculpture and Painting* (1780–94) which had illustrated the minor arts in addition to sculptures and paintings.

He may have left out the minor arts because he had not enough time in the lecture. But he may have wished to concentrate his listener's attention on the more transcendental qualities of monumental sculptures consistent with his Christian piety. He referred in the lecture to 'such noble and magnificent efforts of art, in raising which the intention of our ancestors was to add a solemnity to religious worship, to impress on the mind those virtues which adorn and exalt humanity'. For all the patriotism in the lecture, it is apparent from the examples chosen and the adjectives selected, that Flaxman's views were those of a Christian with a successful studio that supplied church monuments. He praised subject-matter because it was 'useful', performing a didactic role for the benefit of the laity. The stylistic qualities that he most admired were sentiment, grace and delicacy, as well as that most frequently mentioned characteristic, simplicity. The characteristics of medieval art which he most admired were the very ones which formed part of his own style in church monuments, even if they were overtly designed for the most part using a classical vocabulary.

In his tenth and last published lecture, 'Modern Sculpture', Flaxman's likes and dislikes determined the character of his discourse to a very marked degree; some of his comments were unusually outspoken for him, as well as being idiosyncratic.[9] The most interesting part of the lecture is the long section devoted to Michelangelo, whose name occurs throughout the lectures on more occasions than any other modern artist. Flaxman concentrated on the frescoes, since he preferred them to the sculptures which for him lacked 'the chaste simplicity of Grecian art'. He made an exception however of the *Madonna and Child* in the Medici Chapel, and stressed an aspect of Michelangelo's art that was largely unfamiliar to Flaxman's contemporaries. This group, he said, was 'endowed with a sentiment of maternal affection never found in Greek sculpture, but frequently in the works of this artist, particularly in his paintings, and that of the most tender kind'. In an earlier lecture he had already emphasised this maternal affection in Michelangelo's art whilst discussing the figure of *Charity*—nowadays identified as Joram with three of her children—in one of the lunettes of the Sistine Chapel, and which was illustrated amongst the plates in the *Lectures* (Plate 201). Flaxman had been drawing distinctions between ancient and modern subject-matter, and continued by saying that 'an additional distinction between the subjects of ancient and modern composition is occasioned by parental affection, and domestic charities, being cherished in the Christian dispensation much more powerfully than in the Grecian codes: to these graces of benevolence we owe those lovely groups—the Holy Families of Raphael and Correggio, and the Charity of Michelangelo, unequalled in any ancient composition of a mother and children, and one of the finest groups in existence.'[10] Such comments are directly relevant to Flaxman's own art, in which parental affection and domestic charities are important themes in both sculptures and drawings, often conceived within a Christian context.

Flaxman discussed other frescoes by Michelangelo in this last lecture, including the ceiling and the *Last Judgment* of the Sistine Chapel which were for him, as for so many other artists before him, supreme works of art. In describing them he used such well-tried adjectives as 'sublime' and 'extraordinary', and said the *Last Judgment* was unrivalled in either ancient or modern art, but excused himself from making a detailed analysis on the grounds that Fuseli had already done so in his recent lectures on painting at the Royal Academy. Flaxman was more specific and more original in discussing the prophets, sybils and ancestors, which were 'choice selections of piety and love, in sentiments and forms unknown to the ancients, and unattempted by the moderns before his time; the naked figures are new and admirable; the prophets, sybils and the four corners of the ceiling taken separately, will afford matter for contemplation and study, not to be found in whole galleries by other masters'. Flaxman also had interesting comments to make on the Pauline Chapel *Conversion*: 'The groups of angels surrounding the descending Saviour, whilst calling his apostles, are luxuriantly ecstatic, and offer an internal testimony that Correggio's ideas of the celestial ministry, in his celebrated *Nativity* [*La Notte*, in Dresden], were probably awakened by the sight of some sketches from this picture'. Flaxman's admiration for the two artists has made him blind to a proper sense of chronology (Michelangelo's fresco was painted after Correggio's death), but his desire to comment on the similar treatment of angels by the two artists is pertinent to his own treatment of them, suggesting that Michelangelo and Correggio have inspired some of his own images of crowded, fluttering angels.

In view of the importance of the Trecento and Quattrocento to his own art, his comments on these centuries in his tenth lecture are not as full as one could wish. The Nicola and Giovanni Pisano pulpits in Pisa, Pistoia and Siena are 'most magnificant' and Giovanni's statues of the *Virgin and Child* are 'elegant'. They both 'improved sculpture by study of the antique basso-relievos in the Camposanto; in their own works the compositions are simple and intelligible; the female figures are frequently elegant in their movements and their drapery. In them are occasionally seen an originality of idea and force of thought seldom met with when schools of art are in the habit of copying from each other'. All he said of Andrea Pisano's Baptistry doors in Florence was that their compositions had 'a Gothic and simple grandeur'.

Amongst the Quattrocento sculptors Flaxman admired Donatello above all others, although whilst in Italy he seems to have spent more time making sketches after Ghiberti. Now, in the last lecture Donatello's work was 'placed beside the best productions of ancient Greece without discredit'. He started by praising a relief panel from the *cantoria* for its 'extraordinary beauty in sentiment, character, drawing and drapery', and then continued with the *St. George*, in which he admired its 'simple and forcible' sentiment. The San Lorenzo pulpit panels, from which he had made sketches whilst in Italy, were also cited because they 'abound in noble conceptions'. Brunelleschi then received a summary mention, followed by a fuller discussion of Ghiberti. No other Quattrocento sculptors are mentioned. In discussing Ghiberti, Flaxman ignored the first bronze Baptistry doors from which he made so many drawings in Florence, and concentrated on the second, a 'beautiful and laborious work', but which had a basic defect in its compositions because so much space was devoted to landscape and architecture, contrary to the principles of classical bas-reliefs, an adverse criticism which Flaxman took from Reynolds's discourses. In view of his admiration for the first door it is surprising to find Flaxman in this lecture merely following in Reynolds's footsteps, and not striking out on a more original path. The comments at least explain why Flaxman himself had found the first door more attractive.

After a lengthy and enthusiastic discussion of Michelangelo, Flaxman continued with Giambologna, whose versions of the antique theme of a crouching Venus, *Woman bathing, kneeling*, he admired for their 'delicacy and grace', and his famous bronze *Mercury* (in the Museo Nazionale, Florence) because it was 'energetic and original'. But again he omitted comments on a work he had drawn whilst in Florence, the *Rape of the Sabines*. Cellini's *Perseus*, which he had also drawn several times, is merely mentioned in passing. Thereafter, according to Flaxman, the seventeenth century witnessed the debasement of sculpture. He lambasted Bernini's larger works because they were 'remarkable for presuming airs, affected grace and unmeaning flutter'. He made an exception, however, of the early *Apollo and Daphne* (in the Galleria Borghese, Rome), and the 'ease and nature' of his portrait busts.

Flaxman concluded this lecture with practical advice on subject-matter. He started his list with the 'severely beautiful personages and events' in Homer and Hesiod, continued with the 'terrific and afflicting' scenes of Greek tragedies, and followed these with the 'innocent simplicity' of the pastoral poets. To these literary sources he added the Bible, which, said Flaxman, in spite of its frequent use in the past had been overlooked in large parts of the Old Testament, notably the Psalms and the Prophets. Flaxman concluded his list with *Paradise Lost*, lamenting that a poem so full of subject-matter had been largely ignored by British artists, whilst Milton's merits 'have been vindicated and illustrated by the liberal mind and genius of a foreigner'; a reference to Fuseli's Milton Gallery exhibited in London in 1799 and 1800. It is unexpected that Flaxman's closing remarks should be on Milton, but his aim was to encourage his partially student audience to be just as resourceful in their use of all aspects of the past as in striving to create works of art which posterity should value. Although his lectures were largely historical in content, Flaxman never overlooked their main didactic aim addressed to students who would be the practising artists of the next generation.

Flaxman's other comments on modern art are to be found mainly in his addresses delivered at the Academy on the deaths of Banks in 1805 and Canova in 1822, in both of which Flaxman is fairly outspoken.[11] In the address on Banks the passages of particular interest are those in which he discussed Baroque and early eighteenth century sculpture, together with a detailed assessment of the works of Banks himself.

Bernini's success as a young man with his *Apollo and Daphne* had the unfortunate consequence, as far as Flaxman was concerned, that he had 'captivated' public taste, and caused the antique, Michelangelo and nature itself to be forgotten for the next hundred years. Bernini's later works were dismissed by Flaxman with a bluntness characteristic of several passages in the Banks address, showing that Flaxman's comments represented the more extreme and uncompromising Neoclassical attitude towards the Baroque. The postures of Bernini's figures, he said, were 'much twisted, the heads turned with a meretricious grace, the countenances simper affectedly, or are deformed by low passions: the poor and vulgar limbs and bodies are loaded with draperies or such protruding or flying folds, as equally expose the unskilfulness of the artist and the solidity of the material on which he worked; his groups have an unmeaning connection, and his basreliefs are filled up with buildings in perspective, clouds, water, diminished figures, and attemps to represent such aerial effects, as break down the boundaries of painting and sculpture, and confound the two arts.' Flaxman also blamed Bernini for debasing the type of monument which consisted of a sarcophagus in front of a niche or architectural setting, accompanied by statues of the deceased and of allegories, citing Michelangelo's *Julius II* and *Medici* tombs. As Flaxman himself on several occasions used this type of monument, he was naturally indignant about Bernini's treatment of it, denouncing him in general terms because he had 'stripped it of its ancient simple grandeur, leaving it neither group, statue, basrelief, sarcophagus or trophy, but an absurd mixture of all . . . and thus sacrificing all that is valuable in sculpture to what he conceived a picturesque effect.' In Flaxman's eyes, Bernini committed every possible artistic crime, and Flaxman also roundly dismissed Duquesnoy, Mochi and Bolgi, together with works further into the eighteenth century such as the tomb of *Benedict XIV* in St. Peter's by Bracci, and the Trevi Fountain. French sculptors were just as bad, argued Flaxman, dismissing Puget (whom he had liked to a moderate extent when travelling through France), Girardon and later, Bouchardon. The rest of Europe became equally degraded in taste under the malignant influence of Italy and France, Flaxman told his audience.

Later in the address, Flaxman turned his attention to modern British sculpture, starting with a critique of Cibber. The figures of Madness for the gate of Bedlam Hospital he found 'ill drawn', grudgingly conceding they had a 'natural sentiment'; the allegorical relief on the Monument (which commemorates the Fire of London) was 'stiff and clumsy'; and the Royal Exchange figures 'strut like dancing masters'.

Flaxman was so hostile to the seventeenth and the earlier part of the eighteenth centuries that he could be very sweeping and unjust in his assessments. Rysbrack was summarily dismissed with the words: 'a mere workman, too insipid to give pleasure, and too dull to offend greatly'. Presumably Flaxman had the monuments in mind, and may have scarcely been familiar with the busts. Roubiliac was allowed a few more words, but they were no kinder. The virtues of his busts too were overlooked, and the monuments dismissed. 'He copied vulgar nature with zeal', said Flaxman, 'and some of his figures seem alive; but their characters are mean, their expressions grimace, and their forms are frequently bad; his draperies are worked with great diligence and labour, from the most disagreeable examples in nature, the folds being either heavy or meagre.'

All was not lost, however, in the development of art, argued Flaxman, since the excavations at Herculaneum and Pompeii had been helping to arrest the decline. But in a rare attack by Flaxman on the greed of antiquarian collectors, he criticised them with unusual passion for the high prices they paid for pieces, and he also attacked those collectors who on principle had preferred works of ancient art to the encouragement of modern work.

Amongst modern sculptors, Flaxman had a great admiration for Thomas Banks. The address is no mere pious eulogy dutifully made. It is sincere, containing generous praise from a younger man. The works mentioned and the adjectives used to describe them are as revealing about Banks's art as they are about Flaxman's own. Amongst the late artist's works assembled at the Academy as a memorial show at the time of the address, was a model for the *Cupid and Psyche* which Banks had sold to Catherine the Great. Flaxman discussed this work first, and although it is now lost and we have no means of judging its appearance, the way Flaxman described it in sympathetic terms suggests that it could have been influential for his own work. 'The Cupid catching a butterfly on his wing', as he called it, 'is rendered highly interesting to the mind by its philosophical allusion to the power of love, divine or natural, on the soul; nothing can be more graceful than the attitude, the outline is finely varied in the different views; the softness of the form, the character of the face, and the adjustment of the hair, are classically beautiful'. Two other works by Banks are discussed in detail, both of them stylistically relevant to Flaxman's own art. The bas-relief of *Thetis and her Nymphs rising from the Sea to console Achilles for the Loss of Patroclus* (1778; Victoria and Albert Museum) was praised because 'the sentiment and character is beautiful and pathetic, the composition is so unlike any work ancient or modern, that the combination may be considered as the artist's own'. The other work which had no peer in either contemporary Italy or France, and which could be ranked even with the works of antiquity according to Flaxman, was the monument to *Mrs. Margaret Petrie* (1795; in Lewisham parish church) (Plate 204): 'As the situation represented is the most important to humanity, so the expression is most powerfully penetrating, the dying woman is piously resigned, and the theological virtues which surround the bed, are such as you might expect to see,—the departed good, eminent for those qualities in a better state of existence: the son is an admirable human figure absorbed in grief.' Flaxman also admired the monument's architectural composition and its relationship to the wall on which it was placed: 'the architecture and sculpture should always be united in this manner'. By such means the 'church becomes a museum of sacred sculpture.' Flaxman had himself added to that museum in Lewisham in the following year with a monument to *John Petrie*, and in 1798 one of the finest of his wall monuments, to *Mary Lushington* (Plate 165).

Flaxman did not discuss in detail such works as the *Falling Titan* and *Thetis dipping the Infant Achilles in the Styx*, presumably because such sculptures were not directly relevant to Flaxman's own style and taste. Their omission confirms the impression that the address was a very personal selection. His dislike of the nude hero would presumably account for the omission of the *Burgess* monument, but it is surprising that he did not elaborate on the *Penelope Boothby* monument, which is such an epitome of late eighteenth-century sentiment. Flaxman merely called it 'beautiful'. The sculptures that he did choose to discuss, however, clearly reveal the speaker's own preferences, and were described with words that can so easily be used of Flaxman's own works: sentiment, purity, simplicity, grace, softness, outline, 'philosophical allusion' and 'classical beauty'.

On Canova's death in 1822 Flaxman was the obvious person to deliver the Academy's formal address. By now he had already given the main body of his lectures, and he therefore presumably felt it unnecessary to make general comments on the present state of sculpture. He confined his short address entirely to Canova's own work.

Flaxman showed a great admiration for Canova, but he never penetrated deeply in his assessment, and his remarks were often no more than lip-service, even if the feelings expressed were genuine. It is possible that one diarist was correct when he recorded that Flaxman valued Canova's morals more than his art.[12] The only work in the address to which an entire paragraph is devoted is Canova's *Tempio* at Possagno, left unfinished at the time of his death. It is symptomatic of Flaxman's beliefs that he should stress this Christian aspect of Canova's life, but he did not develop this theme when discussing Canova's works since he only chose one religious example, the monument to *Maria Christina of Austria* in Vienna. As Flaxman could not have seen this monument when returning home from Italy, his assessment of its design as 'simple and nobly expressive' would have been based on drawings. Other works are merely listed. He admired the version of the *Three Graces* at Woburn Abbey, and a 'beautiful' recumbent *Nymph* in the Royal Collection. In such works Flaxman presumably admired—although he does not say so explicitly—the sentiment and grace. He summarised Canova's style in general by saying that 'we shall at once acknowledge a poetic fancy which gave a luminous interest to his conversation equally with his composition, his figures are graceful, his forms grand, muscle, tendon or bone most naturally distinguished, and the flesh seems yielding to the touch, by an execution as powerful as delicate.'

Flaxman continued by saying 'it had been observed by some that in Canova's sculptures, we sometimes seek in vain for the severe chastity of Grecian art; this may indeed not be destitute of some foundation in truth, but we must not look for complete perfection in the works of imperfect man.' Flaxman's attitude towards the antique seems here to be ambivalent. On the one hand he excused Canova for not matching up to the perfection of the Greeks. But on the other hand, he argued in the case of both Banks and Canova that in spite of the classical ideal, they had both managed to achieve greatness in contemporary sculptures which lacked antique precedents.

The almost constant stress on classical antiquity throughout the lectures and addresses sometimes overshadowed Flaxman's more fundamental belief in nature and originality. In his last lecture on 'Modern Sculpture', he justified his remarks at one stage by referring to Edward Young's *Conjectures on Original Composition* (1759), that key text in the early development of the Romantic belief in originality. Flaxman agreed with Young that the eighteenth-century artist or writer had access to a far greater store of mental riches than that enjoyed by the ancients, and that such an advantage should therefore be exploited. As Young had written: 'The first ancients had no merit in being originals: they could not be imitators. Modern writers have a choice to make; and therefore have a merit in their power. They may soar in the regions of liberty, or move in the soft fetters of imitation. . . . Rules, like crutches, are a needful aid to the lame, though no impediment to the strong.' Although Flaxman's lectures by their very nature were often concerned with rules, he was also concerned in key passages—notably in the Canova and Banks addresses—with the transgression of those rules.

Elsewhere in the lectures Flaxman reveals occasional insights into his personal preferences, but they are apt to be lost in an overall plan covering the whole history of sculpture.

By the time Flaxman came to deliver his second lecture on 'Egyptian Sculpture', the Egyptian Revival was well under way, especially after the boost it had received as a result of Napoleon's Nile campaign. Knowledge of Egyptian art had greatly increased since the eighteenth-century travellers' accounts by Pococke, Norden and Savary, both through new publications, (notably Baron Denon's lavish volumes of 1802), and the importation of original works of art. It is therefore not surprising that Flaxman should devote most of a lecture to Egyptian sculpture, and should show rather more sympathy towards its characteristics than Winckelmann had done, even if Flaxman still had great reservations about it.

In describing Egyptian art he used adjectives which had become the stock-in-trade of the literature on Egypt, such as 'stupendous' and 'laborious'. Like his contemporaries, Flaxman failed to appreciate the reasons why Egyptian art was stylistically different from that of Greece and Rome, and therefore found the Egyptian style defective: 'In their basreliefs and paintings which require variety of action and situation, are demonstrated their want of anatomical, mechanical and geometrical science'. Flaxman preferred Egyptian statues, finding stylistic similarities with early Greek work. Although Flaxman could not appreciate what he regarded as a lack of anatomical knowledge, he nevertheless admired the 'simplicity of idea, breadth of parts and occasional beauty of form' in Egyptian sculpture.

After a few fleeting remarks on Persepolis, taken from the pages of Le Bruyn and Chardin, Flaxman then looked briefly at Hindu sculpture. Basing his remarks on the text and illustrations in Maria Graham's *Journal of a Residence in India* (1812) and in Edward Moor's *Hindu Pantheon* (1810), and presumably also on the few pieces of sculpture in the museum of the East India Company which had recently been founded in 1801, Flaxman could find nothing to admire. Again he could not appreciate a style which was 'inferior in science and likeness to nature'. In spite of the abstract tendencies of some of his own book illustrations Flaxman could not override his fundamental belief in art based on nature as observed by a European schooled in classical antiquity. He could find no relationship between India and Greek art which might exonerate it, as he had done with some Egyptian examples. He was however more interested in Moghul art, copying miniatures into a sketchbook (Plate 154). These are amongst the prettiest of Flaxman's non-classical drawings, showing he admired in them the same qualities of elegance and linearity which he sought in aspects of Greek and Roman art. Flaxman could well have had access to the large collection of Moghul miniatures bought by the museum of the East India Company as recently as 1807.[13]

Up to this point in his lectures, Flaxman had devoted much space to personal preferences, although feeling obliged to adopt a broad chronological approach, and therefore to include works which in some instances he disliked or failed to understand. His views in general suggest a search for the ideal, which was to become more explicit when he came to discuss Greek sculpture in the third lecture. As a prelude he concluded his second lecture with a discussion of ideal human proportions, starting with the well-known passage in Vitruvius. It is quite clear why Flaxman could not appreciate Egyptian and Hindu art (as well as Mexican and South Sea Island art to which he referred later[14]) when he was able to tell his listeners that: 'Science must attain a certain perfection before the arts of design can be cultivated with success, and that before the human form can be well represented, some system of proportions must be collected from the measurement of man himself.'

Some of Flaxman's lectures are of greater interest for their practical advice than for their historical analysis. He is particularly didactic in his fourth lecture on 'Science,' which he said was intended to 'assist the young artist in forming principles for the course of his studies'. The lecture is devoted to the artist's ability to create 'natural' images in stone, both human and animal. He greatly admired the horses on the Elgin Marbles frieze because the spectator 'can scarcely suffer reason to persuade us they are not alive'. Flaxman then dealt systematically with anatomy, proportion and mechanical motion, making use of Pliny and Vitruvius, and more modern texts by Leonardo and Borelli's *De motu animalium*. As was to be expected, Flaxman came to the conclusion that anatomy, proportion and motion were best understood by artists in fifth and fourth century BC Greece. This was the period the student should always keep before him as his model, so that he did not make the mistake of Giambologna and his contemporaries who showed 'anatomical pedantry and licentious affection of graceful movement', or the earlier mistakes of Gothic nudes which were 'clumsy, mean, insipid'.

The whole of the eighth lecture was devoted to 'Drapery', which the student would find 'an important branch in his future study'. Drapery was of major importance to Flaxman himself, as can be seen in his sketchbook studies in Rome and in his many completed designs and sculptures. In this lecture therefore Flaxman analysed all kinds of drapery, discussing the weight of material, the kinds of folds, and other details from classical times onwards, including an attack on the absurdities of Elizabethan costume which he found 'monstrous and disgusting'. Towards the beginning of the lecture he explained why he thought the study of drapery so important: 'Drapery, as a medium through which the human figure is intelligible, may be compared with speech, by which ideas and thought are perceived. Dignity is expressed by simplicity, grandeur, quantity; action by exertion and succession; grace by those gentle and harmonious undulations peculiar to all the efforts of this quality, and which are inspired by the most grateful and soothing dispositions of the soul. This consistency of the original image with its outward appearance, is proper and decorous, and cannot be violated without inflicting the shock of absurdity and folly; for as the noblest thought would be degraded by low and unbecoming speech, so would the person of a legislator or a prophet by the dress of a buffoon or a bacchanal!'

Practical advice also dominated his sixth lecture on 'Composition', in which he laid down some general principles. If the subject is one of repose, he said, the parts should be 'more simple and rectilinear'; if one of tenderness, then gentle curves should predominate and the person ought to be 'elegant'; but if the subject is one of violent action, then the parts of the composition should be 'more angular'. If the figures are entwined in either love or combat, 'the general curves and views of the limbs should never be exactly and mechanically the same, but partake of the wonderful variety of nature'.

He then listed subjects worthy of the sculptor's chisel, starting with the design of monuments: 'angels, spiritual ministers, embodied virtues, departed worthies, the patriot or general benefactor, shining in the splendour of his deeds, or gloomy and consuming memorials of the great in former ages.' He divided compositions into three categories of the sublime, heroic and tender. Sublime compositions included the Creation, the angels appearing to the shepherds and the Last Judgment, but he regretted that 'the slow and difficult process of sculpture' was hardly ever employed on such subjects, doubtless reflecting a personal regret that he had received so few commissions for this type of composition. His list of sublime Christian subjects omitted the Crucifixion, which had almost disappeared from religious imagery by the turn of the eighteenth century. Flaxman's sublime category also included such pagan subjects as assemblies of the gods and falls of the giants. But whether Christian or pagan, 'the beauty and dignity of the persons should be more than human'. In his heroic category, Flaxman only cited classical precedents, such as battle scenes of Persians and Athenians, or the story of Orestes. Among his tender subjects Flaxman included the death of Meleager, and Michelangelo's *Holy Family* (*Doni Tondo*, Uffizi) and *Charity* in the Sistine Chapel (Plate 201), which although they are paintings were included by Flaxman because they were 'so perfectly sculptural'. Flaxman added a fourth category which he called the 'graceful', which included classical bas-reliefs or 'elegant female figures in the pageants of marine deities, or in the festive choruses'.

The same lecture also provided students with practical advice on light and shade in sculpture: 'if the light be one-third, and shadow two-thirds, the effect will be bold. If the light be one part, and the shade four, it will be still bolder, and will accord with a tragic or terrific action; but the more general effect of sculpture is two thirds of light on the middle of the group, with a small proportion of very dark shadow in the deeper hollows'. In the next paragraph he then made a rare, if brief, comment in his writings on the materials of his art. 'The grey solemn tints of stone', he told his audience, 'the beautiful semi-transparent purity of marble, the golden splendour, or corroding darkened green of bronze, reject as incongruous all subjects and characters which have not some dignity and elevation'.

Flaxman's discussion of classical antiquity in the course of the lectures was often more dutiful than passionate. It is possible that because so much had already been written on classical sculptures, that he felt he had little or nothing new to say, preferring sometimes to give mostly historical information, which could be in the form of summary catalogues. But even these catalogues are conceived in an old-fashioned way, failing to distinguish between genuine works and copies, a distinction that had become widely discussed in archaeological literature by the latter part of the eighteenth century, some of which was readily available in English, including the translation of Mengs's writings in 1796. Flaxman was more careful about distinguishing between original works and copies in his evidence to the House of Commons select committee on Elgin's collection to have been more concerned with a repertoire of visual images than with details of historical accuracy. He was also, unfortunately, unselective in his use of classical examples; by choosing far too many he did not allow himself time to discuss particular pieces in detail.

The third lecture on 'Grecian Sculpture' is the first of six to deal with ancient works of art, which form the core of Flaxman's lectures as one might expect. By 1810 Academy students not only had at their disposal all the visual material available in the eighteenth century, but the British Museum had recently been enriched by the Townley collection, which was soon to be joined by the Parthenon Marbles and the Phigaleian frieze from Bassae. The Academy's own collection had been enriched by a large collection of casts given by the Prince Regent, for which Flaxman expressed gratitude in his introductory lecture.

Flaxman knew very few sculptures of the sixth century BC or earlier at firsthand, and he merely saw them as a 'tasteless and barbarous' prelude to the age of Phidias. Flaxman's rather staccato account of early Greek sculpture was to be superseded by a more enthusiastic one when he reached the fifth century, when sculpture reached 'maturity'. Phidias's 'superior genius', Flaxman told his audience, 'gave a grandeur to his compositions, a grace to his groups, a softness to flesh, and flow to draperies, unknown to his predecessors, the character of whose figures were stiff, rather than dignified; their forms either *maigre* or turgid; the folds of drapery parallel, poor, and resembling geometrical lines, rather than the simple, but ever varying, appearances of nature'. Most of the rest of the third lecture is little more than a short catalogue, with summary comments, on most of the principal statues and groups known from the fifth to the first centuries. His listeners must have been left breathless by the tour. He justified his lack of detailed comment by saying that Fuseli's recent Academy discourses had described them with 'pathos' and 'justness'. Flaxman's modesty is understandable but disappointing; Fuseli's greater scholarly powers and skill as a writer certainly had produced descriptions finer than Flaxman's might have been.

Flaxman frequently referred to examples of Greek and Roman art throughout the next lectures, and later in the series devoted his ninth lecture entirely to 'Ancient Art'. In this lecture he argued that the principal characteristics of such art was the continually 'improved imitation of nature'. In early art, such as the Lion Gate at Mycenae, Greek civilisation had only reached a 'barbarous' stage. But the Greek sculptors then made rapid progress in establishing 'sure principles', created by 'philosophic improvement'. Flaxman thus subscribed to the well-established concept of the history of art as periods of progress followed by ones of decline, which in the context of ancient art meant that the age of Phidias was seen as a peak of achievement which hid in shadow any merits that might exist in the art of preceding generations.

The ninth lecture is disappointing because Flaxman wasted time in a recital of literary evidence, from Pausanias and Pliny, about famous classical statues which no one in modern times had seen, except in copies on a reduced scale. Flaxman then compressed into the rest of the lecture another rapid tour of famous sculptures surviving from classical antiquity. He mentioned obvious sculptures such as the 'sublime' *Apollo Belvedere*, the *Farnese Hercules*, the Cnidian *Venus*, the *Dioscuri* of Monte Cavallo, the *Laocoon* which is described rather oddly as a 'noble concatenation of lines', the *Cupid and Psyche* which represented the 'union of desire and the soul', and so on. Flaxman's comments are too brief to be as revealing as could be wished, except perhaps in the choice of phrase for the *Niobe* group, drawn extensively by him when in Florence, and now mentioned because its 'sentiment is maternal affection'. By selecting this particular characteristic of the *Niobe* group Flaxman suggested another source for the mother and child theme which is so important in his own work, and which, as already mentioned, he singled out for special attention in Michelangelo, Raphael and Correggio.

The list of statues was extended by the addition of bas-reliefs and sarcophagi, all of which should form part of a student's studies. In this category he included Trajan's Column and the Arches of Constantine and Marcus Aurelius, although in an earlier lecture he had summarily dismissed such Roman works because their subject-matter was not epic, but 'mere paragraphs of military gazettes, vulgar in conception, ferocious in sentiment'.[15] But by the ninth lecture these works join the sarcophagi to provide the young artist with the 'true principles of composition'.

He concluded his ninth lecture by reminding his audience that the study of ancient sculpture had the practical advantage of 'guarding against error and false systems', and that if artists wished to attain excellence then 'we cannot proceed by a more certain course than that by which it has been attained before', echoing the beliefs of many earlier commentators.

One other lecture, the seventh on 'Style', contains an interesting section on polychrome sculpture in classical antiquity. Much had been written on the subject by earlier commentators, and most recently in a book to which Flaxman referred in his lecture, by the eminent French antiquarian Quatremère de Quincy, *Le Jupiter Olympien, ou l'art de la sculpture antique considéré sous un nouveau point de vue* (1815). The life-like colouring of Phidias's famous *Jupiter* by the skilful use of ivory, gold and precious stones was the starting point for Flaxman's discussion in this lecture. As he basically disapproved of polychrome sculpture, Flaxman felt he had to justify these apparent anomalies in Greek art. He had been accustomed to white marble copies, and overlooked traces of polychrome on the Elgin Marbles and elsewhere. Flaxman therefore argues that the Olympian *Jupiter* as well as the Athenian *Minerva* had been coloured for a 'higher motive'. He continued by explaining that 'it was the desire of rendering these stupendous forms living and intelligent, to the astonished gaze of the votary, and to confound the sceptical by a flash of conviction, that something of divinity resided in the statues themselves'.

Apart from such examples in ancient Greece, Flaxman associated polychroming with 'early and barbarous' states of society, and cited a curious mixture of examples from South Sea idols and Etruscan monuments to medieval recumbent tomb figures. The sole motive in such works, according to Flaxman, was merely to 'enforce superstition or preserve an exact similitude of the deceased'. Such a motive he found 'perverted', and he concluded his denigration of such works from his customary, Christian viewpoint: 'The real ends of painting, sculpture, and all other arts, are to elevate the mind to the contemplation of truth, . . . and to represent such of our fellow men as have been benefactors to society, not in the deplorable and fallen state of a lifeless and mouldering corpse, but in the full vigour of their faculties when living, or in something correspondent to the state of the good received among the just made perfect.'

Flaxman relied heavily on earlier writers whenever he could in his lectures, especially in the sections dealing with ancient art, which are studded with names and quotations. Most books are historical, few are theoretical or philosophical. For the classical past he used most frequently the obvious sources in Pliny, Pausanias and Vitruvius, supplemented by Herodotus and other texts. He occasionally made use of Homer, Plato and Aristotle, and briefly Horace, as well as other ancient authors. Most of the main modern antiquarian publications feature in his pages, from Bartoli's *Admiranda* and Montfaucon, on to Stuart and Revett and more recent publications by Denon, Visconti and Gell, as well as the folios of engravings of private collections, such as the Pio-Clementino, Capitolino, Giustiniani and others, and the antiquities discovered at Herculaneum. Where Flaxman knew collections at firsthand that had remained unpublished, he makes use of them as well, such as Thomas Hope's. In view of the influence of Greek vase painting it is strange that he referred on only one page to Hamilton's two collections and their publication. But the brief reference to them, together with more recent publications on vases by Millin and Millingen, was nonetheless handsome: they 'form an endless treasure to the artist and the antiquary, supplying every species of example and illustration'.[16]

Winckelmann's name appears in the lectures more than any other eighteenth-century writer; a frequency only out-numbered by the name of Pliny. From the nine references to Winckelmann it is clear that Flaxman mainly knew the *History of Ancient Art* (in an Italian translation), and occasionally used the *Monumenti Antichi Inediti*, both of which he read more for their archaeological material than for their theoretical argument. It is perhaps because Flaxman did not see Winckelmann as a theorist and interpreter, that he made no mention of the early influential, and widely read, essay *On the Imitation of the Painting and Sculpture of the Greeks*. On two occasions Flaxman cited Winckelmann only to disagree with him on points of historical interpretation, but these instances are fairly minor.[17] Far more important was Flaxman's failure to use Winckelmann's historical approach properly. Flaxman did not distinguish clearly between the style of one century and the next, especially between the age of Phidias and that of Praxiteles, as Winckelmann had attempted to do. Flaxman even discussed famous sculptors in the wrong chronological order. As he gave the impression of wanting to achieve an outline historical approach in his lectures on classical art, it can only be assumed that Flaxman had not grasped fully the significance of archaeological writings from the 1790's onwards, merely adding them to earlier titles in which the approach to classical history was more confused.

Writers on later periods of art cited by Flaxman are also fairly standard, ranging from Leonardo and Vasari, to Félibien and Camper (but omitting Shaftesbury) on to such contemporaries, or near-contemporaries, as Mengs, Reynolds and Fuseli (the current Professor of Painting at the Royal Academy).

A complete list of books mentioned throughout the lectures would show Flaxman's familiarity with, if not necessarily a deep understanding of, the main literature. The many names he cited not only showed that he must have attempted to prepare his lectures with care, but that he could provide useful booklists for his partially student audience. As Reynolds had said in his seventh discourse: 'he can never be a great artist who is grossly illiterate'. Flaxman's lectures are a response to such a dictum.

The literary style of Flaxman's lectures was evaluated fairly in the *Edinburgh Review* when they appeared in published form. 'They may be characterised', wrote the critic, 'as the work of a sculptor by profession—dry and hard: a meagre outline, without colouring or adventitious ornament.'[18] Haydon also had a perceptive comment to make when he once said that Flaxman's lectures 'though containing many useful hints . . . display clear evidence of no very high intellectual power'.[19] Haydon's comment would be particularly apt in describing the most disappointing of all the lectures, the fifth on 'Beauty', in which Flaxman ventured on no deep philosophical discussion. For 'intellectual power' Flaxman's lectures are overshadowed by those of Reynolds and Fuseli, or in his own field by the writings of Falconet. But as Flaxman's *Lectures* contain so many passages that are relevant to his own art, they deserve more attention than they have tended to receive. The best assessment of Flaxman's lectures, censuring faults in the content but praising the merits of the man himself, is to be found in Cockerell's diary for 1823: 'Flaxman's lectures are literally but the exposition of beautiful drawings', lacking 'that poetry or perception in his lectures which is so abundantly displayed in his works. So true is it that the critic and the poet are separate beings not to be united'. Cockerell also confided in his diary a possible reason for the disappointment about the content of Flaxman's lectures, which he thought might have resulted from Flaxman's extreme diffidence, which was 'so remarkable that I have some doubt whether he has not restrained himself from giving his notions of principles on this account'.[20] Flaxman himself was well aware of his own limitations, saying on one occasion earlier in life that 'my mind is frequently occupied by objects fitter for the chisel or pencil than the pen'.[21]

Epilogue: Victorian Taste

Flaxman himself is not commemorated by a tomb, ironically enough. He was buried in the churchyard of St. Giles-in-the-Fields, near the northern end of Charing Cross Road in London, and his gravestone disappeared long ago. A later generation of Royal Academicians, however, made amends in the early twentieth century by erecting the memorial plaque that is today in the church. The principal memorial to Flaxman was to be in the form of the Flaxman Gallery at University College, London.

After Flaxman's death, the Victorians continued to admire his work; his classicism was revered as a timeless standard of excellence, and his tombs as important examples of Christian art.

His engravings continued in print throughout the nineteenth century; the most easily available one-volume edition of the classical plates was that edited in 1879 by John Sparkes, the Head Master of the National Art Training Schools in South Kensington, London (the parent of today's Royal College of Art). This edition was a popular channel for the dissemination of the more sentimental interpretation of Flaxman's art; as Sparkes wrote in his preface, 'the charm found in the designs and the works of Flaxman proceeds, no doubt, from the peculiar character of the man and artist who created them. It was a peculiar character, simple, blameless and unselfish. Religious in the best sense, caring for others more than for himself.' This stress on the religious foundation of Flaxman's art, even in the context of works illustrating classical authors, is typical of Victorian commentaries on Flaxman.

The only notable attack on Flaxman's illustrations in the Victorian period came from the pen of John Ruskin, who argued that Flaxman's outlines did not depict adequately the objects they were supposed to represent. In his *Elements of Drawing* (1857) Ruskin attacked the style in general terms because of the varied thickness of lines which not only failed to suggest shading, but also produced inaccurate shapes. In the fourth volume of *Modern Painters* (1856), devoted to mountain scenery, he took one particular scene from the *Inferno* series, that depicting the Pool of Envy, and was highly critical of the delineations of the rocks because they do not convey any sense of mass: 'It is not the outline of a stone, however true, that will make it solid or heavy', he wrote, 'it is the interior markings, and thoroughly understood perspectives of its sides.'

Some of Flaxman's secular sculptures continued to be familiar in the Victorian period, either through exhibitions or reproductions. The transport of gigantic blocks of marble was no obstacle to Victorian exhibition-organisers, and Flaxman's *Fury of Athamas*

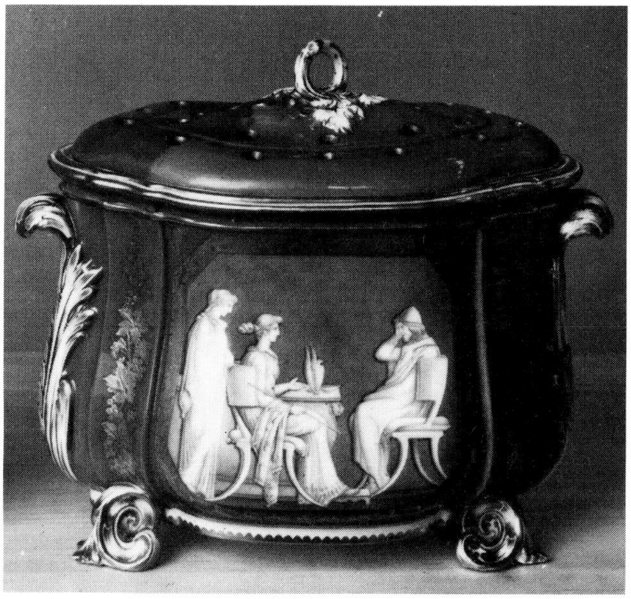

281 Coalport tureen decorated with a copy of *Ulysses at the Table of Circe* after Flaxman. c.1850. Victoria and Albert Museum.

travelled from Suffolk to London for the International Exhibition of 1862. The group was joined there by the *Cephalus and Aurora*, together with a plaster cast of the bas-relief of the parable of the good Samaritan designed for the *William Bosanquet* monument in the parish church at Leyton in Essex. One of the versions of the *Shield of Achilles* was also included in the 1862 Exhibition.

The importance to the Victorians of this classical side of Flaxman's sculpture was demonstrated by the choice of the Petworth *Saint Michael overcoming Satan*, in the form of a reduction by William Wyon, as the first piece of sculpture to be issued to members of the Art Union of London, in 1843. Later in the mid-1850's the same Art Union reproduced the bas-relief of *Mercury transporting Pandora to Earth* on one side of their Flaxman Medal executed by Henry Weigall.

This Victorian homage to Flaxman can also be seen in a range of artefacts which either kept his designs in production as in the case of Wedgwood's factory, or re-used his engravings in new contexts.

Coalport tureens designed about 1850 made use of plates from Flaxman's *Odyssey*, including the iconographically appropriate scene of Ulysses at the table of Circe (Plate 281), one of the rare engravings in the Homer series to represent food. Stripped of its significance in the context of Homer's epic, Circe's offer of refreshment has become merely a charming scene at a table, and a good example of the Victorian love of appropriate narrative detail on household objects.

Flaxman's illustrations of the story of Pandora were also popular. They were re-used on a table in the 1851 Exhibition, made of walnut and inlaid with etched brass. According to the official catalogue entry this manufacturer wanted to show 'an application of the products of high art to the embellishment of ordinary furniture'. Flaxman would doubtless have approved of this ideal, if not necessarily of all the examples of its application by this firm, since he had been one of the few fine artists at the turn of the century actively involved in designing for the decorative arts, and had therefore been an important precursor of the ambitious scheme of Summerley Art Manufactures, launched by Henry Cole shortly before the Crystal Palace exhibition. The catalogue entry for the Pandora table seems to reflect Cole's explicit intention of crossing the barrier between the fine and the applied arts.

The firm of Josiah Wedgwood had a large display at the 1851 Exhibition, representing a revival of interest in eighteenth-century Wedgwood designs. Entries included many of Flaxman's pieces, ranging from an *Apotheosis of Homer* vase to a set of chessmen. Only a few years before, Henry Cole's *Journal of Design* in 1849 had remarked: 'We are glad to see an extensive revival of the beautiful blue and white jasper ornaments which Flaxman designed for Wedgwood'.

A similar view was expressed shortly afterwards in Sir John Charles Robinson's text that accompanied a series of chromolithographs published by Day & Son in 1858 with the title *The Treasury of Ornamental Art*. The choice of plates is almost as wide-ranging as those in Owen Jones's more famous *Grammar of Ornament* published two years before by Day & Son, also embracing medieval, Renaissance and oriental art. But unlike Jones, Robinson included eighteenth-century pieces, such as Flaxman's Wedgwood jasper ware *Blind Man's Buff* on a pair of vases. In the accompanying text Flaxman's contribution to the decorative arts is praised because 'the highest artistic talent this country has ever produced may be seen in intimate alliance with manufacture'.

Flaxman's reputation for funerary art was so extensive that it seemed inevitable that a volume by F. and M. A. Palliser entitled *Mottoes for Monuments, or Epitaphs* (1872) should be illustrated almost entirely by engravings of tombs designed by him. The volume contains a wide range of epitaphs selected from monuments throughout Britain, grouped according to themes, that of the 'Death of the Believer' being illustrated by the engraving reproduced in Plate 282. The engraver has

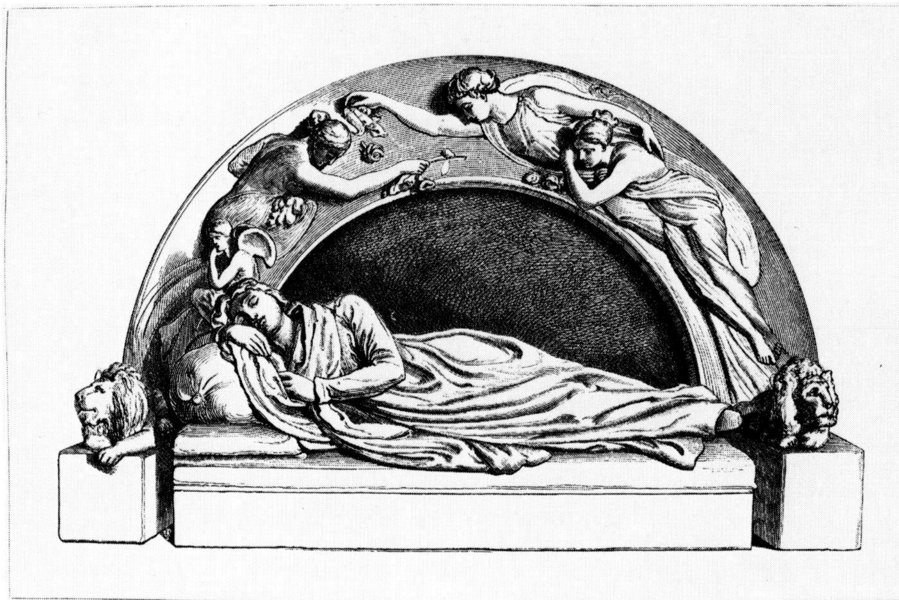

282 Two of Flaxman's monuments combined to form an illustration, *The Sleep of Death*, in F. and M. A. Palliser, *Mottoes for Monuments*, 1872. Aberdeen University Library.

combined two of Flaxman's monuments, placing the recumbent figure of the Irish poetess Mary Tighe in front of the relief lunette of the earlier eighteenth-century writer Isaac Hawkins Browne and adding a pair of lions of his own invention. The corporate image of the engraving contains a superabundance of parts which by their combination have changed Flaxman's original images into an unmistakably Victorian work of art.

Pugin wanted to include Flaxman's monuments in a revival of Christian art, but he felt unable to do so because he found Neoclassicism alien to his ideals. In his polemical treatise *An Apology for the Revival of Christian Architecture* (1843), he wrote: 'Had Flaxman lived a few years later, he would have been a great Christian artist; but in his day men never thought it possible to do any thing fine in art that was not derived from paganism: hence his great powers were unhappily expended in illustrating fables of classic antiquity, instead of embodying edifying truths.' Pugin did however admire the religious aspects of Flaxman's art, basing his assessment on the sculptor's first Royal Academy lecture, which had been partially devoted to extolling the merits of late medieval English tomb sculptures. Pugin found Flaxman's 'observations on the excellence of our Catholic ancestors, and his lamentations on the destruction of their work', both 'heartfelt and eloquent'. 'The Christian artist of the present time must feel grateful for the good he effected by setting forth neglected truth', Pugin concluded.

A description of Flaxman by a later Victorian writer as 'the Fra Angelico of sculpture' epitomises the Victorian assessment of him as a Christian artist, an evaluation which should be set against the background of the Victorian revival of Christian art, associated with such artists as William Dyce and writers like Lord Lindsay. The parallel with Fra Angelico occurs in the most extensive account of the sculptor's work to be published in the Victorian period, a series of articles between 1867 and 1872 in the *Art Journal* by G. F. Teniswood.

These *Art Journal* articles used a new adjective, 'Flaxmanic', which has not found its way into the *Oxford English Dictionary*, but which is defined as being 'synonymous with the highest conceptions of imaginative sublimity, ideal beauty, purity of sentiment and tender pathos'. The *Art Journal* even claimed for Flaxman 'a rank and influence in modern sculpture second not even to Michelangelo', but fortunately admitted that there was a wide disparity between the 'power and style' of the two men. Flaxman's art was 'gentler' and one should look, so we are told, for the 'calmer virtues' associated with the art of Raphael. By putting Flaxman in the same company as Fra Angelico, Raphael and Michelangelo, the writer was according him exaggerated praise typical of Victorian assessments. For a more carefully measured criticism of Flaxman one should turn to Allan Cunningham writing just before the Victorian period, in 1830, in his *Lives*, and also to comments by other contemporaries, or near-contemporaries, in lectures, essays or diaries.

NOTES TO THE TEXT

CHAPTER I Early Career.

1 Disraeli quotation from his *Lothair* (London 1870), ch. XXXIII, describing some gilt cups; and W. B. Yeats, 'Blake and his illustrations to the Divine Comedy' (1897), in *Ideas of Good and Evil* (London and Dublin, third edn. 1907), p. 222. For a more detailed discussion see Epilogue.

2 The most useful contemporary and near-contemporary accounts of Flaxman are in J. T. Smith, *Nollekens and His Times* (London 1828); Allan Cunningham, *Lives* (London 1830), vol. III, together with Maria Denman's corrections published in *The Builder*, 17 and 24 January 1863 (the original manuscript for which forms part of the grangerised Cunningham *Lives*, vol. III, in National Library of Scotland, MS 828); H. C. Robinson, *Diary* (London 1869); and J. Farington, *Diary*, complete manuscript in Royal Library, Windsor, typescript in British Museum Print Room, selections edited by J. Greig (London 1922–28). As the new, complete edition of Farington by K. Garlick and A. MacIntyre (London and New Haven 1978 onwards) has only reached the entry for 31 July 1801 at the time of going to press, I have not altered footnote references in my text to either Greig or to the manuscript.

3 Farington, *Diary*, unpublished entry, 5 October 1798; Cunningham, *op. cit.*, III, p. 361.

4 W. Hayley, *Memoirs* (London 1823), II, p. 121; the pupil was Hayley's son Thomas.

5 The young sculptor Musgrave Lewthwaite Watson, who had received helpful advice from Flaxman when he arrived in London from Cumbria; reported in Reverend Dr. J. Bayley, *New Church Worthies* (London 1884), p. 334, in which the last chapter is devoted to Flaxman.

6 Cunningham, *op. cit.*, III, p. 332.

7 Music, chiefly vocal, was included as items 171–182 in Christie's sale of Flaxman's engravings, etc., 1 July 1828. Frederick Tatham comments for example on his beautiful singing; quoted G. E. Bentley, *Blake Records* (Oxford 1969), p. 521.

8 Cunningham, *op. cit.*, III, p. 275. See also D. Watkin, *C. R. Cockerell* (London 1974), p. 100.

9 Flaxman's interest in Swedenborgianism is discussed in more detail below, Chapter V, Section 4.

10 British Library, Add. MSS. 39780, f. 94, Flaxman to Hayley, 17 December 1805.

11 H. C. Robinson, *op. cit.*, II, p. 229, 7 May 1822.

12 A. Cunningham copy of an extract from a letter by Flaxman to an unnamed correspondent, declining a dedication, in grangerised Cunningham, *Lives*, III, p. 216 v., National Library of Scotland, MS 828.

13 Cunningham, *op. cit.*, III, p. 360, and Smith, *op. cit.*, II, p. 439.

14 Cunningham, *op. cit.*, III, p. 359.

15 D. E. Williams, *Lawrence* (London 1831), I, pp. 446–50.

16 Cunningham, *op. cit.*, III, p. 360.

17 MSS, Gennadius Library, American School, Athens, Flaxman to Hayley, 22 April 1805. Cowper's friend was Samuel Rose.

18 Smith, *op. cit.*, II, p. 448.

19 Cunningham, *op. cit.*, III, p. 360.

20 Same source as n. 5.

21 D. Watkin, *op. cit.*, p. 99.

22 Robinson, *op. cit.*, I, p. 315, part of general entry for 1810. See also Ludwig Schorn in *Kunst-Blatt*, 1827, p. 120, who says Flaxman's eyes 'expressed an animated spirit'.

23 British Library, Add. MSS. 39780, f. 123, Nancy Denman to Flaxman, 19 July [1780].

24 Cunningham, *op. cit.*, III, p. 351.

25 Cunningham, *op. cit.*, III, p. 292.

26 Maria Denman in *The Builder*, 24 January 1863, p. 60, says Flaxman received no training, contradicting Cunningham, *op. cit.*, III, p. 276.

27 Statues of both *Painting* and *Architecture* at Raby Castle, Durham have been attributed to the elder Flaxman, both executed in a late Baroque style, like the example reproduced.

28 R. Gunnis, *Dictionary of British Sculptors* (London 1953; and revised edn. 1968) in the entry on John Flaxman senior, gives his date of death as 1795, following Redgrave's *Dictionary*. However, amongst the MSS in the Birmingham Assay Office Library, is a bill from a John Flaxman to Matthew Boulton, 17 November 1801, giving the Strand as his address. By that date the younger Flaxman was living in Buckingham Street, so the bill must be the father's.

29 S. C. Hutchison, 'The Royal Academy Schools, 1768–1830', *Walpole Society*, XXXVIII, 1960–62, p. 134.

30 A lecture in 1770 in *Dr. William Hunter at the Royal Academy of Arts*, edit. M. Kemp (Glasgow 1975), p. 38.

31 W. Hayley, *op. cit.*, I, p. 309.

32 MSS, Pierpont Morgan Library, New York, Flaxman to Hayley, 24 August 1803.

33 J. Romney, *Memoirs of George Romney* (London 1830), p. 203.

34 Flaxman to Reverend John Romney, 11 August 1821, in J. Romney, *op. cit.*, p. 232.

35 Cunningham, *op. cit.*, III, p. 283 and Smith, *op. cit.*, II, p. 455.

36 Smith, *op. cit.*, II, p. 451.

37 Cunningham, *op. cit.*, III, p. 351.

38 Bentley, *op. cit.*, p. 521, n. 2, quoting J. T. Smith as source.

39 Dated 1792; D. Bindman collection; repr., Bentley, *op. cit.*, pl. VI.

40 D. Bindman, *Blake as an Artist* (London 1977), p. 108.

41 Smith, *op. cit.*, II, p. 456.

42 MSS, Pierpont Morgan Library, Flaxman to Hayley, 26

April [1784]; printed in Bentley, *op. cit.*, pp. 27–28. Hayley's copy, given to him by Flaxman, is now in the Huntington Library, San Marino.

43 Letter already cited in previous footnote, and Bentley, *op. cit.*, p. 24.

44 Flaxman's copy of the Gray *Poems*, now in the Mellon Collection, has been published by Irene Tayler (Princeton 1971) and by Sir G. Keynes (London 1972). The preliminary drawing for the *Arlington Court Picture* is in the Pierpont Morgan Library. Flaxman's name appears on the subscribers' list for the Blair, and the *Job* appears as item 107 in Christie's sale of Flaxman's books on 12 June 1828.

45 A poem in a letter to Flaxman, undated [12 September 1800] in *Complete Writings*, edit. G. Keynes (London 1966 edition), p. 799.

46 D. Erdman, *Blake: Prophet Against Empire* (Princeton 1969 edition), p. 93.

47 Farington, *Diary*, edit. Greig, XII, p. 226.

48 Lady Victoria Manners and G. C. Williamson, *Angelica Kauffmann* (London 1924), p. 156, where Flaxman's name is misspelt in her account-book as 'Mr. Flackenman', and p. 157.

49 MSS, Houghton Library, Harvard University, Flaxman to Hayley, Rome, 17 November 1791.

50 G. E. Bentley, 'A. S. Mathew, Patron of Flaxman and Blake', *Notes and Queries*, 203, 1958, p. 172.

51 These drawings are now lost. Smith, *op. cit.*, II, pp. 435–6 and Cunningham, *op. cit.*, III, pp. 281–82.

52 J. T. Smith, *Book for a Rainy Day* (London 1845), p. 83. See Iolo Williams, 'An Identification of some early drawings by John Flaxman', *Burlington Magazine*, CII, 1960, pp. 246–50. J. T. Smith, *op. cit.*, p. 110 and his *Nollekens*, II, p. 436 says Mrs. Mathew obtained Flaxman's first commission for a sculpture, from Edward Knight of Portland Place for a marble of *Alexander the Great*, now lost. But this cannot be substantiated, especially as the statue may have been executed as late as 1784.

53 MSS, Fitzwilliam Museum, Cambridge, Flaxman letter-volume, f. 4, Flaxman to Hayley, 18 October 1784: '. . . Mr. Romney is the only man fit to paint your portrait in large . . .'. Hayley had known Romney since 1776.

54 MSS, Pierpont Morgan Library, Flaxman to Romney, 20 October 1783, expressing gratitude to Romney for having introduced him to Hayley; cited in Bentley, *Blake Records*, p. 27, n. 2. But for evidence that Flaxman and Hayley met earlier in the year, see below n. 60.

55 M. Bishop, *Blake's Hayley* (London 1951), p. 78; and British Library, Add. MSS. 39780, f. 33, Flaxman to Hayley, 10 February 1784, saying he has already begun the monument, and asking Hayley to produce an inscription. In another letter, MSS, Pierpont Morgan Library, dated 26 April [1784], already quoted, Flaxman twice misspells Hayley's surname as 'Haley', suggesting that the acquaintance is only a recent one. The letter, without the misspelt names, is printed in Bentley, *op. cit.*, pp. 27–28. The name is also misspelt in Flaxman's dedication in the copy of Blake's *Poetical Sketches* that he sent to Hayley; see Bentley, *op. cit.*, p. 27, n. 5.

56 W. Hayley, *op. cit.*, II, p. 399.

57 W. Hayley, *op. cit.*, I, pp. 320–1. Flaxman's contribution has survived, but not Romney's.

58 A drawing of this subject, which seems to be Flaxman's earliest known surviving drawing, and which might relate to the 1768 bas-relief, was included in the *John Flaxman* exhibition, London, Heim Gallery, 1976, no. 40, reproduced in the catalogue and the Hamburg *Flaxman* Exhibition, 1979, no. 6.

59 The medallion is a terracotta. There is a cast in the Soane Museum. The frontal pose is similar to that of the self-portrait drawing reproduced in Plate 6.

60 British Library, Add. MSS. 39780, ff. 29–30, Flaxman to wife, undated [18 June 1783]. The first monument is not specified. The clients are called 'Messrs Romney, Russell and Long', presumably George Romney and Hayley's friends William Russell and William Long. In which case the commission would presumably have been the *Ball* monument, and therefore Flaxman may well have been introduced to Hayley about the early summer of 1783. That was the summer the two men together with Hayley were in Westminster Abbey. The later letter is in the same volume, f. 31, undated [23 June 1783]; again the monuments are unidentified; the first was ordered by Sir Henry Englefield, and the second by Captain Dalrymple.

61 MSS, Keele University, Wedgwood Archive, L 208-1, an account rendered by Flaxman to Mr. Fierville, 12 Edward Street, Portman Square, including for 12 June 1784 'A Tomb to the memory of Rousseau in Portland stone erected on Mr. Fierville's estate near Stanmore', costing £105. 'Monsieur Fierville' has eluded identification, even by Rousseau scholars. I am most grateful to R. A. Leigh and Samuel Taylor for trying to track him down. R. A. Leigh suggests he might be the author of the anonymous *Tour to Ermenonville containing . . . a particular description of the tomb of Rousseau* (London 1785), in which the author says he was an English gentleman who went to Ermenonville in about 1783.

62 British Library, Add. MSS, 39781, f. 362, Bates to Mrs. Flaxman, 4 January 1787. Flaxman's dogmatism, shown by this letter, might further substantiate the role of Flaxman as Steelyard the Lawgiver in Blake's satire 'An Island in the Moon' already mentioned in this chapter.

63 Also used e.g. *Agatha Halsey*, died 1782 (Great Gaddesden, Hertfordshire); *Revd. John Wickins*, died 1783 (Petworth, Sussex); *Medows monument*, three deaths between 1780–95 (paid for 1795; Kingston, Surrey); *John Stuart Wortley*, died 1797 (paid for 1803; Wortley, Yorkshire). No account-books seem to have survived covering Flaxman's commissions before he was in Italy. Two of Flaxman's account-books provide the main documentation on costs, dates of commission, and completion of later monuments and other works. One, covering the period 1794–1810 is British Library, Add. MSS. 39784 B.B., and has been published by E. Croft-Murray in *Walpole Society*, XXVIII, 1939–40, pp. 51 ff. This will be cited as 'Croft-

Murray account-book'. The other remains unpublished, covering the period 1809–26, in Columbia University, New York, Special Collection, D. 430. 394–F. 61. This will be cited as 'Columbia account-book'. Unless otherwise specified, these are the sources used throughout this book for dates and costs, and each reference to these two particular account-books will therefore not be footnoted, unless the source is not clear from the context.

64 As Mrs. Morley only died in May 1784, the work entitled *A Monument of a lady who died a short time before her child* in the Royal Academy's summer exhibition that year cannot be the *Morley* monument, as Constable, *op. cit.*, p. 81, suggested, apart from the fact that the title is incorrect. If a sculptor had to be found, and correspondence travel between India and Britain, it is unlikely that Flaxman completed the *Morley* monument before 1785 at the earliest. He worked on the smaller *Ball* monument for two years.

65 Cunningham, *op. cit.*, III, p. 293.

66 For the origin of the term see D. Irwin, 'Neoclassicism in Art', in Scribner's *Dictionary of the History of Ideas* (New York 1972), III, p. 363–71.

67 John Rylands Library, Manchester, Eng. MS. 341, Flaxman to Hayley, 1 August [1786].

68 The monument was not erected. The idea of a Chatterton monument was raised again in 1792, but seems not to have involved Flaxman at this stage, but at the end of 1812 he sent John Britton a further idea for a monument at the time the project was revived, to once again lapse. Reproduced in Appendix to Britton's *Autobiography* (London 1850), p. 68. See also E. H. W. Meyerstein, *Life of Chatterton* (London 1930), p. 525.

69 Reproduced by Iolo Williams in *Burlington Magazine*, CII, 1960, p. 247.

70 British Library, Add. MSS. 39780, ff. 6-6v., Flaxman to Nancy Denman, 2 August [1780].

71 Cunningham, *op. cit.*, III, p. 283.

72 Early 1780's; exhibited *John Flaxman*, Heim Gallery, London 1976, no. 34, reproduced in catalogue and Hamburg *Flaxman* exhibition, 1979, no. 8.

73 Most of the seven drawings in the Fitzwilliam set (volume 832/1) are not identified. The identifications of the drawings reproduced here are the author's. The story of Judah and Tamar (*Genesis*, ch. 38) is one that most closely fits the Old Testament drawing; it might just possibly be the story of Jephthah's daughter in *Judges*, ch. 11. The Hamburg *Flaxman* catalogue proposes different interpretations. (nos. 10 and 12). Another drawing similar in style and size to this series, in the collection of Walter Brandt, shows *Samuel committed to the care of Eli*.

CHAPTER II Artist and Industry: Wedgwood

1 National Library of Scotland, MS 828, grangerised Cunningham *Lives*, III, p. 217, copy by Cunningham, Flaxman to Wedgwood's nephew Joseph Byerley, 19 January 1795.

2 British Library, Add. MSS. 33610.S., f. 94 v, draft address to George III on John Opie's plan, 28 February 1801.

3 Flaxman to Wedgwood, 13 December 1785, in W. G. Constable, *John Flaxman* (London 1927), p. 108.

4 See D. Irwin, 'Neoclassical Design: Industry Plunders Antiquity', *Apollo*, XCVI, 1972, pp. 288–97.

5 'I am glad you have met with a modeller and that Flaxman is so valuable an artist', Wedgwood to Bentley, 14 January 1775, in E. Meteyard, *Life of Wedgwood* (London 1865–66), II, p. 321.

6 Wedgwood to Bentley, 29 October 1777, in Lady Farrar, *Letters of Wedgwood* (London 1903–6), II, p. 390.

7 Wedgwood to Bentley, 9 July 1776, in Meteyard, *op. cit.*, II, p. 366. In another letter Flaxman asks for technical comments: Flaxman to Wedgwood, 13 December 1785, in Constable, *op. cit.*, p. 108.

8 The 1779 Wedgwood catalogue lists an earlier *Cook* medallion, but this can only be attributed to Flaxman, not on any convincing grounds.

9 MSS, Keele University, Wedgwood Archive, 1339–2, a long account for work rendered to Wedgwood, includes *Herschel* and *Dr. Buchan* (11 July 1783), *Captain Cook* (24 January 1784), *Dr. Johnson* (3 February 1784), *C. Jenkinson* (21 March 1784), *King of Sweden* (23 November [1785]) all at two guineas each; for three guineas are listed *Warren Hastings* (14 January [1785]) and *Queen of Portugal* (1 June 1787). Same archive, L 206–1, a receipt for *Banks* dated 21 August 1779, for two guineas.

10 MSS, Keele University, Wedgwood Archive, 1334–2, an account rendered for work executed for Wedgwood, written by Flaxman's father, dated 28 April 1782, lists 'Moulding a Bust of Mrs. Siddons', for £1.11.6. This receipt raises doubts that the younger Flaxman executed the *Mrs. Siddons* medallion. However, two years later the younger Flaxman writes in a letter to Wedgwood that he has 'repaired the bust of Mrs. Siddons'. As his father was still alive, there seems to be no reason why the son should mend the father's broken model. Same archive, 30188–2, Flaxman to Wedgwood, London, 5 February 1784.

11 Hugh Tait, 'Wedgwood, Flaxman and an English eighteenth-century portrait carver, Silvanus Bevan', *Wedgwood Society Proceedings*, no. 3, 1959, pp. 126–132.

12 Convincing arguments for removing some medallions from Flaxman's oeuvre are provided in R. Reilly and G. Savage, *Wedgwood: Portrait Medallions* (London 1973), e.g. Sir William Hamilton, p. 182.

13 Vol. I, plate 30; sarcophagus relief subsequently bought by Cardinal Albani, and now in the Louvre.

14 Also known as *The Crowning of a Kitharist*, and first called *Homer and Hesiod*.

15 List in full in Meteyard, *op. cit.*, II, p. 231. Keele University, Wedgwood Archive, 31201–1.

16 MS letter in possession of Mrs. Robert D. Chellis, Bentley to Hamilton, 26 February 1779, says the design is copied from a drawing lent by d'Hancarville. Letter published by Vivian J. Scheidemantel, 'The Apotheosis of Homer: A Wedgwood and Bentley Plaque', in *Festschrift Ulrich*

Middeldorf (Berlin 1968), pp. 517–22, reprinted in *American Wedgwoodian*, III, no. 3, June 1969, pp. 68–74.

[17] Wedgwood to Erasmus Darwin, 28 June 1789, in Farrar, *op. cit.*, III, p. 86.

[18] Meteyard, *op. cit.*, II, pp. 380–1.

[19] Amongst Wedgwood's payments to Flaxman is an entry two years later for a 'bas-relief of Hercules in the Hesperian Garden' for £23, dated 10 August 1787. MSS, Keele University, Wedgwood Archive, 1339–2.

[20] MSS, Keele University, Wedgwood Archive, 30191–2, Flaxman to Wedgwood, London, 20 October 1785.

[21] MSS, Keele University, Wedgwood Archive, 1335–2, Flaxman to Wedgwood, London, 28 October 1782.

[22] MSS, Keele University, Wedgwood Archive, 30193–2, Wedgwood to Flaxman, Etruria, 2 November 1786, discussing the division of the design into two; same archive, 1338–2 and 1339–2, Flaxman's letters, 12 and 16 January 1787.

[23] MSS, Keele University, Wedgwood Archive, L 210–1, Flaxman to Byerley, Rome, 15 March 1788.

[24] MSS, Keele University, Wedgwood Archive, 1339–2, entry dated 18 December 1783, 15s. paid for 'Grinding the Edges of 6 snuff-boxes for the Spanish Ambassador'.

[25] Same archive, references between 1781 and 1787 in 1333–2, 1338–2, 1339–2, 30186–2, 30187–2, 30188–2, 30192–2, 30194–2 and unnumbered Mosley Collection, same archive, dated 1782. None of this work survives.

[26] Wedgwood to Hamilton, 16 June 1787, in A. Finer and G. Savage, *Letters of Wedgwood* (London 1965), p. 307.

[27] The author's next book will deal with the relationship of artists to industry, in Britain and on the Continent, from about 1760 to about 1860.

[28] Richard Wornum, 'The Exhibition as a Lesson in Taste', *Art Journal Illustrated Catalogue* (London 1851), p. v***.

CHAPTER III To Italy

[1] British Library, MS. 39784, A., Flaxman account-book entries.

[2] Wedgwood to Sir William Hamilton, 16 June 1787, in Finer and Savage, *op. cit.*, p. 307.

[3] A Mr. Freeman suggested the visit, according to a letter from Wedgwood to Bentley, 7 September 1771, in Finer and Savage, *op. cit.*, p. 114.

[4] The Italian-period commissions for illustrations are discussed below in ch. V.

[5] MSS, Keele University, Wedgwood Archive, 26273–1, list of contents of a box being despatched by Flaxman to Messrs Micali & Son, Leghorn, for transport to Gavin Hamilton in Rome. The list includes the possessions of Mr. and Mrs. Flaxman as well as those of two other people, presumably Dr. and Mrs. Bates. The drawing and modelling equipment can be assumed to be entirely Flaxman's.

[6] Some of this material was published in the author's article 'Flaxman: Italian Journals and Correspondence', *Burlington Magazine*, CI, 1959, pp. 212–17. Further material in this chapter is included in the author's paper at the 5th International Congress of the Enlightenment, Pisa 1979, entitled 'Italian Renaissance Art viewed by an Eighteenth Century Sculptor', to be published in *Studies on Voltaire and the Eighteenth Century*.

[7] The various purchases are listed in account-book entries, British Museum, Add. MS. 39784, E. and F.

[8] J. T. Smith, *Nollekens*, I, pp. 318–19, where the titles of some of the medals are listed.

[9] British Library, Add. MSS. 39786, Flaxman's journal on the way to Italy, as far as Bologna. All quotations for this part of his travels are taken from this source, unless otherwise specified.

[10] MSS, Keele University, Wedgwood Archive, L 26272–1, instructions from the Duc de Bouillon to Flaxman, 28 February 1786, for twelve Wedgwood seals with his coat-of-arms.

[11] British Library, Add. MSS. 39780, f. 43, Flaxman to Hayley, Rome, 17 July 1788.

[12] British Library, Add. MSS. 39780, f. 38 v, Flaxman to parents, Paris, 1 October 1787.

[13] Same letter as the one quoted in the previous note.

[14] British Library, Add. MS. 39780, f. 43 v, Flaxman to Hayley, Rome, 17 July 1788.

[15] Florence is contained in Fitzwilliam Museum notebook 832/5, and all quotations are from this source unless otherwise specified. The Luca della Robbia he copied is a seated figure inscribed 'Luc della Robia' (*sic*), a detail which cannot be identified with precision.

[16] *Memoirs and Recollections of the late Abraham Raimbach*, edit. M. T. S. Raimbach (London 1843), p. 199. Westmacott in his lecture on Flaxman, for example, makes a similar point, in Flaxman's *Lectures*, second edition (London 1823), p. vii. Contemporary British attitudes to Gothic and early Renaissance art are discussed in more detail in D. Irwin, *English Neoclassical Art*, ch. IV. Useful new information on the Uffizi is provided by the second of the 1978 Mellon Lectures by Joseph Alsop, 'Art history and art collecting', in *Times Literary Supplement*, 28 July 1978, p. 852.

[17] See above, Ch. I. Section 1.

[18] See E. Bassi, *Il Museo Civico di Bassano. I Disegni di Antonio Canova* (Venice 1959), pp. 167–80, drawings after Pietro Lorenzetti in the lower church at Assisi, Signorelli at Orvieto, Ghirlandaio in Santa Maria Novella, etc.

[19] The Fitzwilliam Florence notebook in the context of the reference to Giotto includes a mention to the *Navicella* in Rome as 'an astonishing improvement on the works of his predecessors'. Either this is a secondhand comment, as he would not yet have seen this work, or the Florence notebook may have been written later in Flaxman's Italian sojourn, even on the way home again in 1794.

[20] Sketches after works of art mentioned from now onwards are mostly to be found in the two Flaxman sketchbooks in the Victoria and Albert Museum. All sketches are from these sources unless a third sketchbook, now in the Mellon Collection, is being used, in which case—to prevent confusion—it will be named in the text. The contents of

the non-classical works in the Victoria and Albert Museum sketchbooks were usefully identified in the appendix to Margaret Whinney's article, 'Flaxman and the Eighteenth Century', *Journal of the Warburg and Courtauld Institutes*, XIX, 1956, pp. 280–2.

21 British Library, Add. MS. 39780, f. 44, Flaxman to Hayley, Rome, 17 July 1788.

22 See below p. 208.

23 On the basis of Flaxman's sketchbooks, journals and correspondence it is impossible to reconstruct a detailed itinerary with dates for his travels in the area around Florence and north of Rome. Although for example we know that he was visiting Orvieto in 1792 (e.g. British Library Add. MS. 39780, f. 199, Mrs. Flaxman to Mrs. Ann Kirk, 16 December 1792), we do not know if this was his first visit. We do know that he visited Florence on the way south and again on the way north, as has already been mentioned. It is uncertain, however, when and how often he visited other places, such as Siena, Pisa and so on.

24 The *Athamas* is discussed below, Ch. IV.

25 Victoria and Albert Museum sketchbook B.2.c., pages 43 and 45.

26 For the *Divine Comedy*, see below, Ch. V, Section 3.

27 Farington, *Diary*, edit. Greig, I, p. 123.

28 There is a very rough ground plan of Tivoli in the Mellon sketchbook.

29 Flaxman to Sir William Hamilton, undated [1790], in *Collection of Autograph Letters . . . Alfred Morrison. Hamilton and Nelson papers.* I, Letter 237.

30 Entry in Mellon sketchbook, showing a total cost of £28.17s. Edward Knight had already bought a marble *Alexander the Great* (see above Ch. I, no. 52, as well as in 1787, a *Venus and Cupid.*

31 British Library, Add. MS. 39780, f. 44, Flaxman to Hayley, Rome 17 July 1788.

32 J. Romney, *op. cit.*, p. 204, letter dated 25 May 1788.

33 British Library, Add. MS. 39780, f. 41 v, Flaxman to parents, Rome, 2 April 1788.

34 MS in Library, University College London. All quotations about Naples and Portici are from this source, unless otherwise specified. The Portici antiquities were transferred to Naples in 1822, where they now form part of the Museo Nazionale collection.

35 British Library, Add. MS. 39780, f. 45, Flaxman to parents, Rome, 30 August 1788, and same volume, f. 49, same to same, Rome, 7 October 1790.

36 Later in 1791 Flaxman wrote to his parents to say that Romney's casts were to be despatched in the spring, and confirms that 'I shall desire in my letter that he will let my father mould such of them as he chooses'. British Library, Add. MS. 39780, f. 56 v, Flaxman to parents, Rome, 21 November 1791.

37 British Library, Add. MS. 39780, f. 57, Flaxman to parents, Rome, 3 March 1792.

38 J. Romney, *op. cit.*, p. 230. Also British Library, Add. MS. 39784, E., f. 32 v, account-book entries for 1792.

39 British Library, Add. MS. 39784, F., ff. 26 and 31, entries for 1794. Flaxman and Thomas Banks were to be sent by the Royal Academy to Romney's sale in 1801 to buy some of these plasters for the Royal Academy Schools. H. C. Morgan, *History of Royal Academy Schools 1768–1836*, unpublished thesis, Leeds University, 1964, pp. 56–57.

40 British Library, Add. MS. 39780, f. 44 v, Flaxman to Hayley, Rome, 17 July 1788.

41 British Library, Add. MS. 39780, f. 197 v, Mrs. Flaxman to Mary Flaxman, 15 December 1792.

42 British Library, Add. MS. 39780, ff. 49 v–50, Flaxman to parents, Rome, 7 October 1790.

43 British Library, Add. MS. 32491, f. 1, Flaxman to Hayley, Rome, 15 November 1791. *Athamas* reference in same library, Add. MS. 39780, f. 50, Flaxman to parents, Rome, 7 October 1790.

44 British Library, Add. MS. 39784, E, f. 29.

45 John Murray Ltd., London, Flaxman sketchbook 435.

46 British Library, Add. MS. 39780, f. 45 v, Flaxman to parents, Rome, 30 August 1788.

47 Same volume as previous note, f. 186, Mrs. Flaxman to father, Rome, 29 August 1788.

48 Same volume as previous note, f. 53, Mrs. Flaxman to sister, [Rome] 24 April 1792.

49 J. Romney, *op. cit.*, p. 230, Flaxman to Romney, Rome, 12 September 1792.

50 British Library, Add. MS. 39784, F., f. 26, account-book entry, 19 April 1794. Farington, *Diary*, unpublished entry, 25 February 1796, records that Flaxman showed the diarist a letter of thanks he had received from artists in Rome for his work in this campaign, the artists including Gavin Hamilton, Christopher Hewetson, William Theed, Ottley and others.

51 British Library, Add. MS. 39780, f. 47 v, Flaxman to parents, Rome, 26 January [1790].

52 John Murray Ltd., London, Flaxman sketchbook 435.

53 *Collection of Autograph letters . . . Alfred Morrison. Hamilton and Nelson papers*, I, Letter 237.

54 MS, Fitzwilliam Museum, Flaxman letter-volume, f. 49, Flaxman to Percier, London, 2 November 1802.

55 All three drawings are in the Soane Museum. It is possible that Percier was inspired to illustrate Didot's edition of Horace in 1799 by seeing Flaxman's Homer, but he did not adopt the English artist's linear style.

56 British Library, Add. MS. 39780, f. 179, Mrs. Flaxman to sister, [Rome], 22 July 1788.

57 British Library, Add. MS. 39792, A, f. 16 v, Mrs Flaxman's diary, 9 April 1792.

58 Bodleian Library, MSS. Autog. d. 11, ff. 319–20, Rome, 13 March 1792. Playfair's drawings for a London house and for a temple of Neptune contain ideas that stylistically relate to Cairness, the country-house Playfair was designing at the time for an estate in Aberdeenshire.

59 MSS, Fitzwilliam Museum, Flaxman letter-volume, f. 62, Flaxman to parents [1789], and J. Romney, *op. cit.*, p. 208, Flaxman to Romney, Rome, 15 April 1790.

60 British Library, Add. MS. 39780, f. 195, Mrs. Flaxman to James Kirk, [no place] 17 October 1790.

[61] British Library, Add. MS. 39781, f. 372, Mariana Starke to Mrs. Flaxman, Villa Careggi, 27 July 1794. Also next two folios of same volume.

[62] MSS, Houghton Library, Harvard University, Flaxman to Hayley, Rome, 17 November 1791. Mrs. Mathew is also mentioned in British Library, Add. MS. 39780, f. 61 v, Flaxman to parents, Rome, 23 November [1792].

[63] British Library, Add. MS. 39790, f. 110, Flaxman notes on sculpture; the bas-relief is mentioned in Flaxman's article on bas-reliefs in Rees's *Cyclopaedia*. Hawkins is mentioned elsewhere: e.g. Fitzwilliam Museum, Flaxman MS notes on a villa at Pompeii; MSS, Westfield College, London, Mrs. Flaxman to Hayley, 3 July 1805.

[64] In the April number of the *Giornale delle Belle Arti*.

[65] MSS, Pierpont Morgan Library, grangerised Hayley, *Romney*, Flaxman to Hayley, Rome, 28 May 1794.

[66] British Library, Add. MS. 39780, f. 62 v, Flaxman to father, Rome, 23 November [1792].

[67] Same volume as previous note, f. 63 v, Flaxman to father and sister, Carrara, 22 July 1794.

[68] British Library, Add. MS. 39780, f. 53, Mrs. Flaxman to sister, 24 April 1792. Also British Library, Add. MS. 32491, f. 1 v, Flaxman to Hayley, Rome, 15 November, 1791.

[69] Cunningham, *op. cit.*, III, p. 311.

[70] Same volume as previous note, f. 203, Mrs. Flaxman to Mrs. Kirk, Carrara, 26 July [1794].

[71] Same volume as previous note, Flaxman to father and sister, Carrara, 22 July 1794.

[72] British Library, Add. MS. 39790, f. 159 v, wife's journal in northern Italy in 1794.

[73] Augsburg for example is mentioned in British Library, Add. MS. 39781, f. 382, unnamed correspondent to Mrs. Flaxman [4 November 1794] and Kassel in same volume, f. 386, Mrs. G. Hare-Naylor to Mrs. Flaxman, 8 November 1794.

[74] Same letter as quoted at end of previous note.

[75] Cunningham, *op. cit.*, III, p. 330; Farington's *Diary* covers the 1802 visit in some detail, the published parts being in Greig, *op. cit.*, II, pp. 13–17.

CHAPTER IV Sculptures in Italy

[1] The terracotta version of the relief is lost, but a plaster version is in the Soane Museum. The Mellon sketchbook notes a payment of £35 for the frieze. Croft-Murray account-book, 10 March 1802, lists a payment of £157.10s. from Edward Knight for a marble version. The same account-book, under 8 November 1794, lists £200 also from Knight, unspecified. He was also to carve for Knight a marble bust of Homer, which he despatched in 1791. Entry in the Mellon sketchbook, debiting Knight's account £35 for this item, including a pedestal.

[2] British Library, Add. MS. 39780, f. 179, Mrs. Flaxman to sister, [Rome], 22 July 1788. The daughter married Captain Way and went to live in Bath, presumably taking the bust with her. The bust was not included in the sale of the artist's pictures and engravings at Christies's on 15 May 1811, and is now lost. [T. J. Mulvany], 'Memoirs of Native Artists', *Dublin Monthly Magazine*, January-June 1842, pp. 68–69. Information about the subsequent history of the bust kindly supplied by Anne Crookshank.

[3] British Library, Add. MS. 39780, f. 45 v, Flaxman to parents, Rome, 30 August 1788. He does not seem to have begun this project unless it is the untitled relief finished for Knight and mentioned in same volume, f. 47 v, same to same, Rome, 26 January [1790].

[4] Same letter as quoted at end of previous note.

[5] The cast is of the *Nike* bought in Rome in 1777 for the Landgraf's collection in Kassel, and still in the Museum Fridericianum, Kassel.

[6] W. A. Childe-Pemberton, *The Earl Bishop* (London 1925), II, pp. 417–18.

[7] J. Romney, *op. cit.*, p. 208, Flaxman to Romney, Rome, 15 April 1790.

[8] Same letter as quoted in previous note. Wark, *op. cit.*, no. 15 is said to relate to the *Iliad*, but it is much more likely to relate to this project.

[9] British Library, Add. MS. 39780, f. 50, Flaxman to parents, Rome, 7 October 1790.

[10] Flaxman went specially to Carrara to select the block of marble in April 1792, taking a month to complete the transaction. Studio assistants were then set to work on the block, and by mid-December the sculptor's wife was able to report that the 'great group of Athamas is got so forward in the marble that he must begin to put the finishing strokes to it himself'. Same volume as in previous note, f. 197, Mrs. Flaxman to sister, [Rome] 15 December 1792. But in a letter of 23 November that year, Flaxman says that he is 'now actually giving the last touches'; same volume, f. 61.

[11] British Library, Add. MS. 39781, f. 380 v, A. Clark to Mrs. Flaxman, Florence, 1 November 1794.

[12] British Library, Add. MS. 39781, f. 392, Mrs. Hare-Naylor to Mrs. Flaxman, Voldagno, 3 July [1795].

[13] MSS. Bodleian Library, Autog. d. 11, f. 319, Flaxman to Sir William Hamilton, Rome, 13 March 1792.

[14] Croft-Murray account-book, p. 56.

[15] British Library, Add. MS. 39780, f. 197, Mrs. Flaxman to sister, [Rome] 15 December 1792.

[16] Childe-Pemberton, *op. cit.*, II, p. 438.

[17] This was the reason Flaxman later gave to A. W. von Schlegel, included in his 1828 addition to his 1799 essay on Flaxman, in Schlegel, *op. cit.*, p. 154.

[18] Cunningham, *op. cit.*, III, p. 304, where he also incorrectly states that the plaster group had been destroyed.

[19] Flaxman also executed for Hope a black-veined marble copy of the *Apollo Belvedere*. British Library, Add. MS. 39781, f. 16, Hope to Flaxman, 6 December 1794; and C. H. Westmacott, *British Galleries of Painting and Sculpture* (London 1824), p. 213.

[20] The figures are identified by Hayley in a letter to Flaxman, 18 January 1802. Fitzwilliam Museum, Hayley MSS, vol. IX.

[21] Maria Denman, in *The Builder, op. cit.*, p. 60.
[22] W. G. Constable, *op. cit.*, p. 53 says the commission was given before Flaxman went to Italy.
[23] J. T. Smith, *Nollekens*, I, p. 278.
[24] British Library, Add. MS. 36652, f. 123, Lord Mansfield to Flaxman, London, 28 June 1793.
[25] *Collection of Autograph Letters . . . Alfred Morrison. Hamilton and Nelson Papers*, I, Letter 224, Flaxman to Sir William Hamilton, Rome, 30 July 1793. The author has suggested that a hitherto unidentified drawing in the collection of the Hamburg Kunsthalle is almost certainly a design for this wall version of the monument to Mansfield. See the Hamburg *Flaxman* exhibition catalogue, 1979, no. 140.
[26] The origin of the error is in Cunningham, *op. cit.*, III, p. 312.
[27] British Library, Add. MSS. 39784, E. and F.
[28] Lord Buchan to Caleb Whitefoord, 19 January 1808, in W. H. Whitley, *Art in England 1800–1820* (Cambridge 1928), p. 134.
[29] J. S. Memes, *Memoirs of Antonio Canova* (Edinburgh 1825), p. 278.

CHAPTER V Illustrations

[1] Goethe, 'Über die Flaxmanischen Werke', *Propyläen*, 1799, in *Werke* (Weimar 1896), 47, pp. 245–46. When Flaxman's sister visited Weimar a few years later, he asked her to thank Goethe for 'the polite notice of my Homer', which suggests he may not have seen the actual article, since it was largely devoted to Dante. British Library, Add. MSS. 39780, f. 89, Flaxman to Mary Ann Flaxman, London, 23 November 1804.
[2] J. D. Fiorillo, *Geschichte der zeichnenden Künste* (Göttingen 1798–1808), V, p. 851.
[3] Guglielmo della Valle, *Vite dei Pittori Antichi Greci e Latini* (Siena 1795), p. 255.
[4] A. W. von Schlegel, 'Über Zeichnungen zu Gedichten und John Flaxmans Umrissen', *Athenäum, 1799, in Sämmtliche Werke* (Leipzig 1846), IX, pp. 114–15.
[5] British Library, Add. MSS. 39780, f. 197, Mrs. Flaxman to Mary Ann Flaxman, [Rome], 15 December 1792, is the main letter giving information about the Homer illustrations. She lists the works on which her husband is currently engaged, saying that drawings for Homer 'are for Mr. Udny an Englishman, of which he also makes duplicates for Mr. Naylor (husband of the late Bishop of Asaph's daughter), the which are engraving here as Mr. Naylor means to publish them on his return to England. He has promised to give us half a dozen copies'. Plans were subsequently changed, since the engravings were first published whilst the Flaxmans were still in Rome, and Mrs. Naylor was eventually to be accredited with commissioning a set, not her husband. Mr. Udney paid for his drawings at the rate of four crowns each.
[6] MSS, Fitzwilliam Museum, unbound letter, Flaxman to Hayley, Rome, 26 October 1793.
[7] British Library, Add. MSS. 39780, f. 98, Flaxman to Hayley, London, 6 November 1807.
[8] British Library, Add. MSS. 39784, E., f. 21, account-book entry, 1790.
[9] Most of the Homer drawings are in London collections, chiefly the Royal Academy of Arts and the British Museum. Other drawings are widely scattered, including the Fogg Art Museum, Chicago Art Institute, Huntington Library and Art Gallery, York City Art Gallery, etc.
[10] Goethe, *op. cit.*, p. 245.
[11] Cunningham, *op. cit.*, III, p. 296; Maria Denman, in *Builder, loc. cit.*, p. 60.
[12] P. O. Runge, *Hinterlassene Schriften* (Hamburg 1841), I, p. 54, letter dated 23 August 1800. For other references to Greek vases, see for example Goethe, *op. cit.*, p. 246; Koch in a letter dated Rome, 30 January 1802, in Otto R. von Lutterotti, *J. A. Koch* (Berlin 1940), p. 142.
[13] John Flaxman to George Romney, Rome, 25 May 1788, printed in Revd. J. Romney, *op. cit.*, p. 204.
[14] Flaxman to Sir William Hamilton, undated [1790], printed in *Collection of Autograph letters . . . Alfred Morrison. Hamilton and Nelson Papers* (1893), I, Letter 237.
[15] *Collection of Engravings from Ancient Vases . . . in the possession of Sir William Hamilton . . . with remarks on each Vase by the Collector* (Naples 1791–5), I, pp. 32, 46.
[16] Mengs, *Works*, English translation (London 1796), I, p. 200.
[17] Line engravings in scientific and other treatises, from the time of Dürer's volume on human proportion onwards, represent a different tradition that is not relevant to Neoclassicism.
[18] One of the few plates in Flaxman's Homer series that relate to the first folio of Hamilton's collection (1791) is the one in the *Odyssey* depicting Ulysses following the car of Nausicaa, which can be compared with Hamilton plate 24. Both examples are reproduced in D. Irwin, *English Neoclassical Art*, pls. 66, 67.
[19] Flaxman owned a copy of the book, but the date of its acquisition is unknown; it is included in Christie's 1828 auction catalogue of Flaxman's books.
[20] Other relevant archaeological publications in which a linear style was used include Georg Christoph Kilian's engravings in C. G. Murr's *Abbildungen der Gemälde und Alterthümer welche seit 1738 . . . in der verschütteten Stadt Herkulanum*, the first volume of which appeared in 1777.
[21] Koch letter, dated Rome 16 January 1799, in Otto R. von Lutterotti, *op. cit.*, p. 139.
[22] Lord Bristol patronised both Flaxman and Carstens, buying from the latter in 1796 two drawings, now lost, of *Plato's Banquet* and *Fates*. C. L. Fernow, *Carstens* (Leipzig 1806), pp. 209–10.
[23] Farington, *Diary*, edit. Greig, I, p. 184, 12 January 1797.
[24] Farington, *Diary*, unpublished entry, 19 December 1795.
[25] Cowper to Revd. John Johnson, [no place], 2 August 1793, in *Correspondence of Cowper*, edit. T. Wright, vol. IV (London 1904), p. 432.
[26] C. R. Leslie, *Autobiographical Recollections* (London 1860), I, p. 72.

[27] MSS, Fitzwilliam Museum, Flaxman volume of letters, Millin to Flaxman, [Paris], 26 April 1803.

[28] Bentley, *op. cit.*, p. 363.

[29] A. W. Schlegel, *op. cit.*, p. 149.

[30] MSS, Fitzwilliam Museum, Flaxman letter-volume, f. 47, Flaxman to Hayley, London, 8 September 1814.

[31] The dates are inscribed on the proof sheets in the Bodleian Library, Oxford. A. W. von Schlegel in his 1828 addition to the 1799 essay briefly discussed the Hesiod illustrations, saying that on this occasion Flaxman had chosen a 'less talented' engraver than Piroli, but does not even name him, such was Blake's contemporary reputation abroad. Schlegel, *op. cit.*, p. 156.

[32] Bentley, *op. cit.*, p. 377.

[33] W. B. Scott, *David Scott* (London 1850), p. 260.

[34] *Kunst-Blatt*, no. 8, 27 January 1823, p. 30.

[35] British Library, Add. MSS. 39790, f. 30, Flaxman to Revd. William Gunn, 1 October 1814.

[36] Flaxman to Hayley, 8 September 1814; letter already quoted in n. 30.

[37] Fitzwilliam Museum, Flaxman letter-volume, f. 30, Flaxman to Hayley, London, 12 August 1805; and Pierpont Morgan Library, MSS, Flaxman to Hayley, London, 18 October 1805.

[38] A copy of the printed pamphlet is in the Wedgwood Archive, Keele University, L 222–1. The School seems never to have been actually established.

[39] Sir Walter Scott, *Letters*, edit. H. J. C. Grierson (London 1932–6), I, pp. 226–7.

[40] Cunningham, *op. cit.*, III, p. 307.

[41] Hope's volume of drawings is now in the Houghton Library, Harvard University. All Dante drawings reproduced here from the Harvard collection are in this volume. The Hope commission is mentioned in Flaxman's correspondence: e.g. Bodleian Library, MSS. Autog. d. 11, f. 319, Flaxman to Sir William Hamilton, Rome, 13 March 1792; Flaxman to George Romney, Rome, 12 September 1792, printed in Revd. J. Romney, *op. cit.*, p. 231; British Library, Add. MSS. 39780, f. 197, Mrs. Flaxman to Mary Ann Flaxman, [Rome], 15 December 1792; Fitzwilliam Museum, Flaxman letter box no. 3, Mrs. Flaxman to Hayley, Rome, 22 July 1793.

[42] Plates sold in 1806 for £200. G. E. Bentley, *op. cit.*, pp. 48–50.

[43] English reprints of the *Divine Comedy* followed, one in the year of publication, one in 1808, and another in the year of Flaxman's death. Abroad it was published in Rome in 1815–16, and in Milan in 1822.

[44] Generally preferred to the rival translation by Charles Rogers (1782), both of which were to be superseded by the much better version by Henry Francis Cary in 1805–6.

[45] Hayley, *Epic Poetry*, Epistle III, lines 91–2.

[46] Goethe, *op. cit.*, *loc. cit.*; A. W. von Schlegel, *op. cit.*, pp. 127, 132.

[47] H. C. Robinson, *op. cit.*, I, p. 320, 17 January 1811.

[48] These studies of cloaks, mostly in the University College collection, have been cut out of sketchbooks and are not dated. The cloaks are unmistakably Italian, not British, especially in the obviously unposed sketches. The drawings can only have been done abroad, and can stylistically be dated in the early 1790's.

[49] The link is actually made in R. Rosenblum, *Transformations in Late Eighteenth Century Art* (Princeton 1967), p. 171.

[50] Cunningham, *op. cit.*, III, p. 310.

[51] A. W. von Schlegel, *op. cit.*, p. 127.

[52] D. Watkin, *Thomas Hope* (London 1968), p. 33; Croft-Murray account-book, 25 August 1800, p. 68.

[53] British Museum, Print Room, Shakespeare second folio of 1632 with extra illustrations by a variety of artists, including Blake, contains a scene from *Midsummer Night's Dream* and *Shakespeare between Comedy and Tragedy*, both by Flaxman.

[54] British Library, Add. MSS. 32491, f. 1 v, Flaxman to Hayley, Rome, 15 November 1791: 'I have been making several sketches from our honoured bard Milton'; and Fitzwilliam Museum, Hayley MSS, vol. IX, Hayley to Flaxman, Eartham, 31 December 1791.

[55] The drawings are mentioned in a letter from Flaxman to Hayley, London, 6 November 1807, British Library, Add. MSS. 39780, f. 98.

[56] Not executed; plasters in the Soane Museum and University College.

[57] H. C. Robinson, *op. cit.*, I, p. 320.

[58] MSS, Gennadius Library, American School of Classical Studies, Athens, Flaxman to Hayley, London, 22 April 1805.

[59] Some *Shipwreck* drawings are in the British Museum Print Room. The *Oberon* drawings are referred to in a letter to his sister, London, 23 November 1804, British Library, Add. MSS. 39780, f. 89–89 v. The Hayley drawings are mentioned in the letter quoted in the next note.

[60] MSS, Fitzwilliam Museum, Flaxman letter-volume, f. 35, Flaxman to Hayley, London, 10 December 1806; the authors are not specified.

[61] In 1824. Quoted D. Watkin, *Cockerell*, p. 98.

[62] *Athenaeum*, February 1807, p. 173. *The Acts of Mercy*, aquatints by F. C. Lewis, 1831; *The Lord's Prayer*, lithographs by Richard Lane, 1835.

[63] British Library, Add. MSS. 39781, f. 141, Revd. John Clowes to Flaxman, Manchester, 14 November 1816, in which he says he saw and read 'The Knight' when last dining with Flaxman. Clowes's role in the development of Swedenborgianism is discussed below.

[64] *Art Journal*, new series, IV, 1865, p. 61. It was to be published in facsimile in H. N. Morris, *Flaxman, Blake, Coleridge and other men of genius influenced by Swedenborg* (London 1915).

[65] Westfield College, London, MSS, Mrs. Flaxman to Hayley, London, 3 July 1805, '. . . He employs his few leisure hours for me in designing from Hesiod and the Bible . . .'. Although this letter belongs to a decade later, there is no reason to believe that it does not apply to earlier periods. See also Cunningham, *op. cit.*, III, p. 289.

[66] All known drawings are listed and reproduced by G. E. Bentley, 'Flaxman's Drawings for Pilgrim's Progress', in P. Fritz and R. Morton (edits), *Women in the Eighteenth Century and Other Essays* (Toronto 1976), pp. 245–78.

[67] New Testament panels shown by Flaxman at the Royal Academy exhibitions, unless they are connected with a known monument, are lost; e.g. in 1813 'A resurrection; in marble'.

[68] Ludwig Schorn in *Kunst-Blatt*, 1827, p. 123.

[69] Cunningham, *op. cit.*, III, pp. 332–7. Cunningham summarises the whole poem. The MS together with the illustrations is in Houghton Library, Harvard University. Two of the illustrations, different from those reproduced here, are in D. Irwin, *English Neoclassical Art*, plates 141 and 142.

[70] Flaxman did not, however, publish illustrations to *Kehama*. Southey letter of 1811 in *Letters*, edit. J. Wood Carter (London 1856), II, p. 229.

[71] Fitzwilliam Museum, Cambridge, Flaxman notebook 832/3. Discussed below, p. 211–12.

[72] [Revd. Samuel Noble], in *The Intellectual Repository for the New Church*, II, new series, 1827, pp. 434–38. He provides the identification of the anonymous *Times* critic a few days later, mentioned below.

[73] Ludwig Schorn in *Kunst-Blatt*, 1827, p. 124.

[74] Robert Hindmarsh, *The Rise and Progress of the New Jerusalem Church* (London 1861), p. 23.

[75] M. Bishop, *Blake's Hayley* (London 1951), p. 78.

[76] *Intellectual Repository*, p. 438.

[77] It still survives in the Finchley Chapel, a direct descendant of the original Cross Street congregation.

[78] *Reports of Swedenborg Society*, 1811, 1815, 1816, 1817, and 1827. Decline of election in 1811 in manuscript letter K/147, dated 25 June 1811, in archives of Swedenborg Society, London. Also refers to being busy in another letter (in same collection) dated 24 February 1810.

[79] H. C. Robinson, *Diary*, II, p. 263, 22 December 1823.

[80] H. C. Robinson, *op. cit.*, II, p. 300, 1 November 1825.

[81] R. L. Tafel, *Documents concerning the Life and Character of Swedenborg* (Leipzig 1875–77), II, pp. 555–56.

[82] British Library, Add. MSS. 39781, f. 464 v, J. A. Tulk to Mrs. Flaxman, 17 March 1814.

[83] The original marble was saved when St. John's was demolished, but has since disappeared. Plaster models are at University College. The final marble followed the drawing and models closely. The inscription on the marble said it was erected in 1819, but there must have been a delay since Flaxman exhibited it in 1820 at the Royal Academy with the title *Religious Instruction*.

[84] T. Compton, *Life and Correspondence of Reverend John Clowes* (London 1874), pp. 37, 177, 189.

[85] John Clowes, *The Divine Person and Character of Jesus Christ* (Manchester 1813), p. 63.

[86] For a recent contrary view of the Swedenborgian influence on Flaxman's imagery, see H. W. Janson, 'Thorvaldsen and England', in *Thorvaldsen. Untersuchungen zu seinem Werk und zur Kunst seiner Zeit*, edit. G. Bott (Cologne 1977), p. 111.

[87] H. N. Morris, *op. cit.*, passim.

[88] Flaxman owned the first edition of the first part of the *Arcana* of 1749, which he later gave in 1815 to a fellow Swedenborgian, Leonard Cox, who was to be Secretary of the Swedenborg Society 1839–41, by whom in turn it was given to the Society, in whose Library in London the volume still is. The Library also own Flaxman's composite volume containing minor treatises and indexes to Swedenborg.

[89] Tulk's daughter, quoted in Bentley, *Blake Records*, p. 250. The daughter does not say when these readings took place. They could have been before 1810, in which year both men joined the Swedenborg Society, but they may have known each other earlier. Flaxman also knew Tulk's father, J. A. Tulk, who was in Italy together with his wife at the same time as the Flaxmans. Whilst there J. A. Tulk commissioned, under Flaxman's direction, a cameo head of Swedenborg from Giovanni Giuseppe Caputi in Rome. See A. Carter in *New Church Life*, 1928, p. 336. Other links with the Tulks include the donation by the Tulk family of three plaster reliefs, perhaps originally acquired by C. A. Tulk, to the Kensington Chapel, *Deliver us from Evil*, *Lead us not into Temptation* and *Mercury bearing Pandora to Earth.* The panels were sold in 1975 to the Museum of the Academy of the New Church, Bryn Athyn, Pennsylvania. For a recent article on Tulk see R. H. Deck, 'New Light on C. A. Tulk, Blake's Nineteenth-century Patron', *Studies in Romanticism*, 16, no. 2, Spring 1977, pp. 217–36.

[90] Although the passage in the *Arcana* is identified in the inscription, the drawing was reproduced in error as a Miltonic subject in M. Pointon, *Milton and English Art* (Manchester, 1970) pl. 74. Other Swedenborg drawings are reproduced in *John Flaxman*, Heim Gallery, London 1976, numbers 35–39 and in the Hamburg *Flaxman* catalogue, nos. 160 and 161.

[91] British Library, Add. MSS. 39781, f. 92, Monro to Flaxman, Edinburgh, 5 November 1812; same volume ff. 109–112 for Monro's letters of introduction. A reference to the bust is contained in Birmingham Assay Office, Library, MSS, Flaxman to Matthew Boulton's son, 12 August 1812.

[92] Items listed in Christie's auction catalogue of Flaxman's books, 12 June 1828.

[93] British Library, Add. MSS. 39780, ff. 49 v–50, Flaxman to parents, Rome, 7 October 1790. Already quoted above, Ch. III, no. 42.

[94] Richard Redgrave refers to the collection in 'Passages from Lectures on the Study of Botany', in *Journal of Design*, III, 1850, p. 99.

[95] British Library, Add. MSS. 35610.S., f. 90 v, address to the President of the Royal Academy on Opie's plan for the erection of a Gallery of National Glory, 1800.

[96] W. Holman Hunt, *Pre-Raphaelites and the Pre-Raphaelite Brotherhood* (London 1913), II, pp. 60–61. He brackets Flaxman with Stothard, and then goes on to discuss Wilkie.

CHAPTER VI Sculptor of Tombs: after 1794

[1] M. D. George, *Personal and Political Satires . . . in the British Museum*, IX (London, 1949) no. 11952.

[2] MSS, Pierpont Morgan Library, grangerised copy of Hayley's *Romney*, Mrs. Flaxman to Hayley, 23 May [1796].

[3] MSS, Fitzwilliam Museum, Flaxman letter-box no. 4, Flaxman to Hayley, Rome, 26 October 1793.

[4] A. W. von Schlegel, *op. cit.*, p. 154.

[5] Ludwig Schorn, 'Besuch bei Flaxman im Juli 1826', *Kunst-Blatt*, 1827, especially pp. 120 and 123–24. The last page mentions Cockerell's comment.

[6] [Sir Brooke Boothby], *Sorrows, Sacred to the Memory of Penelope* (London 1796), Sonnet XIX.

[7] Parts of this chapter concerned with sentiment in tombs and its relationship to contemporary literature and theology, formed the basis of a paper on 'Sentiment and Piety in Tombs in the late 18th century', treating both English and French examples, read to the joint conference of the Société des Etudes du Dixhuitième Siècle and the British Society for 18th Century Studies held in Paris in 1976. I am grateful to both French and British colleagues for helpful suggestions made on that occasion. That paper is being expanded into a wider treatment of the theme in British and continental tombs as the author's contribution to the volume of essays on *The Sociology of Death*, edited by Joachim Whaley (London 1980).

Good literature on the subject of death in art is scanty. Amongst the items I have found fruitful I would include Erwin Panofsky, *Tomb Sculpture* (London 1964), Henriette s'Jacob, *Idealism and Realism. A Study of Sepulchral Symbolism* (Leiden 1954), Philipp Fehl, *The Classical Monument* (New York 1972), Florence Ingersoll-Smouse, *La Sculpture funéraire en France au XVIIIe siècle* (Paris 1912), and Paul Arthur Memmesheimer, *Das klassizistische Grabmal. Eine Typologie* (Bonn 1969). More recently Nicholas Penny has published *Church Monuments in Romantic England* (New Haven and London 1977), which appeared after this chapter had been written, and which coincidentally uses some similar material.

Other general books are not much more plentiful. In the field of literature I would include the volume by Fairchild mentioned below in n. 19, together with Eleanor M. Sickels, *The Gloomy Egoist* (New York 1932). John McManners gave a stimulating inaugural lecture at Oxford entitled *Reflections at the Death Bed of Voltaire* (Oxford 1975). The writings of Michel Vovelle and Philippe Ariès are always profitable, including *Mourir autrefois* (Paris 1974) by the former, and *Western Attitudes towards Death* (Baltimore and London 1974) by the latter.

[8] G. F. Tenniswood, 'Memorials of Flaxman', *Art Journal*, 1867, p. 102.

[9] The St. Cecilia type of horizontal figure reappears for example on Flaxman's *George Lindsay Johnstone* (1815) in Westminster Abbey.

[10] Farington, *Diary*, edit. Greig, III, p. 109, 13 September 1805.

[11] Other parallels would include Banks's relief of *Thetis and her nymphs rising to console Achilles* (1778; Victoria and Albert Museum) and page 41 of William Blake's engravings to Young's *Night Thoughts* (edition of 1797).

[12] James Dallaway, *A History of the Western Division of the County of Sussex* (London 1815), I, plate opposite p. 137, line engravings of the *Collins* and *Cromwell* monuments, 'Drawn from his original design and contributed by John Flaxman Esqr, R.A.'

[13] British Library, Add. MS. 39780, f. 70 v, Flaxman to Hayley, London, 29 June 1798. The letter says he will copy the relief from one shown at the R.A. in the previous year.

[14] Maria Denman, *The Builder*, *op. cit.*, p. 60.

[15] D. E. Williams, *op. cit.*, p. 448.

[16] e.g. *Mary Harford*, 1800–1, Holy Trinity, Stapleton, near Bristol, and *Harriot Peach*, 1825, St. Peter's, Ketteringham, Norfolk.

[17] Also re-worked on the monument to *Mrs. Ann Bowling*, 1809–11, Croydon, London, destroyed by fire in 1867; and *Mrs. Frances Schutz Drury Hawkins*, 1824, St. Edmund's, Kingsbridge, Devon.

[18] 'Resignation' was to be used on other tombs, e.g. *Bromley Family*, 1813, St. John Baptist, Baginton, Warwickshire, and *Admiral Sir Henry Frankland and his wife*, 1814, another Chichester Cathedral commission.

[19] Discussed for example in H. N. Fairchild, *Religious Trends in English Poetry* (New York 1942), II, especially chapter VIII.

[20] *John Braithwaite*, 1802, St. Michael's Cathedral, Barbados, and *Archdeacon Richard Leslie*, 1806, St. Mary's, Fort St. George, Madras.

[21] The article is signed 'R. H.'

[22] He had experimented with this attractive, and for him unusual, shape a few years before in the slab to William Hayley's son Thomas (1800; St. Margaret's, Eartham, Sussex), and he was to use it again in the same years as the *Redfearn* commission for the monument to *John Blake*, 1803–4, St. Martin's, Salisbury.

[23] If a drawing of *Suffer the little children* in York City Art Gallery relates to this monument, Flaxman originally intended a relief within a rectangular block, Christ standing to one side, with a mother and a group of children to the left.

[24] Cunningham, *op. cit.*, III, p. 321.

[25] MSS, Fitzwilliam Museum, undated, ? speech, in box with letters. He also attacks the 'farago of fashionable allegory' in a letter to Hayley, 12 July 1797, same collection, Flaxman letter-volume, f. 14.

[26] Cunningham, *op. cit.*, III, 325.

[27] Discussed above, Ch. V, Section 4.

[28] John Wooll, quoted by J. M. G. Blakiston, 'Flaxman's monument to Joseph Warton: Its Genesis and Evolution', *Winchester Cathedral Record*, no. 42, 1973, p. 33. The next quotation is from the same source. The article (pp. 22–29) uses documents in the muniments of Winchester College.

[29] Blakiston, *op. cit.*, p. 37.

[30] A similar composition of teacher and pupils, but in reverse,

was used by Flaxman for his monument to *John Lyon* of Harrow School (1815; St. Mary's, Harrow, Middlesex).

31 In the final monument, only the word 'Believe' appears in the inscription.

32 *Asiatick Researches*, III, 1792, pp. 55 ff, and (on gods) I, 1788, pp. 221 ff. His main article on Indian plants is in IV, 1795, pp. 229 ff.

33 Vol. 90, i, 1820, p. 365.

34 Plaster relief panels in the University College collection; model for the freestanding version in the Soane Museum.

35 For the discussion in the *Lectures*, see below Ch. X.

36 See for example J. H. Plumb, 'The New World of Children in Eighteenth-century England', *Past and Present*, 67, 1975, pp. 64–95.

37 D. E. Williams, *op. cit.*, p. 448.

38 Fanny Burney, *Camilla*, first published 1796, Bk. IV, ch. 9.

39 In *Works* (London 1797 edn.), I, pp. 30–31.

40 If one accepts that Flaxman is Steelyard the Lawgiver in Blake's satire (discussed above), he is even described by Blake as reading Hervey and Young.

41 For similar antique imagery in a contemporary death-bed scene see for example the *Samuel Whitbread* monument by the elder and younger Bacon (1799; St. Mary's, Cardington, Bedfordshire).

42 Discussed below, Ch. VIII.

43 Hugh Pearson, *Memoirs of the Life and Correspondence of the Revd. Christian Frederick Schwartz*, third edn. (London 1839), II, pp. 338–40.

44 MSS, Trinity College, Cambridge, Mrs. Dawson Turner to her husband, 15 November 1824. The *Psyche*, which might be related in design to the statuette Flaxman made for Samuel Rogers, does not appear on the model at University College, or the one in the collection of the Hon. Desmond Guinness. Seen from behind, the *Psyche* on the monument is clearly an addition. The whole monument would presumably not have been carved from one block of marble as this would have been wasteful.

45 Reviewers in *Monthly Review* and *Quarterly Review*, both in 1811, quoted in E. V. Weller, *Keats and Mary Tighe* (New York 1928), pp. xix–xx.

46 In the drawing reproduced here, the inscription 'Abercrombie Monument' is not in Flaxman's hand and is incorrect. As Sir Ralph Abercromby was a General, the nautical elements in the design would be inappropriate.

47 Maria Denman in *The Builder*, *op. cit.*, p. 60.

48 John Flaxman in Prince Hoare, *Academic Correspondence* (London 1804), p. 24.

49 Letter signed 'E. A.' in *Monthly Magazine*, 20, no. 137, 1 January 1806, p. 499.

50 Anonymous, in *Luctus Nelsoniani. Poems on the Death of Lord Nelson, in Latin and English, written for the Turtonian Medals* (London 1807), p. 147.

51 Ludwig Schorn in *Kunst-Blatt*, *op. cit.*, p. 114.

52 Southey, *Letters from England of Don Alvarez Espriella*, (London 1807), I, p. 311.

53 Quoted by D. Watkin, *Cockerell*, p. 20.

54 Rossi, Bacon, Westmacott and Flaxman were invited to take part in the Birmingham competition. See Trevor Fawcett, *The Rise of English Provincial Art* (Oxford 1974), p. 149, where Westmacott's design is reproduced.

55 British Library, Add. MSS. 39790, f. 19, Flaxman to Revd. William Gunn, London, February 1806.

56 MSS, Pierpont Morgan Library, New York, Flaxman to Hayley, London, 14 November 1805.

57 British Library, Add. MSS. 39780, f. 92 v, Flaxman to Hayley, London, 1 December 1805. The bust is in the United Services Club, London.

58 Farington, *Diary*, edit. Greig, IV, p. 151, 10 June 1807, quoting West.

59 West's *Apotheosis of Nelson* (1807) is in the Greenwich Hospital Collection in the National Maritime Museum, and another version is in the Paul Mellon collection.

60 British Library, Add. MSS. 39780, f. 69, Flaxman to [? Hayley], 12 May 1798.

61 *Lectures*, p. 145.

62 *Gentleman's Magazine*, 96, ii, 1826, p. 599.

63 C. H. Tatham, *Three Designs for the National Monument proposed to be erected in commemoration of the late glorious victories of the British Navy* (London 1802), reproduces three designs in handcoloured etchings. For Wyatt's design see D. Linstrum, *Wyattville* (Oxford 1972), p. 257.

64 Drawings in Art Museum, Princeton University, published by M. Campbell, 'An Alternative Design for a Commemorative Monument by John Flaxman', *Record of Art Museum*, Princeton, 17, 1958, pp. 65–73.

65 Farington, *Diary*, unpublished entry, 18 December 1799.

66 Flaxman, *A Letter to the Committee for Raising the Naval Pillar or Monument* (London 1799), a 15-page pamphlet, with three plates. The hostile pamphlet was by a minor architect, Alexander Dufour, *Letter to the Nobility and Gentry composing the Committee for raising the Naval Pillar* (London 1800). For a general discussion of colossal statues, including Flaxman's, as a background to New York's Statue of Liberty, see Marvin Trachtenberg, *Statue of Liberty* (London 1976).

67 Both examples in Cunningham, *op. cit.*, pp. 323–4.

68 B. R. Haydon, *Diary*, 23 July 1808 and 19 December 1808.

69 MSS, Fitzwilliam Museum, Hayley MSS, vol. IX, Hayley to Flaxman, [no place] 18 January 1802.

70 MSS, Yale University Library, Flaxman to Hayley, [no place], 20 May 1803.

71 British Library, Add. MSS. 39790, ff. 50 v–51, Mrs. Flaxman to Revd William Gunn, [no place] 15 March 1810.

72 See below, Ch. VII, for a discussion of the Covent Garden frieze, and below, Ch. IX, for the *Shield of Achilles*.

73 The Paddington Canal was used in 1804 for the transport of the *Hon. Evelyn Henry Frederick Pierrepont* monument going to St. Edmund's, Holme Pierrepont, Nottinghamshire. Croft-Murray account-book, p. 75.

74 Croft-Murray account-book, p. 80.

75 MSS, National Library of Scotland, MS. 587, no. 1150, Flaxman to George Thomson, London, 14 October 1823.

76 Croft-Murray account-book, p. 57.

CHAPTER VII Sculpture: Secular Commissions

[1] He had been an Associate since 1797.

[2] MSS, Westfield College, London, Mrs. Flaxman to Hayley, 3 July 1805.

[3] Apollodorus's name appears on the version of the composition in the drawing in the National Gallery of Scotland. This relief used to be dated about 1800. For the dating of 1790–c.1794, see the Hamburg *Flaxman* exhibition catalogue, no. 121.

[4] Same letter as quoted above in n. 2. A marble version exists in the British Royal Collection and another plaster in University College.

[5] It would have cost £500. Columbia account-book, p. 68; undated entry, but from the context is 1826. The plaster reliefs of this subject at University College and Soane Museum presumably relate to this commission.

[6] Statue now lost. It cost £260. Entry of 28 July 1811 in Columbia account-book.

[7] Farington, *Diary*, unpublished entry, 19 July 1809.

[8] Drawings by J. W. Archer in British Museum Print Room; engraving by G. Hawkins, reproduced e.g. J. Summerson, *Architecture in Britain 1530–1830* (Harmondsworth 1955 edn.), pl. 176.

[9] A fragment of a man's and horse's head from the Parthenon frieze, brought back by Chandler, had been drawn by Flaxman at the Society of Dilettanti in 1783. This fragment is now also in the British Museum. L. Cust and S. Colvin, *History of the Society of Dilettanti* (London 1898), p. 105.

[10] A. H. Smith, 'Lord Elgin and His Collection', *Journal of Hellenic Studies*, XXXVI, 1916, p. 298; and W. St. Clair, *Lord Elgin and the Marbles* (London 1967), pp. 152–3.

[11] West cited his *Christ healing the Sick* (1811; Tate Gallery) and *Christ rejected by Caiaphas* (1814; Pennsylvania Academy of Fine Arts, Philadelphia).

[12] Sidney Smith, *Letters*, edit. Smith (London 1953), I, p. 273. The report was published in 1816.

[13] The report of the Radcliffe Camera scheme is in *Gentleman's Magazine*, 77, 1807, p. 706. R. Ackermann's *History of the University of Oxford*, published in 1814, shows the Marbles in the Schools (plate opp. p. 224), and A. Michaelis in his *Ancient Marbles in Great Britain* (Cambridge 1882), reports that the Marbles had until recently been in the Schools.

[14] E. D. Clarke, *Greek Marbles brought from the Shores of the Euxine, . . .* (Cambridge 1809).

[15] Entries for July and 20 November 1826, Columbia account-book. Flaxman died on 7 December. Drawings for the flanking pediments are in Huntington Library and Art Gallery, Wark, *op. cit.*, nos. 48–50.

[16] Canova reference in Columbia account-book, 14 June 1817; and same source lists under 1815 'Hon. Fred. North, St. James's Palace. Payments for restoration wk in plaster—a female fig. in altorelievo, a bust of Euripides, 2 medallions of Demosthenes, Homer'.

[17] The Italian period plaster is in the Soane Museum, and a related drawing is in the Huntington (Wark, no. 51). Other fireplace references will be found in Gunnis, and in Croft-Murray, *op. cit.*, pp. 67–69, 77, 82.

[18] Plaster models for all four works are in the Soane Museum; Lawrence's statuettes are in the collection of the Royal Academy of Arts. Models for the Lawrence statuettes are in the British Museum.

[19] Columbia account-book; payments spread out between 1813 and 1827, the year after the artist's death.

[20] The *St. Michael* finally arrived at Petworth in 1826, which is presumably why that date is given in the inscription on the base. The *Apollo* is actually signed and dated 1826, although it had already been shown at the R.A. the previous year.

[21] D. E. Lawrence, *Life and Correspondence of Sir Thomas Lawrence* (London 1831), I, p. 449.

CHAPTER VIII Portraits

[1] e.g. *Gentleman's Magazine*, March 1827, p. 274.

[2] Croft-Murray account book, entry 7 May 1803. I am very grateful to Mrs. Mildred Archer for information about this statue, and for supplying me with photographs. Edward Croft-Murray has very kindly lent me the photograph, taken in 1939, reproduced here.

[3] R. W. Liscombe, 'Canova, Aberdeen and the Pitt Monument', *Burlington Magazine*, CXIX, 1977, pp. 700–705.

[4] MSS, National Library of Scotland, MS. 2732, Sederunt Book of the Committee of Subscribers, Glasgow, to Sir John Moore's monument, 1809–10.

[5] MSS, National Library of Scotland, MS. 9819, f. 104, Flaxman to Colin Donald of Glasgow, 4 August 1818, says *Moore* finished and ready for transportation.

[6] The *Marquess of Hastings* joined other statues in Calcutta which had been commissioned as a result of earlier public subscriptions: the *Marquess of Wellesley* and *Marquess Cornwallis*, both executed by the younger Bacon (although the design of the latter was by his father), and in due course Westmacott's *Warren Hastings* was to follow. All these statues are in the Victoria Memorial.

[7] L. Schorn in *Kunst-Blatt*, 1827, p. 113.

[8] MSS, National Library of Scotland, MS. 685, f. 35, Thomson to Stothard, Edinburgh, 6 September 1822. The commission eventually materialised as a standing statue by Chantrey, erected in George Street, Edinburgh, in 1831, where it remains. There were insufficient funds to meet the costs of an equestrian statue..

[9] National Library of Scotland, MS. 828, grangerised Cunningham *Lives*, volume 3, p. 209 v, copy of letter, undated, from Flaxman to Thomson, but not earlier than 1820 in which year Mrs. Flaxman died, with further note by Cunningham. Two other letters, also National Library of Scotland, from Flaxman to Thomson, provide additional information about the loan of the portrait, MS. 685, 7 October 1821, and the intended site and completion, MS. 590, no. 1742 A, 4 August 1826.

[10] A payment of £84 in 1803 is recorded in Croft-Murray account-book, p. 80.

[11] The dating of these busts as 'soon after Italy' is provided by Maria Denman in her corrections to Cunningham in *The Builder*, *op. cit.*, p. 60. They have been painted to look like terracottas.

[12] It also appears in Mengs's portrait of Hewetson. Terence Hodgkinson, 'Christopher Hewetson, An Irish Sculptor in Rome', *Walpole Society*, XXXIV, 1952–54, pp. 48–49, points out that there is no evidence to show if the Hewetson *Hamilton* bust, signed and dated 1784, now in the collections of Glasgow University, was the one in Sir William Hamilton's collection, or another version.

[13] MS letters in Assay Office Library, Birmingham, show that the Boulton monument was conceived as a bust from the start: Flaxman to Boulton's son, 29 December 1810 and 12 August 1812, the latter letter stating that his normal price for a bust nowadays is 120 guineas.

[14] Some of the portraits in the Fitzwilliam volume have been published elsewhere, e.g. Banks appears in C. F. Bell, *Annals of Banks* (Cambridge 1938), pl. XLI; Blake in Bentley, *Records*, frontispiece and D. Bindman, *Blake, Catalogue of the Collection in the Fitzwilliam Museum* (1970), pl. 62.

CHAPTER IX Royal Plate and Other Metalwork

[1] N. M. Penzer: *Paul Storr* (London 1954), p. 134, gives the cost of the candelabrum with the Apples of the Hesperides as £2,017.16s.0d., and the companion piece of Mercury presenting the Infant Bacchus as £1,985,19s.0d. Geoffrey de Bellaigue has very kindly looked for me through the bills in the Royal Archives from Rundell, Bridge and Rundell, and tells me there is no bill for the candelabra. The sums quoted are taken from an annotated copy of Garrard's George V Inventory, in the Royal Archives.

[2] Rundell, Bridge & Co., *Descriptive Catalogue of the Various Services of Plate &c. belonging to the Crown* (London 1832), p. 20.

[3] Dr. W. S. Goddard, Headmaster of Winchester, received a cup on his retirement in 1809; whereabouts unknown. Thomas Earle, Liverpool alderman, received his cup in 1811; it is now owned by Merseyside County Museum, Liverpool; reproduced in J. Culme, *Nineteenth-Century Silver* (London 1977), pl. 19 and Hamburg *Flaxman* catalogue, no. 193. The Bishop of Winchester's cup was made in 1811–12 and is now in a private collection in Los Angeles.

[4] See pp. 36 and 208 for Flaxman's comments on the second bronze doors. R. Wark, *op. cit.*, no. 59, is right when he says that the design of the Theocritus Cup is only faintly reminiscent of the group of *Orpheus and Eurydice* in the Villa Albani, which Flaxman had drawn whilst in Rome, in one of his Victoria and Albert Museum sketch-books. There are more differences than similarities in the compositions.

[5] A drawing in the collection of Sir John and Lady Witt, catalogued as 'Design for a Vase', is a preliminary idea for another, untraced or unexecuted, piece of plate also illustrating Hesiod. The relief panel on the vase shows Hesiod dedicating to the Muses on Mount Helikon the tripod which he had won in a poetic contest, watched by the personification of Victory. The incident is described in Hesiod's *Works and Days*, and was later elaborated in classical literature into a contest between Hesiod and Homer.

[6] Soane incorporated two plaster models for panels on the Kemble Cup on either side of the one for a Theocritus Cup on his Breakfast Parlour chimneypiece. One Kemble panel shows a classically draped actor being crowned by Melpomene, and in the other he is wearing contemporary dress, reading, with a bust of Shakespeare in the background, and a naked, winged Genius approaching. The whereabouts of the Kemble Cup itself are now unknown.

[7] Volume in Victoria and Albert Museum. Re-attributions made by Charles Oman, 'A Problem of Artistic Responsibility: The Firm of Rundell, Bridge and Rundell', *Apollo*, 1966, pp. 174–77.

[8] Documentation summarised in Wark, *op. cit.*, no. 58, plus British Library, Add. MSS. 39783, a volume containing Maria Denman's correspondence, f. 281.

[9] Maria Denman's correction to page 353 of Cunningham's biography, in *The Builder*, *op. cit.*, p. 60.

[10] Anonymous, *Memoirs of the late Philip Rundell, Esq.* (London 1827), pp. 22–23. Rather confusingly there are two editions of this publication in 1827 which are not distinguished as separate editions, one of them much briefer than the other. This information is in the longer edition.

[11] Royal Archives 26065 v, 3 September 1823, bill from Rundell, Bridge and Rundell, for £280. The date mark on the piece is 1826. Information kindly supplied by Geoffrey de Bellaigue.

[12] Another example, dated 1826, identical in design but set with more jewels, is in a private collection, and was reproduced in D. Irwin, *English Neoclassical Art*, pl. 113.

[13] Reproduced in Louis, 1st Marquess of Milford Haven, *British Naval Medals* (London 1919), no. 456. See Graham Pollard, 'Matthew Boulton and Conrad Heinrich Küchler', *Numismatic Chronicle*, seventh series, X, 1970, pp. 259–318. For a further discussion of medals by Pollard see his contribution to the Hamburg *Flaxman* exhibition catalogue, pp. 159–64.

[14] Flaxman's finished drawing for the side of the Gold Medal reproduced here is bound into Volume II of Jupp's grangerised R.A. catalogues at the royal Academy of Arts.

[15] House of Commons, *Report from the Select Committee on Arts and their Connection with Manufactures* (London 1836), Flaxman references on pp. 46, 47, 49, 105, 129, 132, and in Part 2, pp. 14, 158.
Another metalwork firm for which Flaxman apparently supplied designs was that of Messenger's in Birmingham. But the evidence is slender, consisting of a mention in the *Journal of Design*, March–August 1850, p. 11, 'Introduction to the Birmingham Exposition'. No products

have been traced. I am grateful to Shirley Bury for the reference to the *Journal*.

CHAPTER X Professor of Sculpture

[1] H. C. Robinson, *Diary*, I, p. 322, 18 February 1811. Some of Flaxman's lectures were collected for publication posthumously in 1829, with a second edition in 1838. All references given here are to the latter edition; pages will only be cited in a footnote when it is not clear from the text which lecture is being quoted. He specifically refers to a drawing, for example, on p. 227.
For a shortened version of Chapter X, see the author's contribution to the *Flaxman* exhibition catalogue, Hamburg Kunsthalle, 1979, pp. 153–6.

[2] Apart from the repetition of material and comments published during his own lifetime in articles contributed to Abraham Rees's *Cyclopaedia* (London 1819). Flaxman's articles are listed below in the Bibliography. Some of the plates were engraved by Blake.

[3] MSS, John Murray Ltd., London, Mary Ann Flaxman to John Murray, London, 3 August 1828. Murray's possess seven letters from her on the subject of the publication of the *Lectures*. Murray's would not buy the work outright, but wanted Flaxman's sister to prepare it for publication, estimating an edition of 750 copies. Maria Denman executed the drawings from which lithographs could be made.

[4] Sketchbooks in Fitzwilliam Museum, 832/2, 832/6, 832/10, 832/11 contain medieval subjects, some drawn 1812–13, including the drawing reproduced here in Plate 238.

[5] Lecture VII, 'Style', pp. 192–3.

[6] British Library, Add. MSS. 39790, f. 111, list left unfinished.

[7] R. Gough, *Sepulchral Monuments* (London 1786–96), I, p. 69.

[8] H. C. Robinson, *op. cit.*, *loc. cit.*

[9] Many of the points he made in this lecture had been used by him a few years earlier in an article he had contributed to Prince Hoare's *The Artist*, entitled 'Cursory Strictures on Modern Art . . .', no. XII, 30 May 1807.

[10] Lecture VI, 'Composition', p. 160.

[11] Both printed in the second edition of the *Lectures*, pp. 271 ff. and pp. 295 ff.

[12] H. C. Robinson, *op. cit.*, II, p. 134.

[13] Now in the India Office Library, London.

[14] *Lectures*, pp. 102, 169 and 213.

[15] *Lectures*, p. 145.

[16] Lecture VII, 'Style', p. 174. On vases see also Lecture X, 'Modern Sculpture', pp. 265–6.

[17] Disagreement in *Lectures*, pp. 56, 242; for other references see pp. 63, 74, 82, 132, 204, 213, 262.

[18] *Edinburgh Review*, 50, October 1829, p. 231.

[19] Haydon, *Lectures* (London 1844–46), II, p. 32.

[20] D. Watkin, *C. R. Cockerell* (London 1974), p. 100.

[21] British Library, Add. MS. 39780, f. 68, Flaxman to [? Hayley], 12 May 1798.

BIBLIOGRAPHY

1 Manuscripts

John Flaxman

ATHENS, GENNADIUS LIBRARY, AMERICAN SCHOOL OF CLASSICAL STUDIES

Correspondence, 1805–15.

Review of Thomas Hope's *Household Furniture*, not dated.

BASSANO, MUSEO CIVICO

Correspondence, 1810. MS. 5899-XII-1192.

BIRMINGHAM, ASSAY OFFICE

Correspondence, 1812.

CAMBRIDGE, FITZWILLIAM MUSEUM

Address on Thomas Banks (complete; the published version omits 7 pages of manuscript).

Correspondence, 1784–1826. Flaxman MSS., letter-volume.

Correspondence, 1793–1801. Flaxman MSS., (unbound).

Correspondence of Flaxman and Mrs. Flaxman with William Hayley, 1791–1820. Hayley MSS., vol. IX.

Introduction on the Death of George III. Flaxman MSS., in Lectures, VII, Style.

Journal in Italy (Florence and Rome, 1787). Flaxman MSS., notebook 832/5.

'The Knight of the Blazing Cross', 1796. (Poem in irregular blank verse, with illustrations.) MS. 236.

Lectures on Sculpture (except no. VIII), including an 'Introduction General' not published. Flaxman MSS.

Note- and sketch-book (including notes on motion, character, anatomy, etc.) Flaxman MSS., notebook 832/7.

Notes on decoration of St. Paul's, and other churches, and on classical architecture. Flaxman MSS.

'Taste in the Perfection of the Beautiful' (unfinished essay). Flaxman MSS.

CAMBRIDGE, TRINITY COLLEGE

Correspondence, 1819–24. Dawson Turner letters, refer to Flaxman.

CAMBRIDGE, MASSACHUSETTS, HARVARD COLLEGE LIBRARY

'The Casket'. (Poem in irregular blank verse, with illustrations.)

Correspondence, 1791–1825.

EDINBURGH, NATIONAL LIBRARY OF SCOTLAND

Cunningham, *Lives*, grangerised copy. MS. 828.

Correspondence, 1823, MS. 587, no. 1150.

Correspondence, 1826. MS. 590, no. 1742A.

Correspondence, 1821. MS. 685, f. 20.

Correspondence, 1810. MS. 4947, ff. 114–116.

Correspondence, 1818. MS. 9819, f. 104.

Sederunt Book of the Committee of Subscribers to Sir John Moore's statue, 1809–10. MS. 2732, ff. 158–68 refer to Flaxman.

EDINBURGH, UNIVERSITY LIBRARY

Correspondence, 1812–18. Laing, II, 641 and 426/170.

KEELE, UNIVERSITY, WEDGWOOD ARCHIVE

Correspondence and receipts, 1781–88. MSS. 1330.2 to 1342.2

Correspondence, receipts and lists, 1786–7. MSS. L. 26272-1 to L. 26273-1.

Correspondence and receipts, 1775–1809. MSS. L. 204-1 to L. 216-1.

Correspondence and receipts, 1781–90. MSS. 30186-2 to 30197-2.

Correspondence, 1782. MS. in Mosley Collection.

LONDON, BRITISH LIBRARY

Address to the President of the Royal Academy, and draft address to George III on John Opie's plan for the erection of a Gallery of National Glory. 1800–1801. Add. MSS. 33610. S.

Business books of J. Flaxman and executors 1789–1833. Add. MSS. 39784. A–CC.

Correspondence, 1780–1825. Add. MSS. 39780.

Correspondence, 1780–1826. Add. MSS. 39781.

Correspondence, 1803–22. Add. MSS. 39790.

Correspondence, 1790–1824. Add. MSS. 36652.I.

Correspondence, 1791–8. Add. MSS. 32491.A.

Correspondence, 1802–3. Add. MSS. 37538.B.

Correspondence, 1804. Add. MSS. 36540, f. 4

Correspondence, 1808. Add. MSS. 37309, f. 220.

Journal on the way to Rome (1787). Add. MSS. 39786.

Notes on the history of sculpture. Add. MSS. 39790. ff. 104–12.

LONDON, JOHN MURRAY LTD.

Sketchbook, c. 1790, no. 435.

Sketchbook, c. 1809, no. 448F.

Sketchbook, c. 1816, no. 448E.

LONDON, SWEDENBORG SOCIETY

Correspondence, 1810–11.

LONDON, UNIVERSITY COLLEGE, LIBRARY

Journal in Naples, 1788.

Notebook (containing notes for Lectures).

LONDON, VICTORIA AND ALBERT MUSEUM

Italian Sketchbook, B.2.C.

Italian Sketchbook, 91.D.7.

LONDON, WESTFIELD COLLEGE

Correspondence, 1805.

MANCHESTER, JOHN RYLANDS UNIVERSITY LIBRARY

Correspondence, 1786. English MSS. 341.

NEW HAVEN, CONNECTICUT, YALE UNIVERSITY LIBRARY
Correspondence, 1797–1803.

NEW HAVEN, CONNECTICUT, YALE CENTER FOR BRITISH ART
Italian sketch- and notebook.

NEW YORK, COLUMBIA UNIVERSITY
Account-book, 1809–26. Special Collection, D. 430.394–F. 61.

NEW YORK, PIERPONT MORGAN LIBRARY
Correspondence, 1794–1819.

NEW YORK, PUBLIC LIBRARY
Correspondence, 1802.

OXFORD, BODLEIAN LIBRARY
Correspondence, 1792–1823. MSS. Autog. d. 11.

PORTLAND, MAINE, MAINE HISTORICAL SOCIETY
Correspondence, 1812.

ROME, ACCADEMIA DI SAN LUCA
Congregazione, vol. 58, p. 46v; and vol. 59, p. 70v (refer to Flaxman).

SAN MARINO, CALIFORNIA, H. E. HUNTINGTON LIBRARY AND ART GALLERY
Correspondence, 1803–14.

Mrs. Flaxman

CHICAGO, ART INSTITUTE
Correspondence, 1802. Gurley Collection.

LONDON, BRITISH LIBRARY
Correspondence, 1792–1820. Add. MSS. 39782.
Journal in Italy, 1787–8. Add. MSS. 39787.
Journal in Italy, 1791–2. Add. MSS. 39792. A.
Journal in Northern Italy, 1794. Add. MSS. 39790. ff. 147 *et seq.*

NEW YORK, PIERPONT MORGAN LIBRARY
Correspondence, 1776.

Mary Ann Flaxman

LONDON, JOHN MURRAY LTD.
Correspondence, 1827–28.

Joseph Farington

WINDSOR, ROYAL LIBRARY
Diary, 1793–1821. (Typescript in British Museum Print Room.)

2 Published Works of John Flaxman

Acts of Mercy. Aquatints by F. C. Lewis. London 1831.
Anatomical Studies of the Bones and Muscles . . . from Drawings by John Flaxman. Engraved by Henry Landseer. London 1833.
Compositions from the Tragedies of Aeschylus. Engraved by Tomaso Piroli. London 1795.
Compositions from the Divine Poem of Dante Alighieri. Engraved by Tomaso Piroli. London 1807 (first edn. 1793).
Compositions from the Works and Days and Theogony of Hesiod. Engraved by William Blake. London 1817.
Eight Illustrations of the Lord's Prayer from the Designs of the late John Flaxman, R.A. Lithographs by Richard Lane. London 1835.
The Iliad of Homer, engraved by T. Piroli from the Compositions of John Flaxman. Rome 1793. Enlarged edition, London 1805.
Lectures on Sculpture . . . As delivered before the President and Members of the Royal Academy. With a brief memoir of the author. London 1829.
Lectures on Sculpture. . . . Second edition. To which are now first added, an introductory lecture and two addresses to the Royal Academy on the death of T. Banks, in 1805, and A. Canova, in 1822, with an Address on the death of Flaxman by Sir R. Westmacott. London 1838.
A Letter to the Committee for Raising the Naval Pillar, or Monument, under the Patronage of his Royal Highness the Duke of Clarence. London 1799.
The Odyssey of Homer, engraved by T. Piroli from the Compositions of John Flaxman. Rome 1793. Enlarged edition, London 1805.
'Armour', 'Basso-Relievo', 'Beauty', 'Bronze', 'Bust', 'Composition', 'Cast', and 'Ceres', articles in Abraham Rees, *Cyclopedia*. London 1819.
'Cursory Strictures on Modern Art, and particularly Sculpture, in England, previously to the Establishment of the Royal Academy', in *The Artist*, no. XII, 30 May 1807 (vol. 1, 1810).
'The Monuments of Captain Montagu and of Admiral Howe', in Prince Hoare, *Academic Correspondence, 1803*, London 1804, pp. 24–25.
'Sketch of Romney's Professional Character', in William Hayley, *Life of George Romney*, London 1809, pp. 305–13.
Correspondence on classical figures, in *Gentleman's Magazine*, LI, 1781, p. 65.
Correspondence with George and John Romney, in Revd. J. Romney, *Romney*, London 1830, pp. 204–7, 207–10, 230–3.
Correspondence with the President and Council of the Royal Academy in London, in *Gentleman's Magazine*, LXVII, pt. 1, 1797, pp. 20–1; LXIX, pt. 1, 1799, pp. 97–9.
'An Account Book of John Flaxman, R.A.' (British Library Add. MS. 39784 BB), edit. E. Croft-Murray, *Walpole Society*, XXVIII, 1939–40, pp. 51–93.

3 Other Published Works

(Anon.) 'National Monuments', *Monthly Magazine*, January 1806, pp. 497–9.
(Anon.) 'John Flaxman, Esq., R.A. Professor of Sculpture at

the Royal Academy, *The Annual Biography and Obituary for the Year 1828*, XII, 1828, pp. 20–25.
(Anon.) *Memoirs of the Life of the late Philip Rundell, Esq., Goldsmith and Jeweller to his Majesty and the Royal Family* [by W. Doran]. London 1827.
(Anon.) 'John Flaxman', *Art Journal*, 1855, pp. 205–9.
ANDREWS, Keith *The Nazarenes: A Brotherhood of German Painters in Rome*. Oxford 1964.
ARTS COUNCIL OF GREAT BRITAIN *The Age of Neoclassicism*. Council of Europe Exhibition Catalogue. London 1972.
The Romantic Movement. Council of Europe Exhibition Catalogue. London 1959.
BATE, W. J. *From Classic to Romantic, Premises of Taste in 18th Century England*. Cambridge, Mass., 1946.
BAYLEY, Revd. Dr. J. *New Church Worthies*. London 1884.
BENTLEY, Gerald E. *Blake Records*. Oxford 1969.
'Flaxman's Drawings for *Pilgrim's Progress*', in Paul Fritz and Richard Morton (edits), *Women in the 18th Century and other Essays*, Toronto and Sarasota 1976, pp. 245–78.
'A. S. Mathew, Patron of Flaxman and Blake', *Notes and Queries*, 203, 1958, pp. 168–78.
'Notes on the Early Editions of Flaxman's Classical Designs', *Bulletin of the New York Public Library*, 68, 1964, pp. 277–307, 361–380. [Published separately as *The Early Engravings of Flaxman's Classical Designs*, New York 1964].
'Blakes's Engravings and his Friendship with Flaxman', *Studies in Bibliography*, 12, 1959, pp. 161–88.
'Blakes Hesiod', *Library*, 20, 1965, pp. 315–20.
BEUTLER, Ernst *John Flaxman's Zeichnungen zu Sagen des klassischen Altertums*. Leipzig 1910.
BINDMAN, David *Blake as an Artist*. Oxford 1977.
'John Flaxman's Funerary Monuments', in *Neoclassicismo. Atti del convegno internazionale promosso dal Comité International d'Histoire de l'Art, Londra 1971*, Genoa 1973, pp. 9–13.
BINYON, Robert Laurence *Catalogue of Drawings by British Artists . . . in the British Museum*. 4 vols. London 1898–1907.
BIRNBAUM, Martin 'An Essay on John Flaxman with Special Reference to his Drawings', *International Studio*, 65, 1918, pp. 65–72.
BISHOP, Morchard *Blake's Hayley. The Life, Works and Friendships of William Hayley*. London 1951.
BLAKE, William *Complete Poetry and Prose*. Edit. Geoffrey Keynes. London, 1957 edn.
Letters. Edit. Geoffrey Keynes. London 1956.
BLAKISTON, J. M. G. 'Flaxman's Monument to Joseph Warton: Its Genesis and Evolution', *Winchester Cathedral Record*, no. 42, 1973, pp. 22–39.
BLUNT, Anthony *The Art of William Blake*. London 1959.
BOASE, T. S. R. *English Art 1800–1870*. Oxford 1959.
'An Extra Illustrated Second Folio of Shakespeare'. *British Museum Quarterly*, XX, no. I, 1955, pp. 4–8.
BOLTON, A. T. *English Eighteenth Century Sculptures in Sir John Soane's Museum*. London 1913.
BOTT, Gerhard (Edit.) *Bertel Thorvaldsen. Untersuchungen zu seinem Werk und zur Kunst seiner Zeit*. Cologne 1977.
BRAY, Anna Eliza *Life of Thomas Stothard, R.A.* London 1851.
BRITTON, John (Edit.) *The Fine Arts of the English School*. 3 parts. London 1812.
BURKE, Joseph *English Art 1714–1800*. Oxford 1976.
BURY, Shirley 'The Lengthening Shadow of Rundell's', *Connoisseur*, CLXI, 1966, pp. 79–85, 152–58, 218–22.
Victorian Electroplate. London 1971.
BUTEN, Harry M. *Wedgwood and Artists*. Merion, Pennsylvania, 1960.
BUXTON, John *The Grecian Taste: Studies in the Literature of the Age of Neo-Classicism*. London 1978.
CAMERON, Roderick 'Flaxman et Wedgwood', *L'Oeil*, no. 53, May 1959, pp. 48–55.
CAMPBELL, Malcolm 'An Alternative Design for a Commemorative Monument by John Flaxman', *Princeton Bulletin*, XVII, no. 2, 1958, pp. 65–73.
CARTER, Arthur 'John Flaxman. Sculptor, Artist and New Churchman', *New Church Life*, XLVIII, 1928, pp. 257–66, 334–49, 427–36.
CHILDE-PEMBERTON, W. A. *The Earl Bishop. The Life of Frederick Harvey, Bishop of Derry, Earl of Bristol*. 2 vols. London 1925.
CHRISTIE, MANSON & WOODS *Catalogue of the small but valuable Library of Books . . . of John Flaxman, Esq., R.A. Dec.*, London, 12 June 1828.
Catalogue of a valuable assemblage of Engravings by ancient and modern Masters . . . the property of the late John Flaxman, Esq., R.A. Dec., London, 1 July 1828.
Catalogue of the remaining Works of John Flaxman, R.A., London, 26 April 1876.
Maria Denman Sale Catalogue, London, 1862.
CICOGNARA, Count Leopoldo *Storia della scultura*, 3 vols. Venice 1813–18. Second edition, 8 vols. Prato 1823–25.
CLARKE, Edward Daniel *Greek Marbles brought from the Shores of the Euxine, Archipeligo and Mediterranean*. Cambridge 1809.
CLARKE, M. L. *Greek Studies in England 1700–1830*. Cambridge 1945.
COLVIN, Sidney *Drawings of Flaxman in the Gallery of University College London*. London 1876.
COMMONS, HOUSE OF *Report from the Select Committee of the House of Commons on the Earl of Elgin's Collection of Sculptured Marbles*. London 1816.
CONSTABLE, William George *John Flaxman 1755–1826*. London 1927.
CORBOULD, Henry and MOSES, Henry *Outline Engraving and Descriptions of the Woburn Abbey Marbles*. London 1822.
CROFT-MURRAY, Edward [See under: Published Works of John Flaxman, 'An Account Book'.]
CROOK, J. Mordaunt *The Greek Revival*. London 1972.
CULME, John *Nineteenth-Century Silver*. London 1977.
CUMBERLAND, George *Thoughts on outline, sculpture, and the system that guided the ancient artists in composing their figures and groups, . . . to which are annexed twenty-four designs of classical subjects invented on the principles recommended in the essay by George Cumberland*. London 1796.
CUNNINGHAM, Allan *Lives of the Most Eminent British Painters, Sculptors and Architects*. 2nd edn. 6 vols. London 1830–3.

CUNNINGHAM, Peter 'New Materials for the Life of John Flaxman' [by Maria Denman], *The Builder*, vol. XXI, 17 and 24 January, 1863, pp. 37–38, 60.

DECK, Raymond H. 'New Light on C. A. Tulk, Blake's Nineteenth-Century Patron', *Studies in Romanticism*, 16, no. 2, Spring 1977, pp. 217–36.

DENMAN, Maria [See Cunningham, Peter].

DETROIT, INSTITUTE OF ARTS, and PHILADELPHIA MUSEUM OF ART *Romantic Art in Britain. Paintings, and Drawings 1760–1860*. Exhibition catalogue by Frederick Cummings, Allen Staley and Robert Rosenblum. Philadelphia 1968.

DOBAI, Johannes *Die Kunstliteratur des Klassizismus und der Romantik in England*. 3 vols. Bern 1974–7.

DOIN, Jeanne 'John Flaxman', *Gazette des Beaux-Arts*, V, 1911, pp. 223–46, 330–42.

DORAN, W. [See Anonymous].

DUFOUR, Alexander *Letter to the . . . committee for raising the Naval Pillar . . . in answer to the letter of John Flaxman on that subject*. London 1800.

ELY, Talfourd *Catalogue of the Works of Art in the Flaxman Gallery, University College, London*. London 1900.

ERDMAN, David V. *Blake: Prophet against Empire*. Princeton 1953. Revised edn. 1969.

ERSKINE, Mrs. Steuart 'Some Flaxman Relics', *Art Journal*, 1912, pp. 81–6.

ESDAILE, Katharine A. *English Church Monuments 1510–1840*. London 1946.

'Flaxman's design for the Monument to Lord Mayor Beckford at the Guildhall', *Burlington Magazine*, 45, 1924, pp. 81–7.

ESSICK, Robert and LA BELLE, Jenijoy (Edits.) *Flaxman's Illustrations to Homer*. New York 1977.

FARINGTON, Joseph *Diary 1793–1821*. Edit. James Greig. 8 vols. London 1922–28. Full text, edit. K. Garlick and A. MacIntyre. London and New Haven 1978.

FARRAR, Lady Katherine Euphemia (Edit.) *Letters of Josiah Wedgwood*. 3 vols. London 1903–6.

FAWCETT, Trevor *The Rise of English Provincial Art*. Oxford 1974.

FINER, Ann and SAVAGE, George (Edits.) *The Selected Letters of Josiah Wedgwood*. London 1965.

FIORILLO, Johann Dominik *Geschichte der zeichnenden Kunste von ihrer Wiederauflebung bis auf die neuesten Zeiten*. 5 vols. Göttingen 1798–1808.

FLORENCE, GABINETTO DISEGNI E STAMPE DEGLI UFFIZI *Luigi Sabatelli. Disegni e Incisioni*. Exhibition catalogue by Beatrice Paolozzi Strozzi and Carlo del Bravo. Florence 1978.

FOSTER, Kate 'Wedgwood and neo-classicism: an exhibition at Ickworth', *Connoisseur*, CLXXI, 1969, pp. 90–93.

FOTHERGILL, Brian *The Mitred Earl. An Eighteenth Century Eccentric*. London 1974.

GAUNT, William 'A set of drawings by John Flaxman', *Connoisseur*, CLIII, 1963, pp. 250–4.

GILCHRIST, Alexander *Life of William Blake*. 2 vols. London and Cambridge 1863. Edit. Ruthven Todd. Revised edn. London 1945.

GILLOW, Norah 'Some Flaxman Drawings at York', *Preview*, XXVI, April 1973, pp. 915–19.

GOETHE, Johann Wolfgang von 'Über die Flaxmanischen Werke', *Propyläen*, 1799, in *Werke*, 47 Weimar 1896, pp. 245–46.

GORLEY, Jean 'Flaxman's Work for Wedgwood', *Antiques*, January 1953.

GRAVES, Algernon *Royal Academy Exhibitors 1776–1904*. 8 vols. London 1905–6.

The Society of Artists of Great Britain; the Free Society of Artists: a Complete Dictionary of Contributors. London 1907.

GUNNIS, Rupert *Dictionary of British Sculptors 1660–1851*. London 1953. Revised edn., London 1968. [See also WHINNEY, Margaret].

HALE, John R. *England and the Italian Renaissance*. London 1954.

HAMBURG, KUNSTHALLE *John Flaxman Mythologie und Industrie*, Exhibition Catalogue by Werner Hofmann, David Bindman, Shirley Bury, David Irwin, Mary Webster, Graham Pollard, Bruce Tattersall. Hamburg 1979 (and subsequently Copenhagen and London).

HARRIS, John 'The Wyatts at Westport, home of the Marquess of Sligo', *Connoisseur*, CLXII, 1966, pp. 224–7.

HASKELL, Francis *Rediscoveries in Art*. London 1976.

HAUTECOEUR, Louis *Rome et la Renaissance de l'Antiquité à la fin du XVIIIe siècle*. Paris 1912.

HAYDON, Benjamin Robert *Diary*. Edit. W. B. Pope. 5 vols. Cambridge, Mass., 1960–63.

HAYLEY, William *Essay on Sculpture in a series of Poetical Epistles to John Flaxman, R.A.* London 1800.

Life of George Romney. Chichester 1809.

Memoirs of the Life and Writings of William Hayley . . . and memoirs of his son Thomas Alphonso Hayley. Edit. J. Johnson. 2 vols. London 1823.

HERVEY, Thomas Kibble *Illustrations of Modern Sculpture*. London 1832.

HINDMARSH, Robert *Rise and Progress of the New Jerusalem Church*. London 1861.

HONOUR, Hugh *Neo-classicism*. Harmondsworth 1968.

Romanticism London 1979.

HOPE, Thomas *Household Furniture and Interior Decoration*. London 1807.

HUNT, William Holman *Pre-Raphaelitism and the Pre-Raphaelite Brotherhood*. London 1905.

HUTCHISON, Sidney C. 'The Royal Academy Schools, 1768–1830', *Walpole Society*, XXXVIII, 1960–62, pp. 123–191.

ICKWORTH, NATIONAL TRUST *British Neoclassical Art*. Exhibition catalogue by David Irwin. Ickworth 1969.

IRWIN, David *English Neoclassical Art: Studies in Inspiration and Taste*. London 1966.

English Neoclassical Art: Views and Tastes of the Principal Artists. Ph.D. Thesis, London University, 1960.

'Flaxman: Italian Journals and Correspondence', *Burlington Magazine*, 101, 1959, pp. 212–17.

'Reviving Interest in Flaxman', *Connoisseur*, 144, 1959,

pp. 104–5.
'Neoclassical Design: Industry plunders Antiquity', *Apollo*, XCVI, 1972, pp. 288–97.
'Neoclassicism in Art' in Scribner's *Dictionary of the History of Ideas* New York 1972, III, pp. 363–71.
'Unclassical Neo-classicism: Sentiment and Gothic', *Connoisseur*, CLXXXI, 1972, pp. 18–24.
'The Industrial Revolution and the Dissemination of Neo-classical Taste', *Studies on Voltaire and 18th Century*, CLIII, 1976, pp. 1087–98.
'John Flaxman's Drawings,' *Burlington Magazine*, CXVIII, 1976, pp. 335–36.
'John Flaxman', *Portfolio*, forthcoming 1979
'Sentiment and Piety in Tombs about 1800', in *Social History of Death*, edit. J. Whaley. Forthcoming London 1980.
[See also: Hamburg, Kunsthalle; Ickworth, National Trust].
IRWIN, David and Francina *Scottish Painters: At Home and Abroad 1700 to 1900*. London 1975.
IVON-JONES, Brian 'Regency Splendour 1810–1820: the Achilles Silver-gilt Shield', *Apollo*, 97, 1973, p. 447.
JONES, E. Alfred *The Gold and Silver of Windsor Castle*. London 1911.
JOSEPH, M. K. 'Charles Aders', *Auckland University College Bulletin*, no. 43, English series no. 6, 1953.
KELLY, Alison *Decorative Wedgwood in Architecture and Furniture*. London 1965.
The Story of Wedgwood. London 1962. Revised edn., London 1975.
LARRABEE, S. A. *English Bards and Grecian Marbles. The Relationship between sculpture and poetry especially in the Romantic period*. New York 1943.
LAWRENCE, Sir Thomas [See Williams, D. E.]
LESLIE, Charles Robert *Autobiographical Recollections*. Edit. Tom Taylor. 2 vols. London 1860.
LONDON, HEIM GALLERY *John Flaxman*. Exhibition catalogue by Christopher Powney and David Bindman. London 1976.
LONDON, IVEAGH BEQUEST *British Artists in Rome 1700–1800*. Exhibition Catalogue, by Lindsay Stainton. London 1974.
LONDON, ROYAL ACADEMY OF ARTS *The First Hundred Years of the Royal Academy 1769–1868*. Exhibition Catalogue. London 1951–52.
LONDON, SCIENCE MUSEUM *Josiah Wedgwood: 'The Arts and Sciences United'*. Exhibition Catalogue by John des Fontaines and others. London 1978.
LONDON, SOANE MUSEUM *A New Description*. Catalogue by John Summerson. London 1955.
LONDON, VICTORIA AND ALBERT MUSEUM *An Exhibition of Royal Plate from Buckingham Palace and Windsor Castle*. Catalogue. London 1954.
LONDON: *see also* ARTS COUNCIL OF GREAT BRITAIN.
LONDSDALE, Henry *The Life and Works of Musgrave Lewthwaite Watson, Sculptor*. London 1866.
LOWERY, M. R. Blake and the Flaxman's, in F. W. Hilles, (edit.) *Age of Johnson. Essays presented to C. B. Tinker*, New Haven 1949, pp. 281–90.
MACHT, Carol M. *Classical Wedgwood Design*. New York 1957.
MACKENDRICK, N. 'Josiah Wedgwood: an eighteenth-century entrepreneur in salesmanship and marketing technique', *Economic History Review*, Second series, XII, 1960, pp. 408–33.
MANKOWITZ, Wolf *Wedgwood*. London 1953.
MARGOLIOUTH, H. M. 'Blake's Mr. Mathew', *Notes and Queries*, 196, 1951, pp. 162–3.
MELCHIORI, Giorgio *Michelangelo nel Settecento Inglese. Un Capitolo di Storia del Gusto in Inghilterra*. Rome 1950.
MEMES, John S. *Memoirs of Antonio Canova, with a critical analysis of his works and an historical view of modern sculpture*. Edinburgh 1825.
MEMMESHEIMER, Paul Arthur *Das klassizistische Grabmal. Eine Typologie*. Bonn 1969.
MERCHANT, W. Moelwyn *Shakespeare and the Artist*. London 1959.
METEYARD, Eliza *The Life of Josiah Wedgwood*. 2 vols. London 1865–66.
MICHAELIS, A. *Ancient Marbles in Great Britain*. Cambridge 1882.
MITTER, Partha *Much Maligned Monster: a History of European Reactions to Indian Art*. Oxford 1977.
MONGAN, Agnes 'Ingres and the Antique', *Journal of the Warburg and Courtauld Institutes*, 10, 1947, pp. 1–13.
MORRIS, H. N. *Flaxman, Blake, Coleridge and other men of Genius influenced by Swedenborg, and Flaxman's Allegory on the Knight of the Blazing Cross*. London 1915.
MORRISON, Alfred *The Collection of Autograph Letters and Historical Documents formed by Alfred Morrison*. (Second Series, 1882–93.) *The Hamilton and Nelson Papers*. 2 vols. Printed for private circulation 1893.
MUSGRAVE, Clifford 'The Treasures of Lloyd's', *Connoisseur*, 174, 1970, pp. 86–98.
NEWCASTLE, HATTON GALLERY *John Flaxman. R.A., Sculptor*. Exhibition Catalogue by Lawrence Gowing. Newcastle, 1958.
OMAN, Charles 'A Problem of Artistic Responsibility: The Firm of Rundell, Bridge and Rundell', *Apollo*, LXXXIII, 1966, pp. 174–183.
'Models for the Royal Plate', *Country Life*, CXV, 1954, p. 945.
OMAN, Charles and PENZER, N. M. 'The galvanic goblet', *Country Life*, CXV, 1954, p. 606.
OTTLEY, William Young *A Series of Plates engraved after the paintings and sculptures of the Most Eminent Masters of the Early Florentine School*. London 1826.
PALLISER, Fanny Bury and M. A. *Mottoes for Monuments . . . Illustrated with Designs by Flaxman and others*. London 1872.
PANOFSKY, Dora and Erwin *Pandora's Box. The Changing Aspects of a Mythical Symbol*. London 1956.
PARIS, MUSÉE DU LOUVRE, CABINET DES DESSINS *Dessins français de 1750 à 1825. Le néo-classicisme*. Exhibition catalogue by Arlette Sérullaz. Paris 1972.
PENNY, Nicholas *Church Monuments in Romantic England*. London and New Haven 1977.
PENZER, N. M. *Paul Storr, the Last of the Goldsmiths*. London

1954.
PEVSNER, Nikolaus *The Englishness of English Art*. London 1956.
The Buildings of England. 40 vols. Harmondsworth 1951–74.
PHYSICK, John *Designs for English Sculpture 1680–1860. Victoria and Albert Museum*. London 1969.
POINTON, Marcia *Milton and English Art*. Manchester 1970.
POLLARD, Graham 'Matthew Boulton and Conrad Heinrich Küchler', *Numismatic Chronicle*, Seventh series, X, 1970, pp. 259–318.
POTTS, Alexander *Winckelmann's Interpretation of the History of Ancient Art in its Eighteenth Century Context*. Ph.D. Thesis, London University, 1977.
PRAZ, Mario *Gusto Neoclassico*. Florence 1940. 2nd edn. Naples 1959. English trans., London 1969.
PREVITALI, Giovanni 'Collezionisti di primitivi nel Settecento', *Paragone*, 113, 1959, pp. 3–32.
REILLY, Robin and SAVAGE, George *Wedgwood: The Portrait Medallions*. London 1973.
ROBINSON, Henry Crabb *Diary, Reminiscences and Correspondence* Ed. T. Sadler, 3 vols, London 1869.
ROMNEY, Rev. John *Memoirs of the Life and Works of George Romney*. London 1830.
ROSCOE, E. S. 'The Career and Work of Flaxman', *Magazine of Art*, IV, 1881.
ROSENBLUM, Robert *Transformations in Late Eighteenth Century Art*. Princeton 1967.
The International Style of 1800: A Study in Linear Abstraction. Ph.D. Thesis, New York University 1956. Published New York 1976.
RUNDELL, BRIDGE & CO. *Descriptive Inventories of the Various Services of Plate, etc. belonging to the Crown*. London 1832.
ST. CLAIR, William L. *Lord Elgin and the Marbles*. London 1967.
SANTA BARBARA, UNIVERSITY ART GALLERIES *William Blake in the Art of His Time*. Exhibition Catalogue by Corlette Walker, and others. Santa Barbara 1976.
SAUERLANDT, Max 'John Flaxman', *Zeitschrift für bildende Kunst*, 19, 1908, pp. 189–97.
SAXL, F. and WITTKOWER, R. *British Art and the Mediterranean*. London 1948.
SCHEIDEMANTEL, Vivian J. 'The Apotheosis of Homer: A Wedgwood and Bentley Plaque', in *Festschrift Ulrich Middeldorf* (Berlin 1968), pp. 517–22; reprinted in *The American Wedgwoodian*, III, no. 3, June 1969, pp. 68–74.
SCHLEGEL, A. W. von 'Über Zeichnungen zu Gedichten und John Flaxmans Umrissen', *Athenäum*, 1799, in *Sammtliche Werke*, Leipzig 1846, IX, pp. 102–57.
SCHORN, Ludwig 'Besuch bei Flaxman in Juli 1826', *Kunst-Blatt*, 1827, pp. 133–15, 118–20, 123–24.
SCHUDT, Ludwig *Le Guide di Roma*. Vienna and Augsburg 1930.
SCOTT, David *British, French and German Paintings: being a reference to the grounds which render the proposed painting of the new Houses of Parliament important as a public Measure*. Edinburgh 1841.
SCOTT, William Bell *The British School of Sculpture illustrated by twenty engravings from the finest works of deceased masters of the art*. London [1872].
SMITH, H. Clifford *Buckingham Palace*. London [1931].
SMITH, John Thomas *Book for a Rainy Day*. London 1845. Edit. W. Whitten. London 1905.
Nollekens and His times. 2 vols. London 1828. Edit. W. Whitten, London 1920.
SPARKES, J. C. L. *Flaxman's Classical Outlines*. London 1879.
SPENCER, T. *Fair Greece Sad Relic*. London 1954.
STEEGMAN, John E. *The Rule of Taste from George I to George IV*. London 1936.
STERN, B. H. *The Rise of Romantic Hellenism in English Literature, 1732–1786*. Menasha, Wisconsin 1940.
STROUD, Dorothy *George Dance, Architect, 1741–1825*. London 1971.
Henry Holland: His Life and Architecture. London 1966.
SUMMERSON, John *Architecture in Britain: 1530–1830*. 2nd edn. Harmondsworth 1955.
John Nash, Architect to George IV. London 1935.
SYMMONS, Sarah *John Flaxman: his engraved illustrations to Dante, Homer, Aeschylus and Hesiod*. M.A. Thesis, London University 1968.
'John Flaxman and Francisco Goya: Infernos Transcribed', *Burlington Magazine*, CXIII, 1971, pp. 508–12.
'The Spirit of Despair: Patronage, Primitivism and the Art of John Flaxman', *Burlington Magazine*, CXVII, 1975, pp. 644–50.
'French Copies after Flaxman's Outlines', *Burlington Magazine*, CXV, 1973, pp. 591–99.
'Gericault, Flaxman and "Ugolino" ', *Burlington Magazine*, CXV, 1973, pp. 671–2.
TAIT, Hugh 'Wedgwood, Flaxman and an Eighteenth-century portrait carver, Silvanus Bevan', *Proceedings of the Wedgwood Society*, no. 3, 1959, pp. 126–32.
TENISWOOD, C. F. 'Memorials of Flaxman', *Art Journal*, 1867, pp. 101–4, 161–4, 201–5, 241–4; 1868, pp. 1–4, 81–4, 145–8, 241–4.
'Flaxman as a Designer', *Art Journal*, 1872, pp. 189–91, 205–7, 221–3, 251–60, 278–80.
THOMAS, John 'John Flaxman', *Journal of the Royal Society of Arts*, CIV, 1955, pp. 43–66.
TODD, Ruthven *Tracks in the Snow*. London 1946.
TOYNBEE, Paget 'Dante in English Art', *38th Annual Report of the Dante Society*, Cambridge, Mass. 1919, Boston 1921.
WARK, Robert R. *Drawings by John Flaxman in the Huntington Collection*. San Marino, California 1970.
British Silver in the Huntington Collection. San Marino, California, 1978.
WATKIN, David *The Life and Work of C. R. Cockerell*. London 1974.
Thomas Hope and the Neoclassical Idea. London 1968.
WATSON, Francis 'Flaxman. The Bicentenary of an English Neo-classicist', *Architectural Review*, 118, 1955, pp. 285–9.
WEDGWOOD, Josiah [See Farrar, Lady; Finer, Ann and Savage, George].
WELLS-COLE, Anthony 'John Flaxman and Benjamin Gott of Armley House, Leeds', *Leeds Art Calendar*, no. 63, 1968, pp. 21–4.

WESTMACOTT, C. M. *British Galleries of Painting and Sculpture*. London 1824.

WHINNEY, Margaret *English Sculpture 1720–1830. Victoria and Albert Museum*. London 1971.

Sculpture in Britain 1530–1830. Harmondsworth 1964.

'Flaxman and the Eighteenth Century: A Commemorative Lecture', *Journal of the Warburg and Courtauld Institutes*, XIX, 1956, pp. 269–82.

'Flaxman at Covent Garden', *About the House* (The Friends of Covent Garden Ltd.), I, no. 10, 1965, p. 24.

WHINNEY, Margaret and GUNNIS, Rupert *The Collection of Models by John Flaxman R.A. at University College, London*. London 1967.

WHITLEY, William T. *Artists and their Friends in England 1700–1799*. 2 vols. London 1928.

Art in England 1800–1820. Cambridge 1928.

Art in England 1821–1837. Cambridge 1930.

WIEBENSON, Dora 'Subjects from Homer's Iliad in Neoclassical Art', *Art Bulletin*, 46, 1964, pp. 23–37.

WILKINSON, Theon *Two Monsoons*. London 1976.

WILLIAMS, D. E. *The Life and Correspondence of Sir Thomas Lawrence*. 2 vols. London 1831.

WILLIAMS, Iolo A. 'An Identification of some early drawings by John Flaxman', *Burlington Magazine*, CII, 1960, pp. 246–50.

YATES, Frances 'Transformation of Dante's Ugolino', *Journal of Warburg and Courtauld Institutes*, XIV, 1951, pp. 92–117.

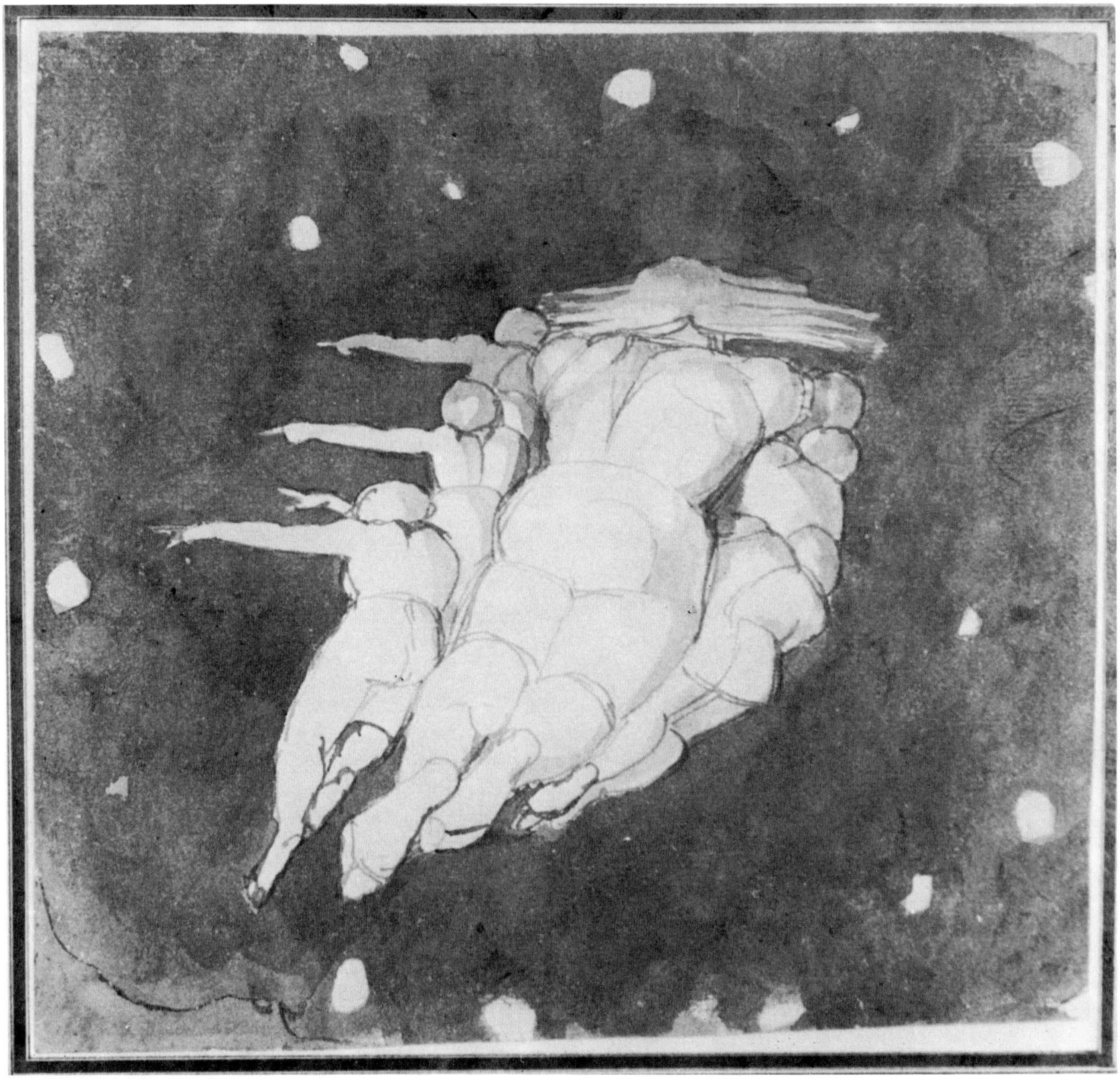

Index of Works

The reference numbers to illustrations are in italics

General Index

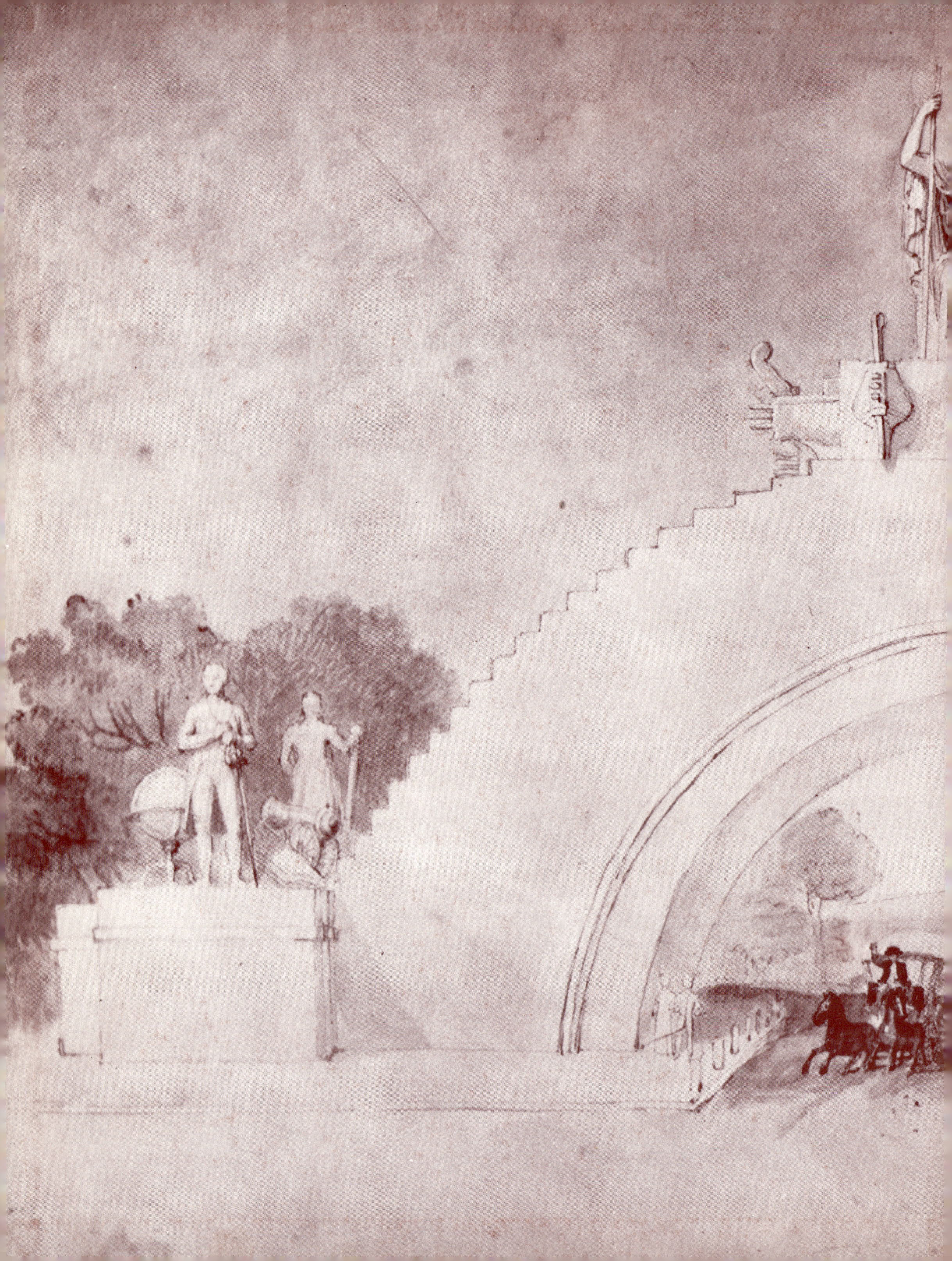